# Lecture Notes in Computer Science 16835

The series Lecture Notes in Computer Science (LNCS), including its subseries Lecture Notes in Artificial Intelligence (LNAI) and Lecture Notes in Bioinformatics (LNBI), has established itself as a medium for the publication of new developments in computer science and information technology research, teaching, and education.

LNCS enjoys close cooperation with the computer science R & D community, the series counts many renowned academics among its volume editors and paper authors, and collaborates with prestigious societies. Its mission is to serve this international community by providing an invaluable service, mainly focused on the publication of conference and workshop proceedings and postproceedings. LNCS commenced publication in 1973.

Yi Li · Frank Stephan · Xiaoming Sun
Editors

# Computing and Combinatorics

32nd International Computing and Combinatorics Conference, COCOON 2026
Singapore, Singapore, July 23–25, 2026
Proceedings

Springer

*Editors*
Yi Li
Nanyang Technological University
Singapore, Singapore

Frank Stephan
National University of Singapore
Singapore, Singapore

Xiaoming Sun
Chinese Academy of Sciences
Beijing, China

ISSN 0302-9743 ISSN 1611-3349 (electronic)
Lecture Notes in Computer Science
ISBN 978-981-92-3308-3 ISBN 978-981-92-3309-0 (eBook)
https://doi.org/10.1007/978-981-92-3309-0



This Springer imprint is published by the registered company Springer Nature Singapore Pte Ltd.
The registered company address is: 152 Beach Road, #21-01/04 Gateway East, Singapore 189721, Singapore

# Preface

This volume contains the papers presented at the 32nd International Computing and Combinatorics Conference (COCOON 2026), held in Singapore during 23–25 July 2026. COCOON 2026 provides an international forum for researchers working in the areas of algorithms, theory of computation, computational complexity, and combinatorics related to computing.

This year, COCOON 2026 received 109 valid submissions from 20 countries and regions, reflecting its broad international participation. Each submission underwent a rigorous peer-review process conducted by the Programme Committee, with the support of external reviewers, and typically received at least three independent double-blind reviews. Following careful evaluation and discussion, 34 papers were selected for presentation, corresponding to an acceptance rate of approximately 31.2%.

The conference also included two invited presentations, delivered by Yuichi Yoshida (National Institute of Informatics, Japan) and Seth Pettie (University of Michigan, USA).

We sincerely thank the authors for their high-quality submissions; the Program Committee members and external reviewers for their careful evaluations; and the invited speakers for their insightful presentations. We are grateful to the School of Physical and Mathematical Sciences at Nanyang Technological University for hosting and supporting COCOON 2026, and to the Steering Committee for their continued guidance and support.

Finally, we thank Springer for publishing the COCOON 2026 proceedings in the Lecture Notes in Computer Science (LNCS) series, making the research presented at the conference widely accessible online.

May 2026

Yi Li
Frank Stephan
Xiaoming Sun

# Organization

## PC Co-chairs

| | |
|---|---|
| Yi Li | Nanyang Technological University, Singapore |
| Frank Stephan | National University of Singapore, Singapore |
| Xiaoming Sun | Chinese Academy of Sciences, China |

## Program Committee

| | |
|---|---|
| Antonios Antoniadis | University of Twente, Netherlands |
| Ioana O. Bercea | KTH Royal Institute of Technology, Sweden |
| Sujoy Bhore | Indian Institute of Technology Bombay, India |
| Jarosław Byrka | University of Wrocław, Poland |
| Armando Castañneda | National Autonomous University of Mexico, Mexico |
| Parinya Chalermsook | University of Sheffield, UK |
| Yi-Jun Chang | National University of Singapore, Singapore |
| Xue Chen | University of Science and Technology of China, China |
| Yu Chen | National University of Singapore, Singapore |
| Rajesh Chitnis | University of Birmingham, UK |
| Bhaskar DasGupta | University of Illinois Chicago, USA |
| Pranjal Dutta | Nanyang Technological University, Singapore |
| Thomas Erlebach | Durham University, UK |
| Takuro Fukunaga | Chuo University, Japan |
| Serge Gaspers | University of New South Wales, Australia |
| Wing-Kai Hon | National Tsing Hua University, Taiwan |
| Zhiyi Huang | University of Hong Kong, China |
| Sanjay Jain | National University of Singapore, Singapore |
| Naonori Kakimura | Keio University, Japan |
| Mong-Jen Kao | National Chiao Tung University, Taiwan |
| Andreas Karrenbauer | Max-Planck Institute for Informatics, Germany |
| Ralf Klasing | CNRS and University of Bordeaux, France |
| Hung Le | University of Massachusetts Amherst, USA |
| Minming Li | City University of Hong Kong, China |
| Chung-Shou Liao | National Taiwan University, Taiwan |
| Markus Lohrey | University of Siegen, Germany |

| | |
|---|---|
| Alantha Newman | Université Grenoble Alpes, France |
| Alexandre Nolin | Télécom SudParis, France |
| Martin Nöllenburg | Technische Universität Wien, Austria |
| André Nusser | CNRS, France |
| Shreyas Pai | Indian Institute of Technology Madras, India |
| Pan Peng | University of Science and Technology of China, China |
| Youming Qiao | University of New South Wales, Australia |
| Saket Saurabh | Institute of Mathematical Sciences, India |
| Dominik Scheder | Chemnitz University of Technology, Germany |
| Daniel Štefankovič | University of Rochester, USA |
| Hanna Sumita | Institute of Science Tokyo, Japan |
| Xiaorui Sun | University of Illinois Chicago, USA |
| Csaba D. Tóth | California State University Northridge, USA |
| Ryuhei Uehara | JAIST, Japan |
| Victor Verdugo | Pontifical Catholic University of Chile, Chile |
| Haitao Wang | University of Utah, USA |
| Michał Włodarczyk | University of Warsaw, Poland |
| Prudence Wong | University of Liverpool, UK |
| Xiaowei Wu | University of Macau, China |
| Yitong Yin | Nanjing University, China |
| Sorrachai Yingchareonthawornchai | Institute for Theoretical Studies, ETH Zurich, Switzerland |
| Christos Zaroliagis | University of Patras, Greece |
| Meirav Zehavi | Ben Gurion University, Israel |

## Local Organizing Committee

| | |
|---|---|
| Xiaohui Bei | Nanyang Technological University, Singapore |
| Yi Li | Nanyang Technological University, Singapore |

## Additional Reviewers

Duncan Adamson
Kevin Kurien Alex
Abolfazl Asudeh
Alexey Barsukov
Mateusz Basiak
Jakob Baumann
Somnath Bhattacharjee
Jackson Bibbens
Lotte Blank
Markus Bläser
Jan Bok
Tiziana Calamoneri
Yixin Cao
Javier Cembrano

Phil Cervenjak
Dibyayan Chakraborty
Prabhat Chand
Jou-Ming Chang
Abhranil Chatterjee
Vincent Chau
Prasad Chaugule
Archit Chauhan
Li-Hsuan Chen
Yanyu Chen
Baolei Cheng
Tsz Chiu Kwok
Jacobus Conradi
Minati De
Sanjana Dey
Paula Navarrete Diaz
Krishnamoorthy Dinesh
Yangjing Dong
Yinhao Dong
Purna Dutta
Prateek Dwivedi
Dor Elimelech
Yiding Feng
Marek Filakovsky
Alexander Firbas
Vincent Froese
Ameet Gadekar
Harmender Gahlawat
Waldo Gálvez
Elaine Gan
Jeff Giliberti
Rahul Goraniya
Svenja Marie Griesbach
Manoj Gupta
Siddharth Gupta
Tesshu Hanaka
Tsubasa Harada
Ramesh Hariharasubramanian
Zhe Hou
Guan-Shieng Huang
Ling-Ju Hung
Ashwin Jacob
Jianhao Jia
Haitao Jiang
Shan Jiang
Kai Jin
Lawqueen Kanesh
Manish Kumar
Dongchen Li
Yinan Li
Zelin Li
Bingkai Lin
Chuang-Chieh Lin
Honghao Lin
Gang Liu
Hsiang-Hsuan Liu
Mingmou Liu
Diptapriyo Majumdar
Sudipta Mallik
Joan Carles Pons Mayol
Kurt Mehlhorn
Lili Mei
Krishna Menon
Pranabendu Misra
Sounak Modak
Kaushik Mondal
Saswata Mukherjee
Yuto Nakashima
Namrata
Frank Neumann
Aikaterini Niklanovits
George Osipov
René Peralta
Matthias Pfretzschner
Théo Pierron
Ashutosh Rai
Xiaobin Rui
Shay Sapir
Gokarna Sharma
Roohani Sharma
Ranran Shen
Nicholas Sieger
Manuel Sorge
Jack Stade
Moritz Stocker
Peter Strulo
Aditya Subramanian
Akira Suzuki
Asahi Takaoka

Yuma Tamura
Johannes Tantow
Agnieszka Tatarczuk
Anamay Tengse
Sergio Thoumi
Hector Tierno
Chhaya Trehan
Meng-Tsung Tsai
Che-Wei Tsao
Soroush Vahidi
Phanu Vajanopath
Vinayak Vinayak
Benyu Wang
Yuyang Wang
Zihe Wang
Wenhao Wu
Hangyu Xu
Jatin Yadav
Mingyang Yang
Peilin Yang
Mingquan Ye
Ryo Yoshinaka
Yixiao Yu
Chuanqi Zhang
Xiao Zhang
Yuhao Zhang
Jiahao Zhao
Mingnan Zhao
Yiming Zhao
Haisheng Zheng
Zihan Zhou

# Contents

# Bi-Perfect Graphs and the Approximability of Maximum Balanced Biclique

Parinya Chalermsook[1], Wanchote Jiamjitrak[2], Ly Orgo[3], and Minoo Zarsav[3](✉)

[1] The University of Sheffield, Sheffield, England
[2] University of Helsinki, Helsinki, Finland
[3] Aalto University, Espoo, Finland
minoo.zarsav@aalto.fi

**Abstract.** In the Maximum Balanced Biclique Problem (MBB), the input is a bipartite graph $G = (U \cup V, E)$, and the goal is to find a complete bipartite subgraph whose two sides have equal size and to maximize this size. The problem is NP-hard and hard to approximate within a factor of $n^{1-o(1)}$ under standard complexity assumptions.

We develop a structural framework for identifying tractable instances of MBB. Motivated by extremal combinatorics, we introduce a bipartite analogue of perfect graphs, which we call bi-perfect graphs. We show that every almost bi-perfect graph class admits a constant-factor estimation algorithm for MBB via a semidefinite programming relaxation.

Furthermore, we prove that (i) known bipartite analogues of perfect graph classes are almost bi-perfect, and (ii) several geometric bipartite graph classes satisfy non-trivial extremal bounds within our framework.

**Keywords:** Bipartite graph classes · Geometric intersection graphs · Maximum balanced biclique · Perfect graphs

## 1 Introduction

We study the *Maximum Balanced Biclique* problem. Given a bipartite graph $G = (U \cup V, E)$, the goal is to find a complete bipartite subgraph $K_{r,r}$ maximizing $r$. We denote by $\omega^{\otimes}(G)$ the maximum such $r$. MBB is among the classical NP-hard problems and exhibits strong hardness across multiple computational regimes, including approximation, parameterized, and fine-grained complexity [5,18,21,22]. Even in the approximation setting, the problem is hard within a factor of $n^{1-o(1)}$ under standard complexity assumptions. On the algorithmic side, the best known results yield only modest improvements over brute-force search [6]. Biclique is practically motivated by VLSI design and computational biology [1,10,24].

Given this landscape, a natural direction is to identify structured graph classes on which MBB becomes tractable or admits meaningful approximation guarantees. This perspective mirrors the development of algorithms for


Y. Li et al. (Eds.): COCOON 2026, LNCS 16835, pp. 1–14, 2027.
https://doi.org/10.1007/978-981-92-3309-0_1

the CLIQUE problem. While CLIQUE is intractable in general [14,27], it admits polynomial-time algorithms on perfect graphs and related structured classes, where structural equalities between clique number and chromatic number lead to efficient optimization via semidefinite programming.

### 1.1 Conceptual Contribution

We develop a structural framework for MBB inspired by this paradigm. The starting point is to reinterpret balanced bicliques through a relation on edges: two edges are considered related if the subgraph induced by their endpoints is a $K_{2,2}$. Under this viewpoint, a balanced biclique corresponds to a set of pairwise-related matching edges, allowing us to define analogues of clique, stable set, and coloring in bipartite graphs. A cross-coloring of $G$ is a partition of $E(G)$ into cross-stable classes

$$E(G) = E_1 \cup E_2 \cup \cdots \cup E_q.$$

The cross-chromatic number of $G$, denoted by $\chi^{\otimes}(G)$, is the minimum integer $q$ for which such a partition exists. Equivalently, $\chi^{\otimes}(G) = \chi(\mathcal{D}[G])$, where $\mathcal{D}[G]$ is the dependency graph whose vertices are the edges of $G$, and where two vertices of $\mathcal{D}[G]$ are adjacent exactly when the corresponding two edges of $G$ have endpoints that induce a $K_{2,2}$ in $G$. The balanced biclique number of $G$ is denoted by $\omega^{\otimes}(G)$. For example, if $G = K_{2,2}$ with bipartition $U = \{u_1, u_2\}$ and $V = \{v_1, v_2\}$, then $\omega^{\otimes}(G) = 2$. The two opposite edges $\{u_1, v_1\}$ and $\{u_2, v_2\}$ are related, since their endpoints induce the whole $K_{2,2}$, and therefore they cannot receive the same color. Similarly, the other pair of opposite edges cannot receive the same color. On the other hand, the partition

$$E_1 = \{\{u_1, v_1\}, \{u_1, v_2\}\}, \qquad E_2 = \{\{u_2, v_1\}, \{u_2, v_2\}\}$$

is a cross-coloring, since each color class consists of two adjacent edges. Hence $\chi^{\otimes}(K_{2,2}) = 2$.

This leads to the notion of bi-perfect graphs. To make the analogy precise, we consider subgraphs generated by edge sets. For an edge set $F \subseteq E(G)$, let $V(F)$ be the set of endpoints of the edges in $F$, and let $G_F := G[V(F)]$ be the subgraph of $G$ induced by these endpoints. A bipartite graph $G$ is bi-perfect if, for every $F \subseteq E(G)$, the maximum balanced biclique number of $G_F$ equals its cross-chromatic number, that is $\chi^{\otimes}(G_F) = \omega^{\otimes}(G_F)$. For example, if $F = \{\{u_1, v_1\}, \{u_2, v_2\}\}$, then $G_F$ is the subgraph induced by the four vertices $\{u_1, u_2, v_1, v_2\}$. If the two cross edges $\{u_1, v_2\}$ and $\{u_2, v_1\}$ are also present in $G$, then $G_F$ is a $K_{2,2}$; otherwise, $G_F$ is the corresponding induced subgraph on these four vertices.

Our main conceptual result establishes that bi-imperfection governs the approximability of MBB.

**Theorem 1 (Informal).** *Let $\mathcal{G}$ be a class of bipartite graphs. If $\mathsf{bim}(G) \leq g(|V(G)|)$ for all $G \in \mathcal{G}$, then MBB admits an $O(g(n))$-approximation algorithm on $\mathcal{G}$ via semidefinite programming.*

In particular, every graph class with bounded bi-imperfection will admit a constant-factor approximation for MBB. The algorithmic connection closely parallels the classical relationship between perfect graphs and LovászâĂŹs theta function, and extends to weighted variants of related extremal parameters.

### 1.2 Our Coloring Results

We next investigate the bi-imperfection of natural bipartite graph classes. Many classical perfect graph classes admit bipartite analogues (e.g., chordal bigraphs, interval bigraphs, permutation bigraphs). Our first collection of results shows that several such analogues are almost bi-perfect.

**Theorem 2.** *For every chordal bigraph $G$, we have $\chi^{\otimes}(G) \leq 2\,\omega^{\otimes}(G)$.*

Since chordal bigraphs subsume interval and permutation bigraphs, the same bound holds for these classes. Moreover, the factor 2 is tight. These results establish that a broad family of bipartite analogues of perfect graphs admit constant bi-imperfection.

We further consider geometric bipartite graph classes that are not perfect in the classical sense but are known to exhibit near-perfect behavior. Our main geometric result concerns grid intersection graphs (GIGs), the bipartite analogue of rectangle intersection graphs.

**Theorem 3.** *For every grid intersection graph $G$, we have $\chi^{\otimes}(G) \leq 6912\,\omega^{\otimes}(G)$.*

This result is particularly interesting in light of the classical open problem of bounding $\chi$ in terms of $\omega$ for rectangle graphs, posed in 1960 by Asplund and Grünbaum and only recently seeing progress [8]. The above theorem may be viewed as a bipartite analogue of this long-standing question.

### 1.3 Overview of Techniques

The most nontrivial content in this paper is the proof of Theorem 3, whose technical ingredients can be used to derive the coloring results for other graph classes as well. We give an overview of this proof, highlighting the new conceptual and technical ideas.

One of the widely used coloring arguments relies on the concept of graph degeneracy. A graph $G$ is $d$-degenerate if every induced subgraph contains a vertex of degree at most $d$. It is easy to see that $d$-degenerate graphs are $(d+1)$-colorable: Produce a **degeneracy ordering** by taking the vertex $v \in V(G)$ of minimum degree, put it last in the ordering, and recurse. Let $v_1 v_2 \ldots v_n$ be the resulting ordering of vertices. The graph can then be colored greedily based on this vertex ordering: For each $i = 1, \ldots, n$, when we consider vertex $v_i$, use a color in $[d+1]$ that has not been used by any of the neighbors $N_G(v_i)$ that precede $v_i$. This greedy coloring works if and only if the graph admits a $d$-degeneracy ordering.

Recently, the graph classes considered in this paper have been shown to be $O(1)$-degenerate [4], so a natural attempt is to use degeneracy properties to derive the upper bounds on $\chi^{\otimes}(G)$. However, our coloring problem seems very different in nature from classical vertex coloring, and graph degeneracy does not suffice for obtaining a strong coloring result in our context.

We introduce a strengthened property of graph degeneracy, which we call **double-degeneracy**, that is suitably and naturally defined for working with bipartite graphs. A graph being $d$-doubly-degenerate admits an ordering of vertices with a nice property, and would ensure that our natural greedy coloring works for our coloring problem. The idea is similar to coloring degenerate graphs: the notion of double degeneracy captures the case in which our greedy algorithm succeeds.

Next, we provide a recipe for proving that an intersection bigraph is doubly degenerate. To this end, we define the notion of **proximity**, which roughly captures the complexity of geometric objects in the intersection bigraph. Intuitively, intervals and 2D segments have low average proximity. We prove that a degenerate graph (with degeneracy $d$) with low average proximity (with parameter $p$) must be $O(pd)$-doubly-degenerate. Therefore, in order to prove that $\chi^{\otimes}(G) \leq O(\omega^{\otimes}(G))$ for all $G$ in graph class $\mathcal{C}$, it suffices to argue that (i) the graph class $\mathcal{C}$ is $O(\omega^{\otimes})$-degenerate and (ii) $\mathcal{C}$ has $O(1)$ average proximity. This illustrates a new application of upper bounding Zarankiewicz numbers of intersection bigraphs.[1]

We hope that our new notions will find further applications to other graph classes (e.g., those whose Zarankiewicz numbers have been bounded [9,11,15]) as well as to other (edge) coloring problems in bipartite graphs.

### 1.4 Further Related Work

Structured instances of biclique have received attention before [1,2,25], but we are not aware of a systematic attempt to understand their tractability.

The graph classes in this paper have received significant attention, including recognition algorithms, optimization, and structures. For instance, chordal bipartite graphs have been considered in [20,23,26]. GIG is known to capture planar bipartite graphs [13] and is equivalent to the intersection graph of rectangles that are bipartite [3].

## 2 Preliminaries

We use the standard notation of the bipartite graphs as $G = (U \cup V, E)$ where $U$ and $V$ are partitions of vertices. For a graph $G$, we refer to its set of vertices as $V(G)$, its set of edges as $E(G)$, and its induced subgraph on $S \subseteq V(G)$ as $G[S]$. For an edge set $F \subseteq E(G)$, let $G[F]$ denote the subgraph induced by the endpoints of edges in $F$. We write $\omega^{\otimes}(G)$ for the maximum integer $k$ such that $K_{k,k} \subseteq G$.

[1] Zarankiewicz numbers relate the number of edges in a graph to its maximum balanced biclique number.

*Intersection Bigraphs:* An intersection bigraph $G = (U \cup V, E)$ is defined by two families of geometric objects $\mathcal{F}_U$ and $\mathcal{F}_V$ where each vertex $u \in U$ (resp. $v \in V$) is associated with an object $O_u \in \mathcal{F}_U$ (resp. $O_v \in \mathcal{F}_V$); an edge $\{u, v\} \in E$ if and only if $O_u \cap O_v \neq \emptyset$. A containment bigraph can be defined similarly, except that we have $\{u, v\} \in E$ if and only if $O_u \subseteq O_v$.

Let $\phi : u \mapsto O_u, v \mapsto O_v$ for $u \in U$ and $v \in V$ be the bijection between vertices and their representations. We say that $(\mathcal{F}_U, \mathcal{F}_V, \phi)$ is an **intersection or containment representation** of $G$. Whenever the mapping $\phi$ is clear from the context, we omit it.

*Freeable Matrix:* Let $P \in \{0, 1, *\}^{r \times c}$ be a pattern. A matrix $M$ *matches* $P$ if for all $i \in [r]$ and $j \in [c]$, we have $P_{ij} = *$ or $M_{ij} = P_{ij}$. A matrix $M$ *contains* $P$ if some submatrix of $M$ matches $P$. We say $M$ is **$P$-free** if and only if it contains no submatrix matching $P$. A bipartite graph $G$ is **$P$-freeable** if there exists a biadjacency matrix of $G$ (i.e., some ordering of its bipartition) that is $P$-free.

*Graph Classes:* A graph is *chordal* if every cycle of length at least 4 has a chord. *Chordal bigraphs* are bigraphs in which every cycle of length at least 6 has a chord. A bipartite graph $G$ is chordal if and only if it is $\left(\begin{smallmatrix} 0 & 1 \\ 1 & 1 \end{smallmatrix}\right)$-freeable [16].

A *grid intersection graph (GIG)* is defined as an intersection bigraph of $\mathcal{F}_U$ and $\mathcal{F}_V$ where the families $\mathcal{F}_U$ and $\mathcal{F}_V$ are horizontal and vertical segments, respectively. We also consider a containment bigraph of bottomless rectangles and segments. We will use this graph class as a warm-up proof for GIG.

## 2.1 Bi-Perfect Graphs

We denote by $\omega^{\otimes}(G)$ the *balanced biclique number* of a bipartite graph $G$, i.e., the largest integer $k$ such that $K_{k,k} \subseteq G$.

When $\omega^{\otimes}(G) = 1$, the graph $G$ contains no copy of $K_{2,2}$ (equivalently, no induced $C_4$). [2]

**An Analogue of Cliques.** We next reformulate balanced bicliques in an edge-based language. For two edges $e, e' \in E(G)$, we write $e \bowtie e'$ if the subgraph induced by their endpoints is a $K_{2,2}$, that is, if $G[e \cup e']$ is a $K_{2,2}$.

A balanced biclique $K_{k,k}$ contains a matching $\{e_1, \ldots, e_k\}$ such that $e_i \bowtie e_j$ for all distinct $i, j$. Conversely, any matching whose edges are pairwise related by $\bowtie$ necessarily induces a balanced biclique. In other words, we are working with a matching representation of a biclique. Thus, balanced bicliques can be viewed as "cliques" in this edge-based language; see Fig. 1.

**An Analogue of Stable Sets.** Given the relation $\bowtie$, the analogue of stable sets is immediate. A set of edges $F = \{e_1, \ldots, e_q\} \subseteq E(G)$ is called *cross-stable* if no two edges in $F$ satisfy $e_i \bowtie e_j$. We denote by $\alpha^{\otimes}(G)$ the maximum size of a cross-stable edge set in $G$.

[2] The classical Zarankiewicz problem seeks to upper bound the number of edges in cross-stable graphs [17].

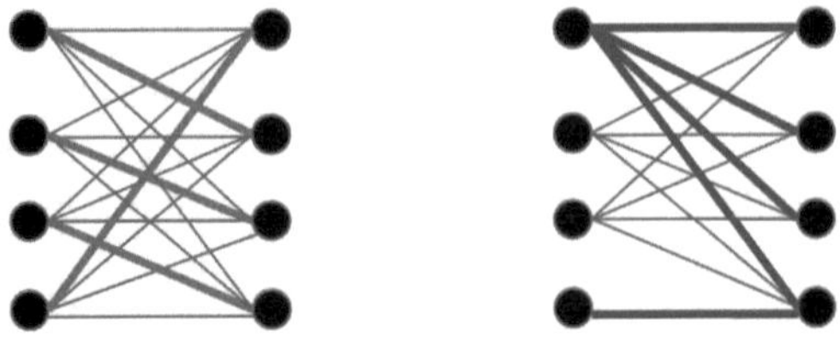

**Fig. 1.** Left: A matching representation of a biclique (red). Right: A cross-stable set (blue) in a graph. (Color figure online)

**An Analogue of Chromatic Number.** A cross-coloring of $G$ is a partition of $E(G)$ into cross-stable classes $E(G) = E_1 \cup E_2 \cup \cdots \cup E_q$. The cross-chromatic number of $G$, denoted by $\chi^{\otimes}(G)$, is the minimum integer $q$ for which such a cross-coloring exists. Equivalently, $\chi^{\otimes}(G) = \chi(\mathcal{D}[G])$, where $\mathcal{D}[G]$ is the dependency graph whose vertices are the edges of $G$ and where adjacency corresponds to $\bowtie$. It is easy to see $\chi^{\otimes}(G) \geq \omega^{\otimes}(G)$. Indeed, if $H$ is a balanced biclique $K_{r,r}$ in $G$, then $H$ contains a perfect matching $M$ of size $r$ such that every two distinct edges of $M$ satisfy $\bowtie$. Hence, each cross-stable color class contains at most one edge of $M$, implying that at least $r$ colors are necessary.

**An Analogue of Perfect Graphs.** For an edge set $F \subseteq E(G)$, let $V(F)$ denote the set of endpoints of the edges in $F$, and let $G_F := G[V(F)]$. We say that $G$ is bi-perfect if, for every $F \subseteq E(G)$, we have $\chi^{\otimes}(G_F) = \omega^{\otimes}(G_F)$. It is easy to verify that bicliques are bi-perfect.

**Proposition 1.** *Every biclique is bi-perfect.*

*Proof.* Notice that an induced subgraph of a biclique on any edge set is a biclique, so we only need to prove that $\chi^{\otimes}(G) = \omega^{\otimes}(G)$ for every biclique $G$. Let $G = (U \cup V, E)$ be a biclique with $|U| < |V|$, so this implies that $|U| = \omega^{\otimes}(G)$. We partition the edges $E$ into $\{E_u\}_{u \in U}$ where $E_u$ contains all the edges incident to $u$. Notice that each set $E_u$ is cross-stable in $G$. This implies that $\chi^{\otimes}(G) \leq |U|$.

**Definition 1.** *The bi-imperfection of a bipartite graph $G$ is*

$$\mathsf{bim}(G) = \max_{F \subseteq E(G)} \frac{\chi^{\otimes}(G_F)}{\omega^{\otimes}(G_F)}$$

A class of graphs $\mathcal{G}$ is said to be bi-perfect if every $G \in \mathcal{G}$ is bi-perfect. It is *almost bi-perfect* if there is a constant $C_0$ such that $\mathsf{bim}(G) \leq C_0$ for all $G \in \mathcal{G}$. More generally, we say that a function $g$ is an (imperfection) upper-bounding for a graph class $\mathcal{G}$ if $\mathsf{bim}(G) \leq g(|V(G)|)$ for all $G \in \mathcal{G}$.

The following proposition connects bi-perfect graphs to estimation algorithms for MBB:

**Proposition 2.** *Let $\mathcal{G}$ be a graph class and let $g$ be an imperfection upper-bounding function for $\mathcal{G}$. Then there exists an $O(g(n))$-estimation algorithm for MBB on graphs $G \in \mathcal{G}$, where $n = |V(G)|$.*

The proof closely follows the connection between perfect graphs and Lovász Theta [12,19]. The full proof is deferred to the full version. A similar algorithmic implication holds for $\alpha^{\otimes}$.

**Proposition 3.** *Let $\mathcal{G}$ be a class of bipartite graphs closed under the biclique replacement operation. If $g$ is an imperfection upper-bounding function for $\mathcal{G}$, then there exists an $O(g(n))$-estimation algorithm for the maximum-weight cross-stable subset problem on graphs $G \in \mathcal{G}$, where $n = |V(G)|$.*

The proof of Proposition 3 closely follows [7].

## 3 Double-Degeneracy Coloring: Structure and Algorithms

Fix a bipartite graph class $\mathcal{C}$, and let $G = (U \cup V, E) \in \mathcal{C}$. We introduce a proximity notion that controls how pairs of vertices can be simultaneously "covered" by adding a new vertex while remaining inside $\mathcal{C}$.

*t-coverage.* For $u, u' \in U$ and an integer $t \geq 2$, we say that $u$ and $u'$ are *$t$-covered* if there exists a set $S \subseteq U$ with $|S| = t$ and $\{u, u'\} \subseteq S$, together with a vertex $v^*$ such that the graph

$$G^* = \big(U \cup V \cup \{v^*\},\ E \cup \{\{v^*, x\} : x \in S\}\big)$$

still belongs to $\mathcal{C}$. We call $v^*$ a *witness* for the $t$-coverage of $u$ and $u'$. The definition is symmetric for pairs of vertices in $V$. See Fig. 2.

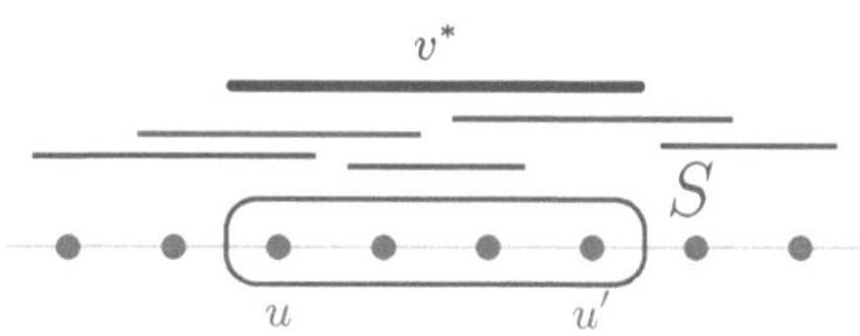


**Fig. 2.** By adding a new segment $v^*$, we have a new graph that belongs to the class of segments and points containment. In this case, the interval representation of $v^*$ must cover all the points between $u$ and $u'$, and therefore the minimum cover for them must have size at least 4.

### 3.1 Proximity

For $u, u' \in U$, define the *proximity* $\mathsf{prox}(u, u')$ as the minimum integer $t$ such that $u$ and $u'$ are $(t + 1)$-covered. For $t \in \mathbb{N}$, let

$$P_t = \{\{u, u'\} \subseteq U : \mathsf{prox}(u, u') \leq t\}$$

be the set of pairs with proximity at most $t$.

**Definition 2 (Average proximity).** *A vertex set* $W \subseteq U$ *has* factor-$\alpha$ average proximity *if for all* $t \in \mathbb{N}$,

$$|P_t| \leq \alpha |W| t.$$

*A graph class* $\mathcal{C}$ *has* $\alpha$-bounded proximity *if in every graph* $G = (U \cup V, E) \in \mathcal{C}$, *both sides* $U$ *and* $V$ *satisfy factor-*$\alpha$ *average proximity.*

**Proximity in Bottomless Rectangle–Segment Containment Graphs.** Let $G = (U \cup V, E)$ be a bipartite graph admitting a bottomless rectangle–segment containment representation $(\mathcal{B}, \mathcal{S}, \phi)$, where $\mathcal{B}$ is a family of bottomless rectangles, $\mathcal{S}$ is a family of horizontal segments, and $\phi$ maps each vertex to its corresponding geometric object. See Fig. 3.

For each segment $\sigma \in \mathcal{S}$, let $\sigma.y$ denote its $y$-coordinate and let $\sigma.x = [\sigma.\ell, \sigma.r]$ be its projection onto the $x$-axis, with endpoints $\sigma.\ell < \sigma.r$.

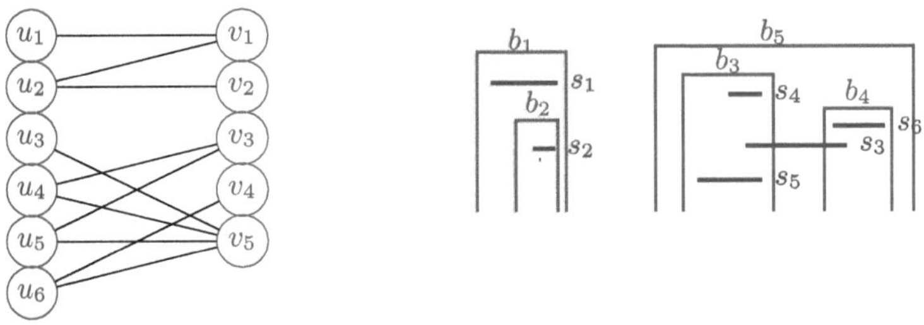


**Fig. 3.** The right-hand side is the bottomless rectangle and segment containment representation of the bipartite graph on the left.

**Lemma 1.** *Every bottomless rectangle–segment containment graph* $G = (U \cup V, E)$ *has factor-3 average proximity on the segment side* $V$.

*Proof (Proof sketch).* Fix $t \in \mathbb{N}$ and count all pairs of segments $\{\sigma, \sigma'\}$ with $\mathsf{prox}(\sigma, \sigma')$ at most $t$. If $\sigma.x$ contains $\sigma'.x$, then for each $\sigma$ only the $t$ lowest such segments can have proximity at most $t$, contributing at most $|\mathcal{S}|t$ pairs. Otherwise, the projections cross; the corresponding proximity graph on $\mathcal{S}$ is $2t$-degenerate, giving at most $2|\mathcal{S}|t$ additional pairs. Hence $|P_t| \leq 3|\mathcal{S}|t$, proving factor-3 average proximity on $V$. The full proof is deferred to the full version.

**Lemma 2.** *Let* $G = (U \cup V, E)$ *admit a bottomless rectangle–segment containment representation* $(\mathcal{S}, \mathcal{B}, \phi)$ *with* $\phi(U) \subseteq \mathcal{B}$ *and* $\phi(V) \subseteq \mathcal{S}$. *Then* $G$ *also admits a bottomless rectangle–segment containment representation* $(\mathcal{S}', \mathcal{B}', \phi')$ *such that* $\phi'(U) \subseteq \mathcal{S}'$ *and* $\phi'(V) \subseteq \mathcal{B}'$.

*Proof.* This follows from the construction in [4, Appendix C].

**Corollary 1.** *Let* $G = (U \cup V, E)$ *be a bottomless rectangle–segment containment graph. Then both* $U$ *and* $V$ *have factor-3 average proximity.*

*Proof.* By Lemma 1, the segment side has factor-3 average proximity, and by Lemma 2, $G$ also admits a representation in which the roles of $U$ and $V$ are exchanged, so the same argument applies to the other side.

**Proximity in Grid Intersection Graphs.** Let $G = (U \cup V, E)$ be a GIG graph with an intersection representation $(\mathbf{X}, \boldsymbol{\Upsilon}, \phi)$, where $\mathbf{X}$ is a set of horizontal segments and $\boldsymbol{\Upsilon}$ is a set of vertical segments in $\mathbb{R}^2$.

For a horizontal segment $\chi \in \mathbf{X}$, let $\chi.y$ denote its $y$-coordinate and let $\chi.x = [\chi.\ell, \chi.r]$ be its projection onto the $x$-axis. We bound the average proximity on the horizontal side $\mathbf{X}$ via a counting argument. Fix $t \in \mathbb{N}$ and consider pairs of horizontal segments $\{\chi, \chi'\}$ with $\mathsf{prox}(\chi, \chi') \leq t$. Such a pair can only occur if $\chi$ and $\chi'$ can be simultaneously intersected by a vertical segment while crossing at most $t$ intermediate horizontals. This implies that, for each endpoint $\chi.\ell$ or $\chi.r$, only the $t$ nearest horizontal segments above and below $\chi$ can participate in a proximity-$t$ pair. Consequently, the number of pairs with proximity at most $t$ is $O(|\mathbf{X}|t)$. We state this formally below.

**Lemma 3.** *Let $G = (U \cup V, E)$ be a* GIG *graph with an intersection representation $(\mathbf{X}, \boldsymbol{\Upsilon}, \phi)$. Then $G$ has factor-8 average proximity on the horizontal side $\mathbf{X}$.*

*Proof (Proof sketch).* Fix $t \in \mathbb{N}$. If $\mathsf{prox}(\chi, \chi') \leq t$, then $\chi$ and $\chi'$ can be intersected by a vertical witness segment meeting at most $t+1$ horizontal segments in total. Such a witness can be assumed to pass through an endpoint of one of the two segments.

For a fixed segment $\chi$ and an endpoint $p \in \{\chi.\ell, \chi.r\}$, only the $t$ closest horizontals above $\chi$ and the $t$ closest below $\chi$ crossing the vertical line $x = p$ can form such a pair. Thus, each endpoint participates in at most $2t$ proximity-$t$ pairs. Summing over both endpoints of all $\chi \in \mathbf{X}$ yields at most $8|\mathbf{X}|t$ pairs. The full proof is deferred to the full version.

By symmetry, the same bound holds on the vertical side $\boldsymbol{\Upsilon}$.

**Corollary 2.** *Every grid intersection graph has factor-8 average proximity on both partitions.*

## 3.2 Double Degeneracy Concept

An ordering of the vertices of an $n$-vertex graph $G$ is a bijection $\sigma : V(G) \to [n]$. The rank of a vertex $v$ is $\sigma(v)$. For $v \in V(G)$, define

$$N^{\sigma}_{<}(v) = \{w \in N(v) : \sigma(w) < \sigma(v)\} \text{ and } N^{\sigma}_{>}(v) = \{w \in N(v) : \sigma(w) > \sigma(v)\}.$$

When the ordering is clear from the context, we write $N_{<}(v)$ and $N_{>}(v)$.

**Definition 3.** *An ordering $\sigma$ is a $d$-*degeneracy ordering *if for every $v \in V(G)$ we have $|N_{<}(v)| \leq d$.*

We now introduce the notion of double degeneracy. Let $G = (U \cup V, E)$ be a bipartite graph. For $u \in U$, let $N^*(u)$ be the set of vertices $u' \in U$ such that

1. $\sigma(u') < \sigma(u)$, and

2. there exists a vertex $v \in N_>(u) \cap N_>(u')$.

The definition is symmetric for vertices in $V$.

**Definition 4.** *An ordering $\sigma$ is a $d$-*double-degeneracy ordering *if for every $w \in V(G)$ we have $|N^*(w)| \leq d$.*

The next lemma shows that double degeneracy is a stronger requirement than ordinary degeneracy.

**Lemma 4.** *If a bipartite graph admits a $d$-double-degeneracy ordering, then it is $(d+1)$-degenerate.*

*Proof.* Let $\sigma$ be a $d$-double-degeneracy ordering. We claim that $\sigma$ is also a $(d+1)$-degeneracy ordering. Fix any vertex $w \in V(G)$ and let $w^*$ be the vertex of maximum rank in $N_<(w)$. Then every vertex in $N_<(w) \setminus \{w^*\}$ lies in $N^*(w^*)$: indeed, it has smaller rank than $w^*$ and shares the common higher-ranked neighbor $w$ with $w^*$.

Since $|N^*(w^*)| \leq d$, we obtain

$$|N_<(w)| \leq |N^*(w^*)| + 1 \leq d + 1,$$

as required.

**Lemma 5.** *Let $\mathcal{C}$ be an intersection bigraph class that has factor $p$ proximity and is $d$-degenerate. Then every graph in $\mathcal{C}$ admits a $16pd$-double-degeneracy ordering.*

*Proof.* Let $G \in \mathcal{C}$ with $n = |V(G)|$. We construct an ordering $\sigma$ iteratively from last to first. In iteration $i$, let $G_i$ be the subgraph induced by the vertices not yet assigned a rank.

Since $G_i$ is $d$-degenerate, its average degree is at most $2d$, and by Markov's inequality, at least half of its vertices have degree at most $4d$.

On the other hand, factor-$p$ proximity implies that for every $t \in \mathbb{N}$, $|\mathcal{P}_t| \leq pt\,|V(G_i)|$. Set $t = 4d$. Then the total participation in $\mathcal{P}_t$ is at most $2|\mathcal{P}_t| \leq 2pt\,|V(G_i)| = 8pd\,|V(G_i)|$. By averaging, at least half of the vertices of $G_i$ participate in at most $16pd$ pairs of $\mathcal{P}_t$.

Therefore, there exists a vertex $w \in V(G_i)$ such that

1. $\deg_{G_i}(w) \leq 4d$, and
2. $w$ belongs to at most $16pd$ pairs $\{w, w'\} \in \mathcal{P}_t$.

Assign $w$ the next highest rank in $\sigma$.

Let $\mathcal{P}_{t,w}$ denote the set of pairs $\{w, w'\} \in \mathcal{P}_t$. We claim that $|N^*(w)| \leq |\mathcal{P}_{t,w}|$, which yields $|N^*(w)| \leq 16pd$.

Indeed, if $w' \in N^*(w)$, then $w$ and $w'$ share a common neighbor

$$v \in N_>(w) \cap N_>(w')$$

whose rank has already been assigned. When $v$ was selected, it had degree at most $t = 4d$, so $v$ witnesses a $t$-cover of $\{w, w'\}$. Thus $\{w, w'\} \in \mathcal{P}_{t,w}$. Therefore, every vertex in $N^*(w)$ corresponds to a distinct pair in $\mathcal{P}_{t,w}$, proving the claim.

Thus, the resulting ordering $\sigma$ satisfies

$$|N^*(w)| \leq 16pd$$

for every vertex $w$. Hence, $\sigma$ is a $16pd$-double-degeneracy ordering.

**Theorem 4.** *Let $G = (U \cup V, E)$ be a bottomless rectangle–segment containment graph, and let $k = \omega^{\otimes}(G)$. Then $G$ admits an $864k$-double-degeneracy ordering.*

*Proof.* By [4, Theorem 18], every such graph satisfies

$$|E(G)| \leq (3|U| + 6\,V|)k \leq 6(|U| + |V|)k = 6\,V(G)|k.$$

Hence the average degree of $G$ is at most

$$\frac{2|E(G)|}{|V(G)|} \leq 12k.$$

In particular, $G$ is $d$-degenerate for some $d \leq 12k$; certainly, we may use the weaker bound $d \leq 18k$.

Moreover, Lemma 1 shows that this class has factor-$p$ average proximity with $p = 3$. Applying Lemma 5 yields a

$$16pd \leq 16 \cdot 3 \cdot 18k = 864k$$

double-degeneracy ordering.

**Theorem 5.** *Let $G = (U \cup V, E)$ be a grid intersection graph, and let $k = \omega^{\otimes}(G)$. Then $G$ admits a $3456k$-double-degeneracy ordering.*

*Proof.* By [4, Observation 20], every GIG graph with $\omega^{\otimes}(G) \leq k$ contains a vertex of degree at most $27(k-1)$. Since every induced subgraph of a grid intersection graph is again a grid intersection graph, and every induced subgraph $H$ of $G$ satisfies $\omega^{\otimes}(H) \leq \omega^{\otimes}(G) \leq k$, it follows that every induced subgraph of $G$ contains a vertex of degree at most $27(k-1)$. Therefore $G$ is $d$-degenerate for

$$d \leq 27(k-1) \leq 27k.$$

Furthermore, Corollary 2 gives factor-$p$ proximity with $p = 8$. Applying Lemma 5 gives a

$$16pd \leq 16 \cdot 8 \cdot 27k = 3456k$$

double-degeneracy ordering.

### 3.3 The Greedy Algorithm

**Theorem 6.** *If a bipartite graph $G = (U \cup V, E)$ admits a d-double-degeneracy ordering $\sigma$, then $\chi^{\otimes}(G) \leq 2d$.*

*Proof.* Let $w_1, \ldots, w_n$ be the vertices in the order given by $\sigma$. We construct a cross-coloring of $E(G)$ using at most $2d$ colors.

Assign each vertex $w_i$ a color from a palette of $2d$ colors so that no color is used by more than $d-1$ vertices in $N^*(w_i)$. This is always possible since $|N^*(w_i)| \leq d$.

Now color every edge $\{w_i, w_j\}$ with $j < i$ by the color of its earlier endpoint $w_j$. Thus, every edge receives exactly one color.

It remains to check that each color class is cross-stable. Suppose two conflicting edges receive the same color. Then they are colored by two distinct vertices $x$ and $y$ on the same side of the bipartition, and there exists a later vertex $z$ adjacent to both $x$ and $y$. Without loss of generality, assume $x$ appears before $y$ in $\sigma$. Then $x \in N^*(y)$, contradicting the choice of colors for vertices in $N^*(y)$. Hence, no conflicting edges share a color, and we obtain a valid cross-coloring with at most $2d$ colors.

The following corollaries follow from Theorems 4 and 5.

**Corollary 3.** *If G is a bottomless rectangle–segment containment graph, then*

$$\chi^{\otimes}(G) \leq 1728\,\omega^{\otimes}(G).$$

**Corollary 4.** *If G is a grid intersection graph, then $\chi^{\otimes}(G) \leq 6912\,\omega^{\otimes}(G)$.*

## 4 Chordal Bipartite Graphs

We prove Theorem 2 for chordal bipartite graphs.

**Theorem 7.** *A bipartite graph $G = (U \cup V, E)$ is chordal bipartite if and only if both U and V admit orderings such that every prefix neighborhood induces a chain graph.*

*Proof (Proof sketch).* This follows from the forbidden submatrix characterization of chordal bipartite graphs and the fact that removing the last row/column yields a chain graph. Full details are deferred to the full version.

**Theorem 8.** *If G is chordal bipartite, then*

$$\chi^{\otimes}(G) \leq 2\,\omega^{\otimes}(G).$$

*Proof (Proof sketch).* Using the partitional orderings from Theorem 7, each induced chain subgraph can be optimally cross-colored by coloring one side and extending to the incident edges. Applying this procedure on both partitions yields a $2k$ cross-coloring, where $k = \omega^{\otimes}(G)$. The full proof is deferred to the full version.

## References


1. Arbib, C., Mosca, R., et al.: Polynomial algorithms for special cases of the balanced bipartite subgraph problem. JCMCC J. Comb. Math. Comb. Comput. **30**, 3–22 (1999)
2. Atminas, A., Lozin, V.V., Razgon, I.: Linear time algorithm for computing a small biclique in graphs without long induced paths. In: Fomin, F.V., Kaski, P. (eds.) SWAT 2012. LNCS, vol. 7357, pp. 142–152. Springer, Heidelberg (2012). https://doi.org/10.1007/978-3-642-31155-0_13
3. Bellantoni, S., Hartman, I.B.A., Przytycka, T., Whitesides, S.: Grid intersection graphs and boxicity. Discret. Math. **114**(1–3), 41–49 (1993)
4. Chalermsook, P., Orgo, L., Zarsav, M.: On geometric bipartite graphs with asymptotically smallest zarankiewicz numbers. In: Proceedings of the 33rd International Symposium on Graph Drawing and Network Visualization (GD 2025) (2025, to appear)
5. Chalermsook, P., et al.: From gap-eth to FPT-inapproximability: clique, dominating set, and more. In: 2017 IEEE 58th Annual Symposium on Foundations of Computer Science (FOCS), pp. 743–754. IEEE (2017)
6. Chalermsook, P., Jiamjitrak, W.P., Orgo, L.: On finding balanced bicliques via matchings. In: Adler, I., Müller, H. (eds.) WG 2020. LNCS, vol. 12301, pp. 238–247. Springer, Cham (2020). https://doi.org/10.1007/978-3-030-60440-0_19
7. Chalermsook, P., Vaz, D.: A note on fractional coloring and the integrality gap of LP for maximum weight independent set. Electron. Notes Discret. Math. **55**, 113–116 (2016)
8. Chalermsook, P., Walczak, B.: Coloring and maximum weight independent set of rectangles. In: Proceedings of the 2021 ACM-SIAM Symposium on Discrete Algorithms (SODA), pp. 860–868. SIAM (2021)
9. Chan, T.M., Keller, C., Smorodinsky, S.: On Zarankiewicz's problem for intersection hypergraphs of geometric objects. In: Aichholzer, O., Wang, H. (eds.) 41st International Symposium on Computational Geometry, SoCG 2025, 23–27 June 2025, Kanazawa, Japan. LIPIcs, vol. 332, pp. 33:1–33:14. Schloss Dagstuhl - Leibniz-Zentrum für Informatik (2025). https://doi.org/10.4230/LIPIcs.SoCG.2025.33
10. Cheng, Y., Church, G.M.: Biclustering of expression data. In: ISMB, vol. 8, pp. 93–103 (2000)
11. Fox, J., Pach, J., Sheffer, A., Suk, A., Zahl, J.: A semi-algebraic version of Zarankiewicz's problem. J. Eur. Math. Soc. **19**(6), 1785–1810 (2017). https://doi.org/10.4171/JEMS/705
12. Grötschel, M., Lovász, L., Schrijver, A.: Geometric Algorithms and Combinatorial Optimization, vol. 2. Springer (2012)
13. Hartman, I.B.-A., Newman, I., Ziv, R.: On grid intersection graphs. Discret. Math. **87**(1), 41–52 (1991)
14. Håstad, J.: Clique is hard to approximate within $n^{1-\varepsilon}$. In: Proceedings of the 37th Annual Symposium on Foundations of Computer Science, pp. 627–636. IEEE (1996)
15. Keller, C., Smorodinsky, S.: Zarankiewicz's problem via $\epsilon$-t-nets. In: Mulzer, W., Phillips, J.M. (eds.) 40th International Symposium on Computational Geometry, SoCG 2024, 11–14 June 2024, Athens, Greece. LIPIcs, vol. 293, pp. 66:1–66:15. Schloss Dagstuhl - Leibniz-Zentrum für Informatik (2024). https://doi.org/10.4230/LIPIcs.SoCG.2024.66

16. Klinz, B., Rudolf, R., Woeginger, G.J.: Permuting matrices to avoid forbidden submatrices. Discret. Appl. Math. **60**(1–3), 223–248 (1995)
17. Kővári, T., Sós, V.T., Turán, P.: On a problem of K. Zarankiewicz. Colloq. Math. **3**, 50–57 (1954). http://eudml.org/doc/210011
18. Lin, B.: The parameterized complexity of the k-biclique problem. J. ACM (JACM) **65**(5), 1–23 (2018)
19. Lovász, L.: On the Shannon capacity of a graph. IEEE Trans. Inf. Theory **25**(1), 1–7 (1979)
20. Lubiw, A.: Doubly lexical orderings of matrices. In: Proceedings of the Seventeenth Annual ACM Symposium on Theory of Computing, pp. 396–404 (1985)
21. Manurangsi, P.: Inapproximability of maximum biclique problems, minimum k-cut and densest at-least-k-subgraph from the small set expansion hypothesis. Algorithms **11**(1) (2018). http://www.mdpi.com/1999-4893/11/1/10. https://doi.org/10.3390/a11010010
22. Manurangsi, P., Rubinstein, A., Schramm, T.: The strongish planted clique hypothesis and its consequences. In: ITCS (2021)
23. Müller, H., Brandstädt, A.: The NP-completeness of Steiner tree and dominating set for chordal bipartite graphs. Theoret. Comput. Sci. **53**(2–3), 257–265 (1987)
24. Ravi, S.S., Lloyd, E.L.: The complexity of near-optimal programmable logic array folding. SIAM J. Comput. **17**(4), 696–710 (1988)
25. Shrestha, A.M.S., Tayu, S., Ueno, S.: On orthogonal ray graphs. Discret. Appl. Math. **158**(15), 1650–1659 (2010)
26. Uehara, R.: Linear time algorithms on chordal bipartite and strongly chordal graphs. In: International Colloquium on Automata, Languages, and Programming, pp. 993–1004. Springer (2002)
27. Zuckerman, D.: Linear degree extractors and the inapproximability of max clique and chromatic number. In: Proceedings of the Thirty-Eighth Annual ACM Symposium on Theory of Computing, pp. 681–690 (2006)

# Single-Shuffle Full-Open Card-Based Secure Computation Protocols for Any Function

Reo Eriguchi[1(✉)] and Kazumasa Shinagawa[1,2,3]

[1] National Institute of Advanced Industrial Science and Technology, Tokyo, Japan
eriguchi-reo@aist.go.jp
[2] University of Tsukuba, Ibaraki, Japan
shinagawa@cs.tsukuba.ac.jp
[3] Kyushu University, Fukuoka, Japan

**Abstract.** A card-based secure computation protocol is a method for $n$ parties to compute a function $f$ on their private inputs $(x_1, \ldots, x_n)$ using physical playing cards, in such a way that the suits of revealed cards leak no information beyond the value of $f(x_1, \ldots, x_n)$. A *single-shuffle full-open* protocol is a minimal model of card-based secure computation in which, after the parties place face-down cards representing their inputs, a single shuffle operation is performed and then all cards are opened to derive the output. Despite the simplicity of this model, the class of functions known to admit single-shuffle full-open protocols has been limited to a few small examples. In this work, we prove for the first time that every function admits a single-shuffle full-open protocol. We present two constructions that offer a trade-off between the number of cards and the complexity of the shuffle operation. These feasibility results are derived from a novel connection between single-shuffle full-open protocols and a cryptographic primitive known as *Private Simultaneous Messages* protocols, which has rarely been studied in the context of card-based cryptography. We also present a variant of single-shuffle protocols in which only a subset of cards are revealed. These protocols reduce the complexity of the shuffle and opening operations compared to existing protocols in the same setting.

## 1 Introduction

A *secure computation* protocol [31] is a fundamental primitive in cryptography and has been studied extensively in the literature (e.g., [11] and references therein). This primitive enables $n$ parties, each holding a private input $x_i$, to evaluate a function $f$ on $(x_1, \ldots, x_n)$ without revealing any information beyond the value of $f(x_1, \ldots, x_n)$. *Card-based secure computation* [2,3,14] studies implementations of secure computation protocols using physical playing cards. In this work, we focus on binary cards with suits ♡ or ♣, which is the most standard setting in the literature. This visual implementation not just serves as an accessible tool that helps non-experts understand the mechanisms of secure


Y. Li et al. (Eds.): COCOON 2026, LNCS 16835, pp. 15–27, 2027.
https://doi.org/10.1007/978-981-92-3309-0_2

computation protocols, but also has found interesting theoretical connections to discrete mathematics and other cryptographic primitives [21,25,26]. Many works have proposed different card-based secure computation protocols for both general and specific functions, e.g., [9,15,23,28].

Most of the existing card-based secure computation protocols proceed as follows. First, the parties place face-down cards encoding their inputs[1]. They then apply a random shuffle, which is unknown to any party, to the sequence of cards and reveal the suits of certain cards at positions specified by the protocol. After possibly multiple rounds of shuffle and opening operations, the parties derive an output $f(x_1, \ldots, x_n)$ from the suits revealed so far.

Note that the security of such protocols relies on two conditions: the permutation chosen by every shuffle must be hidden from all parties, and the suits of cards that are not designated to be opened must remain secret. In other words, the parties need to be careful whenever performing such operations, as improper operations can immediately compromise the privacy of their inputs. It is therefore important to minimize the number of shuffle operations and simplify opening operations, when designing card-based protocols.

In this work, we consider the simplest setting for card-based secure computation protocols, referred to as *single-shuffle full-open protocols* [24,25]. Specifically, in such protocols, a single shuffle operation is performed after the parties place face-down cards corresponding their inputs, and then all cards are turned face up. The output is subsequently computed from the fully revealed sequence of suits. This model assumes the minimum possible number of shuffle operations and the simplest form of opening, namely, turning over all cards. Thus, single-shuffle full-open protocols are important in that they minimize the complexity of both shuffling and opening operations.

Some feasibility results have been shown in this setting. The first card-based secure computation protocol, known as "Five-Card Trick" [2], is a single-shuffle full-open protocol that computes the two-input AND function. It is also known that several specific functions such as three-input equality, majority, and XOR functions can be computed by single-shuffle full-open protocols [6,10,22,27,29]. However, prior to this work, the fundamental question of whether every function $f : \{0,1\}^n \to \{0,1\}$ admits a single-shuffle full-open protocol remained open. Surprisingly, even the three-input AND function is not known to have a single-shuffle full-open protocol. Note that if a more advanced operation—namely, opening only a *subset* of cards—is allowed, then every function can be computed with a single shuffle [17,23,30]. However, it is not straightforward to extend such protocols to the full-open setting since revealing even a single additional card may compromise privacy.

[1] In the standard input model, at most two cards in the sequence representing $x_i$ depend on $x_i$, while the remaining cards are independent of $x_i$. In contrast, we consider a more general setting where any number of cards in the sequence representing $x_i$ may depend on $x_i$.

### 1.1 Our Results

In this work, we prove that every function $f : \{0,1\}^n \to \{0,1\}$ admits a single-shuffle full-open protocol. Our constructions are based on a novel connection between single-shuffle full-open protocols and a cryptographic primitive known as *Private Simultaneous Messages (PSM)* protocols, which has rarely been studied in the context of card-based cryptography. We also present a variant of single-shuffle protocols in which only a subset of cards are opened. These protocols reduce the complexity of the shuffling and opening operations compared to the previous single-shuffle protocols [17,23,30]. We show a comparison of single-shuffle protocols in Table 1. Below, we elaborate on our results.

**Table 1.** Comparison of single-shuffle card-based secure computation protocols

| Protocol | Function | Opening | Shuffle | # cards |
|---|---|---|---|---|
| [2] | 2-input AND | full | RC $\times$ 1 | 5 |
| [22] | 2-input XOR | full | RC $\times$ 1 | 4 |
| [27] | 3-input XOR | full | RC $\times$ 1 | 8 |
| [6,22] | 3-input equality | full | RC $\times$ 1 | 6 |
| [29] | 3-input majority | full | RC $\times$ 1 & RBC $\times$ 1 | 6 |
| [10] | $n$-input XOR | full | RBC $\times$ $(n-1)$ | $2n$ |
| [10] | $n$-input XOR | full | PSc $\times$ 2 | $O(n \log n)$ |
| Ours (Theorem 1) | any | full | PSh $\times$ 1 & CS $\times$ 1 | $2^{O(n^3 2^{n/2})}$ |
| Ours (Theorem 5) | any | full | PSh $\times$ $O(n2^n)$ & PSc $\times$ 1 | $O(n^2 2^n)$ |
| Ours [4] | symmetric | full | PSh $\times$ $n$ | $O(n^3 2^{2n})$ |
| Ours (Theorem 4) | $n$-input AND | full | PSh $\times$ $n$ | $O(n^2)$ |
| [13] | 2-input AND | adaptive | RC $\times$ 1 & RBC $\times$ 1 | 4 |
| [10] | $n$-input AND | adaptive | RBC $\times$ $(n-1)$ | $4n-2$ |
| [10] | $n$-input AND | adaptive | PSc $\times$ 2 | $O(n \log n)$ |
| [17,23,30] | any | adaptive | PSc $\times$ $O(C_f + n)$ | $O(C_f + n)$ |
| Ours (Theorem 2) | any | static | RC $\times$ 1 | $2^{O(n^3 2^{n/2})}$ |

$n$ refers to the number of inputs. "CS" refers to a complete shuffle, "PSc" refers to a pile-scramble shuffle, "RC" refers to a random cut, "PSh" refers to a pile-shifting shuffle, and "RBC" refers to a random bisection cut, which is a pile-shifting shuffle performed on two piles of cards. In each protocol, these shuffles are composed into a single shuffle. $C_f$ refers to the minimum number of gates in any circuit computing $f$. Note that the protocols except for [27] and ours follow the standard input model.

**Single-Shuffle Full-Open Protocols for Any Function.** We present two constructions of single-shuffle full-open protocols that offer a trade-off between the number of cards and the complexity of the shuffle operation. To describe our constructions, we introduce basic shuffle operations. A *complete shuffle* applies a uniformly random permutation to a sequence of cards. A *pile-scramble shuffle* divides a sequence of cards into multiple piles and applies a complete shuffle to these piles. A *random cut* applies a uniformly random shift to a sequence of cards. A *pile-shifting shuffle* divides a sequence of cards into piles and applies a random cut to the piles. All our protocols use a composition of the above four shuffle operations[2]. We consider that a complete shuffle (resp. a random cut) is preferable to a pile-scramble (resp. a pile-shifting) shuffle since the latter requires additional items such as envelopes or sleeves to make piles.

For any function $f : \{0,1\}^n \to \{0,1\}$, our first construction requires $2^{O(n^3 2^{n/2})}$ cards and uses a composition of one pile-shifting shuffle and one complete shuffle. Our second construction reduces the number of cards to $O(n^2 2^n)$, but at the cost of a more complex shuffle: a composition of $O(n2^n)$ pile-shifting shuffles and one pile-scramble shuffle. Along the way, we also obtain single-shuffle full-open protocols with fewer cards tailored to the $n$-input AND function and any symmetric function[3].

**Single-Shuffle Protocols with Partial Opening.** We show a variant of our first construction that reduces the complexity of the shuffle operation by relaxing the requirement that all cards are revealed. When a subset of cards are opened, we distinguish two types of opening: (1) *static opening*, where a fixed subset of cards are revealed; (2) *adaptive opening*, where the next card to reveal is determined by the suits of the cards that have already been revealed. We consider that static opening is preferable to the adaptive one in terms of simplicity.

We show a single-shuffle static-open protocol for any function using a random cut only. Technically, our full-open protocol requires a composition of a pile-shifting shuffle and a complete shuffle. The complete shuffle is required to "erase" information encoded in a specific subset of cards. If we modify the protocol in such a way that the cards except those in that subset are revealed, we obtain a single-shuffle static-open protocol using only a pile-shifting shuffle. Note that the pile-shifting shuffle is used to reveal one pile selected uniformly at random from multiple piles. We propose a novel protocol to realize such a functionality using a random cut, which may be of independent interest. As a result, we obtain a single-shuffle static-open protocol for any function $f$ using a random cut. This variant requires additional cards but the total number of cards remains asymptotically the same as our full-open protocol, i.e., $2^{O(n^3 2^{n/2})}$.

We compare our protocol with the previous single-shuffle protocols in [17,23,30]. Our protocol reduces the complexity of the shuffle operation: the protocols in [17,23,30] require a composition of $O(C_f + n)$ pile-scramble shuffles, where $C_f$ is the minimum number of gates in any circuit computing $f : \{0,1\}^n \to \{0,1\}$, whereas ours uses a random cut only. Our protocol simplifies the opening operation as well: the protocols in [17,23,30] require adaptive opening whereas ours needs static opening. As a trade-off, the number of cards required by our

---

2 We treat any composition of shuffles as a single shuffle.

3 We say that a function is symmetric if its output is independent of the order of inputs.

protocol is larger than those of the previous protocols [17,23,30] with $O(C_f + n)$ cards, which are upper bounded by $2^{O(n)}$ in the worst case.

*Remark 1.* Notably, a converse implication was shown in [25]: Any single-shuffle full-open protocol for a function $f$ can be transformed into a PSM protocol for $f$. Combining the result of [25] with ours, we can relate the minimum number of cards required by any single-shuffle full-open protocol for $f$, to the minimum communication complexity and the minimum randomness complexity of any PSM protocol for $f$. See the full version [4] for details.

### 1.2 Related Works

We provide a brief summary of existing works on card-based secure computation protocols.

**Single-Shuffle Protocols.** Prior to this work, the class of functions known to admit single-shuffle full-open protocols were limited to a few small examples: two-input AND [2], XOR [10,22,27], three-input equality [6,22], and three-input majority [29]. We are the first to prove that every function can be computed by a single-shuffle full-open protocol. The protocols in [17,23,30] can compute any function with a single shuffle but they require a more advanced operation when opening cards, namely adaptive opening. Furthermore, the complexity of the shuffle operation is sub-optimal: the protocols in [17,23,30] require a composition of many pile-scramble shuffles proportional to the number of gates plus the number of input wires in a circuit computing the function. In contrast, our single-shuffle static-open protocol uses only one random cut.

**Protocols Using More Than One Shuffles.** There are card-based secure computation protocols that apply multiple rounds of shuffling and partial opening of cards. In this model, Nishida, Mizuki, and Sone [15] showed that any function $f : \{0,1\}^n \to \{0,1\}$ can be computed using $O(2^n)$ rounds of shuffle and reveal operations. The protocol achieves a constant number of cards (i.e., six) in addition to those representing inputs. For symmetric functions, tailor-made constructions by [15,20,28] reduce the number of operations and the number of cards. Several works have also focused on minimizing the number of cards and shuffle operations for small functions (e.g., [12,16,18,19]).

## 2 Preliminaries

**Notations.** For a natural number $n \in \mathbb{N}$, we denote $[n] = \{1, 2, \ldots, n\}$. Let $\mathfrak{S}_N$ denote the set of all permutations over $[N]$. For an integer $m \geq 2$, we denote the ring of integers modulo $m$ by $\mathbb{Z}_m$ and identify it with $\{0, 1, \ldots, m-1\}$ as a set. Let $\mathbb{Z}_m^*$ denote the multiplicative group of integers modulo $m$ and naturally identify it with a subset of $\{0, 1, \ldots, m-1\}$. We define $\mathsf{AND}_n : \{0,1\}^n \to \{0,1\}$ as $\mathsf{AND}_n(x_1, \ldots, x_n) = 1$ if and only if $x_i = 1$ for all $i \in [n]$.

**Card-Based Protocols.** In this paper, we use *binary cards* whose front sides are either ♣ or ♡ and back sides are both ?. We assume that two cards with the same suit are indistinguishable.

A shuffle is an operation that applies a random permutation to a sequence of $\ell$ face-down cards, where the permutation is chosen from some probability distribution over $\mathfrak{S}_\ell$. We allow a shuffle to be applied not only to the entire sequence of cards but also to a subsequence of cards. We assume that no party guesses which permutation is chosen during the shuffle. Below, we introduce basic shuffles. A *complete shuffle* is a shuffle that applies a uniformly random permutation to a sequence of $\ell$ face-down cards, which is denoted by $[\cdot]$. A *pile-scramble shuffle* [8] is a shuffle that divides a sequence of cards into multiple *piles* of the same number of cards and applies a random permutation to the sequence of the piles, which is denoted by $[\cdot|\cdots|\cdot]$. A *random cut* is a shuffle that applies a cyclic shift to a sequence of cards a uniformly random number of times, which is denoted by $\langle\cdot\rangle$. A *pile-shifting shuffle* is a shuffle that divides a sequence of cards into multiple piles of the same number of cards and applies a random cyclic shift to the sequence of the piles, which is denoted by $\langle\cdot|\cdots|\cdot\rangle$. We allow arbitrary deterministic rearrangements of cards before each shuffle and these are not included in the shuffle complexity. A *composition* of two shuffles is an operation that applies two shuffles to a sequence consecutively. We regard any composition of shuffles as a single shuffle.

We briefly introduce single-shuffle card-based protocols (see [14] for details). A single-shuffle card-based protocol $\Pi$ for a function $f : \{0,1\}^n \to \{0,1\}$ specifies $2n$ sequences of suits $(L_i^b)_{i\in[n],b\in\{0,1\}}$, where $L_i^0$ and $L_i^1$ have the same length. Each party with input $x_i \in \{0,1\}$ puts face-down cards whose suits correspond to $L_i^{x_i}$. Then, a random permutation $\pi$ sampled from a probability distribution $\mathcal{D}$ is applied to the face-down cards, where $\pi$ is unknown to any party. Finally, parties turn over cards at positions specified by the protocol $\Pi$, and obtain an output $y = f(x_1,\ldots,x_n)$ from the revealed suits. The privacy requirement is that the sequence of the revealed suits leaks nothing about $(x_i)_{i\in[n]}$ beyond what follows from $y$. If the suits of all the cards are revealed, then we say that $\Pi$ is a single-shuffle *full-open* protocol. If only the cards at pre-determined positions are revealed, then we call $\Pi$ a single-shuffle *static-open* protocol. We also introduce a single-shuffle *adaptive-open* protocol, in which the position of the next card to be turned face up is determined based on the suits of the cards that have already been revealed.

**Private Simultaneous Messages Protocols.** As mentioned in Sect. 1, our single-shuffle protocols are based on a cryptographic primitive known as PSM protocols [5,7]. This primitive enables $n$ parties each holding an input $x_i$ to reveal $f(x_1,\ldots,x_n)$ to an external party called a referee without revealing any extra information. Specifically, a PSM protocol $\Sigma$ consists of three algorithms: A randomness generation algorithm $\mathsf{Gen}$ takes no input and outputs a random string $\rho$, which is shared among all parties except for the referee; An encoding algorithm $\mathsf{Enc}$ takes a party's index $i \in [n]$, a party's input $x_i$, and shared randomness $\rho$ as inputs, and outputs a message $\mu_i$, which is sent to the referee; A decoding algorithm $\mathsf{Dec}$ takes $n$ messages $(\mu_i)_{i\in[n]}$ as input and outputs $y = f(x_1, \ldots, x_n)$. The privacy requirement is that the messages $(\mu_i)_{i\in[n]}$ reveal nothing about $(x_i)_{i\in[n]}$ other than $y = f(x_1, \ldots, x_n)$. We define the randomness complexity of $\Sigma$ as the bit-length of $\rho$ and the communication complexity of $\Sigma$ as the total bit-length of $(\mu_i)_{i\in[n]}$. See [5,7] or the full version [4] for the formal definition. For any function $f : \{0,1\}^n \to \{0,1\}$, there exists a PSM protocol for $f$ with communication and randomness complexity $O(n^3 2^{n/2})$ [1], which is the currently best known result.

## 3 Single-Shuffle Protocols for Any Function

### 3.1 Full-Open Protocols

First, we show a single-shuffle full-open protocol for a function $f : \{0,1\}^n \to \{0,1\}$ based on a PSM protocol for $f$. In retrospect, our construction is quite simple. Here, we provide a high-level overview and refer the reader to the full version [4] for the formal description and proofs.

Let $\Sigma = (\mathsf{Gen}, \mathsf{Enc}, \mathsf{Dec})$ be a PSM protocol for the function $f$. To simplify the exposition, we here assume that the randomness $\rho$ sampled by $\mathsf{Gen}$ is uniformly distributed over $\{0,1\}^r$, where $r$ is the randomness complexity of $\Sigma$. Our construction allows $\rho$ to be sampled from an arbitrary distribution over $\{0,1\}^r$.

For each $i \in [n]$, each $b \in \{0,1\}$, and each random string $\rho \in \{0,1\}^r$, we define a sequence of card suits $m_i^b(\rho)$ as the encoding of a party $i$'s message $\mathsf{Enc}(i, b, \rho)$ under an input $b$ and shared randomness $\rho$. We follow an encoding rule $\heartsuit\clubsuit = 1$, $\clubsuit\heartsuit = 0$ and encode a bit string into a sequence of suits bit by bit. For example, a string 101 is encoded into $\heartsuit\clubsuit\clubsuit\heartsuit\heartsuit\clubsuit$. Let $L_i^b$ be a sequence of suits obtained by concatenating the $m_i^b(\rho)$'s over all possible $\rho$'s. Here, we enumerate the set of all $\rho$'s as $\{\rho_1, \ldots, \rho_{2^r}\}$ according to the lexicographical order.

Suppose that each party $i$ places a sequence of face-down cards whose suits correspond to $L_i^{x_i}$. These $n$ sequences can be rearranged into the concatenation of $M(\rho) := (m_1^{x_1}(\rho), \ldots, m_n^{x_n}(\rho))$ over all $\rho$n's. Note that it suffices to open only the set of cards corresponding to $M(\rho)$ for a uniformly random $\rho$, since this is equivalent to revealing the messages that the referee receives in the PSM protocol $\Sigma$. We then apply a pile-shifting shuffle to obtain a sequence of cards with suits $M(\rho_s), M(\rho_{s+1}), \ldots, M(\rho_{s-1})$, where $s$ is a uniformly random shift. We here emphasize that the parties must not know which $\rho_s$ is selected, as they play the role of the referee in the PSM protocol. Since the parties must also not observe any messages other than $M(\rho_s)$, we apply a complete shuffle to the remaining cards $M(\rho_{s+1}), \ldots, M(\rho_{s-1})$ to eliminate all information except that of $M(\rho_s)$. As a result, we obtain a sequence of face-down cards whose suits consist of $M(\rho_s)$ followed by a uniformly random arrangement of suits. Finally, we turn over all cards and compute $y = f(x_1, \ldots, x_n)$ by applying the decoding algorithm of $\Sigma$ to the bit string $(\mathsf{Enc}(i, x_i, \rho_s))_{i\in[n]}$ encoded in $M(\rho_s)$. If the communication and randomness complexity of $\Sigma$ are $c$ and $r$, respectively, then the number of cards required to encode each $M(\rho)$ is $2c$ and hence the total number of cards is $2c \cdot 2^r = c2^{r+1}$. Therefore, we obtain the following theorem.

**Theorem 1.** *Assume that there exists a PSM protocol $\Sigma$ for a function $f : \{0,1\}^n \to \{0,1\}$ with randomness complexity $r$ and communication complexity $c$. Then, there exists a single-shuffle full-open protocol $\Pi$ for $f$ such that the number of cards is at most $c2^{r+1}$ and the shuffle is a composition of a pile-shifting shuffle and a complete shuffle. In particular, the number of cards is upper bounded by $2^{O(n^3 2^{n/2})}$ if $\Sigma$ is instantiated with the PSM protocol in [1].*

### 3.2 Static-Open Protocols

Next, we show a variant of the construction in Theorem 1, which uses a simpler shuffle at the price of giving up full-opening. Consider a modification of the construction in which only the pile of cards corresponding to $p_s := M(\rho_s)$ are revealed in the output phase. Then, it is no longer necessary to apply a complete shuffle to the remaining cards in the shuffling phase. Since the positions of cards to be revealed are fixed, this leads to a single-shuffle static-open protocol that only requires a pile-shifting shuffle.

Furthermore, we observe that the pile-shifting shuffle is applied to the sequence to select a pile $p_s$ uniformly at random from the sequence of piles $(p_1, \ldots, p_{2^r})$. We refer to this functionality as *uniform selection*. We show that with some additional cards, uniform selection can be implemented using a random cut only. As a result, we obtain the following theorem, whose proof is provided in the full version [4].

**Theorem 2.** *Under the same assumption as Theorem 1, there exists a single-shuffle static-open protocol $\Pi$ for $f$ such that the number of cards is $c2^{r+1} + 2^{r+2}$ and the shuffle is a random cut. In particular, the number of cards is upper bounded by $2^{O(n^3 2^{n/2})}$ if $\Sigma$ is instantiated with the PSM protocol in [1].*

## 4 Single-Shuffle Full-Open Protocols with Fewer Cards

In this section, we show a different single-shuffle full-open protocol reducing the number of cards at the cost of requiring more complicated shuffles.

### 4.1 Reduction to AND Functions

Let $f : \{0,1\}^n \to \{0,1\}$ be a function and $f^{-1}(1) = \{\boldsymbol{a}^{(1)}, \ldots, \boldsymbol{a}^{(N)}\}$, where $\boldsymbol{a}^{(j)} = (a_1^{(j)}, \ldots, a_n^{(j)}) \in \{0,1\}^n$ is an input on which $f$ evaluates to 1. For each $i \in [n]$, each $j \in [N]$, and each $x_i \in \{0,1\}$, we define $b_i^{(j)}(x_i) \in \{0,1\}$ as $b_i^{(j)}(x_i) = 1$ if and only if $x_i = a_i^{(j)}$. For any $\boldsymbol{x} = (x_1, \ldots, x_n) \in \{0,1\}^n$ with $f(\boldsymbol{x}) = 1$, there exists a unique $j \in [N]$ such that $\boldsymbol{x} = \boldsymbol{a}^{(j)}$; and if $f(\boldsymbol{x}) = 0$, then $\boldsymbol{x} \neq \boldsymbol{a}^{(j)}$ for all $j \in [N]$. Thus, it holds that $f(x_1, \ldots, x_n) = \sum_{j \in [N]} \mathsf{AND}_n(b_1^{(j)}(x_1), \ldots, b_n^{(j)}(x_n))$ for any $(x_1, \ldots, x_n) \in \{0,1\}^n$.

Assume that we are given a single-shuffle full-open protocol $\Pi_0$ for $\mathsf{AND}_n$. Then, we can construct a single-shuffle full-open protocol $\Pi$ for $f$ as follows.

Each party $i$ with input $x_i$ computes bits $b_i^{(j)}(x_i)$ for all $j \in [N]$. Then, for each $j \in [N]$, parties execute $\Pi_0$ on inputs $(b_i^{(j)}(x_i))_{i\in[n]}$. That is, each party $i$ places a sequence of face-down cards corresponding to $b_i^{(j)}(x_i)$ following the instructions of $\Pi_0$, and then apply a shuffle specified by $\Pi_0$. At this point, if $f(\boldsymbol{x}) = 1$, then the resulting card sequence consists of a single pile of cards corresponding to an output 1 and $N-1$ piles of cards corresponding to an output 0, where the position of the unique pile is determined by $j \in [N]$ such that $\boldsymbol{a}^{(j)} = \boldsymbol{x}$. If $f(\boldsymbol{x}) = 0$, then the card sequence consists of $N$ piles of cards corresponding to an output 0. Thus, we can determine $f(\boldsymbol{x})$ from the revealed cards. Note that before turning over cards, we need to apply a pile-scramble shuffle to ensure that the position of the pile corresponding to 1 is independent of $\boldsymbol{x}$. Then, the privacy of $\Pi$ directly follows from that of $\Pi_0$. If $\Pi_0$ uses $\ell$ cards, then $\Pi$ uses $\ell N \leq \ell 2^n$ cards. In summary, we obtain the following theorem, whose formal proof is provided in the full version [4].

**Theorem 3.** *Let $\Pi_0$ be a single-shuffle full-open protocol for the $n$-input AND function. Then, there exists a single-shuffle full-open protocol $\Pi$ for a function $f : \{0,1\}^n \to \{0,1\}$ such that the number of cards is $N\ell$, where $N = |f^{-1}(1)| = |\{\boldsymbol{a} \in \{0,1\}^n : f(\boldsymbol{a}) = 1\}|$ and $\ell$ is the number of cards of $\Pi_0$, and the shuffle is a composition of $N$ independent shuffles for $\Pi_0$ and a pile-scramble shuffle.*

### 4.2 A Single-Shuffle Full-Open Protocol for the AND Function

From the above observation, it remains to construct a single-shuffle full-open protocol for $\mathsf{AND}_n$. It is possible to instantiate it with our general protocol in the previous section. Since there exists a PSM protocol for $\mathsf{AND}_n$ with communication and randomness complexity $O(n \log n)$ [5], we obtain a single-shuffle full-open protocol for $\mathsf{AND}_n$ using $\ell = O(n \log n) \cdot 2^{O(n \log n)} = 2^{O(n \log n)}$ cards. Thus, the total number of cards required for computing a general function $f$ is $2^{O(n \log n)} \cdot 2^n = 2^{O(n \log n)}$, which reduces the number of cards $2^{O(n^3 2^{n/2})}$ in our previous protocol. In the following, we show a single-shuffle full-open protocol tailored to computing $\mathsf{AND}_n$ that uses only $\ell = O(n^2)$ cards. This leads to a more efficient protocol for general $f$ using $O(n^2 2^n)$ cards.

A key observation is that the PSM protocol for $\mathsf{AND}_n$ in [5] has a special algebraic structure, which we refer to as *additive PSM*. Let $m$ be a prime. We call a PSM protocol additive over $\mathbb{Z}_m$ if shared randomness consists of an element $u$ sampled uniformly at random from a subgroup $U \subseteq \mathbb{Z}_m^*$ and additive shares $(r_i)_{i\in[n]} \in \mathbb{Z}_m^n$ of zero, which means that $(r_i)_{i\in[n]}$ are sampled uniformly at random conditioned on $\sum_{i\in[n]} r_i = 0 \bmod m$. Furthermore, a message of each party $i$ with input $x_i \in \{0,1\}$ has the form of $uy_i - r_i$, where $y_i \in \mathbb{Z}_m$ is determined by $x_i$. The output is computed based on $\sum_{i\in[n]}(uy_i - r_i) = u\sum_{i\in[n]} y_i$.

We show a construction of single-shuffle full-open protocols from additive PSM protocols. For several functions including $\mathsf{AND}_n$, this can improve the number of cards in our previous construction from arbitrary PSM protocols. Our construction takes two steps: First, we transform $n$ piles of face-down cards each encoding $y_i$ into $n$ piles each encoding $z_i := uy_i$ for a uniformly random element $u \in U$, which is unknown to any party. Second, we transform the resulting $n$ piles into $n$ piles each encoding $z_i - r_i \bmod m$, where $(r_i)_{i \in [n]}$ are random additive shares of zero. Here, we use a different encoding rule: $x \in \mathbb{Z}_m$ is encoded into a sequence $E_m^{\heartsuit}(x)$ of suits such that $\heartsuit$ is placed at $x$-th position and $\clubsuit$ is placed elsewhere, i.e., $E_m^{\heartsuit}(x) := \overset{0}{\boxed{\clubsuit}} \cdots \overset{x}{\boxed{\heartsuit}} \cdots \overset{m-1}{\boxed{\clubsuit}}$.

To describe the first procedure, we here assume for simplicity that $U = \mathbb{Z}_m^* = \{1, 2, \ldots, m-1\}$ (see the full version [4] for the general case). Since $m$ is a prime, $U$ is a cyclic group with a generator $\alpha$ and we can write $U = \{\alpha, \alpha^2, \ldots, \alpha^{m-1}\}$. Each party with input $x_i$ computes $y_i \in \mathbb{Z}_m$ and places face-down cards with suits $E_m^{\heartsuit}(y_i)$. For each $\gamma \in \mathbb{Z}_m$, let $c_{i,\gamma}$ denote the $\gamma$-th suit of $E_m^{\heartsuit}(y_i)$, that is, $c_{i,\gamma} = \heartsuit$ if and only if $\gamma = y_i$. We rearrange the face-down cards and construct $m$ piles $p(1), \ldots, p(m-1)$, where each $p(j)$ consists of the $\alpha^j$-th cards of $E_m^{\heartsuit}(y_i)$ for all $i \in [n]$, i.e., $p(j) = (c_{i,\alpha^j})_{i \in [n]}$. We apply a pile-shifting shuffle to $p(1), \ldots, p(m-1)$ and denote the resulting piles by $p'(1), \ldots, p'(m-1)$. Then, there exists a uniformly random shift $\Delta$ such that $p'(j) = p(j - \Delta)$ for all $j$, where indices are modulo $m-1$. We define $c'_{i,0} = c_{i,0}$ and for $\gamma \neq 0$, define $c'_{i,\gamma}$ as the $i$-th card of $p'(\log_\alpha \gamma)$. Here, we define $\log_\alpha \gamma$ for $\gamma \in \mathbb{Z}_m \setminus \{0\}$ as $j$ such that $\gamma = \alpha^j$. Finally, we output $(c'_{1,\gamma})_{\gamma \in \mathbb{Z}_m}, \ldots, (c'_{n,\gamma})_{\gamma \in \mathbb{Z}_m}$ with all cards face down. It holds that $c'_{i,\gamma} = c_{i,\alpha^{\log_\alpha \gamma - \Delta}} = c_{i,\gamma u^{-1}}$, where $u := \alpha^{\Delta}$. Thus, $c'_{i,\gamma} = \heartsuit$ if and only if $\gamma = y_i u$, which means that each output pile $(c'_{i,\gamma})_{\gamma \in \mathbb{Z}_m}$ is equal to $E_m^{\heartsuit}(y_i u)$. Since $\Delta$ is uniformly distributed over $\{1, \ldots, m-1\}$, $u$ is uniformly distributed over $U = \mathbb{Z}_m^*$.

The second procedure transforms $n$ piles of cards each with suits $E_m^{\heartsuit}(z_i)$ into $n$ piles each with suits $E_m^{\heartsuit}(z_i - r_i)$, where $(r_i)_{i \in [n]}$ are random additive shares of zero. We first transform $E_m^{\heartsuit}(z_1)$ into $E_m^{\heartsuit}(-z_1)$ simply by reversing the order of the last $m-1$ cards: $\underbrace{\overset{0}{\boxed{?}}\overset{1}{\boxed{?}}\overset{2}{\boxed{?}} \cdots \overset{m-1}{\boxed{?}}}_{E_m^{\heartsuit}(z_1)} \to \underbrace{\overset{0}{\boxed{?}}\overset{m-1}{\boxed{?}} \cdots \overset{2}{\boxed{?}}\overset{1}{\boxed{?}}}_{E_m^{\heartsuit}(-z_1)}$. We then pair two sequences $E_m^{\heartsuit}(-z_1)$ and $E_m^{\heartsuit}(z_n)$, and apply a pile-shifting shuffle:

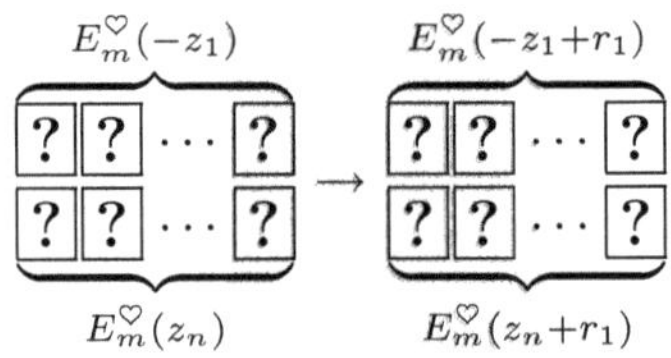


Here, $r_1$ is a uniformly random shift. Finally, we reverse the order of the last $m-1$ cards of $E_m^{\heartsuit}(-z_1 + r_1)$. As a result, we obtain two sequences $E_m^{\heartsuit}(z_1 - r_1)$ and $E_m^{\heartsuit}(z_n + r_1)$. We apply the same procedure to a pair of $E_m^{\heartsuit}(z_2)$ and $E_m^{\heartsuit}(z_n + r_1)$, and obtain $E_m^{\heartsuit}(z_2 - r_2)$ and $E_m^{\heartsuit}(z_n + r_1 + r_2)$, where $r_2$ is another uniformly random shift. By continuing these procedures, we finally obtain $E_m^{\heartsuit}(z_1 - r_1), \ldots, E_m^{\heartsuit}(z_n - r_n)$, where $r_1, \ldots, r_{n-1}$ are uniformly at random and $r_n = -\sum_{i=1}^{n-1} r_i$.

Now, we can transform an additive PSM protocol $\Sigma$ for $f$ into a single-shuffle full-open protocol $\Pi$ for $f$. After performing the above two procedures, we obtain face-down cards with suits $E_m^{\heartsuit}(uy_1 - r_1), \ldots, E_m^{\heartsuit}(uy_n - r_n)$, where $u$ is a uniformly random element of $U$ and $(r_i)_{i \in [n]}$ are random additive shares of zero. We turn over all cards and run the decoding algorithm of $\Sigma$ on $(uy_i - r_i)_{i \in [n]}$. The correctness of $\Sigma$ ensures that the output is $f(x_1, \ldots, x_n)$ and the privacy of $\Sigma$ ensures that the revealed suits leak nothing but $f(x_1, \ldots, x_n)$. The number of cards in $\Pi$ is $mn$. Since $\mathsf{AND}_n$ admits an additive PSM protocol over $\mathbb{Z}_m$ such that $m = O(n)$ [5], we obtain a single-shuffle full-open protocol for $\mathsf{AND}_n$ using $O(n^2)$ cards. In summary, we obtain the following theorem, whose formal proof is provided in the full version [4].

**Theorem 4.** *There exists a single-shuffle full-open protocol $\Pi$ for $\mathsf{AND}_n$ such that the number of cards is $O(n^2)$ and the shuffle is a composition of $n$ pile-shifting shuffles.*

### 4.3 Putting It All Together

By plugging the protocol for $\mathsf{AND}_n$ into the general-to-AND reduction, we obtain a single-shuffle full-open protocol for any function $f : \{0,1\}^n \to \{0,1\}$ using at most $O(n^2) \cdot 2^n = O(n^2 2^n)$ cards. This improves upon our previous construction, which requires $2^{O(n^3 2^{n/2})}$ cards. It is important to note that this comes with a trade-off: this protocol requires a composition of $O(n2^n)$ pile-shifting shuffles followed by one pile-scramble shuffle, while our previous protocol needs only one pile-shifting shuffle and one complete shuffle. In summary, we obtain the following theorem.

**Theorem 5.** *There exists a single-shuffle full-open protocol for $f : \{0,1\}^n \to \{0,1\}$ such that the number of cards is $O(n^2 2^n)$ and the shuffle is a composition of at most $n2^n$ pile-shifting shuffles and a pile-scramble shuffle.*

**Acknowledgements.** This work was partially supported by JST CREST Grant Number JPMJCR22M1, JST K Program Grant Numbers JPMJKP24U2 and JPMJKP24U3, and JSPS KAKENHI Grant Numbers 21K17702, 24K20775 and 26K21162.

## References

1. Beimel, A., Kushilevitz, E., Nissim, P.: The complexity of multiparty PSM protocols and related models. In: Nielsen, J.B., Rijmen, V. (eds.) EUROCRYPT 2018. LNCS, vol. 10821, pp. 287–318. Springer, Cham (2018). https://doi.org/10.1007/978-3-319-78375-8_10
2. Boer, B.: More efficient match-making and satisfiability *the five card trick*. In: Quisquater, J.-J., Vandewalle, J. (eds.) EUROCRYPT 1989. LNCS, vol. 434, pp. 208–217. Springer, Heidelberg (1990). https://doi.org/10.1007/3-540-46885-4_23

3. Crépeau, C., Kilian, J.: Discreet solitary games. In: Stinson, D.R. (ed.) CRYPTO 1993. LNCS, vol. 773, pp. 319–330. Springer, Heidelberg (1994). https://doi.org/10.1007/3-540-48329-2_27
4. Eriguchi, R., Shinagawa, K.: Single-shuffle full-open card-based protocols for any function (2025). https://arxiv.org/abs/2510.17308
5. Feige, U., Kilian, J., Naor, M.: A minimal model for secure computation (extended abstract). In: Proceedings of the Twenty-Sixth Annual ACM Symposium on Theory of Computing, STOC 1994, pp. 554–563 (1994)
6. Heather, J., Schneider, S., Teague, V.: Cryptographic protocols with everyday objects. Formal Aspects Comput. **26**(1), 37–62 (2014)
7. Ishai, Y., Kushilevitz, E.: Private simultaneous messages protocols with applications. In: Fifth Israel Symposium on Theory of Computing and Systems, ISTCS 1997, pp. 174–184. IEEE Computer Society (1997)
8. Ishikawa, R., Chida, E., Mizuki, T.: Efficient card-based protocols for generating a hidden random permutation without fixed points. In: Unconventional Computation and Natural Computation, pp. 215–226 (2015)
9. Kastner, J., et al.: The minimum number of cards in practical card-based protocols. In: Takagi, T., Peyrin, T. (eds.) ASIACRYPT 2017. LNCS, vol. 10626, pp. 126–155. Springer, Cham (2017). https://doi.org/10.1007/978-3-319-70700-6_5
10. Kuzuma, T., Toyoda, K., Miyahara, D., Mizuki, T.: Card-based single-shuffle protocols for secure multiple-input AND and XOR computations. In: ACM ASIA Public-Key Cryptography Workshop, pp. 51–58 (2022)
11. Lindell, Y.: Secure multiparty computation. Commun. ACM **64**(1), 86–96 (2020)
12. Miyahara, D., Hayashi, Y., Mizuki, T., Sone, H.: Practical card-based implementations of Yao's millionaire protocol. Theoret. Comput. Sci. **803**, 207–221 (2020)
13. Mizuki, T., Kumamoto, M., Sone, H.: The five-card trick can be done with four cards. In: Wang, X., Sako, K. (eds.) ASIACRYPT 2012. LNCS, vol. 7658, pp. 598–606. Springer, Heidelberg (2012). https://doi.org/10.1007/978-3-642-34961-4_36
14. Mizuki, T., Shizuya, H.: A formalization of card-based cryptographic protocols via abstract machine. Int. J. Inf. Secur. **13**(1), 15–23 (2014)
15. Nishida, T., Hayashi, Y., Mizuki, T., Sone, H.: Card-based protocols for any Boolean function. In: Theory and Applications of Models of Computation, pp. 110–121 (2015)
16. Odaka, S., Komano, Y.: Card-based arithmetic operations and application to statistical data aggregation. In: Innovative Security Solutions for Information Technology and Communications (2024)
17. Ono, T., Shinagawa, K., Nakai, T., Watanabe, Y., Iwamoto, M.: Single-shuffle card-based protocols with six cards per gate. In: Information Security and Cryptology, pp. 157–169 (2024)
18. Ruangwises, S.: Using five cards to encode each integer in Z/6Z. In: Innovative Security Solutions for Information Technology and Communications, pp. 165–177 (2022)
19. Ruangwises, S., Itoh, T.: Securely computing the $n$-variable equality function with $2n$ cards. In: Theory and Applications of Models of Computation, pp. 25–36 (2020)
20. Shikata, H., Toyoda, K., Miyahara, D., Mizuki, T.: Card-minimal protocols for symmetric Boolean functions of more than seven inputs. In: Theoretical Aspects of Computing - ICTAC 2022, pp. 388–406 (2022)
21. Shinagawa, K., Kanai, K., Miyamoto, K., Nuida, K.: How to covertly and uniformly scramble the 15 puzzle and rubik's cube. In: Broder, A.Z., Tamir, T. (eds.) Fun with Algorithms. LIPIcs, vol. 291, pp. 30:1–30:15, Dagstuhl, Germany. Schloss Dagstuhl (2024)

22. Shinagawa, K., Mizuki, T.: The six-card trick: Secure computation of three-input equality. In: Information Security and Cryptology, pp. 123–131 (2018)
23. Shinagawa, K., Nuida, K.: A single shuffle is enough for secure card-based computation of any Boolean circuit. Discret. Appl. Math. **289**, 248–261 (2021)
24. Shinagawa, K., Nuida, K.: Single-shuffle full-open card-based protocols imply private simultaneous messages protocols. Cryptology ePrint Archive, Paper 2022/1306 (2022)
25. Shinagawa, K., Nuida, K.: Card-based protocols imply PSM protocols. In: 42nd International Symposium on Theoretical Aspects of Computer Science (STACS 2025). Leibniz International Proceedings in Informatics (LIPIcs), vol. 327, pp. 72:1–72:18 (2025)
26. Shinagawa, K., Nuida, K.: Cyclic equalizability of words and its application to card-based cryptography. In: Jez, A., Otop, J. (eds.) Fundamentals of Computation Theory. LNCS, vol. 16106, pp. 406–419. Springer, Singapore (2025)
27. Shinagawa, K., Nuida, K.: A note on single-cut full-open protocols (2025)
28. Takahashi, Y., Shinagawa, K., Shikata, H., Mizuki, T.: Efficient card-based protocols for symmetric functions using four-colored decks. In: ACM ASIA Public-Key Cryptography Workshop, pp. 1–10 (2024)
29. Toyoda, K., Miyahara, D., Mizuki, T.: Another use of the five-card trick: card-minimal secure three-input majority function evaluation. In: Progress in Cryptology—INDOCRYPT 2021, pp. 536–555 (2021)
30. Tozawa, K., Morita, H., Mizuki, T.: Single-shuffle card-based protocol with eight cards per gate. In: Unconventional Computation and Natural Computation, pp. 171–185 (2023)
31. Yao, A.C.: Protocols for secure computations. In: Proceedings of the 23rd Annual Symposium on Foundations of Computer Science, SFCS 1982, pp. 160–164 (1982)

# The Heterogeneous Rural Postman Problem

Pengxiang Pan[1,2], Suding Liu[3], and Hongtao Zhu[4(✉)]

[1] School of Artificial Intelligence, Taizhou University, Taizhou 318000, Zhejiang, China
pengxiang@tzc.edu.cn
[2] School of Mathematics and Statistics, Yunnan University, Kunming 650504, Yunnan, China
[3] School of Science, Xihua University, Chengdu 610039, Sichuan, China
suding314@xhu.edu.cn
[4] Faculty of Engineering, Universiti Malaya, Lembah Pantai, 50603 Kuala Lumpur, Malaysia
htZhu86@outlook.com

**Abstract.** We address the heterogeneous rural postman problem, which extends the rural postman problem to a multi-vehicle setting with nonuniform speeds $\lambda_1, \lambda_2, \ldots, \lambda_k$. In this model, we are asked to find $k$ tours in a given graph $G$ for $k$ vehicles, each starting and ending at a common depot $r$, such that every required edge is covered by at least one of these tours. The objective is to minimize the maximum completion time among all vehicles, where the completion time for a vehicle is computed as the length of its tour divided by its speed. The main contribution of our paper is designing a constant-factor approximation algorithm to solve the heterogeneous rural postman problem.

**Keywords:** Heterogeneous · Rural postman · Approximation algorithm · Time complexity

## 1 Introduction

The tour cover problem represents a fundamental class of combinatorial optimization problems with ubiquitous applications, spanning multi-vehicle routing [2,8,15], nurse station location [6], and data collection in wireless sensor networks [16,17]. A predominant objective in these scenarios is the minimization of the maximum service time (the min-max criterion). Consequently, substantial academic effort has been channeled into optimizing tour cover models under this min-max framework.

In the context of route planning, Frederickson et al. [7] studied the $k$-traveling salesman problem ($k$-TSP) in 1978, which can be viewed as the cycle cover problem with a depot, where the cycle is a tour whose vertices cannot be repeated. This problem considers covering all vertices of a given complete graph using


Y. Li et al. (Eds.): COCOON 2026, LNCS 16835, pp. 28–40, 2027.
https://doi.org/10.1007/978-981-92-3309-0_3

several cycles, each starting from a fixed depot. The objective is to minimize the maximum length among these cycles, where the length of a cycle is the sum of the lengths of the edges on that cycle. By employing a splitting technique, Frederickson et al. [7] proposed a $(\frac{5}{2} - \frac{1}{k})$-approximation algorithm for the $k$-TSP. When $k = 1$, the $k$-TSP reduces to the metric traveling salesman problem (metric TSP), which is to find a minimum length cycle visiting all vertices in a complete graph with edge lengths satisfying the triangle inequality. Using a technique for converting a tour into a cycle, Christofides [3] developed a $\frac{3}{2}$-approximation algorithm for the metric TSP in 1976. More recently, Karlin et al. [11] designed a new approximation algorithm for the metric TSP in 2023, achieving an approximation ratio of $\frac{3}{2} - \epsilon$, where $\epsilon > 10^{-36}$ is a positive constant.

Correspondingly, Frederickson et al. [7] also studied the $k$-Chinese postman problem ($k$-CPP) in 1978, which considers covering all edges of an undirected graph using $k$ tours starting from a fixed depot. The objective is to minimize the maximum length among these tours. Using a splitting technique, Frederickson et al. [7] designed a $(2 - \frac{1}{k})$-approximation algorithm for the $k$-CPP. In particular, the 1-Chinese postman problem corresponds to the classical Chinese postman problem proposed by Guan [10] in 1960. By employing an optimal algorithm for the maximum weight matching problem [12], Edmonds and Johnson [4] developed a polynomial time optimal algorithm for solving the Chinese postman problem in 1973.

It is worth noting that in practical route planning scenarios, the service vehicles may have different speeds. In 2016, Gørtz et al. [9] first introduced the heterogeneous traveling salesman problem (HTSP), which can be viewed as the heterogeneous cycle cover problem with a depot. The problem is defined as follows: Given an undirected complete graph $G = (V, E; w)$, a fixed depot $r \in V$, and $k$ vehicles with respective speeds $\lambda_1, \lambda_2, \ldots, \lambda_k$, where the edge length function $w : E \to \mathbb{R}^+$ satisfies the triangle inequality, it is asked to find $k$ cycles, each starting at the depot $r$, such that the union of these cycles visits all vertices in $V$. The objective is to minimize the maximum completion time among all vehicles, where the completion time of a vehicle is defined as the total length of its assigned cycle divided by its speed. When all vehicle speeds are identical, the problem reduces to the $k$-TSP. By using a technique that guesses the optimal value along with a layered assignment strategy, Gørtz et al. [9] developed a $90(1 + \delta)$-approximation algorithm for the HTSP, where $\delta > 0$ is any constant. Other heterogeneous cycle cover problems can be found in [1,14,18].

Drawing an analogy to the motivation behind the HTSP, Li et al. [13] in 2022 considered a heterogeneous version of the $k$-CPP, referred to as the heterogeneous Chinese postman problem (HCPP). The problem is defined as follows: Given an undirected graph $G = (V, E; w)$, a fixed depot $r \in V$, and $k$ vehicles with respective speeds $\lambda_1, \lambda_2, \ldots, \lambda_k$, where the length function $w : E \to \mathbb{R}^+$ satisfies the triangle inequality, it is asked to find $k$ tours, each starting at the depot $r$, such that the union of these tours traverses all edges in $E$. The objective is to minimize the maximum completion time among all vehicles, where the completion time of a vehicle is defined as the total length of its assigned tour divided by its speed. When all vehicle speeds are identical, the problem reduces to the $k$-CPP. By guessing the optimal value and applying a layered assignment technique, Li et al. [13] developed a $20.8765(1+\delta)$-approximation algorithm for solving the HCPP, where $\delta > 0$ is any constant.

According to the HCPP description, it can be observed that in this problem, all edges are required to be served. However, in practical route planning scenarios, it is often unnecessary to serve all edges; instead, only a specified subset of edges needs to be traversed. For example, in post-disaster road reconstruction, construction teams need to be dispatched to repair and rebuild damaged roads. The route planning for these teams only needs to ensure that the damaged roads are serviced, while other roads, which remain passable, do not require intervention.

Based on the motivations of the HTSP and the HCPP, as well as the above practical observation, it is natural for us to consider the heterogeneous rural postman problem (HRPP). The HRPP is defined as follows: Given an undirected graph $G = (V, E; w; E')$ with a subset of required edges $E' \subseteq E$, a depot $r \in V$, a length function $w : E \to \mathbb{R}^+$ that satisfies the triangle inequality, and $k$ vehicles having speeds $\lambda_1, \lambda_2, \ldots, \lambda_k$, we are asked to find $k$ tours $C_1, \ldots, C_k$, denoted by $\mathcal{C} = \{C_i \mid i = 1, 2, \ldots, k\}$, such that each tour starts at the depot $r$, and the union of all tours collectively traverses every required edge $e \in E'$ at least once. The objective is to minimize the maximum completion time among all vehicles, i.e., $\min_{\mathcal{C}} \max \left\{ \frac{w(C_i)}{\lambda_i} \mid i = 1, 2, \ldots, k \right\}$, where the completion time of a vehicle is defined as the total length of its assigned tour divided by its speed.

The HRPP generalizes several well-known routing problems, including the rural postman problem (RPP) [5], the heterogeneous Chinese postman problem (HCPP) [13], and the heterogeneous traveling salesman problem (HTSP) [9]. When the number of vehicles is $k = 1$, the HRPP reduces to the RPP. When the set of required edges satisfies $E' = E$, the HRPP becomes the HCPP. Furthermore, if $G$ is a complete graph, the required edges in $E'$ are pairwise disjoint, and each required edge in $E'$ is sufficiently short and can be regarded as a vertex, then the HRPP reduces to the HTSP.

To the best of our knowledge, the HRPP introduced above has not yet been explored in existing literature. We anticipate that this novel model and its related variants could lead to a wide range of practical applications. In what follows, for any small constant $\delta > 0$, we propose a $134.4434(1+\delta)$-approximation algorithm for the HRPP, which runs in time polynomial in both the input size and $\frac{1}{\delta}$.

## 2 Algorithm Description

In this section, we focus on the heterogeneous rural postman problem (HRPP), which extends the classical rural postman problem (RPP). Since the RPP [5] is known to be NP-hard, the HRPP naturally inherits this computational complexity. Consequently, we aim to develop an approximation algorithm to tackle the HRPP. Without loss of generality, we assume that all given graphs are connected; otherwise, the HRPP admits no feasible solution.

When designing an approximation algorithm for the HRPP, the following concept plays a key role.

**Definition 1.** (Gørtz et al. [9]) *Let $G = (V, E; w)$ be a weighted graph with $w : E \to \mathbb{R}^+$, and let $M > 0$ and $\varepsilon > 0$ be two given constants. For each integer $i \geq 0$, let $\mathcal{T}_i$ denote a set of tours in $G$, each starting from the depot $r$. The union $\bigcup_{i\geq 0} \mathcal{T}_i$ is called $(\alpha, \beta)_{M,\varepsilon}$-*assignable *if the following two conditions are satisfied:*

(1) *$w(C) \leq \alpha \cdot (1+\varepsilon)^i M$ holds for each $i \geq 0$ and every $C \in \mathcal{T}_i$;*
(2) *$\sum_{j\geq i} w(\mathcal{T}_j) \leq \beta M \cdot \Lambda((1+\varepsilon)^{i-1})$ holds for each $i \geq 0$, where $w(\mathcal{T}_j) = \sum_{C\in\mathcal{T}_j} w(C) = \sum_{C\in\mathcal{T}_j}\sum_{e\in C} w(e)$, and $\Lambda((1+\varepsilon)^{i-1})$ denotes the sum of all speeds no less than $(1+\varepsilon)^{i-1}$.*

For simplicity, we denote the collection by $\{\mathcal{T}_i\}_{i\geq 0}$ instead of writing the full union $\bigcup_{i\geq 0} \mathcal{T}_i$. Based on Definition 1 and the algorithm proposed by Gørtz et al. [9], denoted as $\mathcal{A}_{assign}$, we have the following result.

**Lemma 1.** (Gørtz et al. [9]) *Given a $(\alpha, \beta)_{M,\varepsilon}$-assignable collection of tours $\{\mathcal{T}_i\}_{i\geq 0}$, where each tour starts from the depot $r$, the algorithm $\mathcal{A}_{assign}$ can assign the tours to $k$ vehicles in $O(n^6 + \log w(E))$ time, such that the completion time of any vehicle is at most $((1+\varepsilon)\alpha + \beta)M$.*

Based on Lemma 1, we use the following two-stage strategy to design an approximation algorithm for the HRPP:

(1) For a given graph $G = (V, E; w; E')$, construct a $(\alpha, \beta)_{M,\varepsilon}$-assignable collection of subtours such that every required edge $e \in E'$ is covered by at least one subtour;
(2) Assign the collection of subtours obtained in (1) to $k$ vehicles, aiming to minimize the maximum completion time among them.

Let $G = (V, E; w; E')$ be a given weighted undirected graph, and define $V' = V(G[E']) \cup \{r\}$. As a preprocessing step in our algorithm, using two parameters $M$ and $\varepsilon$ (to be specified later), we partition $V'$ and $E'$ as follows:

- The vertex set $V'$ is partitioned into subsets $V'_0, V'_1, V'_2, \ldots$, where $V'_0 = \{v \in V' \mid d(r, v) \leq M\}$, and for each $i \geq 1$, $V'_i = \{v \in V' \mid (1+\varepsilon)^{i-1}M < d(r, v) \leq (1+\varepsilon)^i M\}$, where $d(r, v)$ denotes the shortest-path distance from $r$ to $v$ in graph $G$.
- Similarly, the edge set $E'$ is partitioned into subsets $E'_0, E'_1, E'_2, \ldots$, where $E'_0 = \{rv \in E' \mid d(r, v) \leq M\}$, and for each $i \geq 1$, $E'_i = \{vv' \in E' \mid d(r, v) \leq (1+\varepsilon)^i M$ and $(1+\varepsilon)^{i-1}M < d(r, v') \leq (1+\varepsilon)^i M\}$.

For each $i \geq 1$, define the cumulative sets of vertices and edges as follows:

$$V'_{\leq i} := \bigcup_{j\leq i} V'_j, \quad V'_{\geq i} := \bigcup_{j\geq i} V'_j, \quad E'_{\leq i} := \bigcup_{j\leq i} E'_j, \quad E'_{\geq i} := \bigcup_{j\geq i} E'_j.$$

Following this layered structure, we now design an approximation algorithm for the HRPP, as described below:

Algorithm: $\mathcal{A}_{HRP}$

Input: A weighted undirected graph $G = (V, E; w; E')$, a subset of required edges $E' \subseteq E$, a depot $r \in V$, a length function $w : E \rightarrow \mathbb{R}^+$, $k$ vehicles with speeds $\lambda_1$, $\lambda_2$, ..., $\lambda_k$ respectively, and a constant $\varepsilon > 0$.

Output: A set $\mathcal{C} = \{C_i \mid i = 1, 2, \ldots, k\}$ of $k$ tours corresponding to the $k$ vehicles.

Begin

Step 1 Set $M = \max_{vv' \in E'} \left\{\frac{d(r,v)+w(vv')+d(v',r)}{\lambda_{\max}}\right\}$, where $\lambda_{\max} = \max\{\lambda_i \mid i = 1, 2, \ldots, k\}$;

Step 2 Using $M$ and $\varepsilon$ (to be specified later), partition $V'$ into $V'_0, V'_1, \ldots$, and $E'$ into $E'_0, E'_1, \ldots$, according to the partitioning method described above; For convenience, assume the number of subsets in the partition is $t + 1$, i.e., $(1 + \varepsilon)^{t-1}M \leq \max\{d(r, v) \mid v \in V'\} \leq (1 + \varepsilon)^t M$;

Step 3 Construct an auxiliary complete graph $\widetilde{G} = (V', \widetilde{E}; \widetilde{w})$ from the graph $G = (V, E; w; E')$, where $\widetilde{E} = \{uv \mid u, v \in V'\}$, and the weight function $\widetilde{w}$ for any edge $uv \in \widetilde{E}$ is defined as follows:
- If the edge $uv \in E'$, then $\widetilde{w}(uv) = w(uv)$;
- Otherwise, $\widetilde{w}(uv)$ is defined as the length of the shortest path between $u$ and $v$ in the graph $G$;

(Note: Each edge $uv \in E'$ in $\widetilde{G}$ corresponds to the edge $uv$ in the original graph $G$, and each edge $uv \in \widetilde{E} \setminus E'$ corresponds to a shortest path between $u$ and $v$ in $G$.)

Step 4 Find a layered spanning tree $\mathcal{H} = \bigcup_{i=0}^{t} H_i$ in the complete graph $\widetilde{G}$, where $H_i$ is the edge set of a minimum spanning tree of the graph obtained by contracting the vertex subset $V'_{<i}$ in $\widetilde{G}[V'_{\leq i}]$; For each $i = 0, 1, \ldots, t$, set $H'_i = H_i \cup E'_i$;

Step 5 If (there exists $l \in \{1, 2, \ldots, t\}$ such that $\sum_{j \geq l} \widetilde{w}(H'_j) > (7 + 6/\varepsilon) \cdot M \cdot \Lambda((1 + \varepsilon)^{l-1})$) then

Set $M := (1 + \delta)M$, where $\delta$ is a small constant; Go to Step 2;

Step 6 Set $\mathcal{S}_0^m$ $(= \mathcal{S}_0) = \{r\} \cup \widetilde{G}[H'_0]$, and $\gamma = \frac{\varepsilon}{(2+\varepsilon)(1+\varepsilon)}$;

Step 7 For all $i \in \{1, 2, \ldots, t\}$, let $\mathcal{S}_i$ be the set of all connected components in $\widetilde{G}[H'_i]$, and set $\mathcal{S}_i^m = \emptyset$ and $\mathcal{S}_i^u = \emptyset$;

Step 8 For all $i \in \{1, 2, \ldots, t\}, \eta \in \mathcal{S}_i$ do:

If $(\widetilde{w}(\eta) \geq \gamma \cdot (1 + \varepsilon)^i M)$ then

Set $\mathcal{S}_i^m := \mathcal{S}_i^m \cup \{\eta\}$;

Else

Set $\mathcal{S}_i^u := \mathcal{S}_i^u \cup \{\eta\}$;

Step 9 For all $i \in \{1, 2, \ldots, t\}, \sigma \in \mathcal{S}_i^u$ do:

Find a connected component $\pi(\sigma)$ in $\widetilde{G}[H'_{i-1}]$ such that $\pi(\sigma) \cap \sigma \neq \emptyset$;

Step 10 For all $i \in \{0, 1, 2, \ldots, t - 1\}, \tau \in \mathcal{S}_i^m$ do:

(10.1) Set Dangle$(\tau) = \{\sigma \in \mathcal{S}_{i+1}^u : \pi(\sigma) = \tau\}$;

(10.2) Find an Eulerian tour in the Eulerian graph $(\tau \cup \text{Dangle}(\tau)) + (\tau \cup \text{Dangle}(\tau))$, partition this tour into maximal paths of length at most $2(1 + \varepsilon)^{i+1}M$, and convert these into corresponding paths in $G$, denoted as $P_1, P_2, \ldots, P_q$;

(10.3) For each $j \in \{1, \ldots, q\}$, augment $P_j$ by connecting $r$ to both endpoints of $P_j$ via shortest paths (if $q = 1$, define both endpoints as the vertex in $P_j$ closest to $r$), to obtain a set of subtours, denoted as $\mathcal{T}_i(\tau)$;

Step 11 For each $i \in \{0, 1, \ldots, t-1\}$, set $\mathcal{T}_i = \bigcup_{\tau \in \mathcal{S}_i^m} \mathcal{T}_i(\tau)$; Use the algorithm $\mathcal{A}_{assign}$ [9] to combine $\{\mathcal{T}_i\}_{i \geq 0} = \bigcup_{i \geq 0} \mathcal{T}_i$ into $k$ tours $C_1, \ldots, C_k$ corresponding to the $k$ vehicles;

Step 12 Output the set $\mathcal{C} = \{C_i \mid i = 1, 2, \ldots, k\}$ of $k$ tours for the $k$ vehicles.

End

According to the algorithm $\mathcal{A}_{HRP}$, we first obtain the following lemmas.

**Lemma 2.** *Given an instance $G = (V, E; w; E')$ of the HRPP with a constant $M > 0$, if $OPT \leq M$, then for each $l \geq 0$, we have*

$$w(E'_{\geq l}) \leq M \cdot \Lambda((1+\varepsilon)^{l-1}),$$

*where $OPT$ denotes the optimal value of the instance $G = (V, E; w; E')$ for the HRPP, and $\Lambda((1+\varepsilon)^{l-1})$ denotes the sum of the speeds of all vehicles with speed at least $(1+\varepsilon)^{l-1}$.*

*Proof.* According to the definition of $E'_{\geq l}$, it is clear that for any edge $e = vv' \in E'_{\geq l}$, we have $\max\{d(r,v), d(r,v')\} \geq (1+\varepsilon)^{l-1}M$. Now consider any edge $e = vv' \in E'_{\geq l}$. Without loss of generality, assume that the edge $e = vv'$ is traversed by a vehicle with speed $\lambda'$ in an optimal solution for the HRPP. Since $\max\{d(r,v), d(r,v')\} \geq (1+\varepsilon)^{l-1}M$, it follows that $\lambda' \cdot OPT \geq (1+\varepsilon)^{l-1}M$. By assumption, since $OPT \leq M$, each vehicle with speed $\lambda'$ travels at most $\lambda' \cdot OPT \leq \lambda' \cdot M$. Therefore, we can deduce that

$$\lambda' \cdot M \geq \lambda' \cdot OPT \geq (1+\varepsilon)^{l-1}M,$$

which implies $\lambda' \geq (1+\varepsilon)^{l-1}$. In other words, the speed of any vehicle that traverses an edge in $E'_{\geq l}$ is at least $(1+\varepsilon)^{l-1}$.

Since in any feasible solution of the problem, all vehicles must traverse all edges in $E'_{\geq l}$, we have

$$w(E'_{\geq l}) \leq OPT \cdot \Lambda((1+\varepsilon)^{l-1}).$$

Since $OPT \leq M$, it is easy to see that $OPT \cdot \Lambda((1+\varepsilon)^{l-1}) \leq M \cdot \Lambda((1+\varepsilon)^{l-1})$, which implies

$$w(E'_{\geq l}) \leq OPT \cdot \Lambda((1+\varepsilon)^{l-1}) \leq M \cdot \Lambda((1+\varepsilon)^{l-1}),$$

that is, $w(E'_{\geq l}) \leq M \cdot \Lambda((1+\varepsilon)^{l-1})$. □

**Lemma 3.** *Given an instance $G = (V, E; w; E')$ of the HRPP with a constant $M > 0$, if $OPT \leq M$, then for every $l \geq 0$, we have*

$$\widetilde{w}(T^{MS}_{\widetilde{G}/V'_{<l}}) \leq M \cdot \Lambda((1+\varepsilon)^{l-1}),$$

*where OPT denotes the optimal value of the instance* $G = (V, E; w; E')$, $T^{MS}_{\widetilde{G}/V'_{<l}}$ *is a minimum spanning tree of the graph* $\widetilde{G}/V'_{<l}$ *obtained by contracting the vertex subset* $V'_{<l}$ *in* $\widetilde{G}$, *and* $\Lambda((1+\varepsilon)^{l-1})$ *denotes the sum of all speeds at least* $(1+\varepsilon)^{l-1}$.

*Proof.* Similar to the definition of the edge set $E'_{\geq l}$ in the partition process, we define $E_{\geq l}$, meaning that $\max\{d(r,v), d(r,v')\} \geq (1+\varepsilon)^{l-1}M$ holds for any edge $e = vv' \in E_{\geq l}$. In any optimal solution $\mathcal{C}^*$ of the HRPP, now consider an arbitrary edge $e = vv' \in \mathcal{C}^* \cap E_{\geq l}$. Without loss of generality, assume that edge $e = vv'$ is traversed by a vehicle with speed $\lambda'$ in $\mathcal{C}^*$. Since $\max\{d(r,v), d(r,v')\} \geq (1+\varepsilon)^{l-1}M$, we have $\lambda' \cdot OPT \geq (1+\varepsilon)^{l-1}M$, where $OPT$ denotes the optimal value of the instance $G = (V, E; w; E')$ for the HRPP. By assumption, since $OPT \leq M$, the total distance traveled by any vehicle with speed $\lambda'$ is at most $\lambda' \cdot OPT \leq \lambda' \cdot M$. Therefore, we can deduce that

$$\lambda' \cdot M \geq \lambda' \cdot OPT \geq (1+\varepsilon)^{l-1}M,$$

which implies $\lambda' \geq (1+\varepsilon)^{l-1}$. In other words, any vehicle that traverses an edge in $\mathcal{C}^* \cap E_{\geq l}$ must have a speed of at least $(1+\varepsilon)^{l-1}$. This means $w(\mathcal{C}^* \cap E_{\geq l}) \leq OPT \cdot \Lambda((1+\varepsilon)^{l-1})$.

In the optimal solution $\mathcal{C}^*$, since the length function $w(\cdot)$ satisfies the triangle inequality, and all vehicles start from the depot and jointly traverse all vertices in $V'_{\geq l}$, it follows that the optimal solution can be transformed into a tour $C$ covering all vertices in the graph $G/V'_{<l}$, and having $w(C) \leq w(\mathcal{C}^* \cap E_{\geq l})$. Furthermore, according to the construction of the graph $\widetilde{G}$, the tour $C$ can be transformed into a Hamiltonian cycle $\widetilde{C}$ in $\widetilde{G}/V'_{<l}$, satisfying $\widetilde{w}(\widetilde{C}) \leq w(C)$, which implies

$$\widetilde{w}(\widetilde{C}) \leq w(\mathcal{C}^* \cap E_{\geq l}).$$

Since the subgraph corresponding to $\widetilde{C}$ contains a spanning tree, we can conclude that $\widetilde{w}(T^{MS}_{\widetilde{G}/V'_{<l}}) \leq \widetilde{w}(\widetilde{C})$, which implies

$$\widetilde{w}(T^{MS}_{\widetilde{G}/V'_{<l}}) \leq w(\mathcal{C}^* \cap E_{\geq l}).$$

Because $w(\mathcal{C}^* \cap E_{\geq l}) \leq OPT \cdot \Lambda((1+\varepsilon)^{l-1})$, we obtain

$$\widetilde{w}(T^{MS}_{\widetilde{G}/V'_{<l}}) \leq OPT \cdot \Lambda((1+\varepsilon)^{l-1}).$$

Since $OPT \leq M$, it is easy to see that $OPT \cdot \Lambda((1+\varepsilon)^{l-1}) \leq M \cdot \Lambda((1+\varepsilon)^{l-1})$, which implies

$$\widetilde{w}(T^{MS}_{\widetilde{G}/V'_{<l}}) \leq OPT \cdot \Lambda((1+\varepsilon)^{l-1}) \leq M \cdot \Lambda((1+\varepsilon)^{l-1}),$$

that is, $\widetilde{w}(T^{MS}_{\widetilde{G}/V'_{<l}}) \leq M \cdot \Lambda((1+\varepsilon)^{l-1})$. □

By executing Step 4 of the algorithm $\mathcal{A}_{HRP}$, we can find a layered spanning tree $\mathcal{H} = \bigcup_{i=0}^{t} H_i$ in the graph $\widetilde{G}$, where $H_i$ is the edge set of a minimum spanning tree of the graph obtained from $\widetilde{G}[V'_{\leq i}]$ by contracting the vertex subset $V'_{<i}$. According to the arguments in [9], the following result holds.

**Lemma 4.** [9] *Given a weighted complete graph $\widetilde{G} = (V', \widetilde{E}; \widetilde{w})$ and constants $M > 0$ and $\varepsilon > 0$, the layered spanning tree $\mathcal{H} = \bigcup_{i=0}^{t} H_i$ generated in Step 4 of the algorithm $\mathcal{A}_{HRP}$ satisfies the following conditions:*

- *Along every path from depot to leaf, the vertex levels are non-decreasing;*
- *For every $i \geq 0$, we have $\sum_{j \geq i} \widetilde{w}(H_j) \leq (6+6/\varepsilon) \cdot \widetilde{w}(T^{MS}_{\widetilde{G}/V'_{<i}})$, where $T^{MS}_{\widetilde{G}/V'_{<l}}$ denotes a minimum spanning tree of the graph $\widetilde{G}/V'_{<l}$ obtained from $\widetilde{G}$ by contracting the vertex subset $V'_{<l}$.*

According to Lemma 3 and Lemma 4, it is easy to see that for every $i \geq 0$, $\sum_{j \geq i} \widetilde{w}(H_j) \leq (6+6/\varepsilon) \cdot M \cdot \Lambda((1+\varepsilon)^{l-1})$. From the algorithm $\mathcal{A}_{HRP}$, it follows that for any $i \in \{0, 1, \dots, t\}$, we have $H'_i = H_i \cup E'_i$, where for any edge $e \in E'_i$, it holds that $\widetilde{w}(e) = w(e)$. By applying Lemma 2, we further obtain the following result.

**Lemma 5.** *The layered spanning tree $\mathcal{H} = \bigcup_{i=0}^{t} H_i$ generated in Step 4 of the algorithm $\mathcal{A}_{HRP}$ satisfies the following conditions:*

- *Along every path from depot to leaf, the vertex levels are non-decreasing.*
- *If $OPT \leq M$, then for every $i \geq 0$, we have $\sum_{j \geq i} \widetilde{w}(H'_j) \leq (7 + 6/\varepsilon) \cdot M \cdot \Lambda((1+\varepsilon)^{l-1})$.*

According to Steps 6–9 of the algorithm $\mathcal{A}_{HRP}$, we obtain the following conclusion.

**Lemma 6.** *For any $i \geq 1$ and $\sigma \in \mathcal{S}_i^u$, we have $\pi(\sigma) \in \mathcal{S}_{i-1}$, and moreover, $\pi(\sigma) \in \mathcal{S}_{i-1}^m$.*

*Proof.* First, we prove that $\pi(\sigma) \in \mathcal{S}_{i-1}$. Since $\sigma \in \mathcal{S}_i^u$, we have $\widetilde{w}(\sigma) < \gamma \cdot (1+\varepsilon)^i M$. By the definition of $\mathcal{S}_i^u$, it follows that for any vertex $v \in V'(\sigma)$, we have $v \in V'_{\leq i}$. Furthermore, we can deduce that $v \in V'_i \cup V'_{i-1}$. Otherwise, assume there exists an edge $vv' \in \widetilde{E}(\sigma)$ with $v \in V'_i$ and $v' \in V'_{<i-1}$. Then $\widetilde{w}(\sigma) \geq \widetilde{w}(vv') \geq d(r,v) - d(r,v') > (1+\varepsilon)^{i-1}M - (1+\varepsilon)^{i-2}M > \gamma \cdot (1+\varepsilon)^i M$, which contradicts the assumption that $\sigma \in \mathcal{S}_i^u$. Therefore, for any vertex $v \in V'(\sigma)$, we have $v \in V'_i \cup V'_{i-1}$.

Without loss of generality, assume there exists a vertex $x' \in V'(\sigma)$ with $x' \in V'_i$. Since the graph $\mathcal{H} \cup E'$ is connected, there exists an edge $yx \in \widetilde{E}$ such that $yx \in \widetilde{E}(P_{r,x'})$, where $P_{r,x'}$ denotes a shortest path in $\mathcal{H} \cup E'$ from $r$ to $x'$, and $x \in V'_i$, $y \in V'_{\leq i-1}$. It follows that $y \in V'_{i-1}$. Therefore, there exists $\pi(\sigma) \in \mathcal{S}_{i-1}$ such that $\pi(\sigma) \cap \sigma \neq \emptyset$.

Next, we prove that $\pi(\sigma) \in \mathcal{S}_{i-1}^m$. When $i = 1$, by algorithm $\mathcal{A}_{HRP}$, it is clear that $\pi(\sigma) = \{r\} \cup \widetilde{G}[H_0'] = \mathcal{S}_0$, and $\pi(\sigma) \in \mathcal{S}_0^m$. When $i \geq 2$, by the above discussion we know that $\pi(\sigma) \in \mathcal{S}_{i-1}$. Using a similar argument, since the graph $\mathcal{H} \cup E'$ is connected, there exists a vertex $z \in \pi(\sigma)$ such that $z \in V_{<i-1}'$. By applying the triangle inequality twice, we have

$$d(z,y) + d(y,x) \geq d(z,x) \geq d(r,x) - d(r,z).$$

Since $x \in V_i'$ and $z \in V_{<i-1}'$, it follows that

$$d(r,x) - d(r,z) > (1+\varepsilon)^{i-1}M - (1+\varepsilon)^{i-2}M = \varepsilon(1+\varepsilon)^{i-2}M,$$

that is, $d(r,x) - d(r,z) > \varepsilon(1+\varepsilon)^{i-2}M$, which implies $d(z,y) + d(y,x) > \varepsilon(1+\varepsilon)^{i-2}M$. Since $\sigma$ is unmarked, i.e., $\sigma \in \mathcal{S}_i^u$, we have

$$d(y,x) = \widetilde{w}(yx) \leq \widetilde{w}(\sigma) < \gamma \cdot (1+\varepsilon)^i M.$$

Therefore, we obtain

$$\widetilde{w}(\pi(\sigma)) \geq d_{\pi(\sigma)}(z,y) \geq d(z,y) > \varepsilon(1+\varepsilon)^{i-2}M - \gamma\cdot(1+\varepsilon)^i M = \gamma\cdot(1+\varepsilon)^{i-1}M,$$

which shows that $\pi(\sigma)$ is marked, i.e., $\pi(\sigma) \in \mathcal{S}_{i-1}^m$. □

According to Step 10 of the algorithm $\mathcal{A}_{HRP}$, by employing a similar discussion process as in [9], the following two lemmas can be easily obtained.

**Lemma 7.** *For any $C \in \mathcal{T}_i(\tau)$, we have $w(C) \leq (4+4\varepsilon)(1+\varepsilon)^i M$.*

*Proof.* For any $C \in \mathcal{T}_i(\tau)$, according to the algorithm $\mathcal{A}_{HRP}$, it is clear that $C$ contains some path $P_j$ $(1 \leq j \leq q)$ together with two shortest paths from $r$ to the two endpoints of $P_j$, where $q$ is computed in Step 10 of the algorithm $\mathcal{A}_{HRP}$. By the construction of $P_j$, we have

$$w(P_j) \leq 2(1+\varepsilon)^{i+1}M.$$

Moreover, since $P_j$ contains only edges from $E_{\leq i+1}$, the total length of the two added shortest paths is at most $2(1+\varepsilon)^{i+1}M$. Therefore, it follows that $w(C) \leq 4(1+\varepsilon)^{i+1}M = (4+4\varepsilon)(1+\varepsilon)^i M$. □

**Lemma 8.** $\sum_{C\in\mathcal{T}_i(\tau)} w(C) \leq \max\{4+\frac{4}{\varepsilon}, 10\} \cdot \widetilde{w}(\tau \cup \mathrm{Dangle}(\tau))$.

*Proof.* We prove this result by considering two cases according to the value of $q$, where $q$ is computed in Step 10 of the algorithm $\mathcal{A}_{HRP}$.

**Case 1:** $q = 1$, i.e., $\mathcal{T}_i(\tau)$ contains only one subtour.

When $i = 0$, since $\tau$ contains the depot $r$, we have $w(C) \leq 2\widetilde{w}(\tau \cup \mathrm{Dangle}(\tau))$. When $i > 0$, by Lemma 6, there exists a vertex $u \in \tau$ such that $u \in V_{<i}'$. By the construction of the tour, we obtain

$$w(C) \leq 2(1+\varepsilon)^{i-1}M + 2\widetilde{w}(\tau \cup \mathrm{Dangle}(\tau)).$$

Since $\tau \in \mathcal{S}_i^m$, by the algorithm $\mathcal{A}_{HRP}$ we know that $\widetilde{w}(\tau) \geq \gamma \cdot (1+\varepsilon)^i M$, implying

$$(1+\varepsilon)^{i-1} M \leq \frac{2+\varepsilon}{\varepsilon} \cdot \widetilde{w}(\tau).$$

Therefore,

$$\begin{aligned} w(C) &\leq 2(1+\varepsilon)^{i-1} M + 2\widetilde{w}(\tau \cup \text{Dangle}(\tau)) \\ &\leq (2 \cdot \frac{2+\varepsilon}{\varepsilon} + 2) \cdot \widetilde{w}(\tau \cup \text{Dangle}(\tau)) \\ &= (4 + \frac{4}{\varepsilon}) \cdot \widetilde{w}(\tau \cup \text{Dangle}(\tau)), \end{aligned}$$

which implies $\sum_{C \in \mathcal{T}_i(\tau)} w(C) = w(C) \leq (4 + \frac{4}{\varepsilon}) \cdot \widetilde{w}(\tau \cup \text{Dangle}(\tau))$.

**Case 2:** $q \geq 2$.

According to Step 10, we have $4\widetilde{w}(\tau \cup \text{Dangle}(\tau)) > (q-1) \cdot 2(1+\varepsilon)^{i+1} M$, i.e.,

$$(1+\varepsilon)^{i+1} M < \frac{2\widetilde{w}(\tau \cup \text{Dangle}(\tau))}{q-1}.$$

Since $\widetilde{E}(\tau \cup \text{Dangle}(\tau)) \subseteq \widetilde{E}_{\leq i+1}$, it follows that $V'(\tau \cup \text{Dangle}(\tau)) \subseteq V'_{\leq i+1}$. This means that the length of each added shortest path from $r$ is at most $(1+\varepsilon)^{i+1} M$. Hence,

$$\begin{aligned} \sum_{C \in \mathcal{T}_i(\tau)} w(C) &\leq 2q \cdot (1+\varepsilon)^{i+1} M + 2\widetilde{w}(\tau \cup \text{Dangle}(\tau)) \\ &\leq \left(\frac{4q}{q-1} + 2\right) \cdot \widetilde{w}(\tau \cup \text{Dangle}(\tau)) \\ &\leq 10 \cdot \widetilde{w}(\tau \cup \text{Dangle}(\tau)). \end{aligned}$$

Combining Case 1 and Case 2, we conclude that $\sum_{C \in \mathcal{T}_i(\tau)} w(C) \leq \max\{4 + \frac{4}{\varepsilon}, 10\} \cdot \widetilde{w}(\tau \cup \text{Dangle}(\tau))$. □

Based on Lemmas 6–8, we obtain the following lemma.

**Lemma 9.** *If for any $i \geq 0$, it holds that $\sum_{j \geq i} \widetilde{w}(H'_j) \leq (7 + 6/\varepsilon) \cdot M \cdot \Lambda((1+\varepsilon)^{l-1})$, then the collection $\{\mathcal{T}_i\}_{i \geq 0}$ obtained in Step 10 of the algorithm $\mathcal{A}_{HRP}$ is $(\alpha, \beta)_{M,\varepsilon}$-assignable, where $\alpha = 4 + 4\varepsilon$, $\beta = (7 + 6/\varepsilon) \cdot \max\{10, 4 + \frac{4}{\varepsilon}\}$, and $\mathcal{T}_i = \bigcup_{\tau \in \mathcal{S}_i^m} \mathcal{T}_i(\tau)$.*

*Proof.* By Definition 1, to prove that the collection $\{\mathcal{T}_i\}_{i \geq 0}$ is $(\alpha, \beta)_{M,\varepsilon}$-assignable, it suffices to show that $\{\mathcal{T}_i\}_{i \geq 0}$ satisfies the two conditions stated in Definition 1. Without loss of generality, consider any $i \geq 0$. By Lemma 7, condition (1) is satisfied. According to the assumption, it remains to prove that $\sum_{j \geq i} w(\mathcal{T}_j) \leq \max\{10, 4 + \frac{4}{\varepsilon}\} \cdot \sum_{j \geq i} \widetilde{w}(H'_j)$.

From the algorithm $\mathcal{A}_{HRP}$, it is clear that $\{\text{Dangle}(\tau) : \tau \in \mathcal{S}_j^m\}$ is a partition of $\mathcal{S}_{j+1}^u$. Hence,

$$\sum_{j\geq i} \left(\widetilde{w}(\mathcal{S}_j^m) + \widetilde{w}(\mathcal{S}_{j+1}^u)\right) \leq \sum_{j\geq i} \widetilde{w}(\mathcal{S}_j) = \sum_{j\geq i} \widetilde{w}(H_j').$$

By Lemma 6, we have $\sum_{\tau\in\mathcal{S}_j^m} \widetilde{w}(\tau \cup \text{Dangle}(\tau)) = \widetilde{w}(\mathcal{S}_j^m) + \widetilde{w}(\mathcal{S}_{j+1}^u)$. By Lemma 8, it follows that $w(\mathcal{T}_j) = \sum_{\tau\in\mathcal{S}_j^m} w(\mathcal{T}_j(\tau)) = \sum_{\tau\in\mathcal{S}_j^m} \sum_{C\in\mathcal{T}_j(\tau)} w(C) \leq \max\{4+\frac{4}{\varepsilon}, 10\} \cdot \sum_{\tau\in\mathcal{S}_j^m} \widetilde{w}(\tau \cup \text{Dangle}(\tau))$, which implies

$$w(\mathcal{T}_j) \leq \max\{4+\tfrac{4}{\varepsilon}, 10\} \cdot \left(\widetilde{w}(\mathcal{S}_j^m) + \widetilde{w}(\mathcal{S}_{j+1}^u)\right).$$

Therefore,

$$\sum_{j\geq i} w(\mathcal{T}_j) \leq \max\{4+\tfrac{4}{\varepsilon}, 10\} \cdot \sum_{j\geq i} \left(\widetilde{w}(\mathcal{S}_j^m) + \widetilde{w}(\mathcal{S}_{j+1}^u)\right) \leq \max\{4+\tfrac{4}{\varepsilon}, 10\} \cdot \sum_{j\geq i} \widetilde{w}(H_j').$$

□

By Lemma 1 and Lemma 9, we obtain the following theorem.

**Theorem 1.** *For any constant $\delta > 0$, the algorithm $\mathcal{A}_{HRP}$ is a $134.4434(1+\delta)$-approximation algorithm for the HRPP, with the time complexity of $O\big(n^4(n^2 + \frac{1}{\delta}) + \log(w(E))\big)$, where $w(E) = \sum_{e\in E} w(e)$.*

*Proof.* By Lemma 5, when $M \geq OPT$, the stopping condition in Step 5 is not satisfied, and Steps 6–12 continue to be executed. By the updating rule of $M$, it is easy to see that during Steps 6–12, we always have $M \leq (1+\delta)\cdot OPT$.

When we take $\varepsilon = 1.6746$, Lemma 9 implies that the collection of sub-tours $\{\mathcal{T}_i\}_{i\geq 0}$ is $(10.6984, 105.8295)_{M,1.6746}$-assignable. By Lemma 1, Step 11 can assign $\{\mathcal{T}_i\}_{i\geq 0}$ to $k$ vehicles in polynomial time $O(n^6 + \log(w(E)))$, such that the travel time of each vehicle is at most $134.4434 \cdot M$. Therefore, the output value satisfies $OUT \leq 134.4434 \cdot M \leq 134.4434(1+\delta)\cdot OPT$.

From the algorithm $\mathcal{A}_{HRP}$, it is clear that each step of the algorithm can be executed in polynomial time. Next, we analyze the number of iterations. As mentioned above, before $M$ exceeds $(1+\delta)OPT$, the algorithm $\mathcal{A}_{HRP}$ terminates, where

$$\begin{aligned}(1+\delta)OPT &\leq (1+\delta)\cdot \frac{\sum_{uv\in E'}(d(r,u) + w(uv) + d(v,r))}{\lambda_{\max}} \\ &\leq (1+\delta)|E'| \cdot \frac{\max_{uv\in E'}(d(r,u) + w(uv) + d(v,r))}{\lambda_{\max}}.\end{aligned}$$

Since $M$ starts from the initial value $\frac{\max_{uv\in E'}(d(r,u)+w(uv)+d(v,r))}{\lambda_{\max}}$ and is multiplied by $(1+\delta)$ in each iteration, we can conclude that the number of iterations is at most $O(\frac{1}{\delta}\log|E'|)$. This means that Steps 1–4 run in at most time $O(\frac{n^3}{\delta}\log|E'|)$. By Lemma 1, Steps 6-12 can be executed in time $O(n^6 + \log(w(E)))$. Therefore, the overall time complexity of the algorithm $\mathcal{A}_{HRP}$ is $O\big(n^4(n^2 + \frac{1}{\delta}) + \log(w(E))\big)$. □

## 3 Conclusion and Further Work

In this paper, we study the heterogeneous rural postman problem, and design a $134.4434(1+\delta)$-approximation algorithm to solve the problem, with the time complexity of $O\big(n^4(n^2+\frac{1}{\delta})+\log(w(E))\big)$, where $w(E)=\sum_{e\in E} w(e)$.

In further work, it is a challenge for us to design some constant factor approximation algorithms in strongly polynomial time to solve the heterogeneous rural postman problem, and we plan to study other versions of the tour cover problems with nonuniform speeds.

**Acknowledgments.** These authors are grateful to the three anonymous reviewers for their insightful comments and for their suggested changes that improve the current presentation greatly.

**Disclosure of Interests.** The authors have no competing interests to declare that are relevant to the content of this article.

## References


1. Bae, J., Rathinam, S.: A primal-dual approximation algorithm for a two depot heterogeneous traveling salesman problem. Optim. Lett. **10**(6), 1269–1285 (2016)
2. Campbell, A.M., Vandenbussche, D., Hermann, W.: Routing for relief efforts. Transp. Sci. **42**(2), 127–145 (2008)
3. Christofides, N.: Worst-case analysis of a new heuristic for the travelling salesman problem. Report 388, Graduate School of Industrial Administration, Carnegie Mellon University (1976)
4. Edmonds, J., Johnson, E.L.: Matching, Euler tours and the Chinese postman. Math. Program. **5**(1), 88–124 (1973)
5. Eiselt, H.A., Gendreau, M., Laporte, G.: Arc routing problems, part II: the rural postman problem. Oper. Res. **43**(3), 399–414 (1995)
6. Even, G., Garg, N., Könemann, J., Ravi, R., Sinha, A.: Min-max tree covers of graphs. Oper. Res. Lett. **32**(4), 309–315 (2004)
7. Frederickson, G., Hecht, M., Kim, C.: Approximation algorithms for some routing problems. SIAM J. Comput. **7**(2), 178–193 (1978)
8. Golden, B.L., Raghavan, S., Wasil, E.A.: The Vehicle Routing Problem: Latest Advances and New Challenges. Springer, New York (2008)
9. Gørtz, I.L., Molinaro, M., Nagarajan, V., Ravi, R.: Capacitated vehicle routing with nonuniform speeds. Math. Oper. Res. **41**(1), 318–331 (2016)
10. Guan, M.: Graphic programming using odd and even points. Acta Math. Sinica **10**, 263–266 (1960). (in Chinese)
11. Karlin, A., Klein, N., Oveis Gharan, S.: A (slightly) improved approximation algorithm for metric TSP. Oper. Res. **72**(6), 2543–2594 (2024)
12. Korte, B., Vygen, J.: Combinatorial Optimization: Theory and Algorithms. Springer (2018)
13. Li, J., Pan, P., Lichen, J., Cai, L., Wang, W., Liu, S.: Approximation algorithms for solving the heterogeneous Chinese postman problem. J. Comb. Optim. **45**(1), 17 (2023)

14. Prasad, A., Choi, H.L., Sundaram, S.: Min-max tours and paths for task allocation to heterogeneous agents. IEEE Trans. Control Netw. Syst. **7**(3), 1511–1522 (2020)
15. Toth, P., Vigo, D.: Vehicle Routing: Problems, Methods and Applications. MOS-SIAM, Philadelphia (2014)
16. Wu, W., Zhang, Z., Lee, W., Du, D.: Optimal Coverage in Wireless Sensor Networks. Springer, Heidelberg (2020)
17. Xu, W., Liang, W., Lin, X.: Approximation algorithms for min-max cycle cover problems. IEEE Trans. Comput. **64**(3), 600–613 (2015)
18. Yadlapalli, S., Rathinam, S., Darbha, S.: 3-approximation algorithm for a two depot, heterogeneous traveling salesman problem. Optim. Lett. **6**(1), 141–152 (2012)

# Sorting Sequences by Symmetric Reversals

Yu-Heng Su, Jhih-Ming Yang, and Wing-Kai Hon(✉)

National Tsing Hua University, Hsinchu, Taiwan
wkhon@cs.nthu.edu.tw

**Abstract.** Tong et al. (2023) initiated the use of symmetric reversal operations to sort a sequence, and showed that the *decision* problem of sorting a signed sequence can be solved in quadratic time. In this paper, we focus on unsigned sequences, and show that the corresponding decision problem can be solved in linear time. We also show that the corresponding *optimization* problem, which computes the fewest number of operations for the sorting, is NP-hard in general. In the special case where each number in the sequence occurs at most three times, we present a polynomial-time approximation algorithm with ratio 4.

**Keywords:** Symmetric reversal · Genome rearrangement · Breakpoint graph · Minimum common string partition

## 1 Introduction

In the late 1980s, Palmer et al. [8] found that different species such as *Brassica oleracea* (cabbage) and *Brassica campestris* (turnip) contain the same set of genes but in different order. Since then, sorting genes within genomes, which may uncover the evolutionary distance of different species, became a topic that was being studied frequently.

For genome rearrangement, operations involved in the sorting usually have some biological meaning. Example operations include reversals, transpositions, or double-cut-and-joins, where they correspond to possible errors that may occur during the DNA copying process. In general, the goal is to find the fewest number of operations so that one can transform a permutation of genes to the other. Such a number is referred to as the *minimum distance* between the two permutations.

The structure of a DNA consists of two complementary strands that are twisted into a double helix. Each strand is a directional 1D sequence (with a 5′ end and a 3′ end), carrying genetic information. Genes among a genome could appear in any of the strands, so sometimes the genes are labeled with directions. In such a case, the input permutation of a genome rearrangement problem could be *signed* (when directions are considered) or *unsigned* (otherwise). Kececioglu

This research is supported in part by Taiwan NSTC grant 113-2221-E-007-139-MY3.


Y. Li et al. (Eds.): COCOON 2026, LNCS 16835, pp. 41–54, 2027.
https://doi.org/10.1007/978-981-92-3309-0_4

and Sankoff [6] first proposed the minimum distance problem using reversals, and derived lower and upper bounds for unsigned permutation.

Later on, Bafna and Pevzner [1] improved Kececioglu and Sankoff's algorithm for both signed and unsigned permutations, and also introduced the notion of *breakpoint graph* to aid the distance calculation. However, as we now know, the time complexity of a problem highly depends on whether the input permutation is signed or unsigned. Hannenhalli and Pevzner [5] showed that computing the minimum distance using reversals between signed permutations can be done in polynomial time. Yet, when the input is unsigned, Caprara [3] showed that the problem becomes NP-hard; currently, the best approximation factor is achieved by Berman et al. [2], which is 1.375.

Recently, inspired by the "breakpoint reuse" phenomenon reported from comparing genomes of human and mouse [9], Tong et al. [10] proposed a new operation called *symmetric reversal* and devised an $O(n^2)$-time method to *decide* if one can transform a signed sequence to the other by such an operation. Note that it is not required to compute the *fewest* number of operations here. Lai et al. [7] proposed an $O(n)$-time algorithm for the decision problem in a special case of unsigned sequences in which each element appears at most twice, and achieved an approximation ratio of 1.5 for the corresponding optimization problem.

In this paper, we focus on the unsigned case and give an $O(n)$-time algorithm for the *decision* problem (Sect. 3). In contrast, for the *optimization* version of the problem, where we want to compute the minimum symmetric-reversal distance, we show that the problem is NP-hard, via a reduction from the classical sorting-by-reversals problem (Sect. 4). For the special case where each element appears at most three times in a sequence, we give a polynomial-time algorithm to compute the distance within a factor of 4 from the optimal (Sect. 5).

Technically speaking, our results stem from a combination of various existing techniques. First, we define the notion of *outliers* which allows us to extend the results of Lai et al. [7]. Next, we notice a close relation of our problem with the Minimum Common String Partition problem; this inspires us to re-use the idea of Goldstein et al. [4] to design our approximation algorithm; then, by the specific property of our problem, the approximation factor is further improved from 8 to 4. Due to the space constraints, we defer most proofs to the full paper.

## 2 Preliminaries

### 2.1 Problem Definition

We use a sequence of characters to represent the arrangement of genes within a genome, where each character in the sequence represents a gene. Characters may be the same, indicating that they correspond to the same gene. Moreover, the sequence does *not* have a direction, so that if one sequence reads the same as the other one from either ends, then the two sequences are considered the same. For instance, the sequence $[0, 1, 2, 1, 4, 0]$ is considered to be the same as the sequence $[0, 4, 1, 2, 1, 0]$. We additionally assume that adjacent characters in these sequences are different, and the characters in the sequence are already coordinate compressed (i.e., characters are integers between 0 and $n$ where $n$ is the length of the sequence).

A *reversal* is an operation that reverses the order of a substring (i.e., a contiguous subsequence). Furthermore, a *symmetric reversal* requires that the substring begins and ends with the same character. For instance, by a symmetric reversal, we can transform

$$[0, 1, \underline{2, 4, 5, 2}, 4, 0] \quad \text{into} \quad [0, 1, \underline{2, 5, 4, 2}, 4, 0].$$

Note that if the original sequence has adjacent characters to be different, so does the sequence after the symmetric reversal.

Given a sequence $S$, we define a *neighbor* to be an unordered pair of adjacent elements in $S$. The multi-set of all neighbors is called the *neighbor set* $N(S)$ of $S$. For instance, the neighbor set of the sequence $\pi = [0, 2, 1, 2, 0]$ is the multi-set

$$N(\pi) \ = \ \{ \ \langle 0, 2\rangle, \ \langle 2, 1\rangle, \ \langle 1, 2\rangle, \ \langle 2, 0\rangle \ \}.$$

Note that a neighbor is an unordered pair, so we will consider $\langle 2, 1\rangle$ and $\langle 1, 2\rangle$ in the above example as the **same**.

**Definition 1.** *Two sequences $\pi$ and $\tau$ are* related *if and only if $N(\pi) = N(\tau)$.*

In this paper, we are interested in the following *decision* problem:

Given two sequences $\pi$ and $\tau$, is it possible to transform $\pi$ to $\tau$ by a series of symmetric reversal operations?

Surprisingly, the answer is very simple, as stated in the following theorem.

**Theorem 1.** *Two sequences can be transformed from one to the other by symmetric reversals if and only if they are related.*

However, the *optimization* problem of finding the *fewest* number of symmetric reversals needed to transform a sequence to the other may not be easy:

**Theorem 2.** *Finding the fewest number of symmetric reversal operations to transform one sequence to the other is* NP*-hard.*

### 2.2 Breakpoint Graph

*Breakpoint graph* is a common tool for analyzing the minimum number of operations in genome-rearrangement problems. Let $\pi$ and $\tau$ be two related sequences, each of length $n$. For ease of discussion, we denote the characters of $\pi$ and $\tau$ as $[\pi_1, \pi_2, \ldots, \pi_n]$ and $[\tau_1, \tau_2, \ldots, \tau_n]$, respectively. Furthermore, without loss of generality, we assume $\pi_1 = \pi_n = \tau_1 = \tau_n = 0$, such that 0 does not appear elsewhere in these two sequences (we call 0 an *end marker*). The breakpoint graph for $\pi$ and $\tau$ is constructed as follows.[1]

[1] We only consider related sequences here, as two sequences can be transformed to one another only if they are related (Lemma 5).

1. Define a matching function (i.e., a bijection) $F(x)$ that maps each neighbor $x$ in the sequence $\tau$ to an identical neighbor in $\pi$.
2. For each character $\pi_i$ in $\pi$ (excluding 0), create two vertices above $\pi_i$: a **left** and a **right** vertex. These are the vertices of the breakpoint graph.
   Next, connect each pair of left and right vertices of the same element with a red edge. This forms $n-2$ red edges in total.
3. For each character $\tau_i$ in $\tau$ (excluding 0), let $x_{i-1}$ and $x_i$ be the neighbors $\langle\tau_{i-1},\tau_i\rangle$ and $\langle\tau_i,\tau_{i+1}\rangle$ in the sequence $\tau$. Then, for the neighbor $F(x_{i-1})$ in $\pi$, it corresponds to a 'dot' formed by $\langle\pi_{j-1},\pi_j\rangle$ for some $j$. Exactly one of these $\pi_{j-1}$ and $\pi_j$ is equal to $\tau_i$. Similarly, for the neighbor $F(x_i)$ in $\pi$, it corresponds to a 'dot' formed by $\langle\pi_{k-1},\pi_k\rangle$ for some $k$, and exactly one of these $\pi_{k-1}$ and $\pi_k$ is equal to $\tau_i$.
   We take the above characters of $\pi$ that are equal to $\tau_i$, and join their 'corresponding' left/right vertices together with a blue edge. More precisely, if the character of $\pi$ is on the left of the corresponding 'dot', we take its *right* vertex; else, we take its *left* vertex.

After constructing the blue edges for all the characters of $\tau$, we obtain the desired breakpoint graph. See Fig. 1 for an example.

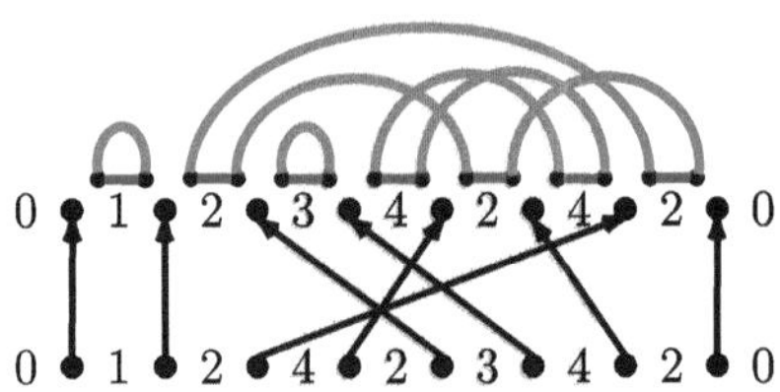


**Fig. 1.** A breakpoint graph between $\pi$ (top sequence) and $\tau$ (bottom sequence)

The breakpoint graph is uniquely determined by the neighbor matching function $F$. Also, each component of the graph is a red–blue alternating cycle.

Let us now call a red-blue alternating cycle a *$k$-cycle* if it contains $k$ red and $k$ blue edges. Then, we have the following lemma.

**Lemma 1.** *If all components of the breakpoint graph are* 1*-cycles, then $\pi$ and $\tau$ are the same (possibly in reverse order).*

*Proof.* Since the character 0 appears either as $\tau_1, \tau_n, \pi_1$, or $\pi_n$, so for the matching function $F$ of the breakpoint graph, the first dot of $\tau$ is either matched with the first dot of $\pi$, or the last dot of $\pi$.

In the former case, the second dot of $\tau$ must be matched with the second dot of $\pi$, as all components are 1-cycles. Repeating the argument, the $j$th dot of $\tau$ must be matched with the $j$th dot of $\pi$, for all $j$. Consequently, the corresponding characters in $\tau$ and $\pi$ must be the same.

In the latter case, the second dot of $\tau$ must be matched with the second last dot of $\pi$, as all components are 1-cycles. Repeating the argument, the $j$th dot of $\tau$ must be matched with the $j$th last dot of $\pi$, for all $j$. Consequently, the corresponding characters in $\tau$ and the reverse of $\pi$ must be the same. This completes the proof. □

## 2.3 Symmetric Reversal

A symmetric reversal can be interpreted as a specific *rematching* of a contiguous region of the matching. See Fig. 2 for an example of a symmetric reversal, and the corresponding region of matching being rematched.

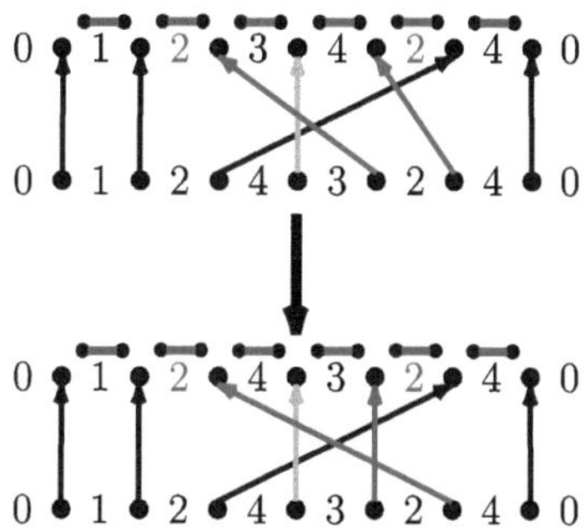


**Fig. 2.** Symmetric reversal and a region of matching that is rematched.

Suppose a symmetric reversal acts on a pair of elements $\pi_i$ and $\pi_j$ of $\pi$ with the same nonzero value. Let $e_i$ and $e_j$ be the red edges in the breakpoint graph corresponding to these two elements. Let $b(v)$ be the vertex such that $(v, b(v))$ forms a blue edge before the symmetric reversal operation. Let $v_{i,\ell}, v_{i,r}$ be the left and right vertices of $e_i$, respectively, before the symmetric reversal operation. Similarly, let $v_{j,\ell}, v_{j,r}$ be the left and right vertices of $e_j$, respectively, before the symmetric reversal operation. Without loss of generality, assume that $e_i < e_j$.[2] Then, the operation can be viewed as performing the following two steps successively (see Fig. 3):

1. *Internal mirroring.* The vertices of all red edges between $e_i$ (exclusive) and $e_j$ (exclusive) are relocated such that their relative positions are all reversed. The breakpoint graph remains structurally unchanged.
2. *Endpoint swapping.* The edges $(v_{i,r}, b(v_{i,r}))$ and $(v_{j,\ell}, b(v_{j,\ell}))$ break at $v_{i,r}$ and $v_{j,\ell}$, and are reconnected to form $(v_{j,\ell}, b(v_{i,r}))$ and $(v_{i,r}, b(v_{j,\ell}))$.

Then, we have the following lemma.

[2] Here, we use $v < u$ to indicate $v$ is on the left of $u$.

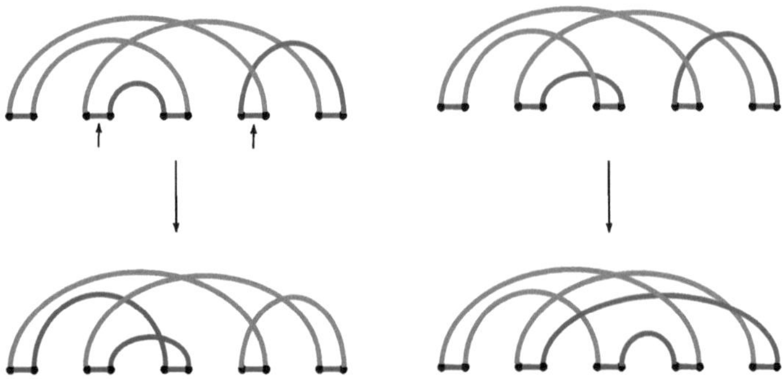

**Fig. 3.** Symmetric reversal as internal mirroring (left) then endpoint swapping (right).

**Lemma 2.** *Let $C$ be any cycle in the breakpoint graph that does not contain the edges $e_i$ and $e_j$. After the symmetric reversal, the structure of $C$ is unchanged.*

Thus, a symmetric reversal may only affect the cycle(s) containing the red edges $e_i$ and $e_j$. The following lemmas show the effect in such a case.

**Lemma 3.** *Suppose the red edges $e_i$ and $e_j$ are on the same cycle $C$ of the breakpoint graph. After the reversal, the red edges in $C$ either stay in the same cycle, or are split into two cycles.*

*Remark.* For the above lemma, the right endpoint of $e_i$ and the left endpoint of $e_j$ (where $e_i$ is on the left of $e_j$) are separated by an even number of edges in $C$ if and only if the red edges of $C$ are split into two disjoint cycles after the symmetric reversal.

**Lemma 4.** *Suppose the red edges $e_i$ and $e_j$ are on different cycles $C_i$ and $C_j$ of the breakpoint graph, respectively. After the symmetric reversal, the red edges in $C_i$ and $C_j$ are merged into the same cycle.*

**Corollary 1.** *After a symmetric reversal, the total number of cycles will either increase by 1, decrease by 1, or remain the same.*

## 3 Feasibility

**Lemma 5.** *Any symmetric reversal will not change the neighbor set.*[3]

As an immediate consequence, any sequence obtainable from $\pi$ via symmetric reversals must be related to $\pi$. This implies the only-if part of Theorem 1.

Next, we show the if part of Theorem 1. Let us fix a matching function $F$ for their neighbors, and construct the corresponding breakpoint graph $G$. We will now show that if there is some long cycle (i.e., non-1-cycle) in $G$, then there is always a sequence of symmetric reversals on some long cycles such that the total number of cycles will be increased by 1. Iterating this process ultimately yields a breakpoint graph $G'$ with only 1-cycles, making $\tau$ and the resulting $\pi$ identical by Lemma 1.

[3] This appears as a claim in Lemma 1 of [7].

*Handling the Favorable Case:* We begin by investigating the simplest way to increase the total number of cycles. From the remark of Lemma 3, when there are $e_i$ and $e_j$ with $e_i < e_j$ in a long cycle $C$, such that the right endpoint of $e_i$ and the left endpoint of $e_j$ are separated by an even number of edges in $C$, then the red edges of $C$ are split into two disjoint cycles after the symmetric reversal operation on $e_i$ and $e_j$. Consequently, the total number of cycles will be increased by 1 (as the remaining cycles are unaffected by Lemma 2) as desired. Let us call the above scenario the *favorable* case, as it gives us a way to increase the total number of cycles just by performing one symmetric reversal operation. To summarize, we have the following.

**Lemma 6.** *If there is a long cycle that satisfies the favorable case, we can increase the total number of cycles by* 1 *using one symmetric reversal operation.*

*Handling the Unfavorable Case:* In the other scenarios (the *unfavorable* cases), we will use different approaches. Indeed, when such scenarios happen, the blue edges in the long cycles are restricted, as shown in the following lemma.

**Lemma 7.** *A long cycle $C$ does not contain red edges $e_i$ and $e_j$ with $e_i < e_j$ such that the right endpoint of $e_i$ and the left endpoint of $e_j$ are separated by an even number of edges in $C$ if and only if all the blue edges in $C$ are joining a left vertex of some red edge and a right vertex of some red edge.*

Yet, we have the following lemma.

**Lemma 8.** *In the unfavorable case, we can increase the total number of cycles by* 1 *using two symmetric reversal operations.*

In summary, as long as the breakpoint graph contains a long cycle, we can always increase the total number of cycles by 1 using one or two symmetric reversal operations. This completes the proof of if part of Theorem 1.

Consequently, we have the following corollary.

**Corollary 2.** *Deciding whether a sequence can be transformed to another sequence by symmetric reversal operations can be done in linear time.*

## 4 NP-Hardness

The classical Sorting By Reversals (SBR) problem for unsigned permutations is known to be NP-complete [3]. In this problem, the input consists of two permutations $X$ and $Y$ on the integers $[1, n]$, and a number $t$ (with $t \leq n$), such that when each of the two permutations is viewed as an ordered length-$n$ sequence, our target is to determine if we can transform one sequence into the other using at most $t$ reversal operations.

We show that the SBR problem can be reduced to our Sorting By Symmetric Reversals (SBSR) problem in polynomial time. Specifically, for the sequence $X$, we perform the following steps to construct a sequence $\pi$:

1. Insert a new symbol $\star$ at the front of the sequence.
2. Insert a new symbol \$ between every two adjacent characters (including the newly added $\star$) and at the back of the sequence.

Similarly, we perform the above steps on $Y$, and construct a sequence $\tau$.

**Example:** If $X = [1, 3, 4, 5, 2]$ and $Y = [1, 2, 3, 4, 5]$, then

$$\pi = [\star, \$, 1, \$, 3, \$, 4, \$, 5, \$, 2, \$] \quad \text{and} \quad \tau = [\star, \$, 1, \$, 2, \$, 3, \$, 4, \$, 5, \$].$$

It is easy to verify that any reversal operation on the sequence in the SBR problem corresponds uniquely to a symmetric reversal operation on the sequence in the SBSR problem; the converse is also true. This implies Theorem 2.

## 5 Approximation

We use $d(\pi, \tau)$ to denote the fewest number of symmetric reversal operations needed to transform $\pi$ into $\tau$ (or the reverse of $\tau$). We call $d(\pi, \tau)$ the *symmetric reversal distance* (or simply, the *distance*) between $\pi$ and $\tau$.

### 5.1 Bounding Distance in the General Case

For a breakpoint graph $G$, let $\kappa(G)$ denote the number of cycles in $G$. For a red-blue alternating cycle $C$, let $n(C)$ denote the number of red edges in $C$. Based on the above, we define an important parameter, called *measure*, to estimate how hard it is to transform $\pi$ to $\tau$ with respect to a breakpoint graph $G$.

**Definition 2 (Measure).** *Let $G$ be a breakpoint graph between sequences $\pi$ and $\tau$. The* measure *of $G$, denoted by $\mu(G)$, is defined as*

$$\mu(G) \;=\; \sum_{\text{cycle } C \in G} (n(C) - 1) \;=\; n - \kappa(G),$$

*where $n$ denotes the total number of red edges in $G$.*

**Lemma 9.** *Let $G$ be a breakpoint graph between $\pi$ and $\tau$. Then,*

$$d(\pi, \tau) \;\leq\; 1.5\, \mu(G).$$

Among all the possible breakpoint graphs $G$, let $G^*$ be the one such that it contains the maximum number of cycles. That is,

$$G^* \;=\; \operatorname*{argmax}_{\text{breakpoint graph } G} \kappa(G).$$

Then, we have the following result.

**Lemma 10.** *The distance $d(\pi, \tau)$ between $\pi$ and $\tau$ is bounded by the following:*

$$\mu(G^*) \;\leq\; d(\pi, \tau) \;\leq\; 1.5\, \mu(G^*).$$

*Remark.* The above lemma implies that if we can find a breakpoint graph $G^*$ that maximizes the number of cycles, we obtain a 1.5-approximate solution for $d(\pi, \tau)$. However, it is still unknown how to find $G^*$ efficiently. Instead, we pose further restrictions on the input $\pi$ and $\tau$, so that we can adapt the above lemma, thereby allowing an efficient approximation algorithm for computing $d(\pi, \tau)$.

### 5.2 Bounding Distance in the Special Case

In the remainder of this paper, we focus on the special case where each element of $\pi$ occurs at most three times. We call this the 3-*bounded case.* To approximate $d(\pi, \tau)$ in such a case, we define an alternative parameter, called the *number of outliers*, that acts similarly to the measure of a breakpoint graph.

**Definition 3 (Outliers).** *Let $G$ be a breakpoint graph between sequences $\pi$ and $\tau$. A red edge is an* outlier *if it is not in a* 1*-cycle. The* number of outliers *of $G$, denoted by $\omega(G)$, is defined as*

$$\omega(G) \;=\; n - \kappa_1(G),$$

*where $n$ denotes the total number of red edges in $G$, and $\kappa_1(G)$ denotes the number of* 1*-cycles in $G$.*

Among all the possible breakpoint graphs $G$, let $G^+$ be the one such that it contains the maximum number of 1-cycles, or equivalently, it contains the minimum number of outliers. That is,

$$G^+ \;=\; \operatorname*{argmax}_{\text{breakpoint graph } G} \;\kappa_1(G) \;=\; \operatorname*{argmin}_{\text{breakpoint graph } G} \;\omega(G).$$

Then, we have the following lemma.

**Lemma 11.** *In the* 3*-bounded case,*

$$\kappa_1(G^+) + \left\lceil \frac{\omega(G^+)}{3} \right\rceil \;\le\; \kappa(G^*) \;\le\; \kappa_1(G^+) + \left\lfloor \frac{\omega(G^+)}{2} \right\rfloor.$$

**Corollary 3.** *In the* 3*-bounded case, $d(\pi, \tau) \ge \lceil \omega(G^+)/2 \rceil$.*

The above corollary establishes a lower bound on $d(\pi, \tau)$ based on $\omega(G^+)$. This provides us a way to design approximation algorithms for $d(\pi, \tau)$, as shown in the following lemma.

**Lemma 12.** *In the* 3*-bounded case, suppose there is a breakpoint graph $G'$ between $\pi$ and $\tau$ such that $\omega(G') \le \rho \cdot \omega(G^+)$, for some $\rho \ge 1$. Then,*

$$d(\pi, \tau) \;\le\; 1.5 \times \left\lfloor \frac{2\rho \cdot \omega(G^+)}{3} \right\rfloor.$$

*Furthermore, if such a graph $G'$ can be obtained in polynomial time, then we have a polynomial-time $2\rho$-approximation algorithm for $d(\pi, \tau)$.*

In the next subsection, we show how to obtain a desired breakpoint graph $G'$ with $\omega(G') \le 2 \cdot \omega(G^+)$ in polynomial time. This implies the following result.

**Theorem 3.** *Let $\pi$ and $\tau$ be two related sequences in the* 3*-bounded case. We can use polynomial time to compute a sequence $S$ of symmetric reversal operations to transform $\pi$ into $\tau$; moreover, $|S| \le 4 \cdot d(\pi, \tau)$.*

### 5.3 Approximating $\omega(G^+)$

We will now show how to construct a breakpoint graph $G'$, in polynomial time, such that $\omega(G') \leq 2 \cdot \omega(G^+)$. To begin with, let us examine the property of a red edge in the breakpoint graph $G$ which forms a 1-cycle. Then, for the 2 neighbors (i.e., 'dots') surrounding the character corresponding to the red edge, say $y_1$ and $y_2$, there must be 2 contiguous neighbors $x_1$ and $x_2$ in $\tau$ such that the matching function $F$ (w.r.t. $G$) either maps the neighbors *forwardly* (i.e., $F(x_1) = y_1$ and $F(x_2) = y_2$), or *backwardly* (i.e., $F(x_1) = y_2$ and $F(x_2) = y_1$).

To describe the above effect more precisely, suppose each neighbor in $\pi$ or $\tau$ is represented by an *ordered* tuple of the two characters surrounding it. Furthermore, we perform a *consistent* relabeling of the tuples with characters in some alphabet $\Sigma$ together with a + or a − sign, such that:

- if two tuples are the same, they are relabeled with the same character and the same sign; and
- if one tuple is the reverse of the other, these two tuples are relabeled with the same character but with opposite signs.

**Example:** Suppose that

$$\pi = [0, 1, 2, 4, 5, 2, 4, 0] \qquad \tau = [0, 1, 2, 5, 4, 2, 4, 0].$$

The following is a possible consistent relabeling of the neighbors:

$$\begin{aligned}\sigma_\pi &= [+a, +b, +c, +e, +f, +c, +g],\\ \sigma_\tau &= [+a, +b, -f, -e, -c, +c, +g].\end{aligned}$$

Let us call a length-2 substring in the relabeled neighbor sequence a *duo*. For a duo $[x, y]$, we call $[-y, -x]$ its reverse form. We regard a duo as *equivalent* to itself or its reverse form. Then, we have the following lemma.

**Lemma 13.** *Let $\sigma_\pi$ and $\sigma_\tau$ be the sequences of neighbors of $\pi$ and $\tau$ after a consistent relabeling. For a breakpoint graph $G$ with matching function $F$, a red edge forming a 1-cycle corresponds to a duo $Y$ of $\sigma_\pi$. Also, the two neighbors of $\tau$ mapped to $Y$ by $F$ correspond to a duo $X$ of $\sigma_\tau$ with $Y$ and $X$ equivalent.*

**The Conflict Graph.** To obtain the desired graph $G'$ whose number of outliers is at most twice that of $G^+$, we use the idea of Goldstein, Kolman, and Zheng [4] for solving a related problem called the MINIMUM COMMON STRING PARTITION (MCSP) problem. Here, we construct a so-called *conflict graph* $K$ based on $\sigma_\pi$ and $\sigma_\tau$. Specifically, each vertex of $K$ corresponds to a *local* matching that creates a 1-cycle. For this to occur, a vertex corresponds to a duo $X$ in $\sigma_\tau$ and a duo $Y$ in $\sigma_\pi$ such that $Y$ is identical to $X$ or the reverse form of $X$.

Next, we join two vertices of $K$ if their corresponding local matching cannot coexist. This happens when a certain neighbor in a sequence is used in both local matchings, but the counterpart neighbors in the other sequence are different in the two local matchings. See Fig. 4 for an example.

$$\sigma_\pi = [+a, +b, +c, +a, +b, +e] \qquad \sigma_\tau = [+a, +b, +e, -e, -b, -a]$$

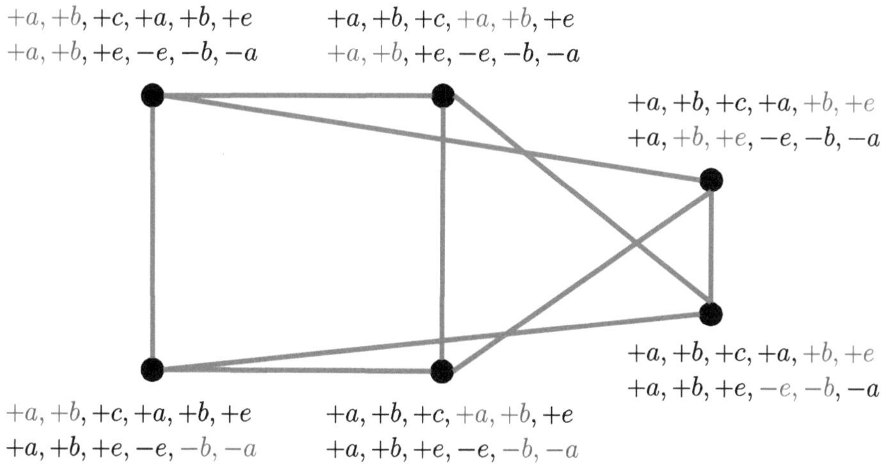


**Fig. 4.** Conflict graph for $\sigma_\pi$ and $\sigma_\tau$ (for each vertex, the corresponding length-2 substrings in the local matching are marked in red). (Color figure online)

Each vertex of the conflict graph corresponds to a 1-cycle that we can form. An independent set of vertices corresponds to a set of 1-cycles that can be formed, given the matching $F$ includes all the corresponding local matchings of these vertices. Thus, finding the *maximum* independent set in $K$ corresponds to a breakpoint graph $G^+$ that contains the maximum number of 1-cycles.

**Simplification.** When $\pi$ and $\tau$ are sequences in the 3-bounded case, we can perform some modifications on $\sigma_\pi$ and $\sigma_\tau$ before we construct the conflict graph, so that the problem becomes simpler. In particular, for some duo $[x, y]$, if equivalent duos appear more than once in $\sigma_\pi$ and the same number of times in $\sigma_\tau$, then we can safely replace the equivalent duos consistently by a single new character, say $+z$ and $-z$ (depending on the direction), solve the problem on the updated $\sigma_\pi$ and $\sigma_\tau$, and finally add back the 1-cycles corresponding to these duos.

**The Final Step.** After the simplification step, we obtain the simplified sequences $\sigma_\pi$ and $\sigma_\tau$. At this point, we will create the conflict graph $K$ on these simplified sequences, and proceed to find a 'large enough' independent set of vertices in $K$, such that the corresponding graph $G'$ satisfies $\omega(G') \leq 2 \times \omega(G^+)$.

Let us begin with a property of the simplified sequences, as this allows us a way to tighten the analysis of the approximation ratio.

**Lemma 14.** *In the 3-bounded case with $\pi$ and $\tau$ related, it is impossible for equivalent duos of a duo to occur exactly three times in $\sigma_\pi$ while only exactly two times in $\sigma_\tau$. The same is true when the roles of $\sigma_\pi$ and $\sigma_\tau$ are exchanged.*

Also, it is trivial that no equivalent duos can appear four or more times in $\sigma_\pi$ or in $\sigma_\tau$; otherwise, the corresponding character surrounded by the neighbors of the duo will appear four or more times. Thus, for equivalent duos to appear in both sequences (so that there will be at least one vertex in the conflict graph corresponding to the duo), the following table summarizes the possible scenarios (labeled by blue ticks) that can occur after the simplification step:

| | 1 | 2 | 3 |
|---|---|---|---|
| 1 | ✓ | ✓ | ✓ |
| 2 | ✓ | △ | × |
| 3 | ✓ | × | △ |

In the table, each row corresponds to the number of times equivalent duos occurring in $\sigma_\tau$, and each column corresponds to the number of times the same equivalent duos occurring in $\sigma_\pi$. The red crosses are the impossible scenarios. The green triangles are the cases that cannot occur after the simplification step.

Next, we will look into the conflict graph $K$ constructed from the simplified sequences. We are going to remove vertices in $K$ so that eventually all vertices are isolated, in which we select all the vertices as our desired independent set.

Recall that each vertex in $K$ corresponds to a *local* matching of a pair of equivalent duos in $\sigma_\pi$ and $\sigma_\tau$. We proceed in three phases based on the number of times a duo occurs in the two sequences and the number of vertices in $K$ corresponding to the same pair of duos:

- **Phase I:** Whenever there is an equivalent duo occurring with different number of times in $\sigma_\pi$ and $\sigma_\tau$, we call them *bad* duos. The possible cases are 2 or 3 times in one sequence, and only once in the other. We remove all the vertices in $K$ whose local matching are between these duos.
- **Phase II:** After Phase I, each vertex remaining in $K$ corresponds to a duo, such that it or its reverse occurs exactly once in each sequence $\sigma_\pi$ and $\sigma_\tau$. If there are two vertices $u$ and $v$ corresponding to the same duo, then the duo must be of the form $[a, -a]$. It can be shown that, apart from $u$ and $v$ themselves, there cannot be a vertex $u'$ in $K$ that conflict with $u$ but not $v$ and another vertex $v'$ that conflict with $v$ but not $u$. Therefore, we remove one of $u$ and $v$ that is in conflict with more vertices. If $u$ and $v$ are in conflict with the same number of vertices, we can remove either of them arbitrarily.
- **Phase III:** After Phase II, each duo whose equivalent duos appear exactly once in each of $\sigma_\pi$ and $\sigma_\tau$ corresponds to exactly one vertex in $K$. While there are remaining edges in $K$, pick an arbitrary edge and remove both its endpoints from $K$.

*Remark.* After Phase III, all the vertices in $K$ do not have conflicts, and we select all of them as the desired independent set.

**Lemma 15.** *The effect of Phase I and Phase III can be summarized as follows.*

- *If Phase I creates $3\,\omega_1$ outliers in our final breakpoint graph, then the optimal breakpoint graph $G^+$ must contain at least $2\,\omega_1$ corresponding outliers.*
- *If Phase III creates $2\,\omega_2$ outliers in our final breakpoint graph, then the optimal breakpoint graph $G^+$ must contain at least $\omega_2$ corresponding outliers.*

Finally, if the duo of a red edge does not have a corresponding vertex in the conflict graph initially, then such a red edge must be an outlier in any matching. Note that some of these red edges will be counted as outliers during Phase I. Let $\omega_0$ denote the remaining number of such red edges that are not yet counted. Summarizing, we have:

$$\omega(G') \;\leq\; \omega_0 + 3\,\omega_1 + 2\,\omega_2\,; \qquad \omega(G^+) \;\geq\; \omega_0 + 2\,\omega_1 + \omega_2\,.$$

Thus, $\omega(G') \;\leq\; 2\,\omega(G^+)$ as desired.

*Remark.* The conflict graph contains a polynomial number of vertices. Next, from the construction and the simplification of neighbor sequences, to the construction of the conflict graph $K$, Phase I to Phase III, every step runs in polynomial time. Thus, the proposed algorithm runs in polynomial time.

## 6 Conclusion and Future Work

In this paper, we established that two sequences can be transformed into one another by a series of symmetric reversals if and only if they are related, and this relation can be verified in linear time. We further proved that the problem of sorting unsigned sequences by symmetric reversals, when minimizing the number of operations, is NP-hard. For a restricted setting where each element appears at most three times, we developed a polynomial-time algorithm with a 4-approximation ratio. However, the exact complexity and tighter approximation bounds for the general case remain unresolved.

Future research can build upon these findings in several directions. First, it is unclear whether the symmetric-reversal distance problem remains NP-hard or becomes APX-hard when each element occurs at most three times. Second, the existing NP-hardness reductions for the 2-MCSP problem (e.g., from cubic graphs) cannot be directly applied to our constrained input model, leaving open the possibility that an exact polynomial-time solution may exist under these restrictions. Addressing these questions would further clarify the computational boundary of sorting by symmetric reversals and deepen our understanding of its approximation complexity.

## References

1. Bafna, V., Pevzner, P.A.: Genome rearrangements and sorting by reversals. SIAM J. Comput. **25**(2), 272–289 (1996)
2. Berman, P., Hannenhalli, S., Karpinski, M.: 1.375-Approximation algorithm for sorting by reversals. In: Proceedings of European Symposium on Algorithms (ESA), pp. 200–210 (2002)

3. Caprara, A.: Sorting permutations by reversals and Eulerian cycle decompositions. SIAM J. Discret. Math. **12**(1), 91–110 (1999)
4. Goldstein, A., Kolman, P., Zheng, J.: Minimum common string partition problem: hardness and approximations. Electron. J. Combinatorics **12** (2005)
5. Hannenhalli, S., Pevzner, P.: Transforming cabbage into turnip: polynomial algorithm for sorting signed permutations by reversals. J. ACM **46**, 1–27 (1999)
6. Kececioglu, J., Sankoff, D.: Exact and approximation algorithms for sorting by reversals with application to genome rearrangement. Algorithmica **13**(1–2), 180–210 (1995)
7. Lai, W., Jiang, H., Zhu, D., Zhu, B.: On sorting by unsigned symmetric reversals. In: Proceedings of Annual International Conference on Computing and Combinatorics (COCOON), pp. 421–432 (2025)
8. Palmer, J.D., Herbon, L.A.: Plant mitochondrial DNA evolved rapidly in structure, but slowly in sequence. J. Mol. Evol. **28**(1–2), 87–97 (1988)
9. Pevzner, P., Tesler, G.: Human and mouse genomic sequences reveal extensive breakpoint reuse in mammalian evolution. Proc. Natl. Acad. Sci. **100**(13), 7672–7677 (2003)
10. Tong, X., et al.: Cabbage can't always be transformed into turnip: decision algorithms for sorting by symmetric reversals. In: Proceedings of Annual International Conference on Computing and Combinatorics (COCOON), pp. 279–294 (2023)

# Parameterized Approximation Algorithms for Dominating Set and Power Dominating Set By Using Leafage

Peihua Li and Jiong Guo(✉)

School of Department of Computer Science, Shandong University, Qingdao, China
peihuali@mail.sdu.edu.cn, jguo@sdu.edu.cn

**Abstract.** We study parameterized approximation algorithms for the Dominating Set (DS) and Power Dominating Set (PDS) problems. Given a graph $G = (V, E)$, DS asks for a minimum-size subset $S \subseteq V$, such that each vertex in $V \setminus S$ has at least one neighbor in $S$. PDS is an extension of DS. Unless P=NP, they are not polynomial-time approximable better than $\Theta(\log n)$, even on chordal graphs [7,12]. Our algorithms use the number $k_1$ of vertices, whose removal transforms the input graph $G$ to a chordal graph with leafage $l$, as parameter. The leafage $l$ of a chordal graph $G$ is the minimum integer, such that $G$ can be represented as the intersection graph of the subtrees of a rooted tree with $l$ leaves. Interval graphs are chordal graphs with $l = 2$. Given a size-$k_1$ vertex deletion set from the input graph $G$ to a chordal graph with leafage $l$, we achieve a $[l(l-1)+1]$-ratio $O(2^{2k_1} \cdot n^{O(1)})$-time parameterized approximation algorithm for DS and a $[l(l-1)+2]$-ratio $O(2^{O(k_1 \cdot k_1)} \cdot n^{O(1)})$-time parameterized approximation algorithm for PDS. As a byproduct, we show that DS is fixed-parameter tractable with respect to the number $k_2$ of vertices, whose removal transforms $G$ to an interval graph, and PDS admits a 2-ratio $O(2^{O(k_2 \cdot k_2)} \cdot n^{O(1)})$-time parameterized approximation algorithm.

**Keywords:** Combinatorial Optimization · Parameterized Approximation · Dominating Set · Power Dominating Set

## 1 Introduction

Given an undirected graph $G = (V, E)$, Dominating Set (DS) aims to find a minimum-size subset $S \subseteq V$, such that each vertex in $V \setminus S$ has at least one neighbor in $S$. Power Dominating Set (PDS) is a "non-local" variant of DS and is motivated by monitoring an electric power network [3,14], where one is asked to place a minimum number of so-called phase measurement units (PMU) at some locations in the network to measure the state variables. The graph-theoretical study of PDS is initiated by Haynes et al. [14]. Given an undirected graph $G = (V, E)$, PDS aims to find a minimum-size subset $S \subseteq V$, such that all vertices in $V$ are "observed" by the vertices in $S$ according to two rules, R1


Y. Li et al. (Eds.): COCOON 2026, LNCS 16835, pp. 55–67, 2027.
https://doi.org/10.1007/978-981-92-3309-0_5

and R2. Initially, R1 is applied once: each vertex in $S$ observes itself and all its neighbors. Then, R2 is applied exhaustively: if an observed vertex has exactly one unobserved neighbor, then that neighbor becomes observed as well. DS is a scaled-down version of PDS, where R2 is not applied.

DS and PDS are both NP-hard [10,14], even on chordal graphs [2,14], but are polynomial-time solvable on interval graphs [17,21]. To the best of our knowledge, we are not aware of any graph class where DS and PDS exhibit different complexity statuses. Unless P=NP, they are not polynomial-time approximable better than $\Theta(\log n)$, even on chordal graphs [7,12]. Therefore, unless P=NP, there are no parameterized $f(k_3)$-ratio approximation algorithm for DS and PDS with respect to $k_3$, the number of vertices, whose removal transforms a graph to a chordal graph, for any computable function $f(\cdot)$. Moreover, DS and PDS are W[2]-hard with respect to the solution size $\widehat{k}$ [12,19]. Assuming W[1]$\neq$FPT, there is no parameterized $g(\widehat{k})$-approximation algorithm for DS with respect to $\widehat{k}$ for any computable function $g(\cdot)$ [5,6,22]. Therefore, in order to derive reasonable parameterized approximation algorithms for DS and PDS, we need to switch to other parameters. In this direction, Inamdar et al. [15] derived a $(1+\epsilon)$-ratio $h(p,\epsilon)\cdot n^{O(1)}$-time parameterized approximation algorithm for DS for any $\epsilon > 0$, where $p$ is the size of a vertex modulator to apex-minor-free graphs and $h(p,\epsilon) = \max\{2^{O(p+\sqrt{\frac{p}{\epsilon}})}, 2^{O(\frac{1}{\epsilon})}\}$. Moreover, Koutis et al. [16] derived a 2-ratio $O(\sqrt{8}^{\mathrm{tw}}\cdot \mathrm{tw}^{O(1)}\cdot n)$-time algorithm and a 2-ratio $O(2^{\mathrm{tw}_d}\cdot n)$-time algorithm for Weighted Dominating Set. Here, tw refers to the treewidth and $\mathrm{tw}_d$ to the size of a vertex modulator to a graph of treewidth $d$.

Due to the inapproximability of DS and PDS on chordal graphs, we focus on a special subclass of chordal graphs, chordal graphs with leafage $l$ for a constant integer $l$, and use the number $k_1$ of vertices as parameter, whose removal transforms the input graph to a chordal graph with leafage $l$. Note that each chordal graph $G$ can be represented as the intersection graph of a collection of subtrees of a rooted tree, the so-called tree representation of $G$. Therefore, for each chordal graph $G=(V,E)$, there exists a pair $(T,M)$ with $T=(Q,F)$ being a rooted tree and $M$ being a collection of subtrees of $T$. Each vertex $v\in V$ is in one-to-one correspondence with a subtree in $M$ and two vertices are adjacent if and only if their corresponding subtrees intersect. The pair $(T,M)$ is called a tree representation of $G$. The leafage $l$ of a chordal graph $G$ is the minimum integer, such that $G$ can be realized as an intersection graph of a collection of subtrees of a rooted tree, which has $l$ leaves. Interval graphs have $l=2$. Habib et al. [13] showed that for any chordal graph, we can construct a corresponding tree representation with the minimum leafage in polynomial time. Recently, researchers have studied various graph problems on chordal graphs with leafage $l$. It is known that Dominating Set [8,9], Connected Dominating Set [9], Steiner Tree [9] and Graph Isomorphism [1] on chordal graphs are fixed-parameter tractable (FPT) parameterized by the leafage. However, Subset FVS [20] and Multicut With Undeletable Terminals [9] are W[1]-hard and Multicut With Deletable Terminals [11] on chordal graphs is para-NP-hard when parameterized by the leafage.

Note that Chordal Vertex Deletion [18] and Interval Vertex Deletion [4] are both FPT with respect to the solution size. However, computing a size-$k_1$ vertex deletion set $V^-$ from the input graph $G$ to a chordal graph with leafage $l$ (for constant $l$) involves a different structural property. Whether this problem is FPT (or even XP) parameterized by the solution size is not known, and the known results for chordal deletion do not directly apply. We leave this as an open question. In this paper, we assume $V^-$ is given as part of the input. Given a size-$k_1$ vertex deletion set $V^-$ from the input graph $G$ to a chordal graph with leafage $l$, we achieve a $[l(l-1)+1]$-ratio $O(2^{2k_1} \cdot n^{O(1)})$-time parameterized approximation algorithm for DS and a $[l(l-1)+2]$-ratio $O(2^{O(k_1 \cdot k_1)} \cdot n^{O(1)})$-time parameterized approximation algorithm for PDS. These two algorithms rely on an FPT algorithm for DS and an FPT 2-ratio approximation algorithm for PDS, respectively. Hereby, the parameter is the number $k_2$ of vertices, whose removal transforms the input graph to an interval graph.

## 2 Preliminaries

For an undirected graph $G = (V, E)$, we use $V$ (or $V(G)$) and $E$ (or $E(G)$) to represent the vertex set and the edge set of $G$, respectively. Let $n := |V|$ and $m := |E|$. We use $(u, v)$ to denote an undirected edge between vertices $u$ and $v$. For $v \in V$, $N_G(v) := \{u : (u, v) \in E\}$ denotes the open neighbourhood of $v$ and $N_G[v] := N_G(v) \cup \{v\}$ denotes the closed neighbourhood of $v$. For a vertex subset $V' \subseteq V$, $N_G(V') := \left(\bigcup_{v \in V'} N_G(v)\right) \setminus V'$ denotes the open neighbourhood of $V'$ and $N_G[V'] := N_G(V') \cup V'$ denotes the closed neighbourhood of $V'$. Let $G - V'$ denote the subgraph obtained from $G$ by deleting all vertices in $V'$ and $G[V']$ denote the subgraph of $G$ induced by $V'$. For an edge subset $E' \subseteq E$, $G - E'$ denotes the subgraph obtained from $G$ by deleting all edges in $E'$.

In a tree $T = (Q, F)$ with root node $r$, $Q$ denotes the set of tree nodes and $F$ the set of tree edges. For each node $q \in Q$, $T_q$ denotes the subtree rooted at $q$. The set $Q_{=1}(T)$ contains all nodes of degree one in $T$ and is called the set of leaves. The set $Q_{\geqslant 3}(T)$ contains all nodes of degree at least three in $T$ and is called the set of branching nodes. Note that $|Q_{\geqslant 3}(T)| \leqslant |Q_{=1}(T)| - 1$.

A chordal graph is a simple graph, in which every cycle of length at least four has a chord. Each chordal graph $G$ can be represented as the intersection graph of a collection of subtrees of a rooted tree, the so-called tree representation of $G$. Therefore, for each chordal graph $G = (V, E)$, there exists a pair $(T, M)$ with $T = (Q, F)$ being a rooted tree and $M$ being a collection of subtrees of $T$. Each vertex $v \in V$ is in one-to-one correspondence with a subtree in $M$ and two vertices are adjacent if and only if their corresponding subtrees intersect. The pair $(T, M)$ is called a tree representation of $G$. The leafage of a chordal graph $G$, denoted by $l$ or $l(G)$, is the minimum number of leaves in all tree representations $(T, M)$ of $G$. For any chordal graph $G$, Michel et al. [13] provided an algorithm running in $O(n^3)$ time to compute a tree representation $(T, M)$ of $G$ with leafage $l$.

Interval graphs form a special subclass of chordal graphs. Every interval graph $G = (V, E)$ can be represented as the intersection graph of a collection of intervals on a real line, the so-called interval representation of $G$. Thus, for every interval graph $G = (V, E)$, there exists a pair $(I, W)$ with $I$ being a line and $W$ being a collection of intervals on $I$. Each vertex $v \in V$ is in one-to-one correspondence with an interval in $W$ and two vertices are adjacent if and only if their corresponding intervals intersect. The pair $(I, W)$ is called an interval representation of $G$. Note that in the special case where a chordal graph $G$ is an interval graph, its tree representation degenerates into an interval representation, meaning $l(G) = 2$.

Given an undirected graph $G = (V, E)$, Power Dominating Set (PDS) asks for a minimum-size set $S \subseteq V$, which observes all vertices in $V$ according to Definition 1.

**Definition 1.** *Given an undirected graph $G = (V, E)$ and a subset $S \subseteq V$, we use $P^i(S)$ to denote the set of vertices observed by $S$ for $i = 0, 1, 2, ..., |V|$, whose computation is done by applying the following two rules:*

- *Observation Rule 1 (R1) $P^0(S) := N_G[S]$;*
- *Observation Rule 2 (R2) For $i \geqslant 0$, $P^{i+1}(S) := \bigcup\{N_G[v] : v \in P^i(S), |N_G[v] \setminus P^i(S)| \leqslant 1\}$.*

*If $P^{|V|}(S) = V$, we say that $S$ observes all vertices in $V$.*

## 3 FPT Approximation Algorithm for DS by $k_1$

In this section, we present the parameterized approximation algorithm for Dominating Set (DS). The parameter is the number $k_1$ of vertices, whose removal transforms the input graph $G$ to a chordal graph with leafage $l$. The set $V^-$ of these $k_1$ vertices is called the vertex deletion set. We assume $V^-$ is given as part of the input. Here, we study a more general version of DS, denoted as DS$^+$. Given an undirected graph $G = (V, E)$ and a subset $V_L \subseteq V$ labeled as dominated, DS$^+$ asks for a minimum-size set $S \subseteq V$, such that each $v \in V \setminus S$ has a neighbor in $S$ or $v \in V_L$. Clearly, DS is a special version of DS$^+$ with $V_L = \varnothing$.

The FPT approximation algorithm for DS$^+$ works as follows. First, apply the algorithm in [13] to compute the tree representation $(T = (Q, F), M)$ of $\widehat{G} := G - V^-$. Then, at each branching node $q \in Q_{\geqslant 3}(T)$, greedily add some vertices to $S_1$, which is initialized as an empty set, in order to satisfy $N_{\widehat{G}}[V_{\geqslant 3}] \subseteq N_G[S_1]$ with $V_{\geqslant 3} := \{v \in V(\widehat{G})$ : the corresponding subtree $T(v)$ of $v$ contains at least one branching node in $Q_{\geqslant 3}(T)\}$. Then, delete the edge set $E^- := \{e \in E(\widehat{G})$ : $e$ is incident to some vertex in $V_{\geqslant 3}\}$ from $G$ to obtain $\overline{G} := G - E^-$. Note that, after deleting all edges in $E^-$ from $\widehat{G}$, the remaining graph has the property that no subtree in its tree representation contains any branching node, i.e., the tree representation $(T = (Q, F), M)$ of $\widehat{G}$ degenerates into an interval representation. Thus, $V^-$ is not only a vertex deletion set from $G$ to a chordal graph with leafage $l$, but also a vertex deletion set from $\overline{G}$ to an interval graph, since $\overline{G} - V^- = G - E^- - V^- = G - V^- - E^- = \widehat{G} - E^-$. Finally, we apply

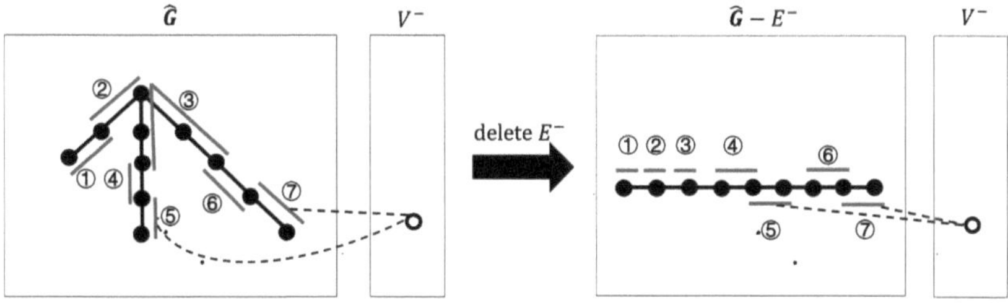


**Fig. 1.** An illustration of the FPT approximation algorithm for DS$^+$. The input graph $G$ has eight vertices and can be transformed to a chordal graph $\widehat{G}$ with leafage $l = 3$ by deleting the vertex in $V^-$. The remaining seven vertices correspond to the subtrees in the tree representation of $\widehat{G}$, i.e., ① ... ⑦, and denoted as $v_1, ..., v_7$. The vertex in $V^-$ is denoted as $v_8$ and is connected in $G$ with $v_5$ and $v_7$. The only branching node in the tree representation of $\widehat{G}$ is the root node, which is contained in the subtrees corresponding to $v_2$ and $v_3$. Thus, $V_{\geqslant 3} = \{v_2, v_3\}$. Since $v_2$ and $v_3$ are adjacent to $v_1, v_3$ and $v_2, v_4, v_6$, respectively, $E^- = \{(v_1, v_2), (v_2, v_3), (v_3, v_4), (v_3, v_6)\}$. The graph $\widehat{G} - E^-$ has only two edges $(v_4, v_5)$ and $(v_6, v_7)$ and is thus an interval graph.

the FPT algorithm in Subsect. 3.1 to solve DS$^+$ on $\overline{G}$ with $\overline{V}_L := N_G[S_1] \cup V_L$ labeled as dominated with respect to $k_2 := |V^-|$, the number of vertices, whose removal transforms $\overline{G}$ to an interval graph. See Figure 1 for an illustration. Note that in the final step, we do not need to consider the domination of $N_G[S_1]$ and thus, we introduce DS$^+$.

### 3.1 FPT Algorithm for DS$^+$ by $k_2$

In this subsection, we present an FPT algorithm for DS$^+$ on $\overline{G}$ with $\overline{V}_L$ labeled as dominated with respect to $k_2 := |V^-|$, the number of vertices, whose removal transforms $\overline{G}$ to an interval graph. As argued above, $V^-$ is also a size-$k_2$ vertex deletion set from $\overline{G}$ to an interval graph.

For convenience, we add an isolated undominated vertex $v^*$ to $\overline{G}$ to obtain $G^*$. Since an isolated vertex does not induce any cycle, $V^-$ is also a vertex deletion set from $G^*$ to an interval graph. Then, we compute in polynomial time an interval representation $(I, W)$ of $G^* - V^-$, where $W$ is a set of $n^*$ sorted intervals labeled by $1, ..., n^*$ in increasing order of their left endpoints and the corresponding interval of $v^*$ has the maximum index. For each interval $i$, its corresponding vertex in $G^*$ is relabeled by $v_i$. Moreover, the vertices in $V^-$ are relabeled as $v_1^-, ..., v_{k_2}^-$ in an arbitrary order. Let $V_0 := \varnothing$ and $V_i := \{v_1, ..., v_i\}$ for each $i \in \{1, ..., n^*\}$. Then, for each $i \in \{0, ..., n^*\}$, let $G_i$ denote the graph obtained from $G^*$ by deleting the vertices in $V(G^*) \setminus (V^- \cup V_i)$. Moreover, let $p_i$ be the vertex in $V_i$, whose corresponding interval has the maximum right endpoint among all intervals of the vertices in $V_i$. For each $V' \subseteq V(G^*)$, $\mathcal{L}(V')$ denotes the maximum right endpoint among all intervals of the vertices in $V'$ and is called the "length" of $V'$. See Fig. 2 for a DS$^+$-instance $(G^*, \overline{V}_L, V^-)$.

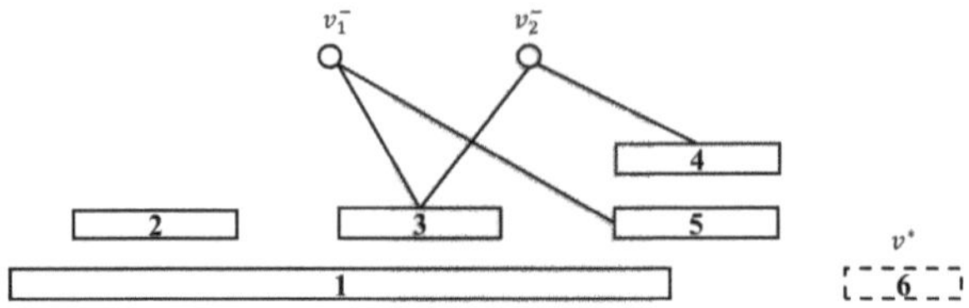


**Fig. 2.** A DS$^+$-instance $(G^*, \overline{V}_L, V^-)$ with $\overline{V}_L = \varnothing$. The dots represent the vertices in $V^-$, i.e., $V^- = \{v_1^-, v_2^-\}$. The rectangles represent the intervals of $G^* - V^-$, corresponding to the vertices $v_1, ..., v_5, v_6 = v^*$. The lines represent the edges between the vertices in $V^-$ and the vertices in $G^* - V^-$. The optimal solution is $\{v_1, v_3, v_6\}$, where the interval of $v_1$ "covers" the interval of $v_3$, which is used to dominate $V^-$.

The FPT algorithm is based on dynamic programming. Here, we need the following data structure. For each $i \in \{0, ..., n^*\}$ and for each two subsets $X, Y \subseteq V^-$, we define $S_Y^X(i)$ as a subset of $V(G_i)$, which has the following properties: ① containing $\{v_i\}$ and its intersection with $V^-$ equal to $X$; ② dominating $Y \cup V_i$ on $G_i$ with $V(G_i) \cap \overline{V}_L$ labeled as dominated; ③ having the minimum size; ④ having the maximum length among all subsets of $V(G_i)$, satisfying ①, ② and ③. If no such subset exists, we set $S_Y^X(i) := \perp$ with its cardinality equal to $\infty$ and the results of all set operations of $\perp$ and any set are $\perp$. Let $C_Y^X(i)$ be the collection of all subsets of $V(G_i)$, which fulfill ① and ②. Thus, $S_Y^X(i) \in C_Y^X(i)$ and for any $\widehat{S} \in C_Y^X(i)$, we have $|S_Y^X(i)| \leqslant |\widehat{S}|$ and in the case $|S_Y^X(i)| = |\widehat{S}|$, it holds $\mathcal{L}(S_Y^X(i)) \geqslant \mathcal{L}(\widehat{S})$.

The computation of $S_Y^X(i)$ is done by an iteration from $i = 0$ to $i = n^*$. For each $0 \leqslant i \leqslant n^*$ and for each two subsets $X, Y \subseteq V^-$, $S_Y^X(i)$ is initialized as $\perp$. If $i = 0$, then we have $V_0 = \varnothing$ and $G_0 = G^*[V^-]$. Then, for each two subsets $X, Y \subseteq V^-$, we set $S_Y^X(0) := X$, if $X$ dominates $Y$ on $G_0$ with $V(G_0) \cap \overline{V}_L$ labeled as dominated; otherwise $S_Y^X(0) := \perp$. If $i > 0$, then we iterate from $j = 0$ to $j = i - 1$ and set $Y' := Y \setminus N_{G_i}[v_i]$. If $S_{Y'}^X(j) \cup \{v_i\}$ dominates $Y \cup V_i$ on $G_i$ with $V(G_i) \cap \overline{V}_L$ labeled as dominated, then set $Z_j := S_{Y'}^X(j) \cup \{v_i\}$; otherwise, if $S_{Y'}^X(j) \cup \{v_i, p_j\}$ dominates $Y \cup V_i$ on $G_i$ with $V(G_i) \cap \overline{V}_L$ labeled as dominated, then set $Z_j := S_{Y'}^X(j) \cup \{v_i, p_j\}$; otherwise $Z_j := \perp$. Recall that $p_j$ is a vertex in $V_j$, whose corresponding interval has the maximum right endpoint among all intervals of the vertices in $V_j$. Finally, set $S_Y^X(i)$ to the set $Z_j$, whose size is minimum and whose length is maximum among the sets with the minimum size.

The FPT algorithm for DS$^+$, called FPT-DS$^+$, consists of three steps. First, add an isolated, undominated vertex $v^*$ to $\overline{G}$ to obtain $G^*$. Second, compute $S_Y^X(i)$ for each $0 \leqslant i \leqslant n^*$ and for each two subsets $X, Y \subseteq V^-$ by the above dynamic programming. Third, output $S := S_{V^-}^{X^*}(n^*) \setminus \{v^*\}$ with $X^* = \arg\min_{X \subseteq V^-} |S_{V^-}^X(n^*) \setminus \{v^*\}|$.

**Theorem 1.** *FPT-DS$^+$ solves DS$^+$ exactly in $O(2^{2k_2} \cdot n^{O(1)})$ time on $\overline{G}$ with $\overline{V}_L$ labeled as dominated. Here, $k_2 = |V^-|$ is the number of vertices, whose removal transforms $\overline{G}$ to an interval graph.*

*Proof.* First, we analyze the running time of FPT-DS$^+$. The first step clearly runs in $O(n^{O(1)})$ time. Since $|V^-| = k_2$, there are at most $2^{2k_2} \cdot (n^* + 1)$ many $S_Y^X(i)$'s. For each $S_Y^X(i)$, its computation needs $O(n^*)$ time. Since $n^* \leqslant n + 1$, the second step runs in $O(2^{2k_2} \cdot n^{O(1)})$ time. The third step enumerates all subsets $X$ of $V^-$ and needs $O(2^{k_2} \cdot n^{O(1)})$ time. Thus, the running time of FPT-DS$^+$ is $O(2^{2k_2} \cdot n^{O(1)})$.

We now show that the output $S$ of FPT-DS$^+$ is an optimal solution for the given DS$^+$-instance $(\overline{G}, \overline{V}_L, V^-)$. It follows from the claim, that for each $0 \leqslant i \leqslant n^*$ and for each two subsets $X, Y \subseteq V^-$, $S_Y^X(i)$ is correctly computed, i.e., $S_Y^X(i)$ is a subset of $V(G_i)$ having the properties ① - ④ mentioned above. The reason is as follows. Let $OPT$ be an optimal solution for the given DS$^+$-instance $(\overline{G}, \overline{V}_L, V^-)$ and $X^\circ := OPT \cap V^-$. Then, $OPT \cup \{v^*\}$ dominates $V(G^*)$ on $G^*$ with $V(G^*) \cap \overline{V}_L$ labeled as dominated. Moreover, one of the subsets $X$ of $V^-$ enumerated in the third step of FPT-DS$^+$ must be $X^\circ$. Then, $|S| = |S_{V^-}^{X^*}(n^*) \setminus \{v^*\}| \leqslant |S_{V^-}^{X^\circ}(n^*) \setminus \{v^*\}|$. If $S_{V^-}^{X^\circ}(n^*)$ is correctly computed, it holds that $X^\circ \cup \{v^*\} \subseteq S_{V^-}^{X^\circ}(n^*)$ and $S_{V^-}^{X^\circ}(n^*)$ dominates $V^- \cup V_{n^*}$ on $G_{n^*}$ with $V(G_{n^*}) \cap \overline{V}_L$ labeled as dominated. By $G^* = G_{n^*}$ and $V(G^*) = V(G_{n^*}) = V^- \cup V_{n^*}$, $OPT \cup \{v^*\}$ dominates $V^- \cup V_{n^*}$ on $G_{n^*}$ with $V(G_{n^*}) \cap \overline{V}_L$ labeled as dominated. Since $OPT \cup \{v^*\}$ also fulfills the properties ① and ②, we have $|S_{V^-}^{X^\circ}(n^*)| \leqslant |OPT \cup \{v^*\}|$ and $|S_{V^-}^{X^\circ}(n^*) \setminus \{v^*\}| \leqslant |OPT|$. Then, $|S| \leqslant |S_{V^-}^{X^\circ}(n^*) \setminus \{v^*\}| \leqslant |OPT|$. Clearly, $S = S_{V^-}^{X^*}(n^*) \setminus \{v^*\}$ is a solution for the given DS$^+$-instance $(\overline{G}, \overline{V}_L, V^-)$, since $G^* = G_{n^*}$ is obtained from $\overline{G}$ by adding an isolated undominated vertex $v^*$. Thus, $S$ is also an optimal solution for the given DS$^+$-instance $(\overline{G}, \overline{V}_L, V^-)$.

We now prove the claim, that for each $0 \leqslant i \leqslant n^*$ and for each two subsets $X, Y \subseteq V^-$, $S_Y^X(i)$ is correctly computed. We prove by an induction on $i$. For $i = 0$, the correctness of $S_Y^X(0)$ follows directly from the description of FPT-DS$^+$. For $i > 0$, we suppose that for each $j \in \{0, ..., i-1\}$ and for each two subsets $X, Y \subseteq V^-$, $S_Y^X(j)$ is correctly computed, i.e., $S_Y^X(j)$ is a subset of $V(G_j)$ having the properties ① - ④. Suppose $\widehat{S}$ is a subset of $V(G_i)$ having the properties ① - ④. Let $v_j$ be the vertex in $\widehat{S} \setminus (V^- \cup \{v_i\})$ with the largest index among all vertices in $\widehat{S} \setminus (V^- \cup \{v_i\})$ and $Y' := Y \setminus N_{G_i}[v_i]$. Note that the interval of any vertex in $V_j \setminus \{v_j\}$, which intersects the interval of a vertex in $V_i \setminus V_j$, also intersects the interval of $v_j$. That is, any vertex in $V_j \setminus \{v_j\}$, which is adjacent to a vertex in $V_i \setminus V_j$, is also adjacent to $v_j$. By $v_j \in \widehat{S} \setminus \{v_i\}$ and $v_i \in V_i \setminus V_j$, any vertex in $V_j$, which is dominated by $v_i$, is also dominated by $\widehat{S} \setminus \{v_i\}$. Thus, $\widehat{S} \setminus \{v_i\}$ is a subset of $V(G_j)$, which contains $X \cup \{v_j\}$ and dominates $Y' \cup V_j$ on $G_j$ with $V(G_j) \cap \overline{V}_L$ labeled as dominated. Thus, $\widehat{S} \setminus \{v_i\} \in C_{Y'}^X(j)$. Since $S_{Y'}^X(j)$ is correctly computed, we have

$$|S_{Y'}^X(j)| \leqslant |\widehat{S} \setminus \{v_i\}| \tag{1}$$

and in the case $|S_{Y'}^X(j)| = |\widehat{S} \setminus \{v_i\}|$, it holds

$$\mathcal{L}(S_{Y'}^X(j)) \geqslant \mathcal{L}(\widehat{S} \setminus \{v_i\}) \tag{2}$$

. We distinguish four situations based on whether $|S_{Y'}^{X}(j)| = |\widehat{S} \setminus \{v_i\}|$ and $S_{Y'}^{X}(j) \cup \{v_i\}$ dominates $Y \cup V_i$ on $G_i$ with $V(G_i) \cap \overline{V}_L$ labeled as dominated.

(I) If $|S_{Y'}^{X}(j)| = |\widehat{S} \setminus \{v_i\}|$ and $S_{Y'}^{X}(j) \cup \{v_i\}$ dominates $Y \cup V_i$ on $G_i$ with $V(G_i) \cap \overline{V}_L$ labeled as dominated, we have $|S_{Y'}^{X}(j) \cup \{v_i\}| = |\widehat{S}|$. By Inequality (2), $\mathcal{L}(S_{Y'}^{X}(j) \cup \{v_i\}) \geqslant \mathcal{L}(\widehat{S})$. Thus, $S_{Y'}^{X}(j) \cup \{v_i\}$ is also a subset of $V(G_i)$ having the properties ① - ④. Thus, $S_{Y}^{X}(i) := S_{Y'}^{X}(j) \cup \{v_i\}$ is correctly computed.

(II) If $|S_{Y'}^{X}(j)| < |\widehat{S} \setminus \{v_i\}|$ and $S_{Y'}^{X}(j) \cup \{v_i\}$ dominates $Y \cup V_i$ on $G_i$ with $V(G_i) \cap \overline{V}_L$ labeled as dominated, then we have $|S_{Y'}^{X}(j) \cup \{v_i\}| < |\widehat{S}|$. Then, $\widehat{S}$ is not a subset of $V(G_i)$ having the properties ① - ④, contradicting the definition of $\widehat{S}$.

(III) The situation, that $|S_{Y'}^{X}(j)| = |\widehat{S} \setminus \{v_i\}|$ and $S_{Y'}^{X}(j) \cup \{v_i\}$ does not dominate $Y \cup V_i$ on $G_i$ with $V(G_i) \cap \overline{V}_L$ labeled as dominated, cannot happen. The reason is as follows. By $Y' = Y \setminus N_{G_i}[v_i]$ and the definition of $S_{Y'}^{X}(j)$, $S_{Y'}^{X}(j) \cup \{v_i\}$ dominates $Y \cup V_j$ on $G_i$ with $V(G_i) \cap \overline{V}_L$ labeled as dominated. Thus, $S_{Y'}^{X}(j) \cup \{v_i\}$ does not dominate $V_i \setminus V_j$ on $G_i$. That is, there is a vertex $v_a \in V_i \setminus V_j$ with $j < a < i$, such that $S_{Y'}^{X}(j) \cup \{v_i\}$ does not dominate $v_a$ on $G_i$. By the definitions of $\widehat{S}$ and $v_j$, there is a vertex $v_b \in \widehat{S} \setminus \{v_i, v_j\}$ with $b < j < i$ dominating $v_a$ on $G_i$. That is, $b < j < a < i$ and the interval of $v_b$ intersects the interval of $v_a$. Since $|S_{Y'}^{X}(j)| = |\widehat{S} \setminus \{v_i\}|$, by Inequality (2), $S_{Y'}^{X}(j)$ contains a vertex $v_c$ with $c \leqslant j$, whose corresponding interval has a right endpoint larger than or equal to that of the interval of $v_b$. By $c \leqslant j < a$ and $b < j < a < i$, the interval of $v_c$ intersects the interval of $v_a$. That is, $S_{Y'}^{X}(j)$ dominates $v_a$ on $G_i$. It contradicts that $S_{Y'}^{X}(j) \cup \{v_i\}$ does not dominate $v_a$ on $G_i$.

(IV) If $|S_{Y'}^{X}(j)| < |\widehat{S} \setminus \{v_i\}|$ and $S_{Y'}^{X}(j) \cup \{v_i\}$ does not dominate $Y \cup V_i$ on $G_i$ with $V(G_i) \cap \overline{V}_L$ labeled as dominated, we have $|S_{Y'}^{X}(j) \cup \{v_i\}| < |\widehat{S}|$. We first show that $S_{Y'}^{X}(j) \cup \{v_i, p_j\}$ dominates $Y \cup V_i$ on $G_i$ with $V(G_i) \cap \overline{V}_L$ labeled as dominated, implying $|S_{Y'}^{X}(j) \cup \{v_i, p_j\}| \leqslant |\widehat{S}|$, and then show that in the case of $|S_{Y'}^{X}(j) \cup \{v_i, p_j\}| = |\widehat{S}|$, $\mathcal{L}(S_{Y'}^{X}(j) \cup \{v_i, p_j\}) \geqslant \mathcal{L}(\widehat{S})$. We prove by contradiction. Suppose $S_{Y'}^{X}(j) \cup \{v_i, p_j\}$ does not dominate $Y \cup V_i$ on $G_i$ with $V(G_i) \cap \overline{V}_L$ labeled as dominated. By $Y' = Y \setminus N_{G_i}[v_i]$ and the definition of $S_{Y'}^{X}(j)$, $S_{Y'}^{X}(j) \cup \{v_i, p_j\}$ dominates $Y \cup V_j$ on $G_i$ with $V(G_i) \cap \overline{V}_L$ labeled as dominated. Then, $S_{Y'}^{X}(j) \cup \{v_i, p_j\}$ does not dominate $V_i \setminus V_j$ on $G_i$. Thus, there is a vertex $v_a \in V_i \setminus V_j$ with $j < a < i$, such that $S_{Y'}^{X}(j) \cup \{v_i, p_j\}$ does not dominate $v_a$ on $G_i$. By the definitions of $\widehat{S}$ and $v_j$, there is a vertex $v_b \in \widehat{S} \setminus \{v_i, v_j\}$ with $b < j < i$ dominating $v_a$ on $G_i$. That is, $b < j < a < i$ and the interval of $v_b$ intersects the interval of $v_a$. By the definition of $p_j$, $p_j$ is a vertex in $V_j$, whose corresponding interval has the maximum right endpoint among all intervals of the vertices in $V_j$. Since $v_b \in V_j$, the interval of $p_j$ has a right endpoint greater than or equal to that of the interval of $v_b$. Since $b < j < a < i$, the interval of $p_j$ also intersects the interval of $v_a$. That is, $p_j$ dominates $v_a$ on $G_i$. It contradicts that $S_{Y'}^{X}(j) \cup \{v_i, p_j\}$ does not dominate $v_a$ on $G_i$. Thus, $S_{Y'}^{X}(j) \cup \{v_i, p_j\}$ dominates $Y \cup V_i$ on $G_i$ with $V(G_i) \cap \overline{V}_L$ labeled as dominated and $|S_{Y'}^{X}(j) \cup \{v_i, p_j\}| \leqslant |\widehat{S}|$. If $|S_{Y'}^{X}(j) \cup \{v_i, p_j\}| = |\widehat{S}|$, by Inequality (2), $\mathcal{L}(S_{Y'}^{X}(j) \cup \{v_i, p_j\}) \geqslant \mathcal{L}(\widehat{S})$. Thus,

**Algorithm 1.** FPT Approximation Algorithm for $\text{DS}^+$ by $k_1$

**Input:** An undirected graph $G = (V, E)$, a subset $V_L \subseteq V$ labeled as dominated, a size-$k_1$ vertex deletion set $V^-$ from $G$ to a chordal graph with leafage $l$;
**Output:** A set $S \subseteq V$;

Apply the algorithm in [13] to compute the tree representation $(T = (Q, F), M)$ of $\widehat{G} := G - V^-$;
Let $S := S_1 := S_2 = \varnothing$;
**for** each branching node $q \in Q_{\geqslant 3}(T)$ **do**
  **for** each branching direction $q \xrightarrow{T} q'$ **do**
    Find the node $\overline{q}$, which is the farthest node related to $q$ in the branching direction $q \xrightarrow{T} q'$;
    Select an arbitrary subtree $T' \in M(\overline{q}) \cap M(q)$;
    $S_1 := S_1 \cup \{v\}$; //The vertex $v$ corresponds to $T'$;
  **end for**
**end for**
Let $V_{\geqslant 3} := \{v \in V(\widehat{G}) :$ the corresponding subtree $T(v)$ of $v$ contains at least one branching node in $Q_{\geqslant 3}(T)\}$, $E^- := \{e \in E(\widehat{G}) : e$ is incident to some vertex in $V_{\geqslant 3}\}$ and $\overline{G} := G - E^-$;
Apply the algorithm FPT-$\text{DS}^+$ in Subsection 3.1 to solve $\text{DS}^+$ on $\overline{G}$ with $\overline{V}_L := N_G[S_1] \cup V_L$ labeled as dominated with respect to $k_2 := |V^-|$ and obtain a vertex subset $S_2$ of $V(\overline{G})$;
**return** $S := S_1 \cup S_2$.

$S^X_{Y'}(j) \cup \{v_i, p_j\}$ is also a subset of $V(G_i)$ having the properties ① - ④. Thus, $S^X_Y(i) := S^X_{Y'}(j) \cup \{v_i, p_j\}$ is correctly computed. □

### 3.2 FPT Approximation Algorithm for $\text{DS}^+$ by $k_1$

Before presenting the parameterized approximation algorithm for $\text{DS}^+$, we give some notations about the tree representation $(T = (Q, F), M)$ of $\widehat{G} = G - V^-$ with $T = (Q, F)$ being a rooted tree and $M$ being a collection of subtrees of $T$. For each vertex $v \in V(\widehat{G})$, the corresponding subtree of $v$ is denoted by $T(v)$. For each node $q \in Q$, $M(q)$ denotes the collection of all subtrees in $M$ containing $q$. For each branching node $q \in Q_{\geqslant 3}(T)$, the branching direction of $q$ to a leaf node $q'$, denoted by $q \xrightarrow{T} q'$, is the direction of the path from $q$ to $q'$. For each branching direction $q \xrightarrow{T} q'$, let $X_T(q, q')$ be the set of all nodes $q''$ on the path from $q$ to $q'$ satisfying $M(q'') \cap M(q) \neq \varnothing$ and let $\overline{q}$ be the node in $X_T(q, q')$ with the maximal distance from $q$. We call $\overline{q}$ the farthest node related to $q$ in the branching direction $q \xrightarrow{T} q'$.

See Algorithm 1 for the FPT approximation algorithm for $\text{DS}^+$ with respect to the number $k_1 := |V^-|$ of vertices, whose removal transforms a graph to a chordal graph with leafage $l$. The rest of this subsection is dedicated to proving the following theorem.

**Theorem 2.** *Given a size-$k_1$ vertex deletion set $V^-$ from the input graph $G$ to a chordal graph with leafage $l$, Algorithm 1 is a $[l(l-1)+1]$-ratio $O(2^{2k_1} \cdot n^{O(1)})$-time algorithm for DS$^+$ on $G$ with $V_L$ labeled as dominated.*

*Proof.* First, we analyze the running time of Algorithm 1. In line 1 of Algorithm 1, we apply the algorithm in [13] to compute the tree representation in $O(n^3)$ time. Line 2 of Algorithm 1 runs in $O(1)$ time. Note that for each $q \in Q_{\geqslant 3}(T)$ and for each branching direction $q \xrightarrow{T} q'$, we can find the node $\overline{q}$ (in line 5) in $n$ time. Since $|Q_{\geqslant 3}(T)| \leqslant |Q_{=1}(T)| - 1 = l - 1$, there are at most $l \cdot (l-1)$ iterations in lines 3–9 of Algorithm 1. Thus, lines 3–9 of Algorithm 1 run in $l(l-1) \cdot n$ time. Line 10 of Algorithm 1 runs in $O(n)$ time. By Theorem 1, line 11 of Algorithm 1 runs in $O(2^{2k_2} \cdot n^{O(1)}) = O(2^{2|V^-|} \cdot n^{O(1)}) = O(2^{2k_1} \cdot n^{O(1)})$ time. In summary, the running time of Algorithm 1 is $O(2^{2k_1} \cdot n^{O(1)})$.

The correctness and the ratio of Algorithm 1 for the DS$^+$-instance $(G, V_L, V^-)$ follow from the claim, that the DS$^+$-instance $(G, N_G[S_1] \cup V_L, V^-)$ has a solution $S'$ iff the DS$^+$-instance $(\overline{G}, N_G[S_1] \cup V_L, V^-)$ has a solution $S'$. We prove this claim by the end of this proof. Concerning the correctness, in line 11 of Algorithm 1, by Theorem 1, the output $S_2$ of the algorithm FPT-DS$^+$ is a solution for the DS$^+$-instance $(\overline{G}, N_G[S_1] \cup V_L, V^-)$. By the above claim, $S_2$ is also a solution for the DS$^+$-instance $(G, N_G[S_1] \cup V_L, V^-)$. Since $S_1$ dominates $N_G[S_1]$, $S = S_1 \cup S_2$ (in line 12 of Algorithm 1) is solution for the given DS$^+$-instance $(G, V_L, V^-)$. Thus, Algorithm 1 outputs a solution for the input. We consider now the approximation ratio. Suppose $OPT$ is an optimal solution for the DS$^+$-instance $(G, V_L, V^-)$ and $\overline{OPT}$ is an optimal solution for the DS$^+$-instance $(G, N_G[S_1] \cup V_L, V^-)$. Since $OPT$ is also a solution for the DS$^+$-instance $(G, N_G[S_1] \cup V_L, V^-)$, $|\overline{OPT}| \leqslant |OPT|$. In line 11 of Algorithm 1, by Theorem 1, the output $S_2$ of FPT-DS$^+$ is an optimal solution for the DS$^+$-instance $(\overline{G}, N_G[S_1] \cup V_L, V^-)$. By the above claim, $S_2$ is also an optimal solution for the DS$^+$-instance $(G, N_G[S_1] \cup V_L, V^-)$. Thus, $|S_2| = |\overline{OPT}| \leqslant |OPT|$. As for $|S_1|$, in lines 3–9 of Algorithm 1, there are at most $l(l-1)$ iterations and at each iteration, we add one vertex to $S_1$. Thus, $|S_1| \leqslant l(l-1)$ and in line 12 of Algorithm 1, $|S| = |S_1 \cup S_2| \leqslant |S_1| + |S_2| \leqslant l(l-1) + |OPT| \leqslant [l(l-1)+1] \cdot |OPT|$.

Before proving the above claim, we need the following observation.

**Observation 1** $N_{\widehat{G}}[V_{\geqslant 3}] \subseteq N_G[S_1]$.

*Proof.* It suffices to show that for each $v' \in V_{\geqslant 3}$ and for each $v'' \in N_{\widehat{G}}[v']$, $v'' \in N_G[S_1]$. Let $T(v')$ denote the subtree of $v'$, $T(v'')$ denote the subtree of $v''$, and $q$ denote a branching node contained in $T(v')$. Since $v'' \in N_{\widehat{G}}[v']$, there is a leaf node $q'$, such that the path from $q$ to $q'$ passing through some nodes in $T(v'')$. In lines 5–7 of Algorithm 1, for the branching direction $q \xrightarrow{T} q'$, we add the vertex $v$ to $S_1$, whose corresponding subtree $T(v)$ contains the farthest node related to $q$ in the branching direction $q \xrightarrow{T} q'$. Then, $T(v)$ intersects $T(v'')$ and $v'' \in N_{\widehat{G}}[v] \subseteq N_G[v] \subseteq N_G[S_1]$. Thus, $N_{\widehat{G}}[V_{\geqslant 3}] \subseteq N_G[S_1]$. □

Finally, we prove the claim, that the DS$^+$-instance $(G, N_G[S_1] \cup V_L, V^-)$ has a solution $S'$ iff the DS$^+$-instance $(\overline{G}, N_G[S_1] \cup V_L, V^-)$ has a solution $S'$.

$\Rightarrow$: Suppose that the DS$^+$-instance $(G, N_G[S_1] \cup V_L, V^-)$ has a solution $S'$. For each $v \in V(\overline{G}) \setminus S'$, we distinguish two cases: $v \in N_{\widehat{G}}[V_{\geqslant 3}]$ and $v \notin N_{\widehat{G}}[V_{\geqslant 3}]$. If $v \in N_{\widehat{G}}[V_{\geqslant 3}]$, then by Observation 1, $v \in N_{\widehat{G}}[V_{\geqslant 3}] \subseteq N_G[S_1] \cup V_L$. If $v \notin N_{\widehat{G}}[V_{\geqslant 3}]$, then we show that there is a vertex $u \in S'$ with $(u, v) \in E(\overline{G})$ or $v \in N_G[S_1] \cup V_L$. We prove by contradiction. Suppose $(u, v) \notin E(\overline{G})$ for all $u \in S'$ and $v \notin N_G[S_1] \cup V_L$. Note that for each $v' \in V(G) \setminus S'$, in the DS$^+$-instance $(G, N_G[S_1] \cup V_L, V^-)$, there is a vertex $u' \in S'$ with $(u', v') \in E(G)$ or $v' \in N_G[S_1] \cup V_L$. Since $v \in V(\overline{G}) \setminus S' = V(G) \setminus S'$, there is a vertex $u \in S'$ with $(u, v) \in E(G)$ or $v \in N_G[S_1] \cup V_L$. By the assumption, this implies that $(u, v) \in E(G) \setminus E(\overline{G}) = E^-$. By the definition of $E^-$, we have $(u, v) \in E(\widehat{G})$, $u, v \in V(\widehat{G})$ and $u \in V_{\geqslant 3}$. Then, $v \in N_{\widehat{G}}[V_{\geqslant 3}]$. It contradicts that $v \notin N_{\widehat{G}}[V_{\geqslant 3}]$. In summary, for each $v \in V(\overline{G}) \setminus S'$, there is a vertex $u \in S'$ with $(u, v) \in E(\overline{G})$ or $v \in N_G[S_1] \cup V_L$. Thus, $S'$ is also a solution for the DS$^+$-instance $(\overline{G}, N_G[S_1] \cup V_L, V^-)$.

$\Leftarrow$: Suppose that the DS$^+$-instance $(\overline{G}, N_G[S_1] \cup V_L, V^-)$ has a solution $S'$. Thus, for each $v \in V(\overline{G}) \setminus S'$, there is a vertex $u \in S'$ with $(u, v) \in E(\overline{G})$ or $v \in N_G[S_1] \cup V_L$. Note that $V(\overline{G}) = V(G)$ and $E(\overline{G}) \subseteq E(G)$. Thus, in $(G, N_G[S_1] \cup V_L, V^-)$, for each $v \in V(G) \setminus S'$, there is a vertex $u \in S'$ with $(u, v) \in E(G)$ or $v \in N_G[S_1] \cup V_L$. Then, $S'$ is also a solution for DS$^+$-instance $(G, N_G[S_1] \cup V_L, V^-)$. □

## 4 FPT Approximation Algorithm for PDS by $k_1$

In this section, we present a parameterized approximation algorithm for a more general version of Power Dominating Set (PDS), denoted as PDS$^+$. Given an undirected graph $G = (V, E)$ and a subset $V_L \subseteq V$ labeled as observed, PDS$^+$ asks for a minimum-size set $S \subseteq V$, which observes all vertices in $V$ according to a modified version of Definition 1, where $P^0(S) := N_G[S]$ is modified to $P^0(S) := N_G[S] \cup V_L$. Clearly, PDS is a special version of PDS$^+$ with $V_L = \varnothing$. The FPT approximation algorithm FPTA-PDS$^+$ for PDS$^+$ is the same as Algorithm 1 for DS$^+$, except that in line 11, we apply the 2-ratio $O(2^{O(k_2 \cdot k_2)} \cdot n^{O(1)})$-time algorithm (see the full version of the paper) to solve PDS$^+$ on $\overline{G}$ with $\overline{V}_L := N_G[S_1] \cup V_L$ labeled as observed with respect to $k_2 := |V^-|$ to obtain a vertex subset $S_2$ of $V(\overline{G})$. The 2-ratio algorithm follows a similar strategy to the FPT algorithm FPT-DS$^+$ in Subsection 3.1. The main difference from DS$^+$ is that PDS$^+$ involves an additional rule R2, which introduces dependency cycles. To handle this, our algorithm for PDS$^+$ relies on the concept of valid orientations [12] and achieves an approximation ratio of 2 instead of an exact solution, even though both DS and PDS are polynomially solvable on interval graphs [17,21]. Thus, we have the following theorem.

**Theorem 3.** *Given a size-$k_1$ vertex deletion set from the input graph $G$ to a chordal graph with leafage $l$, FPTA-PDS$^+$ is a $[l(l-1)+2]$-ratio $O(2^{O(k_1 \cdot k_1)} \cdot n^{O(1)})$-time algorithm for PDS$^+$ on $G$ with $V_L$ labeled as observed.*

# 5 Conclusion

Given a size-$k_1$ vertex deletion set from the input graph $G$ to a chordal graph with leafage $l$, we present a $[l(l-1)+1]$-ratio $O(2^{2k_1} \cdot n^{O(1)})$-time parameterized approximation algorithm for DS and a $[l(l-1)+2]$-ratio $O(2^{O(k_1 \cdot k_1)} \cdot n^{O(1)})$-time parameterized approximation algorithm for PDS. The parameter is the number $k_1$ of vertices, whose removal transforms $G$ to a chordal graph with leafage $l$. As a byproduct, we also show that DS is fixed-parameter tractable with respect to the number $k_2$ of vertices, whose removal transforms $G$ to an interval graph, and PDS admits a 2-ratio $O(2^{O(k_2 \cdot k_2)} \cdot n^{O(1)})$-time parameterized approximation algorithm. It remains four open questions: (1) whether it is FPT to compute the vertex deletion set from general graphs to chordal graphs with leafage $l$ with respect to $k_1$; (2) whether the $[l(l-1)+1]$-ratio $O(2^{2k_1} \cdot n^{O(1)})$-time parameterized approximation algorithm for DS can be improved, since when $l = 2$ the ratio is 3 while we have an exact algorithm for deletion to interval graphs; (3) whether DS is fixed-parameter tractable parameterized by $k_1$ and $l$; (4) whether the 2-ratio $O(2^{O(k_2 \cdot k_2)} \cdot n^{O(1)})$-time algorithm for PDS can be improved to an exact algorithm, i.e., whether PDS is fixed-parameter tractable with respect to $k_2$.

**Acknowledgements.** The work was supported by the National Natural Science Foundation of China (No. 61772314, 61761136017, and 62072275).

# References

1. Arvind, V., Nedela, R., Ponomarenko, I., Zeman, P.: Testing isomorphism of chordal graphs of bounded leafage is fixed-parameter tractable (extended abstract). In: Proceedings of the Forty-Eighth International Workshop on Graph-Theoretic Concepts in Computer Science, WG 2022, vol. 13453, pp. 29–42 (2022)
2. Booth, K.S., Johnson, J.H.: Dominating sets in chordal graphs. SIAM J. Comput. **11**(1), 191–199 (1982)
3. Brueni, D.J., Heath, L.S.: The PMU placement problem. SIAM J. Discret. Math. **19**(3), 744–761 (2005)
4. Cao, Y., Marx, D.: Interval deletion is fixed-parameter tractable. In: Proceedings of the Twenty-Fifth Annual ACM-SIAM Symposium on Discrete Algorithms, SODA 2014, pp. 122–141 (2014)
5. Chen, Y., Lin, B.: The constant inapproximability of the parameterized dominating set problem. In: Proceedings of the Fifty-Seventh Annual Symposium on Foundations of Computer Science, FOCS 2016, pp. 505–514 (2016)
6. Downey, R.G., Fellows, M.R., McCartin, C., Rosamond, F.: Parameterized approximation of dominating set problems. Inf. Process. Lett. **109**(1), 68–70 (2008)
7. Feige, U.: A threshold of ln N for approximating Set Cover (preliminary version). In: Proceedings of the Twenty-Eighth Annual ACM Symposium on the Theory of Computing, STOC 1996, pp. 314–318 (1996)
8. Fomin, F.V., Golovach, P.A., Raymond, J.: On the tractability of optimization problems on H-graphs. Algorithmica **82**(9), 2432–2473 (2020)

9. Galby, E., Marx, D., Schepper, P., Sharma, R., Tale, P.: Domination and cut problems on chordal graphs with bounded leafage. Algorithmica **86**(5), 1428–1474 (2024)
10. Garey, M.R., Johnson, D.S.: Computers and Intractability: A Guide to the Theory of NP-Completeness. Freeman, W. H (1979)
11. Guo, J., Hüffner, F., Kenar, E., Niedermeier, R., Uhlmann, J.: Complexity and exact algorithms for vertex multicut in interval and bounded treewidth graphs. Eur. J. Oper. Res. **186**(2), 542–553 (2008)
12. Guo, J., Niedermeier, R., Raible, D.: Improved algorithms and complexity results for power domination in graphs. Algorithmica **52**(2), 177–202 (2008)
13. Habib, M., Stacho, J.: Polynomial-time algorithm for the leafage of chordal graphs. In: Proceedings of the Seventeenth Annual European Symposium, ESA 2009, vol. 5757, pp. 290–300 (2009). https://doi.org/10.1007/978-3-642-04128-0_27
14. Haynes, T.W., Hedetniemi, S.M., Hedetniemi, S.T., Henning, M.A.: Domination in graphs applied to electric power networks. SIAM J. Discret. Math. **15**(4), 519–529 (2002)
15. Inamdar, T., Kanesh, L., Kundu, M., Ramanujan, M.S., Saurabh, S.: FPT approximations for packing and covering problems parameterized by elimination distance and even less. In: Proceedings of the Forty-Third Foundations of Software Technology and Theoretical Computer Science, FSTTCS 2023, vol. 284, pp. 28:1–28:16 (2023)
16. Koutis, I., Wlodarczyk, M., Zehavi, M.: Sidestepping barriers for dominating set in parameterized complexity. In: Proceedings of the Eighteenth International Symposium on Parameterized and Exact Computation, IPEC 2023, vol. 285, pp. 31:1–31:17 (2023)
17. Liao, C.-S., Lee, D.-T.: Power domination problem in graphs. In: Proceedings of the Eleventh Annual International Conference, COCOON 2005, vol. 3595, pp. 818–828 (2005). https://doi.org/10.1007/11533719_83
18. Marx, D.: Chordal deletion is fixed-parameter tractable. Algorithmica **57**(4), 747–768 (2010)
19. Niedermeier, R.: Invitation to Fixed-Parameter Algorithms. Oxford University Press (2006)
20. Papadopoulos, C., Tzimas, S.: Computing a minimum subset feedback vertex set on chordal graphs parameterized by leafage. Algorithmica **86**(3), 874–906 (2024)
21. Ramalingam, G., Rangan, C.P.: A unified approach to domination problems on interval graphs. Inf. Process. Lett. **27**(5), 271–274 (1988)
22. Karthik, C.S., Laekhanukit, B., Manurangsi, P.: On the parameterized complexity of approximating dominating set. In: Proceedings of the Fiftieth Annual ACM SIGACT Symposium on the Theory of Computing, STOC 2018, pp. 1283–1296 (2018)

# The Min-Max Clustered General Routing Problem with a Depot

Pengxiang Pan[1] and Hongtao Zhu[2(✉)]

[1] School of Artificial Intelligence, Taizhou University, Taizhou 318000, Zhejiang, China
pengxiang@tzc.edu.cn
[2] Faculty of Engineering, Universiti Malaya, Lembah Pantai 50603, Kuala Lumpur, Malaysia
htZhu86@outlook.com

**Abstract.** In the paper, we investigate a generalization of the min-max clustered traveling salesman problem and the clustered general routing problem, referred to as the min-max clustered general routing problem with a depot. For the problem, we design a strongly polynomial time 35/6-approximation algorithm to solve it.

**Keywords:** Combinatorial optimization · Min-max · Clustered · General routing · Approximation algorithm

## 1 Introduction

The clustered traveling salesman problem (CTSP) is an important routing problem involving heterogeneous service targets. In this setting, service conflicts exist between targets with different attributes, requiring that all targets of one attribute (i.e., within a cluster) must be served consecutively before serving any targets of another attribute. Formally, given a complete graph $G = (V, E; w)$ with edge weights obeying the triangle inequality, and with the vertex-set $V$ partitioned into $h$ clusters, the CTSP is to find a Hamiltonian cycle $C$ where all vertices in the same cluster must be visited consecutively. The objective is to minimize the sum of edge weights in $C$.

The CTSP and its variants arise naturally in real-world applications [12], such as parcel delivery, disk defragmentation, examination timetabling, computer program restructuring, and integrated circuit testing. Since the CTSP reduces to the metric TSP when $h = 1$, which is known to be NP-hard, much of the research has focused on designing approximation algorithms to solve it. The first approximation algorithm for the CTSP was proposed by Arkin et al. [1] in 1997, achieving a 7/2-approximation ratio. Then, by leveraging known results on the minimum Hamiltonian path problem [9] and the rural postman problem [6], Guttmann-Beck et al. [8] in 2000 designed an improved 11/4-approximation algorithm to solve the CTSP. Later, using a combination strategy, Bao and Liu [2] in 2012 reconsidered the CTSP and developed a 13/6-approximation algorithm.


Y. Li et al. (Eds.): COCOON 2026, LNCS 16835, pp. 68–80, 2027.
https://doi.org/10.1007/978-981-92-3309-0_6

Building upon previous work in the CTSP, Bao et al. [3] in 2022 introduced a multi-vehicle extension of the CTSP, called the min-max CTSP with a depot (min-max CTSP-D). The problem is to find $k$ cycles in a given complete graph $G = (V, E; w; r)$ with a depot $r$ such that each cycle starts at the depot, all vertices in $V$ are visited, and all vertices in the same cluster must be visited consecutively. The objective is to minimize the maximum cycle weight. For the min-max CTSP-D, Bao et al. [3] developed a 11/2-approximation algorithm to solve it.

Considering that service targets may be located on edges rather than solely on vertices, Zhang et al. [13] in 2022 proposed the clustered general routing problem (CGRP), which is described as follows. Given a complete graph $G = (V, E, w)$ with required elements $V' \subseteq V$ and $E' \subseteq E$, where the vertex-set $V$ is partitioned into $h$ clusters $V_1, \ldots, V_h$, the CGRP is to find a tour $C$ that covers $V'$ exactly once and $E'$ at least once, and visits vertices in $V(C) \cap V_i$ (for each $i \in \{1, \ldots, h\}$) consecutively, and the objective is to minimize the tour weight. For the CGRP, Zhang et al. [13] developed a 11/4-approximation algorithm. A special case of the CGRP is the general routing problem (GRP), where the number of clusters is $h = 1$. By analogy with techniques used in solving the metric TSP, Jansen [10] in 1992 proposed a 3/2-approximation algorithm for the general routing problem.

Motivated by the progression from the CTSP to the min-max CTSP-D, it is natural to consider the multi-vehicle extension of the CGRP. However, to the best of our knowledge, no prior work has addressed the multi-vehicle version of the CGRP. The paper initiates a formal study of such an extension, namely the min-max clustered general routing problem with a depot (min-max CGRP-D). Formally, given an undirected complete graph $G = (V, E; w; r)$ with a positive integer $k$, a depot $r \in V$, a required vertex-subset $V' \subseteq V \setminus \{r\}$ and a required edge-subset $E' \subseteq E$, where $V \setminus \{r\}$ is partitioned into $h$ clusters $V_1, \ldots, V_h$, and the weight function $w : E \to \mathbb{R}^+$ satisfying the triangle inequality, this problem is to find $k$ tours $\mathcal{C} = \{C_1, \ldots, C_k\}$, each starting at the depot $r$, such that

- each required vertex $v \in V'$ is visited exactly once across all tours,
- each required edge $e \in E'$ is covered by at least one tour,
- all visited vertices $V(\mathcal{C}) \cap V_i$ appear consecutively in $\mathcal{C}$ for each $i \in \{1, \ldots, h\}$.

The objective is to minimize the maximum tour weight.

It is easy to see that the min-max CGRP-D generalizes the GRP, implying that the min-max CGRP-D is NP-hard. Therefore, this study focuses on designing an approximation algorithm to solve it. Our primary innovation involves modifying the splitting technique to match the min-max CGRP-D. In particular, we solve a critical subproblem called the general traveling walk problem, which is used to solve the min-max CGRP-D.

This paper is organized as follows. In Sect. 2, we propose an important subproblem called the general traveling walk problem, and design an algorithm to solve it; In Sect. 3, we present an approximation algorithm to solve the min-max CGRP-D; In Sect. 4, we provide our conclusion and further research.

## 2 The General Traveling Walk Problem

In this section, we consider the general traveling walk problem (GTWP). It will be used as a sub-problem to solve the min-max CGRP-D. Specifically, given a complete graph $G = (V, E; w)$ with a required vertex-subset $V' \subseteq V$ and a required edge-subset $E' \subseteq E$, where the edge weight function $w : E \to \mathbb{R}^+$ satisfies the triangle inequality. Let $X \subseteq V$ be a set of designated vertices, which may be one of the following: the empty set $\emptyset$, a singleton set $\{s\}$, or a pair of vertices $\{s, t\}$. A general traveling walk $P$ with endpoints $a$ and $b$ is a walk that visits each required vertex exactly once and visits each required edge at least once, and satisfying $X \subseteq \{a, b\}$. The objective of the GTWP is to find such $P$ with minimum weight.

For convenience, let $G' = (\{v \mid v \in e \in E'\} \cup V' \cup X, E')$. Upon analysis, we can conclude that the GTWP has no feasible solution only in the following cases: (1) There exists a vertex $v \in V'$ such that $d_{G'}(v) > 2$, where $d_{G'}(v)$ is the degree of $v$ in $G'$. (2) There exists a vertex $x \in X \cap V'$ such that $d_{G'}(x) \geq 2$. (3) There exists a connected component $Y$ in $G'$ such that $V(Y) \subseteq V'$ and $d_{G'}(v) = 2$ for every vertex $v \in V(Y)$.

Now we focus on instances where a feasible solution exists.

**Definition 1.** (*Wrong-Degree Vertex-Set*) Given an undirected weighted graph $G = (V, E; w)$, a connected spanning subgraph $\hat{G}' = (V, E_{\hat{G}'})$, and a designated vertex-set $X$ (where $X = \emptyset$, $\{s\}$, or $\{s, t\}$), the *wrong-degree vertex-set* of $\hat{G}'$ is defined as

$$wrong(\hat{G}') := odd(\hat{G}') \triangle X = (odd(\hat{G}') \setminus X) \cup (X \setminus odd(\hat{G}')),$$

where $odd(\hat{G}')$ denotes the set of odd-degree vertices in the graph $\hat{G}'$.

Subsequently, by modifying the algorithmic framework proposed in [9], we design an algorithm $\mathcal{A}_{GTW}$ (Algorithm 1) to solve the GTWP.

For convenience, let $P^*$ denote any optimal solution to the GTWP on instance $G$, and let $OPT$ denote the corresponding optimal value. Using the algorithm $\mathcal{A}_{GTW}$, we obtain the following results.

**Lemma 1.** *Given an instance $G = (V, E; w)$, if the designated vertex-set $X = \emptyset$, then the algorithm $\mathcal{A}_{GTW}$ can output a feasible walk $P$ such that $w(P) \leq \frac{3}{2} \cdot OPT$.*

*Proof.* If the designated vertex-set $X = \emptyset$, it is easy to see that the algorithm $\mathcal{A}_{GTW}$ can output a feasible solution. Since any optimal solution must traverse all vertices and edges in the subgraph $G'$, it follows that $w(\hat{G}') = w(G') + w(T) \leq OPT = w(P^*)$. Therefore, it remains to prove that $w(M) \leq \frac{1}{2} w(P^*)$.

Assume that the sequence in which all odd-degree vertices in $\hat{G}'$ first appear in $P^*$ is $v_1, \ldots, v_{2q}$. Then, we can construct two (non-perfect) matchings $M_1 = \{v_{2i-3}v_{2i-2} \mid i = 2, \ldots, q\}$ and $M_2 = \{v_{2i-2}v_{2i-1} \mid i = 2, \ldots, q\}$ in the complete graph $G$. Furthermore, we can construct two perfect matchings $M_1' = M_1 \cup \{z_1 v_{2q-1}, z_2 v_{2q}\}$ and $M_2' = M_2 \cup \{z_1 v_1, z_2 v_{2q}\}$ in the auxiliary graph $H_{S,2}$.

According to the construction of the graph $H_{S,2} = (S \cup \{z_1, z_2\}, E_S \cup E_2; w_2)$ in the algorithm, we know that each edge $e \in E_S$ has weight $w_2(e) = w(e)$, and each edge $e \in E_2$ has weight $w_2(e) = 0$. Thus, it follows that $w_2(M_1') = w(M_1)$, $w_2(M_2') = w(M_2)$, and $w_2(M') = w(M)$, where $M'$ and $M$ are generated at Step 4 of the algorithm. Since $M'$ is a minimum weight perfect matching in the graph $H_{S,2}$, we have $w_2(M') \leq \min\{w_2(M_1'), w_2(M_2')\}$, which implies $w(M) \leq \min\{w(M_1), w(M_2)\}$.

Because the weight function $w(\cdot)$ satisfies the triangle inequality, it follows that $w(M_1) + w(M_2) < w(P^*)$, and thus $w(M) \leq \min\{w(M_1), w(M_2)\} \leq \frac{w(M_1)+w(M_2)}{2} < \frac{1}{2}w(P^*)$, which yields $w(M) \leq \frac{1}{2}w(P^*)$. □

---

**Algorithm 1** : $\mathcal{A}_{GTW}$

---

**Input**: A complete graph $G = (V, E; w)$, required vertices $V' \subseteq V$, required edges $E' \subseteq E$, a weight function $w : E \to \mathbb{R}^+$, and a designated set $X \subseteq V$ (where $X = \emptyset$, $X = \{s\}$, or $X = \{s, t\}$);

**Output**: A walk $P$ that visits each required vertex exactly once, visits each required edge at least once, and whose endpoints $a, b$ satisfy $X \subseteq \{a, b\}$.

---

**Begin**

**Step 1**: Construct the graph $G' = (\{v \mid v \in e \in E'\} \cup V' \cup X, E')$ and find all its connected components, denoted as $H_1, H_2, \ldots, H_t$;

**Step 2**: Let $U = \{v \in V \mid d_{G'}(v) \in \{0, 1\}$ or $v \notin V'\}$; Construct a complete graph $H = (V_H, E_H; w_H)$, where $V_H = \{u_1, \ldots, u_t\}$, and the weight of each edge $u_i u_j \in E_H$ is $w_H(u_i u_j) = \min\{w(xy) \mid x \in V(H_i) \cap U, y \in V(H_j) \cap U\}$;

**Step 3**: Find a minimum spanning tree $T$ of $H$; Add the corresponding edges of $T$ to $G'$ to obtain a new graph $\hat{G}'$; Determine the wrong-degree vertex-set $S = wrong(\hat{G}') = odd(\hat{G}') \triangle X$;

**Step 4**: If $X = \emptyset$, then construct an auxiliary graph $H_{S,2} = (S \cup \{z_1, z_2\}, E_S \cup E_2; w_2)$, where $z_1, z_2 \notin S$ are new vertices, $E_S = \{xy \mid x, y \in S\}$, $E_2 = \{z_1 v, z_2 v \mid v \in S\}$, $w_2(e) = w(e)$ for each $e \in E_S$ and $w_2(e) = 0$ for each $e \in E_2$; Find a minimum weight perfect matching $M'$ in $H_{S,2}$ and let $M = M' \cap E_S$;

**Step 5**: If $X = \{s\}$, then construct a complete graph $H_{S,1} = (S \cup \{z_1\}, E_S \cup E_1; w_1)$, where $z_1 \notin S$ is a new vertex, $E_S = \{xy \mid x, y \in S\}$, $E_1 = \{z_1 v \mid v \in S\}$, $w_1(e) = w(e)$ for each $e \in E_S$ and $w_1(e) = 0$ for each $e \in E_1$; Find a minimum weight perfect matching $M'$ on $H_{S,1}$ and let $M = M' \cap E_S$;

**Step 6**: If $X = \{s, t\}$, then construct a complete graph $H_{S,0} = (S, E_S; w_0)$, where $E_S = \{xy \mid x, y \in S\}$, and $w_0(e) = w(e)$ for each $e \in E_S$; Find a minimum weight perfect matching $M$ on $H_{S,0}$;

**Step 7**: If the graph $\hat{G}' \cup M$ contains no odd-degree vertex (implying $X = \{s\} \subseteq S$ and $\delta_G(s) \cap M = \emptyset$), then remove any non-required edge incident to $s$ from $\hat{G}' \cup M$ and find an Eulerian walk $P'$ in the resulting graph; Otherwise, find an Eulerian walk $P'$ in $\hat{G}' \cup M$;

**Step 8**: Use the "shortcutting" technique to convert $P'$ into a feasible walk $P$ which visits each $v \in V'$ exactly once and covers $E'$;

**Step 9**: Output the walk $P$.

**End**

---

**Lemma 2.** *Given an instance $G = (V, E; w)$, if the designated vertex-set $X = \{s\}$, then the algorithm $\mathcal{A}_{GTW}$ can output a feasible walk $P$ such that $w(P) \leq \frac{3}{2} \cdot OPT$.*

*Proof.* Assume that the two endpoints of an optimal solution $P^*$ are $s$ and $b$, and the sequence in which all odd-degree vertices in $\hat{G}'$ first appear in $P^*$ is $v_1, \dots, v_{2q}$. We now consider the following two cases:

**Case 1.** The vertex $s$ is an odd-degree vertex in the graph $\hat{G}'$, implying that $s$ is not a wrong-degree vertex (i.e., $s \notin S$). Without loss of generality, we assume $v_1 = s$.

In this case, it is evident that the algorithm $\mathcal{A}_{GTW}$ can produce a feasible solution. Since any optimal solution must traverse all vertices and edges of the subgraph $G'$, we have $w(\hat{G}') = w(G') + w(T) \leq OPT = w(P^*)$. Thus, it suffices to show that $w(M) \leq \frac{1}{2}w(P^*)$.

Based on $P^*$, we can construct two (non-perfect) matchings $M_1 = \{v_{2i-2}v_{2i-1} \mid i = 2, \dots, q\}$ and $M_2 = \{v_{2i-1}v_{2i} \mid i = 2, \dots, q\}$ in the complete graph $G$. From these, we can further construct two perfect matchings $M_1' = M_1 \cup \{z_1 v_{2q}\}$ and $M_2' = M_2 \cup \{z_1 v_2\}$ in the complete graph $H_{S,1}$. According to the construction of $H_{S,1}$ in the algorithm, each edge $e \in E_S$ has weight $w_1(e) = w(e)$, and each edge $e \in E_1$ has weight $w_1(e) = 0$. Therefore, we have $w_1(M_1') = w(M_1)$, $w_1(M_2') = w(M_2)$, and $w_1(M') = w(M)$, where $M'$ and $M$ are obtained at Step 5 of the algorithm.

Since $M'$ is a minimum weight perfect matching in $H_{S,1}$, it follows that $w_1(M') \leq \min\{w_1(M_1'), w_1(M_2')\}$, which implies $w(M) \leq \min\{w(M_1), w(M_2)\}$. Because the weight function $w(\cdot)$ satisfies the triangle inequality, we derive the inequality $w(M_1) + w(M_2) < w(P^*)$. Therefore,

$$w(M) \leq \min\{w(M_1), w(M_2)\} \leq \frac{w(M_1) + w(M_2)}{2} < \frac{1}{2}w(P^*),$$

which establishes that $w(M) \leq \frac{1}{2}w(P^*)$.

**Case 2.** The vertex $s$ is an even-degree vertex in the graph $\hat{G}'$, implying that $s$ is a wrong-degree vertex (i.e., $s \in S$).

We first show that the algorithm $\mathcal{A}_{GTW}$ can produce a feasible solution. If $s$ is covered by $M$, it is straightforward to verify that a feasible solution can be produced; Otherwise, $M$ covers only all odd-degree vertices in $\hat{G}'$, meaning that the connected graph $\hat{G}' \cup M$ has no odd-degree vertices. In this case, we have $\delta_{\hat{G}' \cup M}(s) \geq 2$, and a feasible solution can be constructed using Steps 7–8 of the algorithm $\mathcal{A}_{GTW}$. Moreover, from the algorithm and the structure of the optimal solution, it follows that

$$w(\hat{G}') = w(G') + w(T) \leq OPT = w(P^*) \quad \text{and} \quad w(P) \leq w(G') + w(T) + w(M),$$

where $P$ denotes the solution outputted by the algorithm $\mathcal{A}_{GTW}$. Thus, it remains to prove that $w(M) \leq \frac{1}{2}w(P^*)$.

Based on $P^*$, we can construct two (non-perfect) matchings $M_1 = \{sv_1\} \cup \{v_{2i-2}v_{2i-1} \mid i = 2, \dots, q\}$, $M_2 = \{v_{2i-1}v_{2i} \mid i = 1, \dots, q\}$ in the complete graph $G$. These yield two perfect matchings $M_1' = M_1 \cup \{z_1 v_{2q}\}$, $M_2' = M_2 \cup \{z_1 s\}$ in the complete graph $H_{S,1}$. According to the construction of $H_{S,1}$ in the algorithm, each edge $e \in E_S$ has weight $w_1(e) = w(e)$, and each edge $e \in E_1$ has weight $w_1(e) = 0$. Therefore, we obtain $w_1(M_1') = w(M_1)$, $w_1(M_2') = w(M_2)$, and $w_1(M') = w(M)$, where $M'$ and $M$ are obtained at Step 5 of the algorithm.

Since $M'$ is a minimum weight perfect matching in the graph $H_{S,1}$, we have $w_1(M') \leq \min\{w_1(M_1'), w_1(M_2')\}$, which implies $w(M) \leq \min\{w(M_1), w(M_2)\}$. As the weight function $w(\cdot)$ satisfies the triangle inequality, we obtain $w(M_1) + w(M_2) < w(P^*)$, and thus,

$$w(M) \leq \min\{w(M_1), w(M_2)\} \leq \frac{w(M_1) + w(M_2)}{2} < \frac{1}{2}w(P^*),$$

which proves that $w(M) \leq \frac{1}{2}w(P^*)$.

In summary, for both cases regarding vertex $s$, we have shown that $w(P) \leq \frac{3}{2} \cdot OPT$. □

For the case where the designated vertex-set $X$ contains two vertices, the following lemma can be derived by applying the same arguments as those presented in [13].

**Lemma 3.** [13] *Given an instance $G = (V, E; w)$, if the designated vertex-set is $X = \{s, t\}$, then the algorithm $\mathcal{A}_{GTW}$ can output a feasible walk $P$ such that $w(P) \leq \frac{5}{3} \cdot OPT$.*

Furthermore, the time complexity of the algorithm $\mathcal{A}_{GTW}$ is analyzed as follows: (1) Steps 1–2 need $O(n^2)$ time to construct the auxiliary graph $H$, where $n$ is the number of vertices in the given graph; (2) Using Prim's algorithm [11], Step 3 takes $O(n^2)$ time to find a minimum weight spanning tree in $H$; (3) Using Edmonds' algorithm [5], Steps 4–6 each require $O(n^3)$ time to find a minimum weight perfect matching; (4) Using an exact algorithm for finding an Eulerian walk [4], Steps 7–8 require $O(n^2)$ time to construct a feasible walk $P$. Therefore, the overall time complexity of the algorithm $\mathcal{A}_{GTW}$ is $O(n^3)$.

## 3 The Min-Max Clustered General Routing Problem with a Depot

Without loss of generality, assume that $k \geq 2$; Otherwise, when $k = 1$, a 11/4-approximation solution to the clustered general routing problem can be obtained using an algorithm presented in [13]. Note that the min-max clustered general routing problem with a depot (min-max CGRP-D) involves two possible cases:

(1) Every edge $e \in E'$ connects two vertices within the same cluster;
(2) There exists at least one edge $e \in E'$ that connects vertices from two different clusters.

### 3.1 Case (1)

We first consider Case (1), where each edge $e \in E'$ has both endpoints in the same cluster. For convenience, let $\bar{H} = (\bar{V}, \bar{E}) = (\{v \mid v \in e \in E'\} \cup V', E')$. For each $i \in \{1, 2, \ldots, h\}$, we define $V_i' = V' \cap V_i$, $E_i' = E' \cap E(G[V_i])$, $\bar{H}_i = (\bar{V}_i, \bar{E}_i) = (\{v \mid v \in e \in E_i'\} \cup V_i', E_i')$. Through analysis, we find that the min-max CGRP-D has no feasible solution only in the following two situations:

(1) There exists a vertex $v \in V'$ such that $d_{\bar{H}}(v) > 2$, implying that there is no solution in which $v$ is traversed exactly once;
(2) There exists a connected component $Y$ in $\bar{H}$ such that $V(Y) \subseteq V'$ and every vertex $v \in V(Y)$ satisfies $d_{\bar{H}}(v) = 2$.

Therefore, we only consider instances for which feasible solutions exist. The solution strategy is described as follows:

(1) In the induced subgraph corresponding to each cluster $V_i$, find a minimum weight general traveling walk $P_i$ that visits each required vertex exactly once and visits each required edge at least once;
(2) In the original graph, find a minimum weight tour $C$ that traverses all the walks $P_1, P_2, \ldots, P_h$ obtained in (1);
(3) Split and reconstruct the tour $C$ obtained in (2) into $k$ tours such that the maximum weight among these tours is minimized.

Based on the above strategy, an algorithm $\mathcal{A}_D$ (Algorithm 2) for the min-max CGRP-D is designed as follows.

Without loss of generality, we may assume that $k \leq h$; Otherwise, we can construct $h$ feasible tours by directly connecting the depot to the endpoints of each walk $P_i$ $(i = 1, \ldots, h)$, and supplement the remaining $k - h$ cycles with trivial cycles that only include the depot. This construction produces a feasible solution of the min-max CGRP-D. Since the vertices within each cluster must be visited consecutively, it follows that the objective value of this feasible solution will not exceed that produced by the algorithm $\mathcal{A}_D$. Therefore, the assumption $k \leq h$ is reasonable.

For convenience, let $\mathcal{C}^* = \{C_i^* \mid i = 1, 2, \ldots, k\}$ denote any optimal solution to the min-max CGRP-D on instance $G$, and $OPT$ its optimal value. By the algorithm $\mathcal{A}_D$, we have the following result.

**Lemma 4.** *At Step 3 of the algorithm $\mathcal{A}_D$, the generated tour $C$ satisfies*

$$w(C) \leq (\rho_P + \rho_R) \cdot k \cdot OPT,$$

*where $\rho_P$ denotes the approximation ratio of the algorithm for the GTWP, and $\rho_R$ denotes the approximation ratio of the algorithm for the rural postman problem.*

*Proof.* By the algorithm $\mathcal{A}_D$, we know that $w(C) \leq w\left(\bigcup_{i=1}^{h} P_i\right) + w(\hat{C})$. Then we will prove separately that $w\left(\bigcup_{i=1}^{h} P_i\right) \leq \rho_P \cdot k \cdot \mathrm{OPT}$ and $w(\hat{C}) \leq \rho_R \cdot k \cdot \mathrm{OPT}$.

**Algorithm 2** : $\mathcal{A}_D$

**Input**: A complete graph $G = (V, E; w)$, a depot $r \in V$, required vertices $V' \subseteq V$, required edges $E' \subseteq E$, a function $w : E \to \mathbb{R}^+$ satisfying the triangle inequality, a positive integer $k$, and a partition of $V \setminus \{r\}$ into $h$ clusters $V_1, \ldots, V_h$;

**Output**: A set of $k$ tours $\mathcal{C} = \{C_i \mid i = 1, 2, \ldots, k\}$, each starting and ending at the depot $r$.

**Begin**

**Step 1**: For each $i = 1, 2, \ldots, h$, let $X = \emptyset$, and use the algorithm $\mathcal{A}_{GTW}$ described in Section 2 to find a $\rho_P$-approximate general traveling walk $P_i$ in the subgraph $G[\bar{V}_i]$, with endpoints denoted $a_i$ and $b_i$; Let $V_R = \{r\} \cup A \cup B$, where $A = \{a_i \mid i = 1, \ldots, h\}$ and $B = \{b_i \mid i = 1, \ldots, h\}$;

**Step 2**: Treat $\{a_i b_i \mid i = 1, \ldots, h\}$ as the required edge-subset, and use an algorithm for the rural postman problem (denoted $\mathcal{A}_{RP}$) to find a $\rho_R$-approximate tour in $G[V_R]$ starting at $r$ and visiting each required edge at least once; Then, apply the "shortcutting" technique to obtain a cycle $\hat{C}$ that visits each required edge exactly once;

**Step 3**: For each $i = 1, 2, \ldots, h$, replace the subsequence $(a_i, b_i)$ in $\hat{C}$ with $P_i$ to obtain a clustered general tour $C = (r, v_1^s, \ldots, v_1^t, \ldots, v_h^s, \ldots, v_h^t, r)$, where $v_i^s$ and $v_i^t$ are the entry and exit vertices in cluster $V_i$ respectively; Let $w_{\max} = \max\{w(r, v) \mid v \in \bar{V}\}$, $V_0 = \{r\}$, $v_0^t = v_{h+1}^s = r$, $v_{s(1)} = v_{t(k)} = r$;

**Step 4**: If $w(C) \leq (2\rho_P + 2)w_{\max}$, then:

- Set $C_1 := C$; For each $i \in \{2, \ldots, k\}$, set $C_i := \emptyset$; Go to Step 7;

**Step 5**: For $j = 1$ to $k - 1$ do:

- Set $L_j = \frac{j}{k}(w(C) - 4w_{\max}) + 2w_{\max}$, and find an edge $e_j = x_j y_j \in E$ such that $w(C[r, x_j]) \leq L_j$ and $w(C[r, y_j]) > L_j$, where $C[r, v]$ denotes the sub-walk from $r$ to $v$ along $C$; Let $R_j = L_j - w(C[r, x_j])$;
- If $x_j$ and $y_j$ belong to different clusters $V_i$ and $V_{i+1}$ respectively, then:

-- If $v_i^t \prec v_{s(j)}$ (meaning that $v_i^t$ appears no later than $v_{s(j)}$ along $C$), then:

Set $v_{s(j)} := r$, $v_{t(j)} := r$, $v_{s(j+1)} := v_{i+1}^s$;

-- Else:

Set $v_{t(j)} := v_i^t$, $v_{s(j+1)} := v_{i+1}^s$;

- Else if $x_j$ and $y_j$ belong to the same cluster $V_i$, then:

-- If $R_j + w(C[v_i^s, x_j]) + w(r, v_i^s) \leq w(e_j) - R_j + w(C[y_j, v_i^t]) + w(v_i^t, r)$, then:

If $v_{i-1}^t \prec v_{s(j)}$, then:

Set $v_{s(j)} := r$, $v_{t(j)} := r$, $v_{s(j+1)} := v_i^s$;

Else:

Set $v_{t(j)} := v_{i-1}^t$, $v_{s(j+1)} := v_i^s$;

-- Else:

If $v_i^t \prec v_{s(j)}$, then:

Set $v_{s(j)} := r$, $v_{t(j)} := r$, $v_{s(j+1)} := v_{i+1}^s$;

Else:

Set $v_{t(j)} := v_i^t$, $v_{s(j+1)} := v_{i+1}^s$;

**Step 6**: For each $j = 1, \ldots, k$, construct $j$th sub-tour $C_j$ by connecting $r$ with both endpoints of the sub-walk $C[v_{s(j)}, v_{t(j)}]$;

**Step 7**: Output the set of $k$ tours $\mathcal{C} = \{C_i \mid i = 1, 2, \ldots, k\}$.

**End**

For any optimal solution $\mathcal{C}^*$, by removing the depot $r$ and all edges connecting different clusters, we can obtain $h$ general traveling walks $P'_1, \ldots, P'_h$, where each walk $P'_i$ $(i = 1, \ldots, h)$ is a feasible solution to the GTWP with $X = \emptyset$ in the corresponding subgraph $G[\bar{V}_i]$. Since each walk $P_i$ $(i = 1, \ldots, h)$ is a $\rho_P$-approximate general traveling walk in its respective subgraph $G[\bar{V}_i]$, we have $w\left(\bigcup_{i=1}^h P_i\right) \leq \rho_P \cdot w\left(\bigcup_{i=1}^h P_i^*\right) \leq \rho_P \cdot w\left(\bigcup_{i=1}^h P'_i\right)$, where $P_i^*$ $(i = 1, \ldots, h)$ denotes an optimal solution to the GTWP with $X = \emptyset$ on $G[\bar{V}_i]$. Moreover, since $w\left(\bigcup_{i=1}^h P'_i\right) \leq w(\mathcal{C}^*)$, it follows that $w\left(\bigcup_{i=1}^h P_i\right) \leq \rho_P \cdot w(\mathcal{C}^*) \leq \rho_P \cdot k \cdot \mathrm{OPT}$, which completes the proof that $w\left(\bigcup_{i=1}^h P_i\right) \leq \rho_P \cdot k \cdot \mathrm{OPT}$.

It remains to show that $w(\hat{C}) \leq \rho_R \cdot k \cdot OPT$. By the triangle inequality property and the "shortcutting" technique, the optimal solution $\mathcal{C}^*$ can be transformed into a clustered general tour $C'$ such that $w(C') \leq w(\mathcal{C}^*) \leq k \cdot OPT$. Applying the "shortcutting" technique again, we skip all vertices in $C'$ except those in the set $\{r, a_i, b_i \mid i = 1, \ldots, h\}$ to obtain a tour $\hat{C}'$ in $G[V_R]$ that visits each edge $e \in \{a_i b_i \mid i = 1, \ldots, h\}$ exactly once, with the total weight satisfying $w(\hat{C}') \leq w(C')$. Since $\hat{C}$ is a $\rho_R$-approximate tour in $G[V_R]$ that visits each edge $e \in \{a_i b_i \mid i = 1, \ldots, h\}$ exactly once, it follows that $w(\hat{C}) \leq \rho_R \cdot w(\hat{C}') \leq \rho_R \cdot w(C') \leq \rho_R \cdot k \cdot OPT$, which proves that $w(\hat{C}) \leq \rho_R \cdot k \cdot OPT$.

The preceding lemma directly yields the following result.

**Theorem 1.** *The algorithm $\mathcal{A}_D$ is a $(\rho_R + 2\rho_P + 1 - \frac{2}{k})$-approximation algorithm for solving the min-max CGRP-D in Case (1), and its time complexity is $O(n^3 h + f_R(n))$, where $\rho_P$ denotes the approximation ratio of the algorithm $\mathcal{A}_{GTW}$, $\rho_R$ and $f_R(n)$ denote the approximation ratio and runtime of an algorithm for the rural postman problem respectively, $n$ is the number of vertices in the given graph, and $h$ is the number of clusters.*

*Proof.* Since the edge weight function satisfies the triangle inequality, and by the definition of $w_{\max}$, it follows that $2w_{\max} \leq OPT$. If the tour $C$ generated in Step 3 satisfies $w(C) \leq (2\rho_P + 2)w_{\max}$, then, under the assumption $k \geq 2$, we have for any $j \in \{1, \ldots, k\}$,

$$\begin{aligned} w(C_j) &\leq (2\rho_P + 2) \cdot w_{\max} \\ &\leq (\rho_P + 1) \cdot OPT \\ &\leq \left(\rho_R + 2\rho_P + 1 - \frac{2}{k}\right) \cdot OPT. \end{aligned}$$

Now, suppose that the tour $C$ generated at Step 3 satisfies $w(C) > (2\rho_P + 2)w_{\max}$. We first consider the $j$th tour $C_j$ outputted by the algorithm $\mathcal{A}_D$, where $j \in \{2, \ldots, k-1\}$.

According to the algorithm $\mathcal{A}_D$, the worst-case (in which the length of tour $C_j$ is maximized) occurs when $C_j$ starts from the depot $r$, travels along the shortest path to the vertex $v_{s(j)} = v_{i_1}^s$ $(\in V_{i_1})$, then follows the tour $C$ to reach the vertex $v_{t(j)} = v^t_{i_2}$ ($\in V_{i_2}$), and finally returns to the depot $r$ via the shortest path. In this case, the following two inequalities are satisfied:

$$w(r, v^s_{i_1}) + w(C[v^s_{i_1}, x_{j-1}]) + R_{j-1} \le w(e_{j-1}) - R_{j-1} + w(C[y_{j-1}, v^t_{i_1}]) + w(v^t_{i_1}, r)$$

and

$$w(r, v^s_{i_2}) + w(C[v^s_{i_2}, x_j]) + R_j > w(e_j) - R_j + w(C[y_j, v^t_{i_2}]) + w(v^t_{i_2}, r).$$

Since $P_{i_1} = C[v^s_{i_1}, v^t_{i_1}]$ and $P_{i_2} = C[v^s_{i_2}, v^t_{i_2}]$ are both $\rho_P$-approximate general traveling walks within the clusters $V_{i_1}$ and $V_{i_2}$, respectively, and the optimal tour $\mathcal{C}^*$ includes general traveling walks within the clusters, we have

$$w(C[v^s_{i_1}, v^t_{i_1}]) \le \rho_P \cdot OPT \quad \text{and} \quad w(C[v^s_{i_2}, v^t_{i_2}]) \le \rho_P \cdot OPT.$$

This implies that

$$w(r, v^s_{i_1}) + w(C[v^s_{i_1}, v^t_{i_1}]) + w(v^t_{i_1}, r) \le 2w_{\max} + \rho_P \cdot OPT$$

and

$$w(r, v^s_{i_2}) + w(C[v^s_{i_2}, v^t_{i_2}]) + w(v^t_{i_2}, r) \le 2w_{\max} + \rho_P \cdot OPT.$$

From this, it can be further deduced that

$$\begin{aligned}
&w(r, v^s_{i_1}) + w(C[v^s_{i_1}, x_{j-1}]) + R_{j-1} \\
&= \min\{w(r, v^s_{i_1}) + w(C[v^s_{i_1}, x_{j-1}]) + R_{j-1}, w(e_{j-1}) - R_{j-1} + w(C[y_{j-1}, v^t_{i_1}]) + w(v^t_{i_1}, r)\} \\
&\le \frac{1}{2}(w(r, v^s_{i_1}) + w(C[v^s_{i_1}, x_{j-1}]) + w(x_{j-1}y_{j-1}) + w(C[y_{j-1}, v^t_{i_1}]) + w(v^t_{i_1}, r)) \\
&= \frac{1}{2}(w(r, v^s_{i_1}) + w(C[v^s_{i_1}, v^t_{i_1}]) + w(v^t_{i_1}, r)) \\
&\le \frac{1}{2}(2w_{\max} + \rho_P \cdot OPT) = w_{\max} + \frac{1}{2}\rho_P \cdot OPT,
\end{aligned}$$

and

$$\begin{aligned}
&w(e_j) - R_j + w(C[y_j, v^t_{i_2}]) + w(v^t_{i_2}, r) \\
&= \min\{w(r, v^s_{i_2}) + w(C[v^s_{i_2}, x_j]) + R_j, w(e_j) - R_j + w(C[y_j, v^t_{i_2}]) + w(v^t_{i_2}, r)\} \\
&\le \frac{1}{2}(w(r, v^s_{i_2}) + w(C[v^s_{i_2}, x_j]) + w(x_j y_j) + w(C[y_j, v^t_{i_2}]) + w(v^t_{i_2}, r)) \\
&= \frac{1}{2}(w(r, v^s_{i_2}) + w(C[v^s_{i_2}, v^t_{i_2}]) + w(v^t_{i_2}, r)) \\
&\le \frac{1}{2}(2w_{\max} + \rho_P \cdot OPT) = w_{\max} + \frac{1}{2}\rho_P \cdot OPT.
\end{aligned}$$

Therefore, by applying Lemma 4, we obtain

$$\begin{aligned}
w(C_j) &\le w(r, v_{s(j)}) + w(C[v_{s(j)}, v_{t(j)}]) + w(v_{t(j)}, r) \\
&= w(r, v^s_{i_1}) + w(C[v^s_{i_1}, x_{j-1}]) + R_{j-1} \\
&\quad -R_{j-1} + w(e_{j-1}) + w(C[y_{j-1}, x_j]) + R_j \\
&\quad -R_j + w(e_j) + w(C[y_j, v^t_{i_2}]) + w(v^t_{i_2}, r) \\
&\le w_{\max} + \frac{1}{2}\rho_P \cdot OPT + \frac{1}{k}(w(C) - 4w_{\max}) + w_{\max} + \frac{1}{2}\rho_P \cdot OPT \\
&\le \frac{1}{k}w(C) + \rho_P \cdot OPT + 2w_{\max} - \frac{4}{k}w_{\max} \\
&\le (\rho_R + 2\rho_P + 1 - \frac{2}{k}) \cdot OPT.
\end{aligned}$$

Similarly, for each $j \in \{1, k\}$, by analyzing $C_j$, we have

$$\begin{aligned}
w(C_j) &\le \frac{1}{k} \cdot (w(C) - 4w_{\max}) + 2w_{\max} + w_{\max} + \frac{1}{2}\rho_P \cdot OPT \\
&\le \frac{1}{k}w(C) + \left(3 - \frac{4}{k}\right) w_{\max} + \frac{1}{2}\rho_P \cdot OPT \\
&\le \left(\rho_R + \frac{3}{2}\rho_P + \frac{3}{2} - \frac{2}{k}\right) \cdot OPT \\
&\le \left(\rho_R + 2\rho_P + 1 - \frac{2}{k}\right) \cdot OPT.
\end{aligned}$$

In conclusion, for any $j \in \{1, \ldots, k\}$, it holds that $w(C_j) \le (\rho_R + 2\rho_P + 1 - \frac{2}{k}) \cdot OPT$.

The time complexity analysis of the algorithm $\mathcal{A}_D$ is as follows: (1) Step 1, which applies the algorithm $\mathcal{A}_{GTW}$, requires $O(n^3 h)$ time; (2) Steps 2–3 apply a $\rho_R$-approximation algorithm for the rural postman problem, which takes $f_R(n)$ time; (3) Since $k \le h$ by assumption, Steps 4–5 require $O(mh)$ time, where $m$ is the number of edges in the given graph; (4) Step 6 requires $O(m)$ time to construct a set of tours $\mathcal{C} = \{C_i \mid i = 1, 2, \ldots, k\}$. Therefore, the total running time of the algorithm $\mathcal{A}_D$ is $O(n^3 h + f_R(n))$. □

In Case (1), $X = \emptyset$, so the approximation ratio of the algorithm $\mathcal{A}_{GTW}$ is 3/2 according to Lemma 1. Applying the 3/2-approximation algorithm for the rural postman problem given in [7], which has a time complexity of $O(n^3)$, we obtain the following corollary.

**Corollary 1.** *Case (1) of the min-max CGRP-D admits a* 11/2*-approximation algorithm running in* $O(n^3 h)$ *time.*

### 3.2 Case (2)

In Case (2), we can infer that there is at most one required edge connecting any two different clusters (while there is no restriction on non-required edges);

Otherwise, no feasible solution exists. We now show that Case (2) can be reduced to Case (1):

Assume two distinct clusters $V_i$ and $V_j$ are connected by a required edge $e = b_i a_j$, implying that a cluster is associated with one (or two) required edges not in the cluster. Without loss of generality, let the intersection vertices of clusters $V_i$ and $V_j$ with the required edges be $\{b_i\}$ (or $\{a_i, b_i\}$) and $\{a_j\}$ (or $\{a_j, b_j\}$) respectively. We can set $X = \{b_i\}$ (or $\{a_i, b_i\}$) and $X = \{a_j\}$ (or $\{a_j, b_j\}$) respectively, and apply the algorithm $\mathcal{A}_{GTW}$ to obtain general traveling walks within the two clusters, denoted as the $a_i - b_i$ walk and the $a_j - b_j$ walk. Then, we construct a combined walk $a_i \to b_i \to a_j \to b_j$ over $V_i \cup V_j$ and treat it as a single unit. By iteratively repeating the above process, the constraints of Case (1) can be satisfied. However, if a cluster is associated with two required edges not in the cluster, implying that a general traveling walk with two fixed endpoints must be found in such a cluster, the approximation ratio $\rho_P$ increases from 3/2 to 5/3 according to Lemmas 2-3.

Based on the above induction and the result of Theorem 1, we conclude that the algorithm $\mathcal{A}_D$ is an approximation algorithm with ratio at most 35/6 for the min-max CGRP-D in Case (2) and Case (1).

**Theorem 2.** *The min-max CGRP-D admits a* 35/6*-approximation algorithm running in* $O(n^3 h)$ *time.*

## 4 Conclusion and Further Work

We investigate the min-max CGRP-D, mainly yielding the following result. By first identifying suitable walks within the induced subgraphs corresponding to each cluster, then integrating these walks into a single tour followed by partitioning, a constant factor approximation algorithm is designed for the min-max CGRP-D.

Some important open problems remain the design of more efficient approximation algorithms for solving the min-max CGRP-D, as well as their generalization to heterogeneous vehicle fleets.

**Acknowledgments.** These authors are grateful to the three anonymous reviewers for their insightful comments and for their suggested changes that improve the current presentation greatly.

**Disclosure of Interests.** The authors have no competing interests to declare that are relevant to the content of this article.

## References

1. Arkin, E., Hassin, R., Klein, L.: Restricted delivery problems on a network. Networks **29**, 205–216 (1997)
2. Bao, X., Liu, Z.: An improved approximation algorithm for the clustered traveling salesman problem. Inf. Process. Lett. **112**, 908–910 (2012)
3. Bao, X., Xu, L., Yu, W., Song, W.: Approximation algorithms for the min-max clustered $k$-traveling salesmen problems. Theoret. Comput. Sci. **933**, 60–66 (2022)
4. Corberán, A., Laporte, G.: ARC routing: problems, methods, and applications. MOS-SIAM Series on optimization (vol. 20). Society for industrial and applied mathematics, Philadelphia (2014)
5. Edmonds, J., Johnson, E.L.: Matching, Euler tours and the Chinese postman. Math. Program. **5**, 88–124 (1973)
6. Eiselt, H.A., Gendreau, M., Laporte, G.: Arc routing problems, part II: the rural postman problem. Oper. Res. **43**, 399–414 (1995)
7. Frederickson, G.N.: Approximation algorithms for some postman problems. J. ACM **26**, 538–554 (1979)
8. Guttmann-Beck, N., Hassin, R., Khuller, S., Raghavachari, B.: Approximation algorithms with bounded performance guarantees for the clustered traveling salesman problem. Algorithmica **28**, 422–437 (2000)
9. Hoogeveen, J.A.: Analysis of Christofides' heuristic: some paths are more difficult than cycles. Oper. Res. Lett. **10**, 291–295 (1991)
10. Jansen, K.: An approximation algorithm for the general routing problem. Inf. Process. Lett. **41**, 333–339 (1992)
11. Korte, B., Vygen, J.: Combinatorial Optimization: Theory and Algorithms (The Sixth Edition). Springer, Berlin (2018)
12. Laporte, G., Palekar, U.: Some applications of the clustered travelling salesman problem. J. Oper. Res. Soc. **53**, 972–976 (2002)
13. Zhang, X., Du, D., Gutin, G., Ming, Q., Sun, J.: Approximation algorithms with constant ratio for general cluster routing problems. J. Comb. Optim. **44**(4), 2499–2514 (2022)

# Distance Recoloring

Niranka Banerjee[1], Christian Engels[2], and Duc A. Hoang[3(✉)]

[1] Mie University, Tsu, Japan
banerjee@eng.mie-u.ac.jp
[2] National Institute of Informatics, Tokyo, Japan
[3] VNU University of Science, Vietnam National University, Hanoi, Vietnam
hoanganhduc@hus.edu.vn

**Abstract.** Reconfiguration problems ask whether one feasible solution can be transformed into another by a sequence of local moves while maintaining feasibility throughout. For integers $d \geq 1$ and $k \geq d+1$, the Distance Coloring problem asks if a given graph $G$ has a $(d, k)$-coloring, i.e., a coloring of the vertices of $G$ by $k$ colors such that any two vertices within distance $d$ from each other have different colors.

For ordinary proper colorings ($d = 1$), the $k$-Coloring Reconfiguration problem is polynomial-time solvable for $k \leq 3$ [Cereceda, van den Heuvel, and Johnson, *J. Graph Theory* 67(1):69–82, 2011] but is PSPACE-complete for every fixed $k \geq 4$, even on bipartite graphs [Bonsma and Cereceda, *Theor. Comput. Sci.* 410(50):5215–5226, 2009]. In this work, we initiate a study of the distance-$d$ analogue, for $d \geq 2$. We show that even for planar, bipartite, and 2-degenerate graphs, $(d, k)$-Coloring Reconfiguration remains PSPACE-complete for every $d \geq 3$ via a reduction from the well-known Sliding Tokens problem. Our construction uses $k = k_0 + 2 + n(\lceil d/2 \rceil - 1)$ colors on instances of size $n$, where $k_0 \in \{3d+3, 3d+6\}$ (depending on the parity of $d$). For $d = 2$, the same reduction scheme can be adapted to show that the problem is PSPACE-complete on planar and 2-degenerate graphs with same values of $k$.

**Keywords:** Reconfiguration problem · $d$-Distance $k$-Coloring · Computational complexity · PSPACE-completeness

## 1 Introduction

For the last few decades, *reconfiguration problems* have emerged in various areas of computer science, including computational geometry, recreational mathematics, and constraint satisfaction [15,16,18]. Given a *source problem* $\mathcal{P}$ (e.g., Satisfiability, Coloring, Independent Set), one can define its *reconfiguration variants*. In such a variant, two *feasible solutions* (e.g., satisfying truth assignments, proper vertex-colorings, independent sets) $S$ and $T$ of $\mathcal{P}$ are given along with a prescribed *reconfiguration rule* that usually describes a "small" change in a solution. The question is to decide if there is a sequence of feasible solutions


Y. Li et al. (Eds.): COCOON 2026, LNCS 16835, pp. 81–94, 2027.
https://doi.org/10.1007/978-981-92-3309-0_7

that transforms $S$ into $T$, where each intermediate member is obtained from its predecessor by applying the reconfiguration rule exactly once. Such a sequence, if it exists, is called a *reconfiguration sequence.*

**Distance Coloring** The concept of $(d, k)$-*coloring* (or $d$-*distance* $k$-*coloring*) was introduced in 1969 by Kramer and Kramer [8,9]. For a graph $G = (V, E)$ and integers $d \geq 1$ and $k \geq d+1$, a $(d, k)$-*coloring* of $G$ is an assignment of $k$ colors to the vertices of $G$ such that no two vertices within distance $d$ share the same color. In particular, the classic *proper* $k$-*coloring* is the case when $d = 1$. The $(d, k)$-COLORING problem, which asks if a given graph $G$ has a $(d, k)$-coloring, is known to be NP-complete for any fixed $d \geq 2$ and large $k$ [12,14]. For every fixed $d \geq 2$, Sharp [17] proved the following complexity dichotomy: $(d, k)$-COLORING can be solved in polynomial time for $k \leq \lfloor 3d/2 \rfloor$ but is NP-hard for $k > \lfloor 3d/2 \rfloor$. We refer readers to the survey [10] for more details on related $(d, k)$-COLORING problems.

**Coloring Reconfiguration** $k$-COLORING RECONFIGURATION has been extensively studied in the literature [13,15,16]. In $k$-COLORING RECONFIGURATION, we are given two proper $k$-colorings $\alpha$ and $\beta$ of a graph $G$ and want to decide if there exists a way to recolor vertices one by one, starting from $\alpha$ and ending at $\beta$, such that every intermediate coloring is still a proper $k$-coloring. It is well-known that $k$-COLORING RECONFIGURATION is PSPACE-complete for any fixed $k \geq 4$ on bipartite graphs, for any fixed $4 \leq k \leq 6$ on planar graphs, and for $k = 4$ on bipartite planar graphs (and thus 3-degenerate graphs) [2]. A further note from Bonsma and Paulusma [3] shows that $k$-COLORING RECONFIGURATION is PSPACE-complete even on $(k-2)$-connected bipartite graphs for $k \geq 4$. Indeed, the problem remains PSPACE-complete even on planar graphs of bounded bandwidth and low maximum degree [19]. On the other hand, for $1 \leq k \leq 3$, $k$-COLORING RECONFIGURATION can be solved in linear time [4,7]. Additionally, $k$-COLORING RECONFIGURATION is solvable in polynomial time on planar graphs for $k \geq 7$ and on bipartite planar graphs for $k \geq 5$ [2,18]. With respect to graph classes, $k$-COLORING RECONFIGURATION is solvable in polynomial time on 2-degenerate graphs (which contains graphs of treewidth at most two such as trees, cacti, outerplanar graphs, and series-parallel graphs) and several subclasses of chordal graphs [3,6].

### 1.1 Our Problem and Results

In this paper, for $d \geq 2$ and $k \geq d + 1$, we study the $(d, k)$-COLORING RECONFIGURATION problem, a generalized variant of $k$-COLORING RECONFIGURATION. In $(d, k)$-COLORING RECONFIGURATION, we are given two $(d, k)$-colorings $\alpha$ and $\beta$ of a graph $G$ and want to decide if there exists a way to recolor vertices one by one, starting from $\alpha$ and ending at $\beta$, such that every intermediate coloring is still a $(d, k)$-coloring.

Recall that the $d$-*th power* of a graph $G$, denoted by $G^d$, is the graph with $V(G^d) = V(G)$ and $E(G^d) = \{uv \mid u, v \in V(G) \text{ and } \mathsf{dist}_G(u, v) \leq d\}$, where $\mathsf{dist}_G(u, v)$ denotes the *distance* (i.e., the length of a shortest path) between $u$ and

$v$ in $G$. It is well known that $\alpha$ is a $(d,k)$-coloring of a graph $G$ if and only if $\alpha$ is a $(1,k)$-coloring of $G^d$. At first glance, this relationship suggests a straightforward proof of PSPACE-completeness for $(d,k)$-Coloring Reconfiguration: since the problem is already known to be PSPACE-complete for $d=1$ and $k \geq 4$ [2], one might attempt to reduce $(1,k)$-Coloring Reconfiguration to $(d,k)$-Coloring Reconfiguration. However, we emphasize that *such a reduction fails.*

For a valid polynomial-time reduction, given any instance $(G,\alpha,\beta)$ of $(1,k)$-Coloring Reconfiguration, one would need to construct a corresponding instance $(H,\alpha,\beta)$ of $(d,k)$-Coloring Reconfiguration where $H$ is a *$d$-th root* of $G$ (i.e., $H^d \simeq G$). The problem lies in finding such a root: deciding whether a graph $G$ has a $d$-th root is NP-complete for all fixed $d \geq 2$ in chordal graphs and remains NP-complete even on bipartite graphs for all fixed $d \geq 3$ [11]. Therefore, unless P = NP, this reduction cannot be computed in polynomial time, invalidating this approach for proving PSPACE-completeness.

Our major contribution, shown in Sect. 3, is that for every $d \geq 3$ and $k \geq d+1$, $(d,k)$-Coloring Reconfiguration is PSPACE-complete even on graphs that are bipartite, planar, and 2-degenerate. Additionally, when $d = 2$, the same reduction scheme can be adapted to show that the problem is PSPACE-complete on planar and 2-degenerate graphs. In this context, recall that $k$-Coloring Reconfiguration was PSPACE-complete on bipartite graphs for $k \geq 4$ and planar graphs for $4 \leq k \leq 6$ but was polynomial time solvable on planar graphs for $k \geq 7$ and 2-degenerate graphs.

**Theorem 1.** *For every integer $d \geq 2$, given two $(d,k)$-colorings $\alpha,\beta$ of a graph $G$ (where $k$ is part of the input), it is* PSPACE*-complete to decide if there is a reconfiguration sequence that transforms $\alpha$ into $\beta$ and vice versa, even if either*

*(i) $d \geq 3$ and $G$ is bipartite, planar, and 2-degenerate, or*
*(ii) $d = 2$ and $G$ is planar and 2-degenerate.*

*Moreover, in case (i) our reduction produces instances with $k = k_0+2+n(\lceil d/2\rceil - 1) = \Theta(nd + k_0)$ colors, where $k_0 \in \{3d+3, 3d+6\}$.*

Due to space constraints, several statements and proofs (marked with ($\star$)) are deferred to the full version [1].

## 1.2 On the Technical Contributions of Our Main Result

In this section, we outline the main technical obstacles that arise in proving our main theorem (Theorem 1), and we summarize the ideas used to overcome them.

**Scope of the Main Hardness Statement.** Our primary contribution, presented in Sect. 3, shows that for every fixed $d \geq 3$, the $(d,k)$-Coloring Reconfiguration problem is PSPACE-complete even when restricted to graphs that are bipartite, planar, and 2-degenerate, with $k$ given as part of the input (in particular, the number of colors produced by our reduction is $k = \Theta(nd)$). For

$d = 2$, the same reduction scheme yields PSPACE-completeness on planar 2-degenerate graphs. The case $d = 1$ was settled by Bonsma and Cereceda [2]; our contribution is the extension to distance-$d$ constraints under strong structural restrictions.

**Two-Step Strategy.** Our approach follows the high-level template of [2] but requires additional ideas to handle the fact that constraints are imposed at distance $d \geq 2$ rather than only on adjacent vertices. We proceed via two reductions.

1. **List-to-nonlist reduction (Section 3.2).** We give a polynomial-time reduction from LIST $(d, k)$-COLORING RECONFIGURATION to $(d, k')$-COLORING RECONFIGURATION with $k' = k + 2 + n(\lceil d/2 \rceil - 1) = \Theta(nd + k)$, where $n$ is the number of vertices in the input list-instance.
2. **Hardness of the list version (Section 3.4).** We show that LIST $(d, k)$-COLORING RECONFIGURATION is PSPACE-complete on bipartite, planar, and 2-degenerate graphs for every fixed $d \geq 2$ and sufficiently large fixed $k$ (namely $k \geq 3d + 3$ if $d$ is odd and $k \geq 3d + 6$ if $d$ is even). This is obtained by first introducing, in Sect. 3.3, a variant of the SLIDING TOKENS problem that remains PSPACE-complete even on planar 2-degenerate graphs, and then giving a polynomial-time reduction from this variant to LIST $(d, k)$-COLORING RECONFIGURATION.
   Finally, combining these two steps yields our main PSPACE-hardness statement for $(d, k)$-COLORING RECONFIGURATION by transforming the resulting list-instance into a non-list instance via the list-to-nonlist reduction of Sect. 3.2. In particular, this final transformation uses $k' = \Theta(nd + k)$ colors, and Lemma 7 shows that the dependence on $n$ is inherent for the present scheme.

**Why Distance-$d$ Creates New Difficulties.** To highlight the technical differences with [2], we describe the key locality properties exploited when $d = 1$ and explain why they fail for $d \geq 2$. For $j \in \{1, 2\}$, let $G_j$ denote the graph of the source instance of Reduction ($j$) and let $G'_j$ denote the graph of the produced target instance.

**Reduction (1): Simulating Lists via Frozen Graphs.** In Reduction (1), each vertex $v$ of $G_1$ is assigned a list of admissible colors $L(v) \subseteq \{1, \dots, k\}$, and all vertices of $G_1$ remain present in $G'_1$. Bonsma and Cereceda [2] enforce the restriction "$c \notin L(v)$" (for $d = 1$) as follows: for each pair $(v, c)$ with $c \notin L(v)$ they attach to $v$ a pre-colored frozen graph $F_{v,c}$ containing all $k$ colors, and they join $v$ to a vertex of $F_{v,c}$ colored $c$. Since the coloring of $F_{v,c}$ is frozen, $v$ can never take color $c$, thereby simulating the forbidden color. The crucial locality property is that, when $d = 1$, the attachment vertex $v$ acts as a separator: vertices of $G_1$ other than $v$ are not constrained by vertices inside $F_{v,c}$.

For $d \geq 2$, this locality is no longer automatic. Indeed, if a vertex $w \in V(G_1)$ lies within distance $d$ of some vertex $x \in V(F_{v,c})$ colored $c_x$, then the distance-$d$ rule forbids $w$ from receiving color $c_x$ in $G'_1$. This may inadvertently remove colors that are allowed at $w$ in the original list instance (i.e., it may happen that $c_x \in L(w)$), so the naive frozen-gadget attachment fails. Consequently, to correctly simulate lists at distance $d$, we must (i) introduce additional auxiliary colors and (ii) design the frozen gadgets so that they forbid exactly the intended colors and do not "leak" constraints to unrelated vertices of $G_1$.

A second obstacle is global: once auxiliary colors are introduced, every frozen graph must use *all* colors in the palette (both original and auxiliary) in its frozen coloring. Since our construction introduces auxiliary colors that depend on the vertex set of $G_1$, each frozen graph attached to a vertex must be able to realize all these colors while remaining frozen, planar, bipartite (for $d \geq 3$), and sparse, and while still ensuring that auxiliary colors cannot be used on the original vertices of $G_1$. In Sect. 3.2, we present a dedicated family of frozen graphs that overcomes these issues. In particular, unlike the frozen graphs in [2] (which are either bipartite or planar), our gadgets are bipartite (for $d \geq 3$), planar, and even 2-degenerate, while still supporting the required frozen colorings under the distance-$d$ constraint.

**Reduction (2): Enforcing Token Constraints via Forbidding Paths.** In Reduction (2), Bonsma and Cereceda [2] reduce from Sliding Tokens by encoding token placements as list colorings. Their Sliding Tokens instances consist of token triangles and token edges. Each token triangle $i$ (with vertices $t_{i1}, t_{i2}, t_{i3}$) is contracted to a vertex $t_i$ in $G'_2$ with list $\{1, 2, 3\}$, and each token edge $j$ (with vertices $e_{j1}, e_{j2}$) is contracted to a vertex $e_j$ with list $\{1, 2\}$. A token move within a gadget (e.g., from $t_{i1}$ to $t_{i2}$) corresponds to recoloring the corresponding vertex (e.g., recoloring $t_i$ from 1 to 2).

Adjacency constraints between tokens are enforced using *$(a, b)$-forbidding paths*: if the vertex $t_{ia}$ of triangle $i$ is adjacent (in the Sliding Tokens instance) to the vertex $t_{\ell b}$ of triangle $\ell$, then one must ensure that $t_i$ and $t_\ell$ are never simultaneously colored $a$ and $b$. This is achieved by placing an $(a, b)$-forbidding path between $t_i$ and $t_\ell$ whose internal vertices use auxiliary colors outside $\{1, 2, 3\}$. Again, for $d = 1$ a key locality property holds: recoloring an internal vertex of a forbidding path does not affect vertices outside the path, because the endpoints separate the internal auxiliary recolorings from the rest of the graph.

For $d \geq 2$, however, internal vertices of distinct forbidding paths can lie within distance $d$ in $G'_2$, causing unintended interactions between gadgets. This destroys the intended "local simulation" of token moves, unless one carefully arranges both graph distances and auxiliary palettes. In Sect. 3.4, we extend the forbidding-path framework by introducing buffer structure and a controlled assignment of auxiliary colors so that recolorings inside one forbidding path remain local with respect to the distance-$d$ constraint, even in the presence of many nearby gadgets. This refinement is essential for the correctness of the reduction at distance $d$.

**A Degeneracy Dichotomy.** Our constructions also imply PSPACE-completeness on 2-degenerate graphs for every $d \geq 2$. Together with the known fact that the problem is in P for $d = 1$ on 2-degenerate graphs [6], this yields an appealing complexity dichotomy on this sparse graph class.

## 2 Preliminaries

We refer readers to [5] for the concepts and notations not defined here. Unless otherwise mentioned, we always consider simple, undirected, connected graphs. For two vertices $u, v$ of a graph $G$, we denote by $\mathsf{dist}_G(u, v)$ the *distance* (i.e., the length of the shortest path) between $u$ and $v$ in $G$. The *diameter* of a graph $G$, denoted by $\mathsf{diam}(G)$, is the maximum distance between any pair of vertices in $G$. We denote by $\Delta(G)$ and $\delta(G)$ the maximum and minimum degrees of a vertex of $G$, respectively. We define $N_d(v)$ for a given graph $G$ to be the set of all vertices of distance at most $d$, i.e., $N_d(v) = \{u \in V \mid \mathsf{dist}_G(u, v) \leq d\}$. An *s-degenerate* graph is an undirected graph in which every induced subgraph has a vertex of degree at most $s$.

**$(d, k)$-Coloring.** For two positive integers $d \geq 1$ and $k \geq d+1$, a $(d, k)$*-coloring* of a graph $G$ is a function $\alpha\colon V(G) \to \{1, \dots, k\}$ such that for any pair of distinct vertices $u$ and $v$, $\alpha(u) \neq \alpha(v)$ if $\mathsf{dist}_G(u, v) \leq d$. In particular, a $(1, k)$-coloring of $G$ is also known as a *proper $k$-coloring*. If a graph $G$ has a $(d, k)$-coloring, we say that it is $(d, k)$*-colorable*. In this paper, we focus on the case $d \geq 2$.

One can generalize the concept of $(d, k)$-coloring to list $(d, k)$-coloring as follows. A given function $L$ assigns to each vertex $v \in V(G)$ a list of possible colors $L(v) \subseteq \{1, \dots, k\}$. A $(d, k)$-coloring $\alpha$ of $G$ is called a *list* $(d, k)$*-coloring* if for every $v$, we have $\alpha(v) \in L(v)$. In particular, if $L(v) = \{1, \dots, k\}$ for every $v \in V(G)$, then any list $(d, k)$-coloring of $G$ is also a $(d, k)$-coloring of $G$ and vice versa.

**(List) $(d, k)$-Coloring Reconfiguration.** Two (list) $(d, k)$-colorings $\alpha$ and $\beta$ of a graph $G$ are *adjacent* if there exists exactly one $v \in V(G)$ such that $\alpha(v) \neq \beta(v)$ and $\alpha(w) = \beta(w)$ for every $w \in V(G) - v$. If $\beta$ is obtained from $\alpha$ (and vice versa) by recoloring only one $v$, we say that such a recoloring step is *valid*. Given two different (list) $(d, k)$-colorings $\alpha, \beta$ of a graph $G$, the (List) $(d, k)$-Coloring Reconfiguration problem asks if there is a sequence of (list) $(d, k)$-colorings $\langle \alpha_0, \alpha_1, \dots, \alpha_\ell \rangle$ where $\alpha = \alpha_0$ and $\beta = \alpha_\ell$ such that $\alpha_i$ and $\alpha_{i+1}$ are adjacent for every $0 \leq i \leq \ell - 1$. Such a sequence, if exists, is called a *reconfiguration sequence* (i.e., a sequence of valid recoloring steps) between $\alpha$ and $\beta$. An instance of List $(d, k)$-Coloring Reconfiguration is usually denoted by the 4-tuple $(G, \alpha, \beta, L)$ and an instance of $(d, k)$-Coloring Reconfiguration by the triple $(G, \alpha, \beta)$.

## 3 PSPACE-Completeness on Bipartite, Planar, and 2-Degenerate Graphs

In this section, we will prove Theorem 1. Let us restate the theorem here.

**Theorem 1.** *For every integer $d \geq 2$, given two $(d, k)$-colorings $\alpha, \beta$ of a graph $G$ (where $k$ is part of the input), it is* PSPACE*-complete to decide if there is a reconfiguration sequence that transforms $\alpha$ into $\beta$ and vice versa, even if either*

*(i)* $d \geq 3$ *and* $G$ *is bipartite, planar, and* 2*-degenerate, or*
*(ii)* $d = 2$ *and* $G$ *is planar and* 2*-degenerate.*

*Moreover, in case (i) our reduction produces instances with* $k = k_0+2+n(\lceil d/2 \rceil - 1) = \Theta(nd + k_0)$ *colors, where* $k_0 \in \{3d+3, 3d+6\}$.

### 3.1 Outline

In Sect. 3.2, we describe a polynomial-time reduction from List $(d,k)$-Coloring Reconfiguration to $(d,k')$-Coloring Reconfiguration, where $k' = \Theta(nd + k)$ and $n$ is the number of vertices in the input graph. In Sect. 3.3, we introduce a PSPACE-complete variant of Sliding Tokens. In Sect. 3.4, we complete our reduction by describing a polynomial-time reduction from our variant to List $(d,k)$-Coloring Reconfiguration.

### 3.2 Reduction to $(d,k')$-Coloring Reconfiguration

In this section, we present a polynomial-time reduction from List $(d,k)$-Coloring Reconfiguration to $(d,k')$-Coloring Reconfiguration, where $k' = n(\lceil d/2 \rceil - 1) + 2 + k$ and $n = |V(G)|$. In particular, for every fixed integer $d \geq 2$, this implies that $(d,k)$-Coloring Reconfiguration is PSPACE-complete when $k$ is part of the input. Specifically, we prove the following theorem.

**Theorem 2.** *For any fixed integer* $d \geq 2$*, given an instance* $(G, \alpha, \beta, L)$ *of* List $(d,k)$-Coloring Reconfiguration*, we can construct in polynomial time an instance* $(G', \alpha', \beta')$ *of* $(d,k')$-Coloring Reconfiguration *where* $k' = n(\lceil d/2 \rceil - 1) + 2 + k$ *and* $n = |V(G)|$*, such that* $(G, \alpha, \beta, L)$ *is a yes-instance if and only if* $(G', \alpha', \beta')$ *is a yes-instance.*

Note that any $(d,k)$-coloring of a graph $G$ is a list $(d,k)$-coloring of $G$ where $L(v) = \{1, \ldots, k\}$ for every $v \in V(G)$.

**Proof Sketch.** To simulate the behavior of a list $(d,k)$-coloring, we need to constrain the available colors for each vertex $v$ to those in $L(v)$. We do this by attaching to $v$ a *frozen graph.* A graph $F$ with a $(d,k)$-coloring $\alpha$ is called a frozen graph if no vertex in $F$ can be recolored—that is, there exists no reconfiguration sequence between $\alpha$ and any other $(d,k)$-coloring $\beta$ of $F$. For each vertex $v$ in $G$, the construction adds a corresponding frozen graph $F_v$. The vertices of $F_v$ use all colors in the new palette, but their distances from $v$ are chosen according to the list of $v$. If a color $i$ does not belong to $L(v)$, then a vertex of color $i$ in $F_v$ is placed at distance at most $d$ from $v$. Thus $v$ can never receive color $i$ in a $(d,k')$-coloring of the constructed graph. If $i \in L(v)$, then the corresponding vertex of color $i$ in $F_v$ is placed at distance $d+1$ from $v$, and hence this occurrence of color $i$ does not by itself forbid color $i$ at $v$. In this way, the frozen graph attached to $v$ blocks exactly the colors outside $L(v)$.

The distance-$d$ condition makes the construction less local than the usual coloring case. A color used inside a gadget can also interact with vertices outside the gadget if it is placed too close to them. For this reason, the attachment paths and auxiliary colors are chosen so that each gadget enforces the list of its own anchor vertex and does not remove allowed colors from other original vertices. The formal distance checks in the appendix verify this point separately for vertices in the original graph, vertices inside one frozen graph, and vertices in two different frozen graphs. The same checks also show that the structural properties needed later are preserved: the gadget is planar and 2-degenerate for $d = 2$, and is planar, bipartite, and essentially a tree for $d \geq 3$.

It remains to explain why the reduction preserves reconfigurability. First suppose that the original list instance has a reconfiguration sequence from $\alpha$ to $\beta$. We obtain a sequence in the constructed graph by recoloring the same original vertex at each step and leaving all frozen graphs unchanged. Since the gadgets forbid precisely the colors outside the lists, every step that is valid in the list instance is valid in the constructed instance. Conversely, suppose that there is a reconfiguration sequence in the constructed graph. Every vertex of every $F_v$ is frozen: within $F_v$, all colors of the new palette occur within distance at most $d$ of that vertex. Adding the rest of the graph can only add distance-$d$ constraints, so no vertex of a frozen graph becomes recolorable after the gadget is attached to $G$. Therefore the sequence changes only vertices of the original graph. Restricting the sequence to $V(G)$ gives a list $(d, k)$-reconfiguration from $\alpha$ to $\beta$, because the attached gadgets prevent exactly the colors not in the corresponding lists. This proves the equivalence of the two instances.

**Frozen Graphs.** We begin by describing how a (precolored) frozen graph $F_v$ and its $(d, k')$-coloring $\alpha_v$ can be constructed for a vertex $v \in V(G)$, where $k' = n(\lceil d/2 \rceil - 1) + 2 + k$ and $n = |V(G)|$. The gadget is illustrated in Fig. 1. We emphasize that $v$ does not belong to its corresponding frozen graph $F_v$.

For $d \geq 3$, our construction is as follows. First, for each $v \in V(G)$, we create a central vertex $c_v$. We then construct a path $T_v$ which includes $c_v$ as an endpoint and has length $\lceil d/2 \rceil - 1$. Suppose that $T_v = c_v c_{v,1} \cdots c_{v,\lceil d/2 \rceil - 1}$. Let $c'_v = c_{v,\lceil d/2 \rceil - 1}$ be the endpoint of $T_v$ other than $c_v$. Let $C_0 \notin \{1, \ldots, k\}$ be a fixed color. We color the vertices of $T_v$ starting from $c_v$ by using the color $C_0$ for $c_v$ and $\lceil d/2 \rceil - 1$ other distinct new colors $C_{v,1}, C_{v,2}, \ldots, C_{v,\lceil d/2 \rceil - 1}$ for the remaining vertices $c_{v,1}, \ldots, c_{v,\lceil d/2 \rceil - 1}$, respectively. In particular, $c'_v$ has color $C_{v,\lceil d/2 \rceil - 1}$. We also remark that none of $C_{v,1}, C_{v,2}, \ldots, C_{v,\lceil d/2 \rceil - 1}$ is in $\{1, \ldots, k\}$. At this point, so far, for each $v \in V(G)$, we have used $\lceil d/2 \rceil - 1$ distinct colors for vertices other than $c_v$ in each $T_v$ and one fixed color $C_0$ for every $c_v$. Thus, in total, $n(\lceil d/2 \rceil - 1) + 1$ distinct colors have been used.

Next, for each $v \in V(G)$ and each vertex $u \neq v$, we construct a (possibly trivial) path $T^v_u$ which includes $c_v$ as an endpoint and has length $t := \lfloor d/2 \rfloor - 1$. If $t = 0$ (equivalently, $d = 3$), then $T^v_u$ consists only of the vertex $c_v$ and we define $c'^v_u := c_v$. Otherwise, we write $T^v_u = c_v c^v_{u,1} \cdots c^v_{u,t}$ and denote by $c'^v_u = c^v_{u,t}$ the endpoint of $T^v_u$ other than $c_v$.

- When $d$ is even, we have $\lceil d/2 \rceil - 1 = \lfloor d/2 \rfloor - 1$, i.e., the number of vertices in $T_u - c_u$ is equal to the number of vertices in $T^v_u - c_v$. In this case, we color the vertices of $T_u^v$ starting from $c_v$ by using the color $C_0$ for $c_v$ and the $\lceil d/2 \rceil - 1 = \lfloor d/2 \rfloor - 1$ other distinct colors $C_{u,1}, C_{u,2}, \dots, C_{u,\lfloor d/2 \rfloor - 1}$ respectively for the remaining vertices $c_{u,1}^v, \dots, c_{u,\lfloor d/2 \rfloor - 1}^v$. In particular, the endpoint $c'^v_u$ has color $C_{u,\lfloor d/2 \rfloor - 1}$. (We note that all these colors are used to color vertices in $T_u$ for $u \in V(G)$.)

- When $d$ is odd, we have $\lceil d/2 \rceil - 1 = (\lfloor d/2 \rfloor - 1) + 1$, i.e., the number of vertices in $T_u - c_u$ is equal to the number of vertices in $T_u^v - c_v$ plus one. In this case, we color the vertices of $T_u^v$ starting from $c_v$ by using the color $C_0$ for $c_v$ and the $\lfloor d/2 \rfloor - 1$ other distinct colors $C_{u,2}, C_{u,3}, \dots, C_{u,\lceil d/2 \rceil - 1}$ respectively for the remaining vertices $c_{u,1}^v, \dots, c_{u,\lfloor d/2 \rfloor - 1}^v$, leaving one color $C_{u,1}$ that has not yet been used. To handle this situation, we add a new vertex $c^{\star v}_u$ adjacent to $c_v$ and color it by the color $C_{u,1}$.

To finish our construction of $F_v$ and $\alpha_v$ for each $v \in V(G)$, we pick some vertex $u_0$ in $G$ other than $v$. Additionally, we add $k+1$ extra new vertices labelled $c_v^\star, w_{v,1}, \dots, w_{v,k}$. We then join $c_v^\star$ to any $w_{v,i}$ where $i \in L(v) \subseteq \{1, \dots, k\}$ and join the endpoint $c'^v_{u_0}$ of $T_{u_0}^v$ to $c_v^\star$ and to any $w_{v,i}$ where $i \notin L(v)$. Let $C_1$ be a fixed color that is different from any colors that have been used. We finally color $c_v^\star$ by $C_1$, and each $w_{v,i}$ by the color $i \in \{1, \dots, k\}$. At this point, $k+1$ extra distinct colors are used. In total, we use $k' = (n(\lceil d/2 \rceil - 1) + 1) + (k+1) = n(\lceil d/2 \rceil - 1) + 2 + k$ colors. This concludes our construction for $d \geq 3$.

For $d = 2$, we construct $F_v$ and $\alpha_v$ as follows. We create a central vertex $c_v$ and color it by a fixed color $C_0$. We create a new vertex $c_v^\star$ adjacent to $c_v$ and color it by a fixed color $C_1$. We then add $k$ extra vertices $w_{v,1}, \dots, w_{v,k}$ and color them by the colors $1, \dots, k$ respectively. Next, we join $c_v^\star$ to any $w_{v,i}$ $(1 \leq i \leq k)$ and join $c_v$ to any $w_{v,i}$ where $i \notin L(v)$. In total, we use $k+2$ colors, which is equal to $n(\lceil d/2 \rceil - 1) + 2 + k$ when $d = 2$.

**Lemma 3** ($\star$). *Our construction correctly produces a frozen graph $F_v$ with its $(d, k')$-coloring $\alpha_v$.*

One can verify that our construction indeed can be done in polynomial time.

**Construction of An Instance $(G', \alpha', \beta')$ of $(d, k')$-Coloring Reconfiguration.** Given an instance $(G, \alpha, \beta, L)$ of List $(d, k)$-Coloring Reconfiguration, we now describe how to construct $G'$ and its two $(d, k')$-colorings $\alpha', \beta'$, where $k' = n(\lceil d/2 \rceil - 1) + 2 + k$. To construct $G'$, we start from the original graph $G$, and we construct $F_v$ for each $v \in V(G)$ as described before. Then, for $d \geq 3$, we simply join $v$ to $c'_v$—the endpoint of $T_v$ other than $c_v$. For $d = 2$, we join $v$ to $c_v$. To construct $\alpha'$ from $\alpha$, we simply assign $\alpha'(v) = \alpha(v)$ for any $v \in V(G)$ and $\alpha'(w) = \alpha_v(w)$ for any $w \in V(F_v)$. The construction of $\beta'$ is similar. One can verify that for any $v \in V(G)$, no vertex in $F_v$ can be recolored in $G'$. Again, to see this, observe that $(F_v, \alpha_v)$ is frozen by Lemma 3. Since $F_v$ is an induced subgraph of $G'$, adding vertices outside $F_v$ can only introduce additional distance-$d$ constraints, and therefore no vertex of $F_v$ becomes recolorable in $G'$. One can also verify that our construction can be done in polynomial time.

The following simple observation will be useful later in our proof.

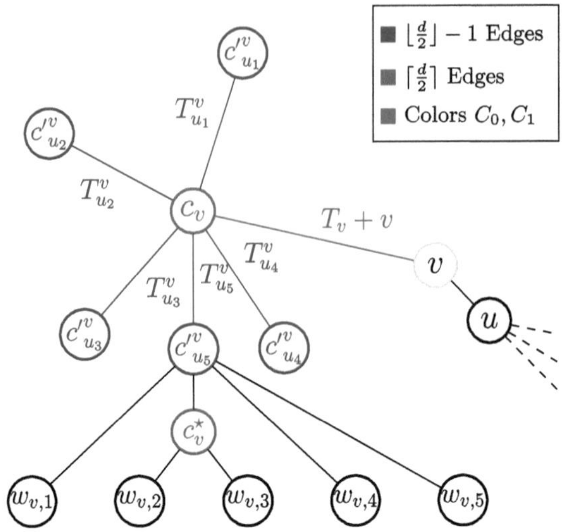


**Fig. 1.** An example of a vertex $v$ joining to its corresponding frozen graph $F_v$. Here $d$ is even, $k = 5$, $G$ is some list $(d, k)$-colorable graph having six vertices labelled $v, u_1, u_2, \ldots, u_5$ (note that here we selected $u_0 = u_5$), and $L(v) = \{2, 3\} \subseteq \{1, \ldots, 5\}$.

**Lemma 4** (⋆). *Suppose that $G$ is planar, bipartite, and 2-degenerate. The constructed graph $G'$ is planar, bipartite, and 2-degenerate if $d \geq 3$, and is planar and 2-degenerate but not necessarily bipartite if $d = 2$.*

In the following lemma, we show that our construction correctly produces an instance of $(d, k')$-Coloring Reconfiguration.

**Lemma 5** (⋆). *$\alpha'$ is a $(d, k')$-coloring of $G'$. Consequently, so is $\beta'$.*

**The Correctness of Our Reduction.** We are now ready to prove the correctness of our reduction which will prove Theorem 2.

**Lemma 6** (⋆). *$(G, \alpha, \beta, L)$ is a yes-instance if and only if $(G', \alpha', \beta')$ is a yes-instance.*

To conclude this section, we show that the palette size $k'$ in our reduction is asymptotically tight up to constant factors.

**Lemma 7** (⋆). *Assume $d \geq 3$ and let $F_v$ be the gadget constructed above for some $v \in V(G)$. Then $\mathsf{diam}(F_v) \leq d$, and hence every two distinct vertices of $F_v$ are at distance at most $d$. Consequently, in any $(d, \ell)$-coloring of $F_v$ all vertices must receive pairwise distinct colors, and therefore $\ell \geq |V(F_v)| = k'$. In particular, within the present list-to-nonlist reduction scheme, the palette size $k' = k + 2 + n(\lceil d/2 \rceil - 1) = \Theta(nd + k)$ in Theorem 2 is asymptotically tight up to constant factors.*

### 3.3 SLIDING TOKENS

In this section, we first revisit a variant of SLIDING TOKENS used by Bonsma and Cereceda [2] and then describe and prove PSPACE-completeness of our restricted variant. In particular, this will help prove the following theorem.

**Theorem 8 (⋆).** *SLIDING TOKENS is* PSPACE*-complete on graphs that are planar and 2-degenerate.*

### 3.4 Reduction to List $(d, k)$-COLORING RECONFIGURATION

In this section, we describe a reduction from our variant of SLIDING TOKENS to LIST $(d, k)$-COLORING RECONFIGURATION. In particular we show,

**Theorem 9.** LIST $(d, k)$ *COLORING RECONFIGURATION is* PSPACE*-complete even on planar, bipartite and 2-degenerate graphs, for any fixed* $d \geq 2$ *and* $k \geq 3d + 3$ *if* $d$ *is odd or* $k \geq 3d + 6$ *if* $d$ *is even.*

The encoding is as follows. Each token triangle or token edge of the SLIDING TOKENS instance becomes one vertex of the list-coloring instance, and the color of this vertex records the position of the unique token inside the corresponding gadget. For every link edge that forbids two token positions from being occupied simultaneously, we insert a forbidding path between the two corresponding list-coloring vertices. Thus, a token slide becomes a recoloring of one such vertex, and the forbidding paths enforce exactly the independent-set condition for tokens. The extra work for distance-$d$ recoloring is to keep different forbidding paths from interacting accidentally. We do this by using buffer vertices and three auxiliary palettes, so that recoloring inside one forbidding path can be treated as a local operation in the whole constructed graph. The correctness proof follows the same correspondence. Given a token-sliding sequence, we recolor the vertex representing the gadget whose token moves, and then reconfigure only the forbidding paths incident with that vertex. The path gadgets are designed so that this local update is possible whenever the token move is valid. Conversely, in any list-coloring reconfiguration sequence, a vertex representing a token gadget can only use colors corresponding to positions inside that gadget. The forbidding paths ensure that two adjacent token positions are never selected at the same time. Therefore each coloring of the constructed instance encodes an independent set with exactly one token in each token gadget, and each recoloring step projects to either no token move or one valid token slide. The buffer vertices are used only to separate these local simulations. They carry auxiliary colors and do not encode token positions; their role is to prevent a recoloring inside one forbidding path from creating a distance-$d$ conflict with a different forbidding path. This is why the construction uses several auxiliary palettes while keeping the graph planar, bipartite, and 2-degenerate.

Combining our construction in Theorem 2 and proofs of Theorems 8 and 9, we finally have Theorem 1.

**Theorem 1.** *For every integer $d \geq 2$, given two $(d, k)$-colorings $\alpha, \beta$ of a graph $G$ (where $k$ is part of the input), it is* PSPACE*-complete to decide if there is a reconfiguration sequence that transforms $\alpha$ into $\beta$ and vice versa, even if either*

*(i) $d \geq 3$ and $G$ is bipartite, planar, and 2-degenerate, or*
*(ii) $d = 2$ and $G$ is planar and 2-degenerate.*

*Moreover, in case (i) our reduction produces instances with $k = k_0+2+n(\lceil d/2 \rceil - 1) = \Theta(nd + k_0)$ colors, where $k_0 \in \{3d + 3, 3d + 6\}$.*

*Proof.* The PSPACE-completeness follows by combining Theorems 2, 8 and 9. The instance from Theorem 9 is planar, bipartite, and 2-degenerate. By Lemma 4, the frozen graphs used in Theorem 2 are planar and 2-degenerate for $d = 2$, and are also bipartite for $d \geq 3$. Thus the constructed graph is planar and 2-degenerate for $d = 2$, and planar, bipartite, and 2-degenerate for $d \geq 3$. Finally, applying Theorem 2 to the LIST $(d, k_0)$-COLORING RECONFIGURATION instance of Theorem 9, where $k_0 \in \{3d + 3, 3d + 6\}$, gives $k' = k_0 + 2 + n(\lceil d/2 \rceil - 1) = \Theta(nd + k_0)$. □

### 3.5 The Case $d = 2$ and Bipartiteness

Lemma 4 shows that, although our reduction preserves planarity and 2-degeneracy for all $d \geq 2$, it preserves bipartiteness only when $d \geq 3$. To briefly explain why such a limitation exists, we show that within the present list-to-nonlist interface for $d = 2$, any frozen list-enforcement gadget that remains planar and 2-degenerate cannot also be bipartite.

**Lemma 10 (⋆).** *Fix $d = 2$ and let $v$ be a vertex whose list $L(v)$ is a proper subset of $\{1, \ldots, k\}$. Consider the interface of Sect. 3.2, where $v$ is attached by a single edge to an anchor $c_v$ of a precolored frozen gadget $F_v$ whose coloring uses all colors. If $F_v$ is required to be planar and 2-degenerate, then $F_v$ cannot be bipartite.*

## 4 Concluding Remarks

We proved $(d, k)$-COLORING RECONFIGURATION is PSPACE-complete for $d \geq 2$ on graphs that are planar and 2-degenerate (and also bipartite when $d \geq 3$). Following the natural hierarchy of graph degeneracy, a logical next open direction is to examine 1-degenerate graphs (forests). Notably, the complexity of $(d, k)$-COLORING RECONFIGURATION ($d \geq 2$) remains unresolved even for trees. This case seems to require ideas different from the gadgets used here. Our reductions use 2-degenerate structures to remember unavailable colors and to connect many local forbidding paths. In a tree, these two roles cannot be separated by the same local interfaces, so the present proof does not directly extend to forests. Another natural direction is to understand the role of the number of colors. Our non-list hardness result uses a number of colors that grows with the size of the intermediate list instance, while the list version is hard already for a number of colors depending only on $d$. It remains open whether the non-list problem is PSPACE-complete for a number of colors depending only on $d$, or whether additional polynomial-time cases appear when the color set is small. A full dichotomy in the parameters $d$ and $k$ therefore remains open. One possible way to attack this question is to make the list-simulation step more economical. In our proof, the reduction to the non-list setting uses frozen gadgets to exclude colors that are not in a list. These gadgets preserve planarity and 2-degeneracy, but they introduce many auxiliary colors because different original vertices may have different lists. A construction that simulates these local lists with a bounded palette would strengthen the main theorem, while a limitation for small $k$ may lead to additional polynomial-time cases. Thus, the current result should be viewed as a hardness boundary for planar 2-degenerate graphs, rather than as a complete classification. It also identifies the two main obstacles left by the reduction: removing the extra degeneracy used by the gadgets, and controlling the palette size in the non-list setting.

**Acknowledgments.** We thank the anonymous reviewers for their useful comments. A part of this work was done when Niranka was at RIMS, Kyoto University and Duc was at the Vietnam Institute for Advanced Study in Mathematics (VIASM). Duc A. Hoang's research was partially supported by the Vietnam National University, Hanoi under the project QG.25.07 "A study on reconfiguration problems from algorithmic and graph-theoretic perspectives".

## References

1. Banerjee, N., Engels, C., Hoang, D.A.: Distance recoloring. arXiv preprint arXiv:2402.12705 (2024)
2. Bonsma, P.S., Cereceda, L.: Finding paths between graph colourings: PSPACE-completeness and superpolynomial distances. Theoret. Comput. Sci. **410**(50), 5215–5226 (2009). https://doi.org/10.1016/j.tcs.2009.08.023
3. Bonsma, P.S., Paulusma, D.: Using contracted solution graphs for solving reconfiguration problems. Acta Informatica **56**, 619–648 (2019). https://doi.org/10.1007/s00236-019-00336-8
4. Cereceda, L., van den Heuvel, J., Johnson, M.: Finding paths between 3-colorings. J. Graph Theory **67**(1), 69–82 (2011). https://doi.org/10.1002/jgt.20514
5. Diestel, R.: Graph theory, graduate texts in mathematics, vol. 173. Springer, 5th edn. (2017). https://doi.org/10.1007/978-3-662-53622-3
6. Hatanaka, T., Ito, T., Zhou, X.: The coloring reconfiguration problem on specific graph classes. IEICE Trans. Inf. Syst. **E102.D**(3), 423–429 (2019). https://doi.org/10.1587/transinf.2018FCP0005
7. Johnson, M., Kratsch, D., Kratsch, S., Patel, V., Paulusma, D.: Finding shortest paths between graph colourings. Algorithmica **75**(2), 295–321 (2016). https://doi.org/10.1007/s00453-015-0009-7
8. Kramer, F., Kramer, H.: Ein färbungsproblem der knotenpunkte eines graphen bezüglich der distanz p. Rev. Roumaine Math. Pures Appl. **14**(2), 1031–1038 (1969)

9. Kramer, F., Kramer, H.: Un probleme de coloration des sommets d'un graphe. CR Acad. Sci. Paris A **268**(7), 46–48 (1969)
10. Kramer, F., Kramer, H.: A survey on the distance-colouring of graphs. Discret. Math. **308**(2–3), 422–426 (2008). https://doi.org/10.1016/j.disc.2006.11.059
11. Le, V.B., Nguyen, N.T.: Hardness results and efficient algorithms for graph powers. In: Paul, C., Habib, M. (eds.) WG 2009. LNCS, vol. 5911, pp. 238–249. Springer, Heidelberg (2010). https://doi.org/10.1007/978-3-642-11409-0_21
12. Lin, Y.L., Skiena, S.S.: Algorithms for square roots of graphs. SIAM J. Discret. Math. **8**(1), 99–118 (1995). https://doi.org/10.1137/S089548019120016X
13. Mahmoud, R.: Graph coloring reconfiguration. Ph.D. thesis, virginia commonwealth university (2024). https://scholarscompass.vcu.edu/etd/7564/
14. McCormick, S.T.: Optimal approximation of sparse hessians and its equivalence to a graph coloring problem. Math. Program. **26**(2), 153–171 (1983). https://doi.org/10.1007/BF02592052
15. Mynhardt, C., Nasserasr, S.: Reconfiguration of colourings and dominating sets in graphs. In: Chung, F., Graham, R., Hoffman, F., Mullin, R.C., Hogben, L., West, D.B. (eds.) 50 years of Combinatorics, Graph Theory, and Computing, pp. 171–191. CRC Press, 1st edn. (2019). https://doi.org/10.1201/9780429280092-10
16. Nishimura, N.: Introduction to reconfiguration. Algorithms **11**(4), 52 (2018). https://doi.org/10.3390/a11040052
17. Sharp, A.: Distance Coloring. In: Arge, L., Hoffmann, M., Welzl, E. (eds.) ESA 2007. LNCS, vol. 4698, pp. 510–521. Springer, Heidelberg (2007). https://doi.org/10.1007/978-3-540-75520-3_46
18. van den Heuvel, J.: The complexity of change. In: Surveys in Combinatorics, London Mathematical Society Lecture Note Series, vol. 409, pp. 127–160. Cambridge University Press (2013). https://doi.org/10.1017/cbo9781139506748.005
19. van der Zanden, T.C.: Parameterized complexity of graph constraint logic. In: Proceedings of IPEC 2015. LIPIcs, vol. 43, pp. 282–293. Schloss Dagstuhl – Leibniz-Zentrum für Informatik (2015). https://doi.org/10.4230/LIPIcs.IPEC.2015.282

# Graph Partitioning Games

Xinyao Wang(✉) and Zihui Liang(✉)

University of Electronic Science and Technology of China, Chengdu, China
xinyao@std.uestc.edu.cn, zihuiliang.tcs@gmail.com

**Abstract.** This paper introduces a new class of combinatorial games, termed graph partitioning games, played on graphs. These games model the influence of two competing parties attempting to partition a given graph. In such a game, given the graph, the players take turns moving. On each turn, a player selects an unclaimed vertex and claims the vertex along with its unclaimed neighbors. The players must ensure that all vertices claimed by each player remain connected. The objective is to determine which player claims the majority of the vertices at the end of the game. We prove that finding an optimal strategy is a PSPACE-complete problem. Furthermore, we resolve the graph partitioning games on weighted chordal graphs by identifying the winners and computing winning strategies on these graphs. This result advances our understanding of combinatorial games played on graphs.

**Keywords:** combinatorial games · strategies · PSPACE

## 1 Introduction

### 1.1 Problem Statement

Let $G = (V, E)$ be a finite, undirected, and connected graph. We assume the graph is simple, meaning the edge set $E$ consists of two-element subsets of $V$. The edge between vertices $u$ and $v$ is denoted by $uv$. A **weighted graph** $G = (V, E, f)$ is a graph equipped with a vertex-weight function $f : V \to \mathbb{R}^+$. The **weight** of a subset $S \subseteq V$ is given by $f(S) = \sum_{v \in S} f(v)$. If a graph lacks vertex weights, it can be treated as a weighted graph with each vertex assigned a weight of 1.

Let $x \in V$. The **neighborhood** of $x$, denoted by $N(x)$, is defined as: $N(x) = \{x\} \cup \{v \mid xv \in E\}$. Vertices in $N(x)$ are called **neighbors** of $x$. Similarly, for a subset $X \subseteq V$, the neighborhood of $X$ is given by $N(X) = \bigcup_{v \in X} N(v)$.

We now define **Graph Partitioning Games** played on $G = (V, E, f)$. There are two players: Player 1 and Player 2. Player $\varepsilon$ is the opponent of Player $\overline{\varepsilon}$, i.e., $\overline{\varepsilon} = 1$ if and only if $\varepsilon = 2$, where $\varepsilon \in \{1, 2\}$. The game proceeds in rounds. In odd-numbered rounds, Player 1 makes a move. In even-numbered rounds Player 2 makes a move. Player 1 starts the first round. In round 1, Player 1 selects a vertex $x_1$ and claims all vertices in $N(x_1)$. Set $X_1 = N(x_1)$. Player 2 starts in


Y. Li et al. (Eds.): COCOON 2026, LNCS 16835, pp. 95–106, 2027.
https://doi.org/10.1007/978-981-92-3309-0_8

round 2 by selecting a vertex $x_2$ in $V \setminus X_1$, and claims all vertices in $N(x_2) \setminus X_1$. Set $X_2 = N(x_2) \setminus X_1$.

Let $X_{2i-1}$ and $X_{2i}$ denote the sets of vertices claimed by Player 1 and Player 2, respectively, after round $2i-1$ and round $2i$ ($i > 0$). In round $2i+1$, Player 1 must expand the region $X_{2i-1}$ so that it remains connected. Formally, Player 1 selects a vertex $x_{2i+1} \in N(N(X_{2i-1}) \setminus X_{2i}) \setminus (X_{2i-1} \cup X_{2i})$, and claims $x_{2i+1}$ together with its unclaimed neighbors. Thus, $X_{2i+1} = X_{2i-1} \cup (N(x_{2i+1}) \setminus X_{2i})$. If no valid vertex $x_{2i+1}$ exists for Player 1 to select, then Player 1 selects no vertex and passes the control to Player 2. Symmetrically, in round $2i+2$, Player 2 expands the region $X_{2i}$ by selecting $x_{2i+2} \in N(N(X_{2i}) \setminus X_{2i+1}) \setminus (X_{2i} \cup X_{2i+1})$, and claims $x_{2i+2}$ together with its unclaimed neighbors. Hence, $X_{2i+2} = X_{2i} \cup (N(x_{2i+2}) \setminus X_{2i+1})$. If no vertex $x_{2i+2}$ exists for Player 2 to select, then Player 2 selects no vertex and passes the control to Player 1.

We now provide more details when one of the players has no vertex to select. Suppose Player $\varepsilon$ has no vertex to select in round $t$. If $X_{t-1} \cup X_{t-2} = V$, then the play ends. If $X_{t-1} \cup X_{t-2} \neq V$, then we say that Player $\overline{\varepsilon}$ **blocks** Player $\varepsilon$ in round $t-1$. In this case, Player $\varepsilon$ ceases claiming vertices, and Player $\overline{\varepsilon}$ will eventually claim all remaining vertices since the game graph is connected.

To define a winner, we introduce the following notations. Let $C_1$ and $C_2$ represent the sets of all vertices claimed by Player 1 and Player 2, respectively, at the end of the play.

**Definition 1.** *Player* $\varepsilon$ **wins** *the play if and only if* $\sum_{v \in C_\varepsilon} f(v) > \sum_{u \in C_{\overline{\varepsilon}}} f(u)$. *If* $\sum_{v \in C_\varepsilon} f(v) = \sum_{u \in C_{\overline{\varepsilon}}} f(u)$, *then the play is a* **draw**.

The sets $C_1$ and $C_2$ form a partition of $G$. Moreover, both $C_1$ and $C_2$ are connected subgraphs of $G$. Hence, we refer to these as *graph partitioning games.*

Given a weighted connected graph $G$, we aim to solve the graph partitioning game on $G$ which involves two objectives. First, we seek to design an algorithm that given a weighted graph $G$, determines the winner of the graph partitioning game on $G$. Second, we aim to extract a winning strategy for the winner.

We present three examples to illustrate both winning and drawing scenarios. To do this, we recall three specific classes of graphs. The **path graph** of order $n$, denoted $P_n$, consists of vertices $\{1, \ldots, n\}$ with edges connecting consecutive integers. The **cycle graph** of order $n \geq 3$, denoted $C_n$, is obtained from $P_n$ by adding an edge between vertices 1 and $n$. The **hypercube graph** of dimension $n$, denoted $Q_n$ [33], has $2^n$ vertices $\{0, \ldots, 2^n - 1\}$, where an edge exists between any two vertices if and only if their binary representations differ by exactly one bit. In Examples 1, 2 and 3 below each vertex has weight 1.

*Example 1.* Consider the path graph $P_n$. Player 1's first move is to select the vertex $\lceil \frac{n}{2} \rceil$ which is a middle vertex of $P_n$, thereby forcing Player 2 into a component with fewer than $\frac{n}{2}$ vertices. Then Player 1 wins on $P_n$.

*Example 2.* Consider the hypercube graph $Q_n (n \geq 3)$. Player 2 always selects the vertex with the binary representation $\overline{a_0}\ \overline{a_1} \ldots \overline{a_{n-1}}$ after Player 1 selects the vertex with the binary representation $a_0 a_1 \ldots a_{n-1}$ where $a_i + \overline{a}_i = 1$ for $i \in [0, n-1]$. Hence, Player 2 guarantees a draw.

Path graphs represent a straightforward scenario in which Player 1 can guarantee a win, while Hypercube graphs present a scenario where Player 1 can never win. The following example illustrates how the parity of the number of vertices influences the outcomes of the games. For the games on cycle graph $C_n$, where $3 \leq n \leq 5$, Player 1 clearly wins. We now turn to the case when $n \geq 6$.

*Example 3.* Consider the cycle graph $C_n$ $(n \geq 6)$. The following results hold:

1. Player 1 never loses.
2. If $n$ is odd, Player 1 wins.
3. If $n$ is even, Player 2 guarantees a draw.

### 1.2 Brief Background and Motivation

The graph partitioning problem, in its various formulations, is a fundamental problem in graph theory with numerous applications in areas such as parallel computing, network design, and data clustering. In its most general setting, the problem involves partitioning a given graph $G$ into two disjoint sets of vertices $X$ and $Y$ that satisfy certain specifications. For instance, one may seek to minimize or maximize the edge cut between the two sets $X$ and $Y$ [37]. Another common objective is to ensure that the sets $X$ and $Y$ are connected and have close cardinalities, i.e., $|X| \approx |Y|$, which is important in balanced partitioning problems [4,23]. Additionally, maximizing modularity [32] is a well-known objective in community detection, where the goal is to partition the graph into communities that are more tightly connected internally than externally.

Game theory is a powerful mathematical tool used to study the nature of struggle or competition, with widespread applications in network analysis. In particular, Z. Liang, B. Khoussainov, and M. Xiao introduced network control games [26], which explore graph partitioning problems through a game-theoretic lens. In these games, two competing players take turns claiming vertices in a given graph. On each turn, a player selects an unclaimed vertex and automatically claims all its unclaimed neighbors. The player who ultimately claims the most vertices wins the game. Note that the players are free to choose any unclaimed vertex during the play. In particular, there are no connectivity type of requirements on the sets of claimed vertices.

The topological network control game [28–30] extends the framework of network control games by imposing the connectivity requirement on the claimed vertices, namely that the set of all claimed vertices must remain connected throughout the game. In these works, the authors further left as future work the study of a variant in which, instead of requiring global connectivity, each player must maintain connectivity of their own claimed vertex set. This viewpoint naturally interprets the process as a competitive partition of a connected graph into two connected subgraphs.

Motivated by this direction, we introduce a refined game-theoretic variant of the graph partitioning problem in which each player is required to preserve the connectivity of their claimed vertex set at every stage of the game. We formally define this model and provide a systematic investigation of its structural and strategic properties.

In contrast to graph partitioning games, topological network-control games and network-control games lack the connectivity constraint on each player's claimed vertices set. As a result, blocks do not occur in topological network-control games and network-control games – that is, there are no situations where one player has no available vertex to claim while the other player still does. This distinction implies that strategies effective in graph partitioning games may differ fundamentally from those used in the two aforementioned game types. For example, in Sect. 4.1 we show that on any tree, Player 1 can force a win in the graph partitioning game precisely by blocking the opponent. In this sense, this refinement is closer to certain real-world scenarios.

Potentially one relevant application lies in network security and epidemic control. In globally connected networks, virus can cause severe losses in both time and resources. Therefore, it is crucial to act swiftly to contain the spread and protect the network [38]. A virus may be introduced at certain nodes through external means and then spread through the network connections [9]. Conversely, protectors can be placed at certain nodes to shield them and guard neighboring nodes via the connections. Given limited protection capabilities, the challenge is to determine the optimal placement of a limited number of protectors to maximize the number of safeguarded vertices [2].

In network security research, networks are often represented as graphs. Assuming there is only one protector and one virus, we model this scenario as a graph partitioning game, where Player 1 acts as the protector and Player 2 as the virus. The players take turns influencing vertices: The protector player selects an uninfluenced vertex, shielding it and its uninfluenced neighbors, while the virus player selects an uninfluenced vertex to infect, spreading to all uninfluenced neighbors. Each player's goal is to strategically claim vertices to either maximize influence (through infection or shielding) or block the opponent's spread, reflecting the trade-offs in real-world network defense strategies. Eventually, all infected and protected vertices naturally partition the original network.

This research falls within the domain of combinatorial games, which are typically of finite durations and played on spaces with finite configurations. Combinatorial games can generally be categorized into two types: scoring games and non-scoring games. In scoring games, players aim to accumulate a certain number of points to guarantee a win. Examples of such games include the graph-grabbing game [15,31], the median game [14], the orthogonal coloring game [3], the Vertex-Capture Game [8] and the largest connected subgraph game [6,7], Network control games [26], Topological network control games [28–30]. On the other hand, in non-scoring games, the objective is to force the opponent into a position where he cannot make a legal move. Examples of non-scoring games are GRIM [1], Nim on graphs [12,16], Kayles on graphs [10,11,17–19,34], game

0.33 [5], and EF games [21]. More broadly, they are related to regular games [13,24,25,27]. For the majority of combinatorial games, determining the winner in general scenarios is PSPACE-hard, and analyzing games on simple graph structures (such as path graphs, cycle graphs, and trees) often poses a significant bottleneck. These bottlenecks are partly addressed in this work through our graph partition games.

### 1.3 Our Contributions

Our games are scoring games since the winner is determined by which player claims more vertices. We develop a prototypical theory for solving such games based on partitioning behaviors. Many of our ideas extend to scoring games on trees and more general graphs. Our key contributions are summarized as follows.

1. We introduce graph partitioning games. These games model the influence of competing parties to partition a given graph. In these games, each player must ensure that the set of vertices claimed by the player remains connected.
2. We prove that finding optimal strategies is a PSPACE-complete problem. The proof involves two key challenges: first, the cardinalities of the neighborhoods of unclaimed vertices are dependent on specific configurations, unlike in the Competitive Facility Allocation problem, where encoding a quantified Boolean formula is straightforward. Second, the connectivity requirement for the set of claimed vertices adds another layer of complexity. These conditions make it challenging to encode PSPACE-complete problems into our graph partitioning game framework.
3. We analyze games played on trees and chordal graphs, demonstrating that Player 1 has a winning strategy in both cases. As previously mentioned, solving scoring games on general trees has been a significant challenge in earlier works. However, we overcome this obstacle by extending techniques developed for assured graphs. In partitioning games on weighted trees, we resolve the problem by proving that the median vertices of a tree are assured vertices. For partition games on weighted chordal graphs, we show that any vertex in the median of the corresponding weighted clique-tree is also an assured vertex. It is important to note that all of our proofs employ non-trivial graph-theoretical methods.

## 2 Preliminaries

In this section, we introduce the basic definitions and notations, and show that finding an optimal strategy is in PSPACE, which lays the groundwork for Sect. 3. We also define assured graphs, a structural property ensuring a win for Player 1, which will be essential in Sect. 4 for analyzing weighted chordal graphs.

Assume the players play the game on graph $G$. We denote a move by $(v, S)$ where Player $\varepsilon$ selects vertex $v$ and claims the set of vertices $S$ on $G$. Thus, a play is a sequence $(v_1, S_1), \ldots, (v_{i-1}, S_{i-1})$ of selected vertices and claimed sets from round 1 to round $i-1$. The configuration determined by this play is the tuple $(G_i, (C_{i,0}, C_{i,1}))$, where

1. The set $G_i$ is the subgraph of $G = (V, E)$ induced by all unclaimed vertices at the end of the play, i.e., $V(G_i) = V \setminus (S_1 \cup S_2 \cup \ldots S_{i-1})$.
2. Let $\varepsilon \in \{1, 2\}$ denote the player who begins in configuration $(G_i, (C_{i,0}, C_{i,1}))$. The set $C_{i,0}$ contains the vertices Player $\varepsilon$ can select in $G_i$, while the set $C_{i,1}$ contains the vertices Player $\overline{\varepsilon}$ can select in $G_i$. Thus,

$$(C_{i,0}, C_{i,1}) = \begin{cases} (V, V) & \text{if } i = 1 \\ (V \setminus S_1, N(N(S_1)) \cap G_2) & \text{if } i = 2 \\ (N(N(S_1) \setminus S_2) \cap G_3, N(N(S_2) \setminus S_1) \cap G_3) & \\ & \text{if } i = 3 \\ (N(N(S_2 \cup S_4 \cup \cdots \cup S_{i-2}) \setminus (S_1 \cup S_3 \cup \cdots \cup S_{i-1})) \cap G_i, & \\ \quad C_{i-1,0} \cup N(N(v_{i-1}) \setminus (S_2 \cup S_4 \cup \cdots \cup S_{i-2}))) & \\ & \text{if } i > 3 \text{ and } i \text{ is even} \\ (N(N(S_1 \cup S_3 \cup \cdots \cup S_{i-2}) \setminus (S_2 \cup S_4 \cup \cdots \cup S_{i-1})) \cap G_i, & \\ \quad C_{i-1,0} \cup N(N(v_{i-1}) \setminus (S_1 \cup S_3 \cup \cdots \cup S_{i-2}))) & \\ & \text{if } i > 3 \text{ and } i \text{ is odd.} \end{cases}$$

Note that the configuration $(G, (V, V))$ in round 1 indicates that Player 1 begins the game by selecting any vertex $x$ from the vertex set $V$. Additionally, if $G_i \neq \emptyset$ then $C_{i,0} \cup C_{i,1} \neq \emptyset$.

Now we define optimal strategies. Intuitively, an optimal strategy is one for the given player that, given a game configuration, guarantees the best result under all possible behaviors of the opponent. Optimality is determined by the number of vertices claimed by the player. Here is a formal definition.

**Definition 2.** *Let $w \geq 0$ be an integer and $G$ be a weighted graph. A strategy for Player $\varepsilon$ played on $G$ is called $w$-**optimal** if the following conditions hold:*

1. *The strategy can guarantee that Player $\varepsilon$ claims at least $w$ more weights than the opponent, regardless of the opponent's strategies.*
2. *The opponent, Player $\overline{\varepsilon}$, has a strategy that guarantees claiming at most $w$ fewer weights than Player $\varepsilon$, regardless of Player $\varepsilon$'s strategies.*

Let $(G, (C_0, C_1))$ be a configuration where $G = (V, E, f)$ and $\varepsilon \in \{1, 2\}$ such that Player $\varepsilon$ begins the game in configuration $(G, (C_0, C_1))$. We define the integer $Opt(G, (C_0, C_1))$ as the maximum guaranteed weights advantage Player $\varepsilon$ can secure when starting from the configuration.

1. If $G = \emptyset$ then $Opt(G, (C_0, C_1)) = 0$.
2. If $C_0 = \emptyset$ then $Opt(G, (C_0, C_1)) = -Opt(G, (C_1, C_0)) = f(V)$ where $V$ is the vertex set of $G$.

3. Let $(v_1, S_1)$ ,..., $(v_m, S_m)$ be all possible moves of Player $\varepsilon$ at $(G, (C_0, C_1))$. Let $(G_i, (C_{i,0}, C_{i,1}))$ be updated configuration after move $(v_i, S_i)$ and $f(S_i)$ be the weights of $S_i$, $i = 1, \ldots, m$. Set

$$Opt(G, (C_0, C_1)) = \max_{1 \leq i \leq m} \{f(S_i) - Opt(G_i, (C_{i,0}, C_{i,1}))\}.$$

We first establish the computational complexity of finding optimal strategies.

**Lemma 1.** *Player $\varepsilon$ has an $Opt(G, (C_0, C_1))$-optimal strategy at $(G, (C_0, C_1))$, and the computation of $Opt(G, (C_0, C_1))$ is in PSPACE.*

Lemma 1 establishes the general complexity of computing optimal strategies, and in Sect. 3. we will show that this problem is PSPACE-hard. To further investigate the structural conditions under which Player 1 is guaranteed to win, we now introduce a new class of graphs that will serve as a key tool in our later proofs.

**Definition 3.** *A vertex $v$ in a weighted graph $G = (V, E, f)$ is called an* **assured vertex** *if the weight of every component of $G \setminus N(v)$ is less than $f(V)/2$. Thus, if $G$ contains an assured vertex, we refer to $G$ as an* **assured graph**.

Here is a sufficient condition on graphs that guarantee a win for Player 1.

**Lemma 2.** *Player 1 can guarantee a win on any assured graph.*

It follows directly that any weighted path graph is an assured graph, and thus we have the following result:

**Corollary 1.** *Player 1 can guarantee a win on any weighted path graph.*

For weighted cycle graphs, the following lemma applies:

**Lemma 3.** *There exists an algorithm that given a weighted cycle graph $G = (V, E, f)$, computes $Opt(G, (V, V))$ in time $O(|V|^4)$.*

## 3 PSPACE-Hardness

The 3-*TQBF* problem involves determining whether the fully quantified Boolean formula $\psi = \exists x_1 \forall x_2 \exists x_3 \ldots \exists x_n \phi(x_1, x_2, \ldots, x_n)$ is true, where $\phi$ is a conjunction of clauses, each with three literals. This problem is known to be PSPACE-complete [36].

Let $\phi$ be a 3-*CNF* formula $\phi$ with clauses $C_1, \ldots, C_m$ and variables $x_1, \ldots, x_n$. We may assume that for any pair of distinct variables $x_i$ and $x_j$, neither $x_i \vee \overline{x_i} \vee x_j$ nor $x_i \vee \overline{x_i} \vee \overline{x_j}$ are in $\{C_i\}_{i \leq m}$ since such clauses can be removed from $\{C_i\}_{i \leq m}$ in polynomial time. Without loss of generality, we further assume that $n$ is odd and $m \geq 6$ (if $n$ is even, we can introduce a new variable together with a clause containing this variable).

We then build a weighted graph $G_\psi$ with $2n + m + 10$ vertices and $5n + m(m-1)/2 + 7m + 12$ edges along with the vertex-weighted function $f$ such that the formula $\psi = \exists x_1 \forall x_2 \exists x_3 \ldots \exists x_n \phi(x_1, x_2, \ldots, x_n)$ is true if and only if $Opt(G_\psi, (V(G_\psi), V(G_\psi))) \geq (3^{n+3} + 1)m/2$. Therefore, we can state the following theorem.

**Theorem 1.** *Computing $Opt(G, (C_0, C_1))$ is PSPACE-hard.*

# 4 Graph Partitioning Games on Weighted Chordal Graphs

In this section, we prove that weighted chordal graphs are assured graphs. Chordal graphs form a broad and important class of graphs that generalize trees while retaining a tree-like structural property. Our strategy is to first establish the result for weighted trees, which are both chordal graphs themselves and serve as a foundation for understanding the general case. We then extend the argument to chordal graphs via their clique-tree representations.

## 4.1 Graph Partitioning Games on Weighted Trees

Trees are the simplest non-trivial chordal graphs. We begin by introducing the notion of the weighted median of a tree, which captures the balance of vertex weights across its components. Using properties of the weighted median, we prove that weighted trees are assured graphs, meaning Player 1 always has a winning strategy.

**Definition 4.** *Given a weighted graph $G = (V, E, f)$, let $d(u, v)$ be the distance between vertices $u$ and $v$ in $G$. The* **vertex-weighted distance-sum** *of vertex $x$ is defined as $ds^w(x) = \sum_{v \in V} d(x, v) \cdot f(v)$. The* **median** *of the weighted graph $G$ is the set of vertices that minimize the vertex-weighted distance-sum. This set is denoted by $MC(G) = \{v \in V \mid ds^w(v) \leq ds^w(u) \text{ for all } u \in V\}$.*

Recall that a **tree** is a connected graph with no cycles. We denote a weighted tree by $\mathcal{T} = (T, E, f)$. The **subtree** of a vertex $x$ with respect to an edge $xy \in E$, denoted $S_y^x$, is the subgraph induced by all the vertices whose paths to $y$ pass through $x$. The following lemma and corollary summarize important properties of weighted trees.

**Lemma 4.** *Given a tree $\mathcal{T} = (T, E, f)$, for any two vertices $x, y \in T$ such that $xy \in E$, the following equality holds: $ds^w(x) + f(S_y^x) = ds^w(y) + f(S_x^y)$.*

**Corollary 2.** *Given a tree $\mathcal{T} = (T, E, f)$, for all vertices $v \in MC(\mathcal{T})$, the weight of any component of $\mathcal{T} \setminus \{v\}$ is no greater than $f(T)/2$.*

From Corollary 2, it follows that in games played on a tree, the choice made in the first round is crucial, and controlling the median of the tree is key to winning. The next lemma provides a characterization of the median of weighted trees.

**Lemma 5.** *In a weighted tree, the median consists of either a single vertex or two adjacent vertices.*

Intuitively, if Player 1 claims all the vertices in the median in the first round, Player 1 will win. Otherwise, Player 2 can guarantee at least a draw. We are now ready to present the following theorem.

**Theorem 2.** *Weighted trees are assured graphs, and all vertices in $MC(\mathcal{T})$ are assured vertices of $\mathcal{T}$. Hence, Player 1 wins the game on any weighted tree.*

### 4.2 From Trees to Chordal Graphs

Having established the result for trees, we now turn to chordal graphs. The key insight is that chordal graphs admit clique-tree representations, which provide a bridge to the tree case. We first recall the definition of chordal graphs and introduce clique-trees.

**Definition 5.** *A graph is* **chordal** *if every cycle of length at least 4 has a chord, which is an edge between two non-consecutive vertices in the cycle.*

Examples of chordal graphs include trees and $k$-trees. In general, chordal graphs exhibit a 'tree-like' structure and can be represented by clique-trees [35] which we now define. Recall that the vertex set of $\mathcal{T}$ is denoted by $T$.

**Definition 6.** *A* **clique-tree** *of a graph $G$ is a triplet $(\mathcal{T}, \mathcal{E}, \xi)$ such that*

1. *$\mathcal{T}$ is a tree (we call elements of it nodes),*
2. *$\mathcal{E} = \{\mathcal{C}_1, \mathcal{C}_2, \ldots\}$ is the set of all maximal cliques in $G$, and*
3. *$\xi : \mathcal{E} \to T$ is a bijective map that has the following* **subtree property***:*

*For all $v \in V(G)$, the set $\{x \mid v \in \mathcal{C}$ and $\xi(\mathcal{C}) = x\}$ induces a subtree of $\mathcal{T}$.*

The following is a well-known proposition.

**Proposition 1** ([20,22])**.** *A graph is chordal if and only if it has a clique-tree.*

Let $(\mathcal{T}, \mathcal{E}, \xi)$ be a clique-tree of $G$. For $v \in V$ we define the following:

1. $\mathcal{E}(v) = \{\mathcal{C} \mid \mathcal{C} \in \mathcal{E}$ *and* $v \in \mathcal{C}\}$.
2. $\mathcal{T}(v)$ is a subtree of $\mathcal{T}$ induced by vertex set $\{x \mid v \in \mathcal{C}$ *and* $\xi(\mathcal{C}) = x\}$.

We will also need the following operation. Let $\mathcal{T}_1 = (T_1, E_1)$ and $\mathcal{T}_2 = (T_2, E_2)$ be subtrees of a tree $\mathcal{T}$. Then $\mathcal{T}_1 \sqcup \mathcal{T}_2$ is the sub-forest of $\mathcal{T}$ with the nodes set $T_1 \cup T_2$ and the edge set $E_1 \cup E_2$. Now, we are ready to present the following lemma.

**Lemma 6.** *Let $G = (V, E, f)$ be a weighted graph with a clique tree $(\mathcal{T}, \mathcal{E}, \xi)$. Suppose $\mathcal{C} \in \mathcal{E}$, $x = \xi(\mathcal{C})$ and $V'$ is a component of $G \setminus \mathcal{C}$. Then the set $\mathcal{T}' = \bigsqcup_{v \in V'} \mathcal{T}(v) \setminus \{x\}$ forms a subtree in the forest $\mathcal{T} \setminus \{x\}$.*

Now, we move on to weighted chordal graphs and their tree representations.

**Definition 7.** *Let $G = (V, E, f)$ be a weighted chordal graph, and let $(\mathcal{T}, \mathcal{E}, \xi)$ be its clique-tree representation. Let $x_1, \ldots, x_k$ be an ordering of nodes of $\mathcal{T}$ and $\mathcal{C}_i = \xi^{-1}(x_i)$. Then the* **node-weighted function based on the ordering** *is the function $g$ defined as follows:*

$$g(x_i) = \sum_{\substack{v \in \mathcal{C}_i \text{ and} \\ v \notin \mathcal{C}_j,\ j<i}} f(v).$$

*We call the quadruplet $(\mathcal{T}, \mathcal{E}, \xi, g)$* ***weighted clique-tree*** *of $G = (V, E, f)$.*

Note that the weighted clique-tree depends on the order $x_1, \ldots, x_k$. Additionally, the value of $g$ is defined so that $f(v)$ contributes to the weight of exactly one node in $\mathcal{T}$.

For weighted chordal graphs and their corresponding weighted clique-trees, we have the following two lemmas that show the relationship between their weights.

**Lemma 7.** *Let $(\mathcal{T}, \mathcal{E}, \xi, g)$ be a weighted clique-tree of the weighted chordal graph $G = (V, E, f)$. Then we have $f(V) = g(\mathcal{T})$.*

**Lemma 8.** *Let $V'$ be a component of $G \setminus \mathcal{C}$ and $\mathcal{T}' = \bigsqcup_{v \in V'} \mathcal{T}(v) \setminus \{x\}$, where $x = \xi(\mathcal{C})$. Then we have $f(V') \leq g(\mathcal{T}')$.*

We now state the following theorem.

**Theorem 3.** *Let $G = (V, E, f)$ be a weighted chordal graph, and $(\mathcal{T}, \mathcal{E}, \xi, g)$ be its weighted clique-tree. Then $\bigcap_{x \in MC(\mathcal{T})} \xi^{-1}(x) \neq \emptyset$ and any vertex in the set $\bigcap_{x \in MC(\mathcal{T})} \xi^{-1}(x)$ is an assured vertex of $G$.*

Thus, by Corollary 2, we obtain the following result.

**Theorem 4.** *All chordal graphs are assured graphs, and Player 1 wins graph partitioning game on any chordal graph.*

## 5 Conclusion

This paper presents a complete solution to graph partitioning games on chordal graphs. As highlighted in the introduction, such comprehensive solutions are rare in combinatorial game theory, as most scoring games fall into the PSPACE-complete class. Interestingly, it remains open whether there exist graph partitioning games in which Player 2 has a winning strategy. It will also be interesting to push the ideas of this paper into infinite regular games setting such as McNaughton games, Büchi games, and Muller games.

## References

1. Adams, R., Dixon, J., Elder, J., Peabody, J., Vega, O., Willis, K.: Combinatorial analysis of a subtraction game on graphs. Int. J. Combin. **2016** (2016)
2. Agrawal, S.K.: Models for Virus Detection in Contact Networks. The University of Texas at Austin (2021)
3. Andres, S.D., Huggan, M., Mc Inerney, F., Nowakowski, R.J.: The orthogonal colouring game. Theoret. Comput. Sci. **795**, 312–325 (2019)
4. Arora, S., Rao, S., Vazirani, U.: Expander flows, geometric embeddings and graph partitioning. J. ACM (JACM) **56**(2), 1–37 (2009)
5. Beaudou, L., et al.: Octal games on graphs: the game 0.33 on subdivided stars and bistars. Theoret. Comput. Sci. **746**, 19–35 (2018)
6. Bensmail, J., Fioravantes, F., Mc Inerney, F., Nisse, N.: The largest connected subgraph game. Algorithmica **84**(9), 2533–2555 (2022)
7. Bensmail, J., Fioravantes, F., Mc Inerney, F., Nisse, N., Oijid, N.: The maker-breaker largest connected subgraph game. Theoret. Comput. Sci. **943**, 102–120 (2023)
8. Bensmail, J., Mc Inerney, F.: On a vertex-capturing game. Theoret. Comput. Sci. **923**, 27–46 (2022)
9. Besse, C., Faye, G.: Dynamics of epidemic spreading on connected graphs. J. Math. Biol. **82**, 1–52 (2021)
10. Bodlaender, H.L., Kratsch, D.: Kayles and nimbers. J. Algorithms **43**(1), 106–119 (2002)
11. Brown, S., et al.: Nimber sequences of node-kayles games. J. Integer Sequences **23** (2020)
12. Calkin, N.J., et al.: Computing strategies for graphical NIM. In: Proceedings of the Forty-First Southeastern International Conference on Combinatorics, Graph Theory and Computing, vol. 202, pp. 171–185. Citeseer (2010)
13. Calude, C.S., Jain, S., Khoussainov, B., Li, W., Stephan, F.: Deciding parity games in quasipolynomial time. In: Proceedings of the 49th Annual ACM SIGACT Symposium on Theory of Computing, pp. 252–263 (2017)
14. Changat, M., Lekha, D.S., Peterin, I., Subhamathi, A.R., Špacapan, S.: The median game. Discret. Optim. **17**, 80–88 (2015)
15. Cibulka, J., Kynčl, J., Mészáros, V., Stolař, R., Valtr, P.: Graph sharing games: complexity and connectivity. Theoret. Comput. Sci. **494**, 49–62 (2013)
16. Duchêne, É., Renault, G.: Vertex NIM played on graphs. Theoret. Comput. Sci. **516**, 20–27 (2014)
17. Fleischer, R., Trippen, G.: Kayles on the way to the stars. In: van den Herik, H.J., Björnsson, Y., Netanyahu, N.S. (eds.) CG 2004. LNCS, vol. 3846, pp. 232–245. Springer, Heidelberg (2006). https://doi.org/10.1007/11674399_16
18. Guignard, A., Sopena, É.: Compound node-kayles on paths. Theoret. Comput. Sci. **410**(21–23), 2033–2044 (2009)
19. Huggan, M.A., Stevens, B.: Polynomial time graph families for arc kayles. Integers **16**, A86 (2016)
20. Ibarra, L.: The clique-separator graph for chordal graphs. Discret. Appl. Math. **157**(8), 1737–1749 (2009)
21. Khoussainov, B., Liu, J.: On complexity of Ehrenfeucht-Fraïssé games. Ann. Pure Appl. Logic **161**(3), 404–415 (2009)
22. Kloks, T., Xiao, M.: A Guide to Graph Algorithms. Springer, Singapore (2022). https://doi.org/10.1007/978-981-16-6350-5

23. Krauthgamer, R., Naor, J., Schwartz, R.: Partitioning graphs into balanced components. In: Proceedings of the Twentieth Annual ACM-SIAM Symposium on Discrete Algorithms, pp. 942–949. SIAM (2009)
24. Liang, Z., Khoussainov, B., Xiao, M.: Two new algorithms for solving m\" uller games and their applications. arXiv preprint arXiv:2311.04655 (2023)
25. Liang, Z., Khoussainov, B., Xiao, M.: Deciding regular games: a playground for exponential time algorithms. In: 50th International Symposium on Mathematical Foundations of Computer Science (MFCS 2025), pp. 66–1. Schloss Dagstuhl–Leibniz-Zentrum für Informatik (2025)
26. Liang, Z., Khoussainov, B., Xiao, M.: Network control games played on graphs. Theoret. Comput. Sci. 115123 (2025)
27. Liang, Z., Khoussainov, B., Xiao, M.: Exponential time algorithms for deciding regular games. Inf. Comput. 105443 (2026)
28. Liang, Z., Khoussainov, B., Yang, H.: Topological network-control games. In: Wu, W., Tong, G. (eds.) COCOON 2024. LNCS, vol. 15162, pp. 144–156. Springer, Cham (2024). https://doi.org/10.1007/978-981-96-1093-8_2
29. Liang, Z., Khoussainov, B., Yang, H.: Topological network-control games played on graphs. In: Chen, Y., Gao, X., Sun, X., Zhang, A. (eds.) COCOON 2024. LNCS, vol. 15162, pp. 15–26. Springer, Singapore (2025). https://doi.org/10.1007/978-981-96-1093-8_2
30. Liang, Z., Khoussainov, B., Yang, H.: Topological network-control games. Theoret. Comput. Sci. **1068**, 115793 (2026)
31. Micek, P., Walczak, B.: A graph-grabbing game. Comb. Probab. Comput. **20**(4), 623–629 (2011)
32. Newman, M.E.: Finding and evaluating community structuring networks. Phys. Rev. E **69**(26113), 1–16 (2004)
33. Saad, Y., Schultz, M.H.: Topological properties of hypercubes. IEEE Trans. Comput. **37**(7), 867–872 (1988)
34. Schaefer, T.J.: On the complexity of some two-person perfect-information games. J. Comput. Syst. Sci. **16**(2), 185–225 (1978)
35. Shibata, Y.: On the tree representation of chordal graphs. J. Graph Theory **12**(3), 421–428 (1988)
36. Stockmeyer, L.J., Meyer, A.R.: Word problems requiring exponential time (preliminary report). In: Proceedings of the Fifth Annual ACM Symposium on Theory of Computing, pp. 1–9 (1973)
37. Stoer, M., Wagner, F.: A simple min-cut algorithm. J. ACM **44**(4), 585–591 (1997)
38. Van Mieghem, P., Omic, J., Kooij, R.: Virus spread in networks. IEEE/ACM Trans. Network. **17**(1), 1–14 (2008)

# Maximizing the Margin Between Desirable and Undesirable Elements in a Covering Problem

Sophie Boileau[1,2], Andrew Hong[1,3], David Liben-Nowell[1](✉), Alistair Pattison[1,4], Anna N. Rafferty[1], and Charlie Roslansky[1]

[1] Carleton College, Northfield, MN 55057, USA
{dln,arafferty}@carleton.edu
[2] University of Minnesota, Minneapolis, MN 55455, USA
[3] Stony Brook University, Stony Brook, NY 11794, USA
[4] Opportunity Insights, Harvard University, Cambridge, MA 02138, USA

**Abstract.** In many covering settings, it is natural to consider the presence both of elements that we seek to include and of elements that we seek to avoid. This paper introduces a novel combinatorial problem formalizing this tradeoff: from a collection of sets containing both "desirable" and "undesirable" items, pick the subcollection that maximizes the *margin* between the number of desirable and undesirable elements covered. We call this the *Target Approximation Problem* (TAP) and argue that many real-world scenarios are naturally modeled via this objective. We exhibit an efficient 0.5-approximation for the case of TAP where each of the given subsets contains only one undesirable element, derived through a tight connection to the greedy algorithm for Unweighted Set Cover. We then show that TAP is hard, even when restricted to cases where the given sets are small or where elements appear in only a small number of sets. We also provide exact polynomial-time algorithms for other restricted cases, but show that, in a large swath of instances, TAP is hard even to approximate.

**Keywords:** Target Approximation Problem · desirable and undesirable elements · partial covering · approximation · inapproximability

## 1 Introduction

In a well-studied class of combinatorial problems, we face a collection $\mathcal{S}$ of subsets of some groundset, and we must select some subcollection $\mathcal{S}' \subseteq \mathcal{S}$. Typically, the measure of benefit of $\mathcal{S}'$ is the size (or weight) of the union of $\mathcal{S}'$—i.e., we seek to cover all or most of the groundset—and the cost of $\mathcal{S}'$ is the number (or

A number of proofs in this paper have been omitted due to space constraints. They are available in the extended version of this paper [8].


Y. Li et al. (Eds.): COCOON 2026, LNCS 16835, pp. 107–119, 2027.
https://doi.org/10.1007/978-981-92-3309-0_9

weight) of the chosen sets. For example, Set Cover requires us to cover every groundset element while minimizing the number (or weight) of chosen sets [21]. Max-$k$-Cover requires us to cover as many groundset elements as possible using only $k$ sets [17]. There is also the complementary cost-focused formulation, Min-$k$-Union, in which we seek to *avoid* groundset elements: we must cover as *few* groundset elements as possible while choosing at least $k$ sets [13].

More rarely, but intriguingly, there are applications that merge these maximization and minimization views: we are given a set of *desirable* elements and a separate set of *undesirable* elements. The benefit of $\mathcal{S}' \subseteq \mathcal{S}$ comes from the former; the cost comes from the latter. (Thus, the groundset contains both "good" and "bad" elements, and we seek to cover many good and few bad elements.)

As a motivating example, consider a company that seeks to leverage its existing customers' social connections to expand its market share. The company might advertise a shareable "friends and family" discount code to a selected set of its existing customers, giving a discount to (a few) existing clients while trying to influence (many) new potential customers to consider buying the company's product. The more distinct people who are friends of those people in the seed set, the better—but, too, the smaller the seed set itself, the better. Concretely, one might formulate this as a viral marketing problem: we are given a social network with a set of "target" nodes and a set of "nontarget" nodes, and we must choose a set of influencers/seed nodes to reach many targets and few nontargets [28].

*A Novel Computational Formulation: The Target Approximation Problem (TAP).* Although there has been less attention to this combined view in the literature, this dual minimization/maximization perspective has appeared in certain combinatorial formulations. For example, Red-Blue Set Cover [10,30] asks us to choose $\mathcal{S}' \subseteq \mathcal{S}$ covering all desired ("blue") elements while minimizing the number of undesired ("red") elements. Positive-Negative Partial Set Cover [26] drops the hard requirement to cover all blue elements, instead seeking to minimize the number of errors in either direction—i.e., the number of false negatives (uncovered blue elements) plus the number of false positives (covered red elements).

In many of the applications in which this formulation is apt, though, this objective function does not seem to capture the intuitive goal. For example, take the viral marketing scenario above [28]: if an influencer-based discount campaign reaches $b$ potential new customers and $r$ current customers, then, up to constant multipliers, the profit from the campaign is determined by $b - r$. That is, the *margin* between the number of true positives and the number of false positives is what characterizes success, not the total number of "errors." (Failing to reach a potential new customer may be a missed opportunity, but it's not a loss.)

In this paper, we formulate a new optimization problem, which we call the *Target Approximation Problem (TAP)*, which takes this margin-based view. Concretely, we are given a *groundset* $U$ and a *target* $B \subseteq U$ of desirable ("blue") elements. The remaining groundset elements $R = U - B$ are undesirable ("red"). We are also given a collection of sets $\mathcal{S} = \{S_1, \ldots, S_m\}$, with each $S_j \subseteq U$. We select some of the given subsets, yielding a benefit from every covered blue element and a cost from every red element. Formally, we must find a set $\mathcal{S}' \subseteq \mathcal{S}$ maximizing the *margin* of $\mathcal{S}'$:

$$\text{(the number of blue elements in } \mathcal{S}') - \text{(the number of red elements in } \mathcal{S}').$$

Note that we only measure the margin between true positives and false positives; there is no benefit to true negatives (uncovered red elements), nor any cost for false negatives (uncovered blue elements).

*Our Results: One-Red TAP.* Consider a bipartite graph representation of the viral marketing problem described above. The nodes in the left column are all red, and represent existing customers. The nodes in the right column are all blue, and represent new customers. Edges represent friendship. In this formulation, then, we must choose a set $R$ of red nodes, which has a set $\Gamma(R)$ of neighbors (all of which are blue). We seek the set $R$ such that $|\Gamma(R)| - |R|$ is maximized.

This bipartite graph implicitly represents a TAP instance: the subsets from which we choose take the form $\{r\} \cup \Gamma(r)$ for each red node $r$, i.e., each set consists of a single node $r$ and all of its (blue) neighbors. Because each subset contains exactly one red element—i.e., the subsets are of the form $\{r, b_1, b_2, \ldots, b_k\}$—we refer to this instance as a *one-red* instance of TAP.

We first establish hardness for one-red TAP, by showing that an optimal solution to a one-red instance yields an optimal solution to Red-Blue Set Cover (which is known to be hard [10]). We are nonetheless able to give an efficient 0.5-approximation algorithm for one-red instances. This is our most technically involved result, based on careful analysis of the greedy algorithm for Unweighted Set Cover. Specifically, we leverage the results of Parekh [29] and Slavík [31] that lower bound the number of elements covered by the $i$th iteration of the greedy algorithm for Set Cover.

*Our Results: The General TAP Problem.* Absent the one-red restriction—e.g., in a social network that is not bipartite (so a subset in $\mathcal{S}$ might contain multiple red nodes)—our first results are unsurprisingly negative: TAP is NP-hard in general, and hard to $\Theta(1)$-approximate. As a result, we focus on two natural special cases of TAP that may be tractable: (i) *restricted occurrence,* in which each groundset element occurs in $k$ or fewer of the given subsets; and (ii) *restricted weight,* in which each subset contains $w$ or fewer elements. (Intuitively and, often, technically, these restrictions correspond to well-studied special cases of CNF-SAT in which clauses only contain a small number of literals or where variables only occur in a limited number of clauses.)

We establish an intriguing interplay between the occurrence and weight constraints: TAP is hard when *either* is nontrivial—but, perhaps surprisingly, TAP can be solved efficiently when *both* are tightly constrained. That is, there is an efficient, exact algorithm when $k = 1$ or $w = 1$, but TAP is NP-hard even with a 2-occurrence or 2-weight constraint if the other quantity is unrestricted. And yet when *both* quantities are constrained, the problem becomes tractable again: an efficient algorithm for 2-occurrence, 2-weight TAP emerges from an efficient solution to Independent Set on a collection of cycles and paths [3].

Based on these results, we explore two further avenues. First, we consider the boundary between tractability and intractability for small $k$ and $w$. Using the known hardness for Vertex Cover even for low-degree graphs [2,16], we show that 2-weight, $k$-occurrence TAP is hard for $k \geq 3$, as is 2-occurrence, $w$-weight TAP for $w \geq 4$. (The tractability of 2-occurrence, 3-weight TAP remains open; see Sect. 7.)

Second, we derive concrete inapproximability results when $k \geq 3$ or $w \geq 5$, even with constraints on the other quantity. Our proofs use the known hardness of $k$DM-$k$ ($k$-dimensional matching with at most $k$ occurrences of each element) [14] and $a$-OCC-Max-2-SAT (Max-2-SAT where variables are limited to occurring in $a$ clauses) [6].

*Other Related Work.* Other applications of the dual minimization/maximization scenario abound; regrettably, it is all too common for that which we seek to be bundled with that which we seek to avoid. Some example problems follow. Given a set of paths in a graph, choose a subset covering many distinct edges but few distinct nodes (relevant to network reliability [33]). Given a collection of papers, choose some authors who cover a large number of universities/institutions but a small number of individual conferences (relevant to group fairness [24]). Given a set of participants who might be hired to collect data by following any of a given set of routes through a collection of points of interest (POIs), choose some routes that cover many POIs but a small number of participants [20]. Further applications have been identified in, e.g., record linkage in data mining [7], online review collation [27], and motif identification in computational biology [23].

To the best of our knowledge, the Target Approximation Problem is a novel formulation, but it has some aspects that echo classical combinatorial problems. We previously mentioned Max-$k$-Cover, where we maximize the number of covered blue elements given a ceiling $k$ on the number of sets (e.g., [17]), and the less-studied (and seemingly much harder) Min-$k$-Union, where we minimize the number of covered red elements given a floor $k$ on the number of chosen sets [12]. Some variations have relaxed these problems with broadly similar motivations to ours: e.g., in $k$-Partial Set Cover, we must cover at least $k$ groundset elements (though not necessarily all of them) with the smallest number of sets (e.g., [32]; see also [15]). As previously detailed, perhaps the closest matches are Red-Blue Set Cover [10,30] and Positive-Negative Partial Set Cover [26], both of which incorporate the dual desired/undesired perspective; the difference in objective functions, though, means that these results yield few direct implications for TAP.

Although the problem itself is very different, in some ways TAP is most reminiscent of Correlation Clustering [5], in which we are asked to cluster the nodes of a graph whose given $\pm 1$-weighted edges represent the reward/penalty for grouping the corresponding endpoints in the same cluster. The intuitive similarity stems from the fact that Correlation Clustering does not specify the number of clusters, just as a TAP algorithm is free to choose how many, and which, blue elements to cover. Indeed, a modification of Correlation Clustering called Overlapping Correlation Clustering is a generalization of Positive-Negative Partial Set Cover [9]. The objective functions studied in correlation clustering (minimize errors, or maximize the number of correct answers) are analogous to Positive-Negative Partial Set Cover, but a version of Correlation Clustering where we maximize the total intracluster margin—i.e., ignoring intercluster edges, regardless of whether they are labeled +1 or −1—is a closer, interesting relative of our problem.

## 2 Preliminaries

As described in Sect. 1, we start with a fixed groundset $U$ of $n$ *elements* and a specified *target* $B \subseteq U$. Elements in $B$ are called *blue*; elements in $R = U - B$ are called *red.* We are also given a collection $\mathcal{S} = \{S_1, \ldots, S_m\}$ of $m$ *subsets* of $U$. We are asked to select $\mathcal{S}' \subseteq \mathcal{S}$, and the set of elements in $\mathcal{S}'$—that is, $\bigcup_{S_i \in \mathcal{S}'} S_i$—is then compared to $B$. A blue element in $\mathcal{S}'$ is *correct;* red elements in $\mathcal{S}'$ are *incorrect.* (Again, elements not in $\mathcal{S}'$ play no role in the objective; there is no benefit to uncovered red elements nor any cost for uncovered blue elements.)

**Definition 1 (Target Approximation Problem [TAP]).**

**Input:** *A groundset $U$ of $n$ elements, a target $B \subseteq U$, and a collection $\mathcal{S} = \{S_1, \ldots, S_m\}$ of subsets of $U$.*
**Output:** *A subset $\mathcal{S}' \subseteq \mathcal{S}$ that maximizes the* margin *of $\mathcal{S}'$:*

$$\left|\left\{i \in B : i \in \bigcup_{S_i \in \mathcal{S}'} S_i\right\}\right| - \left|\left\{i \in U - B : i \in \bigcup_{S_i \in \mathcal{S}'} S_i\right\}\right|.$$

*To avoid trivialities, we assume that every element appears in at least one subset in $\mathcal{S}$; that $B$ and each $S_j$ are nonempty; and that the subsets in $\mathcal{S}$ are distinct.*

By the *weight* of $S_i \in \mathcal{S}$, we mean $|S_i|$. A subset $S_i$'s *blue-weight* (respectively, *red-weight)* is the number of blue (respectively, red) elements it contains. We say a TAP instance is *one-red* if each given subset contains exactly one red element.

By the number of *occurrences* of a groundset element $i$, we mean the number of subsets in $\mathcal{S}$ in which $i$ appears.

## 3 TAP with Restricted Weight

We start with special cases of TAP in which each subset contains at most $w$ elements, establishing a sharp transition in hardness based on $w$. We first show that TAP is efficiently solvable when each subset's weight is 1 (or, slightly more generally, when there is no subset containing both blue and red elements). We then establish TAP's hardness with the mildest relaxation of this constraint, even if subsets have a 2-weight restriction. We begin with a useful fact:

*Remark 2.* Let $\mathcal{S}' \subseteq \mathcal{S}$. Let $S^+$ be any subset with zero red-weight, and let $S^-$ be any subset with zero blue-weight. Then the margin of $\mathcal{S}' \cup \{S^+\}$ is never worse than the margin of $\mathcal{S}'$, and the margin of $\mathcal{S}' \cup \{S^-\}$ is never better.

The tractability of 1-weight TAP follows from Remark 2 (we simply take all and only those subsets with zero red-weight; see [8] for details):

**Theorem 3.** *The case of TAP in which every subset has either zero blue-weight or zero red-weight (which includes* 1*-weight TAP) is solvable in polynomial time.*

We also use Remark 2 to preprocess TAP instances to simplify their structure. Specifically, we henceforth assume that there are no zero-red-weight subsets: we might as well take all of them, so we delete them along with deleting from the groundset the elements that they cover. Similarly, we delete any zero-blue-weight subsets: we would never take these subsets, so we simply delete them from $\mathcal{S}$. Thus, from here on, every subset contains both blue and red elements.

Next, we show that 1-weight TAP is the limit of tractability.

**Lemma 4.** *Consider a one-red instance. Let $\mathcal{S}'$ be a collection of subsets that fails to cover at least one blue element. Then there exists a subset $S_i \notin \mathcal{S}'$ such that the margin of $\mathcal{S}' \cup \{S_i\}$ is no worse than the margin of $\mathcal{S}'$.*

*Thus, for any one-red TAP instance, there is an optimal set of subsets that includes every blue element. Furthermore, given any optimal solution, we can efficiently compute another optimal solution that includes every blue element.*

The result follows from the fact that adding any one-red subset that contains an uncovered blue element never hurts the margin; see [8] for details.

Note that, after preprocessing, any 2-weight TAP instance satisfies the one-red constraint; thus the conclusions of Lemma 4 apply to 2-weight TAP. As a result, efficiently solving 2-weight TAP implies an efficient solution to the problem of finding the set of subsets covering all blue elements while covering as few red elements as possible in the same (one-red) instance: that is, the Red-Blue Set Cover problem [10]. Carr et al.'s reduction from Set Cover to (one-red) Red-Blue Set Cover can be applied essentially unchanged to show the hardness of 2-weight TAP:

**Theorem 5.** *It is NP-hard to solve $w$-weight TAP for any $w \geq 2$.*

(For the argument, see the proof of Theorem 12, in Sect. 5, deferred to the extended version of this paper [8]. Theorem 12 establishes hardness of TAP for $w \geq 2$ even with an additional occurrence constraint.)

## 4 One-Red TAP (and 2-Weight TAP) is 0.5-Approximable

We now give an efficient approximation algorithm for one-red TAP, which includes the 2-weight case. Specifically, we show that the classic greedy Set Cover algorithm yields a 0.5-approximation for one-red TAP instances.

Recall that an instance is one-red if each subset contains exactly one red element. In a one-red instance, we can speak of a red element "covering" a blue element. Under the one-red constraint, the choice to absorb the cost of any particular red element $r$ then allows us to reap the benefit of any blue element that appears in a subset with it. So a subset like $\{r, b_1, b_2\}$, with the one-red form, means that $r$ covers $b_1$ and $b_2$. (It might also cover other blue elements because of a different subset that also contains the same element $r$.)

In the context of one-red TAP, GREEDY behaves as follows: in each iteration, it picks the red element that covers the largest number of (currently uncovered) blue elements, repeating until all blue elements are covered.

To analyze the performance of GREEDY, we appeal to existing literature on the performance of this same algorithm on the Set Cover problem. The key fact is the following result, due independently to Parekh [29] and Slavík [31]:

**Lemma 6 (Parekh [29], Slavík [31]).** *Let $m_i$ denote the number of elements covered by the ith iteration of* GREEDY *applied to* (Unweighted) *Set Cover. Then*

$$m_i \geq \left\lceil \frac{n - \sum_{j=1}^{i-1} m_j}{\mathtt{OPT}_{SC}} \right\rceil, \tag{1}$$

*where the groundset has size $n$ and the size of the optimal set cover is* $\mathtt{OPT}_{SC}$.

Or, to restate this in the TAP context: let $m_i$ denote the number of blue elements covered in the $i$th iteration of GREEDY applied to one-red TAP, and let $\mathtt{OPT}_{\mathrm{SC}}$ denote the number of red elements in the optimal TAP solution that covers all $n$ blue elements. Then (1) holds.

We leverage Lemma 6 to prove our main result: GREEDY is a $\frac{1}{2}$-approximation for one-red TAP (including 2-weight TAP). It turns out that showing that GREEDY covers "enough" elements in its first "few" iterations will be sufficient to establish our efficient 0.5-approximation. Specifically, we first prove the following lemma (where the value of $K$ formalizes the notion of "few," which, critically, depends on the instance's structure):

**Lemma 7.** *Let $K := \left\lceil \frac{1}{2}(n - \mathtt{OPT}_{SC}) \right\rceil$. Then* GREEDY *covers at least $2K$ blue elements in its first $K$ moves.*

*Proof (sketch; see [8] for details).* We argue by induction on $k$ that, for any $k \leq K$, the first $k$ iterations of GREEDY cover at least $2k$ blue elements. The base case ($k = 1$) is immediate by Lemma 6 if $\mathtt{OPT}_{\mathrm{SC}} < n$ (and if $\mathtt{OPT}_{\mathrm{SC}} = n$ then $K = 0$ and the lemma is vacuous). For the inductive case, we consider two possibilities (which are exhaustive by the inductive hypothesis):

*Case 1:* GREEDY is "ahead of schedule," having covered at least $2k - 1$ blue elements in its first $k - 1$ iterations. Then GREEDY need only cover one additional blue element in its $k$th iteration, which it must do (unless the algorithm already terminated before the $k$th iteration).

*Case 2:* GREEDY is "right on schedule," having covered exactly $2k - 2$ blue elements in its first $k - 1$ iterations. In this case, the lemma requires GREEDY to cover at least two elements on its current iteration. Here, we appeal to Lemma 6's lower bound on $m_k$—noting that by the definition of Case 2 we know that the summation in the numerator in (1) is exactly $2k - 2$—and algebraic manipulation (and the fact that $k \leq K$) to establish the result. □

**Theorem 8.** GREEDY *is a $\frac{1}{2}$-approximation for the one-red TAP problem (and therefore* GREEDY *is a $\frac{1}{2}$-approximation for 2-weight TAP).*

*Proof (sketch; see* [8] *for details).* Lemma 7 implies that, after the first $K$ "good" moves (averaging at least two blue elements per move), only $n - 2K$ additional iterations are required (each covering at least one of the $\leq n - 2K$ as-yet-uncovered blue elements). The careful choice of $K$ ensures that covering all $n$ blue elements with only $K + (n - 2K) = n - K$ red elements is within a $\frac{1}{2}$ factor of optimal. □

The bound on the approximation ratio is tight: there are 2-weight TAP instances in which GREEDY achieves only $\frac{1}{2} \cdot$ OPT (see [8] for an example).

*Note 9.* Following Lemma 6, write $m_i$ to denote the number of elements covered by the $i$th iteration of the greedy algorithm for Set Cover. Write $g$ to denote the number of iterations before GREEDY terminates. Then we have that $m_1 \geq m_2 \geq \cdots \geq m_g$ (and $\sum_{i=1}^{g} m_i = n$), by the definition of GREEDY. (Parekh [29] observes this fact explicitly.) Thus $m_1 = \max_i m_i$.

If $m_1 = 2$, then, the sequence $m_{1,\ldots,g}$ takes the form $\langle 2, \cdots, 2, 1, \cdots 1 \rangle$: that is, GREEDY makes a sequence of "2-moves" (each covering two new elements) followed by a sequence of "1-moves" (each covering one new element), until it terminates. Case 2 of the proof of Lemma 7 arises precisely when $m_1 = m_2 = \cdots = m_{k-1} = 2$; our proof argues that $m_k$ must also equal 2 (under the assumption that $k \leq K$). (Case 1 of the proof can arise only if $m_1 \geq 3$. This case corresponds to an instance in which GREEDY at some point "gets ahead" of the 2-move pace—i.e., $m_1 + m_2 + \cdots m_i > 2i$ for some $i$—and, because $i < K$, we still had to argue that $m_1 + m_2 + \cdots m_{i+1} \geq 2i + 2$. But because the $m$ values are nonincreasing, GREEDY at some point gets ahead of the 2-move pace if and only if its *first* move is ahead of the 2-move pace.)

## 5 TAP with Restricted Occurrence

We next consider the occurrence constraint on TAP: each element appears in at most $k$ subsets. As with weight, we show a sharp transition in hardness based on $k$: TAP can be solved efficiently when elements occur only once, but TAP is hard if elements can occur even twice.

**Theorem 10.** *Under the $k$-occurrence restriction (and no weight restriction), TAP is solvable exactly in polynomial time for $k = 1$, and is NP-hard for $k \geq 2$.*

The algorithm for 1-occurrence TAP simply takes all and only those subsets that have higher blue weight than red weight; the hardness result for $(k \geq 2)$-occurrence TAP follows from the hardness of Max $k$-SAT (even for $k = 2$ [16]). Proofs are omitted due to space constraints; see [8].

Together, Theorems 5 and 10 establish the hardness of 2-weight TAP and 2-occurrence TAP. But, perhaps surprisingly, the combination of these constraints yields instances that *can* be solved efficiently:

**Theorem 11.** *2-occurrence, 2-weight TAP can be solved exactly in polynomial time.*

*Proof.* By Theorem 3 (and the preprocessing described immediately after), we assume that each subset has exactly one blue and one red element. We can solve this TAP instance by turning it into a graph in which each node corresponds to a red element and each edge to a blue element. Specifically, $\{r, b\} \in \mathcal{S}$ corresponds to a half-edge (or "stub") connecting node $r$ with half of the edge $b$. Thus an edge and its endpoints correspond to a pair of subsets with a shared blue element between two distinct red elements. (We may assume there is no unmatched half-edge: if some blue element $b$ occurs only once, then, by Lemma 4, there exists an optimal solution that includes $b$'s sole subset. Thus we augment our preprocessing to delete such subsets and both their red and blue elements.)

By the 2-occurrence constraint, each node in this graph has degree at most two; as a result, the graph consists only of connected components that are cycles and paths. By Lemma 4, it suffices to choose a collection of subsets that covers all blue elements while minimizing the number of red elements. It follows that an optimal set of subsets corresponds directly to a minimum vertex cover of the graph. Because our graph consists of a collection of disjoint cycles and paths, finding a minimum vertex cover is easy: take an alternating set of nodes (i.e., skipping every other node), starting from an arbitrary node in a cycle, or from the penultimate node of a path. (See, e.g., [3].) The resulting set of nodes and their incident edges yields an optimal set of subsets. □

Thus $k$-occurrence, 2-weight TAP is hard for general $k$, but tractable for $k = 2$. It is then natural to ask for the smallest $k$ for which this problem is hard. Similarly, what is the smallest $w$ for which 2-occurrence, $w$-weight TAP is hard? Unfortunately, the answer to the first question is negative: even 3-occurrence, 2-weight TAP is hard. We have not been able to fully answer the second question, but we establish that 2-occurrence, 4-weight TAP is hard (leaving $w = 3$ open).

**Theorem 12.** *Both* 3*-occurrence,* 2*-weight and* 2*-occurrence,* 4*-weight TAP are NP-hard.*

The proof follows from Carr et al.'s hardness proof for Red-Blue Set Cover [10], reducing from Set Cover, and invoking Lemma 4. The weight and occurrence restrictions follow from the fact that Set Cover remains hard even when each groundset element occurs in exactly two sets (i.e., Vertex Cover) and, further, even when the resulting graph has a maximum degree of three [2,16]. Following Carr et al.'s construction on such an instance yields a 3-occurrence and 2-weight TAP instance. The 2-occurrence, 4-weight result follows by merging together all subsets that share the same red element; the optimal solution is not affected. (See [8] for the detailed proof.)

## 6 Inapproximability Results

We now turn to inapproximability, even under restrictions on occurrence and weight. Our results follow from, first, a tightening of Theorem 10, and, second, another hardness derivation based on the $k$-dimensional matching problem.

**Theorem 13.** *2-occurrence, 5-weight TAP is hard to $\frac{2011}{2012}$-approximate, and 2-occurrence, 12-weight TAP is hard to $\frac{667}{668}$-approximate.*

Our proof begins by recalling $a$-OCC-MAX-$k$-SAT, which is MAX-$k$-SAT with the further restriction that variables are limited to occurring in only $a$ clauses. Following the approach of Theorem 10, but with a tightened construction and more careful bookkeeping, we show that an $\alpha$-approximation of $(a+2\cdot\lfloor\frac{a}{2}\rfloor)$-weight $k$-occurrence TAP yields an $\alpha$-approximation of $a$-OCC-MAX-$k$-SAT. Known inapproximability results due to Berman and Karpinski [6] for 3-Occ-Max-2-SAT and 6-Occ-Max-2-SAT imply the stated hardness. For details, see the extended version of the paper [8].

We derive a second set of inapproximability results using the $k$-*dimensional matching* problem: we are given sets $S_1, S_2, \ldots, S_k$, and a collection of $k$-tuples $C \subseteq S_1 \times S_2 \times \cdots \times S_k$; we must find the largest subcollection of $C$ so that no element of any $S_i$ appears more than once in the subcollection. (Indeed, 3-dimensional matching was one of Karp's original NP-hard problems [21].)

**Theorem 14.** *Unconstrained TAP is hard to c-approximate, for any constant $c > 0$. Further, 3-occurrence, 3-weight TAP is hard to $\frac{94}{95}$-approximate and 4-occurrence, 4-weight TAP is hard to $\frac{47}{48}$-approximate.*

Denote by MAX-$k$DM-$k$ the $k$-dimensional matching problem with the additional restriction that each element occurs in at most $k$ sets. We show that an $\alpha$-approximation of $k$-occurrence, $k$-weight TAP implies an $\alpha$-approximation of MAX-$k$DM-$k$. (Given sets $S_1, S_2, \ldots, S_k$, and $k$-tuples $C \subseteq S_1 \times S_2 \times \cdots \times S_k$, construct a TAP instance with one blue element for each element of $\bigcup_i S_i$ and $k-1$ red elements for each $k$-tuple $c \in C$. Build $k$ subsets corresponding to $c$, one for each index $i$, each containing these $k-1$ red elements and the blue element corresponding to the element of $S_i$ found in $c$.) Known hardness results by Hazan, Safra, and Schwartz [19]; Lee, Svensson, and Thiery [22]; and Chlebík and Chlebíková [14] for MAX-$k$DM-$k$ imply the stated hardness results. (Again, details are in the extended version of the paper [8].)

## 7 Future Work

Our results on TAP—including hardness, efficient exact algorithms, and efficient approximation algorithms—are summarized in Fig. 1. These leave several interesting open problems, which we briefly outline.

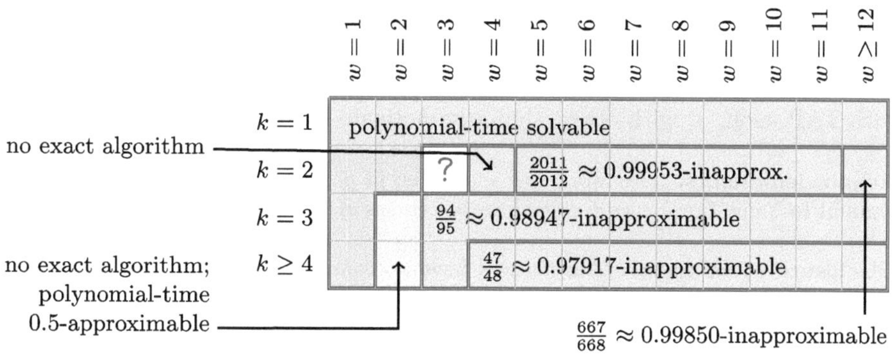


**Fig. 1.** Summary of results for $k$-occurrence, $w$-weight TAP: each of the given subsets contains $\leq w$ elements, and each element appears in $\leq k$ of the given subsets.

*2-Occurrence, 3-Weight TAP.* Some of the essential structural properties that allowed an efficient solution for 2-occurrence, 2-weight TAP—roughly, that here TAP reduces to a Vertex Cover instance in a graph whose connected components are all cycles or paths—seem to have rough analogs in 3-weight TAP. We harbor some hope that an efficient algorithm for 2-occurrence, 3-weight TAP might emerge through this approach, though we have not yet been able to realize that hope (or to find an argument for hardness).

*Generalized (Especially for 3-Weight) or Improved (In)approximability.* Thus far, we have been unable to generalize our 0.5-approximation for 2-weight, arbitrary-occurrence TAP to broader settings. Still, as noted above, the 3-weight constraint leaves intact some of the helpful structural properties that enabled our approximation. Is it possible to efficiently approximate 3-weight TAP? One possible approach involves semi-definite programming: the classic Goemans–Williamson SDP for MAX-2-SAT [18] has some structural similarities to an SDP for MIN-2-SAT [4]; might it be possible to combine them (using the former for blue elements and the latter for red elements)? Relatedly, there are sizable gaps between our algorithmic and inapproximability results; might these gaps be closed?

*Efficient Exact Algorithms for Additional Cases of TAP.* We concentrated in this paper on restricted-occurrence and restricted-weight instances of TAP. But there are other tractable special cases For example, under the one-red constraint it suffices to find the optimal Red-Blue Set Cover (Lemma 4), which is efficiently solvable in certain geometric settings [1,11,25]We might hope to find broader sets of TAP instances that are efficiently solvable.

*Margin-Based Formulations.* Finally, and most broadly, we see as a primary contribution of this paper the introduction of a (to the best of our knowledge) novel problem with an understudied *style* of objective function for covering-type problems. First, we both seek to reap reward (for desirable elements) and to avoid cost (for undesirable elements). Second, we have the freedom to ignore "regions" of the input where the costs outweigh the benefits; our algorithms have the choice of how much to try to explain. We see TAP as a fascinating combinatorial problem with these two properties. What other applications can we address, either with TAP itself, or with other, similarly motivated combinatorial problems?

**Acknowledgments.** This work was supported in part by Carleton College. We are grateful to Yang Tan for work during earlier stages of this project.

**Disclosure of Interests.** The authors have no competing interests to declare that are relevant to the content of this article.

## References

1. Abidha, V., Ashok, P.: Red blue set cover problem on axis-parallel hyperplanes and other objects. Inf. Process. Lett. **186**, 106485 (2024)
2. Alimonti, P., Kann, V.: Hardness of approximating problems on cubic graphs. In: Bongiovanni, G., Bovet, D.P., Di Battista, G. (eds.) CIAC 1997. LNCS, vol. 1203, pp. 288–298. Springer, Heidelberg (1997). https://doi.org/10.1007/3-540-62592-5_80
3. Arnborg, S., Proskurowski, A.: Linear time algorithms for NP-hard problems restricted to partial $k$-trees. Discret. Appl. Math. **23**(1), 11–24 (1989)
4. Avidor, A., Zwick, U.: Approximating MIN $k$-SAT. In: ISAAC (2002)
5. Bansal, N., Blum, A., Chawla, S.: Correlation clustering. In: FOCS (2002)
6. Berman, P., Karpinski, M.: On some tighter inapproximability results. In: ICALP (1999)
7. Bilenko, M., Kamath, B., Mooney, R.J.: Adaptive blocking: learning to scale up record linkage. In: IEEE ICDM (2006)
8. Boileau, S., Hong, A., Liben-Nowell, D., Pattison, A., Rafferty, A.N., Roslansky, C.: Maximizing the margin between desirable and undesirable elements in a covering problem (2025). https://arxiv.org/abs/2507.03817
9. Bonchi, F., Gionis, A., Ukkonen, A.: Overlapping correlation clustering. Knowl. Inf. Syst. **35**, 1–32 (2013)
10. Carr, R.D., Doddi, S., Konjevod, G., Marathe, M.: On the red-blue set cover problem. In: SODA (2000)
11. Chan, T.M., Hu, N.: Geometric red–blue set cover for unit squares and related problems. Comput. Geom. **48**(5), 380–385 (2015)
12. Chen, H., Chen, L., Ye, S., Zhang, G.: On extensions of Min-$k$-Union$^\star$. In: COCOON (2024)
13. Chlamtác, E., Dinitz, M., Konrad, C., Kortsarz, G., Rabanca, G.: The densest $k$-subhypergraph problem. SIAM J. Discrete Math. **32**(2), 1458–1477 (2018)
14. Chlebík, M., Chlebíková, J.: Inapproximability results for bounded variants of optimization problems. In: Proceedings of Fundamentals Computation Theory (FCT) (2003)
15. Dimant, S.M., Krumke, S.O.: On approximating partial scenario set cover. Theoret. Comput. Sci. **1023**, 114891 (2025)
16. Garey, M.R., Johnson, D.S., Stockmeyer, L.: Some simplified NP-complete graph problems. Theoret. Comput. Sci. **1**(3), 237–267 (1976)
17. Garey, M.R., Johnson, D.S.: Computers and Intractability: A Guide to the Theory of NP-Completeness. W. H. Freeman and Company (1979)

18. Goemans, M.X., Williamson, D.P.: .879-approximation algorithms for MAX CUT and MAX 2SAT. In: STOC (1994)
19. Hazan, E., Safra, S., Schwartz, O.: On the complexity of approximating $k$-dimensional matching. In: RANDOM/APPROX (2003)
20. Huang, P., Zhu, W., Liao, K., Sellis, T., Yu, Z., Guo, L.: Efficient algorithms for flexible sweep coverage in crowdsensing. IEEE Access **6**, 50055–50065 (2018)
21. Karp, R.: Reducibility among combinatorial problems. In: Complexity of Computer Computations, vol. 40, pp. 85–103. Plenum (1972)
22. Lee, E., Svensson, O., Thiery, T.: Asymptotically optimal hardness for $k$-set packing and $k$-matroid intersection. In: STOC (2025)
23. Li, Y., Liu, Y., Juedes, D., Drews, F., Bunescu, R., Welch, L.: Set cover-based methods for motif selection. Bioinformatics **36**(4), 1044–1051 (2019)
24. Ma, H., Guan, S., Toomey, C., Wu, Y.: Diversified subgraph query generation with group fairness. In: WSDM (2022)
25. Madireddy, R.R., Nandy, S.C., Pandit, S.: On the geometric red-blue set cover problem. In: WALCOM (2021)
26. Miettinen, P.: On the positive-negative partial set cover problem. Inf. Process. Lett. **108**(4), 219–221 (2008)
27. Nguyen, T.S., Lauw, H.W., Tsaparas, P.: Review selection using micro-reviews. IEEE Trans. Knowl. Data Eng. **27**(4), 1098–1111 (2014)
28. Padmanabhan, M.R., Somisetty, N., Basu, S., Pavan, A.: Influence maximization in social networks with non-target constraints. In: IEEE BigData (2018)
29. Parekh, A.K.: A note on the greedy approximation algorithm for the unweighted set covering problem. Technical report, LIDS, MIT (1988)
30. Peleg, D.: Approximation algorithms for the label-cover$_{\mathrm{MAX}}$ and red-blue set cover problems. J. Discrete Algorithms **5**, 55–64 (2007)
31. Slavík, P.: A tight analysis of the greedy algorithm for set cover. In: STOC (1996)
32. Slavík, P.: Improved performance of the greedy algorithm for partial cover. Inf. Process. Lett. **64**(5), 251–254 (1997)
33. Yuan, S., Varma, S., Jue, J.: Minimum-color path problems for reliability in mesh networks. In: INFOCOM (2005)

# Asymptotically Optimal Collaborative Caching in Edge Computing Systems

Hongjie Guo(✉), Jinchao Wu, Jianxu Shen, and Hanchun Yuan

School of Computer Science and Technology, Zhejiang Normal University, Jinhua, Zhejiang, China
{guohongjie,wujinchao,shenjianxu,hanchunyuan}@zjnu.edu.cn

**Abstract.** This paper investigates the fundamental problem of latency-minimization in collaborative edge caching systems. We formalize the task as a combinatorial optimization problem, **P0**, characterized by non-linearizable existential constraints and a non-convex objective. We prove that **P0** is not only NP-hard but also resistant to standard gradient-based optimization due to its structural irregularities. We reformulate **P0** into an equivalent integer linear programming problem, denoted as **P1**, using McCormick envelopes and logical linearization. We propose a dual-algorithm framework: an exact branch-and-bound algorithm for global optimality in moderate-scale instances, and a randomized rounding-based approximation algorithm for large-scale deployments. Through rigorous theoretical analysis, we prove that our approximation algorithm is asymptotically optimal. While we establish a robust 2-approximation factor for the general case, our refined analysis using Bernstein-type concentration inequalities yields a tighter bound of $1 + \mathcal{O}(\sqrt{s_{\max}/S_{\min}})$. In practice, the ratio $s_{\max}/S_{\min}$ is often very small. This tighter bound proves that under this common condition, the algorithm's performance converges toward optimality.

**Keywords:** Edge caching · Asymptotic optimality · Integer linear programming · Randomized rounding

## 1 Introduction

The exponential growth of data-intensive applications, such as high-definition video streaming, augmented reality, and autonomous driving, has placed unprecedented strain on core network infrastructures [1,9]. Edge Caching has emerged as a pivotal paradigm to alleviate this congestion by storing popular content at the network edge, thereby reducing backhaul traffic and system latency [16,18,23]. Unlike traditional content delivery networks, edge servers

This work was supported in part by the National Natural Science Foundation of China under Grant Nos. U22A2025 and 62402450, and the Zhejiang Provincial Natural Science Foundation of China under Grant No. LQ24F020024.


Y. Li et al. (Eds.): COCOON 2026, LNCS 16835, pp. 120–133, 2027.
https://doi.org/10.1007/978-981-92-3309-0_10

are characterized by limited storage capacities and highly localized request patterns [15,17].

To maximize the utility of these constrained resources, collaborative caching allows neighboring edge servers to share their cached content via low-latency side-links [19]. While collaboration significantly expands the virtual storage available to each user, it introduces complex decision dependencies. Mathematically, this optimization is notoriously difficult. The objective function is typically non-convex and discontinuous, as the latency "jumps" between local, neighbor, and cloud tiers. Furthermore, the logic governing neighborhood access, which is characterized by existential quantifiers, cannot be directly handled by standard optimization solvers.

Existing works often addresses these challenges through swarm intelligence [6], reinforcement learning [23], or game theory [4]. However, these approaches have distinct limitations: swarm intelligence lacks theoretical optimality guarantees, reinforcement learning suffers from state-space explosion, and game-theoretic models often incur prohibitive computational complexity for Nash equilibrium convergence. Approximation algorithms [8,13] offer a promising alternative, yet most existing works rely on simplified assumptions or yield loose constant-factor ratios that fail to characterize the behavior of large-scale systems.

In this paper, we address these gaps by providing a comprehensive theoretical and algorithmic framework. We reformulate the problem into an Integer Linear Programming (ILP) problem and derive tight approximation bounds based on the concentration of measure.

Our contributions are summarized as follows:

- We formalize the collaborative edge caching problem (**P0**) and identify three critical structural barriers: non-linearizable existential constraints, decision coupling, and non-convexity. We rigorously prove the NP-hardness of **P0**.
- We propose a systematic transformation of **P0** into an equivalent ILP (**P1**). Using auxiliary variables and McCormick envelopes, we eliminate discontinuities, enabling the application of global optimization techniques.
- We develop an exact Branch and Bound (BnB) algorithm with $\mathcal{O}(2^{NK} \cdot (NK)^{3.5})$ complexity for optimal benchmarking, and a polynomial-time randomized approximation algorithm with $\mathcal{O}((NK)^{3.5})$ complexity for large-scale deployments.
- The core theoretical contribution is the proof that our approximation algorithm is asymptotically optimal. By deriving a bound of $1 + \mathcal{O}(\sqrt{s_{\max}/S_{\min}})$ via concentration inequalities, we show that the rounding gap vanishes as minimum server capacity $S_{\min}$ grows relative to maximum content size $s_{\max}$.

## 2 Related Work

Methods for developing edge caching strategies can be classified into four main categories: swarm intelligence, reinforcement learning (RL), game theory, and approximation algorithms.

Yuan *et al.*. [21] utilized particle swarm optimization to minimize long-term average latency, while Jiang *et al.*. [6] optimized cooperative caching using a bat algorithm. For RL, Yang *et al.*. [20] and Zhou *et al.*. [22] proposed Dueling Double Deep Q-Networks and federated DRL, respectively. While effective for dynamic scenarios, these methods are often "black-box" in nature and lack the provable performance guarantees required for mission-critical theoretical analysis. Fan *et al.*. [4] presented a method based on contract theory and Stackelberg games to solve storage allocation. While game theory effectively models competition, the computational cost of reaching equilibrium often scales poorly with the number of content items and nodes.

Approximation algorithms provides the most rigorous performance bounds. Ricardo *et al.*. [13] proposed a 2-approximation algorithm for small cell networks, while Kwak *et al.*. [8] utilized submodular properties to achieve a ratio of $\frac{e}{e-1}$ for file caching. In multi-tier edge networks, He *et al.*. [5] established an online caching strategy with a ratio determined by hop counts and transmission overheads. Other researchers have identified topology-dependent bounds; for instance, Jin *et al.*. [7] derived a ratio of $\ln(\Theta_{limit}+1)$, where $\Theta_{limit}$ is the maximum number of neighbors within the hop limit, and Luo *et al.*. [10] achieved a $\ln N$ factor for encoded data retrieval. Furthermore, Chen *et al.*. [3] extended this to online competitive analysis, deriving a ratio based on the balance of switching and communication costs.

While these studies provide valuable worst-case guarantees through constant or logarithmic approximation ratios, such bounds are often static and do not capture the performance gains inherent in large-scale system parameters. In contrast, our work establishes an asymptotically optimal bound of $1+\mathcal{O}(\sqrt{s_{\max}/S_{\min}})$. This indicates that while we maintain a robust constant-factor guarantee in the worst case, the actual performance gap vanishes as the server capacity scales relative to content size. This refined analysis provides a more optimistic and precise characterization of algorithm performance in modern high-capacity edge environments compared to traditional fixed-ratio bounds.

## 3 Preliminaries

As illustrated in Fig. 1, the considered edge-cloud system comprises a cloud server, $N$ edge servers, $M$ end devices, and a collaborative management unit. The cloud server maintains a repository of $K$ distinct content types, denoted by $\mathcal{O}=\{o_1,\ldots,o_K\}$, where each content $o_k$ has a specific storage size $s_k$. Each edge server $e_j$ ($j\in\{1,\ldots,N\}$) possesses an independent storage capacity $S_j$ to cache a subset of the repository. The cloud server is connected to all edge servers via high-capacity fiber links, while edge servers are interconnected through wireless communication channels. End devices are geographically distributed within the coverage of their respective base stations, maintaining cellular connectivity for content retrieval. At the beginning of each decision epoch, the collaborative unit collects request patterns from all edge servers and executes the caching algorithm to determine the optimal placement matrix $\mathbf{Z}$.

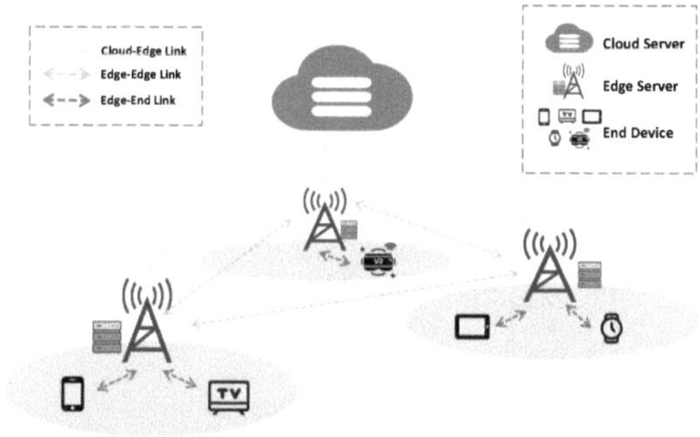


**Fig. 1.** Illustration of edge caching architecture.

### 3.1 Content Caching and Latency Models

The caching state of edge server $e_j$ is represented by a binary vector $\mathbf{z}_j = [z_{j,1}, \ldots, z_{j,K}]$, where $z_{j,k} \in \{0,1\}$ indicates whether content $o_k$ is locally cached. The global caching state is denoted by the matrix $\mathbf{Z} = \begin{bmatrix} \mathbf{z}_1 \\ \vdots \\ \mathbf{z}_N \end{bmatrix} \in \{0,1\}^{N \times K}$. The retrieval of content $o_k$ by a device associated with $e_j$ incurs a latency $t_{j,k}$ composed of three possible components: backhaul delay ($t_{c2e}$), collaborative (edge-to-edge) delay ($t_{e2e}$), and delivery (edge-to-device) delay ($t_{e2d}$). Based on the Shannon-Hartley theorem, the transmission rates are modeled as:

$$R_{e2e} = B\log_2\left(1 + \frac{P \cdot g_{e2e}}{\theta^2}\right), \quad R_{e2d} = B\log_2\left(1 + \frac{P \cdot g_{e2d}}{\theta^2 + I}\right), \tag{1}$$

where $P$ is the transmission power, $g_{e2e}$ and $g_{e2d}$ respectively represents the channel gains between edge and edge, and edge and end, $\theta^2$ is the noise power, and $I = (M-1)P \cdot g_{e2d}$ denotes the intra-cell interference. The corresponding delays are $t_{e2e} = s_k/R_{e2e}$ and $t_{e2d} = s_k/R_{e2d}$.

The total latency for an end device associated with edge server $e_j$ to retrieve content $o_k$ is modeled as:

$$t_{j,k} = t_{e2d} + \begin{cases} 0 & \text{if } z_{j,k} = 1, \\ t_{e2e} & \text{if } z_{j,k} = 0 \text{ and } \exists l, z_{l,k} = 1, \\ t_{c2e} & \text{otherwise.} \end{cases} \tag{2}$$

Note that Eq. (2) introduces non-linearity due to the logical dependencies between caching decisions.

### 3.2 Problem Formulation

The total network latency $L$ is the weighted sum of retrieval delays: $L(\mathbf{Z}) = \sum_j \sum_k p_{j,k} t_{j,k}$, where $p_{j,k}$ is the request frequency.

Our objective is to minimize $L(\mathbf{Z})$ subject to storage constraints:

$$\mathbf{P0}: \quad \min_{\mathbf{Z}} \quad \sum_{j=1}^{N}\sum_{k=1}^{K} p_{j,k} t_{j,k} \tag{3}$$

$$\text{s.t.} \quad \sum_{k=1}^{K} z_{j,k} s_k \le S_j, \quad \forall j \in 1, \ldots, N, \tag{4}$$

$$t_{c2e} \gg t_{e2e}, \tag{5}$$

$$z_{j,k} \in \{0,1\}, \quad \forall j, k. \tag{6}$$

The decision variables $z_{j,k}$ in Eq. (6) are binary-valued, the objective function in Eq. (3) is a nonlinear function of these decision variables, and Eq. (4) represents a knapsack-type constraint. Equation (5) ensures that the delay of obtaining resources from the cloud server will be much greater than the interaction delay between the edge servers. Problem **P0** is an Integer Nonlinear Programming (INLP) problem. Minimizing total latency inherently maximizes the cache hit rate, as local and collaborative hits significantly reduce retrieval time compared to cloud fetching.

### 3.3 Problem Hardness

To establish a theoretical foundation for algorithm design and justify the necessity of a sophisticated solution framework, we first analyze the computational complexity and structural characteristics of problem **P0**.

**Theorem 1.** *Problem* **P0** *is NP-Hard.*

*Proof.* We establish the NP-hardness of **P0** by performing a polynomial-time reduction from the Multiple Knapsack Problem (MKP), a well-known NP-hard combinatorial optimization problem [11]. Due to space limitations, the detailed reduction and proof are omitted.

Beyond its NP-hardness, **P0** exhibits distinctive structural irregularities that impede the direct application of standard optimization solvers. These properties are summarized as follows:

**Theorem 2.** *The optimization problem* **P0** *possesses three critical structural barriers: (a) non-linearizable logical dependencies arising from neighborhood access; (b) complex coupling of decision variables across the edge network; and (c) a non-convex, discontinuous objective landscape.*

*Proof.* **(a) Non-linearizable existential constraints.** The term $\exists l : z_{lk} = 1$ encodes a logical OR over binary variables. A linear representation $a^\top z + c$ cannot capture the discontinuous jumps of existential logic: for a two-server example, matching three points forces a prediction for $(1, 1)$ that contradicts the physical OR outcome. Hence, no single hyperplane suffices.

**(b) Decision variable coupling.** The latency at server $e_j$ depends on caching states $\mathbf{z}_l$ of its neighbors. In a fully connected cluster of $N$ servers, the joint decision space for a single content $o_k$ grows as $\mathcal{O}(2^N)$, preventing per-server decomposition.

**(c) Non-convexity.** The objective $L$ is defined on a discrete domain; its continuous relaxation inherits step changes from the "if-else" structure. As shown in (a), the gradient is zero almost everywhere and the Hessian is undefined at transition boundaries, confirming non-convexity. □

# 4 Solution

To overcome the inherent computational intractability of problem **P0**, we propose a hierarchical solution framework. We first reformulate the non-linear objective and existential constraints into a tractable ILP problem. Building upon this, we develop a dual-algorithm strategy: an exact BnB algorithm to provide optimal benchmarks for moderate-scale networks, and a randomized rounding-based approximation algorithm to ensure scalability for large-scale deployments with provable performance guarantees.

## 4.1 Problem Reformulation

The structural complexity of **P0** stems from the non-linear coupling of decision variables and the discontinuous nature of neighborhood-aware caching. We transform **P0** into an equivalent ILP model, denoted as **P1**, by employing logical linearization and McCormick envelopes.

We introduce an auxiliary binary variable $x_{j,k} \in \{0,1\}$ to represent the state of the neighborhood cache. Let $x_{j,k} = 1$ if content $o_k$ is available in at least one neighboring server $l \in \mathcal{N}(j)$. This logic is enforced by the following linear inequalities:

$$\begin{cases} x_{j,k} \geq z_{l,k} & \forall l \in \mathcal{N}(j) \\ x_{j,k} \leq \sum_{l \in \mathcal{N}(j)} z_{l,k}. \end{cases} \tag{7}$$

The latency $t_{j,k}$ involves the product of $(1 - z_{j,k})$ and $(1 - x_{j,k})$. We define a second auxiliary variable $y_{j,k} = (1 - z_{j,k})(1 - x_{j,k})$. For $z_{j,k}, x_{j,k} \in \{0,1\}$, this product is exactly linearized using McCormick envelopes:

$$\begin{cases} y_{j,k} \leq 1 - z_{j,k} \\ y_{j,k} \leq 1 - x_{j,k} \\ y_{j,k} \geq 1 - z_{j,k} - x_{j,k}, \end{cases} \tag{8}$$

here, $y_{j,k} = 1$ if and only if the content is neither in the local cache nor in the neighbor's cache, forcing a cloud access.

Using these variables, the expected latency $t_{j,k}$ in Eq. (2) can be rewritten as a linear combination:

$$t_{j,k} = t_{e2d} + (1 - z_{j,k})t_{e2e} + y_{j,k}(t_{c2e} - t_{e2e}). \tag{9}$$

Let $\mathbf{X} = \{x_{j,k}\}_{N \times K}$ and $\mathbf{Y} = \{y_{j,k}\}_{N \times K}$ denote the auxiliary decision matrices for neighborhood states and joint cache misses, respectively. By integrating these variables, the reformulated problem **P1** is expressed as follows:

$$\mathbf{P1}: \min_{\mathbf{Z},\mathbf{X},\mathbf{Y}} \sum_{j=1}^{N}\sum_{k=1}^{K} p_{j,k} t_{j,k} \tag{10}$$

$$\text{Eqs. } (4), (5), (7), (8), \tag{11}$$

$$z_{j,k}, x_{j,k}, y_{j,k} \in \{0,1\}, \quad \forall j, k. \tag{12}$$

**Theorem 3.** *The reformulated problem* **P1** *is equivalent to the original problem* **P0** *over the discrete domain* $\mathbf{Z} \in \{0,1\}^{N \times K}$.

*Proof.* For any $(j, k)$, if $z_{j,k} = 1$, then $y_{j,k} = 0$ and $t_{j,k} = t_{e2d}$. If $z_{j,k} = 0$ and $x_{j,k} = 1$, then $y_{j,k} = 0$ and $t_{j,k} = t_{e2d} + t_{e2e}$. If $z_{j,k} = 0$ and $x_{j,k} = 0$, then $y_{j,k} = 1$ and $t_{j,k} = t_{e2d} + t_{c2e}$. This mapping covers all cases in Eq. (2) identically. □

**Reformulation Problem Analysis:** Although **P1** remains NP-hard due to its binary constraints, this reformulation significantly enhances tractability. By transforming **P0** into a standard ILP model, we eliminate logical discontinuities and non-convexities, enabling the use of powerful Branch-and-Cut solvers. Furthermore, the McCormick envelopes provide a tight convex relaxation that facilitates efficient pruning of the search space, while the introduction of auxiliary variables $x_{j,k}$ decouples cross-server dependencies, allowing for global optimality guarantees and potential parallelization via decomposition techniques.

### 4.2 Algorithmic Framework

To address the NP-hard Problem **P1**, we develop a dual-strategy approach: an exact BnB algorithm for moderate-scale instances and a randomized approximation algorithm for large-scale deployments. Both algorithms exploit the convexified structure of **P1** after McCormick reformulation, enabling efficient combinatorial optimization despite the original problem's nonlinearity.

**Exact Solution via Branch and Bound:** The pseudocode of BnB-based exact algorithm is shown in Algorithm 1. Line 1 initializes global upper bound $UB \leftarrow \infty$, the incumbent solution $\mathbf{Z}^* \leftarrow \emptyset$, and a priority queue $Q$ where nodes are ordered in ascending order of their evaluated LP lower bounds ($LB$). Line 2 generates the root node $\mathcal{P}_0$ by relaxing the integrality constraints of Problem **P1**. Line 3 solves the LP relaxation of $\mathcal{P}_0$ to obtain its initial lower bound $LB_0$ and fractional solution $\tilde{\mathbf{Z}}_0$, and Line 4 pushes the evaluated root node into $Q$. While $Q$ is non-empty, Line 6 extracts the subproblem $\mathcal{P}_{\text{curr}}$ that currently holds the minimum $LB$ in the queue. If $LB \geq UB$, Line 8 prunes the current subtree and proceeds to the next subproblem. If $\tilde{\mathbf{Z}}$ is purely integer and $LB < UB$, Line 11 updates $UB \leftarrow LB$ and $\mathbf{Z}^* \leftarrow \tilde{\mathbf{Z}}$. Otherwise, Line 14 selects the branching variable $z_{j,k}$ whose fractional value is closest to 0.5 to balance subtree exploration. Lines 1516 partition the space into child subproblems $\mathcal{P}_{\text{left}}$ and $\mathcal{P}_{\text{right}}$ by fixing $z_{j,k} = 0$ and $z_{j,k} = 1$, respectively, and immediately solve their corresponding LP relaxations to determine their lower bounds. Line 17 inserts these newly evaluated subproblems back into $Q$ to repeat the process. Line 20 returns the optimal solution $\mathbf{Z}^*$ when the queue is exhausted.

**Algorithm 1:** BnB-based Algorithm

**Input**: Content sizes $s_k$, storage capacities $S_j$, request frequency $p_{j,k}$, and transmission delays $\{t_{e2e}, t_{c2e}\}$.

**Output**: Optimal caching matrix $\mathbf{Z}^*$.

1 Initialize $UB \leftarrow \infty$, $\mathbf{Z}^* \leftarrow \emptyset$, $Q \leftarrow$ PriorityQueue();<br>
2 $\mathcal{P}_0 \leftarrow$ LP relaxation of **P1** without integrality constraints;<br>
3 Solve $\mathcal{P}_0$'s LP relaxation via interior-point method $\rightarrow (\tilde{\mathbf{Z}}_0, LB_0)$;<br>
4 $Q$.push($(\mathcal{P}_0, \tilde{\mathbf{Z}}_0, LB_0)$);<br>
5 **while** $Q \neq \emptyset$ **do**<br>
6     $(\mathcal{P}_{\text{curr}}, \tilde{\mathbf{Z}}, LB) \leftarrow Q$.pop();<br>
7     **if** $LB \geq UB$ **then**<br>
8         **continue**;<br>
9     **end**<br>
10     **if** $\tilde{\mathbf{Z}}$ *is integer* **then**<br>
11         $UB \leftarrow LB$; $\mathbf{Z}^* \leftarrow \tilde{\mathbf{Z}}$;<br>
12     **end**<br>
13     **else**<br>
14         $\{j^*, k^*\} \leftarrow \arg\min_{j,k} |\tilde{z}_{j,k} - 0.5|$;<br>
15         $\mathcal{P}_{\text{left}} \leftarrow \mathcal{P}_{\text{curr}}$ with $z_{j^*,k^*} = 0$; Solve $\mathcal{P}_{\text{left}}$'s LP $\rightarrow (\tilde{\mathbf{Z}}_{\text{left}}, LB_{\text{left}})$;<br>
16         $\mathcal{P}_{\text{right}} \leftarrow \mathcal{P}_{\text{curr}}$ with $z_{j^*,k^*} = 1$; Solve $\mathcal{P}_{\text{right}}$'s LP $\rightarrow (\tilde{\mathbf{Z}}_{\text{right}}, LB_{\text{right}})$;<br>
17         $Q$.push($(\mathcal{P}_{\text{left}}, \tilde{\mathbf{Z}}_{\text{left}}, LB_{\text{left}})$); $Q$.push($(\mathcal{P}_{\text{right}}, \tilde{\mathbf{Z}}_{\text{right}}, LB_{\text{right}})$);<br>
18     **end**<br>
19 **end**<br>
20 **return** $\mathbf{Z}^*$

**Time Complexity of BnB-Based Algorithm:** Explores up to $\mathcal{O}(2^{NK})$ nodes in worst case; each node solves an LP with $\mathcal{O}(NK)$ variables and constraints via interior-point method in $\mathcal{O}((NK)^{3.5})$. Total: $\mathcal{O}(2^{NK} \cdot (NK)^{3.5})$.

For large-scale instances where the BnB algorithm becomes prohibitive due to its worst-case exponential time complexity, we propose a randomized rounding-based approximation algorithm that achieves a near-optimal approximation guarantee in polynomial time.

**Randomized Approximate Algorithm via LP Rounding:** The core insight is to relax **P1**'s integrality constraints, solve the resulting LP, and apply randomized rounding with capacity repair. Specifically, the LP relaxation allows variables $z_{j,k}, x_{j,k}, y_{j,k} \in [0, 1]$, after obtaining the fractional solution, we independently round $z_{j,k}$ and $x_{j,k}$ to integers while ensuring $y_{j,k} = (1-z_{j,k})(1-x_{j,k})$ satisfies McCormick envelopes. Capacity violations are resolved via greedy removal based on marginal utility density $\delta_{j,k}$. The pseudocode of approximate algorithm is shown in Algorithm 2. Line 1 solves the convex LP relaxation of **P1** to obtain $\tilde{z}_{j,k}$, $\tilde{x}_{j,k}$ for all $j$, $k$. Lines 2–4 perform independent randomized rounding by setting $z_{j,k} \leftarrow 1$ with probability $\tilde{z}_{j,k}$, otherwise 0, preserving $\mathbb{E}[z_{j,k}] = \tilde{z}_{j,k}$. This step may violate capacity constraints. Lines 5–16 repair capacity violations: for each server $e_j$ violating its storage constraint, we define the marginal utility density $\delta_{j,k}$ as the latency penalty per unit of storage incurred by removing content $o_k$. Specifically, $\delta_{j,k} = \frac{p_{j,k}}{s_k}(t_{j,k}^{miss})$, where $t_{j,k}^{miss}$ is the retrieval latency from the nearest available source (either a cooperative neighbor or the cloud) given the current caching state of other servers. We iteratively evict the item with the minimum $\delta_{j,k}$ until the capacity constraint $S_j$ is restored.

---

**Algorithm 2:** LP Rounding-based Approximation Algorithm

---

**Input**: Content sizes $s_k$, storage capacities $S_j$, request frequency $p_{j,k}$, and transmission delays $\{t_{e2e}, t_{c2e}\}$.

**Output**: Approximate caching matrix $\hat{\mathbf{Z}}$.

`// Phase 1: Solve LP Relaxation`

1 Solve the LP relaxation of **P1** by relaxing $z_{j,k}, x_{j,k}, y_{j,k} \in \{0, 1\}$ to the interval $[0, 1]$ using an interior-point method to obtain $(\tilde{z}_{j,k}, \tilde{x}_{j,k})$;

`// Phase 2: Randomized Rounding`

2 **for** $j = 1$ **to** $N$ ***and*** $k = 1$ **to** $K$ **do**
3     Sample binary decision: $z_{j,k} \leftarrow \text{Bernoulli}(\tilde{z}_{j,k})$;
4 **end**

`// Phase 3: Capacity Repair and State Synchronization`

5 **for** $j = 1$ **to** $N$ **do**
6     Update $x_{j,k} \leftarrow \max_{i \in \mathcal{N}(j)} z_{i,k}, \quad \forall k$;
7     **while** $\sum_k z_{j,k} s_k > S_j$ **do**
8         **for** *each item* $k$ *such that* $z_{j,k} = 1$ **do**
9             $t_{miss} \leftarrow x_{j,k} \cdot t_{e2e} + (1 - x_{j,k}) \cdot t_{c2e}$;
10             $\delta_{j,k} \leftarrow \frac{p_{j,k} \cdot t_{miss}}{s_k}$;
11         **end**
12         $k^* \leftarrow \arg\min_{k: z_{j,k}=1} \delta_{j,k}$;
13         $z_{j,k^*} \leftarrow 0$;
14         Update neighbor states $x_{i,k^*}$ for all $i \in \mathcal{N}(j)$;
15     **end**
16 **end**
17 **return** $\hat{\mathbf{Z}} = [z_{j,k}]_{N \times K}$;

---

**Time Complexity of Approximate Algorithm**: Dominated by solving one LP relaxation in $\mathcal{O}((NK)^{3.5})$; rounding and repair steps each take $\mathcal{O}(NK)$. Overall: $\mathcal{O}((NK)^{3.5})$.

### 4.3 Approximation Analysis

**Theorem 4 (2-Approximation Guarantee).** *Algorithm 2 achieves an approximation ratio of 2 in expectation. That is,*

$$\mathbb{E}[L_{final}] \leq 2 \cdot \mathrm{OPT} \tag{13}$$

*where* $\mathbb{E}[L_{final}]$ *is the expected total latency of the solution produced by the algorithm and OPT is the optimal latency of problem* **P0**.

*Proof.* Let $L_{\text{round}}$ denote the latency cost of the solution immediately after the randomized rounding phase, and let $\Delta_j$ represent the additional latency penalty incurred by server $e_j$ during the capacity repair phase. The final latency cost $L_{\text{final}}$ can be expressed as:

$$L_{\text{final}} = L_{\text{round}} + \sum_{j=1}^{N} \Delta_j. \tag{14}$$

The penalty $\Delta_j$ is non-zero only if the capacity constraint of server $e_j$ is violated after rounding:

$$\Delta_j = \begin{cases} \text{Latency increase from greedy removal,} & \text{if } W_j > S_j, \\ 0, & \text{otherwise,} \end{cases} \tag{15}$$

where $W_j = \sum_k z_{j,k} s_k$ is the total storage load of server $e_j$ post-rounding. Taking the expectation of Eq. (14), we have:

$$\mathbb{E}[L_{\text{final}}] = \mathbb{E}[L_{\text{round}}] + \sum_{j=1}^{N} \mathbb{E}[\Delta_j]. \tag{16}$$

By the property of randomized rounding, where $\mathbb{E}[z_{j,k}] = \tilde{z}_{j,k}$, the expected latency of the rounded solution (which ignores capacity constraints) is equal to the LP optimal value:

$$\mathbb{E}[L_{\text{round}}] = \mathrm{LP} \leq \mathrm{OPT}. \tag{17}$$

Next, we bound the expected repair penalty $\mathbb{E}[\Delta_j]$. Using the law of total expectation and the fact that $\Delta_j = 0$ for $W_j \leq S_j$:

$$\mathbb{E}[\Delta_j] = \mathbb{E}[\Delta_j \mid W_j > S_j] \cdot P(W_j > S_j). \tag{18}$$

During the repair phase, the algorithm greedily removes items with the minimum utility density $\delta_{j,k}$. Consequently, the average latency penalty per unit of reclaimed storage does not exceed the average utility density of the items assigned to server $e_j$ in the LP solution. Let $\text{Reduction}_j$ be the contribution of server $e_j$ to the total latency reduction in the LP optimal. When $W_j > S_j$, the removal cost satisfies:

$$\Delta_j \le \left(\frac{W_j - S_j}{S_j}\right)\text{Reduction}_j = \frac{R_j}{S_j}\text{Reduction}_j. \tag{19}$$

The conditional expectation of the penalty can thus be bounded as:

$$\mathbb{E}[\Delta_j \mid W_j > S_j] \le \frac{\text{Reduction}_j}{S_j}\mathbb{E}[R_j \mid W_j > S_j]. \tag{20}$$

Using the fundamental property of expectations, $\mathbb{E}[W_j] \ge \mathbb{E}[W_j \mid W_j > S_j]P(W_j > S_j)$, and since $R_j < W_j$, we obtain the following key inequality:

$$\mathbb{E}[R_j \mid W_j > S_j] \le \mathbb{E}[W_j \mid W_j > S_j] \le \frac{\mathbb{E}[W_j]}{P(W_j > S_j)}. \tag{21}$$

Substituting Eq. (21) into Eq. (18), the probability $P(W_j > S_j)$ cancels out:

$$\mathbb{E}[\Delta_j] \le \frac{\text{Reduction}_j}{S_j}\mathbb{E}[W_j]. \tag{22}$$

Since $\mathbb{E}[W_j] = \sum_k \tilde{z}_{j,k}s_k$ and the LP relaxation satisfies the storage constraint $\sum_k \tilde{z}_{j,k}s_k \le S_j$, it follows that:

$$\mathbb{E}[\Delta_j] \le \frac{\text{Reduction}_j}{S_j} \cdot S_j = \text{Reduction}_j. \tag{23}$$

By summing over all servers, $\sum_j \mathbb{E}[\Delta_j] \le \sum_j \text{Reduction}_j \le \sum_j (t_{c2e} - \text{Reduction}_j) = \text{LP}$, where the last inequality holds due to $t_{c2e} \gg t_{e2e}$. Finally, substituting this into Eq. (16):

$$\mathbb{E}[L_{\text{final}}] \le \text{LP} + \text{LP} = 2 \cdot \text{LP} \le 2 \cdot \text{OPT}. \tag{24}$$

The proof is thus complete. □

While the 2-approximation ratio established in Theorem 4 provide a robust worst-case guarantee, the inequality $\mathbb{E}[R_j \mid W_j > S_j] \le \mathbb{E}[W_j \mid W_j > S_j]$ is inherently conservative. In practice, $R_j = W_j - S_j$ is typically an order of magnitude smaller than $W_j$. By directly bounding the expected excess storage $\mathbb{E}[(W_j - S_j)^+]$, we derive a tighter approximation bound that converges to 1 as the ratio of maximum content size $s_{\max}$ to minimum server capacity $S_{\min}$ decreases.

**Theorem 5 (Asymptotic Optimality).** *The expected total latency of Algorithm 2 satisfies:*

$$\mathbb{E}[L_{\text{final}}] \le \left(1 + \mathcal{O}\sqrt{\frac{s_{\max}}{S_{\min}}}\right) \cdot \text{OPT}. \tag{25}$$

*Proof.* We refine the bound on the expected removal penalty $\mathbb{E}[\Delta_j]$. Combining Eq. (18) and Eq. (19), we have:

$$\mathbb{E}[\Delta_j] \leq \mathbb{E}\left[\frac{(W_j - S_j)^+}{S_j}\text{Reduction}_j\right] = \frac{\text{Reduction}_j}{S_j}\mathbb{E}[(W_j - S_j)^+]. \tag{26}$$

Let $X_j = W_j/S_j$ be the normalized storage load. Given the LP constraints, we have $\mathbb{E}[X_j] = \frac{1}{S_j}\sum_k \tilde{z}_{j,k}s_k \leq 1$. To bound the expected violation $\mathbb{E}[(X_j-1)^+]$, we treat $X_j$ as a sum of independent Bernoulli-weighted variables: $X_j = \sum_k a_{j,k}z_{j,k}$, where $a_{j,k} = s_k/S_j \in [0, a_{\max}]$ and $a_{\max} = s_{\max}/S_j$. We bound the expected violation $\mathbb{E}[(X_j - 1)^+]$ by considering the concentration properties of $X_j$. Since $\mathbb{E}[X_j] \leq 1$, we have:

$$\mathbb{E}[(X_j - 1)^+] \leq \mathbb{E}[(X_j - \mathbb{E}[X_j])^+] \leq \mathbb{E}[|X_j - \mathbb{E}[X_j]|]. \tag{27}$$

By applying Jensen's Inequality [14] to the concave function $\sqrt{\cdot}$, we obtain:

$$\mathbb{E}[|X_j - \mathbb{E}[X_j]|] \leq \sqrt{\mathbb{E}[(X_j - \mathbb{E}[X_j])^2]} = \sqrt{\text{Var}(X_j)}. \tag{28}$$

Alternatively, following the Bernstein-type concentration [2] for sums of independent bounded variables, there exists a constant $c \in (0, 1]$ such that [12]:

$$\mathbb{E}[(X_j - 1)^+] \leq c\sqrt{\text{Var}(X_j)}. \tag{29}$$

The variance of $X_j$ is computed as:

$$\begin{aligned}\text{Var}[X_j] &= \sum_k a_{j,k}^2 \text{Var}[z_{j,k}] = \sum_k a_{j,k}^2 \tilde{z}_{j,k}(1 - \tilde{z}_{j,k}) \\ &\leq a_{\max}\sum_k a_{j,k}\tilde{z}_{j,k} = a_{\max}\mathbb{E}[X_j] \leq a_{\max},\end{aligned} \tag{30}$$

where the second equality holds because the $z_{j,k}$ are independent Bernoulli random variables (taking values 0 or 1 with probability $P(z_{j,k} = 1) = \tilde{z}_{j,k}$), the inequality follows from $0 \leq (1 - \tilde{z}_{j,k}) \leq 1$ and $a_{j,k} \leq a_{\max}$. Thus, we obtain:

$$\mathbb{E}[(X_j - 1)^+] \leq c\sqrt{a_{\max}} = c\sqrt{\frac{s_{\max}}{S_j}}. \tag{31}$$

Consequently, the expected marginal penalty for server $j$ is bounded by:

$$\mathbb{E}[\Delta_j] \leq \frac{\text{Reduction}_j}{S_j} \cdot S_j c\sqrt{\frac{s_{\max}}{S_j}} = \text{Reduction}_j c\sqrt{\frac{s_{\max}}{S_j}}. \tag{32}$$

Summing over all $N$ servers and letting $S_{\min} = \min_j S_j$:

$$\sum_j \mathbb{E}[\Delta_j] \leq c\sqrt{\frac{s_{\max}}{S_{\min}}}\sum_j \text{Reduction}_j \leq c\sqrt{\frac{s_{\max}}{S_{\min}}} \cdot \text{LP}. \tag{33}$$

Finally, combining this with $\mathbb{E}[L_{\text{round}}] = \text{LP} \leq \text{OPT}$:

$$\mathbb{E}[L_{\text{final}}] \leq \left(1 + c\sqrt{\frac{s_{\max}}{S_{\min}}}\right) \cdot \text{OPT}. \tag{34}$$

This confirms that the approximation gap vanishes as $s_{\max}/S_{\min} \to 0$. □

Theorem 5 shows that the approximation ratio approaches 1 when $s_{\max} \ll S_{\min}$, explaining the algorithm's excellent practical performance in a real environment.

## 5 Conclusion

This paper presented a comprehensive study on collaborative edge caching, progressing from NP-hard formalization to a provably asymptotically optimal solution framework. By leveraging McCormick linearization, we successfully transformed the non-linear objective into an Integer Linear Programming problem. Our dual-algorithm approach ensures that while global optima can be found for smaller networks, the randomized rounding scheme provides a scalable and near-optimal solution for large-scale systems. The refined theoretical bound established in this work, $1 + \mathcal{O}(\sqrt{s_{\max}/S_{\min}})$, shifts the focus from static approximation ratios to parameter-dependent convergence analysis. This asymptotic optimality suggests that in modern high-capacity edge environments, the proposed rounding mechanism offers a practical yet theoretically sound alternative to exhaustive search.

## References

1. Abbas, N., Zhang, Y., Taherkordi, A., Skeie, T.: Mobile edge computing: a survey. IEEE Internet Things J. **5**(1), 450–465 (2018)
2. Boucheron, S., Lugosi, G., Massart, P.: Concentration Inequalities: A Nonasymptotic Theory of Independence. Oxford University Press, Oxford (2013)
3. Chen, C., Herrera, M., Zheng, G., Xia, L., Ling, Z., Wang, J.: Cross-edge orchestration of serverless functions with probabilistic caching. IEEE Trans. Serv. Comput. **17**(5), 2139–2150 (2024)
4. Fan, Y., Zhang, Z., Hu, Z., Wu, W., Du, D.: Contract theory and Stackelberg-game-based storage resource allocation in edge caching systems. IEEE Internet Things J. **11**(19), 32284–32295 (2024)
5. He, X., et al.: Online caching with delayed hits in multi-server edge networks. IEEE Trans. Mob. Comput. 1–16 (2026) (Early Access). https://doi.org/10.1109/TMC.2025.3650474
6. Jiang, H., Cai, J., Xiao, Z., Yang, K., Chen, H., Liu, J.: Vehicle-assisted service caching for task offloading in vehicular edge computing. IEEE Trans. Mob. Comput. **24**(7), 6688–6700 (2025)
7. Jin, H., Luo, R., He, Q., Wu, S., Zeng, Z., Xia, X.: Cost-effective data placement in edge storage systems with erasure code. IEEE Trans. Serv. Comput. **16**(2), 1039–1050 (2023)

8. Kwak, J., Le, L.B., Kim, H., Wang, X.: Two time-scale edge caching and BS association for power-delay tradeoff in multi-cell networks. IEEE Trans. Commun. **67**(8), 5506–5519 (2019)
9. Li, Y., Wang, X., Gan, X., Jin, H., Fu, L., Wang, X.: Learning-aided computation offloading for trusted collaborative mobile edge computing. IEEE Trans. Mob. Comput. **19**(12), 2833–2849 (2020)
10. Luo, R., et al.: Popularity-aware data placement in erasure coding-based edge storage systems. IEEE Trans. Parallel Distrib. Syst. **36**(12), 2733–2746 (2025)
11. Martello, S., Toth, P.: Knapsack Problems: Algorithms and Computer Implementations. Wiley, Chichester, UK (1990)
12. Mitzenmacher, M., Upfal, E.: Probability and Computing: Randomized Algorithms and Probabilistic Analysis. Cambridge University Press, Cambridge (2005)
13. Ricardo, G.I., Tuholukova, A., Neglia, G., Spyropoulos, T.: Caching policies for delay minimization in small cell networks with coordinated multi-point joint transmissions. IEEE/ACM Trans. Network. **29**(3), 1105–1115 (2021)
14. Rudin, W.: Real and Complex Analysis, 3rd edn. McGraw-Hill, New York (1987)
15. Su, Z., Hui, Y., Xu, Q., Yang, T., Liu, J., Jia, Y.: An edge caching scheme to distribute content in vehicular networks. IEEE Trans. Veh. Technol. **67**(6), 5346–5356 (2018)
16. Tang, M., Wong, V.W.S.: Deep reinforcement learning for task offloading in mobile edge computing systems. IEEE Trans. Mob. Comput. **21**(6), 1985–1997 (2022)
17. Wang, X., Han, Y., Wang, C., Zhao, Q., Chen, X., Chen, M.: In-edge AI: Intelligentizing mobile edge computing, caching and communication by federated learning. IEEE Netw. **33**(5), 156–165 (2019)
18. Wang, Y., et al.: A survey on metaverse: fundamentals, security, and privacy. IEEE Commun. Surv. Tutorials **25**(1), 319–352 (2023)
19. Yang, H., Xiong, Z., Zhao, J., Niyato, D., Xiao, L., Wu, Q.: Deep reinforcement learning-based intelligent reflecting surface for secure wireless communications. IEEE Trans. Wirel. Commun. **20**(1), 375–388 (2021)
20. Yang, M., et al.: Deep reinforcement learning-based joint caching and routing in AI-driven networks. IEEE Trans. Mob. Comput. **24**(3), 1322–1337 (2025)
21. Yuan, J., Xiang, Y., Deng, Y., Zhou, Y., Min, G.: UPOA: a user preference based latency and energy aware intelligent offloading approach for cloud-edge systems. IEEE Trans. Cloud Comput. **11**(2), 2188–2203 (2023)
22. Zhou, H., Wang, H., Yu, Z., Bin, G., Xiao, M., Wu, J.: Federated distributed deep reinforcement learning for recommendation-enabled edge caching. IEEE Trans. Serv. Comput. **17**(6), 3640–3656 (2024)
23. Zhou, Z., Chen, X., Li, E., Zeng, L., Luo, K., Zhang, J.: Edge intelligence: paving the last mile of artificial intelligence with edge computing. Proc. IEEE **107**(8), 1738–1762 (2019)

# Minimum Sum Set Cover: Structures and Algorithm

Zhongyi Zhang[1] and Yixin Cao[2](✉)

[1] Shandong Provincial Key Laboratory of Computing-Network Integration, School of Computer Science and Technology, Shandong University, Qingdao, China
zhangzhongyi@mail.sdu.edu.cn

[2] Department of Computing, Hong Kong Polytechnic University, Hong Kong, China
yixin.cao@polyu.edu.hk

**Abstract.** A set cover of a hypergraph $H$ is a set of vertices intersecting every hyperedge. In the minimum sum set cover problem, vertices are selected one by one; each edge pays the position of the first vertex that hits it, and the objective is to minimize the total cost. When $H$ is a graph, this is the minimum sum vertex cover problem. A solution is specified by a set cover $S$ together with an ordering of its vertices. While the classical set cover problem seeks to minimize $|S|$, the minimum sum variant favors covering many edges early and may prefer larger covers. This motivates a natural question: how large can the gap between $\overrightarrow{\tau}$ and $\tau$ be?

We prove an upper bound $\overrightarrow{\tau} \leq \tau \log_2 |E(H)|$, and show that for any $n > 0$, there exists a hypergraph $H$ on $n+3$ vertices with $\tau = 3$ and $\overrightarrow{\tau} = n$. For graphs, we obtain stronger bounds: we prove $\overrightarrow{\tau} \leq 2\tau \log_2 \tau$, improving the bound of Liu et al. [Theor. Comput. Sci., 2025], and we construct graphs with $\overrightarrow{\tau} = \Omega\left(\frac{\tau \log \tau}{\log \log \tau}\right)$, nearly matching this upper bound.

On the algorithmic side, we show that minimum sum set cover is fixed-parameter tractable on bounded-rank hypergraphs, parameterized by $\overrightarrow{\tau}$, extending the algorithm of Liu et al. for graphs.

## 1 Introduction

A *hypergraph* $H$ consists of a vertex set $V(H)$ and hyperedge set $E(H)$, where each hyperedge is a nonempty subset of $V(H)$. The *rank* $r(H)$ of a hypergraph $H$ is the maximum cardinality of any of the edges in $H$. A *set cover* of a hypergraph is a set of vertices that intersects every hyperedge.[1] A solution consists of

Supported by NSFC under grant 62372394.

All the omitted proofs can be found at the full version (arXiv:2605.21920).

[1] In the literature, a set of vertices that covers all hyperedges is typically referred to as a *hitting set*, whereas a set cover is a collection of hyperedges whose union encompasses the entire vertex set. These concepts are equivalent because a set cover of a hypergraph corresponds to a hitting set of its dual hypergraph, where the roles of vertices and edges are interchanged. We follow this established convention, as introduced by Feige et al. [3].


Y. Li et al. (Eds.): COCOON 2026, LNCS 16835, pp. 134–148, 2027.
https://doi.org/10.1007/978-981-92-3309-0_11

an ordered set cover. When the $i$th chosen vertex is processed, every previously uncovered hyperedge containing it becomes covered and contributes cost $i$. A *minimum sum set cover* of a hypergraph is a set cover associated with a permutation of its vertices that minimizes the total cost of covering all hyperedges. When the hypergraph is a graph (rank-two hypergraph), we have *vertex covers* and *minimum sum vertex covers*.

The classical set cover problem asks for a set cover of minimum cardinality. In contrast, the minimum-sum variant rewards covering many edges early. Consequently, a minimum sum set cover does not need to be minimum, or even minimal, as a set cover. For example, in the hypergraph on vertex set $\{1, \ldots, 7\}$ and the following eleven hyperedges (blue hyperedges contain vertex 2, and green ones contain vertex 3)

$$\{1, 2, 3\}, \{2, 4, 5\}, \{3, 6, 7\}, \{\{1, 2, i\}, \{1, 3, i\} \mid 4 \leq i \leq 7\}$$

the only minimum set cover is $\{2, 3\}$, while the only minimum sum set cover is $\langle 1, 2, 3 \rangle$, with cost $9 + 2 + 3 = 14$. The first vertex 1 is not needed to achieve a minimum set cover, but it covers many edges early and is therefore beneficial under the sum objective.

Another peculiarity of minimum sum set cover is that isomorphic components of a (hyper)graph does not need to be treated symmetrically by an optimal solution; see Fig. 1.

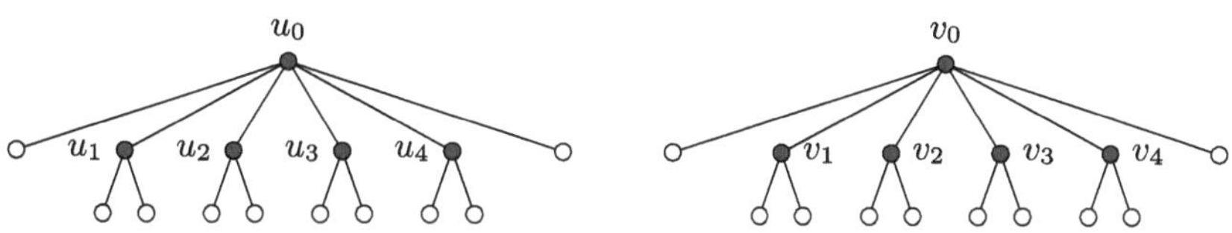


**Fig. 1.** A graph with two identical components. All minimum sum vertex covers of this graph are of the form $\langle u_0, v_1, v_2, v_3, v_4, u_1, u_2, u_3, u_4, v_0 \rangle$, with the sequence of effective coverages $\langle 6, 3, 3, 3, 3, 2, 2, 2, 2, 2 \rangle$. For the left component alone, the only optimal solution is of the form $\langle u_1, u_2, u_3, u_4, u_0 \rangle$.

Let $\tau(H)$ denote the size of a minimum (classical) set cover of $H$. Since a hypergraph may admit multiple optimal minimum sum set covers of varying sizes, we define $\overrightarrow{\tau}(H)$ to be the maximum cardinality of a set cover appearing in an optimal solution. The example above shows that $\overrightarrow{\tau}(H)$ can be strictly larger than $\tau(H)$. This raises a basic structural question: *What is the possible gap between $\overrightarrow{\tau}(H)$ and $\tau(H)$?*

This question is nontrivial even for graphs, where the ordering objective can force optimal solutions to use substantially more vertices than a minimum vertex cover. Liu et al. [5] showed that for all graphs $G$, $\overrightarrow{\tau}(G) = O(\tau(G)^{1.5})$. We significantly improve this upper bound. For hypergraphs, the upper bound has to rely on $|E(H)|$ as well.

**Theorem 1.** – *For any graph $G$ with $\tau(G) \geq 2$, it holds $\overrightarrow{\tau}(G) \leq 2\tau(G)\log_2 \tau(G)$.*
– *For any hypergraph $H$ with $\tau(H) \geq 2$, it holds $\overrightarrow{\tau}(H) < \tau(H)\log_2 |E(H)| \leq r(H)\tau(H)\log_2 |V(H)|$.*

The main observation behind the proof is that at any step, the remaining sub-hypergraph admits a set cover of size at most $\tau(H)$. Consequently, the vertex maximizing immediate coverage must remove at least a $1/\tau(H)$ fraction of the remaining edges. This implies that the number of uncovered edges decays exponentially, by a factor of $(1-1/\tau(H))$ at each step. For graphs $G$, this implies that $|E(G)| \leq \tau(G)^2$ after removing the vertices contained in every minimum vertex cover and every minimum sum vertex cover.

We show by construction that the $|E(H)|$ term for hypergraphs is inevitable. Our construction is based on encoding an $n$-vertex graph $G$ into a hypergraph $H_G$ with three "special" vertices that form the only minimum set cover, while $V(G)$ forms the only other minimal set cover. The minimum sum objective forces almost all vertices in $V(G)$ to be used before those special vertices.

**Theorem 2.** *For any integer $n \geq 3$, there exists a hypergraph $H$ such that $\tau(H) = 3$ and $\overrightarrow{\tau}(H) = n$.*

For graphs, we are only able to furnish an almost tight construction matching the upper bound in Theorem 2, leaving a gap of $\log\log\tau(G)$.

**Theorem 3.** *There are bipartite graphs $G$ such that $\overrightarrow{\tau}(G) = \Omega\left(\frac{\tau(G)\log\tau(G)}{\log\log\tau(G)}\right)$.*

For the lower bound, we use a connected bipartite graph $B_q$ inspired by the seminal construction of Johnson [4] for the degree-greedy algorithm for the vertex cover problem. We start with a matching of $2n^q$ edges on $L$ and $R_0$. The set $L$ is the only minimum vertex cover of the graph. The other side $R$ has $q$ more groups of vertices, $R_1, \ldots, R_q$, each of $n^q$ vertices. They are connected to $L$ in a way that with the removal of the last group, the graph is decomposed into $n$ components, each isomorphic to $B_{q-1}$.

We show that any minimum sum vertex cover proceeds through the graph in a highly constrained way. In particular, it starts with all the vertices in $R_q$, whose removal leaves $n$ copies of $B_{q-1}$. For each of them, we either take the vertices in the $L$ side, or the last group of it (which is a subset of $R_{q-1}$). The same pattern must repeat in the copies $B_{q-2}, \ldots, B_2$, leading to a lower bound $\overrightarrow{\tau}(B_q) = \Omega(n^{q+1})$. The claimed bound follows from these by setting $q = n$.

The approximation and complexity of the minimum sum set cover problem were initiated by Feige et al. [3], who studied approximation algorithms and hardness for the general problem. Their reduction implies that it is NP-hard to compute $\overrightarrow{\tau}$. Recently, Liu et al. [5] complemented this by showing that the problem remains NP-hard even when the vertex set of a minimum sum set cover is provided.

We study the parameterized complexity of the minimum sum set cover problem. Formally, we consider the following decision problem. Given a hypergraph

$H$ and integers $k$ and $w$, does there exist a set cover $S$ of $H$ and a permutation of $S$ such that $|S| \leq k$ and the cost is at most $w$. Parameterizing by $w$ alone is not meaningful, since every yes-instance satisfies $w \geq |E(H)|$. The more natural parameterization is to use $\overrightarrow{\tau}$. Liu et al. [5] showed that the minimum sum vertex cover problem, minimum sum set cover on rank-two hypergraphs, is fixed-parameter tractable (FPT) with respect to $\overrightarrow{\tau}$.

The algorithm of Liu et al. [5] finds the solution set $S$ by extending a minimal vertex cover $S'$, which can be found in FPT time. The most crucial observation behind their low complexity is that for each of the remaining positions of $S \setminus S'$, one only needs to consider a small number of candidates: since $S'$ is a vertex cover, the number of edges effectively covered by any vertex in $S \setminus S'$ depends solely on its position relative to the sequence of $S'$. Heavily relying on the fact that each edge involves precisely two vertices, the algorithm cannot be easily adapted to hypergraphs.

We present a simple branching algorithm for the minimum sum set cover problem on bounded-rank hypergraphs, first using sunflowers to identify a bounded set of candidate vertices, and then exhaustively searching over subsets and permutations of these candidates. The algorithm iteratively applies the Sunflower Lemma [2] to the hypergraph induced by the uncovered edges (i.e., $H - S$): as long as this hypergraph is large, we find a sunflower with more than $k - |S|$ petals and branch on the (at most $r(H)$) vertices in its core, since any set cover of size at most $k$ must contain at least one of them. Once no such sunflower exists, the lemma implies that the remaining instance has size bounded as a function of the parameter, and we can enumerate all ways to complete the solution set to size at most $k$ and all permutations of this set, selecting one of minimum sum cost.

**Theorem 4.** *The minimum sum set cover problem can be solved in time*

$$O\left(r(H)^{r(H)+k}k^{r(H)}|E(H)| + (r(H)k)^{r(H)k}\right).$$

It remains open whether the problem is fixed-parameter tractable when the rank of the input hypergraph is unbounded. See more discussion in Sect. 6.

*Related Work.* Feige et al. [3] showed that a greedy algorithm approximates minimum sum set cover within a ratio of 4, and it becomes NP-hard to achieve a constant-approximation better than 4. On graphs, the approximation ratio can be improved to 16/9 [1], while the lower bound, assuming the Unique Games Conjecture and P $\neq$ NP, is 1.014 [6]. It remains to see whether these ratios can be improved if FPT time is allowed.

## 2 Upper Bounds: Theorem 1

We let $H - S$ denote the subhypergraph of $H$ induced by $V(H) \setminus S$, i.e., the hypergraph with vertex set $V(H) \setminus S$ and hyperedge set $\{e \setminus S \mid e \in E(H), e \cap S = \emptyset\}$, and it is further shortened to $H - v$ when $S$ consists of a single vertex $v$.

The minimum sum set cover problem asks for a set cover $S$ and a permutation of its vertices. It is more convenient to extend this permutation into a bijection $\sigma : V(H) \to \{1, 2, \ldots, |V(H)|\}$ by arbitrarily assigning vertices in $V(H) \setminus S$ into $\{|S|+1, \ldots, |V(H)|\}$. Note that any ordering of $V(H)$ induces a feasible extension of an ordering of a set cover. For an ordering $\sigma : V(H) \to \{1, 2, \ldots, |V(H)|\}$, define the *effective coverage* of the $i$th vertex as

$$r_\sigma(i) = \left|\{e \in E(H) \mid \min_{v \in e} \sigma(v) = i\}\right|.$$

Abusing notation, we also write $r_\sigma(\sigma(v))$ as $r_\sigma(v)$. The cost of minimum sum set covers of $H$, denoted as $\phi(H)$, is

$$\phi(H) = \min_\sigma \sum_{i=1}^{|V(H)|} i \cdot r_\sigma(i) = \min_\sigma \sum_{e \in E(H)} \min_{v \in e} \sigma(v).$$

Throughout the paper, we will consider solutions $(S, \sigma)$ with $r_\sigma(i) > 0$ for all $i = 1, \ldots, |S|$. Indeed, if $r_\sigma(|S|) = 0$, then the last vertex of $S$ is redundant; if $r_\sigma(i) = 0$ for some $i < |S|$, then the vertex at position $i$ does not cover any edge at that position; removing it and shifting all later vertices one step earlier yields another solution with strictly smaller cost. Under this assumption, the set $S$ is implicit from the ordering $\sigma$: its vertices are exactly those that appear before any edge is first covered. Equivalently, $|S| = \max_{e \in E(H)} \min_{v \in e} \sigma(v)$. Henceforth, we will use $\sigma$ to denote a solution, and $S_\sigma$ the implied vertex set.

**Observation 1.** *Let $H$ be a hypergraph on $n$ vertices, and $\langle v_1, v_2, \ldots, v_n\rangle$ a minimum sum set cover of $H$. For all $i = 1, \ldots, n-1$, the ordering $\langle v_i, v_{i+1}, \ldots, v_n\rangle$ is a minimum sum set cover of $H - \{v_1, v_2, \ldots, v_{i-1}\}$.*

In an optimal solution, the numbers $r_\sigma(\cdot)$ are non-increasing.

**Lemma 1.** *In any optimal solution $\sigma$ of $H$, it holds $r_\sigma(1) \geq \cdots \geq r_\sigma(|V(H)|)$.*

*Proof.* By Observation 1, it suffices to show that $r_\sigma(1) \geq r_\sigma(2)$. Let $u$ and $v$ be the vertices with $\sigma(u) = 1$ and $\sigma(v) = 2$. Let $\sigma'$ be obtained from $\sigma$ by switching the order of $u$ and $v$. For each hyperedge containing $u$ but not $v$, the cost is 1 in $\sigma$ and 2 in $\sigma'$. For each hyperedge containing $v$ but not $u$, the cost is 2 in $\sigma$ and 1 in $\sigma'$. All the other hyperedges have the same cost in $\sigma$ and $\sigma'$. By the optimality of $\sigma$, we have $r_\sigma(1) - r_\sigma(2) \geq 0$.

Lemma 1 implies a lower bound for the effective coverage of the first vertex.

**Lemma 2.** *In any minimum sum set cover $\sigma$, it holds $r_\sigma(1) \geq |E(H)|/\tau(H)$.*

*Proof.* Let $S$ be a minimum set cover of $H$, hence $|S| = \tau(H)$. We take an ordering $\pi$ of $V(H)$ such that $\pi(x) \leq \tau(H)$ if and only if $x \in S$, and $r_\pi(1) \geq r_\pi(2) \geq \cdots \geq r_\pi(\tau(H))$. Such an ordering can be produced as follows. Let $H_1 = H$. For $i = 1, \ldots, \tau(H)$, we take a vertex $v_i$ in $S$ with the maximum degree in $H_i$, and let $H_{i+1} = H_i - v_i$. The ordering is $\langle v_1, \ldots, v_{\tau(H)} \rangle$ followed by other vertices in an arbitrary order. For $i = 1, \ldots, \tau(H) - 1$,

$$r_\pi(i+1) = d_{H_{i+1}}(v_{i+1}) \leq d_{H_i}(v_{i+1}) \leq d_{H_i}(v_i) = r_\pi(i).$$

The maximum possible cost of $\pi$ is when $r_\pi(i)$ is either $\left\lceil \frac{|E(H)|}{\tau(H)} \right\rceil$ or $\left\lfloor \frac{|E(H)|}{\tau(H)} \right\rfloor$ for all $i = 1, \ldots, \tau(H)$. If $r_\sigma(1) < |E(H)|/\tau(H)$, then $r_\sigma(i) < |E(H)|/\tau(H)$ for all $i$. By Proposition 1, the cost of $\sigma$ is higher than $\pi$, a contradiction. □

We are now ready to prove Theorem 1.

*Proof (Theorem 1).* We deal with the hypergraph first. Let $\tau = \tau(H)$ and $\overrightarrow{\tau} = \overrightarrow{\tau}(H)$ and $m = |E(H)|$. For $i = 1, \ldots, n$, let $H_i = H - \{v_1, \ldots, v_{i-1}\}$ and $m_i = |E(H_i)|$. Note that $m_1 = m$ and $m_{i+1} = m_i - r_\sigma(i)$ for $i = 1, \ldots, n-1$. By Observation 1 and Lemma 2,

$$r_\sigma(i) \geq \frac{m_i}{\tau(H_i)} \geq \frac{m_i}{\tau}.$$

Thus,$m_{i+1} = m_i - r_\sigma(i) \leq m_i - \frac{m_i}{\tau} = \frac{\tau-1}{\tau} m_i$, which implies

$$m_{\overrightarrow{\tau}} \leq \left(\frac{\tau-1}{\tau}\right)^{\overrightarrow{\tau}-1} m_1 = \left(\frac{\tau-1}{\tau}\right)^{\overrightarrow{\tau}-1} m.$$

Since $\tau \geq 2$ and $m_{\overrightarrow{\tau}} \geq 1$, we have

$$m \geq \left(1 + \frac{1}{\tau-1}\right)^{(\tau-1)\left(\frac{\overrightarrow{\tau}-1}{\tau-1}\right)} \geq 2^{\frac{\overrightarrow{\tau}-1}{\tau-1}},$$

and

$$\overrightarrow{\tau} \leq (\tau-1)\log_2 m + 1 < \tau \log_2 m. \tag{1}$$

Now consider a graph $G$. We fix a minimum vertex cover $S^*$, and a minimum sum vertex cover $\sigma$ of $G$. Let $v$ be the first vertex in $\sigma$. We may assume without loss of generality that $v \notin S^*$, as otherwise we consider the subgraph $G - v$ (Observation 1). Repeating this argument while the first chosen vertex lies in $S^*$, we eventually arrive at a subgraph in which the first chosen vertex is outside a fixed minimum vertex cover, without changing the validity of the bound. As a result, $N(v) \subseteq S^*$, and hence $r_\sigma(1) = d(v) \leq |S^*| = \tau$. By Lemma 2, $m \leq \tau^2$. The statement then follows from (1). □

The proof of Lemma 1 is simple because switching two juxtaposed vertices has no impact on the effective coverages of other vertices. In the later proofs, we will frequently switch two vertices that are not juxtaposed in a solution to obtain another solution. The following arithmetic inequality and its corollary will help us compare their costs.

**Proposition 1.** *Let $\langle s_1, \ldots, s_n \rangle$ and $\langle s'_1, \ldots, s'_n \rangle$ be two non-increasing sequences of nonnegative integers such that $\sum_{i=1}^{n} s_i = \sum_{i=1}^{n} s'_i$. If there exists an integer $t \in \{1, \ldots, n\}$ such that*

$$s_i \le s'_i, \quad i = 1, \ldots, t, \tag{2}$$

$$s_i \ge s'_i, \quad i = t+1, \ldots, n. \tag{3}$$

*then*

$$\sum_{i=1}^{n} i \cdot s_i \ge \sum_{i=1}^{n} i \cdot s'_i,$$

*with equality if and only if all inequalities in* (2) *and* (3) *are equalities.*

**Corollary 1.** *Let $\sigma$ be an ordering of $V(H)$ and let $\sigma'$ be obtained from $\sigma$ by swapping two vertices $u, v$ with $\sigma(u) < \sigma(v)$. Denote $p = \sigma(u)$ and $q = \sigma(v)$. If*

1. *$r_{\sigma'}(p) > r_\sigma(p)$, and*
2. *$r_{\sigma'}(i) \le r_\sigma(i)$ for all $i$ with $p < i \le q$.*

*Then $\sigma'$ has strictly smaller total cost than $\sigma$.*

## 3 The Lower Bound: Theorem 2

Consider a hypergraph on vertex set $A \cup B$ with $|A| = n$ and $|B| = 3$. We will construct hyperedges such that a solution with $A$ preceding $B$ has a cost smaller than a solution with $A$ following $B$, while all other solutions are even worse than the latter. This construction establishes Theorem 2.

Given a graph $G$ on $n$ vertices $\{v_1, \ldots, v_n\}$ and $m$ edges, we define a hypergraph $H_G$ as follows. The vertex set is $A \cup B$, where $A = V(G)$ and $B = \{b_1, b_2, b_3\}$. The hyperedges are constructed based on the subsets of $A$. For each nonempty subset $X$ of $A$ that is not in $\binom{A}{2} \setminus E(G)$ (i.e., $|X| \ne 2$ or $X \in E(G)$), introduce three hyperedges $X \cup \{b_1\}$, $X \cup \{b_2\}$, and $X \cup \{b_3\}$. Formally, the edge set of $H_G$ is:

$$\begin{aligned} E(H_G) = &\{\{v_i, b_k\} \mid i \in \{1, \ldots, n\}, k \in \{1,2,3\}\} \\ &\cup \{\{v_i, v_j, b_k\} \mid v_i v_j \in E(G), k \in \{1,2,3\}\} \\ &\cup \{X \cup \{b_k\} \mid X \subseteq A, |X| \ge 3, k \in \{1,2,3\}\}. \end{aligned}$$

**Proposition 2.** *Both $A$ and $B$ are minimal set covers of $H_G$, and they are the only minimal set covers.*

We now analyze the cost of a solution $\pi_B$ that orders $B$ before $A$, where the order of $b_1, b_2, b_3$ is irrelevant. For $k = 1, 2, 3$,

$$r_{\pi_B}(k) = n + m + \left(2^n - 1 - n - \binom{n}{2}\right) = 2^n - 1 - \binom{n}{2} + m. \tag{4}$$

Since $r_{\pi_B}(k) = 0$ for $k \geq 4$, the cost is

$$\sum_{i=1}^{n+3} i \cdot r_{\pi_B}(i) = \sum_{i=1}^{3} i \cdot r_{\pi_B}(i) = 6\left(2^n - 1 - \binom{n}{2} + m\right). \quad (5)$$

We show that any solution that orders $A$ before $B$ is strictly better than $\pi_B$, while any other solution is strictly worse than $\pi_B$.

**Lemma 3.** *For any graph $G$, every minimum sum set cover of $H_G$ places all vertices of $B$ after all vertices of $A$.*

Theorem 2 now follows immediately from the preceding discussion.

## 4 The Lower Bound for Graphs: Theorem 3

Fix a positive integer $n$. For a positive integer $q \leq n$, let $B_q$ be the bipartite graph with bipartition $L \uplus R$, where $|L| = 2n^q$ and $|R| = (q+2)n^q$. Partition $R$ as $R = R_0 \uplus R_1 \uplus \cdots \uplus R_q$ with $|R_0| = 2n^q$ and $|R_i| = n^q$ for each $i = 1, \ldots, q$.

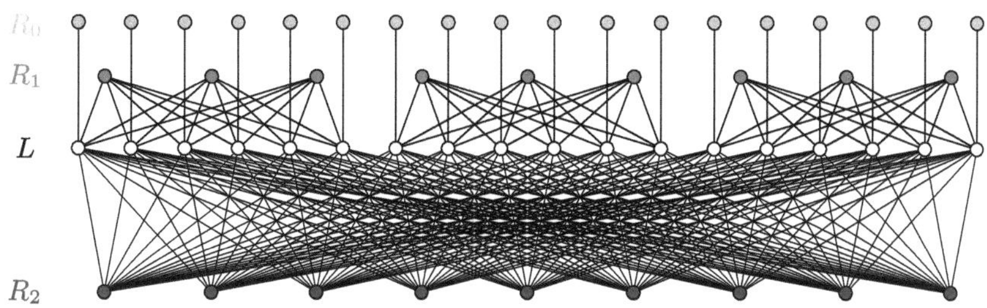


**Fig. 2.** The graph $B_2$ with $n = 3$.

Define the edges as follows. First, add all edges between $L$ and $R_q$, and set $\mathcal{L}_q = \{L\}$. For each $i = q-1, \ldots, 1$, obtain $\mathcal{L}_i$ from $\mathcal{L}_{i+1}$ by evenly refining every part into $n$ subparts; thus $\mathcal{L}_i$ is a partition of $L$ into $n^{q-i}$ parts, each of size $2n^i$. Independently, partition $R_i$ into $n^{q-i}$ parts of equal size, and for each $j$, make the bipartite subgraph between the $j$th part of $\mathcal{L}_i$ and the $j$th part of this partition of $R_i$ complete. Thus every vertex in a part of $\mathcal{L}_i$ has the same neighbors in $R_i$. Finally, index the vertices of $L$ and $R_0$ as $\{1, \ldots, 2n^q\}$, and for each $i = 1, \ldots, 2n^q$, add an edge between the $i$th vertex of $L$ and the $i$th vertex of $R_0$. See Fig. 2 for an illustration.

In summary, $|V(B_q)| = (q+4)n^q$, $|E(B_q)| = 2n^q \frac{n^{q+1}-1}{n-1}$, and the degree of a vertex $v \in V(B_q)$ is

$$d(v) = \begin{cases} \frac{n^{q+1}-1}{n-1} & v \in L, \\ 1 & v \in R_0, \\ 2n^i & v \in R_i, i = 1, \ldots, q. \end{cases}$$

The set $L$ is the only minimum vertex cover of $B_q$: the subgraph induced by $L \cup R_0$ is an induced matching.

**Proposition 3.** *$\tau(B_q) = 2n^q$. The cardinality of a vertex cover of $B_q$ that does not contain $L$ is at least $3n^q$.*

*Proof.* The edges between $L$ and $R_0$ form an induced matching of size $2n^q$. Any vertex cover must contain at least one endpoint of each such edge, so $\tau(B_q) \geq 2n^q$. Taking $L$ itself yields a vertex cover of size $2n^q$, so $\tau(B_q) = 2n^q$.

If a vertex cover $C$ does not contain all vertices of $L$, then there exists $u \in L \setminus C$. The edge between $u$ and its unique neighbor in $R_0$ forces that neighbor into $C$. Repeating this argument shows that $C$ must contain all of $R_0$ and at least $n^q$ vertices of $L$, so $|C| \geq 3n^q$. □

We will show that $\overrightarrow{\tau}(B_n) = \Omega(n^{n+1})$. In the rest, we assume that $n \geq 7$.

Since $N(v_2) \subsetneq L = N(v_1)$ for any $v_1 \in R_q$ and $v_2 \in R \setminus R_q$, a minimum sum vertex cover of $B_q$ will not choose any vertex in $R \setminus R_q$ before $R_q$. In other words, before the first vertex in $R \setminus R_q$, at least one of $L$ and $R_q$ has been exhausted. As we will see, a minimum sum vertex cover will start with $R_q$. After that, the remaining graph $B_q - R_q$ is decomposed into $n$ components, each is a copy of $B_{q-1}$. For a positive integer $p$ and a graph $G$, we use $pG$ to denote the disjoint union of $p$ copies of $G$.

**Observation 2.** *The subgraph $B_q - R_q$ is isomorphic to $nB_{q-1}$.*

As we have seen in Fig. 1, these copies may behave differently in a minimum sum vertex cover. We show that in each of the copies,

1. the vertices in $L$ are selected first (which cover all edges);
2. all vertices of $R_{q-1}$ are selected first, which reduces the remaining copy into $n$ copies of $B_{q-2}$; or
3. vertices of a subset of $L \cup R_{q-1}$ are selected first.

The main technical lemma is that the third case will never happen in a minimum sum vertex cover. Let $G_{p,q} = pB_q$. For $i = 1, \ldots, p$, we use $B_q^i$ to refer to the $i$th copy of $B_q$ in $G_{p,q}$, with vertex set $L^i$, $R_0^i$, ..., $R_q^i$. For a solution $\sigma$ of $G_{p,q}$, let $\sigma^i = \sigma|_{V(B_q^i)}$, the sub-ordering of $\sigma$ induced by $V(B_q^i)$.

We next prove that in each copy, an optimal solution cannot mix a proper prefix of $R_q$ with later vertices in any beneficial way. This forces each copy to begin either with all of $R_q$ or with all of $L$.

**Lemma 4.** *Let $\sigma$ be an optimal solution for $G_{p,q}$. For all $i = 1, \ldots, p$, the subsequence $\sigma^i$ starts with either $R_q^i$ or $L^i$.*

Before presenting the proof of Lemma 4, we use it to prove Theorem 3. We start with bounds on the cost of optimal solutions of $G_{p,q}$, denoted $\phi(G_{p,q})$.

While the lower bound is nearly trivial, we will upper-bound by explicitly constructing a solution and computing its cost. Note that the number of edges in $G_{p,q}$ is

$$|E(G_{p,q})| = 2pn^q \sum_{i=0}^{q} n^i = 2pn^q \frac{n^{q+1}-1}{n-1}. \tag{6}$$

Thus, $\overrightarrow{\tau}(B_n) = \Omega(n^{n+1})$. Combining with Proposition 3, it implies Theorem 3. We prove Lemma 4 in two steps.

**Lemma 5.** *Let $\sigma$ be an optimal solution for $G_{p,q}$. For all $i = 1, \ldots, p$, the subsequence $\sigma^i$ starts with either $R_q^i$ or a proper (possibly empty) subset of $R_q^i$ followed by $L^i$.*

*Proof.* Let $v$ be the first vertex in $\sigma$ from $V(B_q^i) \setminus (L^i \cup R_q^i)$, and let $u$ be the first vertex in $\sigma$ from $L^i$.

In the first case, $v <_\sigma u$ (i.e., $v <_\sigma x$ for all $x \in L^i$). We argue that $x <_\sigma v$ for all $x \in R_q^i$; i.e., $\sigma^i$ starts with $R_q^i$. Suppose for contradiction that there exists a vertex $w \in R_q^i$ such that $\sigma(v) < \sigma(w)$. Let $\sigma'$ be the ordering of $G_{p,q}$ obtained from $\sigma$ by switching $v$ and $w$. Since $N(v) \subsetneq L^i = N(w)$, we have

$$r_{\sigma'}(\sigma(v)) = n^q > r_\sigma(\sigma(v)),$$

and $r_{\sigma'}(j) \leq r_\sigma(j)$ for all $j$ with $\sigma(v) < j \leq \sigma(w)$. It follows from Corollary 1 that $\sigma'$ is strictly better than $\sigma$, contradicting the optimality of $\sigma$.

In the second case, $u <_\sigma v$. Let

$$h = \sigma^i(u) - 1,$$
$$k = \sigma^i(v) - h.$$

By the selection of $u$ and $v$, all the first $h$ vertices in $\sigma^i$ are from $R_q^i$; number them as $w_1, \ldots, w_h$ in order. We note that the next $k$ vertices (from $u$, inclusive, to $v$, exclusive) in $\sigma^i$ are from $L^i$. If there is a vertex $x \notin L^i$ with $u <_\sigma x <_\sigma v$, then $x \in R_q^i$ by the selection of $v$, and switching $x$ with $u$ gives a strictly better solution $\sigma'$ than $\sigma$ by Corollary 1: $r_{\sigma'}(\sigma(u)) = 2n^q > r_\sigma(\sigma(u))$ and $r_{\sigma'}(j) \leq r_\sigma(j)$ for all $j$ with $\sigma(u) < j \leq \sigma(x)$. It remains to show that

$$h = n^q \quad \text{or} \quad k = 2n^q.$$

Suppose that $h < n^q$ and $k < 2n^q$. Let $\sigma'$ be obtained from $\sigma$ by replacing the $(h+1)$st through $(h+2n^q)$th in $\sigma^i$ with the vertices in $L^i$. Since $L^i$ covers all edges in $B_q^i$, the order of the remaining vertices (i.e., $R^i \setminus \{w_1, \ldots, w_h\}$) is immaterial.

Number the vertices in $L^i$ as $u_1, \ldots, u_{2n^q}$ in the order of their occurrence in $\sigma'$, and let $t = \sigma'(u_{2n^q})$. Note that $\sigma'(u_{k+1}) = \sigma(v)$. We have

$$r_{\sigma'}(\sigma'(u_j)) = \frac{n^{q+1}-1}{n-1} - h = r_\sigma(u_1) \geq r_\sigma(\sigma'(u_j)), j = k+1, \ldots, 2n^q.$$

On the other hand, $r_{\sigma'}(x) = 0$ for all $x \in R^i \setminus \{w_1, \ldots, w_h\}$, which come after $u_{2n^q}$ in $\sigma'$, and hence for all $j > t$,

$$r_{\sigma'}(j) \leq r_{\sigma}(j).$$

Let $X$ be the set of the first $(h + 2n^q)$ vertices in $\sigma^i$, and $y$ the $(h + 2n^q + 1)$st vertex in $\sigma^i$; note that $\sigma(y) > t$. Since $h < n^q$, the set $X$ is not a vertex cover of $B_q^i$ by Proposition 3. Thus, $r_\sigma(\sigma(y)) > 0 = r_{\sigma'}(\sigma(y))$, and $\sigma'$ is a strictly better solution than $\sigma$ by Proposition 1, contradicting the optimality of $\sigma$.

Therefore, either $h = n^q$, i.e., the subsequence $\sigma^i$ starts with $R_q^i$, or $h < n^q$ and $k = 2n^q$, i.e., it starts with a proper subset of $R_q^i$ followed by $L^i$. □

We are now ready for the proof of Lemma 4: in the second case of Lemma 5, the proper subset of $R_q^i$ must be empty.

*Proof (Proof of Lemma 4).* In view of Lemma 5, we need to show that for all $i = 1, \ldots, p$, the subset of $R_q^i$ must be empty in the second case. Our strategy is to assume that some copy starts with a nonempty proper prefix of $R_q^i$, and then locally reorder the boundary between this prefix and the subsequent block of $L^i$-vertices. By comparing the change in edge costs under these swaps/rotations, we show that one obtains a strictly better solution, contradicting optimality.

We number the vertices in $L^i$ as $u_1^i, \ldots, u_{2n^q}^i$, and the vertices in $R_q^i$ as $w_1^i, \ldots, w_{n^q}^i$, by their occurrence in $\sigma$; let $h_i$ denote the length of the longest prefix that is a subset of $R_q^i$, and $\ell^i$ the number of consecutive vertices from $L^i$ afterward.

Suppose for contradiction that $\sigma^1$ starts with a proper and nonempty subset of $R_q^1$ followed by $L^1$ (we can always renumber the copies of $B_q$).

We show that at most one copy can behave in this way; otherwise we can locally swap and improve the solution. In the first case, there exists another $b \in \{1, \ldots, p\}$ such that $\sigma^b$ starts with a proper and nonempty subset of $R_q^b$ followed by $L^b$. Again, assume without loss of generality that $b = 2$ and $h_1 \leq h_2$. Hence, $r_\sigma(u_i^1) \geq r_\sigma(u_j^2)$ for all $i, j \in \{1, \ldots, 2n^q\}$. Since $r_\sigma(w_i^1) \geq r_\sigma(w_j^2) = 2n^q$ for all $i, j \in \{1, \ldots, n^q\}$, we may assume that the following vertices in this order in $\sigma$:

$$w_1^1, \ldots, w_{h_1}^1, w_1^2, \ldots, w_{h_2}^2, u_1^1, \ldots, u_{2n^q}^1, u_1^2, \ldots, u_{2n^q}^2.$$

Let $\sigma'$ be obtained from $\sigma$ by swapping $w_{h_1}^1$ and $w_{h_2+1}^1$. Note that $r_{\sigma'}(w_{h_2+1}^1) = r_\sigma(w_{h_1}^1) = 2n^q$ and $r_\sigma(w_{h_2+1}^1) = r_{\sigma'}(w_{h_1}^1) = 0$. For $i = 1, \ldots, 2n^q$, we have

$$r_{\sigma'}(u_i^1) = r_\sigma(u_i^1) + 1 > r_\sigma(u_i^1),$$
$$r_{\sigma'}(u_i^2) = r_\sigma(u_i^2) - 1 < r_\sigma(u_i^2).$$

Let $t = \sigma'(u_{2n^q}^1) = \sigma(u_{2n^q}^1)$. Finally, $r_\sigma(j) = r_{\sigma'}(j) = 0$ for all $j > \sigma(u_{2n^q}^2) = t + 2n^q$. Thus, the solution $\sigma'$ is a strictly better solution than $\sigma$ by Proposition 1, contradicting the optimality of $\sigma$.

In the rest, for all $i = 2, \ldots, p$, the subsequence $\sigma^i$ starts with either $R_q^i$ or $L^i$. We may renumber the copies such that $\sigma^i$ starts with $R_q^i$ when $i = 2, \ldots, a$ and $L^i$ when $i = a + 1, \ldots, p$. Hence, $\sigma$ must start with the following in order

- all vertices in $R_q^2 \cup R_q^3 \cup \cdots \cup R_q^a \cup \{w_1^1, \ldots, w_{h_1}^1\}$, each vertex in it with effective coverage $2n^q$;
- all vertices in $L^{a+1}, L^{a+2}, \ldots, L^p$, each vertex in it with effective coverage $\frac{n^{q+1}-1}{n-1}$; and
- all vertices in $L^1$, each vertex in it with effective coverage $\frac{n^{q+1}-1}{n-1} - h_1$.

We may assume that $w_{h_1}^1$ is the last vertex in $\sigma$ with effective coverage $2n^q$ and $w_{h_1+1}^1$ is the last of $\sigma$, i.e.,

$$\sigma(w_{h_1}^1) = (a-1)n^q + h_1, \qquad \sigma(w_{h_1+1}^1) = p(q+4)n^q.$$

Thus, $\sigma$ has the following structure:

$$\underbrace{[R_q^2, \cdots, R_q^a]}_{\text{full } R_q\text{-blocks}}, \underbrace{[w_1^1, \cdots, w_{h_1}^1]}_{\text{partial prefix}}, \underbrace{[L^{a+1}, L^{a+2}, \ldots, L^p]}_{\text{full } L\text{-blocks}}, \underbrace{[u_1^1, \cdots, u_{2n^q}^1]}_{L^1}, \quad \cdots, \quad w_{h_1+1}^1.$$

We now construct two new solutions $\overrightarrow{\sigma}$ and $\overleftarrow{\sigma}$ by rotating the subsequence between them (both inclusive) of $\sigma$ by one position. Define $\overleftarrow{\sigma}$ by moving $w_{h_1}^1$ to the very end of the sequence, shifting all vertices after $(a-1)n^q + h_1$ one position to the left, and $\overrightarrow{\sigma}$ by moving $w_{h_1+1}^1$ to the position $(a-1)n^q + h_1 + 1$, shifting all other vertices after $(a-1)n^q + h_1$ one position to the right. We show that at least one of $\overrightarrow{\sigma}$ or $\overleftarrow{\sigma}$ is a better solution than $\sigma$.

In the transformation from $\sigma$ to $\overrightarrow{\sigma}$, the costs of the edges between $w_{h_1+1}^1$ and $L^1$ become $\overrightarrow{\sigma}(w_{h_1+1}^1) = (a-1)n^q + h_1 + 1$, while every edge that was originally covered after position $(a-1)n^q + h_1$ and is not incident to $w_{h_1+1}^1$ has its cost increased by 1. Thus, the cost increases by

$$\sum_{i=(a-1)n^q+h_1+1}^{|V(G_{p,q})|} \left(r_\sigma(i) - r_{\overrightarrow{\sigma}}(w_{h_1+1}^1)\right) - \sum_{i=1}^{2n^q} \left(\sigma(u_i^1) - \overrightarrow{\sigma}(w_{h_1+1}^1)\right)$$

$$= (|E(G_{p,q})| - 2n^q((a-1)n^q + h_1) - 2n^q) - \left(\sum_{i=1}^{2n^q} \left(\sigma(u_i^1) - \sigma(w_{h_1}^1)\right) - 2n^q\right).$$

$$= |E(G_{p,q})| - 2n^q((a-1)n^q + h_1) - \sum_{i=1}^{2n^b} \left(\sigma(u_i^1) - \sigma(w_{h_1}^1)\right).$$

In the transformation from $\sigma$ to $\overleftarrow{\sigma}$, the cost of the edge between $w_{h_1+1}^1$ and $u_i^1, i = 1, \ldots, 2n^q$, becomes $\overleftarrow{\sigma}(u_i^1)$, while every edge that was originally covered after position $(a-1)n^q + h_1$ has its cost decreased by 1. Thus, the cost increases by

$$\sum_{i=1}^{2n^q} \left(\overleftarrow{\sigma}(u_i^1) - \sigma(w_{h_1}^1)\right) - \sum_{i=\sigma(w_{h_1}^1)+1}^{|V(G_{p,q})|} r_\sigma(i)$$

$$= \sum_{i=1}^{2n^q} \left(\sigma(u_i^1) - 1 - \sigma(w_{h_1}^1)\right) - \left(|E(G_{p,q})| - 2n^q((a-1)n^q + h_1)\right).$$

Since the summation of these two terms is $-2n^q$, at least one of them is negative. Hence, at least one of $\overrightarrow{\sigma}$ and $\overleftarrow{\sigma}$ is strictly better than $\sigma$, contradicting the optimality of $\sigma$. This concludes the proof. □

## 5 A Parameterized Algorithm

We present a simple fixed-parameter branching algorithm for the minimum sum set cover problem on bounded-rank hypergraphs. Recall that the rank $r(H)$ of a hypergraph $H$ is the maximum cardinality of any of the hyperedges in $H$, and we consider the decision version: given a hypergraph $H$ and integers $k$ and $w$, does there exist a set cover $S$ of $H$ and a permutation of $S$ such that $|S| \leq k$ and the cost is at most $w$.

We say that a solution $\sigma$ of an instance $(H, w, k)$ is *feasible* if $|S_\sigma| \leq k$ and its total cost is at most $w$. For the minimum sum vertex cover problem, the set of any feasible solution must contain all vertices with degree greater than $k$. This is no longer true in our setting. Instead, we require the Sunflower Lemma [2].

A *sunflower* in a hypergraph $H$ consists of a (possibly empty) subset $K \subseteq V(H)$, called the *core*, and a subset $P \subseteq E(H)$, called the *petals*, such that the intersection of every pair of distinct hyperedges in $P$ is exactly $K$. The size of the sunflower is $|P|$.

**Lemma 6 ( [2]).** *If a hypergraph $H$ with no repeated edges has more than $r(H) \cdot r(H)!(k-1)^{r(H)}$ hyperedges, then $H$ contains a sunflower with $k$ petals, and such a sunflower can be computed in time polynomial in $|E(H)|$, $|V(H)|$, and $k$.*

If there is a sunflower with $k+1$ petals, then any set cover of $H$ with at most $k$ vertices must contain at least one vertex from its core $K$. Since $K$ cannot be larger than the size of any petal, we have $|K| \leq r(H)$. Thus, we can branch on choosing a vertex from $K$: this is why our algorithm only works on bounded-rank hypergraphs. We repeat this until there is no sunflower with $k+1$ petals, or $k$ vertices have already been selected. By the Sunflower Lemma, the number of edges, and hence the number of vertices, in the remaining instance is bounded. We can then find the remaining vertices of the solution set by branching, and finally enumerate all possible orderings of this set.

*Proof (Theorem 4).* We use the algorithm described in Fig. 3. Since the algorithm returns "yes" only when a solution is explicitly constructed, it suffices to show that a solution must be returned for every yes-instance. Let $S$ denote the set of elements contained in an optimal solution, and let $r = r(H)$.

The algorithm has two phases: first, finding the vertex set $S$ (steps 1–4), and then computing an ordering of $S$ (step 5). We find the solution set $S$ by branching. During this process, we work with the hypergraph $H - S$: all hyperedges intersecting $S$ have already been covered. If $H - S$ still has more than $r \cdot r!(k-|S|)^r$ hyperedges, then by the Sunflower Lemma we can find a sunflower with $k-|S|+1$ petals [2]. Any solution must contain a vertex from the core of this sunflower; otherwise, it would need to use a distinct vertex to cover each petal, which would

1. $S \leftarrow \emptyset$;
2. **while** $|E(H-S)| > r \cdot r!(k-|S|)^r$ and $|S| \le k$ **do**
2.1. **if** $|S| = k$ **then return** "no";
2.2. find a sunflower of $H - S$ with core $K$;
2.3. **if** $K = \emptyset$ **then return** "no";
2.4. guess a vertex $v \in K$ and add it to $S$;
3. remove all isolated vertices in $H - S$;
4. guess a subset $T \subseteq V(H-S)$ with $|T| \le k - |S|$ and $S \leftarrow S \cup T$;
5. guess an bijective mapping $\sigma \colon S \to \{1, 2, \ldots, |S|\}$;
6. **if** $S$ is a set cover of $H$ and the cost of $\sigma$ is $\le w$ **then return** "yes"; **else return** "no."

**Fig. 3.** The parameterized algorithm for minimum sum set cover.

require more than $k$ vertices and thus be infeasible. Thus, there cannot be a feasible solution when the core is empty. Therefore, either step 2.3 correctly returns "no," or at least one branch in step 2.4 adds a vertex from the optimal solution.

Once the algorithm exits the loop in step 2, we are allowed to add at most $k - |S|$ additional vertices, and these can be found by enumeration: we branch over all subsets $T \subseteq V(H-S)$ with $|T| \le k - |S|$.

We now analyze the running time. The search tree in step 2 has depth at most $k$, and the branching factor is at most the core size, which is bounded by $r$. Thus, this phase takes time $O(r^{|S|+1} \cdot r!(k-1)^r m)$, where $m = |E(H)|$. After step 2, we have $|E(H-S)| \le r \cdot r!(k-|S|)^r$ by the Sunflower Lemma, and hence $|V(H-S)| \le r|E(H-S)| \le r^2 \cdot r!(k-|S|)^r$ because there are no isolated vertices. Thus, there are $O\big((r^2 \cdot r!(k-1)^r)^{k-|S|}\big)$ subsets to be enumerated in step 4. Step 5 takes $O(k!)$ time. Overall, the total running time is $O\left(r^{r+k}k^r m + (rk)^{rk}\right)$. □

# 6 Concluding Remarks

The most compelling open question is to close the $\log\log \tau(G)$ gap between the upper bound in Theorem 1 for graphs and the lower bound given by the construction in Theorem 3. We also leave open the fixed-parameter tractability of minimum sum set cover on general hypergraphs when parameterized solely by $\overrightarrow{\tau}$. Since $\overrightarrow{\tau}$ and $\tau$ are polynomially related (Theorem 1), minimum sum vertex cover is fixed-parameter tractable with respect to $\tau$ [5]. For hypergraphs, this is very unlikely to remain true. In fact, we conjecture that minimum sum set cover is NP-hard even on hypergraphs with bounded minimum set cover number.

## References


1. Bansal, N., Batra, J., Farhadi, M., Tetali, P.: On min sum vertex cover and generalized min sum set cover. SIAM J. Comput. **52**(2), 327–357 (2023). https://doi.org/10.1137/21M1434052
2. Erdős, P., Rado, R.: Intersection theorems for systems of sets. J. Lond. Math. Soc. **35**(1), 85–90 (1960). https://doi.org/10.1112/jlms/s1-35.1.85
3. Feige, U., Lovász, L., Tetali, P.: Approximating min sum set cover. Algorithmica **40**(4), 219–234 (2004). https://doi.org/10.1007/S00453-004-1110-5
4. Johnson, D.S.: Approximation algorithms for combinatorial problems. J. Comput. Syst. Sci. **9**(3), 256–278 (1974). https://doi.org/10.1016/S0022-0000(74)80044-9
5. Liu, J., Cao, Y., Gai, L., Wang, J.: Minimum sum vertex cover: difficulty of ordering. Theor. Comput. Sci. **1049**, 115371 (2025). https://doi.org/10.1016/j.tcs.2025.115371
6. Stanković, A.: Some results on approximability of minimum sum vertex cover. ACM Trans. Comput. Theory **17**(2), 11:1–11:28 (2025). https://doi.org/10.1145/3716551

# Sublinear-Time Algorithms for Diagonally Dominant Systems and Applications to the Friedkin-Johnsen Model

Weiming Feng[1], Zelin Li[2(✉)], and Pan Peng[2]

[1] School of Computing and Data Science, The University of Hong Kong, Hong Kong, China
wfeng@hku.hk

[2] School of Computer Science and Technology, University of Science and Technology of China, Hefei, China
meguru@mail.ustc.edu.cn, ppeng@ustc.edu.cn

**Abstract.** We study sublinear-time algorithms for solving linear systems $Sz = b$, where $S$ is a diagonally dominant matrix, i.e., $|S_{ii}| \geq \delta + \sum_{j \neq i} |S_{ij}|$ for all $i \in [n]$, for some $\delta \geq 0$. We present randomized algorithms that, for any $u \in [n]$, return an estimate $z_u$ of $z_u^*$ with additive error $\varepsilon$ or $\varepsilon \|z^*\|_\infty$, where $z^*$ is some solution to $Sz^* = b$, and the algorithm only needs to read a small portion of the input $S$ and $b$. For example, for the relevant parameter regime where $\varepsilon$ and $\delta$ are constants and $||b||_\infty \leq 1$, our algorithm runs in time $O(S_{\max})$, where $S_{\max} = \max_{i \in [n]} |S_{ii}|$. We also prove a matching lower bound, showing that the linear dependence on $S_{\max}$ is optimal. Unlike previous sublinear-time algorithms, which apply only to symmetric diagonally dominant matrices with non-negative diagonal entries, our algorithm works for general strictly diagonally dominant matrices ($\delta > 0$) and a broader class of non-strictly diagonally dominant matrices ($\delta = 0$). Our approach is based on analyzing a simple probabilistic recurrence satisfied by the solution. As an application, we obtain an improved sublinear-time algorithm for opinion estimation in the Friedkin–Johnsen model.

## 1 Introduction

Solving linear systems is a fundamental computational problem with numerous applications. Given a matrix $S \in \mathbb{R}^{n \times n}$ and a vector $b \in \mathbb{R}^n$, the goal is to find a solution $z \in \mathbb{R}^n$ satisfying $Sz = b$. General algorithms achieve runtimes such as $O(n^\omega)$ (where $\omega < 2.371339$ is the matrix multiplication exponent [1])

Weiming Feng was supported by the ECS grant 27202725 from Hong Kong RGC. Zelin Li and Pan Peng were supported in part by NSFC Grant 62272431 and Quantum Science and Technology – National Science and Technology Major Project (Grant No. 2021ZD0302901).

The authors are listed in alphabetical order by surname. The primary affiliation is University of Science and Technology of China.


Y. Li et al. (Eds.): COCOON 2026, LNCS 16835, pp. 149–162, 2027.
https://doi.org/10.1007/978-981-92-3309-0_12

or $O(\mathrm{nnz}(S) \cdot n)$ (see e.g. [26]), with $\mathrm{nnz}(S)$ denoting the number of nonzeros in $S$. Certain structured systems admit faster solvers. A key example is *symmetric diagonally dominant (SDD)* matrices, where $S_{ii} \geq \sum_{j \neq i} |S_{ij}|$, $S_{ij} = S_{ji}$ for all $i, j$. This class includes graph Laplacians $L_G$ of undirected graphs. Building on the seminal work of Spielman and Teng [27], subsequent research has shown that systems like $L_G z = b$ can be solved in nearly linear time [11,20]. The best known algorithms run in $\tilde{O}(\mathrm{nnz}(S) \log(1/\varepsilon))$ time, where $\varepsilon$ is the error tolerance. More recently, nearly linear-time solvers have also been developed for certain directed Laplacian systems [10].

Solving linear systems with SDD matrices arise naturally in numerous practical settings, such as PageRank or Personalized PageRank (PPR), computing the effective resistance, and machine learning on graphs including semi-supervised learning and label propagation [17,28].

Motivated by advances in fast linear-system solvers under alternative computational models and the challenges posed by modern large-scale datasets, Andoni, Krauthgamer, and Pogrow [3] pioneered *sublinear-time algorithms* for solving SDD linear systems. These algorithms inspect only a sparse subset of the input (the matrix $S$ and vector $b$) while preserving rigorous guarantees on output quality.

The work in [3] addresses settings where only one or a few coordinates of the solution $z^* \in \mathbb{R}^n$ are sought. Focusing on SDD matrices $S$ with non-negative diagonal entries, their algorithm assumes query access to both $S$ and $b$, which corresponds to vertex queries and neighbor queries in the underlying graph. For any index $u \in [n]$, it computes an estimate $\hat{z}_u$ approximating the $u$-th coordinate of a solution $z^*$ to the system $Sz = b$. The runtime is sublinear for a wide class of graphs (see further discussion below). This framework is applicable to a wide range of applications. As noted in [3], estimating effective resistances – central to graph clustering, recommendation systems and network reliability etc. – reduces estimating a few coordinates of the solution to a Laplacian linear system. The algorithm was later improved by Peng et al. [24]. Neumann et al. [23] further showed that such methods can predict the opinions of individual nodes in social networks within the Friedkin–Johnsen (FJ) model. Finally, the development of sublinear-time linear system solvers has been shaped by advances in quantum algorithms for linear systems [2,9,13,16] (see Sect. 1.4).

While powerful, the algorithm in [3] is limited to SDD matrices with non-negative diagonal entries, a special subclass of positive semi-definite (PSD) matrices. The method interprets $S$ as the Laplacian matrix of an undirected graph $G$ and defines estimates via short random walks on $G$. It inherently requires $S$ to be symmetric with non-negative diagonal entries.

In this paper, we present new sublinear-time algorithms for solving linear systems as long as the matrix $S$ is diagonally dominant, i.e., $|S_{ii}| \geq \sum_{j \neq i} |S_{ij}|$ for all $i$. *Note that $S$ is not necessarily symmetric or constrained to have non-negative diagonal entries. In fact, such $S$ is not necessarily PSD.* We also provide a lower bound to demonstrate that our algorithm is nearly optimal. Finally, we apply our algorithm to obtain improved sublinear algorithms for opinion estimation in the Friedkin–Johnsen model.

### 1.1 Main Results

**The Problem and Computational Model.** We study the problem of estimating individual entries of the solution $z^*$ to the linear system $Sz = b$ in sublinear time, where $S \in \mathbb{R}^{n\times n}$ is a $\delta$-diagonally dominant ($\delta$-DD) matrix and $b \in \mathbb{R}^n$. The definition of $\delta$-DD matrix is given below.

**Definition 1 ($\delta$-Diagonally Dominant ($\delta$-DD) Matrix).** *Let $\delta \geq 0$ be a non-negative parameter. A matrix $S \in \mathbb{R}^{n\times n}$ is called* $\delta$-diagonally dominant *(or* $\delta$-DD*) if $\forall i \in [n]$, $|S_{ii}| \geq \delta + \sum_{j:j\neq i} |S_{ij}|$. If $\delta > 0$, we say that $S$ is* strictly DD. *If $\delta = 0$, we say $S$ is* non-strictly DD.

Note that if $S$ is strictly DD, then it is non-singular, so the solution $z^*$ is unique.

We now specify the query model. The algorithm accesses $S$ and $b$ via oracle queries. To define the oracle, we first model $S \in \mathbb{R}^{n\times n}$ as a directed graph $G = G(S) = (V, E)$, where $V = [n]$. For any pair $(u, v)$ with $u \neq v$ and $S_{uv} \neq 0$, there exists a directed edge $(u, v) \in E$ with weight $S_{uv}$. For each vertex $u \in [n]$, define the out-degree $\Delta_u^{\text{out}}$ as the number of out-edges from vertex $u$, and define the out-weighted degree as $d_u^{\text{out}} = \sum_{v\neq u} |S_{uv}|$. Note that $\Delta_u^{\text{out}} = d_u^{\text{out}}$ when $S_{uv} \in \{-1, 0, 1\}$.

**Definition 2 ($(S, b)$-oracle).** *Let $S \in \mathbb{R}^{n\times n}$, $b \in \mathbb{R}^n$, and let $G = ([n], E)$ be the graph defined from $S$. The $(S, b)$-oracle supports the following queries, each with unit query cost: (1)* ***Vertex query:*** *Given $u \in [n]$, return $\Delta_u^{out}$, $d_u^{out}$, $S_{uu}$, and $b_u$. (2)* ***Neighbor query:*** *Given $u \in [n]$ and $i \in [\Delta_u^{out}]$, return the $i$-th out-neighbor $v$ of $u$ (under a fixed but arbitrary ordering). (3)* ***Random walk query:*** *Given $u \in [n]$, return a random out-neighbor $v \neq u$ with probability proportional to $|S_{uv}|$, along with the edge weight $S_{uv}$. If $u$ has no out-neighbors, then return a symbol $\perp$.*

The vertex query and neighbor query can be viewed as a natural extension of local queries on unweighted undirected graphs to the setting of weighted directed graphs [15]. The random walk query has been considered in more recent works [19,23].

We consider the problem of solving the linear system $Sz = b$ in the query model. Given the access to the $(S, b)$-oracle, an input vertex $u \in [n]$, an error bound $\varepsilon > 0$, and possible other additional information such as $\delta$ and $\|b\|_\infty$, the algorithm is required to compute a value $z_u$ in sublinear time such that $|z_u - z_u^*| < \varepsilon$, where $z^*$ is the unique solution satisfying $Sz^* = b$.

**Algorithmic Results.** We first present our result on strictly DD matrices ($\delta$-DD for $\delta > 0$). We define $S_{\max} = \max_{i\in[n]} |S_{ii}|$.

**Theorem 1.** *Let $\delta > 0$, $S \in \mathbb{R}^{n\times n}$ be a $\delta$-DD matrix and $b \in \mathbb{R}^n$. There exists an algorithm with access to the $(S, b)$-oracle such that given $\delta$, $\|b\|_\infty$, an error bound $\varepsilon > 0$ and a vertex $u \in [n]$, it outputs a random value $z_u$ with query* *complexity* $O\left(\frac{\|b\|_\infty^2 S_{\max}}{\delta^3\varepsilon^2}\log\frac{\|b\|_\infty}{\delta\varepsilon}\right)$, *and with probability at least* $2/3$, $z_u$ *satisfies* $|z_u - z_u^*| < \varepsilon$, *where* $z^*$ *is the unique solution satisfying* $Sz^* = b$.

As a corollary, we can also obtain a sublinear-time algorithm that achieves relative error with respect to $\|z^*\|_\infty$.

**Corollary 1.** *Let* $\delta > 0$. *There exists an algorithm with access to* $(S, b)$*-oracle for any* $\delta$*-DD matrix* $S$ *and let* $b \in \mathbb{R}^n$ *be a vector such that for given* $\delta$, $\|b\|_\infty$, *the value of* $S_{\max}$, *an error bound* $\varepsilon > 0$, *and a vertex* $u \in [n]$, *it outputs a random value* $z_u$ *with query complexity* $O\left(\frac{S_{\max}^3}{\delta^3\varepsilon^2}\log\frac{S_{\max}}{\delta\varepsilon}\right)$, *and with probability at least* $2/3$, $z_u$ *satisfies* $|z_u - z_u^*| < \varepsilon\|z^*\|_\infty$, *where* $z^*$ *is the solution satisfying* $Sz^* = b$.

We next consider the case that $S$ is a non-strictly DD matrix, which means for all $i \in [n]$, $|S_{ii}| \geq \sum_{j\in[n]:j\neq i}|S_{ij}|$. We consider matrices $S$ satisfying the following condition.

**Condition 1.** *$S$ is non-strictly DD and $(S, b)$ satisfies one of the following two conditions (i) $S$ is non-singular; (ii) $S$ is symmetric, and all the diagonal entries are non-zero and have the same sign.*

Define $\infty$-norm condition number of $S$ as $\kappa_\infty(S) = \|S\|_\infty\|S^{-1}\|_\infty$, where $S^{-1}$ is the pseudo-inverse of $S$ if $S$ is singular. Let $z^*$ be a solution to $Sz = b$. Under the first condition in Condition 1, $z^*$ is unique. Under the second condition, $S$ is symmetric and we define $z^* = S^{-1}b$, where $S^{-1}$ is the pseudo-inverse of the symmetric matrix $S$.

**Theorem 2.** *There exists an algorithm with access to* $(S, b)$*-oracle for any* $S$ *satisfying Condition 1 and any* $b$ *in the range of* $S$ *such that given* $\kappa_\infty(S)$, $\|b\|_\infty$, $S_{\max}$, *and a vertex* $u \in [n]$, *it returns a random value* $z_u$ *with query complexity* $O\left(\frac{\kappa_\infty(S)^3}{\varepsilon^5}\log\frac{\kappa_\infty(S)}{\varepsilon}\right)$, *and with probability at least* $2/3$, $z_u$ *satisfies* $|z_u - z_u^*| < \varepsilon\|z^*\|_\infty$, *where* $z^* = S^{-1}b$.

**Lower Bound.** Note that when $\|b\|_\infty \leq 1$, the query complexity of the algorithm in Theorem 1 is $O\left(\frac{S_{\max}}{\delta^3\varepsilon^2}\log\frac{1}{\delta\varepsilon}\right)$. The following lower bound shows that the dependence on $S_{\max}$ is optimal.

Assume $S$ is non-singular. We say a sublinear-time algorithm $\mathcal{A}$ with access to a $(S, b)$-oracle solves the system $Sz = b$ with additive error $\varepsilon$ if, for every $u \in [n]$, it outputs $z_u$ such that $|z_u - z_u^*| \leq \varepsilon$ with probability at least $2/3$, where $z^*$ is the unique solution to $Sz = b$. Let $\Delta_{\max}^S = \max_{u\in[n]}\left|\{v \neq u : S_{uv} \neq 0\}\right|$ denote the maximum out-degree of the graph induced by $S$.

**Theorem 3.** *There exists a constant* $\varepsilon_0 > 0$ *such that the following holds: For any sublinear-time algorithm* $\mathcal{A}$ *that solves the linear system* $Sz = b$ *with additive error* $\varepsilon_0$, *there exist a* $1$*-diagonally dominant matrix* $S \in \mathbb{R}^{n\times n}$ *satisfying* $S_{\max} = \Theta(\sqrt{n})$ *and* $\Delta_{\max}^S = O(1)$, *and a Boolean vector* $b \in \{0, 1\}^n$, *such that* $\mathcal{A}$ *must make* $\Omega(S_{\max})$ *queries to the* $(S, b)$*-oracle.*

Taking $\delta = 1$, $\varepsilon = \varepsilon_0 = \Theta(1)$, and $\|b\|_\infty = 1$, the algorithm in Theorem 1 achieves query complexity $O(S_{\max})$, which matches the lower bound in Theorem 3. For the hard instances constructed in Theorem 3, we have $S_{\max} = \Theta(d^S_{\max})$, where $d^S_{\max} = \max_u \sum_{v \neq u} |S_{uv}|$ is the maximum weighted out-degree of the graph $G$ constructed from $S$. This lower bound shows that even when the maximum out-degree $\Delta^S_{\max}$ is constant, the running time must be at least linear in the maximum weighted out-degree $d^S_{\max}$. When expressed in terms of $n$, Theorem 3 establishes an $\Omega(\sqrt{n})$ lower bound on the query complexity.

*Independent Work.* Recently, Kwok et al. [21] give new sublinear-time algorithms for solving some special asymmetric DD system, such as row and column DD (RCDD) matrices or $b$ is nonnegative, and they established a lower bound on the dependence on $\varepsilon$. Our algorithm is mainly based on the property of strictly DD matrices, while our lower bound depends on $S_{\max}$.

**Applications to the Friedkin–Johnsen Opinion Dynamics.** The Friedkin–Johnsen (FJ) model is a popular model for studying opinion formation processes in social networks [14]. Neumann et al. applied the solver from [3] to the opinion estimation problem in the Friedkin–Johnsen model [23]. Let $G_{\mathrm{FJ}} = (V, E, w)$ be an undirected, weighted graph. Each node $u$ has an *innate opinion* $b_u \in [0, 1]$ and an *expressed opinion* $z_u \in [0, 1]$. While the innate opinions are fixed, the expressed opinions evolve over time $t$ according to the update rule:

$$z_u^{(t+1)} = \frac{b_u + \sum_{(u,v)\in E} w_{uv} z_v^{(t)}}{1 + \sum_{(u,v)\in E} w_{uv}}, \tag{1}$$

i.e., each node updates its expressed opinion as a weighted average of its own innate opinion and the expressed opinions of its neighbors. It is known that as $t \to \infty$, the expressed opinions converge to the equilibrium $z^* = (I + L)^{-1} b$, where $I$ is the identity matrix and $L = D - A$ is the graph Laplacian of $G_{\mathrm{FJ}}$, with $D$ as the weighted degree matrix and $A$ as the weighted adjacency matrix.

It was observed by Neumann, Dong and Peng in [23] that $z_u^*$ can be approximated using the sublinear-time solver from [3], yielding an estimate $\tilde{z}_u^*$ such that $|\tilde{z}_u^* - z_u^*| \leq \varepsilon$ with probability $1 - \frac{1}{s}$, where $s = O(\kappa \log(\varepsilon^{-1} n \kappa \max_u w_u))$ and $\kappa$ is an upper bound on the 2-norm condition number of $(I+D)^{-\frac{1}{2}}(I+L)(I+D)^{-\frac{1}{2}}$. This algorithm works if $G_{\mathrm{FJ}}$ is a regular graph and the query complexity is $(W/\varepsilon)^{O(W \log(1/\varepsilon))}$, where $W$ is the weighted degree of the graph $G_{\mathrm{FJ}}$.

We apply our sublinear-time algorithm in Theorem 1 to the Friedkin–Johnsen model. We set $S = I + L$ and define $W$ is the maximum *weighted* degree of the graph $G_{\mathrm{FJ}}$ for Friedkin–Johnsen model such that $W = \max_{u \in V} \sum_{v:\{u,v\}\in E} w_{uv}$. Then, the parameter $S_{\max} = W + 1$. Note that for Friedkin–Johnsen model, $S = I + L$ is 1-diagonally dominant and $\|b\|_\infty \leq 1$. We obtain the following algorithm.

**Theorem 4.** *For the Friedkin–Johnsen model, there exists an algorithm with access to the $(I + L, b)$-oracle such that given an error bound $\varepsilon > 0$ and a vertex $u \in [n]$, the algorithm returns a random value $z_u$ with query complexity*

*$O(\frac{W}{\varepsilon^2}\log\frac{1}{\varepsilon})$ such that with probability at least 2/3, $z_u$ satisfies $|z_u - z_u^*| < \varepsilon$, where $z^*$ is the unique solution satisfying $(I+L)z^* = b$.*

*Worst-Case Optimal Query Complexity.* The query complexity in Theorem 4 is worst-case *optimal* for the Friedkin–Johnsen model. The hard instances $(S, b)$ in Theorem 3 satisfy $S = I + L$ and $b \in \{0,1\}^n$, where $L$ is the Laplacian matrix of an undirected weighted regular graph $G_L$. We can take $G_{\mathrm{FJ}} = G_L$, then the hardness instance becomes a Friedkin–Johnsen model on graph $G_{\mathrm{FJ}}$. The lower bound in Theorem 3 shows that to achieve constant error $\varepsilon = O(1)$, the query complexity is $\Omega(S_{\max}) = \Omega(W)$. For constant error, our algorithm in Theorem 4 achieves the optimal $O(W)$ query complexity.

### 1.2 Comparison to Prior Work

We compare our results with closely related works and highlight key differences in assumptions, guarantees, and complexity.

*Comparison to* [3]. We compare with results in [3], which study a similar problem under different assumptions. Let $D = \mathrm{diag}(S_{11}, \ldots, S_{nn})$ and define $\tilde{S} = D^{-1/2} S D^{-1/2}$. Their algorithm outputs $z_u$ such that $|z_u - z_u^*| < \varepsilon \|z^*\|_\infty$ in time $\tilde{O}(\kappa^3/\varepsilon^2)$, where $\kappa$ is the 2-norm condition number of $\tilde{S}$.

Our algorithm applies to general settings and achieves improved performance on certain classes of matrices. Their algorithm is restricted to symmetric DD matrices with strictly positive diagonal entries, whereas Corollary 1 and Theorem 2 hold for general DD matrices without such restrictions. Furthermore, under the Friedkin–Johnsen model, Theorem 1 yields improved query complexity for networks with small degree variation, such as small-world networks and Erdős–Rényi (ER) networks, since $\|b\|_\infty \le 1$ in this setting.

*Comparison to* [23]. We also compare our results for the Friedkin–Johnsen model with those of [23]. Their randomized algorithm achieves query complexity $\tilde{O}(W^3/\varepsilon^2)$ when $G_{\mathrm{FJ}}$ is a regular graph with uniform edge weights and maximum weighted degree $W$. Their deterministic algorithm has query complexity $(W/\varepsilon)^{O(W\log(1/\varepsilon))}$. Our algorithm achieves a much better query complexity $\tilde{O}(\frac{W}{\varepsilon^2}\log\frac{1}{\varepsilon})$. We also conduct experiments on the Friedkin–Johnsen model and compare the performance of our algorithm with that of [23] on the same dataset. The results show that our algorithm is much faster in practice.

### 1.3 Technical Overview

**Algorithm Overview.** Our main algorithm is based on a probabilistic recursion. Consider the linear system $Sz^* = b$, where $S$ is strictly diagonally dominant. For any $u \in [n]$, it holds that $\sum_{v \neq u} S_{uv} z_v^* + S_{uu} z_u^* = b_u$. Rearranging the terms, the following equation holds for any $u \in [n]$:

$$z_u^* = \frac{b_u - \sum_{v \neq u} S_{uv} z_v^*}{S_{uu}}.$$

Define the following sign function. For any $x \in \mathbb{R}$, define the sign function as $\operatorname{sgn}(x) = 1$ if $x > 0$, $\operatorname{sgn}(x) = 0$ if $x = 0$, and $\operatorname{sgn}(x) = -1$ if $x < 0$. Recall that $d_u^{\text{out}} = \sum_{v \neq u} |S_{uv}|$ is the out-weighted-degree of $u$. Now, $z_u^*$ can be rewritten as

$$z_u^* = \underbrace{\frac{|S_{uu}| - d_u^{\text{out}}}{|S_{uu}|}}_{=P(u,u)} \cdot \frac{\operatorname{sgn}(S_{uu}) b_u}{|S_{uu}| - d_u^{\text{out}}} + \sum_{v \neq u} \underbrace{\frac{|S_{uv}|}{|S_{uu}|}}_{=P(u,v)} \cdot \operatorname{sgn}(-S_{uu} S_{uv}) z_v^*. \tag{2}$$

Let $P(u,u) = \frac{|S_{uu}| - d_u^{\text{out}}}{|S_{uu}|}$ for $u \in [n]$ and $P(u,v) = \frac{|S_{uv}|}{|S_{uu}|}$ for $v \neq u$. Since $S$ is strictly diagonally dominant, the matrix $P$ forms a row-stochastic matrix. Equation (2) can be interpreted as: $z_u^*$ equals the expectation of a random process that, with probability $P(u,u)$, outputs $\frac{\operatorname{sgn}(S_{uu}) b_u}{|S_{uu}| - d_u^{\text{out}}}$, and with probability $P(u,v)$ transitions to vertex $v$ with a sign correction. This interpretation suggests a simple recursive algorithm.

**Proof Overview of the Lower Bound.** Our lower bound is based on the construction of two distributions of $S \in \mathbb{R}^{n \times n}$ and $b \in \mathbb{R}^n$ instances $\mathcal{F}_0$ and $\mathcal{F}_1$. Consider the sublinear-time algorithm interacting with the $(S, b)$-oracle. By choosing a proper $u \in [n]$ as the input, we can show the following two propositions:

- If there is a sublinear-time algorithm that approximates $z_u^*$ with a small constant error, where $z^*$ is the unique solution satisfying $S z^* = b$, then the algorithm can distinguish whether $\mathcal{F} = \mathcal{F}_0$ or $\mathcal{F} = \mathcal{F}_1$.
- Any sublinear-time algorithm that can distinguish whether $\mathcal{F} = \mathcal{F}_0$ or $\mathcal{F} = \mathcal{F}_1$ requires at least $\Omega(S_{\max})$ queries, where $S_{\max} = \max_{i \in [n]} |S_{ii}|$.

Next, we sketch the construction of the hard instances. In both distributions $\mathcal{F}_0$ and $\mathcal{F}_1$, the matrix $S = I + L$ is the same, where $I$ is the identity matrix and $L$ is the Laplacian matrix of a weighted graph $G$. The graph $G$ is constructed by using constant degree expander graphs as building blocks. The vector $b$ takes different values in two distributions $\mathcal{F}_0$ and $\mathcal{F}_1$. The two properties mentioned above can be verified by using some expansion properties of the expanders.

### 1.4 Other Related Work

Random walks have also played a central role in the design of sublinear-time algorithms for various graph problems beyond solving linear systems. They have been used to approximate a variety of local graph centrality measures, such as PageRank and personalized PageRank scores, which are important in ranking and recommendation systems [5]. Random walks are also instrumental in estimating stationary distributions of Markov chains, particularly for fast convergence and mixing time analysis in large networks [4,6]. In addition, random walk techniques have been applied to estimate effective resistances between vertex pairs [3,24], a quantity closely tied to graph connectivity and electrical flow. Another notable application is in designing algorithms for sampling vertices with probability proportional to their degrees, which is useful in streaming and sparsification contexts [12]. These applications demonstrate the versatility of random walks as a tool for designing efficient sublinear and local algorithms in large-scale graphs.

There are also some quantum-inspired classical sublinear-time algorithms for linear system solvers. Chia et al. gave classical sublinear-time algorithms for solving low-rank linear systems of equations [7,8]. Their algorithms are inspired by the HHL quantum algorithm [16] for solving linear systems and the breakthrough by Tang [29] of dequantizing the quantum algorithm for recommendation systems. Their sublinear-time algorithms sample from and estimate entries of $x$ such that $\|x - A^{\dagger}b\| \leq \varepsilon\|A^{\dagger}b\|$ for low-rank $A \in \mathbb{C}^{m\times n}$ in $\mathrm{poly}(k, \kappa, \|A\|_F, 1/\varepsilon)\cdot\mathrm{poly}\log(m,n)$ time per query, assuming length-square sampling access to input $A$ and query access to $b$. Shao and Montanaro [25] gave a slightly improved algorithm.

## 2 The Algorithms for DD Systems

In this section, we present algorithms based on a recursive procedure.

**Algorithm 1:** RECURSIVESOLVER $(u)$

1: **Input:** Current vertex $u$; query access to the $(S, b)$-oracle
2: **Output:** A real-valued random variable
3: Perform a vertex query on $u$ to retrieve $b_u$, $S_{uu}$, and $\mathrm{d}_u^{\mathrm{out}}$
4: **With probability** $\frac{|S_{uu}|-\mathrm{d}_u^{\mathrm{out}}}{|S_{uu}|}$ **do**
5: **return** $\frac{\mathrm{sgn}(S_{uu})\cdot b_u}{|S_{uu}|-\mathrm{d}_u^{\mathrm{out}}}$
6: **Otherwise**
7: Perform a random walk query on $u$ for out-neighbor $v$ and edge weight $S_{uv}$
8: **return** $\mathrm{sgn}(-S_{uu}S_{uv}) \cdot$ RECURSIVESOLVER$(v)$

For any vertex $u$, let $z_u$ denote the random variable returned by RECURSIVESOLVER$(u)$. We have the following lemma.

**Lemma 1.** *For any $u \in [n]$,* RECURSIVESOLVER$(u)$ *returns a random variable $z_u$ with expected query complexity $O\left(\frac{S_{\max}}{\delta}\right)$, where $z_u$ satisfies $\mathbb{E}[z_u] = z_u^*$ and $z^*$ is the unique solution of $Sz = b$.*

*Proof.* First, we show that the random variable $z_u$ returned by the algorithm is well-defined. In each recursion step, the algorithm terminates and output a value with probability $\frac{|S_{uu}|-d_u^{\mathrm{out}}}{|S_{uu}|} \geq \frac{\delta}{|S_{uu}|} > 0$. Otherwise, the algorithm starts a new recursion step. Hence, the number of recursion steps is dominated by a geometric random variable and the algorithm finally terminates with probability 1. This implies the random variable $z_u$ is well-defined. Furthermore, by the expectation of geometric random variable, the expected recursion depth is at most $O\left(\max_{i\in[n]} \frac{|S_{ii}|}{|S_{ii}|-d_i^{\text{out}}}\right) \leq O\left(\frac{S_{\max}}{\delta}\right)$. Since the total query complexity is linear in the total number of recursions, the expected query complexity of RECURSIVESOLVER $(u)$ is $O\left(\frac{S_{\max}}{\delta}\right)$.

Next, we calculate the expectation $\mathbb{E}[z_u]$ of $z_u$. By the definition of the RECURSIVESOLVER$(u)$, $z_u$ takes the value $\frac{\text{sgn}(S_{uu})b_u}{|S_{uu}|-d_u^{\text{out}}}$ with probability $\frac{|S_{uu}|-d_u^{\text{out}}}{|S_{uu}|}$. Otherwise, with probability $\frac{|S_{uv}|}{|S_{uu}|}$, $z_u$ takes the random value $\text{sgn}(-S_{uu}S_{uv})z_v$. By the law of total expectation, we have

$$\begin{aligned}\mathbb{E}[z_u] &= \frac{|S_{uu}|-d_u^{\text{out}}}{|S_{uu}|}\cdot\frac{\text{sgn}(S_{uu})b_u}{|S_{uu}|-d_u^{\text{out}}} + \sum_{v\neq u}\frac{|S_{uv}|}{|S_{uu}|}\cdot\text{sgn}(-S_{uu}S_{uv})\mathbb{E}[z_v].\\ &= S_{uu}^{-1}\left(b_u - \sum_{v\neq u} S_{uv}\mathbb{E}[z_v]\right).\end{aligned}$$

Let $\mathbb{E}[z]$ denote the vector $(\mathbb{E}[z_u])_{u\in[n]}$. Since the above equation holds for any $u \in [n]$, we have $S\mathbb{E}[z] = b$. Since $Sx = b$ has a unique solution $x = z^*$, we have $\mathbb{E}[z] = z^*$. In particular, $\mathbb{E}[z_u] = z_u^*$ for all $u \in [n]$.

*Basic Subroutines.* Using the recursion idea discussed in Sect. 1.3, Equation (2) suggests the following simple recursive procedure Algorithm 1 RECURSIVESOLVER. Furthermore, we need the subroutine Algorithm 2 ESTIMATEZ that outputs the average of estimates from some other procedure **ASolver**.

*An Algorithm with Bounded Expected Running Time.* We first give an algorithm with bounded expected query complexity in the following lemma. Note that $|z_u^{(i)}| \leq \|b\|_\infty/\delta$, we can bound the variance of $z_u^{(i)}$ and get the following lemma.

**Lemma 2.** *With probability at least* $2/3$*, Algorithm 2, where* ***ASolver*** *is instantiated by* RECURSIVESOLVER *(Algorithm 1), returns an estimate* $\tilde{z}_u$ *such that* $|\tilde{z}_u - z_u^*| \leq \varepsilon$*. The expected query complexity of the algorithm is* $O\left(\frac{\|b\|_\infty^2 S_{\max}}{\delta^3\varepsilon^2}\right)$.

---

**Algorithm 2:** ESTIMATEZ $(u, \delta, \varepsilon, \|b\|_\infty)$

---

1: **Input:** The query vertex $u$; parameters $\delta > 0$, $\varepsilon > 0$, and $\|b\|_\infty$; query access to the $(S, b)$-oracle
2: **Output:** The estimate of $z_u^*$
3: Set $t \leftarrow \frac{6\|b\|_\infty^2}{\delta^2\varepsilon^2}$
4: **for** $i = 1$ to $t$ **do**
5: $\quad z_u^{(i)} \leftarrow$ **ASolver**$(u)$
6: **return** $\tilde{z}_u \leftarrow \frac{1}{t}\sum_{i=1}^{t} z_u^{(i)}$

---

*An Algorithm with Bounded Worst-Case Running Time.* The running time of the algorithm in Lemma 2 is randomized without a fixed upper bound. We now present a modified algorithm with a bounded worst-case running time. Specifically, instead of instantiating **ASolver**($u$) with RECURSIVESOLVER($u$) in Algorithm 2, we use TRUNCATEDRECURSIVESOLVER($u, p$), as defined in Algorithm 3. Note that TRUNCATEDRECURSIVESOLVER($u$,$p$) maintains a probability value $p$.

That is, the modified algorithm, denoted by $\mathcal{A}$, is defined as Algorithm 2 ESTIMATEZ, with **ASolver** instantiated by Algorithm 3 TRUNCATEDRECURSIVESOLVER($u, p$), where the initial value of $p$ is set to 1. We use algorithm $\mathcal{A}$ to prove Theorem 1. The key point is that RECURSIVESOLVER($u$) and TRUNCATEDRECURSIVESOLVER($u, 1$) can be coupled using the same randomness; they differ only when the latter is truncated before the former naturally terminates, and we will bound this event to show that the total variation distance between their output distributions is small. Note that $\|D^{-1}b\|_\infty \leq 2\|z\|_\infty$, we can prove Corollary 1 that achieves relative error with respect to $\|z^*\|_\infty$.

For non-strictly diagonally dominant matrix, we prove Theorem 2. The main idea of the proof is given as follows.

- We define a diagonal matrix $I'$ and a small parameter $\sigma$ (detailed definitions are given later). We show that the solution of $Sz = b$ and the solution of $S'z = b$ are close, where $S' = S + \sigma I'$.
- Now, $S'$ is a strictly diagonally dominant matrix. We can use the algorithm in Corollary 1 to solve the system $S'z = b$.

**Algorithm 3:** TRUNCATEDRECURSIVESOLVER($u$, $p$)

**Input:** Current vertex $u$; recursion probability $p$; query access to the $(S, b)$-oracle
**Output:** A real-valued random variable
Set $t' \leftarrow \frac{6\|b\|_\infty^2}{\delta^2 \varepsilon^2}$
Perform a vertex query on $u$ to retrieve $b_u$, $S_{uu}$, and $\mathrm{d}_u^{\mathrm{out}}$
**With probability** $\frac{|S_{uu}| - \mathrm{d}_u^{\mathrm{out}}}{|S_{uu}|}$ **do**
    **return** $\frac{\mathrm{sgn}(S_{uu}) \cdot b_u}{|S_{uu}| - \mathrm{d}_u^{\mathrm{out}}}$
Update $p \leftarrow \frac{\mathrm{d}_u^{\mathrm{out}}}{|S_{uu}|} \cdot p$
**if** $p \leq \frac{1}{6t'}$ **then**
    **return** an arbitrary value (e.g., 0)
**else**
    Perform a random walk query on $u$ to obtain an out-neighbor $v$ and edge weight $S_{uv}$
    **return** $\mathrm{sgn}(-S_{uu}S_{uv}) \cdot$ TRUNCATEDRECURSIVESOLVER($v, p$)

As an application of our main theorem, we prove Theorem 4.

*Proof (**Proof of Theorem** 4).* By the definition of Friedkin–Johnsen model, we have $S = I + L$ and $b \in [0, 1]^n$, where $L$ is the Laplacian matrix of an undirected weighted graph. We can set $\delta = 1$, $\|b\|_\infty \le 1$, and $S_{\max} = W + 1$ in Theorem 1 to obtain the output $z_u$ satisfying $|z_u - z_u^*| < \varepsilon$ with probability at least $\frac{2}{3}$. The query complexity is $O\left(\frac{\|b\|_\infty^2 S_{\max}}{\delta^3 \varepsilon^2} \log \frac{\|b\|_\infty}{\delta\varepsilon}\right) = O\left(\frac{W+1}{\varepsilon^2} \log \frac{1}{\varepsilon}\right)$.

# 3 The Lower Bound

In this section, we prove Theorem 3. We start with the construction of hard instances. For infinitely many $n$, we consider the following hard instance $(S, b)$, where $S \in \mathbb{R}^{n \times n}$ and $b \in \mathbb{R}^n$ are both constructed from a weighted graph $G$. We first define the weighted graph $G$ and show how to construct $S$ and $b$ from $G$.

We use unweighted expander graphs as a basic building block of our hard instances. Let graph $G^{\mathrm{nd}}$ be an undirected, unweighted graph. The Laplacian of $G^{\mathrm{nd}}$ is defined as $L = D - A$, where $D$ is the diagonal matrix of degrees and $A$ is the adjacency matrix of $G^{\mathrm{nd}}$. Let $\bar{L} = D^{-1/2} L D^{-1/2}$ be the normalized Laplacian of $G^{\mathrm{nd}}$. Let $0 = \lambda_1 \le \lambda_2 \le \cdots \le \lambda_n \le 2$ be the eigenvalues of $\bar{L}$. The spectral expansion of $G^{\mathrm{nd}}$ is defined as $\gamma_G = \min(\lambda_2, 2 - \lambda_n)$.

**Proposition 1 (Ramanujan Graphs** [18,22]**).** *Let $d = 98$, where $d - 1$ is a prime number and $(d-1) \mod 4 = 1$. For infinitely many $N \in \mathbb{N}$, there exists a connected unweighted $d$-regular simple graph $G_N^{\mathrm{ex}} = (V, E)$ with $N$ vertices such that $\gamma_{G_N^{\mathrm{ex}}} \ge 1 - \frac{2\sqrt{d-1}}{d} > \frac{2}{3}$.*

In the rest of the proof, we use $d$ to denote the universal constant 98 in Proposition 1. Fix $k \in \mathbb{N}$ and let $n = k^2$. We now construct a distribution $\mu_n$ of graphs and then sample a random graph $G \sim \mu_n$ to construct hard instances. By Proposition 1, there are infinitely many integers $k$. Hence, we can construct the distribution $\mu_n$ for infinitely many $n$. Let graphs $G'$ and $B$ be two disjoint copies of $G_k^{\mathrm{ex}}$. Let $C$ be a set of $n - 2k$ isolated vertices. Note that $G', B$ and $C$ have $n$ vertices in total. A random *weighted* graph $G \sim \mu_n$ is constructed by the following procedure (See Fig. 1 for an illustration of the construction.):

- Let $G$ be obtained by taking the union of $G'$, $B$, and $C$, and adding an unweighted edge between a uniformly random vertex $w_{G'} \in G'$ and a uniformly random vertex $w_B \in B$.
- Assign a uniform random permutation of $[n]$ to relabel the vertices of $G$.
- Assign weight $k$ to every edge.

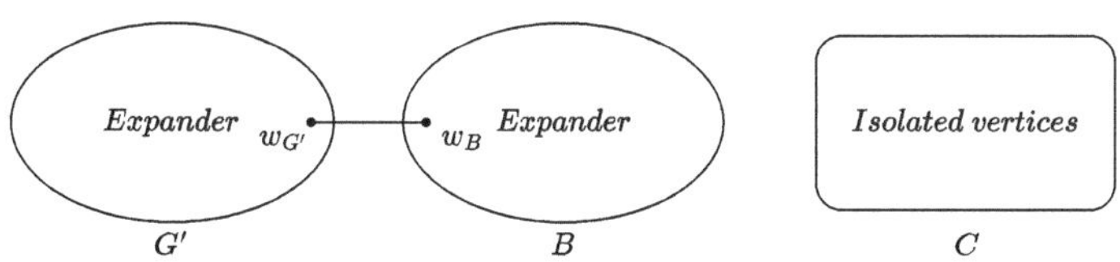


**Fig. 1.** Construction of $G$ with two expanders ($G'$ and $B$) and $n - \Theta(\sqrt{n})$ isolated vertices ($C$).

- For each vertex, independently choose a uniform random permutation of its neighbors for answering neighbor queries.

We now sample a random graph $G \sim \mu_n$ and show how to construct two instances $(S^G, b^{G\text{-}1})$ and $(S^G, b^{G\text{-}0})$ from $G$. Note that two instances share the same matrix $S^G$ but have different vectors $b^{G\text{-}1}$ and $b^{G\text{-}0}$. Let $L^G = D^G - A^G$ be the Laplacian of $G$, where $D^G$ is the diagonal matrix of weighted degrees and $A^G$ is the weighted adjacency matrix of $G$. The input matrix is the following: $S^G = I + L^G$. The following observation follows directly from the definition.

**Observation 1.** *The matrix $S^G$ is 1-DD, $S_{\max} = \Theta(dk) = \Theta(\sqrt{n})$, and $\Delta^S_{\max} = d = O(1)$.*

Given the graph $G$, we define two vectors $b^{G\text{-}0} = \mathbf{0}$ and $b^{G\text{-}1} = \mathbf{1}_B$, where $\mathbf{1}_B$ denotes the indicator vector of the set $B$. Finally, the query vertex $u$ is sampled uniformly at random from $G' \subseteq G$. The following lemma shows that the answers of two instances have a constant gap.

**Lemma 3.** *For the random instances $(S^G, b^{G\text{-}0})$ and $(S^G, b^{G\text{-}1})$ and the random query vertex $u$ sampled uniformly at random from $G' \subseteq G$, the following holds with probability 1:*

- *$z^*_u = 0$ where $z^*$ is the unique solution of $S^G z = b^{G\text{-}0}$.*
- *$z^*_u \geq c_0$ where $z^*$ is the unique solution of $S^G z = b^{G\text{-}1}$ and $c_0 = \frac{1-e^{-\frac{1}{20d}}}{12(d+2)}$ is a constant.*

Next, we show that any sublinear-time algorithm with low query complexity cannot distinguish between the two instances $(S^G, b^{G\text{-}0})$ and $(S^G, b^{G\text{-}1})$ for $G \sim \mu_n$. We first introduce the definition of query-answer history for an abstract sublinear algorithm. Let $\mathcal{A}$ be a sublinear-time algorithm using $\ell$ queries to a given $(S, b)$-oracle. A query-answer history $D^{\mathcal{A}}$ is an ordered tuple $[(q_0, a_0), (q_1, a_1), \cdots, (q_\ell, a_\ell)]$ such that

- $q_0 =$ and $a_0$ is the input of the algorithm;
- For any $1 \leq i \leq \ell$, $q_i$ is the $i_{th}$ query to the $(S, b)$-oracle and $a_i$ is the answer of $q_i$ returned by the oracle. For the $i_{th}$ query, a (possibly probabilistic) mapping maps $\{(q_j, a_j) \mid 0 \leq j < i\}$ to the query $q_i$, where $q_i$ is one of the three types of queries in Definition 2.

Finally, a (possibly probabilistic) mapping maps $\{(q_j, a_j) \mid 0 \leq j < \ell\}$ to the output of $\mathcal{A}$. Abstractly, the algorithm can be viewed as first sampling $x \sim D^{\mathcal{A}}$, and then mapping (possibly probabilistic mapping) $x$ to the output $\mathcal{A}(x)$.

Let $G \sim \mu_n$. Let $u$ be a uniform random vertex in $G' \subseteq G$. Let $P_0$ be the query access oracle of $(S^G, b^{G\text{-}0})$. Let $P_1$ be the query access oracle of $(S^G, b^{G\text{-}1})$. Let $\mathcal{A}$ be a sublinear-time algorithm given $u$ as the input, where $u$ is a uniform random vertex in $G'$. Given the access to an oracle $P \in \{P_0, P_1\}$, consider the algorithm $\mathcal{A}$ that can distinguish whether $P = P_0$ or $P = P_1$, where the algorithm outputs

**Yes** if $P = P_0$ or outputs **No** if $P = P_1$. Define $D_0^{\mathcal{A}}$ and $D_1^{\mathcal{A}}$ as the query-answer histories induced by the interaction of $\mathcal{A}$ and $P_0$ and $P_1$ respectively.

Next, we bound the total variation distance between $D_0^{\mathcal{A}}$ and $D_1^{\mathcal{A}}$. Note that both $D_0^{\mathcal{A}}$ and $D_1^{\mathcal{A}}$ are random variables whose randomness comes from the randomness of $G \sim \mu_n$, the uniform random vertex $u$ sampled from $G'$, and the independent randomness inside $\mathcal{A}$.

**Lemma 4.** *The following result holds for any constant* $\alpha < 1/2$. *For any algorithm* $\mathcal{A}$ *that asks* $m \leq \alpha k$ *queries, the total variation distance between* $D_1^{\mathcal{A}}$ *and* $D_2^{\mathcal{A}}$ *is at most* $6\alpha$.

The lower bound result in Theorem 3 can be proved by combining Lemma 3 and Lemma 4.

## References


1. Alman, J., Duan, R., Williams, V.V., Xu, Y., Xu, Z., Zhou, R.: More asymmetry yields faster matrix multiplication. In: Proceedings of the 2025 Annual ACM-SIAM Symposium on Discrete Algorithms (SODA), pp. 2005–2039. SIAM (2025)
2. Ambainis, A.: Variable time amplitude amplification and quantum algorithms for linear algebra problems. In: 29th Symposium on Theoretical Aspects of Computer Science (STACS), vol. 14, pp. 636–647. LIPIcs (2012)
3. Andoni, A., Krauthgamer, R., Pogrow, Y.: On solving linear systems in sublinear time. In: 10th Innovations in Theoretical Computer Science Conference (ITCS), vol. 124, pp. 3:1–3:19 (2019)
4. Banerjee, S., Lofgren, P.: Fast bidirectional probability estimation in Markov models. In: The 28th Advances in Neural Information Processing Systems (NIPS), pp. 1423–1431 (2015)
5. Bressan, M., Peserico, E., Pretto, L.: Sublinear algorithms for local graph centrality estimation. In: 59th IEEE Annual Symposium on Foundations of Computer Science (FOCS), pp. 709–718 (2018)
6. Bressan, M., Peserico, E., Pretto, L.: On approximating the stationary distribution of time-reversible Markov chains. Theory Comput. Syst. **64**(3), 444–466 (2020)
7. Chia, N.-H., Gilyén, A., Lin, H.-H., Lloyd, S., Tang, E., Wang, C.: Quantum-inspired algorithms for solving low-rank linear equation systems with logarithmic dependence on the dimension. In: 31st International Symposium on Algorithms and Computation (ISAAC), pp. 47–1. Schloss Dagstuhl–Leibniz-Zentrum für Informatik (2020)
8. Chia, N.-H., Lin, H.-H., Wang, C.: Quantum-inspired sublinear classical algorithms for solving low-rank linear systems. arXiv preprint arXiv:1811.04852 (2018)
9. Childs, A.M., Kothari, R., Somma, R.D.: Quantum algorithm for systems of linear equations with exponentially improved dependence on precision. SIAM J. Comput. **46**(6), 1920–1950 (2017)
10. Cohen, M.B., et al.: Solving directed Laplacian systems in nearly-linear time through sparse LU factorizations. In: 2018 IEEE 59th Annual Symposium on Foundations of Computer Science (FOCS), pp. 898–909. IEEE (2018)
11. Cohen, M.B., et al.: Solving SDD linear systems in nearly $m \log^{1/2} n$ time. In: Proceedings of the 46th Annual ACM Symposium on Theory of Computing (STOC), pp. 343–352 (2014)

12. Dasgupta, A., Kumar, R., Sarlos, T.: On estimating the average degree. In: 23rd International World Wide Web Conference (WWW), pp. 795–806 (2014)
13. Dervovic, D., Herbster, M., Mountney, P., Severini, S., Usher, N., Wossnig, L.: Quantum linear systems algorithms: a primer. arXiv preprint arXiv:1802.08227 (2018)
14. Friedkin, N.E., Johnsen, E.C.: Social influence and opinions. J. Math. Sociol. **15**(3–4), 193–206 (1990)
15. Goldreich, O.: Introduction to Testing Graph Properties. Springer, Heidelberg (2010)
16. Harrow, A.W., Hassidim, A., Lloyd, S.: Quantum algorithm for linear systems of equations. Phys. Rev. Lett. **103**(15), 150502 (2009)
17. Holtz, C., Chen, P., Wan, Z., Cheng, C.K., Mishne, G.: Continuous partitioning for graph-based semi-supervised learning. In: The 38th Annual Conference on Neural Information Processing Systems (NeurIPS) (2024)
18. Hoory, S., Linial, N., Wigderson, A.: Expander graphs and their applications. Bull. Am. Math. Soc. **43**(4), 439–561 (2006)
19. Jin, Y., Karmarkar, I., Musco, C., Sidford, A., Singh, A.V.: Faster spectral density estimation and sparsification in the nuclear norm (extended abstract). In: The Thirty Seventh Annual Conference on Learning Theory (COLT). Proceedings of Machine Learning Research, vol. 247, p. 2722. PMLR (2024)
20. Gary, K.I., Miller, L., Peng, R.: Approaching optimality for solving SDD linear systems. SIAM J. Comput. **43**(1), 337–354 (2014)
21. Kwok, T.C., Wei, Z., Yang, M.: On solving asymmetric diagonally dominant linear systems in sublinear time (2025). https://arxiv.org/abs/2509.13891
22. Lubotzky, A., Phillips, R., Sarnak, P.: Ramanujan graphs. Combinatorica **8**(3), 261–277 (1988)
23. Neumann, S., Dong, Y., Peng, P.: Sublinear-time opinion estimation in the Friedkin–Johnsen model. In: Proceedings of the ACM Web Conference 2024 (WWW), pp. 2563–2571 (2024)
24. Peng, P., Lopatta, D., Yoshida, Y., Goranci, G.: Local algorithms for estimating effective resistance. In: Proceedings of the 27th ACM SIGKDD Conference on Knowledge Discovery & Data Mining (KDD), pp. 1329–1338 (2021)
25. Shao, C., Montanaro, A.: Faster quantum-inspired algorithms for solving linear systems. ACM Trans. Quantum Comput. **3**(4), 1–23 (2022)
26. Spielman, D.A.: Algorithms, graph theory, and linear equations in Laplacian matrices. In: Proceedings of the International Congress of Mathematicians 2010 (ICM 2010) (In 4 Volumes) Vol. I: Plenary Lectures and Ceremonies Vols. II–IV: Invited Lectures, pp. 2698–2722. World Scientific (2010)
27. Spielman, D.A., Teng, S.-H.: Nearly-linear time algorithms for graph partitioning, graph sparsification, and solving linear systems. In: Proceedings of the 36th Annual ACM Symposium on Theory of Computing (STOC), pp. 81–90 (2004)
28. Streicher, O., Gilboa, G.: Graph Laplacian for semi-supervised learning. In: International Conference on Scale Space and Variational Methods in Computer Vision (SSVM), pp. 250–262. Springer (2023)
29. Tang, E.: A quantum-inspired classical algorithm for recommendation systems. In: Proceedings of the 51st Annual ACM Symposium on Theory of Computing (STOC), pp. 217–228 (2019)

# Parameterized Complexity of Odd Domination and its Generalization

Toranosuke Kokai, Rin Saito(✉), Tatsuhiro Suga, Takahiro Suzuki, and Yuma Tamura

Graduate School of Information Sciences, Tohoku University, Sendai, Japan
{kokai.toranosuke.s6,rin.saito,suga.tatsuhiro.p5, takahiro.suzuki.q4}@dc.tohoku.ac.jp, tamura@tohoku.ac.jp

**Abstract.** In the Odd Domination problem, given a graph $G$ and a positive integer $k$, the task is to determine whether there exists a vertex subset $D$ of $G$ such that the closed neighborhood of each vertex in $G$ contains an odd number of vertices from $D$. In this paper, we investigate the computational complexity of the problem. When parameterized by the solution size $k$, we establish W[1]-hardness on some restricted graphs and a sharp boundary between fixed-parameter tractability and W[1]-hardness with respect to the girth of the input graph. Then, we address the problem when parameterized by several structural graph parameters. Furthermore, we investigate the parameterized complexity of Parity Domination, which is a generalization of Odd Domination.

**Keywords:** Odd dominating set · Parameterized complexity · Fixed parameter tractability

## 1 Introduction

The Dominating Set problem is a fundamental problem in algorithmic theory. Given a graph $G = (V, E)$ and an integer $k \geq 0$, the task is to decide whether there exists a vertex set $D \subseteq V$ of size at most $k$ such that every vertex of $G$ is contained in the closed neighborhood of some vertex in $D$. The problem is NP-complete and has been central to the development of parameterized complexity theory [8].

One of the generalizations of many domination-type problems is the framework of $(\sigma, \rho)$-dominating sets, introduced in [26,27]. Let $\sigma, \rho \subseteq \mathbb{Z}_{\geq 0}$. A set $D \subseteq V$ is a $(\sigma, \rho)$-dominating set if

- for every vertex $v \in D$, we have $|N_G(v) \cap D| \in \sigma$, and
- for every vertex $v \notin D$, we have $|N_G(v) \cap D| \in \rho$.

This framework captures a wide range of classical graph problems, including Dominating Set, Independent Set, Perfect Code, and Induced Bounded-Degree Subgraph.


Y. Li et al. (Eds.): COCOON 2026, LNCS 16835, pp. 163–176, 2027.
https://doi.org/10.1007/978-981-92-3309-0_13

For many choices of $\sigma$ and $\rho$, the associated optimization problem is NP-hard. Its classical and parameterized complexity has therefore been studied extensively, typically with respect to the solution size $k$ [14,20] and structural graph parameters [6,11,12,18,23]. In particular, when both $\sigma$ and $\rho$ are finite or cofinite (i.e., their complements are finite), the complexity landscape is well understood in many settings [6,18,23].

However, several natural problems arise even when $\sigma$ and $\rho$ are neither finite nor cofinite. A canonical example is the Odd Domination problem [13,24], defined by $\sigma = \{0, 2, 4, \ldots\}$ and $\rho = \{1, 3, 5, \ldots\}$. Equivalently, given a graph $G = (V, E)$ and an integer $k \geq 0$, the task is to decide whether there exists a set $D \subseteq V$ of size at most $k$ such that every vertex in $V$ has an odd number of closed neighbors in $D$.

*Our Contributions.* We investigate the classical and parameterized complexity of Odd Domination. (See also Fig. 1.)

We begin with classical complexity on restricted graph classes. It is known that Odd Domination is NP-complete on bipartite graphs [5]. We show that NP-completeness holds even under strong structural restrictions: Odd Domination is NP-complete on planar bipartite graphs with girth at least $g$, for any fixed integer $g \geq 3$. This result improves the NP-completeness of Odd Domination previously established for bipartite graphs [5], and for planar graphs with maximum degree 3 [3]. This answers an open question posed by Broersma and Li [5].

We next consider parameterized complexity with respect to the solution size $k$. On general graphs, Odd Domination is W[1]-hard when parameterized by $k$ [3]. We strengthen this result by showing that Odd Domination is W[1]-hard even on bipartite graphs of girth 4 and degeneracy 4, and also on split graphs. We then establish a sharp complexity boundary with respect to girth. While Odd Domination is W[1]-hard on graphs of girth 4, we show that it becomes fixed-parameter tractable on graphs of girth at least 5, when parameterized by $k$.

Our W[1]-hardness result is noteworthy from the viewpoint of sparse graph classes (see again Fig. 1(a)). In contrast, Dominating Set is known to be fixed-parameter tractable when parameterized by $k + d$ [1], where $d$ denotes the degeneracy. Moreover, our result complements that Odd Domination is fixed-parameter tractable on nowhere dense graph classes [14], which constitute a broad family of sparse graphs and are incomparable with classes of bounded degeneracy [22].

We also investigate structural parameterizations of Odd Domination. For clique-width cw, the previously known approach, derived from results on the problem called All-Colors, yields an $O^*(16^{\mathrm{cw}})$-time algorithm for Odd Domination [3]. We substantially reduce the base of the exponent from 16 to 4, obtaining an $O^*(4^{\mathrm{cw}})$-time algorithm for Odd Domination.

We complement our algorithmic results with kernelization lower bounds. Specifically, we prove that Odd Domination admits no polynomial kernel when parameterized by the cluster deletion number, tree-depth, or feedback vertex set

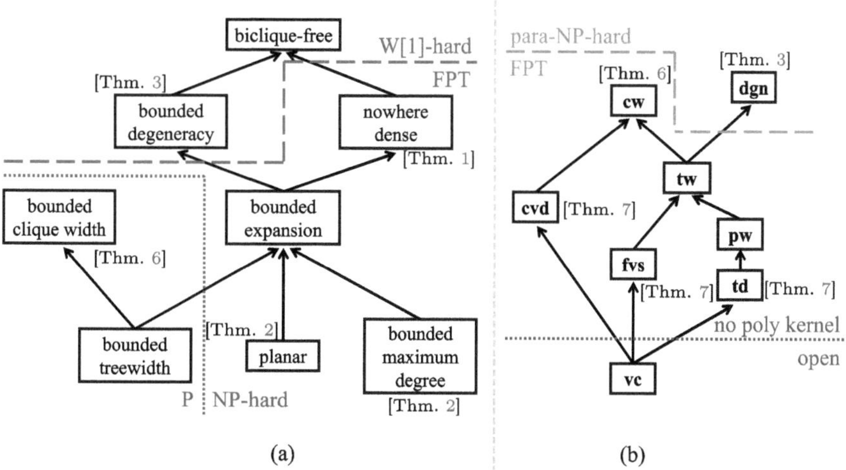


**Fig. 1.** Summary of our results for Odd Domination. (a) Relationships among the graph classes considered in this paper. An arrow $A \to B$ indicates that $A$ is a proper subclass of $B$. The dotted (blue) line separates polynomial-time solvability from NP-hardness, while the dashed (red) line separates fixed-parameter tractability from W[1]-hardness with respect to the solution size. (b) Relationships among the graph parameters considered in this paper. The abbreviations dgn, cw, tw, cvd, fvs, pw, td, and vc denote the degeneracy, clique-width, treewidth, cluster vertex deletion number, feedback vertex set number, pathwidth, tree-depth, and vertex cover number, respectively. An arrow $A \to B$ indicates that $A$ is stronger than $B$, that is, if $A$ is bounded by a constant, then so is $B$. The dashed (orange) line separates fixed-parameter tractability from para-NP-hardness for the corresponding parameters. The dotted (purple) line indicates that the problem admits no polynomial kernel for parameters above the line, whereas the existence of a polynomial kernel parameterized by vc remains open. (Color figure online)

number (see Fig. 1(b)). These lower bounds partially resolve an open question raised in [3].

We also study the complexity of a generalization of Odd Domination called the Parity Domination problem, introduced by Gassner and Hatzl [13]. An instance of Parity Domination consists of a graph $G = (V, E)$, an *offset function* $f\colon V \to \{0,1\}$, a partition $(V_\mathsf{o}, V_\mathsf{c})$ of $V$, and an integer $k \geq 0$. The question is whether there exists a set $D \subseteq V$ with $|D| \leq k$ such that every vertex $v \in V$ satisfies the *parity condition*, defined as follows:

- $|N_G(v) \cap D| + f(v) \equiv 0 \pmod 2$ for every $v \in V_\mathsf{o}$, and
- $|N_G[v] \cap D| + f(v) \equiv 0 \pmod 2$ for every $v \in V_\mathsf{c}$.

We extend several of our results on Odd Domination to Parity Domination. In particular, we show that Parity Domination is fixed-parameter tractable on nowhere dense graph classes when parameterized by $k$, and admits an algorithm running in time $4^{\mathrm{cw}} \cdot n^{O(1)}$. Furthermore, unless coNP $\subseteq$ NP/poly,

PARITY DOMINATION admits no polynomial kernel parameterized by the vertex cover number. This parameter is more restrictive than any parameter considered in our kernelization lower bounds for ODD DOMINATION.

*Related Work.* It is known that PARITY DOMINATION can be solved in linear time on distance-hereditary graphs and on graphs of bounded treewidth [17], both of which have bounded clique-width.

PARITY DOMINATION with $(V_{\mathsf{o}}, V_{\mathsf{c}}) = (\emptyset, V(G))$ and a generalization of ODD DOMINATION have been studied as LIGHTS OUT! on graphs from the viewpoints of graph algorithms, graph-theoretic aspects [17], and linear algebra [2]. LIGHTS OUT! on graphs is derived from the well-known puzzle game of the same name, originally played on a $5 \times 5$ grid. Each cell has a binary state (ON or OFF), and pressing its button toggles the state of both the cell itself and its neighbors. LIGHTS OUT! can be regarded as a $\sigma$-game [24,25], which appears in the context of cellular automata; see the survey by Fleischer et al. [10] for details.

In the standard LIGHTS OUT! setting, each vertex has a binary state, and pressing a button more than once is redundant. In a natural extension called ALL-COLORS [28], each cell has an $m$-ary state, and buttons can be pressed multiple times. Blazej et al. [3] proved that ALL-COLORS is NP-complete on subcubic planar graphs and established lower bounds based on the Exponential Time Hypothesis (ETH) with respect to the solution size.

Another generalization of ODD DOMINATION, called RESIDUE DOMINATION, asks for a $(\sigma, \rho)$-dominating set of size at most $k$, where $\sigma$ and $\rho$ are residue classes modulo $\mathrm{m} \geq 2$ [15]. More precisely, there exist integers $a, b \in \{0, 1, \ldots, \mathrm{m} - 1\}$ such that

$$\sigma = \{x \in \mathbb{Z}_{\geq 0} \mid x \equiv a \pmod{\mathrm{m}}\} \quad \text{and} \quad \rho = \{x \in \mathbb{Z}_{\geq 0} \mid x \equiv b \pmod{\mathrm{m}}\}.$$

Greilhuber et al. [15] showed that RESIDUE DOMINATION can be solved in $\mathrm{m}^{\mathrm{tw}} \cdot n^{O(1)}$ time. They also proved that, under the Strong Exponential-Time Hypothesis (SETH), the problem admits no $(\mathrm{m} - \varepsilon)^{\mathrm{pw}} \cdot n^{O(1)}$-time algorithm for any $\varepsilon > 0$, where pw denotes the pathwidth of the input graph. Consequently, these results imply that ODD DOMINATION admits an $O^*(2^{\mathrm{tw}})$-time algorithm, but no $(2 - \varepsilon)^{\mathrm{pw}} \cdot n^{O(1)}$-time algorithm unless SETH fails.

*Organization.* In Sect. 2, we provide preliminaries and define our problems. In Sects. 3 to 5, we focus on ODD DOMINATION. Specifically, we present NP-completeness in Sect. 3, the W[1]-hardness parameterized by $k$ in Sect. 4, and an FPT algorithm parameterized by $k$ for graphs of girth at least 5 in Sect. 5. In Sect. 6, we present an FPT algorithm for PARITY DOMINATION parameterized by clique-width and kernelization lower bounds with respect to restricted structural parameters. Due to the space limitation, we omit the proofs of statements with the symbol $\star$ marks, which can be found in the full version of this paper.

## 2 Preliminaries

We refer the reader to the book of Cygan et al. [8] for a detailed introduction to parameterized complexity, and give here only the definitions needed in this paper.

For a positive integer $n$, let $[n] := \{1, 2, \ldots, n\}$, and for integers $l$ and $r$ with $l \leq r$, let $[l, r] := \{l, l+1, \ldots, r\}$. The symbol $\equiv_m$ is used for congruence modulo $m$. For $a \in \{0, 1\}$, we write $\overline{a}$ to represent its bit flip $1 - a$.

Let $G$ be a graph. Let $V(G)$ and $E(G)$ denote the vertex set and the edge set of $G$, respectively. For a vertex $v \in V(G)$, let $N_G(v)$ and $N_G[v]$ denote the open and closed neighborhoods of $v$, respectively. For a vertex set $X \subseteq V(G)$, define $N_G(X) := \{v \in V(G) \setminus X \mid uv \in E(G), u \in X\}$ and $N_G[X] := N_G(X) \cup X$. For $X \subseteq V(G)$, let $G[X]$ denote the subgraph of $G$ induced by $X$. The *girth* of a graph $G$ is the length of its shortest cycle. A set $I \subseteq V(G)$ is an *independent set* if no two vertices in $I$ are adjacent, and a set $C \subseteq V(G)$ is a *clique* if every two distinct vertices in $C$ are adjacent. For a nonnegative integer $d$, a graph $G$ is *$d$-degenerate* if every subgraph of $G$ has a vertex of degree at most $d$. The *degeneracy* of $G$ is the minimum such $d$. It is well known that $G$ is $d$-degenerate if and only if it admits an ordering $v_1, v_2, \ldots, v_n$ of $V(G)$ such that each $v_i$ has degree at most $d$ in $G[\{v_i, v_{i+1}, \ldots, v_n\}]$.

Given a graph $G = (V, E)$, an offset function $f \colon V \to \{0, 1\}$, and a partition $(V_{\mathsf{o}}, V_{\mathsf{c}})$ of $V$, a vertex $v$ is said to be *parity-dominated* by a set $D \subseteq V$ if $v$ satisfies the parity condition. A set $D$ satisfying the parity condition for every $v \in V$ is called a *parity dominating set* (PD-set) with respect to $f$. For a given integer $k$, Parity Domination asks whether there exists a PD-set $D$ of $G$ with size at most $k$.

Odd Domination is a special case of Parity Domination by setting $f(v) = 1$ for all $v \in V$ and $(V_{\mathsf{o}}, V_{\mathsf{c}}) = (\emptyset, V)$. In this case, the condition reduces to requiring that $|N_G[v] \cap D|$ is odd for every $v \in V$. Such a set $D$ is called an *odd dominating set* (ODD-set), and a vertex $v$ is said to be *odd-dominated* by $D$ if $|N[v] \cap D|$ is odd.

Following the approach of [14], one can construct a first-order formula $\phi$ expressing the existence of a parity dominating set $D$ of size at most $k$, where the length of $\phi$ depends only on $k$. Consequently, Parity Domination is fixed-parameter tractable on sparse graph classes via FO model checking, for example, on nowhere dense graph classes [16].

**Theorem 1 ($\star$).** *Parity Domination admits an FPT algorithm when parameterized by $k$ on nowhere dense graphs.*

## 3 NP-Completeness

In this section, we prove that Odd Domination remains NP-complete when restricted to planar bipartite graphs of maximum degree 3 and girth at least $g$, for any fixed integer $g \geq 3$. To this end, we give a polynomial-time reduction from the 1-In-3-SAT problem.

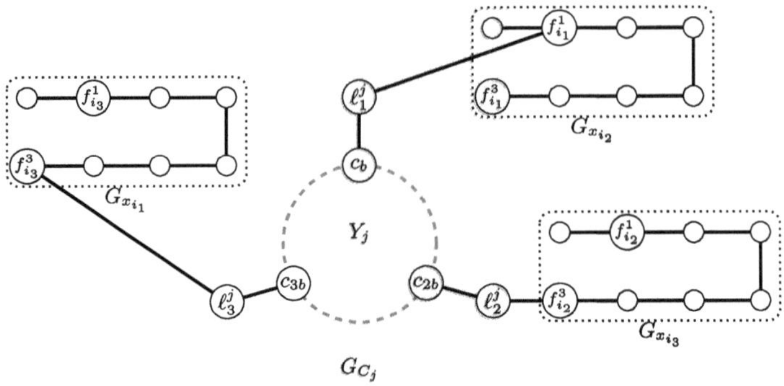


**Fig. 2.** An illustration of the gadgets $G_{x_{i_1}}, G_{x_{i_2}}, G_{x_{i_3}}$, and $G_{C_j}$ corresponding to the clause $C_j = x_{i_1} \vee x_{i_2} \vee x_{i_3}$. Here, $x_{i_1}$ represents the first occurrence of the variable in the formula, while $x_{i_2}$ and $x_{i_3}$ represent its second and third occurrences. The dashed lines between $c_b, c_{2b}$, and $c_{3b}$ denote paths of length $b+1$ connecting the corresponding vertices.

Let $\phi$ be a 3-CNF formula with variable set $X = \{x_1, x_2, \ldots, x_n\}$ and clause set $C = \{C_1, C_2, \ldots, C_m\}$. 1-IN-3-SAT asks whether there exists a truth assignment $\sigma\colon X \to \{\mathsf{true}, \mathsf{false}\}$ such that each clause of $\phi$ contains exactly one true literal. The *incidence graph* of $\phi$, denoted by $G_\phi$, is the bipartite graph with vertex set $X \cup C$, where $x_i$ is adjacent to $C_j$ if and only if $x_i$ occurs in $C_j$. It is known that 1-IN-3-SAT remains NP-complete even if all literals are positive, each variable appears exactly three times, and $G_\phi$ is planar [21].

We now state the main result of this section.

**Theorem 2.** *For every fixed integer $g \geq 3$, ODD DOMINATION is NP-complete on planar bipartite graphs of maximum degree 3 and girth at least $g$.*

*Reduction.* Let $\phi$ be an instance of 1-IN-3-SAT with variables $x_1, x_2, \ldots, x_n$ and clauses $C_1, C_2, \ldots, C_m$. We assume that $\phi$ satisfies the above restrictions. We construct an instance $(G, k)$ of ODD DOMINATION.

For each variable $x_i$ with $i \in [n]$, we introduce a *variable gadget* $G_{x_i}$. The graph $G_{x_i}$ is a path on eight vertices with

$$V(G_{x_i}) = \{t^1_i, f^1_i, z^1_i, t^2_i, f^2_i, z^2_i, t^3_i, f^3_i\}, \text{ and}$$
$$E(G_{x_i}) = \{t^1_i f^1_i, f^1_i z^1_i, z^1_i t^2_i, t^2_i f^2_i, f^2_i z^2_i, z^2_i t^3_i, t^3_i f^3_i\}.$$

We next define a *clause gadget* $G_{C_j}$ for each clause $C_j = (x^j_1 \vee x^j_2 \vee x^j_3)$ with $j \in [m]$. Let $a$ be the smallest integer with $g \leq 2^a$, and set $b := 2^a$. The graph $G_{C_j}$ is defined as follows. (See also Fig. 2) Construct a cycle $Y_j = (c_1, c_2, \ldots, c_{3b})$ of length $3b$ in clockwise order, and add three vertices $\ell^j_1, \ell^j_2, \ell^j_3$ with edges $\ell^j_1 c_b$, $\ell^j_2 c_{2b}$, and $\ell^j_3 c_{3b}$.

To construct the graph $G$, we connect the variable gadgets and clause gadgets as follows. Fix a planar embedding of $G_\phi$. For each variable vertex $x_i$ and clause vertex $C_j$ of $G_\phi$, replace $x_i$ and $C_j$ with the corresponding gadgets $G_{x_i}$ and $G_{C_j}$, respectively. For each variable $x_i$, consider its three occurrences in $\phi$ in an arbitrary but fixed order. Suppose that the $t$-th occurrence ($t \in \{1,2,3\}$) of $x_i$ appears as the $r$-th literal of a clause $C_j$. If $t = 1$, add the edge $f_i^1 \ell_r^j$; otherwise, add the edge $f_i^3 \ell_r^j$. Finally, set $k := 3n + 6m$. This completes the construction of the instance $(G, k)$.

We now verify that $G$ satisfies the required structural properties.

*Claim* $(\star)$. The graph $G$ is planar, bipartite, has maximum degree 3, and girth at least $g$.

To complete our reduction, we show the following lemma.

**Lemma 1** $(\star)$**.** *The instance $\phi$ is a yes-instance of* 1-In-3-SAT *if and only if the instance $(G, k)$ is a yes-instance of* Odd Domination.

# 4 W[1]-Hardness

In this section, we prove that Odd Domination is W[1]-hard parameterized by $k$, even on bipartite graphs with degeneracy 4 and girth 4, and also on split graphs.

## 4.1 W[1]-Hardness on Graphs with Degeneracy 4 and Girth 4

In this subsection, we establish the W[1]-hardness of Odd Domination parameterized by $k$ even on bipartite graphs with degeneracy 4 and girth 4. We also establish a lower bound under the Exponential Time Hypothesis (ETH).

**Theorem 3.** *Odd Domination is* W[1]*-hard when parameterized by $k$ even on bipartite graphs of degeneracy 4 and girth 4. Moreover, unless ETH fails, there is no algorithm solving Odd Domination in time $f(k) \cdot n^{o(k/\log k)}$ for any computable function $f$.*

To prove Theorem 3, we reduce from Partitioned Subgraph Isomorphism. An instance consists of two graphs $H$ and $G$, $V(H) = [|V(H)|]$ and $V(G)$ is partitioned into color classes $V_1, V_2, \ldots, V_{|V(H)|}$. The task is to decide whether there exists an injective mapping $\phi \colon V(H) \to V(G)$ such that (i) $\phi(i) \in V_i$ for every $i \in V(H)$, and (ii) $\phi(i)\phi(j) \in E(G)$ for all $ij \in E(H)$. Such a mapping is called a *colored subgraph isomorphism* from $H$ to $G$. Without loss of generality, we may assume that if $uv \in E(G)$ with $u \in V_i$ and $v \in V_j$, then $ij \in E(H)$, since any edge of $G$ that violates this condition can be deleted. In the remainder of this subsection, we assume $i < j$ whenever we write $ij \in E(H)$.

Partitioned Subgraph Isomorphism is W[1]-hard when parameterized by $m_H := |E(H)|$, and, assuming ETH, there is no algorithm solving $n$-vertex instances of Partitioned Subgraph Isomorphism in time $f(m_H) \cdot n^{o(m_H/\log m_H)}$ for any computable function $f$ [19, Corollary 6.3].

**Construction.** Let $(G, H)$ be an instance of PARTITIONED SUBGRAPH ISOMORPHISM. Denote $n_H := |V(H)|$ and $m_H := |E(H)|$. The vertex set of $G$ is partitioned into $V_1, V_2, \ldots, V_{n_H}$. For each edge $ij \in E(H)$, define $E_{i,j} := \{uv \in E(G) \mid u \in V_i, v \in V_j\}$. By adding isolated vertices and dummy edges if necessary, we may assume that $V_i \neq \emptyset$ for every $i \in V(H)$ and $E_{i,j} \neq \emptyset$ for every $ij \in E(H)$.

We construct an instance $(G', k')$ of ODD DOMINATION. The graph $G'$ consists of a *vertex gadget* $G_i$ for each $i \in V(H)$ and an *edge gadget* $G_{i,j}$ for each $ij \in E(H)$. Finally, let $k' := 4n_H + 4m_H = O(m_H)$.

*Vertex Gadgets.* For each $i \in [n_H]$, the vertex gadget $G_i$ consists of the following vertices: a vertex $q_i$; two disjoint copies $V_i^*$ and $V_i'$ of $V_i$; a set $L_i := \{\ell_{v,i,j} \mid v \in V_i,\ j \in N_H(i)\}$; two vertices $\tilde{x}_i$ and $\tilde{y}_i$; and their respective private neighbors $\tilde{X}_i := \{\tilde{x}_i^r \mid r \in [k'+1]\}$ and $\tilde{Y}_i := \{\tilde{y}_i^r \mid r \in [k'+1]\}$.

The edges of $G_i$ are defined as follows. The vertex $q_i$ is adjacent to every vertex in $V_i^*$. For each $v \in V_i$, let $v^* \in V_i^*$ and $v' \in V_i'$ denote the corresponding copies; add the edge $v^*v'$. For each $v \in V_i$ and each $j \in N_H(i)$, add the edge $v^*\ell_{v,i,j}$. The vertex $\tilde{x}_i$ is adjacent to every vertex in $V_i^*$ and to each vertex in $\tilde{X}_i$. The vertex $\tilde{y}_i$ is adjacent to every vertex in $V_i' \cup L_i \cup \tilde{Y}_i$. Finally, add the edge $\tilde{x}_i\tilde{y}_i$.

*Edge Gadgets.* For each $ij \in E(H)$, the edge gadget $G_{i,j}$ consists of the following vertices: a vertex $q_{i,j}$; two disjoint copies $V_{i,j}^*$ and $V_{i,j}'$ of $E_{i,j}$; two vertices $\tilde{x}_{i,j}$ and $\tilde{y}_{i,j}$; and their respective private neighbors $\tilde{X}_{i,j} :- \{\tilde{x}_{i,j}^r \mid r \in [k'+1]\}$ and $\tilde{Y}_{i,j} := \{\tilde{y}_{i,j}^r \mid r \in [k'+1]\}$.

For each $uv \in E_{i,j}$ with $u \in V_i$ and $v \in V_j$, let $z_{uv}^* \in V_{i,j}^*$ and $z_{uv}' \in V_{i,j}'$ denote the corresponding vertices. The edges of $G_{i,j}$ are defined as follows. The vertex $q_{i,j}$ is adjacent to all vertices in $V_{i,j}^*$. For each $uv \in E_{i,j}$ with $u \in V_i$ and $v \in V_j$, add the edge $z_{uv}^*z_{uv}'$. The vertex $\tilde{x}_{i,j}$ is adjacent to every vertex in $V_{i,j}^*$ and to every vertex in $\tilde{X}_{i,j}$. The vertex $\tilde{y}_{i,j}$ is adjacent to every vertex in $V_{i,j}' \cup \tilde{Y}_{i,j}$. Finally, add the edge $\tilde{x}_{i,j}\tilde{y}_{i,j}$.

For each edge $uv \in E(G)$ with $u \in V_i$ and $v \in V_j$, add the edges $z_{uv}^*\ell_{u,i,j}$ and $z_{uv}^*\ell_{v,j,i}$. This completes the construction of the instance $(G', k')$ of ODD DOMINATION.

We verify the structural properties of the constructed graph.

**Lemma 2** ($\star$). *The graph $G'$ is bipartite, 4-degenerate, with girth at least 4.*

We can show that $(G, H)$ is a yes-instance of PARTITIONED SUBGRAPH ISOMORPHISM if and only if $(G', k')$ is a yes-instance of ODD DOMINATION. Moreover, $|V(G')|$ is bounded by a polynomial in $n_H$ and $|V(G)|$, and $k' = 4n_H + 4m_H = O(m_H)$.

Suppose that ODD DOMINATION can be solved in time $f(k') \cdot |V(G')|^{o(k'/\log k')}$ for some computable function $f$. Then PARTITIONED SUBGRAPH ISOMORPHISM can be solved in time $f'(m_H) \cdot |V(G)|^{o(m_H/\log m_H)}$ for some computable function $f'$, contradicting ETH. Hence, no such algorithm for ODD DOMINATION exists, which completes the proof of Theorem 3.

### 4.2 W[1]-Hardness on Split Graphs

A graph is *split* if its vertex set can be partitioned into a clique and an independent set. We prove the following theorem.

**Theorem 4 (⋆).** *Odd Domination is* W[1]*-hard when parameterized by k even for split graphs.*

## 5 FPT Algorithm on Graphs with Girth at Least 5

In this section, we prove the following theorem.

**Theorem 5.** *Odd Domination can be solved in time $2^{O(k^3)}$ on graphs of girth at least* 5.

To prove Theorem 5, we introduce an annotated variant of Parity Domination. An instance of Annotated Parity Dominationconsists of a graph $G = (V, E)$, a partition $(V_\mathsf{o}, V_\mathsf{c})$ of $V$, a set $F \subseteq V$ of *forbidden vertices*, an offset function $f : V \to \{0, 1\}$, and an integer $k \geq 0$. The question is whether there exists $D \subseteq V \setminus F$ such that $|D \cup F| \leq k$ and $|N_G[v] \cap D| + f(v) \equiv_2 0$ for every $v \in V$.

An instance $(G, k)$ of Odd Domination is transformed into the equivalent annotated instance $(G, V_\mathsf{o}, V_\mathsf{c}, F, f, k)$ by setting $V_\mathsf{o} = \emptyset$, $V_\mathsf{c} = V(G)$, $F = \emptyset$, and $f(v) = 1$ for all $v \in V(G)$. Throughout the remainder of this section, the partition $(V_\mathsf{o}, V_\mathsf{c})$ remains fixed. Accordingly, we abbreviate instances as $(G, F, f, k)$.

We exhaustively apply the following reduction rules in the order listed below.

**Reduction rule 1.** *If $|F| > k$, return "No".*

**Reduction rule 2.** *If $f^{-1}(1) = \emptyset$, return "Yes".*

**Reduction rule 3.** *If there exists a vertex $v$ such that $|N_G(v) \cap f^{-1}(1)| > k$, then return the instance $(G, F', f', k)$, where $F' = F \cup \{v\}$ and*

$$f'(u) = \begin{cases} \overline{f(u)} & \textit{if } u \in N_G[v], \\ f(u) & \textit{otherwise.} \end{cases}$$

Each rule can be applied in polynomial time. Moreover, Rule 3 increases $|F|$ by one while leaving $k$ unchanged. Since Rule 1 immediately rejects any instance with $|F| > k$, Rule 3 can be applied at most $k$ times. Furthermore, as the graph $G$ is never modified, its girth remains at least 5 throughout the reduction process.

The safeness of Rules 1 and 2 is immediate. The following lemma is central to our algorithm.

**Lemma 3 (⋆).** *After exhaustive application of Rules 1 to 3, every vertex not in $F$ has degree at most $2k$.*

We introduce the following branching rule.

**Branching rule 1.** *Suppose that there exists a vertex* $v \in V(G) \setminus F$ *such that* $f(v) = 1$. *Let* $N_G[v] \setminus F = \{v_1, v_2, \ldots, v_d\}$. *For each* $i \in [d]$, *branch into the instance* $(G, F \cup \{v_i\}, f_i, k)$, *where*

$$f_i(u) = \begin{cases} \overline{f(u)} & \text{if } u \in N_G[v_i], \\ f(u) & \text{otherwise,} \end{cases}$$

*for every* $u \in V(G)$.

Each application of Branching Rule 1 increases $|F|$ by one. Hence, the depth of the search tree is at most $k$. By Lemma 3, every vertex in $V(G) \setminus F$ has degree at most $2k$. Therefore, $|N_G[v] \setminus F| \leq \deg_G(v) + 1 \leq 2k + 1$. It follows that each branching step generates at most $2k + 1$ subinstances. Consequently, the total number of instances generated by Branching Rule 1 is at most $(2k + 1)^k$.

After exhaustive application of Rules 1 to 2 and Branching Rule 1, every resulting instance $(G, F, f, k)$ satisfies $|F| \leq k$, $f^{-1}(1) \subseteq F$, and $\deg_G(v) \leq 2k$ for every $v \in V(G) \setminus F$.

We next partition the vertices in $V(G) \setminus F$ according to their neighborhoods in $F$. For each subset $X \subseteq F$, define $C_X := \{v \in V(G) \setminus F \mid N_G(v) \cap F = X\}$. Clearly, the family $\{C_X\}_{X \subseteq F}$ forms a partition of $V(G) \setminus F$.

We iterate over all functions $\mathbf{c} \colon 2^F \to [0, k]$ satisfying

$$|F| + \sum_{X \subseteq F} \mathbf{c}(X) \leq k. \tag{1}$$

Intuitively, the value $\mathbf{c}(X)$ represents the number of vertices to be selected from $C_X$ into the solution. Since $|F| \leq k$, the number of such functions is at most $(2^{|F|} + 1)^{k - |F|} = 2^{O(k^2)}$.

Fix a function $\mathbf{c}$. Our goal is to determine whether there exists a set $S \subseteq V(G) \setminus F$ satisfying the following conditions:

- $|S \cap C_X| = \mathbf{c}(X)$ for each $X \subseteq F$, and
- $S$ is a PD-set for the instance $(G, F, f, k)$.

By Eq. (1), every such set $S$ yields a solution for $(G, F, f, k)$.

To this end, we define the following auxiliary problem. An instance consists of a graph $H$ with maximum degree $\Delta(H) \leq 2k$, a partition $\mathcal{V} = \{V_1, V_2, \ldots, V_\ell\}$ of $V(H)$ with $\ell \leq 2^k$, and a function $\mathbf{c}' \colon \mathcal{V} \to [0, k]$. The objective is to find a set $S \subseteq V(H)$ of size at most $k$ such that: (1) $|N_H(v) \cap S| \equiv_2 0$ for every $v \in V(H)$, and (2) $|S \cap V_i| = \mathbf{c}'(V_i)$ for every $i \in [\ell]$.

We now describe a reduction from our problem to the auxiliary problem. For a vertex $v \in F$, define $\mathcal{X}_v := \{X \subseteq F \mid v \in X\}$. The following reduction rule handles the parity requirements of vertices in $F$.

**Reduction rule 4.** *If there exists a vertex* $v \in F$ *such that*

$$\sum_{X \in \mathcal{X}_v} \mathbf{c}(X) + f(v) \not\equiv_2 0,$$

*then return* "No".

Suppose that Rule 4 does not return "NO". We construct an instance of the auxiliary problem as follows. Let $H := G - F$. The partition of $V(H)$ is $\mathcal{V} = \{C_X\}_{X \subseteq F}$. We further define the function $\mathbf{c}'$ by setting $\mathbf{c}'(C_X) := \mathbf{c}(X)$ for every $X \subseteq F$.

Since $|F| \leq k$, we obtain $|\mathcal{V}| \leq 2^k$, which satisfies the requirements of the auxiliary problem. Furthermore, by Lemma 3, the maximum degree of $H$ is at most $2k$.

**Solving the Auxiliary Problem.** We provide an FPT algorithm for the auxiliary problem parameterized by $k$, which completes the proof of Theorem 5. Our approach employs the *random separation* technique of Cai et al. [7]; see also [8, Section 5.3].

Fix a solution $S \subseteq V(H)$ to the auxiliary problem. Let $\Lambda_S$ denote the set of edges in $H$ incident to vertices in $S$. Furthermore, let $\Gamma_S$ denote the set of edges in $H$ incident to vertices in $N_H(S)$ but not incident to vertices in $S$.

We independently color each edge of $H$ either red or blue uniformly at random. Let $\chi\colon E(H) \to \{\mathsf{red}, \mathsf{blue}\}$ denote the resulting edge-coloring. We say that $\chi$ is *successful* with respect to $S$ if all edges in $\Lambda_S$ are colored red and all edges in $\Gamma_S$ are colored blue. Since $\Delta(H) \leq 2k$ and $|S| \leq k$, we obtain $|N_H(S)| \leq 2k^2$. Thus, the number of possible colorings to the edges in $\Lambda_S \cup \Gamma_S$ is bounded by:

$$|\Lambda_S| + |\Gamma_S| \leq \Delta(G) \cdot (|S| + |N_H(S)|) \leq 2k \cdot (k + 2k^2) = 4k^3 + 2k^2.$$

Therefore, a random coloring $\chi$ is successful with probability at least

$$2^{-(|\Lambda_S|+|\Gamma_S|)} \geq 2^{-(4k^3+2k^2)}.$$

Let $H_R = (V(H), \chi^{-1}(\mathsf{red}))$ be the subgraph of $H$ consisting of all red edges. We call a vertex $v \in V(H)$ *consistent* if every edge incident to $v$ in $H$ is colored red. Observe that if $\chi$ is successful, every vertex $v \in S$ is consistent, since every edge incident to a vertex in $S$ belongs to $\Lambda_S$.

We design a dynamic programming algorithm to find $S$ from $H_R$. Let $\{C_i\}_{i=1}^t$ denote the connected components of $H_R$. and for each $i \in [0, t]$, let $H_R^i$ be the subgraph of $H_R$ induced by $\bigcup_{j=1}^i V(C_j)$, where $H_R^0$ is the empty graph. For each $i \in [0, t]$ and each function $\mathbf{a}\colon [\ell] \to [0, k]$, we define $\mathrm{DP}(i, \mathbf{a}) = \mathsf{true}$ if there exists a set $D \subseteq V(H_R^i)$ such that:

- $|N_H(v) \cap D| \equiv_2 0$ for every $v \in V(H_R^i)$;
- $|D \cap V_j| = \mathbf{a}(j)$ for every $j \in [\ell]$; and
- every vertex in $D$ is consistent.

Otherwise, define $\mathrm{DP}(i, \mathbf{a}) = \mathsf{false}$. The base case is given by $\mathrm{DP}(0, \mathbf{a}) = \mathsf{true}$ if and only if $\mathbf{a}(j) = 0$ for every $j \in [\ell]$.

For $i \geq 1$, we observe that if $|V(C_i)| > k(2k+1)$, then $C_i$ cannot contain any vertex of $S$, since $|N_H[S]| \leq |S| + |N_H(S)| \leq k + 2k^2 = k(2k+1)$. Therefore, in this case, $\mathrm{DP}(i, \mathbf{a}) = \mathrm{DP}(i-1, \mathbf{a})$.

Suppose now that $|V(C_i)| \leq k(2k+1)$. Let $\mathcal{D}_i$ denote the family of all subsets $D \subseteq V(C_i)$ of size at most $k$ such that, for all $v \in V(C_i)$, $v$ is consistent and satisfies $|N_H(v) \cap D| \equiv_2 0$. Since $|V(C_i)| \leq 2k^2+k$, we obtain $|\mathcal{D}_i| \leq \sum_{r=0}^{k} \binom{|V(C_i)|}{r} \leq (2k^2+k+1)^k$. Moreover, $\mathcal{D}_i$ can be computed in time $O((2k^2+k+1)^k) \cdot n^{O(1)}$.

For each $D \in \mathcal{D}_i$, define the function $\mathbf{a}_D(j) = |D \cap V_j|$ for every $j \in [\ell]$. We then update the table according to $\mathrm{DP}(i, \mathbf{a}) = \bigvee_{D \in \mathcal{D}_i} \mathrm{DP}(i-1, \mathbf{a} - \mathbf{a}_D)$.

The number of possible functions $\mathbf{a}$ is at most $2^{O(k^2)}$. Hence, each dynamic programming step can be processed in time $(2k^2+k+1)^k \cdot 2^{O(k^2)} \cdot n^{O(1)} = 2^{O(k^2)} \cdot n^{O(1)}$.

*Running Time and Correctness.* For a fixed coloring $\chi$, the dynamic programming decides in $2^{O(k^2)} \cdot n^{O(1)}$ time whether there exists a set $S$ satisfying the requirements specified by $\mathbf{c}'$. If the given instance is a no-instance, then $\mathrm{DP}(t, \mathbf{c}) = \mathsf{false}$ for any coloring $\chi$. Otherwise, there exists a solution $S$ to the auxiliary problem. As shown above, a random coloring $\chi$ is successful with respect to $S$ with probability at least $2^{-(4k^3+2k^2)}$, in which case the dynamic programming algorithm returns $\mathsf{true}$. Therefore, the auxiliary problem can be solved by a randomized algorithm in $2^{4k^3+2k^2} \cdot 2^{O(k^2)} \cdot n^{O(1)} = 2^{O(k^3)} \cdot n^{O(1)}$ time with constant probability.

By Branching Rule 1, the algorithm generates at most $(2k+1)^k$ instances of Annotated Parity Domination. For each such instance, we consider at most $2^{O(k^2)}$ candidate functions $\mathbf{c}$. For every choice of $\mathbf{c}$, we sample a coloring $\chi$ and solve the auxiliary problem in $2^{O(k^2)} \cdot n^{O(1)}$ time. Therefore, the overall running time is $(2k+1)^k \cdot 2^{O(k^2)} \cdot 2^{O(k^3)} \cdot n^{O(1)} = 2^{O(k^3)} \cdot n^{O(1)}$. The algorithm outputs $\mathsf{true}$ only if it finds a valid solution. Thus, the algorithm is a Monte Carlo algorithm with one-sided error.

Finally, the randomized algorithm can be derandomized using a standard tool called *universal sets*; see, for example, Cygan et al. [8]. This completes the proof of Theorem 5.

# 6 Structural Parameters

## 6.1 Clique-Width

We now state the main result of this subsection.

**Theorem 6 ($\star$).** *Parity Domination is fixed-parameter tractable when parameterized by the clique-width.*

## 6.2 No Polynomial Kernel Parameterized by Structural Parameters

We use the framework of OR-cross-compositions [4], a standard technique for proving kernelization lower bounds. Our proof follows the approach used to establish kernelization lower bounds for Dominating Set parameterized by vertex cover [8,9].

**Theorem 7** ($\star$). *Unless* coNP $\subseteq$ NP/*poly*, *Parity Domination admits no polynomial kernel parameterized by vertex cover. Moreover, Odd Domination admits no polynomial kernel parameterized by cluster vertex deletion, feedback vertex set, or treedepth.*

## References


1. Alon, N., Gutner, S.: Linear time algorithms for finding a dominating set of fixed size in degenerated graphs. Algorithmica **54**(4), 544–556 (2009). https://doi.org/10.1007/S00453-008-9204-0
2. Anderson, M., Feil, T.: Turning lights out with linear algebra. Math. Mag. **71**(4), 300–303 (1998). http://www.jstor.org/stable/2690705
3. Blazej, V., Jana, S., Strulo, P.: A parameterized perspective of All-Colors. Theor. Comput. Sci. **1059**, 115573 (2026). https://doi.org/10.1016/J.TCS.2025.115573
4. Bodlaender, H.L., Jansen, B.M.P., Kratsch, S.: Kernelization lower bounds by cross-composition. SIAM J. Discret. Math. **28**(1), 277–305 (2014). https://doi.org/10.1137/120880240
5. Broersma, H., Li, X.: On the complexity of dominating set problems related to the minimum all-ones problem. Theor. Comput. Sci. **385**(1–3), 60–70 (2007). https://doi.org/10.1016/J.TCS.2007.05.027
6. Bui-Xuan, B., Telle, J.A., Vatshelle, M.: Fast dynamic programming for locally checkable vertex subset and vertex partitioning problems. Theor. Comput. Sci. **511**, 66–76 (2013). https://doi.org/10.1016/J.TCS.2013.01.009
7. Cai, L., Chan, S.M., Chan, S.O.: Random separation: a new method for solving fixed-cardinality optimization problems. In: Parameterized and Exact Computation, Second International Workshop, IWPEC 2006. Lecture Notes in Computer Science, vol. 4169, pp. 239–250. Springer (2006). https://doi.org/10.1007/11847250_22
8. Cygan, M., et al.: Parameterized Algorithms. Springer (2015). https://doi.org/10.1007/978-3-319-21275-3
9. Dom, M., Lokshtanov, D., Saurabh, S.: Kernelization lower bounds through colors and ids. ACM Trans. Algorithms **11**(2), 13:1–13:20 (2014). https://doi.org/10.1145/2650261
10. Fleischer, R., Yu, J.: A survey of the game "lights out!". In: Space-Efficient Data Structures, Streams, and Algorithms - Papers in Honor of J. Ian Munro on the Occasion of His 66th Birthday. Lecture Notes in Computer Science, vol. 8066, pp. 176–198. Springer (2013). https://doi.org/10.1007/978-3-642-40273-9_13
11. Focke, J., et al.: Tight complexity bounds for counting generalized dominating sets in bounded-treewidth graphs - part I: algorithmic results. ACM Trans. Algorithms **21**(3), 27:1–27:45 (2025). https://doi.org/10.1145/3731452
12. Focke, J., et al.: Tight complexity bounds for counting generalized dominating sets in bounded-treewidth graphs part II: hardness results. ACM Trans. Comput. Theory **17**(2), 10:1–10:101 (2025). https://doi.org/10.1145/3708509
13. Gassner, E., Hatzl, J.: A parity domination problem in graphs with bounded treewidth and distance-hereditary graphs. Computing **82**(2–3), 171–187 (2008). https://doi.org/10.1007/S00607-008-0005-8
14. Golovach, P.A., Kratochvíl, J., Suchý, O.: Parameterized complexity of generalized domination problems. Discret. Appl. Math. **160**(6), 780–792 (2012). https://doi.org/10.1016/J.DAM.2010.11.012

15. Greilhuber, J., Schepper, P., Wellnitz, P.: Residue domination in bounded-treewidth graphs. In: 42nd International Symposium on Theoretical Aspects of Computer Science. LIPIcs, vol. 327, pp. 41:1–41:20. Schloss Dagstuhl - Leibniz-Zentrum für Informatik (2025). https://doi.org/10.4230/LIPICS.STACS.2025.41
16. Grohe, M., Kreutzer, S., Siebertz, S.: Deciding first-order properties of nowhere dense graphs. J. ACM **64**(3), 17:1–17:32 (2017). https://doi.org/10.1145/3051095
17. Hatzl, J., Wagner, S.G.: Combinatorial properties of a general domination problem with parity constraints. Discret. Math. **308**(24), 6355–6367 (2008). https://doi.org/10.1016/J.DISC.2007.12.005
18. Jaffke, L., Kwon, O., Strømme, T.J.F., Telle, J.A.: Mim-width III. Graph powers and generalized distance domination problems. Theor. Comput. Sci. **796**, 216–236 (2019). https://doi.org/10.1016/J.TCS.2019.09.012
19. Marx, D.: Can you beat treewidth? Theory Comput. **6**(1), 85–112 (2010). https://doi.org/10.4086/TOC.2010.V006A005
20. Jaffke, L., Kwon, O., Strømme, T.J.F., Telle, J.A.: Mim-width III. Graph powers and generalized distance domination problems. Theor. Comput. Sci. **796**, 216–236 (2019). https://doi.org/10.1016/J.TCS.2019.09.012
21. Moore, C., Robson, J.M.: Hard tiling problems with simple tiles. Discret. Comput. Geom. **26**(4), 573–590 (2001). https://doi.org/10.1007/S00454-001-0047-6
22. Nesetril, J., de Mendez, P.O.: On nowhere dense graphs. Eur. J. Comb. **32**(4), 600–617 (2011). https://doi.org/10.1016/J.EJC.2011.01.006
23. van Rooij, J.M.M., Bodlaender, H.L., Rossmanith, P.: Dynamic programming on tree decompositions using generalised fast subset convolution. In: Fiat, A., Sanders, P. (eds.) Algorithms - ESA 2009, 17th Annual European Symposium. Lecture Notes in Computer Science, vol. 5757, pp. 566–577. Springer (2009). https://doi.org/10.1007/978-3-642-04128-0_51
24. Sutner, K.: Additive automata on graphs. Complex Syst. **2**(6) (1988). http://www.complex-systems.com/abstracts/v02_i06_a03.html
25. Sutner, K.: The $\sigma$-game and cellular automata. Am. Math. Monthly **97**(1), 24–34 (1990). http://www.jstor.org/stable/2323999
26. Telle, J.A.: Complexity of domination-type problems in graphs. Nord. J. Comput. **1**(1), 157–171 (1994)
27. Telle, J.A., Proskurowski, A.: Practical algorithms on partial $k$-trees with an application to domination-like problems. In: Algorithms and Data Structures, Third Workshop, WADS '93. Lecture Notes in Computer Science, vol. 709, pp. 610–621. Springer (1993). https://doi.org/10.1007/3-540-57155-8_284
28. Zhang, X., Wang, C.: Solutions to all-colors problem on graph cellular automata. Complex. **2019**, 3164692:1–3164692:11 (2019). https://doi.org/10.1155/2019/3164692

# A Faster Algorithm for Sorting by Reciprocal Translocations

Xin Tong[1], Haitao Jiang[1(✉)], Tiantian Li[2], Lianrong Pu[1], Binhai Zhu[3], and Daming Zhu[1]

[1] School of Computer Science and Technology, Shandong University, Qingdao, China
xtong@mail.sdu.edu.cn, {htjiang,lianrongpu,dmzhu}@sdu.edu.cn

[2] School of Software and Joint SDU-NTU Centre for Artificial Intelligence Research, Shandong University, Jinan, China
lytt_08@163.com

[3] Gianforte School of Computing, Montana State University, Bozeman, MT 59717, USA
bhz@montana.edu

**Abstract.** Reciprocal translocation is an important genome rearrangement operation that involves swapping non-empty terminal segments between two chromosomes. Given two multi-chromosomal genomes, $A$ and $B$, the problem of sorting by reciprocal translocations aims to find the shortest sequence of reciprocal translocations that can transform $A$ into $B$. This problem can be solved in polynomial time, and, as far as we know, the best time complexity is $O(n^{3/2}\sqrt{\log n})$. In this paper, by leveraging the results on the fully dynamic graph connectivity problem, we improve the time complexity to $O(\frac{n(N^2 \log n+\log^2 n)}{\log\log n})$, where $n$ represents the number of genes and $N$ represents the number of chromosomes. In real evolutionary scenarios, the number of chromosomes involved in rearrangement events is typically small. Consequently, when $N$ is treated as a constant or a polynomial function of $\log n$, our algorithm achieves a time complexity better than $O(n^{3/2}\sqrt{\log n})$.

**Keywords:** Translocations · Fully dynamic graph · Time complexity

## 1 Introduction

In the 1980s, evidence was found that some species share nearly identical set of genes but exhibit distinct gene orders due to genome rearrangements [7,11]. Genome rearrangements reveal the evolutionary events between species. Sankoff et al. [12] formally defined several rearrangement operations: reversal, transposition and translocation. Since then, sorting permutations using rearrangement operations has become a major focus in the field of computational biology. Reciprocal translocations exchange non-empty terminal segments between two chromosomes. For two multi-chromosomal genomes, the problem of *Sorting by Reciprocal Translocations* (abbreviated SRT) seeks the shortest sequence of such translocations required to convert one genome into the other.


Y. Li et al. (Eds.): COCOON 2026, LNCS 16835, pp. 177–191, 2027.
https://doi.org/10.1007/978-981-92-3309-0_14

The problem of SRT was initially introduced by Kececioglu and Ravi [9]. Subsequently, Hannenhalli [4] pioneered the first polynomial-time algorithm for SRT, establishing a critical milestone in the study of this problem. Bergeron et al. [2] later refined Hannenhalli's mathematical proof of the translocation distance formula and presented a new $O(n^3)$ algorithm. Upon these advancements, Wang et al. [16] proposed an $O(n^2)$ algorithm, further reducing the time complexity. The current state-of-the-art algorithm for SRT, achieving a time complexity of $O(n^{3/2}\sqrt{\log n})$, was introduced by Ozery-Flato and Shamir [10].

The problem of SRT exhibits similar research achievements with another genome rearrangement problem: *Sorting by Reversals* (abbreviated SBR). Recently, Dudek et al. advanced SBR with an $O(n \log^2 n/ \log\log n)$ algorithm [3], leveraging breakthroughs in dynamic graph connectivity. This result outperforms the prior same $O(n^{3/2}\sqrt{\log n})$ bound established by Tannier et al. [15]. As demonstrated by Hannenhalli and Pevzner [5], there is a close relationship between reversals and translocations, which motivates us to explore faster algorithms for SRT.

In this paper, we propose an algorithm for SRT in $O(\frac{n(N^2 \log n+\log^2 n)}{\log\log n})$ amortized time, where $n$ is the number of genes and $N$ is the number of chromosomes. We formalize some typical operations involving which translocation should be performed and how to perform a translocation, and show that Ozery-Flato and Shamir's algorithm [10] can be implemented by executing $O(n)$ times of each operation. Performing a translocation is implemented using the splay tree [14] in $O(\log^2 n/ \log\log n)$ time. In order to identify a feasible translocation, we constructively maintain a fully dynamic graph synchronously, convert this task to a connectivity query on the fully dynamic graph, as well as a search for "an active edge" in its spanning forest, which results in an amortized time complexity of $O(\frac{N^2 \log n+\log^2 n}{\log\log n})$. Note that since the input genomes of SRT are multi-chromosomal, the parameter $N$ in the time complexity originates from the pairwise comparison required over all chromosomes in the worst case to determine the existence of a feasible translocation. Moreover, we also have to afford the additional cost for maintaining the fully dynamic graph consisting of edge insertion and deletion operations, which is $O(\log^2 n/ \log\log n)$ amortized time [17]. Consequently, we re-implement Ozery-Flato and Shamir' algorithm in $O(\frac{n(N^2 \log n+\log^2 n)}{\log\log n})$ amortized time, which could be much faster than its original $O(n^{3/2}\sqrt{\log n})$.

## 2 Preliminaries

In the literature on genome rearrangement, we usually have a set $\sigma$ of integers, where each integer represents a gene or a syntenic block. Each integer may appear in two different orientations signed by + and − (for convenience, the sign "+" will be omitted hereafter). A chromosome, which consists of a minimum of two genes, is depicted as a linear sequence of signed integers. Given a chromosome $X = [x_1, x_2, \ldots, x_m]$, $x_i$ denotes the $i$-th element in $X$, and $|x_i|$ denotes the integer while disregarding the sign of $x_i$. An integer $i$ belongs to $X$ if either $i$ or

$-i$ appears in $X$. For each integer $i$ that belongs to $X$, we use $i^{-1}$ to denote the index of $i$, that is, $|x_{i^{-1}}| = i$. For a sequence of signed integers $I = [x_i, \ldots, x_j]$, $-I$ denotes the reversed sequence with flipped signs, i.e., $-I = [-x_j, \ldots, -x_i]$. A chromosome can be viewed from either end to the other; thus, the chromosome $X = [x_1, x_2, \ldots, x_m]$ can also be represented by $-X = [-x_m, -x_{m-1}, \ldots, -x_1]$. We call $x_1$ and $-x_m$ the two *tails* of $X$.

A genome comprises a minimum of two chromosomes, where each integer appears once on the chromosomes. We use $\sigma_A$ to denote the set of integers in a genome $A$. Two genomes $A$ and $B$ are *related* if $\sigma_A = \sigma_B$. A translocation operates on two chromosomes $X$ and $Y$. It splits $X$ into $X_1, X_2$ and $Y$ into $Y_1, Y_2$, then swaps the segments in one of two ways:

- *prefix-prefix* translocation: swaps $X_1$ and $Y_1$, yielding $[Y_1, X_2]$ and $[X_1, Y_2]$;
- *prefix-suffix* translocation: swaps $X_1$ and $Y_2$, yielding $[-Y_2, X_2]$ and $[Y_1, -X_1]$.

A translocation is *reciprocal* if none of $X_1, X_2, Y_1, Y_2$ is empty, which preserves the set of tails of the genome. Genomes are referred to as *co-tailed* when they have an identical set of tails. Thus, genome $A$ cannot be transformed into genome $B$ via reciprocal translocations if $A$ and $B$ are not co-tailed. Note that co-tailed genomes have the same number of chromosomes. We now formally define the problem studied in this paper.

**Definition 1.** *Sorting multi-chromosomal genomes by Reciprocal Translocations, SRT for short.*

***Instance:*** *two related and co-tailed genomes A and B.*

***Question:*** *Is there a sequence of m reciprocal translocations* $S = \rho_1, \rho_2, \ldots, \rho_m$ *that transforms A into B, such that m is minimized.*

The minimum number of reciprocal translocations required to transform $A$ into $B$ is the *translocation distance* between $A$ and $B$, denoted by $d(A, B)$. W.l.o.g., we assume each chromosome in $B$ consists of consecutive positive integers arranged in ascending order, which is achievable by relabeling integers in $B$ with integers in $[n] = \{1, 2, \ldots, n\}$ to enforce this condition, while $A$ changes accordingly. Henceforth, reciprocal translocation is referred to as translocation.

### 2.1 The Cycle Graph

The cycle graph was initially presented in [4]. Consider two related and co-tailed genomes $A$ and $B$, each consisting of $N$ chromosomes such that $\sigma_A = \sigma_B = [n]$. Each signed integer $i$ can be viewed as a pair of ordered nodes $(l(i), r(i))$. If $i$ is positive (+), $l(i) = i^0$ and $r(i) = i^1$; if negative (−), $l(i) = i^1$ and $r(i) = i^0$. The *cycle graph* of $A$ and $B$, denoted by $G(A, B)$, is constructed as follows. The set of nodes is $\bigcup_{i=1}^{n} \{i^0, i^1\}$. For any two consecutive signed integers $i$ and $j$ in a chromosome of $A$ (resp. $B$), connect $r(i)$ and $l(j)$ with a black (resp. gray) edge. Figure 1-(a) gives an example of a cycle graph.

Note that $G(A, B)$ contains $n - N$ black edges and $n - N$ gray edges. All nodes have degree 2 except one node in each tail; thus, the cycle graph consists

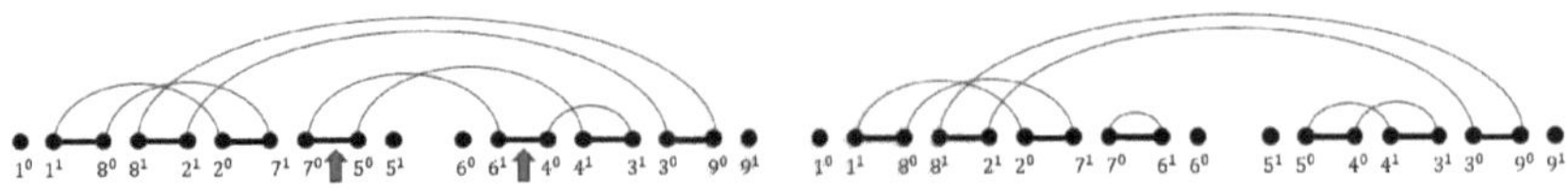

(a) (b)

**Fig. 1.** (a) $G(A, B)$ with $A = \{[1, 8, -2, -7, 5], [6, 4, -3, 9]\}$, $B = \{[1, 2, 3, 4, 5], [6, 7, 8, 9]\}$; thick lines denote black edges, thin arcs denote gray edges. (b) $G(A \cdot \rho, B)$, where $\rho$ (a prefix-suffix translocation) cuts black edges $(7^0, 5^0)$ and $(6^1, 4^0)$, generates new black edges $(7^0, 6^1)$ and $(5^0, 4^0)$, and creates adjacency $\langle 6, 7 \rangle$.

of edge-disjoint cycles with alternating black and gray edges. A cycle containing $k$ black edges and $k$ gray edges is called a $k$-cycle.

Since each chromosome in $B$ is a sequence of integers in increasing order, each gray edge has the form $(i^1, (i+1)^0)$. A gray edge is *internal* if $i$ and $i+1$ belong to the same chromosome of $A$, and *external* if not. The pair of integers $i$ and $i+1$ forms an *adjacency* $\langle i, i+1 \rangle$ if the subsequence $[i, i+1]$ or $[-(i+1), -i]$ is present within any chromosome of $A$. We use $c(A, B)$ to denote the number of cycles in $G(A, B)$. If $A = B$, then $c(A, B) = n - N$ is maximal. Let $\rho$ be a translocation and $A \cdot \rho$ be the genome after performing $\rho$ on $A$, $\Delta c = c(A \cdot \rho, B) - c(A, B)$.

**Lemma 1** ([9]). $\Delta c \in \{-1, 0, 1\}$.

A translocation is *proper* if $\Delta c = 1$. An external edge can help us find a proper translocation. Figure 1-(b) presents an example of a proper translocation.

**Observation 1.** *If there is an external gray edge* $(i^1, (i+1)^0)$ *in* $G(A, B)$, *a proper translocation can be achieved while creating adjacency* $\langle i, i+1 \rangle$.

For simplicity, we refer to the proper translocation that creates the adjacency $\langle i, i+1 \rangle$ as $\rho[i]$. When a proper translocation simultaneously creates two adjacencies, $\langle i, i+1 \rangle$ and $\langle j, j+1 \rangle$, we say that $\rho[i]$ and $\rho[j]$ are *equivalent*.

### 2.2 The Translocation Distance

Consider $\pi_A$ as any random concatenation of chromosomes in $A$, arranged in any sequence and direction. Consequently, $\pi_A = \pi_1, \ldots, \pi_n$ forms a signed permutation of length $n$. Arrange the nodes of $G(A, B)$ linearly following their sequence in $\pi_A$. Two gray edges *intersect* if their associated nodes alternate in the linear sequence. The *overlap graph* $OV(\pi_A)$ of $G(A, B)$ is constructed as follows. Each gray edge corresponds to a vertex in $OV(\pi_A)$. There is an edge between two vertices in $OV(\pi_A)$ iff their corresponding gray edges intersect. Each connected component in $OV(\pi_A)$ corresponds to a set of gray edges that form a *component* in $G(A, B)$. A component in $G(A, B)$ is *external* if it contains at least one external edge; otherwise, it is *internal*. A component in $G(A, B)$ is *trivial* if it is internal and contains exactly one gray edge; otherwise, it is *non-trivial*. For example, Fig. 1-(b) contains one external component and two internal components, one of which is trivial.

The translocation distance formula is somewhat complex, as it involves several parameters [2,4]. However, Ozery-Flato and Shamir investigated a special case of SRT, which they defined as SRTNL (SRT-no leaves) [10]; this case requires that $G(A, B)$ contain no non-trivial internal components. Fortunately, for such instances, the translocation distance is considerably easier to calculate.

**Theorem 1** **([10]).** *Let $A$ and $B$ be related and co-tailed genomes such that there is no non-trivial internal component in $G(A, B)$, then the translocation distance $d(A, B) = n - N - c(A, B)$.*

They also proved that any SRT instance with non-trivial internal components can be optimally transformed into an SRTNL instance by the following theorem.

**Theorem 2** **([10]).** *Given two related and co-tailed genomes $A$ and $B$ with non-trivial internal components in $G(A, B)$, there exists an algorithm to find a sequence of $t$ translocations, such that after applying them to $A$ and obtaining $A'$, $G(A', B)$ does not contain non-trivial internal components and $d(A', B) = d(A, B) - t$. Moreover, the algorithm runs in linear time, except when it calls another algorithm to solve an SRTNL instance of smaller size than $A$.*

A proper translocation is *safe* if it does not create non-trivial internal components, and *unsafe* otherwise. The translocation in Fig. 1-(b) is unsafe. From Theorem 1, any safe translocation $\rho$ satisfies $d(A \cdot \rho, B) = d(A, B) - 1$. Thus, solving SRTNL merely requires identifying a sequence of safe translocations.

## 3 Ozery-Flato and Shamir's Algorithm

Ozery-Flato and Shamir designed an algorithm for SRTNL in $O(n^{3/2}\sqrt{\log(n)})$ [10]. A sequence of translocations $S = (\rho_1, \ldots, \rho_k)$ is *legal* if $\rho_j$ corresponds to an external edge in $G(A \cdot \rho_1 \cdot \cdots \cdot \rho_{j-1}, B)$ for $j = 1, \ldots, k$, where $\rho_0 = \emptyset$. A legal sequence $S$ is *maximal* if $G(A \cdot S, B)$ contains only internal components, and *total* if all the internal components are trivial. Ozery-Flato and Shamir's Algorithm is mostly based on the following important finding.

**Theorem 3** **([10]).** *Let $S = (\rho_1, \ldots, \rho_k)$ be a maximal but not a total sequence of translocations. Let $\rho_l$ be the last unsafe translocation in $S$. Let $S_1 = (\rho_1, \ldots, \rho_{l-1})$ and $S_2 = (\rho_l, \ldots, \rho_k)$. There exists a sequence of nonempty translocations $S'$ such that $S_1, S', S_2$ is a maximal legal sequence and all translocations in $S_2$ are safe.*

The main idea of Ozery-Flato and Shamir's Algorithm is to maintain a maximal legal sequence of translocations and consistently extend it by inserting a nonempty subsequence of translocations before the last unsafe translocation. According to Theorem 3, the length of the safe translocation sequence could be enlarged, provided that unsafe translocations exist. Thus, the algorithm finally returns a sequence of safe translocations that is optimal (Algorithm 1).

To efficiently implement Algorithm 1, we formalize its typical operations.

**Theorem 4.** *Consider a genome composed of $N$ chromosomes on $n$ integers. It is sufficient to implement Algorithm 1 by maintaining the genome and a set of integers $Q \subseteq \{1, 2, \ldots, n-1\}$ allowing the following operations:*

1. *query for $x_i$, where $|x_i|$ belongs to chromosome $X = [x_1, \ldots, x_m]$ in the genome;*
2. *query for $j^{-1}$, where $j$ belongs to chromosome $Y = [y_1, \ldots, y_t]$ in the genome;*
3. *find $v \in Q$ such that $v$ and $v+1$ belong to different chromosomes in the genome;*
4. *apply a given translocation on the genome;*
5. *remove an integer from $Q$.*

*Moreover, Algorithm 1 performs $O(n)$ such operations and additionally takes $O(n)$ time.*

---

**Algorithm 1.** Ozery-Flato and Shamir's Algorithm for solving SRTNL.

Let $V$ be the set of gray edges in $G(A, B)$ that are in non-trivial components
$S_1 \leftarrow \emptyset$, $S_2 \leftarrow \emptyset$
**while** $V \neq \emptyset$ **do**
  **while** there exists an external gray edge $(v^1, (v+1)^0) \in V$ **do**
    Remove $(v^1, (v+1)^0)$ from $V$
    **if** $\rho[v]$ is not equivalent to the first element in $S_2$ **then**
      Append $\rho[v]$ to $S_1$
      $A \leftarrow A \cdot \rho[v]$
    **end if**
  **end while**
  **if** $V = \emptyset$ **then**
    $A \leftarrow A \cdot S_2$
    **return** $S_1, S_2$
  **end if**
  **while** all the gray edges in $V$ are internal **do**
    Remove the last element $\rho[w]$ from $S_1$
    Prepend $\rho[w]$ to $S_2$
    $A \leftarrow A \cdot \rho[w]$
  **end while**
**end while**

---

Initially, $Q = \{v | \ (v^1, (v+1)^0) \in V\}$. Operation 5 (simulates gray edge removal) is implementable in constant time via an $(n-1)$-size array and a counter: initialize the array such that the $i$-th entry is $i$ if $i \in Q$ (0 otherwise), and set the counter to $|Q|$. When removing $i$ from $Q$, update the $i$-th array entry to 0 and decrement the counter by 1; $Q$ is empty iff the counter equals 0. Thus, the runtime of Algorithm 1 depends on the time complexities of operations 1–4.

## 4 Improvement of the Time Complexity

This section introduces data structures that accelerate operations 1–4 in Theorem 4, enabling $O(\frac{n(N^2 \log n+\log^2 n)}{\log\log n})$ amortized time for Ozery-Flato and Shamir's Algorithm ($n$ is the number of genes and $N$ is the number of chromosomes).

### 4.1 A Data Structure for Handling Genomes

Kaplan and Verbin proposed maintaining signed permutations via balanced trees [8]. Here, we use a *splay tree* (first introduced in [14]) with additional node-stored information (see Fig. 2-(a) for an example). The basic operation of a splay tree is *rotation*, which runs in constant time (described in Fig. 2-(b)). While splay trees are not necessarily balanced, their key *splay()* operation—moving a non-root node to the root via amortized $O(\log n)$ *rotation* operations—takes logarithmic amortized time.

**Lemma 2.** *Consider a genome composed of $N$ chromosomes on $n$ integers. There exists a splay tree-based data structure such that querying $x_i$, where $|x_i|$ belongs to $X = [x_1, \ldots, x_m]$ (operation 1), querying $j^{-1}$, where $j$ belongs to $Y = [y_1, \ldots, y_t]$ (operation 2), performing a translocation (operation 4), and determining whether two integers $i$ and $j$ belong to the same chromosome can be implemented in $O(\log n)$ amortized time.*

*Proof.* Each chromosome $X$ in $A$ is represented by a splay tree $T_X$ that ensures the in-order traversal of the nodes in $T_X$ is $X$. The root of $T_X$ is denoted by $r(T_X)$. Additionally, at each node $x$, it stores the size $n_x$ of the subtree rooted at $x$ and a reverse flag. If the reverse flag of $x$ is true, then the subtree rooted at $x$ is read in reverse order, that is—from right to left, and the sign of each integer in it is flipped. Moreover, there is also another array of pointers mapping each integer $i$ ($1 \leq i \leq n$) to the node $v$ in the forest of splay trees where $i$ resides. The splay tree consistently upholds the invariant: the in-order traversal of the tree, taking the reverse flag into consideration, is the current chromosome.

For an internal node $v$, we define *flip(v)* as exchanging its children, flipping the reverse flag of each child, and negating the integer stored in $v$. This operation preserves the invariant. As for the *rotation* operation shown in Fig. 2-(b), it can be ensured that the reverse flags for both $x$ and $y$ are false prior to its execution. After a right rotation from $T_1$ to $T_2$, $n_y = n_b + n_c + 1$ and $n_x = n_a + n_y + 1$; after a left rotation from $T_2$ to $T_1$, $n_x = n_a + n_b + 1$ and $n_y = n_c + n_x + 1$. Recall that each *splay()* operation is implemented by amortized $O(\log n)$ *rotations.*

- **Querying $x_i$:** Search the $i$-th integer of $X$ starting from $r(T_X)$. For node $v$ encountered, execute *flip(v)* if its reverse flag is true. Let $u$ and $w$ be $v$'s left and right children: if $n_u = i-1$, the integer residing at $v$ is $x_i$; if $n_u > i-1$, search the $i$-th integer in the subtree rooted at $u$; if $n_u < i-1$, search the $(i-n_u-1)$-th integer in the subtree rooted at $w$. The time complexity depends on the depth of a splay tree, which is amortized $O(\log n)$.

- **Querying $j^{-1}$:** Locate node $v$ where $j$ resides via the array of pointers, then run *splay(v)* to elevate $v$ to $T_Y$'s root. Let $u$ and $w$ be $v$'s left and right children: if $v$'s reverse flag is false, $j^{-1} = n_u + 1$; otherwise, $j^{-1} = n_w + 1$. The query consists of a call of *splay()*, thus it takes $O(\log n)$ amortized time.
- **Performing a translocation:** For translocation $\rho$ on $A$ operating on chromosomes $X = [X_1, X_2]$ and $Y = [Y_1, Y_2]$, where $X_1 = [x_1, \ldots, x_k]$, $X_2 = [x_{k+1}, \ldots, x_m]$ and $Y_1 = [y_1, \ldots, y_{k'}]$, $Y_2 = [y_{k'+1}, \ldots, y_t]$, let $u, v, u', v'$ be the nodes that $x_k, x_{k+1}, y_{k'}, y_{k'+1}$ reside in, respectively. If $\rho$ is prefix-prefix, run *splay*$(v)$ and *splay*$(v')$, elevating $v$ to the root of $T_X$ and $v'$ to the root of $T_Y$. Use *flip()* to set the reverse flags of $v$ and $v'$ to false if needed. The sub-permutation corresponding to $v$'s left subtree is $X_1$, and the sub-permutation corresponding to $v'$'s left subtree is $Y_1$. Exchange the left subtrees of $v$ and $v'$. If $\rho$ is prefix-suffix, run *splay*$(v)$ and *splay*$(u')$, elevating $v$ to the root of $T_X$ and $u'$ to the root of $T_Y$. Use *flip()* to set the reverse flags of $v$ and $u'$ to false if needed. The sub-permutation corresponding to $v$'s left subtree is $X_1$, and the sub-permutation corresponding to $u'$'s right subtree is $Y_2$. Flip reverse flags of $v$'s left subtree root and $u'$'s right subtree root, then exchange the two subtrees. The translocation operation consists of two calls of *splay()*, thus it takes $O(\log n)$ amortized time.
- **Determine whether two integers $i$ and $j$ belong to the same chromosome:** Locate nodes $u$ and $v$ where $i$ and $j$ reside via the array of pointers. Search upward from $u$ and $v$ to their roots in parallel: $i$ and $j$ belong to the same chromosome iff the roots are identical. The time complexity of the search depends on the depths of the splay trees, which are amortized $O(\log n)$.

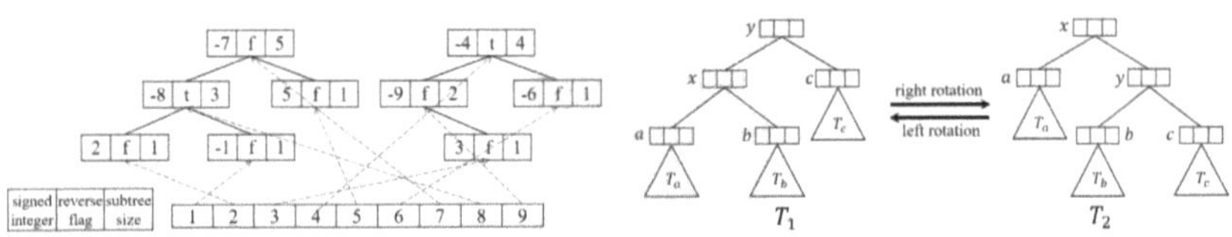


(a) (b)

**Fig. 2.** (a) A representation of $A = \{[1, 8, -2, -7, 5], [6, 4, -3, 9]\}$. The information in each node consists of the signed integer, the status of the reverse flag ($t$ for true and $f$ for false), and the size of subtree rooted at the node. (b) Right rotation: from $T_1$ to $T_2$, and left rotation: from $T_2$ to $T_1$. A *rotation* ascends a node above its parent while keeping the in-order traversal of the tree intact.

## 4.2 Implementation of the Operations via a Fully Dynamic Graph

As a warm-up, we implement operation 3 in $O(\frac{N^2 \log n}{\log \log n} + \log^2 n)$ amortized time. Firstly, we define *underlying graph* $U(A, B) = ([n], E_r \cup E_b)$ for two related and co-tailed genomes $A$ and $B$. Each integer $i \in [n]$ corresponds to a vertex, also denoted by $i$. A blue (resp. red) edge connects two vertices $i$ and $j$ if the integers $i$ and $j$ are adjacent (disregarding their signs) on some chromosome of $A$ (resp. $B$). $E_r$ and $E_b$ are the sets of red and blue edges, respectively. See Fig. 3-(a) as an example. We use $([n], E_b)$ to denote the subgraph that includes all vertices and blue edges. A *blue connected component* is a connected component in the subgraph $([n], E_b)$. The underlying graph of the current genome maintains the invariant: there are $N$ blue connected components, and each blue connected component is a path on which the sequence of vertices is identical to a chromosome (disregarding the signs of integers) in the genome, where $N$ is the number of chromosomes.

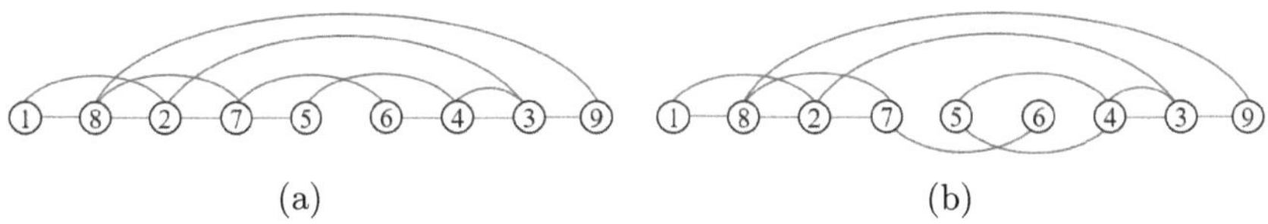


**Fig. 3.** (a) $U(A, B)$ for $A = \{[1, 8, -2, -7, 5], [6, 4, -3, 9]\}$ and $B = \{[1, 2, 3, 4, 5], [6, 7, 8, 9]\}$. (b) The underlying graph after performing the proper translocation corresponding to gray edge $(6^1, 7^0)$ and the removal of 6 from $Q$.

Given two related and co-tailed genomes $A$ and $B$, let $\rho$ be the translocation that occurs on $X = [X_1, X_2]$ and $Y = [Y_1, Y_2]$, where $X_1 = [x_1, \ldots, x_k]$, $X_2 = [x_{k+1}, \ldots, x_m]$ and $Y_1 = [y_1, \ldots, y_{k'}]$, $Y_2 = [y_{k'+1}, \ldots, y_t]$. The underlying graph $U(A \cdot \rho, B)$ can be derived by updating $U(A, B)$ as follows:

1. Remove the two blue edges $(|x_k|, |x_{k+1}|)$ and $(|y_{k'}|, |y_{k'+1}|)$.
2. If $\rho$ is a prefix-prefix translocation, create blue edges connecting $|x_k|$ to $|y_{k'+1}|$ and $|x_{k+1}|$ to $|y_{k'}|$. Alternatively, if $\rho$ is a prefix-suffix translocation, create blue edges connecting $|x_k|$ to $|y_{k'}|$ and $|x_{k+1}|$ to $|y_{k'+1}|$.

The underlying graph will also be changed while performing operation 5. Once an integer $i$ is removed from $Q$, the red edge $(i, i+1)$ is removed from the current underlying graph. See Fig. 3-(b) for an example. The above modifications will not cause the underlying graph to violate the invariant.

A red edge $(i, i + 1)$ is *active* if $i$ and $i + 1$ are in distinct blue connected components of an underlying graph. Thus, implementing operation 3 (find $v \in Q$ such that $v$ and $v+1$ belong to different chromosomes) is equivalent to finding an active edge in the current underlying graph. Actually, the underlying graph is a fully dynamic graph consisting of edge insertion and deletion operations. Thus, determining whether there is an active edge involves solving the connectivity problem on the fully dynamic graph, which is efficiently solved by Holm et al. [6].

**Theorem 5 (Theorem 3, in [6]).** *Given a graph $G$ with $m$ edges and $n$ vertices, there exists a deterministic fully dynamic algorithm that answers connectivity queries in $O(\log n/\log\log n)$ worst-case time, and uses $O(\log^2 n)$ amortized time per edge insertion or deletion.*

In an underlying graph, a true connectivity query between two vertices from distinct blue connected components implies at least one active edge exists on the path connecting the two vertices in the spanning forest of the underlying graph. As shown in [6], a link-cut tree (introduced by Sleator and Tarjan [13]) can be used to maintain the spanning forest of the underlying graph.

A link-cut tree is a data structure for maintaining a forest (a set of rooted trees). The edges of a link-cut tree are split into *solid* and *dashed* types, such that one node has at most one solid edge to its children. A *solid path* is a maximal continuous path of solid edges, or a single node if no solid edge incident with it. The *head* of a solid path is its lowest vertex, and the *tail* is its highest vertex. Each solid path is maintained by a biased binary tree [1]. In each biased binary tree, the external nodes in left-to-right order correspond to the vertices on the solid path from head to tail, and the internal nodes in in-order traversal correspond to edges in the solid path from head to tail.

**Lemma 3** **([13]).** *The depth of a biased binary tree representing a solid path is $O(\log n)$.*

A basic operation on the link-cut tree is *access(v)* for a vertex $v$, which takes $O(\log n)$ amortized time. During execution of *access(v)*, the edges on the path $P$ from $v$ to the root of the tree are set to solid, and the solid edges not in $P$ but incident with the nodes in $P$ are changed into dashed.

**Lemma 4.** *Let $v$ and $w$ be two vertices within the same tree of a link-cut tree. If access(w) is executed immediately following access(v), then the path between $v$ and $w$ is composed of solid edges and potentially at most one dashed edge. Furthermore, the dashed edge (if it exists) connects the end of the solid path that includes $v$ to its parent.*

*Proof.* After the execution of *access(v)* and *access(w)* sequentially, assume that the solid paths containing $v$ and $w$ are $P(v)$ and $P(w)$, respectively. We will explore the three cases based on whether $v$ is an ancestor of $w$, $w$ is an ancestor of $v$, or neither is an ancestor of the other.

- $v$ is an ancestor of $w$. Then executing *access(v)* followed by *access(w)* results in $v$ being included in $P(w)$. Thus, the path from $v$ to $w$ is a subpath of $P(w)$.
- $w$ is an ancestor of $v$. Then after executing *access(v)* and *access(w)* successively, $w$ becomes the head of $P(w)$. The edge connecting $w$ to the tail $v'$ of $P(v)$ is dashed. Thus, the path between $v$ and $w$ is composed of $P(v)$ as well as the dashed edge $(v', w)$.
- Neither $v$ nor $w$ is an ancestor of the other. Assume $u$ is the lowest common ancestor of $v$ and $w$. The edge between the tail $v'$ of $P(v)$ and $u$ is dashed, since otherwise $u$ would associate two solid edges with its children. Thus, the path from $v$ to $w$ consists of $P(v)$, the dashed edge $(v', u)$ and the subpath of $P(w)$ that travels from $u$ to $w$.

Next, we show how to retrieve an active edge using the link-cut tree (equivalently, implementing operation 3) efficiently.

**Lemma 5.** *Given the underlying graph of a genome consisting of $N$ chromosomes on $n$ integers, an active edge can be found in $O(\frac{N^2 \log n}{\log\log n} + \log^2 n)$ amortized time.*

*Proof.* Let $R = \{r_1, r_2, \ldots, r_N\}$ be the set of integers that reside at the roots of the $N$ splay trees. For any $r_a, r_b \in R$, if they are connected in the underlying graph, the path between $r_a$ and $r_b$ in the spanning forest contains at least one active edge. At most $N(N-1)/2$ connectivity queries are needed to either confirm or deny the presence of an active edge. As each query takes $O(\log n/\log\log n)$ by Theorem 5, the queries yield a total cost of at most $O(N^2 \log n/\log\log n)$.

If the query verifies that $r_a$ and $r_b$ are connected, it remains to find an active edge on the path $P = v_0(r_a) - v_1 - \cdots - v_k(r_b)$ within the spanning forest. We first execute $access(r_a)$ and $access(r_b)$ successively, then $P$ has at most one dashed edge (Lemma 4). To verify if a dashed edge exists, we check if the roots of the biased binary trees representing the solid paths containing $r_a$ and $r_b$ differ, which takes $O(\log n)$ by Lemma 3. Once a dashed edge is verified to exist, Lemma 4 indicates that it can be tracked through the tail pointer of the solid path that includes $r_a$. In case $P$ contains a dashed edge $(v_i, v_{i+1})$ with $0 \leq i \leq k-1$, we begin by checking if $v_0$ and $v_i$ belong to the same chromosome. Should they not, we narrow the search to the path $P' = v_0 - \cdots - v_i$ consisting of solid edges. Otherwise, we verify if $v_{i+1}$ and $v_k$ belong to the same chromosome. If not, the search focuses on the path $P'' = v_{i+1} - \cdots - v_k$ consisting of solid edges. Importantly, if both pairs $v_0, v_i$ and $v_{i+1}, v_k$ reside within the same chromosomes, the dashed edge $(v_i, v_{i+1})$ is necessarily an active edge. By Lemma 2, the twice checks yield an overall time complexity of amortized $O(\log n)$.

Until now, the search is refined to a path $P_s = x - \cdots - y$ consisting of solid edges. Recall that each solid path is maintained by a biased binary tree, where leaf nodes represent vertices and internal nodes represent edges. W.l.o.g., assuming $x$ is positioned to the left of $y$ in the biased binary tree. We start a binary search on this tree at the lowest common ancestor of $x$ and $y$ to identify an active edge. At each internal node $(u, w)$, search left if $u$ and $x$ belong to different chromosomes, right if $w$ and $y$ belong to different chromosomes; if both pairs $u$, $x$ and $w$, $y$ are within the same chromosomes, $(u, w)$ is active. The binary search visits at most $O(\log n)$ nodes by Lemma 3, while the check at each node requires $O(\log n)$ amortized time by Lemma 2. Thus, the entire binary search process takes $O(\log^2 n)$ amortized time.

Overall, the time complexity for identifying an active edge is $O(\frac{N^2 \log n}{\log\log n}) + O(\log n) + O(\log^2 n)$, equivalently $O(\frac{N^2 \log n}{\log\log n} + \log^2 n)$.

Figure 4 shows an example of retrieving an active edge. Notably, the update time of the underlying graph must be considered. Then, from Theorems 4 and 5, as well as Lemmas 2 and 5, we have the following theorem.

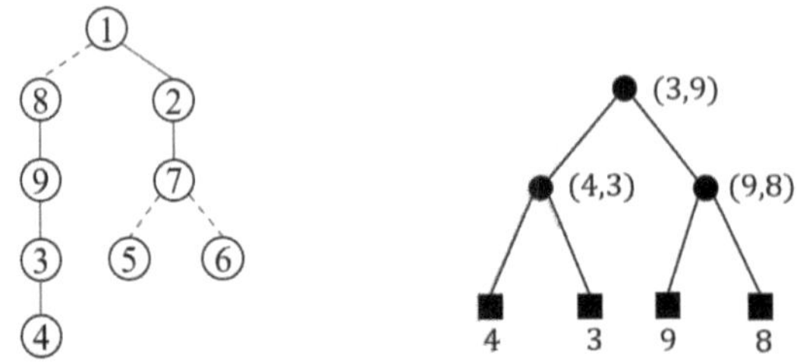


(a) (b)

**Fig. 4.** (a) A spanning forest for $U(A, B)$ in Fig. 3-(a) after *access(4)* and *access(7)*. The path from 4 to 7 contains two solid paths, $P_1 = 4-3-9-8$ and $P_2 = 7-2-1$, and a dashed edge $(8, 1)$. Since 8 and 4 belong to different chromosomes, an active edge can be retrieved from $P_1$. (b) A biased binary tree of $P_1$. The binary search begins at the lowest common ancestor of the endpoints of $P_1$ (4 and 8), which is the node $(3, 9)$. Since 3 and 4 belong to the same chromosome while 9 and 8 belong to different chromosomes, the search descends to the right child.

**Theorem 6.** *Algorithm 1 can be efficiently implemented in* $O(n(\frac{N^2 \log n}{\log\log n} + \log^2 n))$ *amortized time.*

According to Lemma 5's proof, the $\log^2 n$ term in operation 3's time complexity arises from verifying if two integers belong to the same chromosome $O(\log n)$ times. Additionally, Wulff-Nilsen [17] improved the time complexity of edge insertions/deletions in fully dynamic graphs.

**Theorem 7 (Theorem 4.1, in [17]).** *There is a deterministic data structure for fully dynamic graph connectivity which supports edge insertions/deletions in* $O(\log^2 n/\log\log n)$ *amortized time per update and connectivity queries in* $O(\log n/\log\log n)$ *worst case time, where* $n$ *is the number of vertices.*

As stated in [17], their results can be extended to maintain a spanning forest of the fully dynamic graph stored in a link-cut tree. Thus, we can improve the time complexity of operation 3 to $O(\frac{N^2 \log n + \log^2 n}{\log\log n})$, provided that determining whether two integers belong to the same chromosome takes only $O(\log n/\log\log n)$ amortized time. This is achievable by equipping each splay tree node with a shortcut pointer to an ancestor. However, maintaining these shortcut pointers incurs a small slowdown in performing a *rotation*.

**Lemma 6.** *Consider a genome composed of* $N$ *chromosomes on* $n$ *integers. For any* $\varepsilon > 0$*, there exists a splay tree-based data structure such that performing a* rotation *requires* $O(\log^{\varepsilon} n)$ *amortized time, and determining whether two integers belong to the same chromosome takes* $O(\frac{\log n}{\varepsilon \log\log n})$ *amortized time.*

*Proof.* Based on the data structure in Lemma 2, for each node $x$ with depth $d$ in a splay tree, we add a shortcut pointer pointing to its ancestor $w$ with depth $max\{0, d - \lfloor \varepsilon \log\log n \rfloor\}$.

**Determining Whether Two Integers $i$ and $j$ Belong to the Same Chromosome:** We start a search from the node where $i$ resides, ascending to root via shortcut pointers in the splay tree. Given that the depth of $i$ in a splay tree is limited to amortized $O(\log n)$, and each step covers $\varepsilon \log\log n$ nodes, the search encounters at most $O(\frac{\log n}{\varepsilon \log\log n})$ nodes. Thus, the search takes $O(\frac{\log n}{\varepsilon \log\log n})$ amortized time. A similar search for $j$ is also performed, ensuring the same time complexity. Then $i$ and $j$ belong to the same chromosome if and only if the two roots are identical.

**Performing a *Rotation*:** As stated in the proof of Lemma 2, a *rotation* operation can be implemented in constant time, then it suffices to show how the shortcut pointers change after performing a *rotation*. W.l.o.g, assume that the *rotation* from $T_1$ to $T_2$ shown in Fig. 2-(b) is performed. Note that besides $x$ and $y$, only the nodes residing in the subtrees with roots $a$, $b$, and $c$ may alter their shortcut pointers, provided that they are at most $\varepsilon \log\log n$ deeper than $a$, $b$, or $c$. Thus, the number of nodes whose shortcut pointers may be changed is $O(2^{\varepsilon \log\log n}) = O(\log^{\varepsilon} n)$. It is feasible to identify a path $P = v_{-1}(= y), v_0(= x), \ldots, v_k$ of maximum length $\varepsilon \log\log n + 1$ ascending from $y$ in $T_2$ until $y_k$ is the root of $T_2$ or $k = \varepsilon \log\log n$. Then, we can conduct a BFS search beginning with $x$ in the subtree rooted at $x$ of $T_2$, to find all nodes with a distance to $x$ not greater than $\varepsilon \log\log n + 1$ in $O(\log^{\varepsilon} n)$ time. For each node $v$, we record $d(v)$ as the distance from $x$ to $v$ and a boolean variable $b(v)$ that indicates whether $v$ resides in the subtree rooted at $y$. It suffices to consider all nodes $v$ such that $d(v) \leq \varepsilon \log\log n$ or $d(v) = \varepsilon \log\log n + 1$ with $b(v)$ being true. The node to which the shortcut pointer of $v$ points in $T_2$, is changed to $v_{\varepsilon \log\log n - d(v)}$ if $k + d(v) \geq \varepsilon \log\log n$ and $v_k$ otherwise. Thus, it takes $O(1)$ time to change the shortcut pointer of a node, leading to a time complexity of amortized $O(\log^{\varepsilon} n)$ for a *rotation* operation.

Note that if a *rotation* takes $O(\log^{\varepsilon} n)$ amortized time, then *splay()* runs in $O(\log^{1+\varepsilon} n)$ amortized time. By combining Lemma 6 with the proofs of Lemma 2 and Lemma 5, we update the time complexities of operations 1–4 as follows.

**Theorem 8.** *Consider a genome composed of $N$ chromosomes on $n$ integers. For any $\varepsilon > 0$, there exists a splay tree-based data structure that implements operation 1 in $O(\log n)$ amortized time, operation 2 in $O(\log^{1+\varepsilon} n)$ amortized time, operation 3 in $O(\frac{\varepsilon N^2 \log n + \log^2 n}{\varepsilon \log\log n})$ amortized time, and operation 4 in $O(\log^{1+\varepsilon} n)$ amortized time.*

By choosing a proper $0 < \varepsilon < 1$, we have $O(\log^{1+\varepsilon} n) = O(\log^2 n / \log\log n)$. By combining Theorem 4 with the improved time complexities in Theorems 7 and 8, Algorithm 1 can be implemented in $O(\frac{n(N^2 \log n + \log^2 n)}{\log\log n})$ amortized time. Further building on Theorem 2, we state our main contribution as follows.

**Theorem 9.** *The problem of SRT can be efficiently solved in $O(\frac{n(N^2 \log n + \log^2 n)}{\log\log n})$ amortized time.*

## 5 Conclusion

We introduce an algorithm for SRT with an amortized time complexity of $O(\frac{n(N^2 \log n + \log^2 n)}{\log \log n})$. We detail the time complexity analysis of five core operations and integrate fully dynamic connectivity algorithms to implement the operations efficiently. In the real evolution event, the number of chromosomes typically remains constant, making our algorithm considered nearly $O(\frac{n \log^2 n}{\log \log n})$. It is worth improving the time complexity of the operations by using other data structures.

**Acknowledgments.** This research is supported by NSF of China under grant 62272279 and U24A20257.

## References

1. Bent, S.W., Sleator, D.D., Tarjan, R.E.: Biased search trees. SIAM J. Comput. **14**(3), 545–568 (1985)
2. Bergeron, A., Mixtacki, J., Stoye, J.: On sorting by translocations. J. Comput. Biol. **13**(2), 567–578 (2006)
3. Dudek, B., Gawrychowski, P., Starikovskaya, T.: Sorting signed permutations by reversals in nearly-linear time. In: Parter, M., Pettie, S. (eds.) Proceedings of SOSA-2024, pp. 199–214 (2024)
4. Hannenhalli, S.: Polynomial-time algorithm for computing translocation distance between genomes. Discret. Appl. Math. **71**(1–3), 137–151 (1996)
5. Hannenhalli, S., Pevzner, P.A.: Transforming men into mice (polynomial algorithm for genomic distance problem). In: Proceedings of FOCS-1995, pp. 581–592 (1995)
6. Holm, J., de Lichtenberg, K., Thorup, M.: Poly-logarithmic deterministic fully-dynamic algorithms for connectivity, minimum spanning tree, 2-edge, and biconnectivity. J. ACM **48**(4), 723–760 (2001)
7. Hoot, S., Palmer, J.: Structural rearrangements, including parallel inversions, within the chloroplast genome of anemone and related genera. J. Mol. Evol. **38**(3), 274–281 (1994)
8. Kaplan, H., Verbin, E.: Sorting signed permutations by reversals, revisited. J. Comput. Syst. Sci. **70**(3), 321–341 (2005)
9. Kececioglu, J.D., Ravi, R.: Of mice and men: algorithms for evolutionary distances between genomes with translocation. In: Clarkson, K.L. (ed.) Proceedings of SODA-1995, pp. 604–613 (1995)
10. Ozery-Flato, M., Shamir, R.: An $O(n^{3/2}\sqrt{\log(n)})$ algorithm for sorting by reciprocal translocations. J. Discrete Algorithms **9**(4), 344–357 (2011)
11. Palmer, J., Herbon, L.: Tricircular mitochondrial genomes of brassica and Raphanus: reversal of repeat configurations by inversion. Nucleic Acids Res. **14**(24), 9755–9764 (1986)
12. Sankoff, D., Leduc, G., Antoine, N., Paquin, B., Lang, B.F., Cedergren, R.: Gene order comparisons for phylogenetic inference: evolution of the mitochondrial genome. Proc. Nat. Acad. Sci. USA (PNAS) **89**(14), 6575–6579 (1992)
13. Sleator, D.D., Tarjan, R.E.: A data structure for dynamic trees. J. Comput. Syst. Sci. **26**(3), 362–391 (1983)

14. Sleator, D.D., Tarjan, R.E.: Self-adjusting binary search trees. J. ACM **32**(3), 652–686 (1985)
15. Tannier, E., Bergeron, A., Sagot, M.: Advances on sorting by reversals. Discret. Appl. Math. **155**(6–7), 881–888 (2007)
16. Wang, L., Zhu, D., Liu, X., Ma, S.: An $O(n^2)$ algorithm for signed translocation. J. Comput. Syst. Sci. **70**(3), 284–299 (2005)
17. Wulff-Nilsen, C.: Faster deterministic fully-dynamic graph connectivity. In: Khanna, S. (ed.) Proceedings of SODA-2013, pp. 1757–1769 (2013)

# On the Structure of Generalized Flows over Time: Why Storage is Unnecessary

Siyuan Chen[1], Shengminjie Chen[2,3], Suixiang Gao[1,4](✉), Zheyu Jiang[1], Dun Ma[5], and Wenguo Yang[1]

[1] School of Mathematical Sciences, University of Chinese Academy of Sciences, Beijing 100049, China
{chensiyuan221,jiangzheyu24}@mails.ucas.ac.cn, yangwg@ucas.ac.cn

[2] State Key Lab of Processors, Institute of Computing Technology, Chinese Academy of Sciences, Beijing 100190, China
csmj@ict.ac.cn

[3] School of Computer Science and Technology, University of Chinese Academy of Sciences, Beijing 100049, China

[4] Zhongguancun Laboratory, Beijing 100000, China
sxgao@ucas.ac.cn

[5] School of Advanced Interdisciplinary Sciences, University of Chinese Academy of Sciences, Beijing 101408, China
madun21@mails.ucas.ac.cn

**Abstract.** Generalized flows over time constitute a general network flow model that incorporates both transit times and flow losses or gains. For its representative variant, generalized maximum flows over time, existing studies assume that flow can be stored at intermediate nodes. However, due to resource constraints, such storage is typically undesirable or even prohibited. In this paper, we first rule out the possibility of avoiding storage via temporally repeated solutions, proving that finding a maximum temporally repeated flow is NP-hard and inapproximable. We then investigate a broader class of problems, termed optimal generalized flows over time, and establish that intermediate storage is unnecessary. Furthermore, for lossy networks where flow strictly does not increase during transmission, we show that optimal solutions can be achieved by routing flow exclusively along simple paths. These structural insights directly enable the design of a storage-free fully polynomial time approximation scheme via time-condensation techniques.

**Keywords:** Combinatorial Optimization · Network Flow · Structural Property

## 1 Introduction

Network flow is a fundamental class of problems in combinatorial optimization, with widespread applications across logistics, transportation, and telecommunications (see, e.g., [1,17]). Classical network flow models typically assume


Y. Li et al. (Eds.): COCOON 2026, LNCS 16835, pp. 192–205, 2027.
https://doi.org/10.1007/978-981-92-3309-0_15

flow invariance along arcs and instantaneous transmission. However, in practical scenarios such as the long-distance pipeline transmission of oil or gas, the transportation process incurs not only physical losses or leakages but also transit times—characteristics that classical models fail to capture. To address these limitations, two significant generalizations have been established: *generalized flows*, which characterize physical flow changes, and *flows over time*, which account for the temporal dynamics of transmission. While research on these two extensions has historically proceeded in parallel, accurately modeling scenarios like pipeline transmission necessitates the integration of both frameworks.

Groß and Skutella [9] initiated the study of generalized flows over time. In their model, each arc $a$ is associated with a *gain factor* $\gamma_a$ and a *transit time* $\tau_a$. Specifically, $x$ units of flow entering arc $a$ at time $t$ will result in $\gamma_a x$ units exiting at time $t + \tau_a$. Within this framework, they investigated the *generalized maximum flow over time problem* (GMFP), which seeks to maximize the total flow reaching the sink within a fixed time horizon $T$. The authors [9] established that this problem is NP-hard and, utilizing the condensed time-expanded network technique proposed in [3], designed a *fully polynomial time approximation scheme* (FPTAS) for the GMFP on *lossy networks* (where all gain factors are at most 1). However, their model and algorithm rely on the assumption that flow can be stored at intermediate nodes. In many practical scenarios such as traffic networks, limited space or time resources make intermediate stops undesirable or even prohibited. This naturally raises a question:

*Does the GMFP always admit a storage-free optimal solution?*

This work considers a more general problem than the GMFP, demonstrating that optimal solutions indeed do not rely on intermediate storage. To formally analyze the problem, we first present the mathematical definition of generalized flows over time. It is worth noting that while we adopt a continuous-time model for the sake of generality, we utilize discrete tools to solve the problem.

*Model and Problem.* Given a generalized dynamic network $\mathcal{N} = (G, u, \tau, \gamma, s, d, T)$ based on a directed graph $G = (V, A)$ with $n := |V|$ nodes and $m := |A|$ arcs. The network is equipped with capacity, transit time, and gain vectors $u \in \mathbb{R}^m_{\geq 0}$, $\tau \in \mathbb{N}^m_{\geq 0}$, and $\gamma \in \mathbb{R}^m_{>0}$, respectively. Additionally, it includes a time horizon $T \in \mathbb{N}_{\geq 0}$ and distinct nodes $s, d \in V$ acting as the source and sink. We assume w.l.o.g. that $G$ contains no parallel arcs, opposite arcs, or self-loops, and that $\delta^-(s) = \delta^+(d) = \emptyset$, where $\delta^-(i)$ and $\delta^+(i)$ denote the sets of incoming and outgoing arcs of node $i \in V$. A generalized flow over time is a Lebesgue-integrable function $f : A \times [0, T) \to \mathbb{R}_{\geq 0}$ that satisfies, for every $i \in V \setminus \{s, d\}$ and $t \in [0, T)$,

$$\text{(Flow conservation)} \quad \sum_{a \in \delta^-(i)} \int_0^t \gamma_a \, f_a(\theta - \tau_a) \, d\theta \; - \sum_{a \in \delta^+(i)} \int_0^t f_a(\theta) \, d\theta \; \geq \; 0 \tag{1}$$

and

$$\text{(Capacity constraint)} \qquad 0 \leq f_a(t) \leq u_a, \quad \forall\, a \in A,\ t \in [0, T). \tag{2}$$

Here $f_a(t)$ denotes the instantaneous inflow rate entering arc $a$ at time $t$, so inequality (2) bounds this rate by the arc capacity. The flow conservation constraint (1) requires that, up to any time $t$, the cumulative inflow to an intermediate node $i$ must be at least the cumulative outflow from $i$; any surplus is stored at the node. To ensure no flow remains stored at time $T$, we impose equality in (1) at $t = T$. For convenience, we set $f_a(t) = 0$ for $t < 0$ or $t \geq T - \tau_a$, the latter prevents flow that cannot reach the sink $d$ by time $T$. By discretizing the time horizon into the set $\mathcal{T} := \{0, \ldots, T-1\}$, we can also study flows over time in a discrete-time model. In this case, the integral in (1) is replaced by a summation over discrete time steps. As established by Fleischer and Tardos [4], algorithmic results often transfer between these models.

Based on the aforementioned definition, we first restate the GMFP with a given time horizon $T$, proposed in [9], as follows:

$$\text{(GMFP)} \quad v^*(T) := \max_f \sum_{a \in \delta^-(d)} \int_0^T \gamma_a f_a(\theta) d\theta \quad \text{s.t. (1), (2).}$$

Although the GMFP is well-defined, flow gains and losses in generalized dynamic networks may cause a discrepancy between source outflow and sink inflow. For a fixed sink demand $b$ and time horizon $T$, cost efficiency motivates minimizing the total source supply. This leads to the *optimal generalized flow over time problem* (OGFP):

$$\text{(OGFP)} \quad \bar{b} := \min_f \sum_{a \in \delta^+(s)} \int_0^T f_a(\theta) d\theta \quad \text{s.t. (1), (2),} \sum_{a \in \delta^-(d)} \int_0^T \gamma_a f_a(\theta)\, d\theta = b.$$

Since OGFP is determined by the parameter $b$, we sometimes write OGFP($b$) to denote it. This notion of optimality naturally extends to the GMFP: an optimal GMFP is an OGFP instance with demand set to the maximum flow value, i.e., $b := v^*(T)$. Crucially, OGFP serves as a fundamental building block: by embedding an efficient OGFP oracle within a binary search framework over $b$, one can solve the GMFP while ensuring the resulting flow utilizes minimal supply. Consequently, we identify OGFP as the core computational challenge addressed in this work. Note that OGFP inherits the NP-hardness of GMFP.

*Related Work.* Generalized flows were introduced by Kantorovich [11], where each arc is associated with a gain factor to model flow gain or loss. We refer the reader to Wayne [16] and Lin [12] for a comprehensive overview of generalized flow problems and related algorithms. The *generalized maximum flow problem* is the most classic and extensively studied subproblem. Recently, Végh [15] presented the first strongly polynomial time algorithm for this problem and subsequently, with Olver [13], proposed a simpler and faster strongly polynomial time algorithm.

Parallel to the study of physical flow changes, Ford and Fulkerson [5] pioneered the investigation of flows over time (also known as dynamic flows), associating transit times with arcs. For thorough surveys on flows over time, we refer to [2,14]. The *time-expanded network* [6] is a fundamental tool for solving such problems, transforming a dynamic flow problem into an equivalent static flow problem on a larger network. However, since network size depends linearly on the time horizon $T$, algorithms based on it typically exhibit pseudo-polynomial time complexity. To overcome this limitation, Fleischer and Skutella [3] introduced the time-condensation technique, which reduces the network size to polynomial scale at the cost of slightly relaxing the time horizon. Leveraging this technique, they designed FPTASs for numerous dynamic flow problems.

Beyond general algorithmic techniques, a focal point in the study of flows over time is the structure of optimal solutions. This interest is driven not only by practical application requirements but also by the fact that the existence of structurally simple optimal solutions can significantly reduce the search space, thereby facilitating the design of efficient algorithms. Intermediate storage is a key structural property. For the *maximum flow over time problem*, Ford and Fulkerson [5] demonstrated that it admits an optimal solution with a *temporally repeated* structure; specifically, such a solution can be viewed as the decomposition of a static flow into multiple path flows, which are then repeatedly sent along these paths throughout the time horizon. Notably, this construction does not use intermediate storage. Similarly, for the *minimum cost flow over time problem*, Fleischer and Skutella [3] employed the time-expanded network and a proof by contradiction to establish that intermediate storage is not necessary for optimality. However, the landscape differs in the *multicommodity* setting. In certain instances, allowing intermediate storage can indeed strictly improve the optimal solution, although this improvement is shown to be bounded, as discussed in detail in [10].

*Our Contributions and Techniques.* To investigate the necessity of intermediate storage for the OGFP, we first examine whether it admits a temporally repeated optimal solution. However, by constructing a counterexample, we show the GMFP does not admit such a solution, even on a simple *two-terminal series-parallel* network with only three arcs. Since the optimal GMFP is a special case of the OGFP, this implies that the OGFP likewise lacks temporally repeated optimal solutions. Furthermore, via a reduction from the PARTITION problem, we prove finding the maximum temporally repeated flow is NP-hard and inapproximable. Consequently, temporally repeated flows cannot even serve as a viable approximation for generalized maximum flows over time.

These negative results compel us to adopt a direct proof approach. Fleischer and Skutella's proof [3] for the minimum cost flow over time problem relies on the conservation of total flow to derive a structural contradiction—a premise that fails in generalized dynamic networks. Consequently, we must generalize their proof framework. We first transform the OGFP into an equivalent static flow problem, denoted as $\text{OGFP}^T$, on a time-expanded network. In this network, *holdover arcs* model intermediate storage; thus, our goal is to establish the existence of an optimal solution to $\text{OGFP}^T$ that avoids using these arcs. To this end, we construct a function $F$, defined as the sum of the absolute values of the *net flow* (calculated as the difference between inflow and outflow excluding holdover arcs) across all nodes in the time-expanded network. Since $F$ is a convex function and the set of optimal solutions to OGFP$^T$, denoted by $\mathcal{X}^*$, is compact and convex, $F$ necessarily attains its minimum at some point $x^* \in \mathcal{X}^*$. We proceed by contradiction, assuming $F(x^*) > 0$, which implies that strictly positive flow is carried by some holdover arc. It is well-known that a standard static flow decomposes into subflows along paths and cycles; analogous decompositions exist for generalized flows, though the structures involved are significantly more complex. Leveraging generalized flow decomposition, we adjust the flow to construct a new optimal flow $x \in \mathcal{X}^*$ such that $F(x) < F(x^*)$, contradicting the minimality of $x^*$. This leads to the following theorem:

**Theorem 1.** *There exists an optimal solution to the OGFP without intermediate storage.*

Further, we prove that in lossy networks, optimal solutions to the OGFP exhibit an even simpler structure: they not only avoid intermediate storage but also route flow exclusively along simple source-sink paths. This enables us to leverage the time-condensation technique to design FPTAS for the OGFP on lossy networks, yielding solutions that avoid storage.

**Theorem 2.** *In a lossy network $\mathcal{N}$, there exists an optimal solution to the OGFP that uses only simple flow paths and no intermediate storage.*

## 2 Preliminaries

For simplicity of notation, for each arc $a = (i, j) \in A$, we introduce a reverse arc $\overleftarrow{a} = (j, i)$ with capacity $u_{\overleftarrow{a}} := 0$, transit time $\tau_{\overleftarrow{a}} := -\tau_a$, and gain factor $\gamma_{\overleftarrow{a}} := \frac{1}{\gamma_a}$. Let $\overleftarrow{A}$ denote the set of all such reverse arcs.

*Sequence, Path and Cycle.* Let $S = (i_1, a_1, i_2, a_2, \ldots, i_{k-1}, a_{k-1}, i_k)$ be a sequence in $G$ where $a_\ell = (i_\ell, i_{\ell+1}) \in A$ for all $\ell \in \{1, \ldots, k-1\}$ and $i_\ell \in V$ for all $\ell \in \{1, \ldots, k\}$. The *capacity*, *length*, and *gain* of $S$ are defined by $u(S) = \min_{1 \le \ell \le k-1} u_{a_\ell}, \tau(S) = \sum_{\ell=1}^{k-1} \tau_{a_\ell}, \gamma(S) = \prod_{\ell=1}^{k-1} \gamma_{a_\ell}$, respectively. Additionally, for any $a_\ell \in S$ with $1 \le \ell \le k-1$, define $\gamma(a_\ell \mid S) := \prod_{r=1}^{\ell-1} \gamma_{a_r}$, with the conventions $\gamma(a_1 \mid S) = 1$. A *path* $P$ is a sequence that visits no node more than once, i.e., $i_r \neq i_\ell$ for all $1 \le r < \ell \le k$. A *cycle* $C$ is a closed path with $i_1 = i_k$. It is well-known that any sequence $S$ can be decomposed into a collection of paths or cycles in $G$ (possibly empty).

*Generalized Flows.* A generalized flow is a function $x : A \to \mathbb{R}_{\ge 0}$ satisfying the capacity constraints $0 \le x_a \le u_a$ for all $a \in A$, and the flow conservation constraints $\sum_{a \in \delta^-(i)} \gamma_a x_a - \sum_{a \in \delta^+(i)} x_a = 0$ for all $i \in V \setminus \{s, d\}$.

Given a feasible flow $x$ in $G$, the *residual network* is $G_x = (V, A_x = A \cup \overleftarrow{A})$. For every forward arc $a \in A$, the residual capacity is $u_a^x := u_a - x_a \ge 0$, which is the additional flow that can still be sent along $a$. For every reverse arc $\overleftarrow{a}$, set its residual capacity to $u_{\overleftarrow{a}} := \gamma_a x_a \geq 0$, representing the maximum amount of flow that can be pushed back from the head of $a$ to its tail. It is easy to verify that if $y$ is a feasible flow in the residual graph $G_x$, then the sum $x + y$ is again a feasible flow in $G$, with $(x + y)_a := x_a + y_a - \gamma_{\overleftarrow{a}}\, y_{\overleftarrow{a}}$ for any $a \in A$.

We classify cycles in $G$ into three cases: a cycle $C$ is termed *flow-generating* if $\gamma(C) > 1$, *unit-gain* if $\gamma(C) = 1$, and *flow-absorbing* if $\gamma(C) < 1$. Building on the results of Wayne [16] and Gondran and Minoux [7], we obtain the following generalized flow decomposition theorem.

**Lemma 1.** *Let $x$ be a static generalized flow in a directed graph $G = (V, A)$. Then there exists a family of subgraphs $\mathcal{G} = \{G_1, G_2, \ldots, G_k\}$ of $G$ along with flows $x^1, x^2, \ldots, x^k$ in $G$ such that $x_a^\ell = 0$ for all $a \notin A(G_\ell)$ $(\ell = 1, \ldots, k)$, and $x_a = \sum_{\ell=1}^{k} x_a^\ell$ for all $a \in A$. Moreover, there is a choice of $\{G_\ell, x^\ell\}_{\ell=1}^{k}$ with $k \leq |A| = m$, and each $G_\ell$ is one of the following five types: (i) an s-d path, (ii) a unit-gain cycle, (iii) a path from the source to a flow-absorbing cycle, (iv) a flow-generating cycle connected to the sink by a path, or (v) a flow-generating cycle connected to a flow-absorbing cycle by a path.*

*Time-Expanded Network.* Given a generalized dynamic network $\mathcal{N}$, we construct its time-expanded network $\mathcal{N}^T$ as follows. For each $i \in V$ and $\theta \in \mathcal{T} := \{0, 1, \ldots, T-1\}$, create a copy $i_\theta$, then the node set of $\mathcal{N}^T$ is $V^T := \{i_\theta \mid i \in V, \theta \in \mathcal{T}\}$. Define the arc set $A^T := M^T \cup H^T$, where $M^T := \{a_\theta = (i_\theta, j_{\theta+\tau_a}) \mid a = (i,j) \in A, \theta = 0, \ldots, T - \tau_a - 1\}$ is the set of *movement arcs*, and $H^T := \{(i_\theta, i_{\theta+1}) \mid i \in V, \theta = 0, \ldots, T-2\}$ is the set of *holdover arcs*, which are used to model storage. Assign capacities and gains on $\mathcal{N}^T$ by

$$u_{a'} := \begin{cases} u_a, & \text{if } a' = a_\theta \in M^T, \\ \infty, & \text{if } a' \in H^T, \end{cases} \qquad \gamma_{a'} := \begin{cases} \gamma_a, & \text{if } a' = a_\theta \in M^T, \\ 1, & \text{if } a' \in H^T. \end{cases}$$

While all copies of $s$ and $d$ could serve as sources and sinks, for convenience, we treat $s_0$ and $d_{T-1}$ as the unique source and sink of $\mathcal{N}^T$, respectively.

**Lemma 2 (Theorem 1, [9]).** *Given a feasible flow over time $f$ in $\mathcal{N}$, there exists a corresponding feasible static flow $x$ on $\mathcal{N}^T$ such that, by time $T$, the total amount of flow sent by $f$ from the source $s$ (the total amount received at the sink $d$) equals the total amount sent by $x$ from $s_0$ (the total amount received at $d_{T-1}$). Conversely, the same holds.*

This paper proceeds based on the following assumption.

**Assumption 1.** *The network $\mathcal{N}$ contains no zero-length cycles.*

This assumption is without loss of generality: zero-length unit-gain or flow-absorbing cycles neither simulate storage nor increase flow; thus, in our optimization problems, flow particles can avoid traversing such cycles without degrading the solution quality. Moreover, zero-length flow-generating cycles are physically unrealistic, as they create flow without source input.

## 3 The OGFP Without Storage

First, we use a simple example to show that the GMFP does not admit a temporally repeated optimal solution. This indirectly implies that the OGFP does not admit such solutions either.

*Example 1.* Consider a dynamic network $\mathcal{N}$ with three vertices and three arcs: $V = \{s, i, d\}$ and $A = \{a_1, a_2, a_3\}$, where $a_1 = (s, i)$ and $a_2 = a_3 = (i, d)$. Let the time horizon be $T = 2$. Assume all arcs have capacity 1, $\tau_{a_1} = \tau_{a_2} = 0$, $\gamma_{a_1} = \gamma_{a_3} = 1$, $\gamma_{a_2} = 0.5$, and $\tau_{a_3} = 1$. It is easy to see that the maximum flow value $v^*(T) = 1.5$: send flow at rate 1 along $P_1 := (s, a_1, i, a_3, d)$ over time interval $[0, 1)$, and then at rate 1 along $P_2 := (s, a_1, i, a_2, d)$ over time interval $[1, 2)$. For a static flow in $\mathcal{N}$, the possible decompositions fall into three cases: (i) $P_1$ along with flow $x^1$; (ii) $P_2$ along with flow $x^2$; (iii) $P_1, P_2$ along with flows $x^1, x^2$. The value of the temporally repeated flow corresponding to (i) is $(T - \tau(P_1))\, x^1 = x^1 \leq u_{a_1} = 1$, that for (ii) is $(T - \tau(P_2))\, \gamma(P_2)\, x^2 = x^2 \leq u_{a_1} = 1$, and that for (iii) is $(T - \tau(P_1))\, x^1 + (T - \tau(P_2))\, \gamma(P_2)\, x^2 = x^1 + x^2 \leq u_{a_1} = 1$, all strictly less than $v^*(T)$ (Fig. 1).

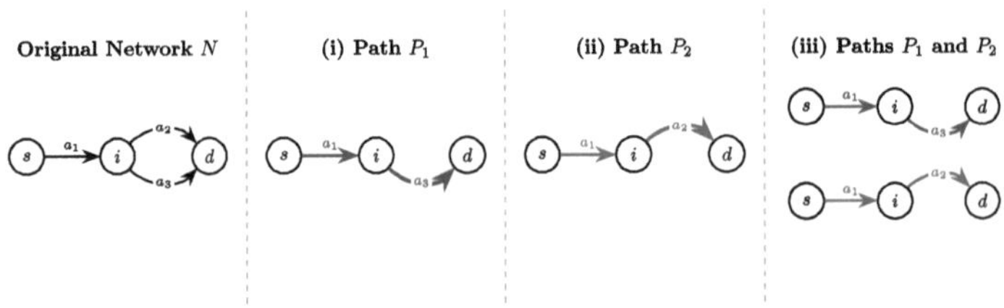


**Fig. 1.** Schematic illustration of the original network $N$ and the three possible decomposition structures of a static flow on $N$.

In fact, even approximating generalized maximum flows over time using temporally repeated flows is infeasible.

**Theorem 3.** *Even on lossy two-terminal series-parallel (TTSP) networks, there is no polynomial-time algorithm or value-approximation algorithm for finding a maximum temporally repeated flow, unless $P = NP$.*

*Proof.* PARTITION. *Input:* Given $n$ elements $e_1, e_2, \ldots, e_n \in \mathbb{N}$ such that $\sum_{\ell=1}^{n} e_\ell = 2K$ for some $K \in \mathbb{N}$.
*Output:* Does there exist a subset $I \subseteq \{1, 2, \ldots, n\}$ with $\sum_{\ell \in I} e_\ell = K$?

Given an instance of PARTITION, we construct a corresponding TTSP dynamic network $N$ with node set $V := \{s = i_1, i_2, \ldots, i_n, d = i_{n+1}\}$, and arc set

$$A := \underbrace{\{a_\ell = (i_\ell, i_{\ell+1}) \mid \ell = 1, \ldots, n\}}_{A_1} \cup \underbrace{\{\hat{a}_\ell = (i_\ell, i_{\ell+1}) \mid \ell = 1, \ldots, n\}}_{A_2}.$$

Let the time horizon be $T := K+1$, and set all arc capacities to 1. Define transit times and gains by

$$\tau_a := \begin{cases} e_\ell, & a = a_\ell \in A_1, \\ 0, & a = \hat{a}_\ell \in A_2, \end{cases} \qquad \gamma_a := \begin{cases} 1, & a = a_\ell \in A_1, \\ 2^{-\alpha e_\ell}, & a = \hat{a}_\ell \in A_2, \end{cases}$$

where $\alpha$ is a positive constant to be chosen. Figure 2 depicts the network $N$ above. We now analyze, for the PARTITION instances with outputs *Yes* and *No*, the amount of flows received at the sink $d$ by a maximum temporally repeated generalized flow in $N$, denoted $v^*$.

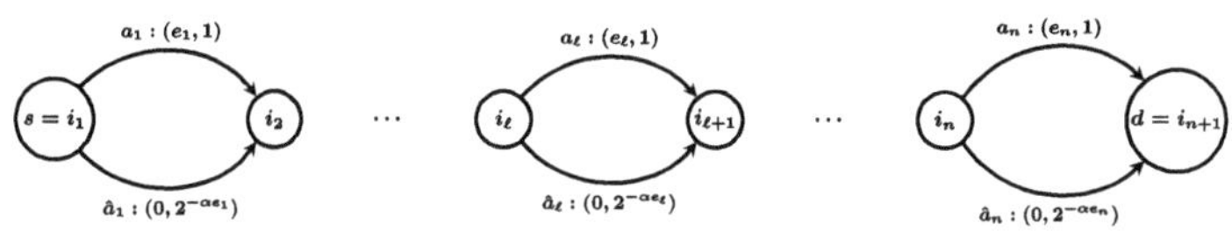


**Fig. 2.** The TTSP dynamic network $\mathcal{N}$ corresponding to a PARTITION instance. Arc labels denote $(\tau, \gamma)$. All capacities are 1.

*Yes-Instance.* There exists a subset $I \subset \{1, 2, \ldots, n\}$ with $\sum_{\ell \in I} e_\ell = K$. For $\ell = 1, \ldots, n$, choose arc $a_\ell$ if $\ell \in I$, and choose arc $\hat{a}_\ell$ otherwise, thereby obtaining an $s$âĂŞ$d$ path $P_1$. Removing $P_1$ from $N$ yields a subgraph that is again an $s$âĂŞ$d$ path, denoted $P_2$. Clearly, $\tau(P_1) = \tau(P_2) = K$ and $\gamma(P_1) = \gamma(P_2) = 2^{-\alpha K}$. Sending flow at rate 1 along both $P_1$ and $P_2$ yields a temporally repeated generalized flow whose amount delivered to $d$ is $\sum_{k=1}^{2} \big(T - \tau(P_k)\big)\, \gamma(P_k) = 2^{\,1-\alpha K} \leq v_Y^*$.

*No-Instance.* We consider an upper bound on the maximum amount of flows received at the sink, $v(T)$; this also upper-bounds $v_N^*$ since $v_N^* \leq v(T)$. At any time $\theta \in [0, T)$, we attempt to send flow at rate 1 along a highest gain path whose length does not exceed $T$. For $\theta \in [0, 1]$, the gain of a highest gain path of length at most $T$ is at most $2^{-\alpha(K+1)}$; for $\theta \in [1, T)$, it is at most $2^{-\alpha(K+\lfloor\theta\rfloor)}$. Therefore,

$$v_N^* \leq \int_0^1 2^{-\alpha(K+1)} d\theta + \sum_{\theta=1}^{K} \int_\theta^{\theta+1} 2^{-\alpha(K+\theta)} d\theta = 2^{-\alpha(K+1)} + 2^{-\alpha K} \frac{1 - 2^{-\alpha K}}{2^\alpha - 1}.$$

In summary, we have

$$\frac{v_Y^*}{v_N^*} \geq \frac{2^{\,1-\alpha K}}{2^{-\alpha(K+1)} + 2^{-\alpha K}\left(\dfrac{1 - 2^{-\alpha K}}{2^\alpha - 1}\right)} = \frac{2\big(2^\alpha - 1\big)}{2 - 2^{-\alpha} - 2^{-\alpha K}} \geq 2^\alpha - 1\,.$$

Since $\alpha$ can be chosen arbitrarily, the theorem follows. □

### 3.1 Proof of Theorem 1

Let $\text{OGFP}^T$ be the counterpart of the OGFP on the time-expanded network $\mathcal{N}^T$. By Lemma 2, an optimal solution to the OGFP can be equivalently transformed into an optimal solution to $\text{OGFP}^T$, and vice versa. Therefore, it suffices to prove that $\text{OGFP}^T$ admits an optimal solution that does not use holdover arcs at intermediate nodes.

*Proof of Theorem* 1. Since $\text{OGFP}^T$ is a linear program, its feasible set $\mathcal{X}$ is a nonempty compact convex polyhedron, and its optimal solution set $\mathcal{X}^*$ is the intersection of $\mathcal{X}$ with a closed convex affine hyperplane, hence $\mathcal{X}^*$ is also a nonempty compact convex set. Given a static flow $x$ on $\mathcal{N}^T$, we examine, at each intermediate node, the "net inflow" through movement arcs: $\widehat{x}(i_\theta) := \sum_{a_\theta \in \delta^-(i_\theta)\cap M^T} \gamma_a x_{a_\theta} - \sum_{a_\theta \in \delta^+(i_\theta)\cap M^T} x_{a_\theta}$, for all $i \in V, \theta \in \mathcal{T}$. Define an auxiliary function $F(x) := \sum_{i\in V\setminus\{s,d\}} \sum_{\theta\in\mathcal{T}} \left|\widehat{x}(i_\theta)\right|$. It is easy to verify that $F(x)$ is convex, therefore $F(x)$ attains a minimum on $\mathcal{X}^*$ at some $x^*$.

We now prove that $F(x^*) = 0$. Assume $F(x^*) > 0$. Let $\theta_1$ be the smallest $\theta \in \mathcal{T}$ such that there exists an intermediate node $l_{\theta_1}$ with $\widehat{x^*}(l_{\theta_1}) > 0$. For the same $l$, let $\theta_2$ be the smallest $\theta \in \mathcal{T}$ with $\widehat{x^*}(l_{\theta_2}) < 0$. This implies that every holdover arc between $l_{\theta_1}$ and $l_{\theta_2}$ has been used. Clearly, $r := \theta_2 - \theta_1 \geq 1$. For any arc $a_\theta = (i_\theta, j_{\theta+\tau_a}) \in M^T$, we call $a_\theta$ an *excess arc* if $x^*_{a_\theta} > x^*_{a_{\theta-r}}$, and a *deficit arc* if $x^*_{a_\theta} < x^*_{a_{\theta-r}}$. To make this definition well defined, assume $x^*_{a_\theta} = 0$ when $\theta < 0$. It follows that there is no deficit arc leaving $i_\theta$ for any $i \in V$ and $\theta \leq r$. In the residual network $\mathcal{N}^T_{x^*}$, for an excess arc $a_\theta$, since $u_a \geq x^*_{a_\theta} > x^*_{a_{\theta-r}} \geq 0$, the reverse arc $\overleftarrow{a_\theta}$ has residual capacity $u^{x^*}_{\overleftarrow{a_\theta}} = \gamma_a x^*_{a_\theta} > 0$, and $a_{\theta-r}$ has residual capacity $u^{x^*}_{a_{\theta-r}} = u_a - x^*_{a_{\theta-r}} > 0$. Similarly, for a deficit arc $a_\theta$, since $0 \leq x^*_{a_\theta} < x^*_{a_{\theta-r}} \leq u_a$, we have $u^{x^*}_{a_\theta} > 0$ and $u^{x^*}_{\overleftarrow{a_{\theta-r}}} > 0$.

Since $\widehat{x^*}(l_{\theta_2}) < 0$ and $\widehat{x^*}(l_{\theta_1}) > 0$, there is at least one deficit arc entering $l_{\theta_2}$ or one excess arc leaving $l_{\theta_2}$. Let $\mathcal{S}$ be the subnetwork induced by all nodes reachable from $l_{\theta_2}$ via a path in the underlying undirected graph that uses only *forward* excess arcs and *backward* deficit arcs. Its arc set is $A(\mathcal{S}) := \left\{ a_\theta = (i_\theta, j_{\theta+\tau_a}) \;\middle|\; i_\theta \in \mathcal{S},\ j_{\theta+\tau_a} \in \mathcal{S} \right\}$. Because there is no deficit arc leaving $i_\theta$ for any $i \in V$ and $\theta < r$, all nodes in $\mathcal{S}$ lie on time layers of $\mathcal{N}^T$ that are at least $r$. Therefore, we can similarly define the subnetwork $\mathcal{S}_{-r}$ with node set $V(\mathcal{S}_{-r}) := \{ i_\theta \mid i_{\theta+r} \in \mathcal{S} \} \subset V^T$.

**Case 1:** The subnetwork $\mathcal{S}$ contains at least one leaf other than $l_{\theta_2}$. Let $k_\theta$ be a leaf of $\mathcal{S}$, i.e., $\left|\delta^+_{\mathcal{S}}(k_\theta) \cup \delta^-_{\mathcal{S}}(k_\theta)\right| = 1$. Without loss of generality, assume there is one excess arc entering $k_\theta$. Clearly, there is neither an excess arc leaving $k_\theta$ nor a deficit arc entering $k_\theta$. Hence, $\widehat{x^*}(k_\theta) - \widehat{x^*}(k_{\theta-r}) > 0$. Let $P$ be a path from $l_{\theta_2}$ to $k_\theta$ that contains only forward excess arcs and backward deficit arcs. In the residual network $\mathcal{N}^T_{x^*}$, for any $a_\theta \in P$, if $a_\theta$ is an excess arc, take the reverse arc $\overleftarrow{a_\theta}$ together with $a_{\theta-r}$; if $a_\theta$ is a deficit arc, take $a_\theta$ together with the reverse arc $\overleftarrow{a_{\theta-r}}$. This yields a directed path $P_1$ from $k_\theta$ to $l_{\theta_2}$ with positive residual capacity, and a directed path $P_2$ from $l_{\theta_1}$ to $k_{\theta-r}$ with positive residual capacity. Consequently, we obtain a directed cycle with positive residual capacity $C := \{k_\theta, P_1, l_{\theta_2}, l_{\theta_1}, P_2, k_{\theta-r}, k_\theta\}$ in $\mathcal{N}^T_{x^*}$, where $l_{\theta_2}$ and $l_{\theta_1}$ are connected by reverse holdover arcs, and $k_{\theta-r}$ and $k_\theta$ are connected by holdover arcs. Since $\gamma(P_1)\gamma(P_2) = 1$, the cycle $C$ is a unit-gain cycle, i.e., $\gamma(C) = 1$. Figure 3 clearly illustrates the construction of cycle $C$. Hence we can place a nonzero circulation $x$ on $C$. Let $\alpha$ be the amount of flow that $x$ sends out of $k_\theta$; then the amount entering $l_{\theta_2}$ and the amount leaving $l_{\theta_1}$ are both $\gamma(P_1)\alpha$, and the amount entering $k_{\theta-r}$ is $\gamma(P_1)\gamma(P_2)\alpha = \alpha$. We restrict $0 < \alpha \leq \min\Big\{-\frac{\widehat{x^*}(l_{\theta_2})}{\gamma(P_1)}, \frac{\widehat{x^*}(l_{\theta_1})}{\gamma(P_1)}, \widehat{x^*}(k_\theta) - \widehat{x^*}(k_{\theta-r})\Big\}$. Clearly, $x^* + x$ is a feasible flow on $\mathcal{N}^T$ and remains an optimal solution to OGFP$^T$. We have

$$\begin{aligned}
F(x^*+x) - F(x) = &\left|\widehat{x^*+x}(l_{\theta_2})\right| + \left|\widehat{x^*+x}(l_{\theta_1})\right| + \left|\widehat{x^*+x}(k_\theta)\right| + \left|\widehat{x^*+x}(k_{\theta-r})\right| \\
&- \left(\left|\widehat{x^*}(l_{\theta_2})\right| + \left|\widehat{x^*}(l_{\theta_1})\right| + \left|\widehat{x^*}(k_\theta)\right| + \left|\widehat{x^*}(k_{\theta-r})\right|\right) \\
= &-2\,\gamma(P_1)\alpha + \left|\widehat{x^*}(k_\theta) - \alpha\right| + \left|\widehat{x^*}(k_{\theta-r}) + \alpha\right| \\
&- \left(\,\left|\widehat{x^*}(k_\theta)\right| + \left|\widehat{x^*}(k_{\theta-r})\right|\,\right) \\
\leq &-2\,\gamma(P_1)\alpha \;<\; 0.
\end{aligned}$$

The penultimate inequality follows from the fact that for any $\alpha, \beta, \mu \in \mathbb{R}$ with $\beta - \mu \geq \alpha > 0$, we have $|\beta| + |\mu| \geq |\beta - \alpha| + |\mu + \alpha|$; therefore, $x^*$ is an optimal solution to OGFP$^T$ that does not use holdover arcs.

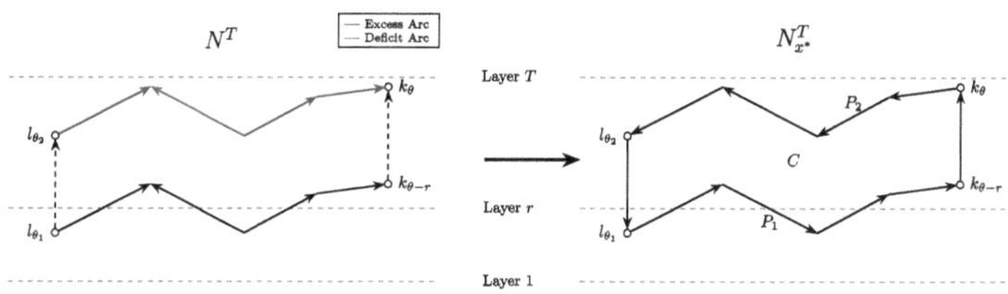


**Fig. 3.** Schematic illustration of the construction of cycle $C$ in Case 1.

**Case 2:** The subnetwork $\mathcal{S}$ contains no leaf nodes other than $l_{\theta_2}$. Starting from $l_{\theta_2}$, we perform a depth-first search in $\mathcal{S}$ to find a path along forward excess arcs or backward deficit arcs. Since $\mathcal{S}$ is finite and contains at most one leaf, $l_{\theta_2}$, only the following two cases can arise.

**Case 2.1:** The search terminates at a node $k_\theta$. Without loss of generality, assume the arc adjacent to $k_\theta$ on the path is an excess arc. This implies there is neither an outgoing excess arc from $k_\theta$ nor an incoming deficit arc to $k_\theta$. Since $k_\theta$ is not a leaf in $\mathcal{S}$, there must exist at least one outgoing deficit arc or incoming excess arc at $k_\theta$. Thus, we have $\widehat{x^*}(k_\theta) - \widehat{x^*}(k_{\theta-r}) > 0$, which reduces to Case 1.

**Case 2.2:** The search encounters a previously visited node. At this point, the path contains a cycle $C$ in the underlying undirected graph. By Assumption 1,

$C$ contains at least one excess arc and at least one deficit arc. Since every excess arc is nonempty (its flow is nonzero), there exists in $\mathcal{N}^T$ a directed nonempty flow path $P_1$ from the source that reaches $C$. For any arc $a_\theta \in C$, take $a_{\theta-r}$ in $\mathcal{N}^T$; this yields an undirected cycle $C'$ in $\mathcal{S}_{-r}$. Because $C$ contains a deficit arc, $C'$ contains at least one nonempty arc, which implies that there is likewise in $\mathcal{N}^T$ a directed nonempty flow path $P_2$ from the source that reaches $C'$. In the residual network $\mathcal{N}^T_{x^*}$, for each $a_\theta \in C$: if $a_\theta$ is an excess arc, take the reverse arc $\overleftarrow{a_\theta}$ together with $a_{\theta-r}$; if $a_\theta$ is a deficit arc, take $a_\theta$ together with the reverse arc $\overleftarrow{a_{\theta-r}}$. In this way we obtain two directed cycles with positive residual capacity, $C_1$ and $C_2$, and it is easy to verify that $C_2$ is equivalent to $C'$ in the undirected sense. Figure 4 illustrates these structures. We now distinguish three cases according to $\gamma(C_1)$.

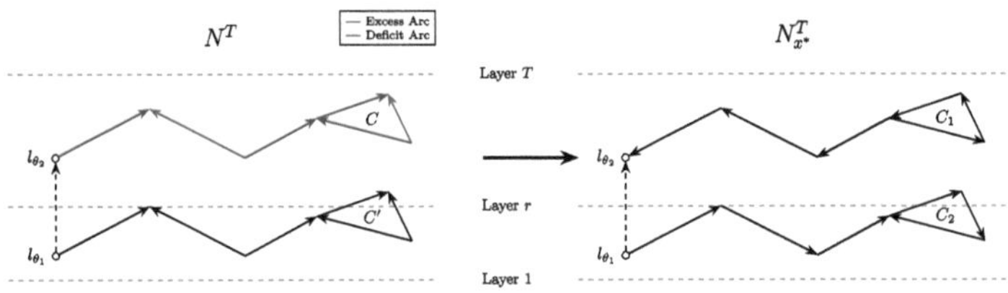


**Fig. 4.** Schematic illustration of the partial structure of $x^*$ in Case 2.2.

(i) $\gamma(C_1) > 1$. Since the reverse path $\overleftarrow{P_1}$ is a directed path in $\mathcal{N}^T_{x^*}$ with positive residual capacity and intersects $C_1$, their union forms a flow-generating cycle connected to the source via a path. We can send a feasible nonzero flow $x$ in this subgraph such that $x^* + x$ remains feasible for OGFP$^T$ but strictly improves the objective, a contradiction.
(ii) $\gamma(C_1) < 1$. Since $\gamma(C_1)\gamma(C_2) = 1$, we have $\gamma(C_2) > 1$. The same argument as in (i) yields a contradiction.
(iii) $\gamma(C_1) = 1$. For any reverse arc $\overleftarrow{a_\theta} \in C_1$, because $a_\theta$ is an excess arc, assign a capacity not exceeding its residual value, $u_{\overleftarrow{a_\theta}} := \gamma_{a_\theta}\left(x^*_{a_\theta} - x^*_{a_{\theta-r}}\right) > 0$. For any deficit arc $a_\theta \in C_1$, assign $u_{a_\theta} := x^*_{a_{\theta-r}} - x^*_{a_\theta} > 0$. Then we can send a feasible nonzero flow $x$ around $C_1$ such that at least one arc on $C_1$ becomes saturated and $x^* + x \in \mathcal{X}^*$. Consequently, in the flow $x^* + x$, at least one excess arc $a_\theta \in C$ has its sent flow reduced by $\gamma_{\overleftarrow{a_\theta}}\gamma_{a_\theta}\left(x^*_{a_\theta} - x^*_{a_{\theta-r}}\right) = x^*_{a_\theta} - x^*_{a_{\theta-r}}$, or at least one deficit arc $a_\theta \in C$ has its sent flow increased by $x^*_{a_{\theta-r}} - x^*_{a_\theta}$. Hence at least one arc of $C$ is removed from $\mathcal{S}$. We call this a *cycle-canceling* operation. Since $\mathcal{S}$ has finitely many arcs, after finitely many cycle-canceling operations the situation reduces to **Case 1**. Combining **Case 1** and **Case 2** completes the proof. □

### 3.2 Proof of Theorem 2

Intuitively, in lossy networks, routing along flow-absorbing cycles incurs flow loss and should be avoided. For networks containing unit-gain cycles, we can slightly perturb all arc gains downwards so that such cycles degenerate into flow-absorbing ones, with an arbitrarily small penalty to the optimal solution.

*Proof of Theorem* 2 Under Assumption 1, it is easy to verify that the time-expanded network $\mathcal{N}^T$ is a directed acyclic graph. Let $\mathcal{P}$ be the set of all source-sink paths in $\mathcal{N}^T$ that do not use holdover arcs at immediate nodes. We can write $\text{OGFP}^T$ in the following formulation based on path decomposition:

$$
\begin{aligned}
(\text{OGFP}^T) \quad \bar{b} = \min\ & \sum_{P\in\mathcal{P}} x_P \\
\text{s.t.}\ & \sum_{P\in\mathcal{P}} \gamma(P)\, x_P \;=\; b \\
& \sum_{P\in\mathcal{P}:\, a_\theta\in P} \gamma(a_\theta \mid P)\, x_P \;\le\; u_a, \quad \forall\, a_\theta \in M^T, \\
& x_P \;\ge\; 0, \quad \forall\, P \in \mathcal{P}.
\end{aligned}
$$

Define $\mathcal{P}_1 := \{\, P \in \mathcal{P} \mid \text{the projection of } P \text{ onto } \mathcal{N} \text{ is an } s\text{-}d \text{ path} \,\}$. Since every $P \in \mathcal{P}$ projects to an $s$-$d$ sequence in the original network $\mathcal{N}$, it suffices to show that restricting $\mathcal{P}$ to $\mathcal{P}_1$ leaves the optimal value of $\text{OGFP}^T$ unchanged.

**Case 1:** $\mathcal{N}$ contains only flow-absorbing cycles. For any optimal solution $\{x_P^*\}_{P\in\mathcal{P}}$ of $\text{OGFP}^T$, we prove by contradiction that $\{\, P \in \mathcal{P} \mid x_P^* > 0 \,\} \subset \mathcal{P}_1$. Suppose there exists $P \in \mathcal{P}$ with $x_P^* > 0$ such that there is a subpath $\Gamma$ of $P$ whose projection onto $\mathcal{N}$ is a flow-absorbing cycle. Write the concatenation $P := P_1 \cdot \Gamma \cdot P_2$. If we send $\gamma(\Gamma)\,\langle x_P^*\rangle$ units of flow along $P$ and, upon entering $\Gamma$, do not traverse it but instead wait along holdover arcs for $\tau(\Gamma)$ units of time before proceeding along $P_2$ to the sink, then the amount received at the sink remains $\gamma(P_1)\gamma(\Gamma)\gamma(P_2)\,\langle x_P^*\rangle \;=\; \gamma(P)\,\langle x_P^*\rangle$. Since $\gamma(\Gamma) < 1$, this modification does not violate arc capacity constraints. By Theorem 1, the existence of this improved flow guarantees the existence of a storage-free flow in $\mathcal{P}$ with an equal or smaller objective value. This contradicts the optimality of $\{x_P^*\}_{P\in\mathcal{P}}$.

**Case 2:** $\mathcal{N}$ contains unit-gain cycles. Fix a sufficiently small $\epsilon > 0$ and scale all arc gains by $\gamma'_a := \left(1 - \frac{\epsilon}{n(T-1)}\right)\gamma_a$ for all $a \in A$. In the scaled network there are no unit-gain cycles, so we reduce to **Case 1**; denote the corresponding problem by $\text{OGFP}_\epsilon^T$. Let $\{x_P^1\}_{P\in\mathcal{P}}$ be an optimal solution to $\text{OGFP}^T(b)$. Then

$$
\begin{aligned}
b > r_1 := \sum_{P\in\mathcal{P}} \gamma'(P)\, x_P^1 &= \sum_{P\in\mathcal{P}} \left(1 - \frac{\epsilon}{n(T-1)}\right)^{|P|} \gamma(P)\, x_P^1 \\
&\ge \left(1 - \frac{\epsilon}{n(T-1)}\right)^{n(T-1)} \sum_{P\in\mathcal{P}} \gamma(P)\, x_P^1 \ge (1-\epsilon) b,
\end{aligned}
$$

where $|P|$ denotes the number of arcs on $P$. Moreover, for any $a_\theta \in M^T$, we have $\sum_{P\in\mathcal{P}:\, a_\theta\in P} \gamma'(a_\theta \mid P)\, x_P^1 \le \sum_{P\in\mathcal{P}:\, a_\theta\in P} \gamma(a_\theta \mid P)\, x_P^1 \le u_a$. Hence $\{x_P^1\}_{P\in\mathcal{P}}$ is feasible for $\text{OGFP}_\epsilon^T(r_1)$. By **Case 1**, there exists an optimal solution for $\text{OGFP}_\epsilon^T(r_1)$ restricted to $\mathcal{P}_1$, denoted by $\{x_P^2\}_{P\in\mathcal{P}_1}$, with $\sum_{P\in\mathcal{P}_1} x_P^2 \le$

$\sum_{P\in\mathcal{P}} x_P^1 = \bar{b}$. Moreover, for any $a_\theta \in M^T$, we have $\sum_{P\in\mathcal{P}:\, a_\theta\in P} \gamma'(a_\theta \mid P)\, x_P^1 \leq \sum_{P\in\mathcal{P}:\, a_\theta\in P} \gamma(a_\theta \mid P)\, x_P^1 \leq u_a$. We also have

$$b > r_2 := \sum_{P\in\mathcal{P}_1} \gamma(P)\,(1-\epsilon)\,x_P^2 \geq \sum_{P\in\mathcal{P}_1} \gamma'(P)\,(1-\epsilon)\,x_P^2 = (1-\epsilon)r_1 \geq (1-\epsilon)^2 b.$$

Thus, $\{(1-\epsilon)x_P^2\}_{P\in\mathcal{P}_1}$ is feasible for $\text{OGFP}^T(r_2)$ with $\sum_{P\in\mathcal{P}_1}(1-\epsilon)\,x_P^2 \leq (1-\epsilon)\bar{b}$. Consequently, given a sequence $\epsilon_k \to 0$ as $k \to \infty$, for each $\epsilon_k$ we obtain a positive number $r^{(k)}$ and a feasible solution $\{x_P^{(k)}\}_{P\in\mathcal{P}_1}$ for $\text{OGFP}^T(r^{(k)})$ satisfying $(1-\epsilon_k)^2 b \leq r^{(k)} < b$ and $\sum_{P\in\mathcal{P}_1} x_P^{(k)} \leq (1-\epsilon_k)\bar{b} < \bar{b}$. Since $\{x_P^{(k)}\}_{P\in\mathcal{P}_1}$ lies in a compact convex polyhedron for all $k \geq 1$, any limit point $\{x_P^*\}_{P\in\mathcal{P}_1}$ is optimal for $\text{OGFP}^T(b)$. Combining **Case 1** and **Case 2** completes the proof. □

By restricting the flow to simple paths as guaranteed by Theorem 2, the cumulative error introduced by rounding transit times is polynomially bounded by the node count $n$. Consequently, applying the time-condensation technique [3] immediately yields an FPTAS for the OGFP on lossy networks without requiring intermediate storage.

## 4 Conclusion

In this paper, we resolved a fundamental structural question regarding generalized flows over time by proving that intermediate storage is not required for optimality. By employing limit arguments, we showed that optimal flows in lossy networks can be strictly decomposed into simple paths. This structural property seamlessly unlocks the design of a storage-free FPTAS. Furthermore, the proposed notion of optimal flows and the storage-free results naturally extend to *quickest flows*, a classic variant of flows over time. An interesting direction for future work is to investigate whether similar storage-free or simple-path properties hold for more complex generalized minimum cost flows over time.

**Acknowledgments.** The authors sincerely thank the editor and anonymous reviewers for their constructive comments that substantially improved the quality of this paper. This work was supported in part by the National Natural Science Foundation of China (Grant Nos. T2341006, 12571382, 12501450, and 2501445) and the National Key R&D Program of China (Grant No. 2022YFA1003900).

## References

1. Ahuja, R.K., Magnanti, T.L., Orlin, J.B.: Network Flows: Theory, Algorithms and Applications. Prentice Hall, Englewood Cliffs, NJ (1995)
2. Aronson, E.J.: A survey of dynamic network flows. Ann. Oper. Res. **20**, 1–66 (1989)
3. Fleischer, L., Skutella, M.: Quickest flows over time. SIAM J. Comput. **36**, 1600–1630 (2007)

4. Fleischer, L., Tardos, E.: Efficient continuous-time dynamic network flow algorithms. Oper. Res. Lett. **23**, 71–80 (1998)
5. Ford, L.R., Fulkerson, D.R.: Constructing maximal dynamic flows from static flows. Oper. Res. **6**(3), 419–433 (1958)
6. Ford, L.R., Fulkerson, D.R.: Flows in Networks. Princeton University Press, Princeton, NJ (1962)
7. Gondran, M., Minoux, M.: Graphs and Algorithms. Wiley, New York (1984)
8. Groß, M.: Approximation algorithms for complex network flow over time problems. PhD thesis, Technical University of Berlin (2014)
9. Groß, M., Skutella, M.: Generalized maximum flows over time. In: Solis-Oba, R., Persiano, G. (eds.) WAOA 2011. LNCS, vol. 7164, pp. 247–260. Springer, Heidelberg (2012). https://doi.org/10.1007/978-3-642-29116-6_21
10. Groß, M., Skutella, M.: A tight bound on the speed-up through storage for quickest multi-commodity flows. Oper. Res. Lett. **43**(1), 93–95 (2015)
11. Kantorovich, L.V.: Mathematical methods of organizing and planning production. Transl. Manag. Sci. **6**, 366–422 (1960). Publication House of the Leningrad State University (1939)
12. Lin, Y.: Algorithms for the Generalized Network Flow Problem. PhD thesis, Columbia University (2001)
13. Olver, N., Végh, L.A.: A simpler and faster strongly polynomial algorithm for generalized flow maximization. J. ACM (JACM) **67**(2), 1–26 (2020)
14. Skutella, M.: An introduction to network flows over time. In: Cook, W., Lovász, L., Vygen, J. (eds.) Research Trends in Combinatorial Optimization, pp. 451–482. Springer, Heidelberg (2009). https://doi.org/10.1007/978-3-540-76796-1_21
15. Végh, L.A.: A strongly polynomial algorithm for generalized flow maximization. In: Proceedings of the Forty-Sixth Annual ACM Symposium on Theory of Computing, pp. 644–653 (2014)
16. Wayne, K.D.: Generalized Maximum Flow Algorithms. PhD thesis, Cornell University (1999)
17. Williamson, D.P.: Network Flow Algorithms. Cambridge University Press, Cambridge, UK (2019)

# An Improved Kernelization Algorithm for Vertex Splitting to Pathwidth-One

Yunlong Liu(✉), Bingyang Wang, and Jingui Huang(✉)

College of Information Science and Engineering, Hunan Provincial Key Laboratory of Intelligent Computing and Language Information Processing, Hunan Normal University, Changsha 410081, People's Republic of China
{ylliu,bywang,hjg}@hunnu.edu.cn

**Abstract.** In this work, we study the Kernelization algorithm for an **NP**-complete problem PATHWIDTH-ONE VERTEX SPLITTING (POVS), which asks whether a graph $G = (V, E)$ with a given vertex subset $S \subseteq V$ can be turned into a graph of pathwidth at most 1 (i.e., a graph admitting a planar 2-layer drawing) using at most $k$ splits on vertices in $S$. We show that the POVS problem admits a kernel of at most $10k$ vertices, which improves the kernel of at most $16k$ vertices (TCS2024). Meanwhile, this kernelization still retains the linear running time.

**Keywords:** Planar 2-layer drawing · Vertex splitting · Kernelization · Reduction rules

## 1 Introduction

The planar 2-layer graph drawing problem has become a trending topic of research in computer science [5,7–9,12]. In a 2-layer drawing of a graph, the vertices are drawn as points on two distinct parallel lines, and edges are drawn as straight-line segments. Moreover, in a planar 2-layer drawing, there are no edge-crossings, i.e., edges intersect only at their common end vertices. Graphs that admit planar 2-layer drawings can be displayed in a more visible, clearer, and more understandable way such that they have a wide range of applications in visual network analysis. A graph has pathwidth at most 1 if and only if it admits a planar 2-layer drawing. So, the problems of constructing graphs admitting 2-layer planar drawings (or constructing graphs having pathwidth at most 1) with the minimum number of modifications have aroused more and more attention in recent years [1–4,6,10].

For a graph that does not admit any planar 2-layer drawing, there are several popular modification approaches to removing edge crossings such as vertex deletion [14], edge deletion [4,6], and vertex explosion [10]. Recently, vertex splitting

This research was supported in part by Hunan Provincial Natural Science Foundation of China (Grant No. 2025JJ50346) and the Key Project of Education Department of Hunan Province (Grant No. 24A0093).


Y. Li et al. (Eds.): COCOON 2026, LNCS 16835, pp. 206–218, 2027.
https://doi.org/10.1007/978-981-92-3309-0_16

has also drawn increasing attention [1,2,13]. Given a vertex $v$ in a graph $G$, a *split* operation on $v$ includes deleting $v$ from $G$, adding two new copies $v_1$ and $v_2$, and distributing the edges originally incident to $v$ between the two new vertices $v_1$ and $v_2$ [13]. Take Fig. 1 as an example, where a graph $G$ admits a planar 2-layer drawing after applying one split to vertex $v_3$ and two splits to vertex $v_9$.

**Fig. 1.** Applying three vertex-splits to a graph (left) such that the resulting graph admits a planar 2-layer drawing (right). Here, two splits are applied to vertex $v_9$.

In this work, we study the problem Pathwidth-One Vertex Splitting (abbreviated as POVS), which was initially posed by Baumann, Pfretzschner, and Rutter in [3] and originated from the problem Crossing Removal with $k$ Splits in [1]. The POVS problem is known to be **NP**-complete [2], which motivates the study of it in the context of parameterized algorithms. When parameterized by the number of splits, the parameterized version of this problem can be described as follows [3].

Pathwidth-One Vertex Splitting
**Input**: An undirected graph $G = (V, E)$, a subset $S \subseteq V$, and a positive integer $k$.
**Parameter**: $k$.
**Question**: Is there a sequence of at most $k$ splits on vertices in $S$ such that the resulting graph has pathwidth at most 1?

Parameterized algorithms for the POVS problem have aroused increasing interest in recent years. Baumann et al. [3] presented a branching algorithm with running time in $\mathcal{O}((6k + 12)^k \cdot m)$, where $m$ is the number of edges of $G$. More recently, it was shown that the POVS problem admits an algorithm with running time in $\mathcal{O}((3k + 11)^k \cdot m)$ [11]. Moreover, Baumann et al. [3] also presented a kernel with at most $16k$ vertices that can be computed in time $\mathcal{O}(m)$.

Let $(G', S', k')$ be the instance obtained from $(G, S, k)$ reduced by the kernelization algorithm in [3]. The graph $G'$ may still contain many vertices of degree 1. More precisely, the number of the vertices of degree 1 is upper bounded by $8k$ (that is, $|V(G')|/2$). Thus, there may be room for obtaining a smaller kernel by reducing such vertices. For a vertex $v$ of $G$, denote by *degree*$^*(v)$ the degree of $v$ ignoring its neighbors with degree 1. Let $x, y$ and $z$ be three degree$^*$-2 vertices. If $y$ is adjacent to both $x$ and $z$ but $x$ is not adjacent to $z$, vertex $y$ is called a *2-enclosed* vertex. The main task of the kernelization in [3] is to reduce the 2-enclosed vertices. When eliminating all 2-enclosed vertices, that kernelization algorithm needs to decide whether a 2-enclosed vertex in $S$ is part of an optimal solution or not. The decision-making procedure includes several steps, such as removing some vertex, contracting some connected component into a single vertex, and computing a spanning tree (see Fig. 5 in [3] for details). In fact, if $(G, S, k)$ is a yes-instance, then any vertex $u \in V(G) \setminus S$ is adjacent to at most two degree*-2 vertices in $V(G) \setminus S$. Based on this fact, these 2-enclosed vertices in $S$ can be eliminated by another simpler approach.

Motivated by these observations, we further focus on the POVS problem and study an improved kernelization algorithm for it. Our work consists of two parts as follows.

1. We obtain a kernel of at most $10k$ vertices by introducing a series of new reduction rules. As mentioned above, an obstacle for obtaining a smaller kernel lies in the vertices of degree 1. Thus, we pay great attention to tackling this obstacle. Based on some new observations, we develop several new reduction rules, by which most of the vertices of degree 1 can be safely eliminated. Moreover, we also introduce two new rules to eliminate the 2-enclosed vertices in $S$. These rules not only simplify the reduction, but also are helpful in analyzing the running time.
2. We adopt a new strategy to schedule the order of the reduction rules such that the kernelization can still be done in $\mathcal{O}(m)$ time, where $m$ is the number of edges of the input graph. As several refined rules are introduced, a chain reaction may occur, namely, applying one reduction rule might make another rule applicable again and vice versa. To control the order of actions that are executed, we use a suitable data structure (i.e., a dynamic list) to store the vertices that satisfy the conditions of some reduction rules.

## 2 Preliminaries

We consider only undirected simple graphs. Given a graph $G = (V, E)$, we let $n = |V|$ and $m = |E|$. Since all isolated vertices of $G$ can be removed, we assume, without loss of generality, that $n \in \mathcal{O}(m)$. For a vertex $v$ in graph $G = (V, E)$, we use $N(v)$ to denote the set of neighbors of $v$, $N^2(v)$ to denote the set of vertices, excluding $\{v\} \cup N(v)$, that are adjacent to a vertex in $N(v)$, and $deg(v)$ to denote the degree of $v$. Moreover, we let $N[v] = N(v) \cup \{v\}$. For a set $S \subseteq V$, let $\overline{S} = V \setminus S$ denote the complementary set of $S$. We also use some notations defined in [3]. The vertices of degree 1 are called *pendant vertices*. If $v$ is a pendant vertex adjacent to $u$, where $\deg(u) \geq 2$, we also refer to the edge $vu$ a *pendant edge* incident to $u$. For a vertex $v \in V(G)$, we let $\deg^*(v) = |\{u \mid u \in N(v)$ and $\deg(u) > 1\}|$ denote the degree of $v$ ignoring its neighbors of degree 1. If $\deg^*(v) = d$, we refer to $v$ as a vertex of *degree* d*. Moreover, we denote by $N^*(v)$ (resp. $N^{2*}(v)$) the set of non-pendant vertices in $N(v)$ (resp. $N^2(v)$). The *potential* of $v$ is defined by $\mu(v) = \max\{\deg^*(v) - 2, 0\}$; the *global potential* of $G$ is defined by $\mu(G) = \sum_{v \in V(G)} \mu(v)$ [3]. In particular, if $(G, S, k)$ is a yes-instance of the

POVS problem, then $\mu(G) \leq 2k$ [3]. Additionally, we denote by $V_3$ the set of all vertices with degree* at least 3. For a vertex $v \in V_3$, let $E_v$ denote the set of non-pendant edges incident to $v$ and let $E_3 = \bigcup_{v \in V_3} E_v$.

A path $P$ connecting two endpoints $u$ and $v$ is denoted by $P_{uv}$. The length of a path $P$ is the number of edges contained in $P$, and is denoted by $|P|$. A path of $G$ is called *isolated* if it contains two vertices of degree 1 as endpoints, and every internal vertex has degree 2. A cycle of $G$ is called *isolated* if it can be seen as resulting from an isolated path $P_{uv}$ by adding edge $vu$. In particular, a path $P$ with length 2 is called a *pendant 2-path* if $P$ contains a vertex of degree* at least 3 and a vertex of degree 1 as endpoints, and a vertex of degree 2 as middle point. Specifically, the endpoint with degree* at least 3 is called the *root* of $P$. See Fig. 2 (left) for an example, where the path induced by vertices $b, t$ and $r$ is a pendant 2-path rooted at $r$.

**Fig. 2.** An $N_2$ substructure rooted at $r$ (left) is eliminated by an operation that splits off the edge $rx$ at $r$ (right).

Baumann et al. [3] characterized that a graph $G$ has pathwidth at most 1 if and only if $G$ is acyclic and contains no $N_2$ substructure. An $N_2$ substructure consists of a root vertex $r$ adjacent to three distinct vertices of degree at least 2. See Fig. 2 (left) for an example.

Let $r$ be a vertex incident to at least three edges, one of them being denoted by $rx$. The operation that we call *splitting off* $rx$ *at* $r$ includes deleting $r$ from $G$ while simultaneously adding two new vertices $r_1$ and $r_2$, and adding some edges such that $r_1$ is adjacent to $x$ and $r_2$ is adjacent to each vertex in $N_G(r) \setminus \{x\}$. See Fig. 2 for an example.

We also say that a sequence $\phi$ of vertex-splits on $S$ is a *pathwidth-one split sequence* (POS-sequence) of $G$ if the graph resulting from applying $\phi$ to $G$ has pathwidth at most 1.

Because of the space limit, most of the proofs are deferred to a full version.

## 3 Reduction Rules

In this section, we present a series of reduction rules one by one. Let $(G = (V, E), S, k)$ be an instance of the POVS problem. Seen from a high level, we take the subgraph induced by $E_3$ as the *core* of the kernel. For this target, we pay great attention to reducing the vertices of degree 1.

We start with giving a rule to reduce some pendant vertex.

**Reduction Rule 1.** Assume that $v$ is a vertex with $deg(v) = 1$ and $deg(w) \geq 3$, where $w$ is the unique neighbor of $v$.

1.1 If $w \notin S$, then remove $v$ from $G$.

1.2 If $w \in S$ and at least one vertex in $N(w) \setminus \{v\}$ has degree* at most 2, then remove $v$ from $G$.

See Fig. 3 for illustrations.

**Fig. 3.** Examples illustrating Reduction Rule 1. The vertices of $S$ are marked in black. Herein, the vertices $v_1$ and $v_2$ are removed by Rule 1.1; the vertices $v_3$ and $v_4$ are removed by Rule 1.2.

**Lemma 1.** *Reduction Rule 1 is safe.*

Let $(G = (V, E), S, k)$ be an instance reduced by Reduction Rule 1 exhaustively. Assume that $vw \in E$ is a pendant edge of $G$, where $\deg(v) = 1$ and $\deg(w) \geq 3$. Then, $w \in S$ and each vertex in $N(w) \setminus \{v\}$ has degree* at least 3. Moreover, by Rule 1, Reduction Rules 2 and 3 in [3] can be simplified as follows.

**Reduction Rule 2.** (// reducing isolated path and isolated cycle)

2.1 If $G$ contains an isolated path $P$, then remove $P$ from $G$ and reduce the instance to $(G - P, S \setminus V(P), k)$.

2.2 Let $G$ contain an isolated cycle $C$. If $V(C) \cap S \neq \emptyset$, then remove $C$ from $G$ and reduce the instance to $(G - C, S \setminus V(C), k - 1)$. Otherwise, reduce to a trivial no-instance.

We employ two rules in [3] to reduce some degree*-2 vertex.

**Reduction Rule 3.** ([3]) (// reducing some 2-enclosed vertex)

Let $v$ denote a 2-enclosed vertex of $G$ with degree*-2 neighbors $x$ and $y$.

3.1 If $\{x, v\} \subseteq S$, then remove $v$ from $G$, add a new edge $xy$, and reduce the instance to $(G - v + xy, S \setminus \{v\}, k)$.

3.2 If $v \notin S$, then remove $v$ from $G$, add a new edge $xy$, and reduce the instance to $(G - v + xy, S, k)$.

**Reduction Rule 4.** ([3]) (// reducing some special degree*-2 vertex)

Let $v$ be a degree*-2 vertex of $G$ with non-pendant neighbors $x$ and $y$, such that $x$ has degree* 1. Remove $v$ from $G$ and add a new edge $xy$. If $v \in S$, reduce to $(G - v + xy, (S \setminus \{v\}) \cup \{x\}, k)$. Otherwise reduce the instance to $(G - v + xy, S \setminus \{x\}, k)$.

To eliminate all 2-enclosed vertices, we shall adopt a new approach, which is simpler than that in [3]. We start with the following auxiliary rule.

**Reduction Rule 5.** Let $u \in \overline{S}$ be a vertex with degree* at least 3. If $|N^*(u) \cap \overline{S}| \geq 3$, then reduce to a trivial no-instance. If $|N^*(u) \cap \overline{S}| = 2$, let $G'$ be the graph obtained from $G$ and $S'$ be the set obtained from $S$ by splitting off each edge $uw$ at $w$, where $w \in N^*(u) \cap S$, reduce the instance to $(G', S', k - |N^*(u) \cap S|)$.

Let $(G, S, k)$ be an instance reduced by Rule 5 exhaustively and let $u$ be an arbitrary vertex of $G$ with degree* at least 3. If $u \in \overline{S}$, then $|N^*(u) \cap \overline{S}| \leq 1$. Based on this observation, we introduce a rule to eliminate the 2-enclosed vertex in $N^{2*}(u) \cap S$ immediately.

**Reduction Rule 6.** Let $(G, S, k)$ be an instance reduced by Rules 1, 2, 3 and 5 exhaustively. If $v \in S$ is a 2-enclosed vertex of $G$ with degree*-2 neighbors $x$ and $y$, then remove $v$ from $G$, add a new edge $xy$, and reduce the instance to $(G - v + xy, S \setminus \{v\}, k)$.

See Fig. 4 for examples.

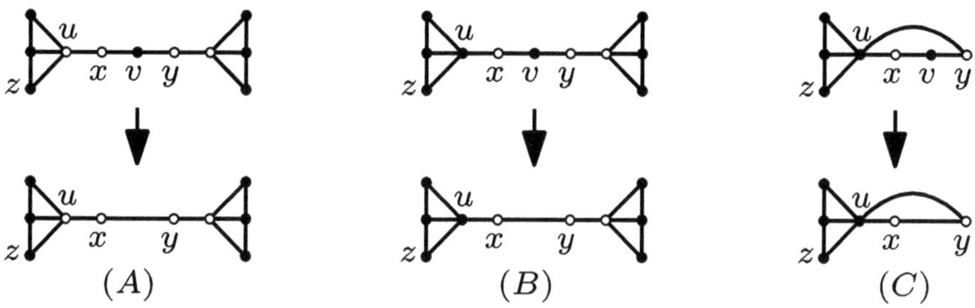


**Fig. 4.** Three examples illustrating Reduction Rule 6.

**Lemma 2.** *Reduction Rule 6 is safe.*

As each pendant 2-path contains a degree-1 vertex, our next task is to reduce it such that $G$ contains as few pendant 2-paths as possible.

We first introduce a rule to reduce some pendant 2-path rooted at the vertices in $\overline{S}$.

**Reduction Rule 7.** Let $(G, S, k)$ be an instance reduced by Rule 5 exhaustively. If a vertex $v \in \overline{S}$ is incident to at least 3 pendant 2-paths, one of them being induced by $\{v, x_3, y_3\}$, where $x_3 \in S$, then remove both $x_3$ and $y_3$, and decrease the parameter by 1.

See Fig. 5 for illustrations.

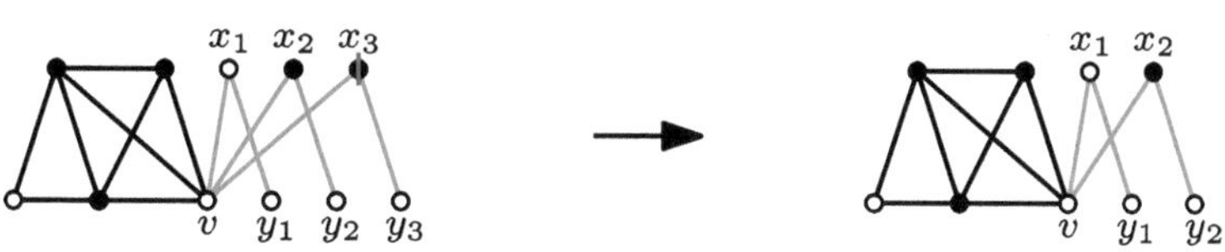


**Fig. 5.** An example of an application of Reduction Rule 7.

**Lemma 3.** *Reduction Rule 7 is safe.*

Our next task is to reduce some pendant 2-path rooted at the vertices in $S$. For ease of presentation, we start with a statement as follows.

**Lemma 4.** *Let $v \in S$ be incident to at least one pendant 2-path. If $\phi$ ($\phi \neq \emptyset$) is a POS-sequence of $G$ with $|\phi| \leq k$, then there exists a non-empty split sequence $\phi' \subseteq \phi$ such that the graph $\hat{G}$ resulting from applying $\phi'$ to $G$ still contains each pendant 2-path of $G$ stemming from $v$. Moreover, if $\phi'$ does not split $v$, then each vertex in $V(\hat{G}) \setminus \{v\}$ has degree* at most 2; otherwise, each vertex in $V(\hat{G}) \setminus \{v'\}$ has degree* at most 2, where $v'$ is the non-pendant vertex split from $v$ by $\phi'$.*

See Fig. 6 for an illustration. Herein, $\phi' = (s_1, s_2, s_3)$, where $s_1$ denotes the operation that splits off $ut$ at $u$; $s_2$ denotes the operation that splits off $gd$ at $d$; and $s_3$ denotes the operation that splits off $vw$ at $v$.

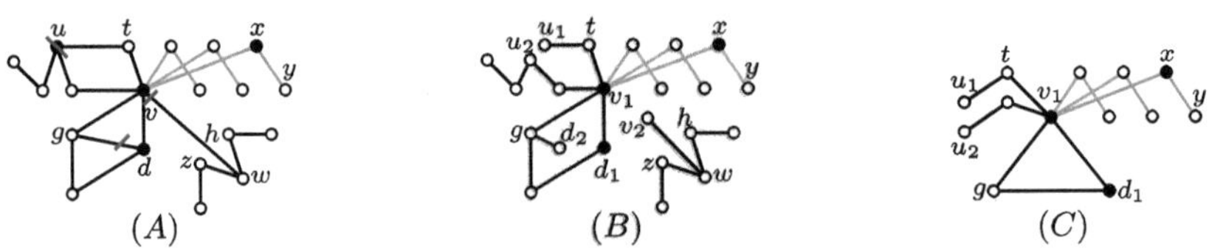


**Fig. 6.** An example illustrating Lemma 4. Graph (B) is obtained from (A) by applying three splits; Graph (C) is obtained from (B) by applying Rules 1–4.

Based on Lemma 4, we introduce a rule to reduce the pendant 2-paths rooted at the vertices in $S$.

**Reduction Rule 8.** If a vertex $v \in S$ is incident to at least three pendant 2-paths, two of them being induced by $\{v, x_i, y_i\}$ (for $i \in \{1, 2\}$), then remove all vertices in $\{x_1, y_1, x_2, y_2\}$ and decrease the parameter by 1.

See Fig. 7 for an illustration.

**Fig. 7.** An example of an application of Reduction Rule 8.

**Lemma 5.** *Reduction Rule 8 is safe.*

Let $(G, S, k)$ be an instance reduced by Rules 7 and 8 exhaustively. If $(G, S, k)$ is a yes-instance, then each vertex in $V_3$ is incident to at most 2 pendant 2-paths.

Furthermore, we introduce a rule to reduce some pendant 2-path rooted at a degree*-3 vertex.

**Reduction Rule 9.** Let a degree*-3 vertex $v$ be incident to exactly two pendant 2-paths induced by $\{v, x_i, y_i\}$ (for $i \in \{1, 2\}$) and denote by $u$ the unique non-pendant vertex in $N(v) \setminus \{x_1, x_2\}$.

9.1 If $u \in S$, then remove all vertices in $(N[v] \setminus \{u\}) \cup \{y_1, y_2\}$ and decrease the parameter by 1. Denote by $G'$ the resulted graph. If $\deg_{G'}(u) = 1$ and the unique vertex $z$ in $N_{G'}(u)$ is incident to two pendant edges, then additionally remove the vertex $u$.

9.2 If $u \notin S$ but $v \in S$, then remove all vertices in $(N(v) \setminus \{u\}) \cup \{y_1, y_2\}$ and decrease the parameter by 1. Denote by $G'$ the resulted graph. If $\deg_{G'}(u) \geq 3$, then additionally remove the vertex $v$.

9.3 If $\{u, v\} \cap S = \emptyset$ but $\{x_1, x_2\} \subseteq S$, then remove all vertices in $(N(v) \setminus \{u, x_1\}) \cup \{y_2\}$, and decrease the parameter by 1.

See Fig. 8 $(A)$, $(B)$, and $(C)$ for illustrations.

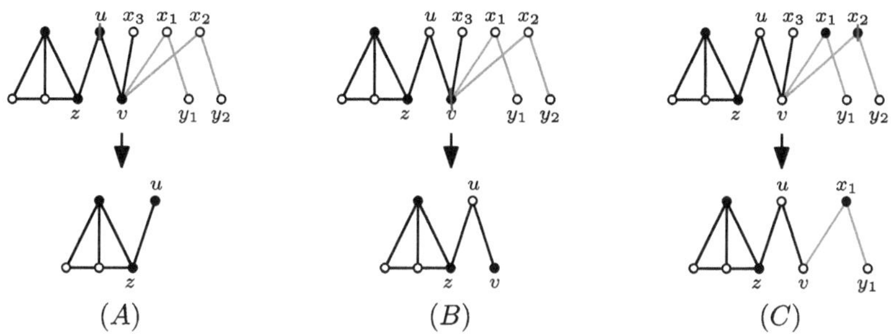


**Fig. 8.** Examples illustrating Reduction Rules 9.1, 9.2, and 9.3 respectively.

**Lemma 6.** *Reduction Rule 9 is safe.*

Notice that one pendant edge may occur in the graph resulted by performing Rule 9.1. However, the additional operation of Rule 9.1 guarantees that this pendant edge will be removed when it is incident to the middle point of a pendant 2-path.

## 4 A Whole Kernelization Algorithm Running in Linear Time

We now present a whole kernelization algorithm based on Reduction Rules 1–9 in Sect. 3 for the POVS problem. Observe that while reducing some pendant 2-paths by Rules 7–9, a chain reaction might occur. For instance, after executing

Rule 8 on a vertex $v \in V_3$, the vertex $v$ might be incident to exactly two pendant 2-paths and thus Rule 9 might become applicable. Furthermore, executing Rule 9 might create a new pendant 2-path such that another vertex is incident to three pendant 2-paths and Rule 8 thus becomes applicable again. To ensure that the reduction rules can be performed efficiently and that the algorithm can be done in linear time, we introduce a list $\mathcal{L}$ to dynamically store some vertices that meet one of the requirements of Rules 3, 4, and 7–9. This list, which is complemented by a while-loop frame, schedules the order of the reduction rules such that they can be executed efficiently.

Based on the above idea, a whole algorithm named as **Kernel-PS** can be described in Fig. 9. Herein, $\mathcal{R}$ denotes the family consisting of Rules 3, 4, and 7–9 in Sect. 3. At Step 7.2.3, a *potential* vertex $w$ that will trigger one rule in $\mathcal{R}$ means that $w$ is either a 2-enclosed vertex, or a degree*-2 vertex, or a degree*-3 vertex, or incident to at least one pendant 2-path.

**Algorithm Kernel-PS**$(G, S, k)$
Input: an undirected graph $G = (V, E)$, a set $S \subseteq V$, and a positive integer $k$;
Output: an equivalent instance $(G' = (V', E'), S', k')$ such that no rule is applicable to $G'$ or an answer saying "no-instance".

1. compute the degree and the degree* for each vertex of degree at least 2, use a proper data structure $\mathcal{D}$ to store them; compute the potential $\mu(G)$;
2. **if** $\mu(G) > 2k$ **then** return "$(G, S, k)$ is a no-instance";
3. reduce the instance with respect to Rule 5 exhaustively;
4. reduce the instance with respect to Rule 1 exhaustively;
5. reduce the instance with respect to Rules 3 and 4 exhaustively;
6. **for** each vertex $v \in V_3$ **do**
6.1 {count the number of pendant 2-paths incident to $v$, and store it to $\mathcal{D}$;
6.2 **if** $v$ meets one of the conditions in Rules 7–9 **then** push $v$ into a list $\mathcal{L}$;}
7. **while** $\mathcal{L}$ is not empty **do**
7.1 { $v \leftarrow$ pop($\mathcal{L}$);
7.2 **if** one rule in $\mathcal{R}$ is applicable to $v$ **then**
7.2.1 {performing the corresponding rule; denote by $G'$ be the resulting graph; and update the data in $\mathcal{D}$;
7.2.2 **if** $v$ is incident to at least one pendant 2-path **then** push $v$ into $\mathcal{L}$;
7.2.3 **if** a vertex $w$ of $G'$ with $w \notin \mathcal{L}$ becomes a potential vertex that will trigger one rule in $\mathcal{R}$ **then** push $w$ into $\mathcal{L}$; } }
8. apply Rule 1 to reduce the excess pendant edges exhaustively;
9. apply Rule 2 to reduce the isolated paths and isolated cycles exhaustively;
10. apply Rule 6 to reduce the remaining 2-enclosed vertices exhaustively;
11. return the resulting instance $(G', S', k')$.

**Fig. 9.** A whole kernelization algorithm running in linear time for the POVS problem.

For ease of analyzing the running time of Algorithm Kernel-PS, we first introduce a lemma for Step 7.2.3 as follows.

**Lemma 7.** *Let $G'$ be the graph obtained from $G$ by applying one rule in $\mathcal{R}$ to $v$. If a vertex $w$ of $G'$ with $w \notin \mathcal{L}$ and $w \neq v$ becomes a potential vertex that will trigger one rule in $\mathcal{R}$, then it can be located in $\mathcal{O}(1)$ time.*

Based on Lemma 7, we arrive at the following conclusion.

**Theorem 1.** *The algorithm Kernel-PS is correct and its running time can be bounded by $\mathcal{O}(m)$, where $m$ is the number of edges of the input graph.*

## 5 Analysis of the Problem Kernel Size

Let $(G = (V, E), S, k)$ be an output of the algorithm Kernel-PS. Assume that $(G, S, k)$ is a yes-instance. In this section, we bound the number of vertices of $G$ by analyzing the structure of $G$.

We start with bounding the number of pendant 2-paths in $G$.

**Lemma 8.** *If $(G = (V, E), S, k)$ is a yes-instance of the POVS problem, then $G$ contains at most $2k$ pendant 2-paths.*

*Proof.* Denote by $\mathcal{P}$ the set of all pendant 2-paths in $G$. Let $v \in V$ and let $\mathcal{P}_v$ denote the set of all pendant 2-paths rooted at $v$. Recall that the potential of $v$ is defined by $\mu(v) = \max\{\deg^*(v) - 2, 0\}$ and that the global potential of $G$ is defined by $\mu(G) = \sum_{v \in V(G)} \mu(v)$.

We now show that, for each vertex $v \in V$, $|\mathcal{P}_v| \leq \mu(v)$. Case (1): $\deg^*(v) \geq 4$. By the definition on the potential of $v$, it follows that $\mu(v) = \deg^*(v) - 2 \geq 2$. On the other hand, since $G$ has been reduced by Rules 7 and 8, there are at most two pendant 2-paths rooted at $v$, namely $|\mathcal{P}_v| \leq 2$. Thus, it holds that $|\mathcal{P}_v| \leq \mu(v)$. Case (2): $\deg^*(v) = 3$. By definition, $\mu(v) = \deg^*(v) - 2 = 1$. On the other hand, since $G$ has been reduced by Rule 9, $v$ is incident to at most one pendant 2-path, namely $|\mathcal{P}_v| \leq 1$. Thus, it also holds that $|\mathcal{P}_v| \leq \mu(v)$. Case (3): $\deg^*(v) \leq 2$. By definition, it holds that $\mu(v) = 0$. On the other hand, since $G$ has been reduced by Reduction Rule 4, each pendant 2-path must stem from a vertex in $V_3$, which means that no pendant 2-path is rooted at $v$, namely, $|\mathcal{P}_v| = 0$. Thus, it holds that $|\mathcal{P}_v| = \mu(v)$. Putting all together, we have that $\sum_{v \in V} |\mathcal{P}_v| \leq \sum_{v \in V} \mu(v)$, namely, $|\mathcal{P}| \leq \mu(G)$.

Moreover, since a single split operation can decrease the global potential by at most 2, it follows that $\mu(G) \leq 2k$ [3]. Thus, it holds that $|\mathcal{P}| \leq 2k$. □

The next task is to investigate the quantitative relationship between the vertices in $V(G) \setminus V_3$ and the edges in $E_3$. Recall that $E_3 = \bigcup_{v \in V_3} E_v$, where $E_v$ denotes the set of non-pendant edges incident to $v$. See Fig. 10, where all edges in $E_3$ are marked in green. For ease of presentation, we introduce some new notations as follows. We first partition the set $E_3$ into three subsets, denoted by $E_{31}, E_{32}$, and $E_{33}$ respectively. More precisely, $E_{31} := \{e \mid e \in E_3$ and the other endpoint of $e$ has degree* 1 but has degree 2}; $E_{32} := \{e \mid e \in E_3$ and the other endpoint of $e$ has degree* 2}; $E_{33} := \{e \mid e \in E_3$ and both endpoints of $e$ have degree* at least 3}. See Fig. 10 for examples, where $w_1z_1 \in E_{31}$, $w_2u_1 \in E_{32}$, and $w_1w_3 \in E_{33}$. Let $V_1 \subseteq V(G)$ (resp. $V_2 \subseteq V(G)$) denote the set of all vertices of $G$ with degree* 1 (resp. degree* 2)[1]. Notice that $G$ contains no vertex of degree* 0 because it has been reduced by Rule 2 exhaustively. Since $G$ has been reduced by Rule 1 exhaustively, it holds, for each vertex $v \in V_1$, that $|N(v)| \leq 2$. If $|N(v)| = 2$, then one vertex in $N(v)$ has degree 1 and another has degree* at least 3 because $G$ has been reduced by Rule 4 exhaustively. Let $V_{10} := \{v \mid v \in V_1$ and $|N(v)| = 2\}$. We also partition the set $V_1 \setminus V_{10}$ into three subsets, denoted by $V_{11}, V_{12}$, and $V_{13}$ respectively. More precisely, $V_{1i} := \{v \mid v \in V_1, |N(v)| = 1$, and the unique vertex in $N(v)$ has degree* $i\}$ for $i \in \{1, 2\}$; $V_{13} := \{v \mid v \in V_1$, $|N(v)| = 1$, and the unique vertex in $N(v)$ has degree* at least 3}. See Fig. 10 for examples, where $V_{10} = \{z_1, z_2\}$, $V_{11} = \{v_1, v_2\}$, $V_{12} = \{v_5\}$, and $V_{13} = \{v_3, v_4\}$.

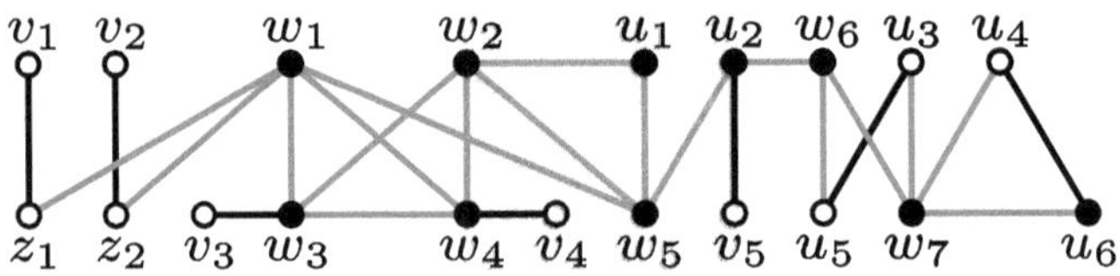


**Fig. 10.** A graph reduced by all reduction rules exhaustively.

**Lemma 9.** *If* $(G = (V, E), S, k)$ *is an instance outputted from Algorithm Kernel-PS, then the following formulas hold: (1)* $|V_{10} \cup V_{11}| = 2 \cdot |E_{31}|$*; (2)* $|V_{12} \cup V_2| \leq |E_{32}|$*; and (3)* $|V_{13}| \leq 2 \cdot |E_{33}|$.

*Proof.* (sketched) We show the soundness of these formulas one by one.

(1). On one hand, let $v \in V_{11}$. Denote by $z$ the unique vertex in $N(v)$. Since $G$ has been reduced by Rule 4 exhaustively, it holds that $z \in V_{10}$. Thus, two vertices $v$ and $z$ lie in a pendant 2-path of $G$, which contains exactly one edge in $E_{31}$. On the other hand, let $e \in E_{31}$. Since $G$ has been reduced by Rule 1 exhaustively, $e$ is contained in a pendant 2-path, whose middle point is in $V_{10}$ and whose end point is in $V_{11}$. Putting them together, we have that $|V_{10} \cup V_{11}| = 2 \cdot |E_{31}|$.

(2). Let $v \in V_2$. Since $G$ has been reduced by Rules 3 and 6 exhaustively, it holds that $1 \leq |N(v) \cap V_3| \leq 2$. Based on this inequality, we further partition $V_2$ into two subsets, denoted by $V_{21}$ and $V_{22}$ respectively. More precisely, $V_{21} := \{v \mid v \in V_2$ and $|N(v) \cap V_3| = 1\}$; $V_{22} := \{v \mid v \in V_2$ and $|N(v) \cap V_3| = 2\}$. Assume that $V_{12} \neq \emptyset$ and let $V'_{22} := \bigcup_{v \in V_{12}} N(v)$. It is clear that $|V'_{22}| = |V_{12}|$ and that $V'_{22} \subseteq V_{22}$. See Fig. 10 for examples, where $V_{21} = \{u_3, u_4, u_5, u_6\}$, $V_{22} = \{u_1, u_2\}$, and $V'_{22} = \{u_2\}$. By these notations, we next bound the size of the

[1] This definition on $V_1$ is slightly different from that in [3], where $V_1$ denotes the set of *non-pendant* degree*-1 vertices of $G$.

set $V_{12} \cup V_2$. Note that $V_{12} \cup V_2 = V_{12} \cup V_{22} \cup V_{21} = (V_{12} \cup V'_{22}) \cup (V_{22} \setminus V'_{22}) \cup V_{21}$. Assume that $V_{12} \neq \emptyset$. Let $v \in V_{12}$ and denote by $u$ the unique vertex in $N(v)$. Denote by $w$ and $h$ the two vertices in $N(u) \setminus \{v\}$ respectively. Then two vertices $v$ and $u$ lie in a subgraph isomorphic to $K_{1,3}$, which contains two edges $uw$ and $uh$ in $E_{32}$. Assume that $V_{22} \setminus V'_{22} \neq \emptyset$. Let $u \in V_{22} \setminus V'_{22}$. Then $u$ is incident to exactly two edges in $E_{32}$. Assume that $V_{21} \neq \emptyset$. Let $u \in V_{21}$. Then $u$ has no pendant neighbor because $G$ has been reduced by Rule 1 exhaustively and thus it is incident to one edge in $E_{32}$. We therefore have that $|V_{12} \cup V_2| \leq |E_{32}|$.

(3). Let $v \in V_{13}$. Denote by $w$ the unique neighbor of $v$ and let $u \in N(w) \setminus \{v\}$. Since $G$ has been reduced by Rule 1 exhaustively, it holds that $u \in V_3$ and that $|N(u) \cap V_{13}| \leq 1$. If $|N(u) \cap V_{13}| = 0$, then vertex $v$ is an endpoint of a 2-path induced by $\{v, w, u\}$, which contains one edge $wu$ in $E_{33}$. Otherwise, let $h$ be the unique vertex in $N(u) \cap V_{13}$. Then, two vertices $v$ and $h$ in $V_{13}$ are the endpoints of a 3-path induced by $\{v, w, u, h\}$, which contains one edge $wu$ in $E_{33}$. Therefore, it follows that $|V_{13}| \leq 2 \cdot |E_{33}|$. □

By Lemma 9, the number of vertices in $V_1 \cup V_2$ can be bounded by $2 \cdot |E_{31}| + |E_{32}| + 2 \cdot |E_{33}|$. Moreover, it follows that $|E_{31}| + |E_{32}| + 2 \cdot |E_{33}| = \sum_{v \in V_3} \deg^*(v)$ because each edge in $E_{33}$ are counted twice. To get an upper bound for $\sum_{v \in V_3} \deg^*(v)$, we directly employ a conclusion obtained in [3] which is restated as follows. Assume that $(G, S, k)$ is a yes-instance. It holds that $|V_3| \leq 2k$ and that $\sum_{v \in V_3} \deg^*(v) \leq 6k$ [3].

Now everything is settled to prove our main result.

**Theorem 2.** *The POVS problem admits a kernel of at most* $10k$ *vertices.*

*Proof.* Assume that $(G = (V, E), S, k)$ is a yes-instance of the POVS problem. We now give a function of $k$ to bound the size of the set $V(G) \setminus V_3$ (i.e., $V_1 \cup V_2$) as follows. By Lemma 8, the number of pendant 2-paths in $G$ is at most $2k$. This means that $|E_{31}| \leq 2k$. By Lemma 9, $|V_1 \cup V_2| \leq 2 \cdot |E_{31}| + |E_{32}| + 2 \cdot |E_{33}|$ $= |E_{31}| + (|E_{31}| + |E_{32}| + 2 \cdot |E_{33}|) = |E_{31}| + \sum_{v \in V_3} \deg^*(v) \leq 2k + 6k = 8k$, that is, $|V(G) \setminus V_3| \leq 8k$. Moreover, it holds that $|V_3| \leq 2k$. It follows that $|V(G)| \leq 8k + 2k = 10k$. □

## 6 Conclusions

In this work, we focus on investigating the kernelization algorithm for the problem PATHWIDTH-ONE VERTEX SPLITTING parameterized by the number of splits. By introducing a series of reduction rules and several techniques, we show that this parameterized problem admits a kernel of at most $10k$ vertices, improving the kernel in [3] with at most $16k$ vertices. Moreover, this kernel can still be obtained in $\mathcal{O}(m)$ time, where $m$ is the number of edges of the input graph.

Improving the kernel is an interesting question for future work. The work we have done mainly lies in reducing the vertices with degree at most two. In the future work, the challenge is to reduce some vertices with high degree.

**Acknowledgements.** We would like to thank the anonymous referees for their helpful comments on improving the presentation of this paper.

## References


1. Ahmed, R., Kobourov, S., Kryven, M.: An FPT algorithm for bipartite vertex splitting. In: Angelini, P., von Hanxleden, R. (eds.) GD 2022, LNCS 13764, pp. 261–268. Springer, Cham (2023). https://doi.org/10.1007/978-3-031-22203-0_19
2. Ahmed, R., Angelini, P., Bekos, M.A., et al.: Splitting vertices in 2-layer graph drawings. IEEE Comput. Graph. **43**(3), 24–35 (2023)
3. Baumann, J., Pfretzschner, M., Rutter, I.: Parameterized complexity of vertex splitting to pathwidth at most 1. Theoret. Comput. Sci. **1021**, 114928 (2024)
4. Dujmović, V., Fellows, M., Hallett, M., et al.: A fixed-parameter approach to 2-layer planarization. Algorithmica **45**, 159–182 (2006)
5. Dujmović, V., Fernau, H., Kaufmann, M.: Fixed parameter algorithms for one-sided crossing minimization revisited. J. Discrete Algorithms **6**(2), 313–323 (2008)
6. Fernau, H.: Two-layer planarization: improving on parameterized algorithmics. J. Graph Algorithms Appl. **9**(2), 205–238 (2005)
7. Fernau, H., Fomin, F.V., Lokshtanov, D., Mnich, M., Philip, G., Saurabh, S.: Social choice meets graph drawing: how to get subexponential time algorithms for ranking and drawing problems. Tsinghua Sci. Technol. **19**(4), 374–386 (2014)
8. Kobayashi, Y., Tamaki, H.: A fast and simple subexponential fixed parameter algorithm for one-sided crossing minimization. Algorithmica **72**(3), 778–790 (2015)
9. Kobayashi, Y., Tamaki, H.: A faster fixed parameter algorithm for two-layer crossing minimization. Inf. Process. Lett. **116**(9), 547–549 (2016)
10. Liu Y., Xiao G., Liu A., Wu D., Huang J.: Improved kernelization and fixed-parameter algorithm for bipartite one-sided vertex explosion. Theoret. Comput. Sci. **1082**, 116149 (2026)
11. Liu Y., Xiao G., Huang J., Wang J.: Parameterized algorithms for planar 2- layer drawing by vertex splitting on a given subset. In: Chen, Y., Gao, X., Sun,X., Zhang, A. (eds.) COCOON 2024. LNCS, vol. 15161, pp. 301–313. Springer, Singapore (2025). https://doi.org/10.1007/978-981-96-1090-7_25
12. Martí, R., Martínez-Gavara, A., Sánchez-Oro, J., Duarte, A.: Tabu search for the dynamic bipartite drawing problem. Comput. Oper. Res. **91**, 1–12 (2018)
13. Nöllenburg, M., Sorge, M., Terziadis, S., Villedieu, A., Wu, H.-Y., Wulms, J.: Planarizing graphs and their drawings by vertex splitting. J. Comput. Geom. **16**(1), 333–372 (2025)
14. Tsur, D.: Faster algorithm for pathwidth one vertex deletion. Theoret. Comput. Sci. **921**, 63–74 (2022)

# Two-Machine Flow Shop Scheduling with One Non-Availability Interval

Hao Lu[1], Xin Han[1(✉)], Yuan Yuan[2], Yaojun Liu[1], and Hanbin Yang[1]

[1] School of Software, Dalian University of Technology, Dalian 116620, Liaoning, China
{luhao,yanghanbin}@mail.dlut.edu.cn, hanxin@dlut.edu.cn
[2] School of Information and Communication Engineering, Dalian Minzu University, Dalian 116600, Liaoning, China

**Abstract.** This paper investigates a two-machine flow shop scheduling problem with one non-availability interval on the first machine. A non-resumable case is considered, that is, if a job cannot be completed before the non-availability interval, then it must be totally restarted. The objective is to minimize the makespan. We propose a $\frac{7}{5}$-approximation algorithm with time complexity $O(n \log n)$, which improves the best-known approximation ratio of $\frac{3}{2}$ in the literature. Furthermore, we present the first fully polynomial-time approximation scheme (FPTAS) with time complexity $O(n^5/\varepsilon^4)$, which outperforms the existing PTAS for this problem.

**Keywords:** Flow shop · Non-availability interval · Fully polynomial-time approximation scheme

## 1 Introduction

Machine scheduling problems incorporating a non-availability interval have been attracting significant research interest in operations research. This paper studies a two-machine flow shop scheduling problem with a non-availability interval on the first machine. This problem was first formally introduced and explored in the foundational work of Lee [11].

We refer to the non-availability interval as maintenance period (MP). MP is categorized into two fundamental variants: **fixed MP** and **flexible MP**. The former is the case where the starting time and completion time of the MP are fixed, while the latter is the case where the MP starts within a given window and the duration is constant.

In the classical scheduling problem, we are given a set $N = \{1, 2, \cdots, n\}$ of jobs that have to be processed on two machines $M_1$ and $M_2$. Each job $i \in N$ comprises two operations: $O_{1,i}$ and $O_{2,i}$, where $O_{1,i}$ is processed on $M_1$ requiring $a_i$ time units, and $O_{2,i}$ is performed on $M_2$ taking $b_i$ time units. In any feasible schedule, the operations of the same job cannot overlap in time, and each machine can process at most one operation at a time. No preemption is allowed


Y. Li et al. (Eds.): COCOON 2026, LNCS 16835, pp. 219–230, 2027.
https://doi.org/10.1007/978-981-92-3309-0_17

in processing any operation. For every job $i$, if $O_{1,i}$ must complete before $O_{2,i}$ starts, the processing system is called a *flowshop*; if the order of operations is not given in advance, and must be chosen, the processing system is called an *openshop*. The objective mentioned in this paper is to minimize the *makespan*, i.e., the maximum completion time of all jobs on two machines.

We extend the classical two-machine flow shop scheduling problem to minimize the makespan by incorporating a fixed MP on the first machine. The MP starts at time $s$ and ends at time $t$, during which the machine is unavailable for processing operations.

Within scheduling literature, three distinct scenarios address fixed MP constraints. During an MP, no job can be processed on that machine. Suppose that some job fails to finish on a certain machine prior to the MP. If the job can be continued after the MP without any penalty, Lee [9] calls this scheduling scenario *resumable*; if the uncompleted job must restart from scratch after the completion time of the MP, the scenario is referred to as *non-resumable* [9]; and if the job will have to partially restart after the machine has become available again, the scenario is referred to as *semi-resumable* [11].

Since the two-machine flow shop scheduling problem with one fixed MP is NP-hard [2], designing and analyzing efficient approximation algorithms with good performance has become an important research direction. A polynomial-time algorithm is called a *$\rho$-approximation algorithm*, for every instance of the problem, if it produces a schedule with makespan at most $\rho$ times the optimal value (where $\rho \geq 1$); where $\rho$ is referred to as *approximation ratio*. A family of $\rho$-approximation algorithms is called a *polynomial-time approximation scheme*, or a PTAS for short, if $\rho = 1 + \varepsilon$ for any fixed $\varepsilon > 0$ and the running time is polynomial in the input size. If additionally the running time of a PTAS is polynomial in $\frac{1}{\varepsilon}$, it is called a *fully polynomial-time approximation scheme*, or an FPTAS for short.

For the two-machine open shop scheduling problem with one fixed MP, Breit et al. [2] proposed a $\frac{4}{3}$-approximation algorithm considering the resumable scenario, while Breit et al. [3] presented a $\frac{4}{3}$-approximation algorithm for the non-resumable scenario. Considering the resumable scenario, Kubzin et al. [8] proposed two PTASes: one for the problem with one fixed MP on each machine and the other for the problem with multiple fixed MPs on one of the machines. Lorigeon et al. [12] developed a pseudo-polynomial time dynamic programming algorithm to solve the two-machine open shop scheduling problem with a fixed MP considering the resumable scenario. Yuan et al. [14] developed a PTAS for the two-machine open shop problem with one fixed MP under the non-resumable scenario.

For the two-machine flow shop scheduling problem with one fixed MP, for the resumable scenario, Lee [10] gives a 4/3-approximation algorithm if the non-availability constraint is on the second machine, and a 3/2-approximation algorithm if the non-availability constraint is on the first machine. For the former problem, Breit [1] develops an improved 5/4-approximation algorithm, while for the latter problem, Cheng and Wang [4] propose an improved 4/3-approximation algorithm. Finally, Ng and Kovalyov [13] provide FPTASes for both problems with time complexity $O(n^5/\varepsilon^4)$.

For the semi-resumable scenario (and also the non-resumable scenario), Lee [11] gives a 3/2-approximation algorithm if the non-availability interval is on the second machine and a 2-approximation algorithm if the non-availability interval is on the first machine. For the latter case, Hadda et al. [5] propose a 3/2-approximation algorithm. For the same setting under the semi-resumable scenario, Kubzin et al. [7] develop a PTAS.

The remainder of this paper is organized as follows. Section 2 introduces some notations and definitions. In Sect. 3, we develop a $\frac{7}{5}$-approximation algorithm. In Sect. 4, we develop an FPTAS. In Sect. 5, we conclude with a short summary.

## 2 Preliminaries

We will use the following notations.

| | |
|---|---|
| $N = \{1, \dots, n\}$ | Set of jobs |
| $J_i$ | Job $i$, $i \in N$ |
| $[s, t]$ | Non-availability period of $M_1$, where $0 \le s \le t$ and $d = t - s$ |
| $a_i, b_i$ | Processing times for $J_i$ on $M_1$ and $M_2$ respectively |
| $\pi = \langle \pi(1), \dots, \pi(n) \rangle$ | Permutation schedule where $\pi(k)$ is the $k$th job in $\pi$ |
| $\pi^*$ | An optimal permutation schedule |
| $A(\pi)$ | Set of jobs that are completed on $M_1$ before or at s in $\pi$ |
| $B(\pi)$ | $B(\pi) = N \setminus A(\pi)$ |
| $F2\|nr - a(M_1)\|C_{max}$ | Two-machine flow shop scheduling problem with a fixed MP on the $M_1$ under non-resumable scenario |
| $F2\|\|C_{max}$ | Two-machine flow shop scheduling problem |
| $C_{\max}(\pi)$ | Makespan of $\pi$ |
| $C^{no}_{\max}(\pi)$ | Makespan of $\pi$ for $F2\|\|C_{\max}$ |
| $S_{j,k}(\pi)$, $C_{j,k}(\pi)$ | Start and finish time of job $\pi(k)$ on machine $j$ in a permutation $\pi$, $j \in \{1, 2\}$, $k \in \{1, \dots, n\}$ |

***Critical Job***: The first job that starts the last busy period on machine $M_2$.

***Johnson Rule(JR)***: $J_i$ precedes $J_j$ if $min(a_i, b_j) < min(a_j, b_i)$. If $min(a_i, b_j) = min(a_j, b_i)$, we break the tie arbitrarily [6]. Let $\pi_{JR}$ be the permutation according to JR. Clearly, we have

$$C^{no}_{max}(\pi_{JR}) \le C_{max}(\pi^*). \tag{1}$$

For problem $F2|nr - a(M_1)|C_{\max}$, we assume $\sum_{i=1}^{n} a_i > s$; otherwise, $\pi_{JR}$ is optimal.

***Ratio Rule(RR)***: $J_i$ precedes $J_j$ if $b_i/a_i > b_j/a_j$. If $b_i/a_i = b_j/a_j$ we break the tie arbitrarily [1]. Let $\pi_{RR}$ be the permutation according to RR and $\pi^*_{no}$ be the optimal permutation for $F_2||C_{\max}$.

**Lemma 1.** *(Lee [11]) There exists an optimal permutation for problem $F2|nr-a(M_1)|C_{\max}$ such that jobs completed on $M_1$ before or at $s$ should follow JR and the remaining jobs also should follow JR.*

## 3 $\frac{7}{5}$-Approximation Algorithm

In this section, we present and analyze a $\frac{7}{5}$-approximation algorithm for minimizing the makespan in a two-machine flow shop, provided that one MP on $M_1$ must start in a given window.

---

**Algorithm 1:** Algorithm H

---

**Input** : Job set $N = \{J_1, J_2, \ldots, J_n\}$; fixed MP $[s, t]$ on $M_1$.
**Output**: Near-optimal schedule $\pi_H$.

**Step 1.** Get the $\pi_{JR}$ according to JR;

**Step 2.** Let $S$ be the set containing the ten jobs with the largest $a_k$ and ten jobs with the largest $b_k$;

**Step 3.** Generate all possible placement combinations of jobs in $S$ (each job is either in $A(\pi)$ or $B(\pi)$), resulting in $2^{|S|}$ combinations denoted as $\{\sigma_1, \sigma_2, \ldots, \sigma_{2^{|S|}}\}$;

**Step 4.** Sort all jobs in the set $N \setminus S$ according to RR;

**Step 5.**
**For each** $\sigma_i \in \{\sigma_1, \sigma_2, \ldots, \sigma_{2^{|S|}}\}$ **do**
  $S' = \sigma_i(A)$;  `// ` $\sigma_i(A)$`: Jobs in ` $\sigma_i$ ` that finish at or before ` $s$ ` on ` $M_1$
  **For each** *job* $J_j \in N \setminus S$ **do**
    **if** $a(S' \cup J_j) > s$ **then**
      **Break**;
    **end**
    **else**
      $S' = S' \cup \{J_j\}$;
    **end**
  **endfor**
  Schedule $S'$ according to $JR$, then schedule the remaining jobs according to $JR$. Let the corresponding schedule be $\pi_{\sigma_i}$;
**endfor**

**Step 6.** $\pi_\sigma = \arg\min_{\sigma_i \in \{\sigma_1, \ldots, \sigma_{2^{|S|}}\}} C_{\max}(\pi_{\sigma_i})$;

**return** $\pi_H = \arg\min\{C_{\max}(\pi_\sigma), C_{\max}(\pi_{JR})\}$

---

### 3.1 The Approximation Algorithm

The core idea of our algorithm consists of three key steps. We first guess the placement of large jobs in the optimal solution, i.e., whether they belong to

$A(\pi^*)$ or $B(\pi^*)$. Next, we sort the remaining small jobs in accordance with the RR and schedule each small job to start processing as early as possible in turn. Finally, we reorder the jobs preceding MP and those succeeding MP by the JR, respectively.

Clearly, the time complexity of the heuristic H is $O(n \log n)$.

### 3.2 Worst Case Analysis

**Theorem 1.** *The relative worst-case error bound of algorithm H is given by* $C_{max}(\pi_H)/C_{max}(\pi^*) \leq \frac{7}{5}$.

*Proof.* If $t \leq \frac{2}{5}C_{\max}(\pi^*)$, we have

$$C_{\max}(\pi_H) \leq C_{\max}(\pi_{JR}) \leq t + C_{max}^{no}(\pi_{JR}) \leq \frac{7}{5}C_{\max}(\pi^*).$$

In what follows, we only consider the case where $t > \frac{2}{5}C_{\max}(\pi^*)$.

We consider the schedule $\pi_r$, which is constructed by sequencing the jobs in $A(\pi_{\sigma_s})$ and $B(\pi_{\sigma_s})$ according to the RR rule, where $\pi_{\sigma_s} \in \{\pi_{\sigma_1}, \dots, \pi_{\sigma_{2^{|S|}}}\}$, $A(\pi_{\sigma_s}) \cap S = A(\pi^*) \cap S$ and $B(\pi_{\sigma_s}) \cap S = B(\pi^*) \cap S$. Clearly, we have

$$A(\pi_r) \cap S = A(\pi^*) \cap S \tag{2}$$

$$B(\pi_r) \cap S = B(\pi^*) \cap S \tag{3}$$

$$C_{max}(\pi_\sigma) \leq C_{max}(\pi_{\sigma_s}) \leq C_{max}(\pi_r) \tag{4}$$

The analysis is divided into two parts according to whether the critical job is located in $A(\pi_r)$ or $B(\pi_r)$. Let $k$ be the critical job in $\pi_r$.

**Lemma 2.** *If* $A(\pi_r) \subseteq S$ *or* $B(\pi_r) \subseteq S$, *then*

$$C_{max}(\pi_H) = C_{max}(\pi^*).$$

*Proof.* Suppose $A(\pi_r) \subseteq S$. By Eqs. (2) and (3), we have $A(\pi_r) = A(\pi^*)$ and $B(\pi_r) = B(\pi^*)$. Furthermore, by Lemma 1, it follows that $\pi_r$ is an optimal solution.

Similarly, the same conclusion holds if $B(\pi_r) \subseteq S$. □

In what follows, we restrict our attention to the case where $A(\pi_r) \setminus S \neq \emptyset$ and $B(\pi_r) \setminus S \neq \emptyset$. For the complementary case, the conclusion holds by Lemma 2.

Let $I$ denote the length of idle interval before MP on $M_1$, i.e. $I = s - a(A(\pi_r))$. We have

$$I \leq \frac{1}{10}C_{max}(\pi^*).$$

Otherwise, from Lines 8–9 of Algorithm H and the condition $B(\pi_r)\setminus S \neq \emptyset$, there exists a job $J_j \in B(\pi_r)\setminus S$ such that $a_j > I > \frac{1}{10}C_{\max}(\pi^*)$. Further, from Line 2 of Algorithm H, we have $a(S) > 10a_j > C_{\max}(\pi^*)$, which yields a contradiction.

Let $\alpha$ denote the first job in $B(\pi_r) \setminus S$ (in the processing order of $\pi_r$). We have

$$b_\alpha \leq \frac{1}{10}C_{max}(\pi^*).$$

**Lemma 3.**

$$b(B(\pi_r)) \leq b(B(\pi^*)) + b_\alpha.$$

**Case 1: The critical job is located in $A(\pi_r)$**

**Lemma 4.** *If the critical job is located in $A(\pi_r)$, then*

$$C_{max}(\pi_r) \leq C_{max}(\pi^*) + \min\{a_k, b_k\}.$$

If $\min\{a_k, b_k\} \leq \frac{2}{5}C^*_{max}$, the result follows from Lemma 4. Otherwise, we have $a_k > \frac{2}{5}C^*_{max}$ and $b_k > \frac{2}{5}C^*_{max}$.

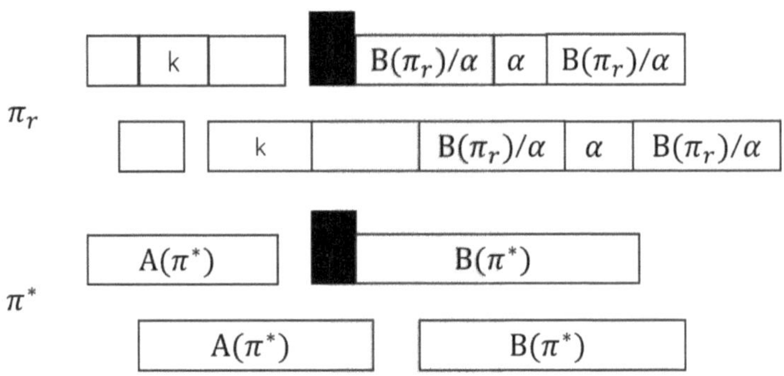


**Fig. 1.** $a_k > \frac{2}{5}C^*_{max}$ and $b_k > \frac{2}{5}C^*_{max}$

As shown in Fig. 1, we have

$$C_{max}(\pi_r) = C_{max}(A(\pi_r)) + b(B(\pi_r))$$

Clearly, $b(B(\pi^*)) \leq \frac{1}{5}C_{\max}(\pi^*)$; otherwise, we would have $C_{\max}(\pi^*) > a_k + b_k + b(B(\pi^*)) \geq C_{\max}(\pi^*)$, which yields a contradiction.

Since $b_\alpha \leq \frac{1}{10}C_{\max}(\pi^*)$, we have

$$\begin{aligned} C_{max}(\pi_r) &= C_{max}(A(\pi_r)) + b(B(\pi_r)) \\ &\leq C_{max}(\pi^*) + b(B(\pi^*)) + b_\alpha \quad \textit{by Lemma 3} \\ &\leq 1.3C_{max}(\pi^*) \end{aligned}$$

**Case 2: The critical job is located in $B(\pi_r)$**

**Lemma 5.** *If the critical job is located in* $B(\pi_r)$*, then*

$$C_{max}(\pi_r) \leq C_{max}(\pi^*) + \frac{1}{10}C_{max}(\pi^*) + \min\{a_k, b_k\}.$$

If $\min\{a_k, b_k\} \leq \frac{3}{10}C^*_{max}$, the result follows from Lemma 5; otherwise, we have $a_k > \frac{3}{10}C_{max}(\pi^*)$ and $b_k > \frac{3}{10}C_{max}(\pi^*)$. Since $C_{max}(\pi^*) \geq t + a_k + b_k > C_{max}(\pi^*)$, this leads to a contradiction.

Combining all the above arguments, we have

$$C_{max}(\pi_H)/C_{max}(\pi^*) \leq \frac{7}{5}$$

□

If in Algorithm H, we select $\lceil\frac{1}{\varepsilon}\rceil$ jobs with the largest $a_k$ and $\lceil\frac{1}{\varepsilon}\rceil$ jobs with the largest $b_k$, respectively. We can readily achieve an approximation ratio of $\frac{4}{3} + \varepsilon$, but its time complexity increases to an exponential function of $\frac{1}{\varepsilon}$.

# 4 FPTAS

In this section, we develop an FPTAS for the problem $F2|nr - a(M_1)|C_{\max}$, with a time complexity of $O(\frac{n^5}{\varepsilon^4})$, where $\varepsilon > 0$. We first propose the dynamic programming (DP) algorithm for the considered problem; subsequently, building upon this DP algorithm, we develop an FPTAS by utilizing the well-known rounding technique.

For the resumable case, Ng and Kovalyov [13] proposed a DP algorithm. Building upon this algorithm, we develop a dedicated DP algorithm for the non-resumable case. The key difference between the two cases is that, in the resumable setting, the first job in $B(\pi^*)$ may start processing before time $t$, whereas in the non-resumable setting, the first job in $B(\pi^*)$ can only start processing at time $t$. To address this critical distinction, we adapt the DP algorithm accordingly. Additionally, we further optimize the state transition equations of the DP algorithm to enhance its suitability for the non-resumable case.

## 4.1 Dynamic Programming Algorithm

We assume that all jobs in $N$ are numbered according to JR. Let $\pi^*$ denote the schedule generated by the DP algorithm. In our DP algorithm, jobs are partitioned into $A(\pi^*)$ and $B(\pi^*)$ following JR's order. For the sake of convenience, these two sets are hereafter referred to as $A$ and $B$, respectively. We define $N_i = \{J_1, \ldots, J_i\}$ and $A_i$ as the set of jobs completed on machine $M_1$ before or at time $s$. We have $A_i \subseteq N_i$, and $B_i = N_i \setminus A_i$.

Define $f_i(u_1, u_2, v_1, v_2)$ as the total processing time of the jobs completed on $M_1$ before or at $s$ if:

1. we have scheduled jobs from $J_1$ up to $J_i$;

2. the completion time of the last job on $M_1$ that finishes before or at s is $u_1$, i.e. $u_1 = a(A_i)$;
3. the total processing time on machine $M_2$ for jobs completed on $M_1$ after $s$ is $u_2$, i.e. $u_2 = b(B_i)$;
4. the makespan of $A_i$ is $v_1$, i.e. $v_1 = C_{max}(A_i)$;
5. the makespan of $B_i$ is $v_2$, i.e. $v_2 = C_{max}(B_i)$.

As shown in Fig. 2,

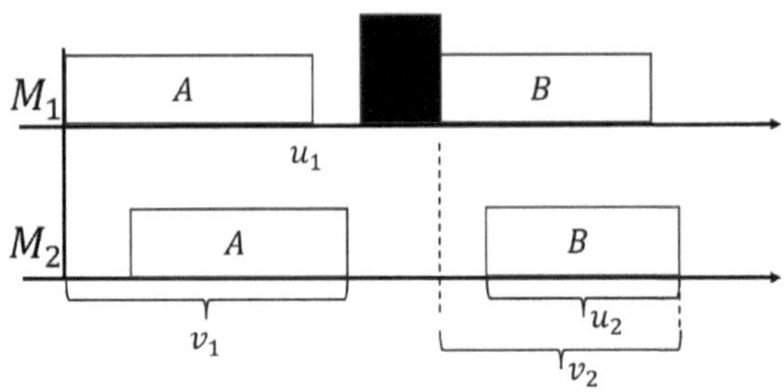


**Fig. 2.** Definitions of $u_1$, $u_2$, $v_1$, and $v_2$.

$$f_i(u_1, u_2, v_1, v_2) = \min \begin{cases} f_{i-1}(u_1 - a_i, u_2, v_1 - b_i, v_2) + a_i, & \text{if} \quad u_1 + b_i \le v_1, \quad (a) \\ f_{i-1}(u_1, u_2 - b_i, v_1, v_2 - b_i), & \text{if} \quad a(N_i) - u_1 + b_i \le v_2. \quad (b) \end{cases}$$

where $i \in [1, n]$; $u_1 \in [0, s]$; $u_2 \in [0, b(N)]$; $v_1 \in [u_1, a(N)+b(N)]$; $v_2 \in [u_2, a(N)+b(N)]$.

During the execution of the DP algorithm, sets $A_i$ and $B_i$ are independent. Their interrelation arises only in the process of computing the makespan.

*Initial Condition*:

$$f_i(u_1, u_2, v_1, v_2) = \begin{cases} 0, & \text{if} \quad (i, u_1, u_2, v_1, v_2) = (0, 0, 0, *, *) \\ +\infty, & \text{otherwise} \end{cases} \tag{5}$$

where $*$ denotes an arbitrary non-negative value.

The study by Ng and Kovalyov [13] distinguishes between the following two cases (as shown in Fig. 3), leading to four transition equations presented in their work, which are explicitly given as follows:

$$f_i(u_1, u_2, v_1, v_2) = \min \begin{cases} f_{i-1}(u_1 - a_i, u_2, v_1 - b_i, v_2) + a_i, & u_1 + b_i < v_1, \quad (1a) \\ \min\limits_{0 \le v_1' \le u_1} f_{i-1}(u_1 - a_i, u_2, v_1', v_2) + a_i, & u_1 + b_i = v_1, \quad (1b) \\ f_{i-1}(u_1, u_2 - b_i, v_1, v_2 - b_i), & a(N_i) - u_1 + b_i < v_2, \quad (2a) \\ \min\limits_{0 \le v_2' \le a(N_i) - u_1} f_{i-1}(u_1, u_2 - b_i, v_1, v_2'), & a(N_i) - u_1 + b_i = v_2. \quad (2b) \end{cases}$$

In contrast, we can merge these two cases by scheduling the operations on $M_2$ in $A_i$ to start as late as possible (without altering the value of $v_1$). Therefore, we adjust the initial condition(Eq. (5)), and such an adjustment does not change the makespan corresponding to this state.

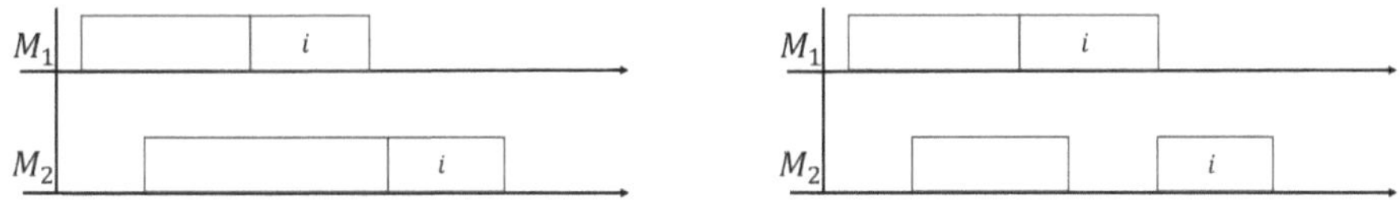


(a) Case (1a) (b) Case (1b)

**Fig. 3.** Two cases for the placement of job $i$ into $A_i$.

**Lemma 6.** *Let $C_{max}^{(u_1,u_2,v_1,v_2)}(f_n)$ denote the makespan of state $(n, u_1, u_2, v_1, v_2)$. For each state $(n, u_1, u_2, v_1, v_2)$, the corresponding makespan is calculated using Eq. (6):*

$$C_{max}^{(u_1,u_2,v_1,v_2)}(f_n) = \max\{v_1 + u_2, t + v_2\} \tag{6}$$

*Proof.* As illustrated in Fig. 4, each state corresponds to two scenarios: either there is a gap between $A$ and $B$, or there is no gap between them. When there exists a gap between $A$ and $B$ (see Fig. 4a), the makespan is equal to $t + v_2$. In contrast, when there is no gap between $A$ and $B$ (see Fig. 4b), the makespan is equal to $v_1 + u_2$. □

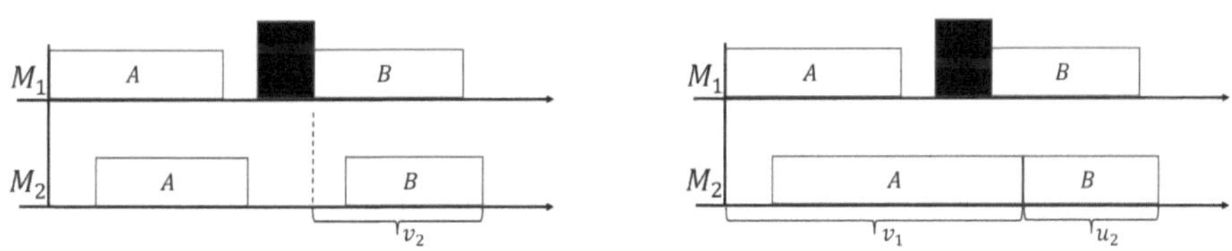


(a) There is a gap between $A$ and $B$ on $M_2$ (b) There is no gap between $A$ and $B$ on $M_2$

**Fig. 4.** Makespan derivation from the state

The first step of the DP algorithm is to sort jobs according to the JR. By Lemma 1, it follows that the optimal solution must be contained in the set of all feasible states.

Thus, the optimal state can be derived from Eq. (7), and the optimal solution can be obtained by backtracking from this optimal state.

$$\min_{u_1,u_2,v_1,v_2} \{\max\{v_1 + u_2, t + v_2\} | f_n(u_1, u_2, v_1, v_2) \leq s\} \tag{7}$$

### 4.2 FPTAS

To derive an FPTAS for problem $F2|nr-a(M_1)|C_{\max}$(hereafter referred to as P for simplicity), we use the well-known rounding technique. Denote $OPT$ as the optimal makespan of problem P. Let $LB$ and $UB$ denote the lower and upper bound of the problem P, respectively, where $UB$ specifically corresponds to the makespan generated by the algorithm proposed by Hadda et al. [5] and satisfies $UB \leq \frac{3}{2}OPT$.

**Lemma 7.** *If $LB = max\{a(N)+d, b(N), t, C_{JR}\}$, then $LB \geq \frac{1}{2}OPT$.*

For a given instance of problem P and fixed $\varepsilon > 0$, we define $\delta = \frac{LB}{n+2}\varepsilon$, and $LB = max\{a(N)+d, b(N), t, C_{JR}\}$. Clearly, $UB \leq 3LB$.

Introduce problem $\mathrm{P}^0$ as problem P, with the processing times defined as

$$d^0 = \lfloor d/\delta \rfloor,\ a_i^0 = \lfloor a_i/\delta \rfloor,\ b_i^0 = \lfloor b_i/\delta \rfloor,\ s^0 = \lfloor s/\delta \rfloor,\ t^0 = \lfloor t/\delta \rfloor \quad i = 1, \ldots, n \quad (8)$$

Let $V^0$ denote the upper bound of the problem $\mathrm{P}^0$. We have:

$$\lceil \frac{UB}{\delta} \rceil \leq \lceil \frac{3LB}{\delta} \rceil \leq \lceil \frac{3(n+2)}{\varepsilon} \rceil := V^0$$

By incorporating the rounded values into the DP, we derive the transition equation for the rounding-based DP as follows:

$$f_i = \min \begin{cases} f_{i-1}(u_1 - a_i^0, u_2, v_1 - b_i^0, v_2) + a_i, & \text{if} \quad u_1 + b_i^0 \leq v_1, \quad (a) \\ f_{i-1}(u_1, u_2 - b_i^0, v_1, v_2 - b_i^0), & \text{if} \quad a(N_i^0) - u_1 + b_i^0 \leq v_2, \quad (b) \\ +\infty, & \text{otherwise.} \end{cases}$$

where $N_i^0 = (J_1^0, \ldots, J_i^0)$; $i \in [1, n]$; $u_1 \in [0, V^0]$; $u_2 \in [0, V^0]$; $v_1 \in [u_1, V^0]$; $v_2 \in [u_2, V^0]$.

When $u_1 + b_i^0 \leq v_1$, we adopt $a_i$ instead of $a_i^0$ to ensure that $f_n(u_1, u_2, v_1, v_2) \leq s$ is still satisfied when the rounded schedule is converted back to the original problem.

**Algorithm FP:**

**Step** 0. Given an $\varepsilon > 0$, renumber jobs by JR.

**Step** 1. Define the instance of problem $\mathrm{P}^0$ by (8).

**Step** 2. For problem $\mathrm{P}^0$, run the rounding-based DP algorithm.

**Step** 3. Get the minimum makespan by (7); Construct optimal permutation $\pi^0$ by backtracking. Call the resulting makespan $C_{max}^0(\pi^0)$.

**Step** 4. Process the jobs from the original instance of problem P according to the permutation $\pi^0$, provided that each operation starts as early as possible. Call the resulting makespan $C_{max}(\pi^0)$. Stop.

**Theorem 2.** *For problem $F2|nr-a(M_1)|C_{\max}$, Algorithm FP is an FPTAS.*

*Proof.* Given an instance of problem $F2|nr-a(M_1)|C_{\max}$, introduce problem P$'$ with the processing times $a_i'$ and $b_i'$ defined as

$$d' = d/\delta,\quad a_i' = a_i/\delta,\quad b_i' = b_i/\delta,\quad s' = s/\delta,\quad t' = t/\delta,\quad i = 1,\ldots,n \tag{9}$$

Let $\pi^*$ be the optimal permutation for problem P.

Firstly, let $C'_{max}(\pi^0)$ be the makespan that process the jobs from the instance of problem P$'$ according to the permutation $\pi^0$. By definition and the scaling property, we have:

$$C_{max}(\pi^0) = \delta C'_{max}(\pi^0) \tag{10}$$

Secondly, as the processing time error for each job is at most 1, encompassing $n+1$ operations and 1 unavailable interval, we have:

$$C'_{max}(\pi^0) \le C^0_{max}(\pi^0) + n + 2 \tag{11}$$

Thirdly, let $C^0_{max}(\pi^*)$ be the makespan that processes the jobs from the instance of problem P$^0$ according to the permutation $\pi^*$. Due to the optimality of $\pi^0$ for P$^0$, we have:

$$C^0_{max}(\pi^0) \le C^0_{max}(\pi^*) \tag{12}$$

Fourthly, by the scaling and rounding property, we have:

$$C^0_{max}(\pi^*) \le C_{max}(\pi^*)/\delta \tag{13}$$

By (10)–(13), we have:

$$\begin{aligned}
C_{max}(\pi^0) &= \delta(C'_{max}(\pi^0)) && \textit{by}\ (10)\\
&\le \delta(C^0_{max}(\pi^0) + (n+2)) && \textit{by}\ (11)\\
&\le \delta(C^0_{max}(\pi^*) + (n+2)) && \textit{by}\ (12)\\
&\le C_{max}(\pi^*) + (n+2)\delta && \textit{by}\ (13)\\
&\le C_{max}(\pi^*) + \varepsilon LB\\
&\le (1+\varepsilon)C_{max}(\pi^*)
\end{aligned}$$

**Time Complexity Analysis.** For problem P$^0$, there are $O(n(V^0)^4)$ distinct states $(i, u_1, u_2, v_1, v_2)$. When $V^0 = \lceil\frac{3(n+2)}{\varepsilon}\rceil$, the overall time complexity is $O\left(\frac{n^5}{\varepsilon^4}\right)$. □

## 5 Conclusion

In this paper, we investigate the non-resumable scheduling model with one non-availability interval on the first machine. We propose an efficient approximation algorithm with a relative worst-case performance ratio of 7/5, as well as the first fully polynomial-time approximation scheme (FPTAS). For future research, we aim to design a 4/3-approximation algorithm with time complexity $O(n\log n)$ for $F2|nr-a(M_1)|C_{max}$.

## References


1. Breit, J.: An improved approximation algorithm for two-machine flow shop scheduling with an availability constraint. Inf. Process. Lett. **90**(6), 273–278 (2004)
2. Breit, J., Schmidt, G., Strusevich, V.A.: Two-machine open shop scheduling with an availability constraint. Oper. Res. Lett. **29**(2), 65–77 (2001)
3. Breit, J., Schmidt, G., Strusevich, V.A.: Non-preemptive two-machine open shop scheduling with non-availability constraints. Math. Methods Oper. Res. **57**(2), 217–234 (2003)
4. Cheng, T.E., Wang, G.: An improved heuristic for two-machine flowshop scheduling with an availability constraint. Oper. Res. Lett. **26**(5), 223–229 (2000)
5. Hadda, H., Dridi, N., Hajri-Gabouj, S.: An improved heuristic for two-machine flow shop scheduling with an availability constraint and nonresumable jobs. 4OR **8**(1), 87–99 (2010)
6. Johnson, S.M.: Optimal two- and three-stage production schedules with setup times included. Nav. Res. Logist. 61–68 (1954)
7. Kubzin, M.A., Potts, C.N., Strusevich, V.A.: Approximation results for flow shop scheduling problems with machine availability constraints. Comput. Oper. Res. **36**(2), 379–390 (2009)
8. Kubzin, M.A., Strusevich, V.A., Breit, J., Schmidt, G.: Polynomial-time approximation schemes for two-machine open shop scheduling with nonavailability constraints. Nav. Res. Logist. **53**(1), 16–23 (2006)
9. Lee, C.Y.: Machine scheduling with an availability constraint. J. Global Optim. **9**(3–4), 395–416 (1996)
10. Lee, C.Y.: Minimizing the makespan in the two-machine flowshop scheduling problem with an availability constraint. Oper. Res. Lett. **20**(3), 129–139 (1997)
11. Lee, C.Y.: Two-machine flowshop scheduling with availability constraints. Eur. J. Oper. Res. **114**(2), 420–429 (1999)
12. Lorigeon, T., Billaut, J., Bouquard, J.: A dynamic programming algorithm for scheduling jobs in a two-machine open shop with an availability constraint. J. Oper. Res. Soc. **53**(11), 1239–1246 (2002)
13. Ng, C., Kovalyov, M.Y.: An FPTAS for scheduling a two-machine flowshop with one unavailability interval. Nav. Res. Logist. **51**(3), 307–315 (2004)
14. Yuan, Y., Lan, Y., Ding, N., Han, X.: A PTAS for non-resumable open shop scheduling with an availability constraint. J. Comb. Optim. **43**(2), 350–362 (2022)

# Algorithms and Bounds for Path Covers of Tree-Structured Graphs

Madhura Dutta[1,2(✉)], Florent Foucaud[3], and Subhas C. Nandy[4]

[1] TCG CREST, Kolkata 700091, India
[2] Academy of Scientific and Innovative Research (AcSIR), Ghaziabad 201002, India
madhura1998kkg@gmail.com
[3] Université Clermont Auvergne, CNRS, Clermont Auvergne INP, Mines Saint-Étienne, LIMOS, 63000 Clermont-Ferrand, France
[4] Dhirubhai Ambani University, Gandhinagar 382007, India

**Abstract.** The path cover problem is a natural graph covering problem that generalizes the Hamiltonian path problem. Given an input graph, it requires to find a minimum-size set of (not necessarily disjoint) paths that cover all the vertices of the graph. In this paper, we give two lower bounds for the path cover number in general graphs and show that they are tight for some graph classes. The second bound uses block-cut trees, a structure that highlights the tree-likeness of the graph. For outerplanar graphs, we use block-cut trees to design a linear-time algorithm for the path cover problem. There already exists a polynomial-time algorithm based on dynamic programming over a tree-decomposition [Foucaud et al., CALDAM 2025] that provides a polynomial-time algorithm for outerplanar graphs, but the exponent is huge.

**Keywords:** Path cover · block-cut tree · outerplanar graph

## 1 Introduction

In the context of graph algorithms, the aim of covering problems is to fully or partially cover the vertices or edges of a given graph. In the case of path covering problems, the graph is required to be covered via paths. (We will use the term *path* to denote simple paths only.) For a given simple undirected graph $G = (V, E)$, in the *path cover problem*, it is asked to find a minimum sized set of paths such that each vertex of the graph lies on at least one path in this set. The cardinality of a minimum path cover is called the *path cover number* of the graph. The case when the paths are required to be vertex-disjoint is called the *path partition problem*. Though this version is also termed as path cover

M. Dutta—Supported by DST INSPIRE PhD Fellowship.
F. Foucaud—This author was supported by the French government IDEX-ISITE initiative 16-IDEX-0001 (CAP 20–25), the International Research Center "Innovation Transportation and Production Systems" of the I-SITE CAP 20–25, by the ANR project GRALMECO (ANR-21-CE48-0004) and by the CNRS IRL ReLaX.


Y. Li et al. (Eds.): COCOON 2026, LNCS 16835, pp. 231–244, 2027.
https://doi.org/10.1007/978-981-92-3309-0_18

in some papers, we reserve the name path partition for vertex-disjoint path cover throughout our work. Here, by the term path cover we will always mean a collection of paths (which need not be vertex-disjoint) that cover all the vertices of the graph (adopting the notation of [17]).

**Definition 1.** *Given a graph $G = (V, E)$, a* path cover *is a set $\mathcal{P}$ of paths in $G$ (not necessarily vertex disjoint) such that for every vertex $v \in V$ there exists a path $P \in \mathcal{P}$ containing $v$. The cardinality of a minimum-size path cover is called the* path cover number *of the graph and is denoted by $\pi_c(G)$.*

We give lower bounds for the path cover number for arbitrary graphs and identify some graph classes that reach these bounds. The class of outerplanar graphs is a well-studied tree-like graph class, where the path cover number can be strictly larger than our given bounds. Our aim is to study the computational complexity of the path cover problem in this class from an algorithmic perspective. We use the concept of *block-cut tree* to provide one lower bound and to design an algorithm.

*Related Work.* Although the path partition problem has been extensively studied in the literature, the path cover problem is less explored. There are numerous applications of the path cover and path partition problems in software testing, bio-informatics, code optimization, database design, VLSI design, and parallel architecture [1,4,18]. The decision version of the path cover problem is NP-complete by reduction from the Hamiltonian path problem. Hence, the path cover problem is NP-hard for all the graph classes for which the Hamiltonian path problem is so, for example planar graphs, chordal graphs, bipartite graphs, chordal bipartite graphs, strongly chordal graphs, etc. [17]. There exist polynomial-time algorithms for the path cover problem for trees and graphs with bounded treewidth [12], block graphs [10] and cographs [16]. For graphs of bounded treewidth at most $t$, the algorithm from [12] runs in time $n^{(10t)!}$ (which places it in the XP complexity class when parameterized by $t$) and it is suspected in [12] that perhaps no algorithm running in time $f(t)n^{O(1)}$ (that is, in FPT time for parameter $t$) exists, but this remains open.

The path cover problem for directed acyclic graphs has been explored in [4]. The version in which the edges of the graph are to be covered has also been explored, where upper bounds on the minimum number of paths have been studied [7]. For covering all the edges of a graph with a minimum number of paths (not necessarily edge-disjoint), some bounds have been given in [13] using the cycle rank of the graph. Other variants of path cover, such as induced path cover [8], isometric path cover [9], identifying path cover [11], etc., have been studied, see the survey [17]. The path partition problem is well-studied in the literature [15,17,19,20,23], including for outerplanar graphs [21].

*Our Results.* In this paper, we first give a lower bound for the path cover number for arbitrary graphs and characterize some graphs for which this lower bound is tight. Although several bounds on path partition were studied, the path cover problem has not been explored much in this regard. In [10], some lower bounds on path cover number were studied for some specific graph classes, using the notion of scattering number of a graph. We give another lower bound for the path cover number for general graphs using the block-cut tree structure. Similar ideas have been used in the PhD thesis [10] to provide an algorithm for solving the path cover problem in block graphs.

In [12], polynomial-time algorithms of the path cover problem for trees and bounded treewidth graphs were studied. Since outerplanar graphs have treewidth at most 2, the results of [12] provide a polynomial-time algorithm to solve the path cover problem for this class. But the time complexity of that algorithm is very high: $n^{t^{O(t)}}$, where $t$ is the treewidth. We give a linear-time algorithm for the path cover problem on outerplanar graphs using the properties of block-cut trees and biconnected outerplanar graphs.

*Preliminaries.* Let $G = (V, E)$ be a simple undirected connected graph.

A *cut-vertex* of $G$ is a vertex $v$ of $G$ such that deleting it (and its incident edges) will result in at least two non-empty disjoint connected components. These obtained connected components are known as *cut components* for $v$.

Assume $U = \{u_1, u_2, \ldots, u_k\} \subset V$ (where $k < n = |V|$) is the set of all cut-vertices of $G$; hence $deg(u_i) \geq 2$ for all $i \in \{1, 2, \ldots, k\}$, where $deg(u_i)$ denotes the degree of the vertex $u_i$ (i.e., the number of vertices adjacent to $u_i$ in $G$). We use $\rho(u_i)$ to denote the number of cut components for $u_i$.

*Block-cut Tree of a Graph.* A *block*, also known as a *biconnected component*, of a graph $G$ is a maximal biconnected subgraph of $G$. Let $G = (V, E)$ be a connected graph. Observe that two blocks of $G$ can share at most one common vertex, which is a cut-vertex. Using this observation, we construct a tree $T_G = (V_T, E_T)$, called the *block-cut tree* of the graph $G$, as follows (See Fig. 1):

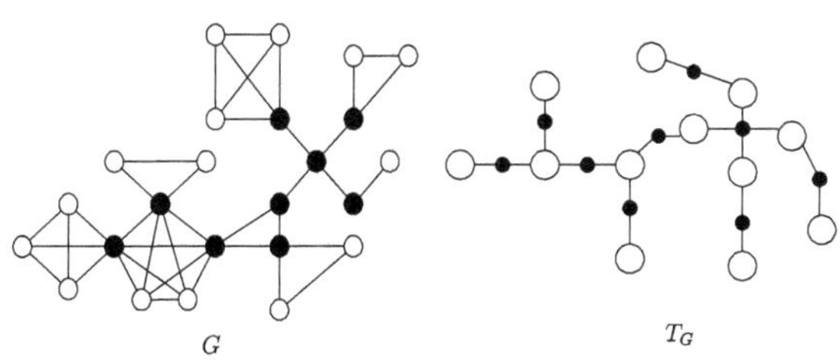


**Fig. 1.** A graph $G$ and its block-cut tree $T_G$

(i) For every block $B_i$ of $G$, create a vertex $b_i \in V_T$. Note that a cut edge (i.e., an edge not contained in any cycle) of $G$ will also be considered by us as a block.
(ii) For every cut-vertex $u_i$ of $G$, we create a vertex $\tilde{u}_i \in V_T$.
(iii) Whenever two blocks $B_i$ and $B_j$ share a common cut-vertex $u_l \in V$, we put two edges $(b_i, \tilde{u}_l), (b_j, \tilde{u}_l) \in E_T$.

Block-cut trees have been well-studied in the literature [3,5,14].

**Lemma 2** ([14]). *A block-cut tree of a connected graph can be constructed in linear time.*

## 2 Lower Bounds for General Graphs

Let $G$ be a connected graph, $U$ and $\rho(u_i)$ are as defined earlier. Observe that at least one path $P$ (say) is required to cover the vertices of $G$. Hence, $\pi_c(G) \geq 1$. Now, each vertex of $U$ may be covered by this path. But then for a fixed $u_i$ in this path $P$, the vertex preceding $u_i$ and post $u_i$ will lie in at most two different components among the $\rho(u_i)$ components corresponding to $u_i$. So, the path $P$ can cover the vertices of at most two components among the $\rho(u_i)$ components corresponding to each $u_i$. So, there are still at least $\sum_{i=1}^{k}\{\rho(u_i) - 2\}$ vertices which are not covered by $P$. This indicates the following result:

**Lemma 3.** *Let $P'$ be a path of $G$. Then there are at least $\sum_{i=1}^{k}\{\rho(u_i) - 2\}$ vertices of $G$ that are not covered by $P'$.*

*Proof.* For a cut-vertex $u_i \in U$ and a path $P'$ in $G$, $P'$ intersects at most two components corresponding to $u_i$. Since the only cut-vertices of $G$ are $u_1, u_2, \ldots, u_k$, the result follows. □

The above lemma gives a lower bound on the path cover number as follows.

**Theorem 4.** *For any graph $G$, we must have $\pi_c(G) \geq 1 + \left\lceil \frac{\sum_{i=1}^{k}\{\rho(u_i)-2\}}{2} \right\rceil$.*

*Proof.* Let $P_1, P_2, \ldots, P_\beta$ be a path cover of $G$. By Lemma 3, at least $\sum_{i=1}^{k}\{\rho(u_i)$ $-2\}$ vertices, which all belong to different blocks of $G$, are not covered by $P_1$. Note that any other path $P_i$, $i > 1$, may cover vertices from at most two distinct blocks among these $\sum_{i=1}^{k}\{\rho(u_i) - 2\}$ blocks in $G$. Hence, in order to cover the vertices uncovered by $P_1$, we need at least $\left\lceil \frac{\sum_{i=1}^{k}\{\rho(u_i)-2\}}{2} \right\rceil \leq \beta - 1$ additional paths, and the result follows. □

### 2.1 Graphs Attaining the Lower Bound

Now, we study some graph classes for which the path cover number is equal to the lower bound given in Theorem 4. We know that a graph $G$ has a Hamiltonian path if and only if $\pi_c(G) = 1$. So, from Theorem 4, we have the following.

**Proposition 5.** *Any graph with a Hamiltonian path reaches the bound.*

Next, consider the class of trees. From [12], we already know the following result.

**Theorem 6** ([12]). *An optimal path cover of a tree with $\ell$ leaves can be found in linear time and it has size $\lceil \frac{\ell}{2} \rceil$.*

The proof of the fact that the size of a minimum path cover of a tree is $\lceil \frac{\ell}{2} \rceil$ was earlier shown in [13].

Here, we show that for a tree, the path cover number is equal to the lower bound.

**Proposition 7.** *Let $T$ be a tree with $n$ vertices, among which there are $\ell$ leaves. Then we have $\lceil \frac{\ell}{2} \rceil = \pi_c(T) = 1 + \lceil \frac{\sum_{i=1}^{k} \{\rho(u_i)-2\}}{2} \rceil$, where $U = \{u_1, \ldots, u_k\}$ is the set of all cut-vertices of the tree $T$.*

*Proof.* Since $T$ is a tree with $n$ vertices and $\ell$ leaves, all $n - \ell$ non-leaf vertices are cut-vertices; thus $k = n - \ell$. Also, $\rho(u_i) = deg(u_i)$ for all $u_i \in U$.

Now, $2(n-1) = \ell + \sum_{i=1}^{k} deg(u_i) \implies 2n - 2 = n - k + \sum_{i=1}^{k} \rho(u_i)$
$\implies n - k - 2 = -2k + \sum_{i=1}^{k} \rho(u_i) \implies \ell - 2 = \sum_{i=1}^{k} \{\rho(u_i) - 2\}$
$\implies \lceil \frac{\ell}{2} - 1 \rceil = \lceil \frac{\sum_{i=1}^{k} \{\rho(u_i)-2\}}{2} \rceil \implies \lceil \frac{\ell}{2} \rceil = 1 + \lceil \frac{\sum_{i=1}^{k} \{\rho(u_i)-2\}}{2} \rceil$ □

**Proposition 8.** *Let $T_G$ be the block-cut tree of a connected graph $G$. If each block of $G$ contains at most two cut vertices, each block containing two cut vertices has a path between its two cut vertices that covers all other vertices of that block, and each block containing one cut vertex has a path starting at the cut vertex and covering all other vertices of that block, then the graph $G$ reaches the lower bound given in Theorem 4.*

*Proof.* By Theorem 6, there is an optimal path cover $\mathcal{P}^T$ of $T_G$ of size $\lceil \frac{\ell}{2} \rceil$, where $\ell$ is the number of leaves of $T_G$.

Note that there is a path associated to each block of $G$ that covers all the vertices of that block. These associated paths have one or both endpoints at the cut-vertices depending on whether the corresponding blocks contain one or two cut vertices. For each path of $\mathcal{P}^T$, construct a path in $G$ by following its trajectory, replacing the $\tilde{u}_i$'s by the corresponding cut vertex $u_i$'s and the $b_j$'s by the path associated to the corresponding block $B_j$'s. Thus, we obtain a path cover of $G$ of size $\lceil \frac{\ell}{2} \rceil$.

Let $deg_H(v)$ denote the degree of the vertex $v$ in the graph $H$. Then, using the notations from the definition of a block-cut tree $T_G$, we have
$\sum_{v \in V_T} deg_{T_G}(v) = 2(|V_T| - 1) = \ell + \sum_{i=1}^{k} deg_{T_G}(\tilde{u}_i) + 2(|V_T| - \ell - k)$
$\implies \ell = 2 + \sum_{i=1}^{k} \{deg_{T_G}(\tilde{u}_i) - 2\} \implies \ell = 2 + \sum_{i=1}^{k} \{\rho(u_i) - 2\}$
$\implies \lceil \frac{\ell}{2} \rceil = 1 + \lceil \frac{\sum_{i=1}^{k} \{\rho(u_i)-2\}}{2} \rceil$
Hence, the result follows. □

*Remark 9.* There exist graphs for which the path cover number is strictly larger than the bound of Theorem 4. For an example, consider the block graph $G$ in Fig. 2; here $\pi_c(G) = 3 > 2 = 1 + \lceil \frac{2+0+0}{2} \rceil$.

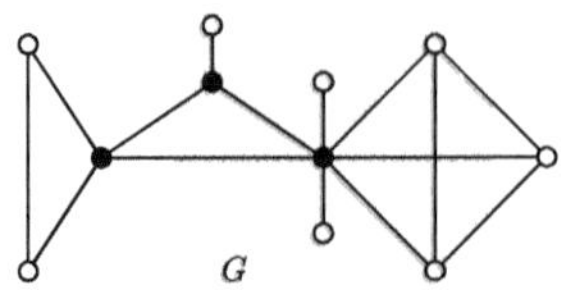


**Fig. 2.** A graph $G$ with $\pi_c(G) = 3$.

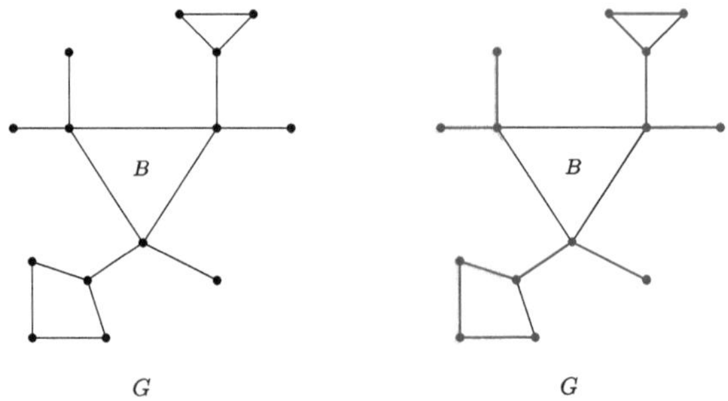


**Fig. 3.** For the graph $G$, no edge of its block $B$ is covered by the optimal path cover shown by blue paths. (Color figure online)

### 2.2 Lower Bound for General Graphs Using Their Block-Cut Tree

Let $G$ be a connected graph with block-cut tree $T_G$. Then we have the following.

**Lemma 10.** $\pi_c(T_G) \leq \pi_c(G)$.

*Proof.* Let $\mathcal{P}$ be an optimal path cover of $G$. Any path of $\mathcal{P}$ may or may not cover all the edges of the block(s) in which its two endpoints lie. We first modify the paths of $\mathcal{P}$ to construct another optimal path cover $\mathcal{P}'$ such that each path of $\mathcal{P}'$ covers at least one edge of the block(s) in which its two endpoints lie.

Now, consider the blocks in $G$. For a block of $G$, the paths in $\mathcal{P}'$ may cover some edges of it or may not cover any edge of the block (See Fig. 3). We first find all those blocks in $G$ for which no edge is covered by the paths of $\mathcal{P}'$. Note that all the vertices of such a block must be cut vertices. Let $(u_i, u_j)$ be an edge of such a block. Since $\mathcal{P}'$ is a path cover, the vertices $u_i$ and $u_j$ will be covered by at least two different paths $P'_1(= P'_{1_l} u_i P'_{1_r}), P'_2(= P'_{2_l} u_j P'_{2_r})$ (say) of $\mathcal{P}'$. We can modify the paths $P'_1, P'_2$ to obtain two new paths $P''_1 = P'_{1_l} u_i u_j P'_{2_l}$ and $P''_2 = P'_{1_r} u_i u_j P'_{2_r}$ so that the paths $P''_1, P''_2$ cover all the vertices and edges covered by $P'_1, P'_2$ as well as the edge $(u_i, u_j)$ (See Fig. 4). Using this method a linear number of times, we construct another optimal path cover $\mathcal{P}''$ such that the paths in $\mathcal{P}''$ cover at least one edge of the block(s) in which their endpoints lie, as well as cover at least one edge of each block of $G$.

From this optimal path cover $\mathcal{P}''$ of $G$, we construct a path cover of $T_G$. A path $P_G$ of $\mathcal{P}''$ starts at some block $B_{x_1}$ of $G$, covers some vertices of that block, and enters into another block $B_{x_2}$ (say) through a cut vertex $u_{x_1 x_2}$ (say) which is shared by $B_{x_1}$ and $B_{x_2}$, and continues similarly. It finally ends at some

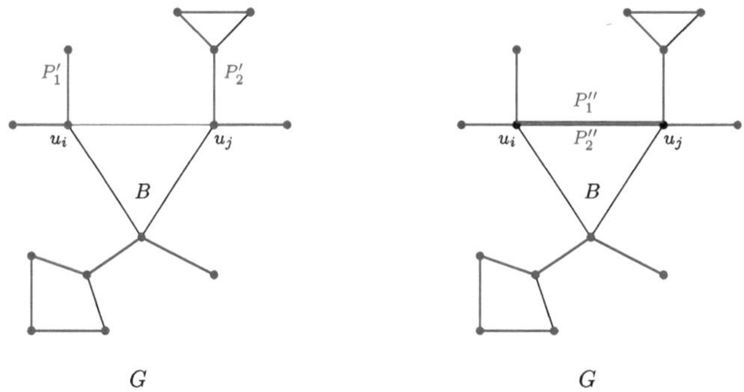


**Fig. 4.** The modified paths $P_1''$ (in green) and $P_2''$ (in brown) cover the edge $(u_i, u_j)$. (Color figure online)

block $B_{x_y}$ covering some vertices of this block. For such a path $P_G$, we get a corresponding path $b_{x_1}\tilde{u}_{x_1x_2}b_{x_2}\dots b_{x_y}$ in $T_G$ by following the trajectory of $P_G$ in $G$. Thus, we get a set $\mathcal{P}_T$ (say) of $|\mathcal{P}''| = \pi_c(G)$ many paths in $T_G$. Due to the construction procedure of $\mathcal{P}''$, the paths of $\mathcal{P}_T$ will cover all the vertices of $T_G$. □

Lemma 10 gives a lower bound for the path cover number in general graphs.

**Theorem 11.** *For a graph $G = (V, E)$, if $T_G$ is its block-cut tree and $\ell$ is the number of leaves of $T_G$, then $\pi_c(G) \geq \lceil \frac{\ell}{2} \rceil$.*

A graph is called a *block graph* if each of its blocks is a clique. The path cover number is equal to the lower bound given in Theorem 11 for trees, graphs having a Hamiltonian path, and block graphs (the latter can be deduced from analyzing the PhD thesis [10]). The sketch of an algorithm to find a minimum path cover of a block graph was also given in [10]. Analyzing this algorithm shows that it runs in linear time.

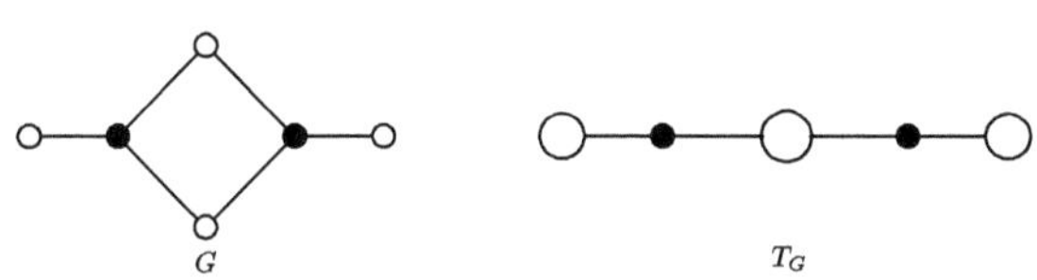


**Fig. 5.** A graph with path cover number strictly greater than the lower bound given using the block-cut tree.

*Remark 12.* There are graphs with path cover number strictly greater than the lower bound given in Theorem 11. See Fig. 5, where $\pi_c(G)(= 2) > 1 = \lceil \frac{\ell}{2} \rceil$, where $\ell$ is the number of leaves of the block-cut tree of the graph $G$.

# 3 A Linear-Time Algorithm for Outerplanar Graphs

We now show that block-cut trees can also lead to a linear-time algorithm to determine optimal path covers of outerplanar graphs. The algorithm is more involved than the one for block graphs [10], because the path cover number of an outerplanar graph is not necessarily equal to the one of its block-cut tree, as seen in Fig. 5.

## 3.1 Lower Bound for Path Cover Number in Outerplanar Graphs

Let $G = (V, E)$ be a connected outerplanar graph. We can construct the block-cut tree $T_G$ of the graph $G$ in linear time using Lemma 2. Let us call the vertices of $T_G$ that correspond to the blocks in $G$ the *block vertices.*

We distinguish between three types of block vertices in $T_G$, namely (i) degree 1 block vertices; we call them leaf block vertices, (ii) degree 2 block vertices, and (iii) degree $> 2$ block vertices. The corresponding blocks of types (i), (ii), and (iii) in $G$ are called Type-1 blocks (or leaf blocks), Type-2 blocks, and Type-3 blocks, respectively. The vertices of $T_G$ corresponding to the cut vertices of $G$ are called (with slight abuse of the nomenclature) cut tree vertices.

Each Type-2 block in $G$ has exactly two cut vertices. For each such block, we check whether there exists a path that covers all the vertices of that block and whose endpoints are the two cut vertices of that block. If no such path exists for a Type-2 block, we mark that block as a special block. The corresponding degree 2 block vertex in $T_G$ is called a special block vertex. Since each Type-2 block of $G$ is a biconnected outerplanar graph $G'$, finding the mentioned path is equivalent to finding a Hamiltonian path of $G'$ with two specified endpoints, which can be done in linear time using standard treewidth-based techniques [2,6], as outerplanar graphs have treewidth at most 2. Hence, finding all special blocks of $G$ can be done in linear time.

**Construction of the Tree $\tilde{T}_G$ from the Block-cut Tree $T_G$:** From each leaf block vertex of $T_G$, move towards the interior of the tree $T_G$ following the path consisting of only the degree 2 cut tree vertices and the degree 2 block vertices (excluding the special block vertices). This process will lead to encounter exactly one of the following four cases: (i) a degree $> 2$ block vertex, (ii) a degree $> 2$ cut tree vertex, (iii) a special block vertex, or (iv) another leaf block vertex. Stop when for the first time one of these four cases is encountered. If in this process, while stopping, case (iii) i.e., a special block vertex is encountered, then we name that special block vertex a bad block vertex. So, in linear time, we can find all bad block vertices[1]. Then, in $T_G$, a dummy leaf vertex is added to each bad block vertex. The tree obtained after adding all the dummy leaf vertices is called $\tilde{T}_G$ (See Fig. 6 for an example).

**Lemma 13.** $\pi_c(G) \geq \pi_c(\tilde{T}_G)$.

[1] After this process, there may remain special block vertices that are not bad. So, every bad block vertex is special, but in general the converse need not be true.

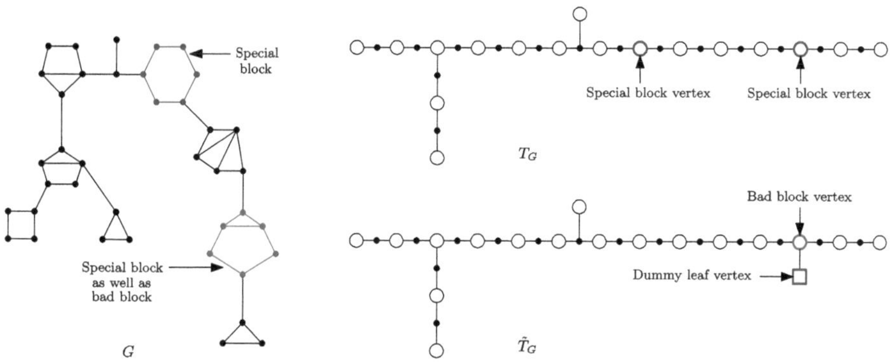


**Fig. 6.** An outerplanar graph $G$, its block cut tree $T_G$ and its corresponding $\tilde{T}_G$. (Color figure online)

*Proof.* Given an optimal path cover of $G$, we will construct a path cover of $\tilde{T}_G$ of the same size. Let $\mathcal{P}$ be an optimal path cover of $G$. By the method used in the proof of Lemma 10, we construct another optimal path cover $\mathcal{P}''$ of $G$ such that the paths in $\mathcal{P}''$ cover at least one edge of the block(s) in which their endpoints lie, as well as cover at least one edge of each block of $G$.

From $\mathcal{P}''$, we will construct a path cover of $\tilde{T}_G$ consisting of $|\mathcal{P}''| = |\mathcal{P}|$ many paths. A path $P_G \in \mathcal{P}''$ begins from some block $B_{x_1}$ of $G$, covers some vertices of that block, and enters into another block $B_{x_2}$ (say) through a cut vertex $u_{x_1x_2}$ (say) which is shared by $B_{x_1}$ and $B_{x_2}$, and continues in a similar way. It ends at some block $B_{x_y}$ after covering some vertices of this block. For such a path $P_G$, a corresponding path $b_{x_1}\tilde{u}_{x_1x_2}b_{x_2}\dots b_{x_y}$ in $\tilde{T}_G$ is constructed by following the trajectory of $P_G$ in $G$. In this manner, we obtain a set $\tilde{\mathcal{P}}_T$ (say) of $|\mathcal{P}''| = \pi_c(G)$ number of paths in $\tilde{T}_G$. The properties of $\mathcal{P}''$ ensure that the paths of $\tilde{\mathcal{P}}_T$ will cover all the vertices of $\tilde{T}_G$ except the dummy leaf vertices.

For a dummy leaf vertex, consider its corresponding bad block vertex. If there is a path in $\tilde{\mathcal{P}}_T$ whose one endpoint is this bad block vertex, we extend that path to cover the dummy leaf vertex. Otherwise, due to the definition of bad block, there exist at least two paths in $\tilde{\mathcal{P}}_T$ passing through the bad block vertex. One of these paths can be extended to cover the branch of $\tilde{T}_G$ emerging from the bad block vertex containing only one leaf block vertex, and the other path can be extended to cover the dummy leaf vertex[2]. Thus, we get a set of $\pi_c(G)$ number of paths in $\tilde{T}_G$ which cover all the vertices of $\tilde{T}_G$. Hence, the result follows. □

[2] Note that in $\tilde{T}_G$, the bad block vertex has three branches emerging from it; one containing only the dummy leaf vertex, one containing only one leaf block vertex, and another containing one or more leaf block vertices.

### 3.2 The Algorithm

An optimal path cover of a connected outerplanar graph $G$ is computed in two steps: (i) Finding an optimal path cover of $\tilde{T}_G$ satisfying some required properties and (ii) Constructing a path cover of $G$ from the computed path cover of $\tilde{T}_G$.

**(i) Optimal Path Cover of $\tilde{T}_G$:** Without loss of generality, assume that $\tilde{T}_G$ contains at least two vertices of degree $\geq 3$. From each leaf vertex of $\tilde{T}_G$[3], move towards the interior of $\tilde{T}_G$ through the path consisting of only degree 2 vertices of $\tilde{T}_G$ and stop as soon as a vertex of degree $\geq 3$ is encountered. Label this degree $\geq 3$ vertex as truncating vertex. In linear time, all the truncating vertices can be found. Also, find a truncating vertex having the least degree in $\tilde{T}_G$ among all truncating vertices; and name it special truncating vertex.

Consider all the branches of $\tilde{T}_G$ emerging from a truncating vertex. Some of these branches contain only degree $\leq 2$ nodes, name them as truncating branches. For each truncating vertex (including the special truncating vertex), we find the corresponding truncating branches. Now, removing all the truncating branches from $\tilde{T}_G$ we obtain a tree $\mathcal{T}$ (say). Observe that a leaf of $\mathcal{T}$ is a truncating vertex of $\tilde{T}_G$ and vice versa. Now, there are two cases:

*Case-1: The number of leaves of $\mathcal{T}$ is odd:* In this case, consider the leaf of $\mathcal{T}$ which was the special truncating vertex of $\tilde{T}_G$. In $\mathcal{T}$, starting from this leaf, move towards the interior of $\mathcal{T}$ through the path consisting of only degree 2 vertices of $\mathcal{T}$ and stop as soon as a vertex with degree $\geq 3$ in $\mathcal{T}$ is encountered; name this vertex trimming branch root and the branch trimming branch. Delete this traversed branch (trimming branch) from $\mathcal{T}$. Thus, we get a subtree of $\mathcal{T}$ with even number of leaves; name it $\mathcal{T}'$.

Now, find an optimal path cover $\mathcal{C}'$ of $\mathcal{T}'$ in linear time using the algorithm from [12]. Extend the paths (if required) so that their endpoints are leaves of $\mathcal{T}'$. Let the optimal path cover thus obtained be denoted by $\mathcal{C}''$.

Now, consider the tree $\mathcal{T}$. Take two copies of each path of $\mathcal{C}''$ in $\mathcal{T}$. Since the trimming branch root has degree at least 2 in $\mathcal{T}'$, two copies of some path $P_r$ (say) of $\mathcal{C}''$ will pass through it. Take one copy of the path $P_r$, cut this path at the trimming branch root and use the two pieces to form two paths $P_{r_1}$ and $P_{r_2}$ both of which cover the trimming branch[4] (See Fig. 7 for an example of the mentioned construction for a tree $\tilde{T}_G$ where the corresponding $\mathcal{T}$ has odd number of leaves). Thus, we get a collection of $2|\mathcal{C}''| + 1$ paths such that each vertex of $\mathcal{T}$ is covered at least twice by these paths and each leaf of $\mathcal{T}$ is endpoint of exactly two paths.

*Case-2: The number of leaves of $\mathcal{T}$ is even:* In this case, find an optimal path cover $\mathcal{C}$ of $\mathcal{T}$ in linear time using the algorithm from [12]. Extend the paths (if required) so that their endpoints are leaves of $\mathcal{T}$. Let the optimal path cover thus obtained be denoted by $\mathcal{C}^*$. Take two copies of each path of $\mathcal{C}^*$. Hence, we

[3] By the leaf vertices of $\tilde{T}_G$, we mean both the original leaf vertices as well as the dummy leaf vertices of $\tilde{T}_G$.

[4] The trimming branch contains the special truncating vertex as one of its endpoint.

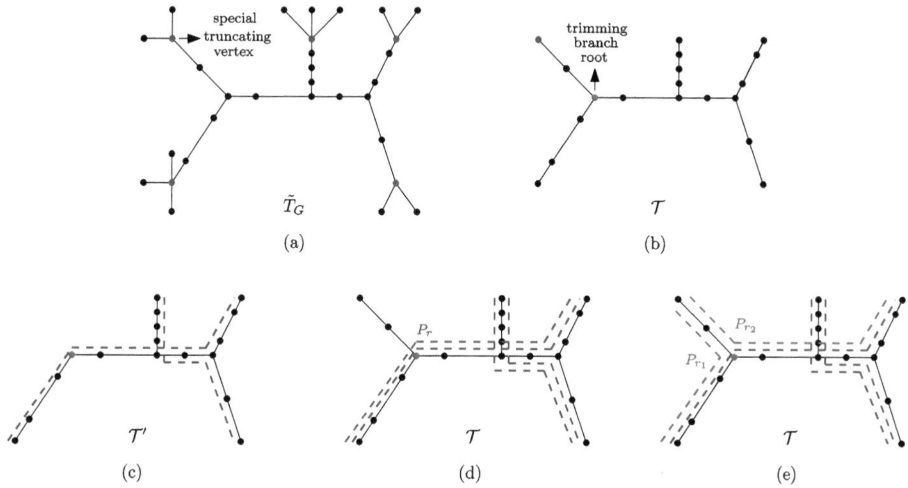


**Fig. 7.** (a) Truncating vertices (marked in blue) of a tree $\tilde{T}_G$, (b) the corresponding $\mathcal{T}$ with odd number of leaves, (c) the path cover $\mathcal{C}''$ of the corresponding $\mathcal{T}'$, (d) two copies of each path of $\mathcal{C}''$ in $\mathcal{T}$, (e) a collection of $2|\mathcal{C}''|+1$ paths that cover each vertex of $\mathcal{T}$ at least two times.(Color figure online)

obtain a collection of $2|\mathcal{C}^*|$ paths such that each vertex of $\mathcal{T}$ is covered at least twice by these paths and each leaf of $\mathcal{T}$ is endpoint of exactly two paths.

Next, in $\mathcal{T}$, add the deleted (truncating) branches to get back $\tilde{T}_G$. Extend the paths ending at each truncating vertex to cover as many of the added branches as possible. After extending all such paths, some added branches may still remain uncovered. If there are $\tilde{l}$ many uncovered branches, then they are covered by $\lceil \frac{\tilde{l}}{2} \rceil$ many paths which can be found in linear time by arbitrarily pairing any two branches and joining them by a truncating vertex when the branches correspond to the same truncating vertex, or by a path joining two truncating vertices (which exists since $\mathcal{T}$ is connected) when the branches correspond to two different truncating vertices.

Thus, the constructed collection $\mathcal{C}_{\mathcal{T}}$ (say) of $l_{\mathcal{T}} + \lceil \frac{\tilde{l}}{2} \rceil$ paths covers all the vertices of $\tilde{T}_G$, where $l_{\mathcal{T}}$ denotes the number of leaves of the tree $\mathcal{T}$. Also, $l_{\mathcal{T}} + \lceil \frac{\tilde{l}}{2} \rceil = \lceil \frac{1}{2} \cdot (\text{no. of leaves of } \tilde{T}_G) \rceil = \pi_c(\tilde{T}_G)$ by our construction. Hence, $\mathcal{C}_{\mathcal{T}}$ is an optimal path cover of $\tilde{T}_G$.

**(ii) Construction of a Path Cover of** $G$: Corresponding to each path of $\mathcal{C}_{\mathcal{T}}$ in $\tilde{T}_G$, we can get a path in $G$ by following the trajectory of the path. We want to form those paths in $G$ in such a way that all the vertices of each block of $G$ are covered. Due to the construction of $\mathcal{C}_{\mathcal{T}}$, at least two paths will pass through each special block and each Type-3 block. So, all the Type-2 blocks and leaf blocks can be covered. For Type-3 blocks, there are two cases:

*Case 1:* There are exactly three cut-vertices $u_1, u_2, u_3$ (say) on the unique Hamiltonian cycle[5] of the Type-3 block $B_i$ (say) under consideration and one path of $\mathcal{C}_T$ passing through $b_i$ traverses as $\ldots \tilde{u}_1 b_i \tilde{u}_3 \ldots$ in $\tilde{T}_G$. Then we create the corresponding path in $G$ by taking the path from $u_1$ to $u_3$ that contains $u_2$ on the unique Hamiltonian cycle (see Fig. 8(a)). The other path passing through $b_i$ covers the vertex $\tilde{u}_2$ and goes through $\tilde{u}_3$ (or $\tilde{u}_1$). In $G$, we take that path from $u_2$ to $u_3$ (or $u_1$) on the unique Hamiltonian cycle which will cover all the remaining uncovered vertices of $B_i$ (see Fig. 8(b)) as its corresponding path.

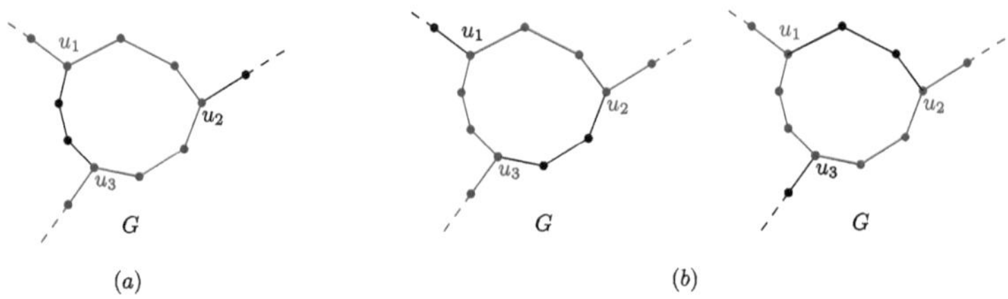


**Fig. 8.** (a) Path (marked in blue) in $G$ which corresponds to the path $\ldots \tilde{u}_1 b_i \tilde{u}_3 \ldots$ of $\tilde{T}_G$. (b) Path (marked in blue) in $G$ which corresponds to the path $\ldots \tilde{u}_2 b_i \ldots$ in the tree $\tilde{T}_G$. (Color figure online)

*Case 2:* There are at least four cut-vertices $u_1, u_2, u_3, u_4$ (say) in this order on the Hamiltonian cycle, and there are two paths in $\mathcal{C}_T$ such that each path uses two of these cut-vertices. Note that there may exist some other cut-vertices in between these four vertices. In this case there are two sub-cases, (i) if one path of $\mathcal{C}_T$ traverses as $\ldots \tilde{u}_1 b_i \tilde{u}_3 \ldots$ and another path as $\ldots \tilde{u}_2 b_i \tilde{u}_4 \ldots$ (see Fig. 9(a)), then we create two new paths $\ldots \tilde{u}_1 b_i \tilde{u}_2 \ldots$ and $\ldots \tilde{u}_3 b_i \tilde{u}_4 \ldots$ in such a way that the vertices of $\tilde{T}_G$ covered by the previous two paths and these two paths are the same. Then the corresponding paths in $G$ are created as a path from $u_1$ to $u_2$ that contains $u_4$ and $u_3$ on the unique Hamiltonian cycle and a path from $u_3$ to $u_4$ that contains $u_2$ and $u_1$ on the unique Hamiltonian cycle (see Fig. 9(b)). (ii) if one path of $\mathcal{C}_T$ traverses as $\ldots \tilde{u}_1 b_i \tilde{u}_2 \ldots$ and another path as $\ldots \tilde{u}_3 b_i \tilde{u}_4 \ldots$, then the paths in $G$ are created in the same manner (see Fig. 9(b)). Hence, we obtain a path cover of $G$ of size $|\mathcal{C}_T| = \pi_c(\tilde{T}_G)$.

**Correctness and Time Complexity of the Algorithm:** From Lemma 13, we already have $\pi_c(\tilde{T}_G) \leq \pi_c(G)$. Also, the constructed path cover of $G$ has $\pi_c(\tilde{T}_G)$ many paths. Hence, the algorithm gives a minimum path cover of $G$.

The constructions of $T_G$ from $G$ and $\tilde{T}_G$ from $T_G$ both require linear time. Finding all the truncating vertices and constructing the tree $\mathcal{T}$ can be done in linear time. Finding $l_\mathcal{T}$ many paths as described in the algorithm requires linear time irrespective of whether $\mathcal{T}$ has odd or even number of leaves. Thus, the path cover $\mathcal{C}_T$ of $\tilde{T}_G$ can be constructed in linear time. Finally, the construction of

[5] Each block of $G$ being biconnected outerplanar has a unique Hamiltonian cycle [22].

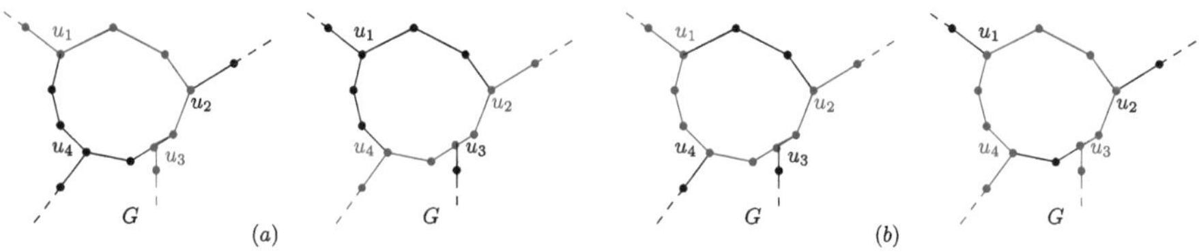


**Fig. 9.** (a) Paths (marked in blue) in $G$ which corresponds to the paths $\ldots\tilde{u}_1 b_i \tilde{u}_3\ldots$ and $\ldots\tilde{u}_2 b_i \tilde{u}_4\ldots$ of $\tilde{T}_G$, respectively. These paths do not cover all the vertices of $B_i$ in $G$. (b) Paths (marked in blue) after transforming the paths of Fig.9.(a). Here the paths correspond to $\ldots\tilde{u}_1 b_i \tilde{u}_2\ldots$ and $\ldots\tilde{u}_3 b_i \tilde{u}_4\ldots$ of the tree $\tilde{T}_G$ and covers all the vertices of $B_i$ in $G$. (Color figure online)

a path cover of $G$ from $\mathcal{C}_T$ requires linear number of steps. Hence, we have the following result.

**Theorem 14.** *An optimal path cover of an outerplanar graph can be constructed in linear time.*

## 4 Conclusion

We have studied some lower bounds for the path cover number in arbitrary graphs. Some graph classes attaining this bound have been explored. A linear-time algorithm for the path cover problem for the class of outerplanar graphs has been proposed. Improving the lower bound and exploring the path cover problem for some other graph classes is an interesting future research direction.

## References

1. Andreatta, G., Mason, F.: Path covering problems and testing of printed circuits. Discret. Appl. Math. **62**(1–3), 5–13 (1995)
2. Beisegel, J., Ratazczak, F., Scheffler, R.: Computing Hamiltonian paths with partial order restrictions. ACM Trans. Comput. Theory **17**(1(5)), 1–24 (2025)
3. Bourneuf, R., Planken, T.: A structural linear-time algorithm for computing the Tutte decomposition (2025). arXiv:2508.06212
4. Cáceres, M., Mumey, B., Toivonen, S., Tomescu, A.I.: Practical minimum path cover. In: Liberti, L., (ed.), 22nd International Symposium on Experimental Algorithms, SEA 2024, Article 3, pp. 1–19. (Leibniz International Proceedings in Informatics, LIPIcs; Vol. 301). Schloss Dagstuhl - Leibniz-Zentrum für Informatik
5. Chakraborty, D., Foucaud, F., Parreau, A., Wagler, A.K.: On three domination-based identification problems in block graphs. Fund. Inform. **191**(3–4), 197–229 (2024)
6. Cygan, M., et al.: Parameterized Algorithms. Springer Cham (2015)
7. Donald, A.: An upper bound for the path number of a graph. J. Graph Theory **4**, 189–201 (1980)
8. Fernau, H., Foucaud, F., Mann, K., Padariya, U., Rao, R.K.N: Parameterizing path partitions; Theoretical Computer Science **1028**, 115029 (2025)

9. Fisher, D.C., Fitzpatrick, S.L.: The isometric path number of a graph, J. Comb. Math. Comb. Comput. **38**, 97–110 (2001)
10. Florkowski, S.F.: Extensions of the Hamiltonian Cycle/Path Problems in Special Families of Graphs. PhD thesis, Lehigh University (2017)
11. Foucaud, F., Kovse, M.: Identifying path covers in graphs. J. Discrete Algorithms **23**, 21–34 (2013)
12. Foucaud, F., Majumder, A., Mömke, T., Roshany-Tabrizi, A.: Polynomial-time algorithms for path cover on trees and graphs of bounded treewidth. In: Proceedings of the 11th International Conference on Algorithms and Discrete Applied Mathematics (CALDAM 2025), Lecture Notes in Computer Science, vol. 15536, pp. 147–159 (2025)
13. Harary, F., Schwenk, A.: Evolution of the path number of a graph: covering and packing in graphs, II. Graph Theory Comput. 39–45 (1972)
14. Hopcroft, J.E., Tarjan, R.E.: Algorithm 447: efficient algorithms for graph manipulation. Commun. ACM **16**(6), 372–378 (1973)
15. Hung, R., Chang, M.: Solving the path cover problem on circular-arc graphs by using an approximation algorithm. Discret. Appl. Math. **154**(1), 76–105 (2006)
16. Lin, R., Olariu, S., Pruesse, G.: An optimal path cover algorithm for cographs. Comput. Math. Appl. **30**(8), 75–83 (1995)
17. Manuel, P.: Revisiting path-type covering and partitioning problems (2018). arXiv:1807.10613
18. Ntafos, S., Hakimi, S.: On path cover problems in digraphs and applications to program testing. IEEE Trans. Softw. Eng. **SE-5**(5), 520–529 (1979)
19. Pan, J., Chang, G.J.: Path partition for graphs with special blocks. Discret. Appl. Math. **145**(3), 429–436 (2005)
20. Peroche, B.: NP-completeness of some problems of partitioning and covering in graphs. Discret. Appl. Math. **8**(2), 195–208 (1984)
21. Sinkovic, J.: Maximum nullity of outerplanar graphs and the path cover number. Linear Algebra Appl. **432**(8), 2052–2060 (2010)
22. Syslo, M.: Characterizations of outerplanar graphs. Discrete Math. **26**, 47–53 (1979)
23. Yeh, H., Chang, G.J.: The path-partition problem in bipartite distance-hereditary graphs. Taiwan. J. Math. **2**(3), 353–360 (1998)

# Ordinal Ranks of $\Delta_2^0$-Measurable Functions

Guohua Wu(✉) and Jia Li Zheng

School of Physical and Mathematical Sciences, Nanyang Technological University, Singapore 637371, Singapore
guohua@ntu.edu.sg

**Abstract.** A function $f : [0, 1] \to \mathbb{R}$ is Baire one if it is the pointwise limit of a sequence of continuous functions. There are several equivalent characterizations of Baire one functions. In particular, Baire one functions are exactly the $\Sigma_2^0$-measurable functions. These equivalent characterizations led Kechris and Louveau [5] to study ordinal ranks of Baire one functions, namely the convergence, separation and oscillation ranks. In this paper, we study the discontinuity rank of $\Delta_2^0$-measurable functions, a subclass of Baire one functions. This rank was introduced by Carroy [1] when he proved the determinacy of Backtrack Games. Our main objective is to investigate the relationship between the discontinuity rank of a $\Delta_2^0$-measurable function and the associated oscillation rank. In particular, we provide conditions under which these two ranks differ. In addition, we introduce a new ordinal rank on this class of functions and show that it coincides with the discontinuity rank.

## 1 Introduction

A function $f : [0, 1] \to \mathbb{R}$ is Baire one if it is the pointwise limit of a sequence of continuous functions. Baire one functions have several equivalent characterizations, each arising from a different point of view.

**Theorem 1 (Kechris [4]).** *Let $f$ be a real-valued function on $[0, 1]$. The following are equivalent:*

*(1) $f$ is Baire one.*
*(2) $f$ is $\Sigma_2^0$-measurable, that is, $f^{-1}(U)$ is $\Sigma_2^0$ for any open set $U$.*
*(3) For any closed set $P$, the restriction $f \restriction P$ has a point of continuity.*

Throughout this paper, $\Sigma_\alpha^0$, $\Pi_\alpha^0$, and $\Delta_\alpha^0$ denote the boldface Borel pointclasses. These equivalences led Kechris and Louveau to study the ordinal ranks of Baire one functions in [5], where they considered convergence ranks, separation ranks (also called Bourgain ranks), and oscillation ranks. Following their work, Elekes, Kiss and Vidnyánszky [2] and Leung, Ng and Tang [7] extended the study of these ranks to Baire $\xi$ functions for $\xi > 1$. We briefly review Kechris and Louveau's use of ordinal ranks to characterize Baire one functions.

Wu is partially supported by MOE Tier 1 grant RG102/23.


Y. Li et al. (Eds.): COCOON 2026, LNCS 16835, pp. 245–258, 2027.
https://doi.org/10.1007/978-981-92-3309-0_19

### A. Convergence rank $\gamma(f)$

The convergence rank is defined for sequences of functions $(f_n)$, which we denote by $\hat{f}$. Fix $\epsilon > 0$, a sequence $\hat{f}$ and a closed subset $P$ of $[0,1]$. Define

$$P'_{\epsilon,\hat{f}} := \{x \in P : \text{for any open neighbourhood } U \text{ of } x \text{ and } k \in \omega, \text{there exists } y \in U \cap P \text{ and } n, m > k \text{ such that } |f_n(y) - f_m(y)| \geq \epsilon\}.$$

$P'_{\epsilon,\hat{f}}$ is obtained from $P$ by removing all the relatively open subsets $U$ of $P$ on which $\hat{f} \restriction (P \cap U)$ is $\epsilon$-uniformly convergent. Since $P'_{\epsilon,\hat{f}}$ is closed, we iterate the process and define the following sets by transfinite induction:

$$\begin{aligned} P^0_{\epsilon,\hat{f}} &= P, \\ P^{\alpha+1}_{\epsilon,\hat{f}} &= (P^{\alpha}_{\epsilon,\hat{f}})'_{\epsilon,\hat{f}}, \\ P^{\lambda}_{\epsilon,\hat{f}} &= \bigcap_{\alpha<\lambda} P^{\alpha}_{\epsilon,\hat{f}}, \qquad \text{if } \lambda \text{ is a limit ordinal.} \end{aligned}$$

Define

$$\gamma(\hat{f}, \epsilon, P) = \begin{cases} \text{the least } \alpha \text{ such that } P^{\alpha}_{\epsilon,\hat{f}} = \emptyset, & \text{if such an } \alpha \text{ exists;} \\ \omega_1, & \text{otherwise,} \end{cases}$$

and let $\gamma(\hat{f}, \epsilon) = \gamma(\hat{f}, \epsilon, [0,1])$. The convergence rank of the sequence $\hat{f}$ is defined as

$$\gamma(\hat{f}) = \sup_{\epsilon>0}\{\gamma(\hat{f}, \epsilon)\}.$$

**Proposition 1 (Kechris and Louveau [5]).** *If $\hat{f}$ is a sequence of continuous functions converging to $f$, then $\gamma(\hat{f}) < \omega_1$.*

Note that here $\gamma(\hat{f})$ depends on the given sequence $\hat{f}$. Since the convergence ranks of different sequences converging to $f$ may not coincide in general, Kechris and Louveau defined the convergence rank of $f$ as

$$\inf\{\gamma(\hat{f}) : \hat{f} \text{ is a sequence of continuous functions converging pointwise to } f\}.$$

### B. Separation rank $\alpha(f)$

By (2) of Theorem 1, for rationals $p < q$, the sets $f^{-1}(-\infty, p]$ and $f^{-1}[q, \infty)$ are disjoint $\Pi^0_2$ sets, and hence can be separated by a $\Delta^0_2$ set. Since any $\Delta^0_2$ set can be expressed as a transfinite difference of closed sets (see [4]), the separation rank provides a measure of the minimal length of such sequences. For $A = f^{-1}(-\infty, p], B = f^{-1}[q, \infty)$, and a closed set $P$, let

$$P'_{A,B} = \overline{P \cap A} \cap \overline{P \cap B}.$$

We define the following sets by transfinite induction:

$$P_{A,B}^0 = P, \quad P_{A,B}^{\alpha+1} = (P_{A,B}^{\alpha})'_{A,B},$$
$$P_{A,B}^{\lambda} = \bigcap_{\alpha<\lambda} P_{A,B}^{\alpha}, \quad \text{if } \lambda \text{ is a limit ordinal.}$$

Define

$$\alpha(P, A, B) = \begin{cases} \text{the least } \alpha \text{ such that } P_{A,B}^{\alpha} = \emptyset, \text{ if such } \alpha \text{ exists,} \\ \omega_1, \qquad\qquad\qquad\qquad \text{otherwise,} \end{cases}$$

and $\alpha(f, p, q) = \alpha([0,1], A, B)$. Define the separation rank of $f$ as

$$\alpha(f) = \sup\{\alpha(f, p, q) : p < q \in \mathbb{Q}\}.$$

**Proposition 2 (Kechris and Louveau [5]).** *A function $f$ is Baire one if and only if $\alpha(f) < \omega_1$.*

## C. Oscillation rank $\beta(f)$

The oscillation rank for Baire one functions is obtained by applying (3) of Theorem 1, which says that $f \restriction P$ has a point of continuity for any closed subset $P$. Equivalently, for any $\epsilon > 0$ and a closed set $P$, there is an open set $U$ such that for any $y, z \in U \cap P$,

$$|f(y) - f(z)| < \epsilon.$$

Fix $\epsilon > 0$, a function $f$, and a closed subset $P$ of $[0,1]$. Define

$$P'_{\epsilon,f} = \{x \in P : \text{for any open neighbourhood } U \text{ of } x,\ U \cap P \text{ contains } y, z$$
$$\text{such that } |f(y) - f(z)| \geq \epsilon\}.$$

This set is obtained from $P$ by removing all relatively open subsets $U$ of $P$ on which $f \restriction (P \cap U)$ is $\epsilon$-continuous. Since $P'_{\epsilon,f}$ is closed, we may iterate this process to define the sets $P_{\epsilon,f}^{\alpha}$ for $\alpha < \omega_1$. We then define

$$\beta(f, \epsilon, P) = \begin{cases} \text{the least } \alpha \text{ such that } P_{\epsilon,f}^{\alpha} = \emptyset, \text{ if such an } \alpha \text{ exists;} \\ \\ \omega_1, \qquad\qquad\qquad\qquad \text{otherwise,} \end{cases}$$

and $\beta(f, \epsilon) = \beta(f, \epsilon, [0,1])$. The oscillation rank of $f$ is defined as

$$\beta(f) = \sup_{\epsilon>0}\{\beta(f, \epsilon)\}.$$

**Proposition 3 (Kechris and Louveau [5]).** *A function $f$ is Baire one if and only if $\beta(f) < \omega_1$.*

### D. Comparison of ordinal ranks

Given ordinal ranks on Baire one functions, it is natural to ask whether they coincide in general, and if not, how far apart they can be. These questions have been studied extensively, and we summarize some of the known properties below.

**Proposition 4.** *For a Baire one function $f : [0,1] \to \mathbb{R}$, the following hold:*

*(1) $\alpha(f) = \beta(f) = \gamma(f)$ if $f$ is the characteristic function of a $\Delta^0_2$ set $A$.* **(Kechris and Louveau** *[5]***)**
*(2) $\alpha(f) \leq \beta(f) = \gamma(f)$. Thus, in general, for a Baire one function, the ordinal ranks proposed do not necessarily coincide.* **(Kechris and Louveau** *[5],* **Leung and Tang** *[6],* **Elekes, Kiss and Vidnyánszky** *[2]***)**
*(3) There exists a bounded upper semi-continuous function $f$ such that $\alpha(f) = 2$ and $\beta(f) = \omega$.* **(Kechris and Louveau** *[5]***)**

In this paper, we focus on the class of $\Delta^0_2$-measurable functions, where $f : [0,1] \to \mathbb{R}$ is $\Delta^0_2$-measurable if the preimage of every open set is $\Delta^0_2$. By (2) of Theorem 1, every $\Delta^0_2$-measurable function is Baire one. Hence, all ordinal ranks introduced by Kechris and Louveau apply to this subclass. For this subclass, we can even consider other ordinal ranks, like the discontinuity rank of these functions, which was introduced by Carroy in [1], when he proved the determinacy of Backtrack Games directly (without referring to the Borel determinacy). We show that the discontinuity rank does not coincide with the oscillation rank in general, and characterize precisely when these two ranks differ.

In addition, we introduce a new ordinal rank in Sect. 4, called the $\rho$-rank, on $\Delta^0_2$-measurable functions. Just as different characterizations of Baire one functions give rise to different ordinal ranks, different characterizations of $\Delta^0_2$-measurable functions also lead naturally to different ordinal ranks. The $\rho$-rank arises from a characterization of piecewise continuous functions due to Császár and Laczkovich in terms of discrete convergence (see Definition 2). We show that the $\rho$-rank coincides with the discontinuity rank.

## 2 Discontinuity Rank on $\Delta^0_2$-Measurable Functions

The notion of the discontinuity rank arose from the study of the Backtrack Game, a type of reduction game generalizing the Wadge Game. The Backtrack Game was introduced by Van Wesep in his PhD thesis [9], and Andretta [11] proved that the Backtrack Game characterizes the piecewise continuous functions, or equivalently, the $\Delta^0_2$-measurable functions. By analyzing the optimality of Player II's winning strategies in the Backtrack Game, Ros [8] and Carroy [1] developed the notion of discontinuity rank for $\Delta^0_2$-measurable functions.

**Definition 1 (Kačena, Ros and Semmes** [3]**).** *A function $f : [0,1] \to \mathbb{R}$ is piecewise continuous if there exists an increasing sequence of closed sets $(A_n)$ such that $[0,1] = \bigcup_{n\in\omega} A_n$ and the restriction $f \upharpoonright A_n$ is continuous for every $n \in \omega$.*

**Theorem 2 (Jayne–Rogers [3]).** *A function $f$ is $\Delta_2^0$-measurable if and only if $f$ is piecewise continuous.*

If $f$ is piecewise continuous, then by Baire's Category Theorem, there exists a non-empty open set $U$ such that $f \restriction U$ is continuous. Using this observation, Carroy introduced the notion of discontinuity rank in his paper [1]. Fix a function $f$ and a closed set $P$. Define

$$P_f^* = \{x \in P : \text{for any open neighbourhood } U \text{ of } x, \text{ there exists } y \in U \cap P \\ \text{such that } f \restriction P \text{ is discontinuous at } y\}.$$

$P_f^*$ is obtained from $P$ by removing all relatively open subsets $U$ of $P$ such that $f \restriction (P \cap U)$ is continuous. Since $P_f^*$ is closed, we define the following sequence of closed sets by transfinite induction.

$$P_f^{*,0} = P, \quad P_f^{*,\alpha+1} = (P_f^{*,\alpha})_f^*,$$
$$P_f^{*,\lambda} = \bigcap_{\alpha<\lambda} P_f^{*,\alpha}, \quad \text{if } \lambda \text{ is a limit ordinal.}$$

We define

$$D(f,P) = \begin{cases} \text{the least } \alpha \text{ such that } P_f^{*,\alpha} = \emptyset, & \text{if such an } \alpha \text{ exists,} \\ \omega_1, & \text{otherwise.} \end{cases}$$

The discontinuity rank of $f$ is defined by $D(f) = D(f,[0,1])$. Since $[0,1]$ is second countable, $D(f)$ is countable for any $\Delta_2^0$-measurable function. In fact, the converse is also true.

**Proposition 5 (Carroy [1] and Ros [8]).** *A function $f$ is $\Delta_2^0$-measurable if and only if $D(f) < \omega_1$.*

## 3 Main Results

Our goal is to compare the discontinuity rank with other ordinal ranks of $\Delta_2^0$-measurable functions. The following proposition is immediate.

**Proposition 6.** *For a $\Delta_2^0$-measurable function $f$, $\beta(f) \leq D(f)$.*

*Proof.* Fix $\epsilon > 0$. We will prove that $\beta(f,\epsilon) \leq D(f)$ by showing that $[0,1]^\alpha_{\epsilon,f} \subseteq [0,1]_f^{*,\alpha}$ for any $\alpha$. For a closed set $P$ and $x \in P$, if $x \in P'_{\epsilon,f}$, then $f \restriction P$ is discontinuous at $x$, and hence $x \in P_f^*$. This shows that $P'_{\epsilon,f} \subseteq P_f^*$. By transfinite induction, $[0,1]^\alpha_{\epsilon,f} \subseteq [0,1]_f^{*,\alpha}$ for any ordinal $\alpha$, and hence $\beta(f,\epsilon) \leq D(f)$ for every $\epsilon > 0$. Therefore, $\beta(f) \leq D(f)$. □

$D(f)$ and $\beta(f)$ are equal for certain functions, for example, for the characteristic functions of $\Delta_2^0$ sets. The next theorem shows that the difference between the discontinuity rank and the oscillation rank of a $\Delta_2^0$-measurable function $f$ can be arbitrarily large.

**Theorem 3.** *For a countable ordinal $\alpha \geq 2$, there exists a $\Delta^0_2$-measurable function $f$ such that $D(f) = \alpha + 1$ and $\beta(f) = 2$.*

*Proof.* We prove this by induction on $\alpha$. First, we show that for each countable ordinal $\alpha \geq 2$, there exists a $\Delta^0_2$-measurable function $f_\alpha$ satisfying the following properties:

(1) $D(f_\alpha) = \alpha + 1$ and $\beta(f_\alpha) = 2$,
(2) $[0,1]^{*,\alpha}_{f_\alpha} = \{0\}$,
(3) $f_\alpha(0) = f_\alpha(1) = 1$, and
(4) $\{0,1\} \subseteq [0,1]^*_{f_\alpha} \cap [0,1]'_{\epsilon, f_\alpha}$ for every $0 < \epsilon < 1$.

For $\alpha = 2$, let $f_2 : [0,1] \to [0,1]$ be defined by

$$f_2(x) = \begin{cases} 1, & \text{if } x = 0, \\ x, & \text{if } x = \dfrac{1}{n} \text{ for some } n > 0, \\ 0, & \text{otherwise.} \end{cases}$$

It is straightforward to verify that $f_2$ satisfies conditions (1)–(4).

Next, we construct a $\Delta^0_2$-measurable function $f_{\alpha+1}$ using scaled copies of $f_\alpha$ as building blocks so that properties (1)–(4) are satisfied. Let $\{[a_n, b_n] : n \in \omega\}$ be a sequence of pairwise disjoint closed intervals such that $b_0 = 1$, $\lim_n a_n = \lim_n b_n = 0$, and $b_{n+1} < a_n < b_n$ for all $n$.

Given a function $f$ and a closed interval $[a,b]$, let $f_{[a,b]} : [a,b] \to \mathbb{R}$ be the function defined by $f_{[a,b]}(x) = f\left(\dfrac{x-a}{b-a}\right)$. $f_{\alpha+1}$ is defined as follows:

(i) $f_{\alpha+1}(0) = f_{\alpha+1}(1) = 1$,
(ii) $f_{\alpha+1} \restriction [a_n, b_n] = \dfrac{1}{2^n}(f_\alpha)_{[a_n,b_n]}$,
(iii) $f_{\alpha+1}$ takes value 0 everywhere else.

Note that by construction, $f_{\alpha+1} \restriction [a_n, b_n]$ is a scaled copy of $f_\alpha$ on the interval $[a_n, b_n]$. Intuitively, we insert scaled copies of $f_\alpha$ into each interval $[a_n, b_n]$ so that $a_n \in [0,1]^{*,\alpha}_{f_{\alpha+1}}$. This ensures $0 \in [0,1]^{*,\alpha+1}_{f_{\alpha+1}}$. We now verify that $f_{\alpha+1}$ satisfies the following properties.

**Claim 1.** $[0,1]^*_{f_{\alpha+1}} = \{0\} \cup \bigcup_{n\in\omega} [a_n, b_n]^*_{f_{\alpha+1}}$.

($\supseteq$): Since $[a_n, b_n] \subseteq [0,1]$ for each $n$, we have $[a_n, b_n]^*_{f_{\alpha+1}} \subseteq [0,1]^*_{f_{\alpha+1}}$ for every $n$. Moreover, $0 \in [0,1]^*_{f_{\alpha+1}}$ since $f_{\alpha+1}$ is discontinuous at 0. Hence,

$$\{0\} \cup \bigcup_{n\in\omega} [a_n, b_n]^*_{f_{\alpha+1}} \subseteq [0,1]^*_{f_{\alpha+1}}.$$

($\subseteq$): Observe that $f_{\alpha+1} \upharpoonright (b_{n+1}, a_n)$ is continuous. Hence, $[0,1]^*_{f_{\alpha+1}} \subseteq \{0\} \cup \bigcup_{n\in\omega}[a_n, b_n]$. Let $x \in (a_n, b_n)$ for some $n$. If $x \in [0,1]^*_{f_{\alpha+1}}$, then $f_{\alpha+1}$ is discontinuous on every neighbourhood $U$ of $x$. Therefore, $f_{\alpha+1}$ is discontinuous on every neighbourhood $U \cap (a_n, b_n)$ of $x$, and $x \in [a_n, b_n]^*_{f_{\alpha+1}}$.

By condition (4) and part (ii) of the construction, $a_n, b_n \in [a_n, b_n]^*_{f_{\alpha+1}}$. Thus,

$$[0,1]^*_{f_{\alpha+1}} \subseteq \{0\} \cup \bigcup_{n\in\omega} [a_n, b_n]^*_{f_{\alpha+1}}.$$

By a similar argument, we obtain the following claim.

**Claim 2.** For $0 < \epsilon < 1$, $[0,1]'_{\epsilon, f_{\alpha+1}} = \{0\} \cup \bigcup_{n\in\omega} [a_n, b_n]'_{\epsilon, f_{\alpha+1}}$.

**Claim 3.** $\beta(f_{\alpha+1}) = 2$.

Observe that if $\frac{1}{2^n} < \epsilon$, then $[a_n, b_n]'_{\epsilon, f_{\alpha+1}} = \emptyset$. Hence, by Claim 2, for $0 < \epsilon < 1$, we have

$$[0,1]'_{\epsilon, f_{\alpha+1}} = \{0\} \cup \bigcup_{n \leq \log_2(\frac{1}{\epsilon})} [a_n, b_n]'_{\epsilon, f_{\alpha+1}}.$$

Since there are only finitely many $n$ with $n \leq \log_2\left(\frac{1}{\epsilon}\right)$, 0 is isolated in $[0,1]'_{\epsilon, f_{\alpha+1}}$ and thus $0 \notin [0,1]''_{\epsilon, f_{\alpha+1}}$. In addition, since $\beta(f_{\alpha+1} \upharpoonright [a_n, b_n]) = \beta(f_\alpha) = 2$ by condition (1), $[a_n, b_n]''_{\epsilon, f_{\alpha+1}} = \emptyset$ for all $n$ and $0 < \epsilon < 1$. Hence, $\beta(f_{\alpha+1}) = 2$.

**Claim 4.** $D(f_{\alpha+1}) = \alpha + 2$.

First, we show that $D(f_{\alpha+1}) \geq \alpha + 2$ by proving that $[0,1]^{*,\alpha+1}_{f_{\alpha+1}}$ contains 0, and hence is non-empty. By condition (2) and part (ii) of the construction, $a_n \in [0,1]^{*,\alpha}_{f_{\alpha+1}}$ for every $n$. Since $a_n \in [0,1]^{*,\alpha}_{f_{\alpha+1}}$ for every $n$ and $(a_n)$ converges to 0, $0 \in [0,1]^{*,\alpha}_{f_{\alpha+1}}$. Moreover, $f_{\alpha+1}(a_n) = \frac{1}{2^n} \to 0$ while $f_{\alpha+1}(0) = 1$, so $f_{\alpha+1} \upharpoonright [0,1]^{*,\alpha}_{f_{\alpha+1}}$ is discontinuous at 0. Hence, $0 \in [0,1]^{*,\alpha+1}_{f_{\alpha+1}}$. Next, we show that $[0,1]^{*,\alpha+1}_{f_{\alpha+1}} = \{0\}$, which implies that $D(f_{\alpha+1}) \leq \alpha + 2$.

By Claim 1, $[0,1]^*_{f_{\alpha+1}} = \{0\} \cup \bigcup_{n\in\omega} [a_n, b_n]^*_{f_{\alpha+1}}$, and a straightforward transfinite induction shows that $[0,1]^{*,\alpha+1}_{f_{\alpha+1}} = \{0\} \cup \bigcup_{n\in\omega} [a_n, b_n]^{*,\alpha+1}_{f_{\alpha+1}}$. By the inductive hypothesis and part (ii) of the construction, $[a_n, b_n]^{*,\alpha+1}_{f_{\alpha+1}} = \emptyset$. Hence, $[0,1]^{*,\alpha+1}_{f_{\alpha+1}} = \{0\}$ and $D(f_{\alpha+1}) = \alpha + 2$.

This completes the successor case.

For a limit ordinal $\alpha$, let $\{\beta_n : n \in \omega\}$ be an increasing sequence of ordinals converging to $\alpha$. We define $f_\alpha$ as follows:

(i) $f_\alpha(0) = f_\alpha(1) = 1$,
(ii) $f_\alpha \upharpoonright [a_n, b_n] = \frac{1}{2^n} (f_{\beta_n})_{[a_n, b_n]}$,

(iii) $f_\alpha$ takes the value 0 everywhere else.

Using the same argument as above, we obtain Claims 1–3 for $f_\alpha$. In order to prove that $D(f_\alpha) = \alpha + 1$, it suffices to show that $[0,1]^{*,\alpha}_{f_\alpha} = \{0\}$. The inclusion $0 \in [0,1]^{*,\alpha}_{f_\alpha}$ follows from the fact that for every $\beta < \alpha$, the sequence $\{a_n : \beta \leq \beta_n\} \subseteq [0,1]^{*,\beta}_{f_\alpha}$. Conversely, as $[a_n, b_n]^{*,\alpha}_{f_\alpha} = [a_n, b_n]^{*,\beta_n+1}_{f_{\beta_n}} = \emptyset$ for every $n$, we have $[0,1]^{*,\alpha}_{f_\alpha} = \{0\}$, and hence $D(f_\alpha) = \alpha + 1$. □

Note that for a continuous function $f$, $D(f) = \beta(f) = 1$. Hence, the functions $f_\alpha$ constructed above have the smallest possible $\beta$-rank among discontinuous functions. Since $\beta(f_\alpha) = 2$ and $f_\alpha$ is discontinuous, it follows that $\alpha(f_\alpha) = 2$ as well. Thus, the same construction also separates the discontinuity rank from the separation rank.

The following theorem provides a characterization of $\Delta^0_2$-measurable functions whose discontinuity rank differs from their oscillation rank.

**Theorem 4.** *Let $f$ be a $\Delta^0_2$-measurable function. Then $D(f) \neq \beta(f)$ if and only if there exists a sequence of functions $(g_n)$ converging uniformly to $f$ such that $\sup_n\{D(g_n)\} < D(f)$.*

We first state a lemma that will be used in the proof of Theorem 4.

**Lemma 1 (Leung and Tang [6]).** *Suppose $P$ is a closed subset of $[0,1]$ and let $f : [0,1] \to \mathbb{R}$ be a Baire one function. For every $\epsilon > 0$, there exists a continuous function $h : P \setminus P'_{\epsilon,f} \to \mathbb{R}$ such that $|h(x) - f(x)| \leq \epsilon$ for all $x \in P \setminus P'_{\epsilon,f}$.*

We now prove Theorem 4.

*Proof.* ($\Leftarrow$) Suppose we have a sequence of functions $(g_n)$ converging uniformly to $f$ such that $\sup_n\{D(g_n)\} < D(f)$. We will show that for each $\epsilon > 0$, there exists $n$ such that $\beta(f,\epsilon) \leq D(g_n)$, which implies that $\beta(f) \leq \sup_n\{D(g_n)\} < D(f)$.

We can assume that for all $x \in [0,1]$, $|g_n(x) - f(x)| < \frac{1}{2^n}$. Fix $\epsilon > 0$ and let $n$ be sufficiently large such that $\frac{1}{2^{n-3}} < \epsilon$. We will show that for any closed set $P$ and open set $U$, if $g_n \upharpoonright (U \cap P)$ is continuous, then for every $x \in U \cap P$ there is an open neighbourhood $V \subseteq U$ of $x$ such that $|f(y) - f(z)| < \epsilon$ for all $y, z \in V \cap P$. As a result, $P'_{\epsilon,f} \subseteq P^*_{g_n}$ holds for any closed set $P$ and consequently $P^\alpha_{\epsilon,f} \subseteq P^{*,\alpha}_{g_n}$ for any ordinal $\alpha$ by transfinite induction. Therefore, $\beta(f,\epsilon) \leq D(g_n)$.

Assume that $g_n \upharpoonright (U \cap P)$ is continuous. For $x \in U \cap P$, choose $\delta_x > 0$ such that for all $y \in U \cap P$ with $|x - y| < \delta_x$, $|g_n(x) - g_n(y)| < \frac{1}{2^n}$. By our assumption on $g_n$,

$$|f(x) - f(y)| < |f(x) - g_n(x)| + |g_n(x) - g_n(y)| + |g_n(y) - f(y)|$$

$$< \frac{1}{2^n} + \frac{1}{2^n} + \frac{1}{2^n} < \frac{1}{2^{n-2}}.$$

Therefore, for any $y, z \in (x-\delta_x, x+\delta_x) \cap (U \cap P)$, we have $|f(y)-f(z)| \leq |f(y)-f(x)| + |f(x)-f(z)| < \dfrac{1}{2^{n-3}}$ and $\beta(f,\epsilon) \leq \beta\left(f, \dfrac{1}{2^{n-3}}\right) \leq D(g_n)$.

($\Rightarrow$) Suppose $D(f) \neq \beta(f)$. Since $D(f) > \beta(f) = \sup_n\{\beta\left(f, \dfrac{1}{2^n}\right)\}$ by Proposition 6, we have $D(f) > \beta\left(f, \dfrac{1}{2^n}\right)$ for each $n$. We will define, for each $n$, a function $g_n$ such that $D(g_n) \leq \beta\left(f, \dfrac{1}{2^n}\right)$ and $|g_n(x) - f(x)| \leq \dfrac{1}{2^n}$ for all $x \in [0,1]$. Suppose $\beta\left(f, \dfrac{1}{2^n}\right) = \alpha + 1$. By Lemma 1, for every ordinal $\theta \leq \alpha$, there exists a continuous function $g_{n,\theta} : [0,1]^{\theta}_{\frac{1}{2^n},f} \setminus [0,1]^{\theta+1}_{\frac{1}{2^n},f} \to \mathbb{R}$ such that

$$|g_{n,\theta}(x) - f(x)| \leq \frac{1}{2^n} \quad \text{for all } x \in [0,1]^{\theta}_{\frac{1}{2^n},f} \setminus [0,1]^{\theta+1}_{\frac{1}{2^n},f}.$$

We then define $g_n : [0,1] \to \mathbb{R}$ to be $\bigcup_{\theta \leq \alpha} g_{n,\theta}$. Since the sets $[0,1]^{\theta}_{\frac{1}{2^n},f} \setminus [0,1]^{\theta+1}_{\frac{1}{2^n},f}$ are pairwise disjoint and partition $[0,1]$, the function $g_n$ is well-defined, and it is clear that for all $x \in [0,1]$, $|g_n(x) - f(x)| \leq \frac{1}{2^n}$. Therefore, $(g_n)$ converges uniformly to $f$.

It remains to show that for each $n$, $D(g_n) \leq \beta\left(f, \dfrac{1}{2^n}\right)$. Fix $x \in [0,1]$. If $x \notin [0,1]'_{\frac{1}{2^n},f}$, then $x \notin [0,1]^*_{g_n}$ as $g_n \restriction \left([0,1] \setminus [0,1]'_{\frac{1}{2^n},f}\right)$ is continuous. Hence $[0,1]^*_{g_n} \subseteq [0,1]'_{\frac{1}{2^n},f}$. By transfinite induction, $[0,1]^{*,\theta}_{g_n} \subseteq [0,1]^{\theta}_{\frac{1}{2^n},f}$ for all ordinals $\theta$, hence $D(g_n) \leq \beta\left(f, \frac{1}{2^n}\right)$. Since $D(g_n) \leq \beta\left(f, \frac{1}{2^n}\right) \leq \beta(f)$ for each $n$, $\sup_n\{D(g_n)\} \leq \beta(f) < D(f)$. □

## 4 Ordinal Rank $\rho$ on $\Delta_2^0$-Measurable Functions

In this section, we introduce a new ordinal rank on $\Delta_2^0$-measurable functions $\rho(f)$, which arises from a characterization of piecewise continuous functions due to Császár and Laczkovich.

**Definition 2 (Császár and Laczkovich [10]).** *Let $(f_n)$ be a sequence of functions. We say that $(f_n)$ converges discretely to $f$ if for every $x$, there exists $n \in \omega$ such that for all $m \geq n$, $f_m(x) = f(x)$.*

**Theorem 5 (Császár and Laczkovich [10]).** *A function $f : [0,1] \to \mathbb{R}$ is piecewise continuous if and only if there exists a sequence of continuous functions $(f_n)$ such that $(f_n)$ converges discretely to $f$.*

Since the piecewise continuous functions are precisely the $\Delta_2^0$-measurable functions, we can use this characterization and the observation in Proposition 7 to define the $\rho$-rank on this class.

**Proposition 7.** *Let $(f_n)$ be a sequence of continuous functions converging discretely to $f$, and let $P$ be a non-empty closed set. Then there exists an open set $U$ and $k \in \omega$ such that for all $m > k$, $f_m \upharpoonright (U \cap P) = f_k \upharpoonright (U \cap P)$.*

*Proof.* We prove it by contradiction. Suppose not. Then for any open $U$ with $U \cap P \neq \emptyset$ and $k \in \omega$, there exists $m > k$ and $y \in U \cap P$ such that $f_m(y) \neq f_k(y)$. Let $A_k := \{x \in P : \text{there exists } m > k \text{ such that } f_m(x) \neq f_k(x)\}$. $A_k$ is relatively open and dense in $P$ for each $k$, hence by Baire's Category Theorem, $\bigcap_k A_k$ is non-empty. Let $x \in \bigcap_k A_k$. Then for every $k$, there exists $m > k$ such that $f_m(x) \neq f_k(x)$. Thus, the sequence $(f_n(x))$ is not eventually constant, a contradiction. □

Given a sequence of functions $\hat{f} = (f_n)$ and a closed subset $P$ of $[0,1]$, define

$$P^{\dagger}_{\hat{f}} := \{x \in P : \text{for every open neighbourhood } U \text{ of } x \text{ and every } k \in \omega, \\ \text{there exist } y \in U \cap P \text{ and } m > k \text{ such that } f_m(y) \neq f_k(y)\}.$$

$P^{\dagger}_{\hat{f}}$ is obtained from $P$ by removing all relatively open subsets $U$ of $P$ for which there exists $k \in \omega$ such that $f_k \upharpoonright (U \cap P) = f_m \upharpoonright (U \cap P)$ for all $m > k$. Note that $P^{\dagger}_{\hat{f}}$ is closed. We can then define the following sequence of closed sets by transfinite induction:

$$P^{\rho,0}_{\hat{f}} = P, \quad P^{\rho,\alpha+1}_{\hat{f}} = (P^{\rho,\alpha}_{\hat{f}})^{\dagger}_{\hat{f}},$$
$$P^{\rho,\lambda}_{\hat{f}} = \bigcap_{\alpha<\lambda} P^{\rho,\alpha}_{\hat{f}}, \quad \text{if } \lambda \text{ is a limit ordinal.}$$

With this, we define

$$\rho(\hat{f}, P) = \begin{cases} \text{the least } \alpha \text{ such that } P^{\rho,\alpha}_{\hat{f}} = \emptyset, & \text{if such an } \alpha \text{ exists;} \\ \omega_1, & \text{otherwise,} \end{cases}$$

and $\rho(\hat{f}) = \rho(\hat{f}, [0,1])$. By Proposition 7 and the second countability of $[0,1]$, $\rho(\hat{f})$ is countable for every sequence of continuous functions $\hat{f}$ that converges discretely. Note that $\rho(\hat{f})$ depends on the sequence $\hat{f}$ and the $\rho$-ranks corresponding to different sequences converging discretely to $f$ may not coincide in general. Hence, we define $\rho(f)$ by

$$\rho(f) = \inf\{\rho(\hat{f}) : \hat{f} = (f_n) \text{ is a sequence of continuous functions} \\ \text{converging discretely to } f\}.$$

Next, we compare the discontinuity rank and the $\rho$-rank of $\Delta^0_2$-measurable functions.

**Proposition 8.** *If $\hat{f} = (f_n)$ is a sequence of continuous functions converging discretely to $f$, then $D(f) \leq \rho(\hat{f})$.*

*Proof.* We will show that for any closed set $P$, $P^*_f \subseteq P^\dagger_{\hat{f}}$. Note that if $x \in P^*_f$, then $f \restriction P$ is discontinuous on every neighbourhood $U \cap P$ of $x$. Since $f_k$ is continuous for all $k$, we have $f_k \restriction (U \cap P) \neq f \restriction (U \cap P)$. Hence, there exists $y \in U \cap P$ such that $f_k(y) \neq f(y)$. As the sequence $(f_n(y))$ is eventually equal to $f(y)$, there exists $m > k$ such that $f_k(y) \neq f_m(y)$. Therefore, $x \in P^\dagger_{\hat{f}}$. We can thus show by induction that $P^{*,\alpha}_f \subseteq P^{\rho,\alpha}_{\hat{f}}$ for all ordinals $\alpha$, and hence $D(f) \leq \rho(\hat{f})$. □

Since Proposition 8 states that $D(f) \leq \rho(\hat{f})$ for any $\hat{f}$ converging discretely to $f$, taking the infimum over all such sequences yields $D(f) \leq \rho(f)$. The next theorem strengthens this result by showing that these two ranks are equal.

**Theorem 6.** *For any $\Delta^0_2$-measurable function $f$, $D(f) = \rho(f)$.*

*Proof.* Let $D(f) = \alpha + 1$. We prove the result by induction on $\alpha$.

For $\alpha = 0$, this is true since $D(f) = 1$ if and only if $f$ is continuous.

For $\alpha = 1$, let $([0,1]^*_f)^c = \bigcup_n C_n$, where each $C_n$ is a finite union of closed intervals and $C_n \subsetneq \mathrm{int}(C_{n+1})$. Such a sequence exists since $([0,1]^*_f)^c$ can be expressed as a countable disjoint union of open intervals, and each open interval is the union of an increasing sequence of closed intervals.

Since $D(f) = 2$, both $f \restriction [0,1]^*_f$ and $f \restriction C_n$ are continuous for every $n$. As $[0,1]^*_f \cup C_n$ is closed, by the Tietze Extension Theorem, there exists a continuous function $f_n : [0,1] \to \mathbb{R}$ extending $f \restriction ([0,1]^*_f \cup C_n)$. We show that $\hat{f} = (f_n)$ has the desired properties.

**Claim 1.** $\hat{f} \to f$ discretely.

If $x \in [0,1]^*_f$, then for all $n$, $f_n(x) = f(x)$ by definition of $f_n$. If $x \notin [0,1]^*_f$, let $k$ be the smallest integer such that $x \in C_k$. For all $m > k$, $f_m(x) = f_k(x) = f(x)$.

**Claim 2.** $\rho(\hat{f}) = 2$.

We will show that $[0,1]^\dagger_{\hat{f}} \subseteq [0,1]^*_f$. Assuming this inclusion, since $f_n \restriction [0,1]^*_f = f \restriction [0,1]^*_f$ for all $n$, we can conclude that $[0,1]^{\dagger\dagger}_{\hat{f}} = \emptyset$ and $\rho(\hat{f}) = 2$. If $x \notin [0,1]^*_f$, let $k$ be the smallest integer such that $x \in \mathrm{int}(C_k)$. Then there exists an open neighbourhood $U$ of $x$ such that for all $m > k$, $f_m \restriction U = f_k \restriction U = f \restriction U$, hence $x \notin [0,1]^\dagger_{\hat{f}}$.

Suppose the theorem holds for all $\Delta^0_2$-measurable functions $g$ with $D(g) \leq \alpha + 1$. We prove the result for functions $f$ with $D(f) = \alpha + 2$. By the inductive hypothesis, if $g$ is a $\Delta^0_2$-measurable function such that $D(g) \leq \alpha + 1$, then there exists a sequence of continuous functions $\hat{g} = (g_n)$ satisfying:

(i) $\hat{g} \to g$ discretely,
(ii) $\rho(\hat{g}) \leq \alpha + 1$,
(iii) $[0,1]^{*,\alpha}_g = [0,1]^{\rho,\alpha}_{\hat{g}}$, and
(iv) for all $n$, $g_n \restriction [0,1]^{*,\alpha}_g = g \restriction [0,1]^{*,\alpha}_g$.

Let $f$ be a $\Delta_2^0$-measurable function such that $D(f) = \alpha + 2$. We will construct $\hat{f} = (f_n)$ that satisfies properties (i)-(iv) with $\alpha + 1$ in place of $\alpha$. Let $([0,1]_f^{*,\alpha+1})^c = \bigcup_n C_n$, where for each $n$, $C_n$ is a finite union of closed intervals and $C_n \subseteq \mathrm{int}(C_{n+1})$. Since $C_n \subseteq ([0,1]_f^{*,\alpha+1})^c$, we have $D(f \restriction C_n) \leq \alpha + 1$. Hence, there exists a sequence of continuous functions $\hat{t}_n = (t_{n,k})_{k\in\omega}$ such that

1. $\hat{t}_n \to f \restriction C_n$ discretely,
2. $\rho(\hat{t}_n, C_n) \leq \alpha + 1$,
3. $(C_n)_f^{*,\alpha} = (C_n)_{\hat{t}_n}^{\rho,\alpha}$,
4. for all $k$, $t_{n,k} \restriction (C_n)_f^{*,\alpha} = f \restriction (C_n)_f^{*,\alpha}$.

Partition each $C_k$ into $C_0, C_1 \setminus C_0, \ldots, C_k \setminus C_{k-1}$. We first define a function piecewise on this partition, using functions from the sequences $\hat{t}_i$ for $i < k$. To ensure that the pieces fit together continuously, we choose the functions appropriately so that they agree on the boundary points of each $C_i$. For each $i$, let $B_i := \overline{C_{i+1} \setminus C_i} \cap C_i$. Note that $B_i$ is finite. Define $n_0 := 0$, and inductively let $n_{i+1}$ be the least integer $n > n_i$ such that

$$(\forall j \leq i)(\forall m \geq n)\big(t_{j,m} \restriction B_j = f \restriction B_j\big).$$

Such an $n_{i+1}$ exists because each $B_j$ is finite and $\hat{t}_j \to f \restriction C_j$ discretely. Define a function $h_k : C_k \cup [0,1]_f^{*,\alpha+1} \to \mathbb{R}$ by:

- $h_k \restriction C_0 = t_{0,n_k}$,
- $h_k \restriction (C_{i+1} \setminus C_i) = t_{i+1,n_k} \restriction (C_{i+1} \setminus C_i)$ for $i < k$, and
- $h_k \restriction [0,1]_f^{*,\alpha+1} = f \restriction [0,1]_f^{*,\alpha+1}$.

By our choice of $n_k$, the functions $t_{i,n_k}$ and $t_{i+1,n_k}$ agree on $B_i$ for every $i < k$. Hence $h_k$ is continuous. Since $C_k \cup [0,1]_f^{*,\alpha+1}$ is closed, by the Tietze Extension Theorem, there exists a continuous extension $f_k : [0,1] \to \mathbb{R}$ of $h_k$. Next, we verify that $\hat{f} = (f_n)$ has the desired properties.

**Claim 1.** $\hat{f} \to f$ discretely.

If $x \in [0,1]_f^{*,\alpha+1}$, then for all $n$, $f_n(x) = f(x)$ by definition of $f_n$. If $x \notin [0,1]_f^{*,\alpha+1}$, let $k$ be the smallest integer such that $x \in C_k$. If $x \in B_k$, then by our choice of $n_{k+1}$, $f_m(x) = t_{k,n_m}(x) = t_{k,n_{k+1}}(x) = f(x)$ for all $m \geq k+1$. If $x \in \mathrm{int}(C_k)$, then by the assumption that $\hat{t}_k \to f \restriction C_k$ discretely, there exists $N$ such that for all $r \geq N$, $t_{k,r}(x) = f(x)$. Since $(n_i)$ is strictly increasing, $f_m(x) = t_{k,n_m}(x) = f(x)$ for sufficiently large $m$.

**Claim 2.** $[0,1]_f^{*,\alpha+1} = [0,1]_{\hat{f}}^{\rho,\alpha+1}$.

The reverse inclusion follows from Proposition 8, thus we will only prove the forward inclusion. Fix $x$. We will show that if $x \notin [0,1]_f^{*,\alpha+1}$ then $x \notin [0,1]_{\hat{f}}^{\rho,\alpha+1}$. Let $k$ be the smallest integer such that $x \in C_k$.

**Subcase a.** $x \in \mathrm{int}(C_k \setminus C_{k-1})$.

Let $V$ be an open neighbourhood of $x$ such that $V \subseteq \overline{V} \subseteq \mathrm{int}(C_k \setminus C_{k-1})$. Since $f_i \restriction \overline{V} = t_{k,n_i} \restriction \overline{V}$ for all $i > k$, the sequence $\hat{f} \restriction \overline{V}$ agrees, up to finitely many terms, with a subsequence of $\hat{t}_k \restriction \overline{V}$. Hence $(\overline{V})^{\rho,\alpha+1}_{\hat{f}} \subseteq (\overline{V})^{\rho,\alpha+1}_{\hat{t}_k}$. By assumption, $(C_k)^{\rho,\alpha+1}_{\hat{t}_k} = \emptyset$, and therefore $(\overline{V})^{\rho,\alpha+1}_{\hat{f}} \subseteq (\overline{V})^{\rho,\alpha+1}_{\hat{t}_k} = \emptyset$. Thus $x \notin [0,1]^{\rho,\alpha+1}_{\hat{f}}$.

**Subcase b.** $x \in B_k$.

Without loss of generality, assume that $x$ is the leftmost point of a closed interval in $C_k$, and the other case is analogous. By assumption, $x \notin (C_k)^{\rho,\alpha+1}_{\hat{t}_k}$, hence there exists an interval $[x, x+\epsilon)$ where $(x, x+\epsilon) \subseteq \mathrm{int}(C_k \setminus C_{k-1})$ and $N_0$ sufficiently large such that for all $m \geq N_0$, $t_{k,m} \restriction \left([x, x+\epsilon) \cap (C_k)^{\rho,\alpha}_{\hat{t}_k}\right) = f \restriction \left([x, x+\epsilon) \cap (C_k)^{\rho,\alpha}_{\hat{t}_k}\right)$. We need the following subclaim.

**Subclaim.** $(x, x+\epsilon) \cap [0,1]^{\rho,\alpha}_{\hat{f}} \subseteq (x, x+\epsilon) \cap (C_k)^{\rho,\alpha}_{\hat{t}_k}$.

We will show that $(x, x+\epsilon) \cap [0,1]^{\rho,\beta}_{\hat{f}} \subseteq (x, x+\epsilon) \cap (C_k)^{\rho,\beta}_{\hat{t}_k}$ for all $\beta \leq \alpha$ by induction on $\beta$. For $\beta = 0$, this is immediate. For $\beta + 1$, let $y \in (x, x+\epsilon) \cap [0,1]^{\rho,\beta+1}_{\hat{f}}$. We show that $y \in (x, x+\epsilon) \cap (C_k)^{\rho,\beta+1}_{\hat{t}_k}$. Fix an open neighbourhood $U$ of $y$ and $s \in \omega$. Choose $r \in \omega$ such that $n_r > s$. Since $y \in (x, x+\epsilon) \cap [0,1]^{\rho,\beta+1}_{\hat{f}}$, there exists $z \in U \cap \left((x, x+\epsilon) \cap [0,1]^{\rho,\beta}_{\hat{f}}\right)$ and $m > r$ such that $f_m(z) \neq f_r(z)$. By construction, $f_m(z) = t_{k,n_m}(z)$ and $f_r(z) = t_{k,n_r}(z)$. By the inductive hypothesis, $z \in U \cap \left((x, x+\epsilon) \cap (C_k)^{\rho,\beta}_{\hat{t}_k}\right)$. Since $n_m > n_r > s$ and $t_{k,n_m}(z) \neq t_{k,n_r}(z)$, it follows that either $t_{k,n_m}(z) \neq t_{k,s}(z)$ or $t_{k,n_r}(z) \neq t_{k,s}(z)$. Thus, $y \in (x, x+\epsilon) \cap (C_k)^{\rho,\beta+1}_{\hat{t}_k}$.

For a limit ordinal $\beta$, the result follows from the inductive hypothesis since

$$(x, x+\epsilon) \cap [0,1]^{\rho,\beta}_{\hat{f}} \subseteq (x, x+\epsilon) \cap \bigcap_{\theta<\beta} (C_k)^{\rho,\theta}_{\hat{t}_k} = (x, x+\epsilon) \cap (C_k)^{\rho,\beta}_{\hat{t}_k}.$$

By the subclaim, for all $m$ such that $n_m \geq N_0$,

$$f_m \restriction \left((x, x+\epsilon) \cap [0,1]^{\rho,\alpha}_{\hat{f}}\right) = t_{k,n_m} \restriction \left((x, x+\epsilon) \cap [0,1]^{\rho,\alpha}_{\hat{f}}\right) = f \restriction \left((x, x+\epsilon) \cap [0,1]^{\rho,\alpha}_{\hat{f}}\right).$$

By a similar argument, we can show the existence of an interval $(x-\delta, x] \subseteq C_{k+1}$ and $N_1$ sufficiently large such that for all $m \geq N_1$, $t_{k+1,m} \restriction \left((x-\delta, x] \cap (C_{k+1})^{\rho,\alpha}_{\hat{t}_{k+1}}\right) = f \restriction \left((x-\delta, x] \cap (C_{k+1})^{\rho,\alpha}_{\hat{t}_{k+1}}\right)$. In addition, we can show analogously that $(x-\delta, x) \cap [0,1]^{\rho,\alpha}_{\hat{f}} \subseteq (x-\delta, x) \cap (C_{k+1})^{\rho,\alpha}_{\hat{t}_{k+1}}$. Hence, for all $m$ such that $n_m \geq N_1$,

$$f_m \restriction \left((x-\delta, x) \cap [0,1]^{\rho,\alpha}_{\hat{f}}\right) = t_{k+1,n_m} \restriction \left((x-\delta, x) \cap [0,1]^{\rho,\alpha}_{\hat{f}}\right) = f \restriction \left((x-\delta, x) \cap [0,1]^{\rho,\alpha}_{\hat{f}}\right).$$

Note that by construction, $f_m(x) = f(x)$ for all $m > k$. Therefore, for all sufficiently large $m$,

$$f_m \restriction \left((x-\delta, x+\epsilon) \cap [0,1]^{\rho,\alpha}_{\hat{f}}\right) = f \restriction \left((x-\delta, x+\epsilon) \cap [0,1]^{\rho,\alpha}_{\hat{f}}\right).$$

Hence the sequence $\hat{f}$ stabilizes on a neighbourhood of $x$ relative to $[0,1]_{\hat{f}}^{\rho,\alpha}$, and therefore $x \notin [0,1]_{\hat{f}}^{\rho,\alpha+1}$.

**Claim 3.** $\rho(\hat{f}) = \alpha + 2$.

By Claim 2, $[0,1]_f^{*,\alpha+1} = [0,1]_{\hat{f}}^{\rho,\alpha+1}$. This set is non-empty since $D(f) = \alpha + 2$, and $f_k \upharpoonright [0,1]_f^{*,\alpha+1} = f \upharpoonright [0,1]_f^{*,\alpha+1}$ for all $k$. Hence, $[0,1]_{\hat{f}}^{\rho,\alpha+2} = \emptyset$, and $\rho(\hat{f}) = \alpha + 2$. By Proposition 8, $\alpha + 2 = D(f) \leq \rho(f) \leq \rho(\hat{f}) \leq \alpha + 2$, hence $\rho(f) = \alpha + 2$. This completes the case for successor ordinals $\alpha$.

For a limit ordinal $\alpha$, let $([0,1]_f^{*,\alpha})^c = \bigcup_n C_n$, such that $D(f \upharpoonright C_n) \leq \beta_n + 1$, where $\{\beta_n : n \in \omega\}$ is an increasing sequence of ordinals converging to $\alpha$. Using the same method as above, we can construct $\hat{f}$ such that $\rho(\hat{f}) = \alpha + 1$ and conclude that $\rho(f) = \alpha + 1$. □

## References


1. Carroy, R.: Playing in the first Baire class. Math. Log. Q. **60**, 118–132 (2014)
2. Elekes, M., Kiss, V., Vidnyánszky, Z.: Ranks on the Baire class $\xi$ functions. Trans. Amer. Math. Soc. **368**, 8111–8143 (2016)
3. Kačena, M., Motto Ros, L., Semmes, B.: Some observations on a new proof of a theorem of Jayne and Rogers. Real Anal. Exchange **38**, 121–132 (2013)
4. Kechris, A.S.: Classical Descriptive Set Theory. Graduate Texts in Mathematics, vol. 156. Springer, New York (1995)
5. Kechris, A.S., Louveau, A.: A classification of Baire class 1 functions. Trans. Amer. Math. Soc. **318**, 209–236 (1990)
6. Leung, D.H., Tang, W.-K.: Functions of Baire class one. Fund. Math. **179**, 225–247 (2003)
7. Leung, D.H., Ng, H.W., Tang, W.-K.: On ordinal ranks of Baire class functions. Fund. Math. **247**, 109–130 (2019)
8. Motto Ros, L.: General Reducibilities for Sets of Reals. PhD thesis, University of Turin (2007)
9. Van Wesep, R.A.: Subsystems of Second-Order Arithmetic, and Descriptive Set Theory under the Axiom of Determinateness. PhD thesis, University of California, Berkeley (1977)
10. Császár, Á., Laczkovich, M.: Some remarks on discrete Baire classes. Acta Math. Acad. Sci. Hungar. **33**, 51–70 (1979)
11. Andretta, A.: More on Wadge determinacy. Ann. Pure Appl. Logic **144**, 2–32 (2006)

# Discrete Homotopy and Promise Constraint Satisfaction Problem

Arash Beikmohammadi(✉) and Andrei A. Bulatov

Simon Fraser University, Burnaby, BC, Canada
{arash_beikmohammadi,abulatov}@sfu.ca

**Abstract.** The Promise Constraint Satisfaction Problem (PCSP for short) is a generalization of the well-studied Constraint Satisfaction Problem (CSP). The PCSP has its roots in such classic problems as the Approximate Graph Coloring and the $(2+\varepsilon)$-Satisfiability problems. The area received much attention recently with multiple approaches developed to design efficient algorithms for restricted versions of the PCSP, and to prove its hardness.

One such approach uses methods from Algebraic Topology to relate the complexity of the PCSP to the structure of the fundamental group of certain topological spaces. In this paper, we attempt to develop a discrete analog of this approach by replacing topological structures with combinatorial constructions and some basic group-theoretic concepts. We consider the 'one-dimensional' case of the approach. We introduce and prove the basics of the framework, show how it is related to the complexity of the PCSP, and obtain several hardness results, including the existing ones, as applications of our approach. The main hope, however, is that this discrete variant of the topological approach can be generalized to the 'multi-dimensional' case needed for further progress.

**Keywords:** Promise Constraint Satisfaction · homotopy · hardness

## 1 Introduction

The Constraint Satisfaction Problem (CSP for short), where the goal is to decide the existence of a homomorphism between relational structures, has been a very successful research area over the last several decades. Developments in the study of the CSP prompted attention to generalizations and variations of the problem. One important such generalizations is the Promise CSP (PCSP) introduced in [1], in which for three relational structures $\mathbf{A}, \mathbf{B}, \mathbf{C}$ such that $\mathbf{A}$ is homomorphic to $\mathbf{B}$, the goal is to decide whether $\mathbf{C}$ is homomorphic to $\mathbf{A}$ or is *not* homomorphic to $\mathbf{B}$. The PCSP has received much attention in recent years.

One of the main special cases that motivated the framework of the PCSP is the *Approximate Graph Coloring Problem* (AGCP): Given a graph $G$, decide whether a graph is $k$-colorable or not even $\ell$-colorable for natural numbers $k, \ell$ with $k \leq \ell$. Overall, the belief is that like the $k$-Coloring problem, the AGCP


Y. Li et al. (Eds.): COCOON 2026, LNCS 16835, pp. 259–272, 2027.
https://doi.org/10.1007/978-981-92-3309-0_20

is hard for almost all combinations of $k$ and $\ell$. The AGCP has been intensively studied even before the introduction of the PCSP, see, e.g., [17,20–22,24,25], although only partial results had been obtained. An instance of the AGCP can be viewed as an instance $(K_k, K_\ell, G)$ of the PCSP, and therefore can also be tackled by the novel approaches developed for the PCSP. This resulted in much improved conditions on $k, \ell$ that guarantee hardness [13,34]. The AGCP can be made more general by replacing $K_k$ and $K_\ell$ in its formulation with arbitrary graphs $G$ and $H$ (provided $G$ is homomorphic to $H$). It was recently proved in [2] that the problem is NP-hard for any pair of non-bipartite 4-colorable graphs $G, H$. The research is ongoing.

When the structures $\mathbf{A}, \mathbf{B}$ are fixed, the restricted version of the PCSP is denoted PCSP$(\mathbf{A}, \mathbf{B})$. Following the success of the program to classify the complexity of restricted versions of the CSP [11,35], the main goal of the research in PCSP is to find a complexity classification for problems of the form PCSP$(\mathbf{A}, \mathbf{B})$. While the PCSP research borrows many ideas from the CSP, it appears that it requires a much more diverse variety of methods. This includes algorithms. While the majority of CSP algorithms are purely algebraic, the PCSP often requires LP- and SDP-based relaxations [7,8,16]. Proving hardness of PCSPs has also proved to be hard. This is witnessed by the AGCP, which, in spite of a range of tools thrown at it, remains widely open [15]. The PCSP also has a number of interesting structural features; see, e.g., [3]. For a recent survey, see [26].

In this paper we attempt to advance the methods of proving the hardness of the PCSP.

**Algebraic Approach.** One of the tools widely used to study the CSP and also applied for the PCSP is the algebraic approach [4,12]. This approach is based on the concept of a *polymorphism* of a pair of relational structures $(\mathbf{A}, \mathbf{B})$ such that $\mathbf{A}$ is homomorphic to $\mathbf{B}$ (also known as a *PCSP-template*). A polymorphism of $(\mathbf{A}, \mathbf{B})$ is a homomorphism $f : \mathbf{A}^n \to \mathbf{B}$, where $\mathbf{A}^n$ denotes the $n$-th direct power of $\mathbf{A}$. It is also often convenient to think of $f$ as a function $f(x_1, \dots, x_n)$ with $n$ input variables taking values from $\mathbf{A}$. The set of all polymorphisms of $(\mathbf{A}, \mathbf{B})$ is denoted Pol$(\mathbf{A}, \mathbf{B})$ and is a *minion*, that is, a set of functions closed under permutation of variables, introduction of dummy variables, and renaming of variables. For two PCSP-templates $(\mathbf{A}_1, \mathbf{B}_1), (\mathbf{A}_2, \mathbf{B}_2)$ a mapping from Pol$(\mathbf{A}_1, \mathbf{B}_1)$ to Pol$(\mathbf{A}_2, \mathbf{B}_2)$ that preserves the arity of the polymorphisms and renaming the variables is called a *minion homomorphism.* Minion homomorphisms are very important in the study of the complexity of the PCSP, because, as is proved in [4], if there exists a minion homomorphism from Pol$(\mathbf{A}_1, \mathbf{B}_1)$ to Pol$(\mathbf{A}_2, \mathbf{B}_2)$ then PCSP$(\mathbf{A}_2, \mathbf{B}_2)$ is polynomial time reducible to PCSP$(\mathbf{A}_1, \mathbf{B}_1)$.

One of the few tools for showing the hardness of a PCSP is the theorem proved in [4] stating that if Pol$(\mathbf{A}, \mathbf{B})$ has *bounded essential arity*, i.e., every function from Pol$(\mathbf{A}, \mathbf{B})$ only depend on a fixed number of variables and Pol$(\mathbf{A}, \mathbf{B})$ does not have a constant function then PCSP$(\mathbf{A}, \mathbf{B})$ is NP-complete. This implies that if there is a minion homomorphism from Pol$(\mathbf{A}_1, \mathbf{B}_1)$ to Pol$(\mathbf{A}_2, \mathbf{B}_2)$ and Pol$(\mathbf{A}_2, \mathbf{B}_2)$ has bounded essential arity and does not have a constant function, then PCSP($\mathbf{A}_1, \mathbf{B}_1$) is also NP-complete. This method was expanded to abstract minors in the place of Pol($\mathbf{A}_2, \mathbf{B}_2$) [9,14,16] and further strengthened in [10].

**Topology.** One of the most interesting ways to apply the approach outlined above is through topology. It was first introduced in [28,29] and then further developed in [34]. As this method is our motivation, we describe the main steps.

Starting from a PCSP template $(G, H)$ (in the literature $G, H$ are almost always graphs), we construct simplicial complexes $\mathrm{Hom}(K_2, G), \mathrm{Hom}(K_2, H)$ on the edge sets of $G, H$. Then the pair $\mathrm{Hom}(K_2, G), \mathrm{Hom}(K_2, H)$ is further converted into a pair of topological spaces $|\mathrm{Hom}(K_2, G)|, |\mathrm{Hom}(K_2, H)|$, and finally we consider the fundamental groups $\pi_1(\mathrm{Hom}(K_2, G)), \pi_1(\mathrm{Hom}(K_2, H))$ of these spaces. All the transformations are fairly standard and can be found in [28,29]. The crucial property of the transformations is that it is possible to define polymorphisms of objects of all four types. Also, all four minions of polymorphisms are related by minion homomorphisms

$$\begin{aligned}\mathrm{Pol}(G, H) &\to \mathrm{Pol}(\mathrm{Hom}(K_2, G), \mathrm{Hom}(K_2, H)) \to \mathrm{Pol}(|\mathrm{Hom}(K_2, G)|, |\mathrm{Hom}(K_2, H)|)\\ &\to \mathrm{Pol}(\pi_1(\mathrm{Hom}(K_2, G)), \pi_1(\mathrm{Hom}(K_2, H))\end{aligned}$$

(the second one is a homomorphism only up to homotopy). Starting from graphs $G, H$ by composing all the minion homomorphisms in the three steps one obtains a homomorphism from $\mathrm{Pol}(G, H)$ to $\mathrm{Pol}(\pi_1(|\mathrm{Hom}(K_2, G)|), \pi_1(|\mathrm{Hom}(K_2, H)|))$. If the graphs $H, G$ satisfy some extra conditions, the minion of group polymorphisms is isomorphic to $\mathrm{Pol}(\mathbb{Z}, \mathbb{Z})$. The latter minion satisfies the condition of bounded essential arity, and therefore one concludes that PCSP$(G, H)$ is NP-complete. In fact, for the method to work simplicial complexes must have an extra symmetry that is a special case of the mapping $\mu$ in our framework.

**Our Results.** In this paper we attempt to develop a discrete analog of the topological approach outlined above by replacing topological structures with combinatorial constructions and some basic group-theoretic concepts. Firstly, we try to isolate the essential components of the approach in order to make them as general as possible, in particular, by extending the technique to relational structures that have more than one predicate and where the predicates are not necessarily binary, making the connection between relational structures and simplicial complexes less rigid, and by relaxing the requirements on $\mathbb{Z}_2$-complexes. Some elements of these have occurred in the literature; see, e.g. [19], however, in a fairly rudimentary way. Secondly, we try to make the approach more elementary by removing several stages from it, and effectively minimizing the use of topology so that it is more accessible for those without a background in topology (ourselves included).

First, let $\mathcal{H}$ be a simplicial complex. We follow [32, Chapter 4] to introduce edge-path groups of $\mathcal{H}$. The set of vertices of $\mathcal{H}$ is converted into a graph $G(\mathcal{H})$, in which two tuples are connected with an edge if they belong to a same face of $\mathcal{H}$. Fixing a vertex $t$ we consider *cycles* in $G(\mathcal{H})$ starting at $t$ that are essentially closed walks in that graph. Let $C = t_1, \ldots, t_m, t_1, t_1 = t$, be a cycle and consider the following transformations of $C$: removing the vertex $t_i$ if $t_{i-1}, t_i, t_{i+1}$ all belong to the same face, and its reverse transformation. Two cycles are *homotopic* if they can be obtained from each other by a sequence of transformations. The set of all cycles homotopic to the cycle $C$ is denoted by $[C]$ and called the *homotopy class* of $C$. The set of all homotopy classes with the operation of concatenation of cycles forms a group $\pi_1(\mathcal{H}, t_1)$ and called the *edge-path group of* $\mathcal{H}$ *at* $t_1$.

Another group related to $\mathcal{H}$ is constructed as follows: Let $\mathcal{T}$ be a spanning tree of the connected component $D$ of $G(\mathcal{H})$ containing $t_1$. By $\mathbb{G}^{\mathcal{H},\mathcal{T}}$ we denote the finitely presented group with the edges from $D$ as generators and a set of relations defined by the faces of $\mathcal{H}$, see Sect. 3. Then by [33, p. 134, Theorem 16], [32, Chapter 4] $\mathbb{G}^{\mathcal{H},\mathcal{T}}$ and $\pi_1(\mathcal{H}, t_1)$ are isomorphic, and thus $\pi_1(\mathcal{H}, t_1)$ is a finitely presented group.

In the next step we replace the last step of the approach from [28] with the following statement[1].

**Theorem 1.** *Let* $(\mathbf{A}, \mathbf{B})$ *be a PCSP-template and* $\mathcal{F}$ *a free group with finitely many generators. If there exists a minion homomorphism* $\varphi : \mathrm{Pol}(\mathbf{A}, \mathbf{B}) \to \mathrm{Pol}(\mathbb{Z}^m, \mathcal{F})$, $m \in \mathbb{N}$, *then there exists a number* $N \in \mathbb{N}$ *such that for any* $f \in \mathrm{Pol}(\mathbf{A}, \mathbf{B})$, *the essential arity of* $\varphi(f)$ *is bounded by* $N$.

In order to apply Theorem 1 we find a free group $\mathcal{F}$ and identify sufficient conditions for the existence of a nontrivial minion homomorphism $\varphi$. Let $(\mathbf{A}, \mathbf{B})$ be a PCSP-template, $R^{\mathbf{A}}, R^{\mathbf{B}}$ a pair of relations primitive positive definable in $\mathbf{A}, \mathbf{B}$ by the same pp-formula, and $\mathcal{H}^{\mathbf{A}}, \mathcal{H}^{\mathbf{B}}$ a pair of simplicial complexes with vertices from $R^{\mathbf{A}}, R^{\mathbf{B}}$, whose faces are preserved by polymorphisms from $\mathrm{Pol}(\mathbf{A}, \mathbf{B})$. The following statement in some cases gives us a free group.

**Lemma 1.** *The group* $\pi_1(\mathcal{H}^{\mathbf{B}}, t_1)$ *is free if any two maximal faces of* $\mathcal{H}^{\mathbf{B}}$ *have at most one common element.*

For the existence of a minion homomorphism we introduce the property of *non-degeneracy* formulated in terms of cycles in $\mathcal{H}^{\mathbf{A}}, \mathcal{H}^{\mathbf{B}}$, see Sect. 4. Combining the two conditions we obtain the main result of the paper.

**Theorem 2.** *Let* $(\mathbf{A}, \mathbf{B})$ *be a non-degenerate template. If* $\pi_1(\mathcal{H}^{\mathbf{B}}, t)$ *is a free group, then* $\mathrm{PCSP}(\mathbf{A}, \mathbf{B})$ *is NP-hard.*

The condition of non-degeneracy is not very natural, so we also offer a weaker, but more natural condition that is similar to $\mathbb{Z}_2$-structures from [28], but applies to a much wider class of structures (see Theorem 8). Finally, in Sect. 5 we give some applications of the main theorems.

We believe that the results of this paper are only the first step in exploring the potential of groups of this kind. One possible direction is to consider groups similar to homotopy groups of higher order.

The full version of the paper is available at [6].

[1] While all the current application of Theorem 1 use the case $m = 1$, we prove it in as general form as possible. In Theorem 6 we prove a more general statement.

## 2 Preliminaries

We assume that the reader is familiar with the basics of the algebraic approach to the (P)CSP (see [5,12]) and also some basic concepts of finitely presented groups [31]. We use the notation $[n] = \{1, 2, \ldots, n\}$ throughout the paper.

**Polymorphisms, Minions, and Primitive-Positive Definitions.** A homomorphism $f : \mathbf{A}^n \to \mathbf{B}$ is called a *polymorphism* of $\mathrm{PCSP}(\mathbf{A}, \mathbf{B})$. The set of all polymorphisms of $\mathrm{PCSP}(\mathbf{A}, \mathbf{B})$ is denoted by $\mathrm{Pol}(\mathbf{A}, \mathbf{B})$ and the set of all polymorphisms of arity $n$ is denoted by $\mathrm{Pol}(\mathbf{A}, \mathbf{B})^{(n)}$. We define $\mathrm{Pol}(\mathbf{A})$ to be $\mathrm{Pol}(\mathbf{A}, \mathbf{A})$. It has been proved that the complexity of $\mathrm{PCSP}(\mathbf{A}, \mathbf{B})$ depends only on the set of all polymorphism of $\mathrm{PCSP}(\mathbf{A}, \mathbf{B})$ [7], that is, if $\mathrm{Pol}(\mathbf{A}, \mathbf{B}) \subseteq \mathrm{Pol}(\mathbf{C}, \mathbf{D})$ then $\mathrm{PCSP}(\mathbf{C}, \mathbf{D})$ is reducible to $\mathrm{PCSP}(\mathbf{A}, \mathbf{B})$.

A function $g : A^m \to B$ is called a *minor* of a function $f : A^n \to B$ if there exists a mapping $\pi : [n] \to [m]$ such that $g(x_1, \ldots, x_m) = f(x_{\pi(1)}, \ldots, x_{\pi(n)})$ for any $x_1, \ldots, x_m \in A$. In such a case, we write $g = f^\pi$ or $f \xrightarrow{\pi} g$.

For two sets $A$ and $B$, let $\mathcal{O}(A, B) = \{f : A^n \to B \,|\, n \geq 1\}$ be the set of all functions from $A^n$ to $B$ for $n \geq 1$. A *(function) minion* $\mathcal{M}$ on a pair of sets $(A, B)$ is a non-empty subset of $\mathcal{O}(A, B)$ that is closed under taking minors: if $f$ is an $n$-ary function in $\mathcal{M}$, then for any $m \in \mathbb{N}$ and any $\pi : [n] \to [m]$, $f^\pi$ is also a function in $\mathcal{M}$. Let $\mathcal{M}^{(n)}$ denote the set of $n$-ary functions in $\mathcal{M}$ for $n \geq 1$.

Our principal example of a minion is the set of polymorphisms of a PCSP template. It is not hard to see that for a template $(\mathbf{A}, \mathbf{B})$ the set $\mathrm{Pol}(\mathbf{A}, \mathbf{B})$ is a minion. Indeed, if $f$ is a polymorphism, then $f^\pi$ is also a polymorphism for any map $\pi : [n] \to [m]$.

Another example of a minion is given by the set of all group polymorphisms. Let $\mathbf{G}$, $\mathbf{H}$ be two groups. Then a function $f : G^n \to H$ is called a *polymorphism* if $f(a_1 \cdot b_1, \ldots, a_n \cdot b_n) = f(a_1, \ldots, a_n) \cdot f(b_1, \ldots, b_n)$ for all $\forall a_i, b_i \in \boldsymbol{G}$. In other words $f$ is a group homomorphism from $G^n$ to $H$. The set of all polymorphisms is a minion denoted by $\mathrm{Pol}(\mathbf{G}, \mathbf{H})$.

Let $\mathcal{M}_1, \mathcal{M}_2$ be two function minions (not necessarily on the same pair of sets). Then a mapping $\xi : \mathcal{M}_1 \to \mathcal{M}_2$ is called a *minion homomorphism* if the following conditions are satisfied:

1. For any $n \in \mathbb{N}$, it maps an $n$-ary function $f \in \mathcal{M}_1$ to an $n$-ary function in $\mathcal{M}_2$, i.e., $ar(f) = ar(\xi(f))$.
2. It preserves minors, i.e., for any $f \in \mathcal{M}_1^{(n)}$ and $\pi : [n] \to [m]$ we have $\xi(f)^\pi = \xi(f^\pi)$, i.e., $\xi(f)(x_{\pi(1)}, \ldots, x_{\pi(n)}) = \xi(f^\pi)(x_1, \ldots, x_m)$.

The notions of a minion and minion homomorphism can be extended to *abstract minions*, in which $\mathcal{M}$ is an arbitrary set partitioned into subsets $\mathcal{M}^{(n)}$, $n \in \mathbb{N}$, with properly defined minor operation. In this paper we almost exclusively use function minions. A homomorphism between minions of polymorphisms of two PCSP templates gives rise to a reduction between PCSPs.

**Theorem 3. ([13],Theorem 3.1).** *Let* $(\mathbf{A}, \mathbf{B})$ *and* $(\mathbf{C}, \mathbf{D})$ *be* PCSP *templates. If there is a minion homomorphism* $\xi : \mathrm{Pol}(\mathbf{A}, \mathbf{B}) \to \mathrm{Pol}(\mathbf{C}, \mathbf{D})$, *then* $\mathrm{PCSP}(\mathbf{C}, \mathbf{D})$ *is log-space reducible to* $\mathrm{PCSP}(\mathbf{A}, \mathbf{B})$.

**Hardness Condition.** A coordinate $i$ of a function $f : A^n \to B$ is called *essential* if there exist $a_1, \ldots, a_n \in A$ and $b_i \in A$ such that

$$f(a_1, \ldots, a_{i-1}, a_i, a_{i+1}, \ldots, a_n) \neq f(a_1, \ldots, a_{i-1}, b_i, a_{i+1}, \ldots, a_n).$$

A minion $\mathcal{M}$ is said to have a *bounded essential arity* if there exists a constant number $k$ such that any function $f$ in $\mathcal{M}$ has at most $k$ essential coordinates.

**Theorem 4.** ([13, Proposition 5.14]). *Let* $(\mathbf{A}, \mathbf{B})$ *be a template. Assume that there exists a minion homomorphism* $\xi : \mathrm{Pol}(\mathbf{A}, \mathbf{B}) \to \mathcal{M}$ *for some minion* $\mathcal{M}$ *on a pair of (possibly infinite) sets such that* $\mathcal{M}$ *has bounded essential arity and does not contain a constant function (i.e., a function without essential coordinates). Then* $\mathrm{PCSP}(\mathbf{A}, \mathbf{B})$ *is NP-hard.*

As an example of an application of Theorem 4 consider the problem $\mathrm{PCSP}(\mathbf{K}_3, \mathbf{K}_4)$. It is possible to construct a minion homomorphism $\xi$ : $\mathrm{Pol}(\mathbf{K}_3, \mathbf{K}_4) \to \mathcal{P}_{\{0,1\}}$, where $\mathcal{P}_{\{0,1\}}$ is the minion of projections on $\{0, 1\}$. Any function $f \in \mathcal{P}_{\{0,1\}}$ has exactly 1 essential coordinate (which also implies $f$ is not constant), so by Theorem 4 $\mathrm{PCSP}(\mathbf{K}_3, \mathbf{K}_4)$ is NP-hard.

## 3 Groups and PCSP Templates

In this section we study how analogues of homotopy groups can be introduced for a relational structure. While [28] first constructs a simplicial complex from a relational structure and then study its properties and how it gives rise to a topological space, we start with an arbitrary simplicial complex (or, equivalently, a hypergraph) on a relation pp-definable in a relational structure and try to extract the conditions essential for our purposes.

### 3.1 Edge-Path Groups

First, we recall the definition of the *edge-path group*[2] of a simplicial complex, see [32]. Let $\mathcal{H} = (V, E)$ be a simplicial complex (a hypergraph). The graph $G(\mathcal{H})$ of $\mathcal{H}$ is defined as follows: the vertex set of $G(\mathcal{H})$ is $V$ and $u, v \in V$ are connected with an edge if and only if $s, t \in A$ for some $A \in E$. We consider paths and cycles in $G(\mathcal{H})$. A cycle $t_1, \ldots, t_k$, $t_1 = t_k$, is called a *null cycle* if $k = 2$. Two paths $P_1 = t_1, \ldots, t_k$ and $P_2 = t'_1, \ldots, t'_r$ are said to be *homotopic*, denoted $P_1 \sim P_2$, if it is possible to transform $P_1$ to $P_2$ by a sequence of transformations of the following two types (called *expansions* and *contractions*): (a) If an element $t \in V$ belongs to the same face as $t_i$, $t_{i+1}$ for some $i \in [k-1]$, then replace $P_1$ by $t_1, \ldots, t_i, t, t_{i+1}, \ldots, t_k$; and (b) if $t_i$, $t_{i+1}$, and $t_{i+2}$ belong to the same face for some $i \in [k-2]$, then replace $P_1$ by $t_1, \ldots, t_i, t_{i+2}, \ldots, t_k$.

Note that if two paths $P_1$ and $P_2$ are homotopic, they have the same initial and terminal elements, i.e., $t_1 = t'_1$ and $t_k = t'_r$ since expansions and contractions

[2] This is also called primal or Gaiffman graph in the literature.

do not change the initial and terminal elements. A cycle $C$ is said to be *null-homotopic* if it is homotopic to a null cycle.

Given two cycles $C_1 = t_1, \ldots, t_k, t_1$ and $C_2 = t'_1, \ldots, t'_r, t'_1$ starting at the same element $t_1 = t'_1$, we define $C_1 \cdot C_2$ to be the concatenation of them, i.e., $C_1 \cdot C_2 = t_1, \ldots, t_k, t_1, t'_2, \ldots, t'_r, t_1$. The *homotopy class* of a cycle $C$ is the set of cycles that are homotopic to $C$. We denote the homotopy class of a cycle $C$ by $[C]$. Multiplication on the set of homotopy classes is defined in the natural way: If $C_1 = t_1, \ldots, t_k, t_1$ and $C_2 = t'_1, \ldots, t'_r, t'_1$ with $t_1 = t'_1$, then $[C_1] \cdot [C_2] := [C_1 \cdot C_2]$. It is not hard to see (cf. [32, Chapter 4]) that the set of homotopy classes along with the operation $\cdot$ is a group denoted $\pi_1(\mathcal{H}, t_1)$. Note that for any $t'$ from the same connected component of $G(\mathcal{H})$ as $t_1$, the groups $\pi_1(\mathcal{H}, t_1)$ and $\pi_1(\mathcal{H}, t')$ are isomorphic. So, we will often use $\pi_1(\mathcal{H})$ rather than $\pi_1(\mathcal{H}, t_1)$, at least when $G(\mathcal{H})$ is connected. (Note that the definitions of homotopic, null-homotopic and $\pi_1$ are similar to the ones in algebraic topology [23].)

Another group related to $\mathcal{H}$ is finitely presented. Fix a vertex $t_1$ of $G(\mathcal{H})$ and let $\mathcal{T}$ be a spanning tree of the connected component of $G(\mathcal{H})$ containing $t_1$. By $V(\mathcal{T})$ and $E(\mathcal{T})$ we denote the vertex set and the edge set of $\mathcal{T}$, respectively. Consider the finitely presented group, denoted by $\mathbb{G}^{\mathcal{H},\mathcal{T}}$, whose generators are the (oriented) edges of the connected component of $G(\mathcal{H})$ that contains $t_1$, the identity element is denoted by $\mathbb{1}$, and the set of relations is: $e = e^{-1} = \mathbb{1}$ for $e \in E(\mathcal{T})$; $(tt) = \mathbb{1}$ for $t \in V(\mathcal{T})$; and $(t_1 t_2) \cdot (t_2 t_3) \cdot (t_3 t_1) = \mathbb{1}$ for $\{t_1, t_2, t_3\} \in V(\mathcal{T})$ that belong to the same face.

The mapping $\rho^{t_1,\mathcal{T}}$ from $\pi_1(\mathcal{H}, t_1)$ to $\mathbb{G}^{\mathcal{H},\mathcal{T}}$ is defined as follows. Let $C = t_1, t_2, \ldots, t_k, t_1$ be a cycle. Then we define $\rho^{t_1,\mathcal{T}}([C]) := (t_1 t_2) \cdot (t_2 t_3) \ldots (t_{k-1} t_k) \cdot (t_k t_1)$. The following lemma can be found in [32, Section 4, Theorem 5].

**Lemma 2.** ([32]). *Let $\mathcal{H} = (V, E)$ be a simplicial complex. For any element $t_1 \in V$ and any maximal tree $\mathcal{T}$ containing $t_1$, the mapping $\rho^{t_1,\mathcal{T}} : \pi_1(\mathcal{H}, t_1) \to \mathbb{G}^{\mathcal{H},\mathcal{T}}$ is a group isomorphism.*

### 3.2 Edge-Path Group of a Relational Structure

Another ingredient of the approach in [28] is the claim that faces of simplicial complexes defined on a PCSP template (graphs in [28]) are preserved under polymorphisms. We introduce a more general version of this connection.

Let $(\mathbf{A}, \mathbf{B})$ be a PCSP template and $\Phi$ a pp-formula with $r$ free variables in the vocabulary of $(\mathbf{A}, \mathbf{B})$. Let $R^{\mathbf{A}}, R^{\mathbf{B}}$ be the $r$-ary relations defined by $\Phi$ in $\mathbf{A}, \mathbf{B}$, respectively. Let also $\mathcal{H}^{\mathbf{A}}, \mathcal{H}^{\mathbf{B}}$ be simplicial complexes on $R^{\mathbf{A}}, R^{\mathbf{B}}$, respectively. The pair $\mathcal{H}^{\mathbf{A}}, \mathcal{H}^{\mathbf{B}}$ is said to be *polymorphism stable* if for any polymorphism $f(x_1, \ldots, x_n)$ of $(\mathbf{A}, \mathbf{B})$ and any faces $\sigma_1, \ldots, \sigma_n$ of $\mathcal{H}^{\mathbf{A}}$ the set $f(\sigma_1, \ldots, \sigma_n) := \{f(t_1, \ldots, t_n) \mid t_i \in \sigma_i\}$ is a face of $\mathcal{H}^{\mathbf{B}}$, where $f(t_1, \ldots, t_n)$ is computed coordinate-wise.

Next, we describe a construction that gives an example of how polymorphism-stable simplicial complexes can be obtained. It includes all the existing applications of the topological method in PCSP. In addition to $\Phi$ and $R$ let $\Psi$ be another pp-formula in the vocabulary of $(\mathbf{A}, \mathbf{B})$, with $2r$ free variables, such that $\Psi$ defines relations $Q^{\mathbf{A}}, Q^{\mathbf{B}}$ in $\mathbf{A}, \mathbf{B}$, respectively, and such that $Q^{\mathbf{A}}, Q^{\mathbf{B}}$ are binary reflexive and symmetric relations on $R^{\mathbf{A}}, R^{\mathbf{B}}$, respectively. A binary reflexive and symmetric relation is often called a *tolerance*. In particular, for $R$ and $Q$ as above, we will say that $Q$ is a tolerance of $R$.

As an example of a tolerance consider a PCSP template $(\mathbf{A}, \mathbf{B})$ where $\mathbf{A}, \mathbf{B}$ are graphs. Let $R^{\mathbf{A}} = E(\mathbf{A}), R^{\mathbf{B}} = E(\mathbf{B})$, i.e., the formula $\Phi$ is just $E(x, y)$. For $\Psi$ consider $\Psi(x_1, y_1, x_2, y_2) = (y_1 = y_2)$. Then $Q^{\mathbf{A}}, Q^{\mathbf{B}}$ consist of pairs $((s_1, t_1), (s_2, t_2))$ of $\mathbf{A}, \mathbf{B}$, respectively, with $t_1 = t_2$.

If $Q$ is a tolerance on a set $A$, a *class* of $Q$ is a subset $B \subseteq A$ such that $(a, b) \in Q$ for any $a, b \in B$. A *maximal class* of $Q$ is defined as a maximal set like this in terms of inclusion. Unlike equivalence classes, maximal classes of a tolerance may overlap.

**Lemma 3.** *Let $R$ be a relation pp-definable in a PCSP template $(\mathbf{A}, \mathbf{B})$ and $Q$ its tolerance. Let also $\mathcal{H}^{\mathbf{A}}, \mathcal{H}^{\mathbf{B}}$ denote simplicial complexes on $R^{\mathbf{A}}, R^{\mathbf{B}}$, respectively, whose faces are classes of the tolerances $Q^{\mathbf{A}}, Q^{\mathbf{B}}$ respectively. Then the pair $\mathcal{H}^{\mathbf{A}}, \mathcal{H}^{\mathbf{B}}$ is polymorphism-stable.*

The approach of [28] uses a specific definition of faces. Let $\mathbf{A} = (A, R^{\mathbf{A}})$ be relational structure with a single $r$-ary relation. A *face* of the relation $R^{\mathbf{A}}$ is a set $\sigma \subseteq R^{\mathbf{A}}$ of the form $\sigma \subseteq X_1 \times \cdots \times X_r \subseteq R^{\mathbf{A}}$ for some $X_1, \ldots, X_r \subseteq A$. As the following statement shows, it also fits into our framework.

**Lemma 4.** *Let $\mathbf{A}$ be as above. Then the binary relation $Q$ on $R^{\mathbf{A}}$ given by $(\mathbf{a}, \mathbf{b}) \in Q$ iff there are $X_1, \ldots, X_r \subseteq A$ such that $X_1 \times \cdots \times X_r \subseteq R$ and $\mathbf{a}, \mathbf{b} \in X_1 \times \cdots \times X_r$, is a tolerance of $R^{\mathbf{A}}$.*

### 3.3 Polymorphisms and Edge-Path Groups

In this section we study the connection between polymorphisms of a PCSP template $(\mathbf{A}, \mathbf{B})$ and edge-path groups of relations pp-definable in $\mathbf{B}$. We fix a relation $R$ pp-definable in $(\mathbf{A}, \mathbf{B})$ and a polymorphism-stable pair $\mathcal{H}^{\mathbf{A}}, \mathcal{H}^{\mathbf{B}}$ of simplicial complexes on $R^{\mathbf{A}}, R^{\mathbf{B}}$ such that $\mathcal{H}^{\mathbf{B}}$ is connected.

Let $(\mathbf{A}, \mathbf{B})$ be as above, fix $t \in R^{\mathbf{B}}$, let $C = t_1, \ldots, t_k, t_1$ be a cycle in $\mathcal{H}^{\mathbf{A}}$, $t \in R^{\mathbf{B}}$, and let $f \in \mathrm{Pol}(\mathbf{A}, \mathbf{B})$ be a polymorphism of arity $n$. Suppose $P = t, \ldots, f(t_1, \ldots, t_1)$ is a path in $\mathcal{H}^{\mathbf{B}}$ from $t$ to $f(t_1, \ldots, t_1)$ (such a path exists since $\mathcal{H}^{\mathbf{B}}$ is connected). Also, let $P^{-1} = f(t_1, \ldots, t_1), \ldots, t$ be the reverse of $P$. Then $P \cdot P^{-1}$ and $P^{-1} \cdot P$ are null-homotopic. For any $i \in [n]$, let

$$C_i = P, f(t_1, \ldots, t_1), f(t_1, \ldots, t_2, \ldots, t_1), \ldots, f(t_1, \ldots, t_k, \ldots, t_1), f(t_1, \ldots, t_1), P^{-1},$$

where the arguments only vary in the $i$-th position. The mapping $\xi_C : \mathrm{Pol}(\mathbf{A}, \mathbf{B}) \to \mathrm{Pol}(\mathbb{Z}, \pi_1(\mathcal{H}^{\mathbf{B}}))$ is as follows. Let $\xi_C(f)_i = \xi_C(f)(0, \ldots, 0, 1, 0, \ldots, 0) = [C_i]$, where the only 1 is in the $i$-th position. Then $\xi_C(f)$ on linear combinations of the basic vectors is obtained by the definition of polymorphisms of $(\mathbb{Z}, \pi_1(\mathcal{H}^{\mathbf{B}}))$.

**Theorem 5.** *The mapping* $\xi_C : \mathrm{Pol}(\mathbf{A}, \mathbf{B}) \to \mathrm{Pol}(\mathbb{Z}, \pi_1(\mathcal{H}^{\mathbf{B}}))$ *constructed above is a minion homomorphism.*

We say that a group $\mathbf{F}$ is *Abelian-bounded* if it satisfies the following two conditions: Every Abelian subgroup of $\mathbf{F}$ is a finitely generated free Abelian group (i.e. $\mathbb{Z}^n$ for some $n$)[3]; and every nontrivial Abelian subgroup is contained in finitely many maximal Abelian subgroups.

**Lemma 5.** *Any finitely generated free group is Abelian-bounded.*

We are in a position to prove the second main result of this section. For vectors $\overline{a}, \overline{b} \in \mathbb{Z}^k$, $\overline{a} = (a_1, \dots, a_k), \overline{b} = (b_1, \dots, b_k)$, let $|\overline{a}|$ denote $|a_1| + \dots + |a_k|$ and let $\overline{a}\overline{b}$ denote $a_1 b_1 + \dots + a_k b_k$.

**Theorem 6.** *Let* $\mathcal{M}$ *be an abstract minion such that* $\mathcal{M}^{(n)}$ *is finite for all* $n$*, and assume that* $\phi : \mathcal{M} \to \mathrm{Pol}(\mathbb{Z}^k, \boldsymbol{F})$ *is a minion homomorphism for an Abelian-bounded group* $\boldsymbol{F}$*. There exist numbers* $P, N \in \mathbb{N}$ *such that for any* $n \in \mathbb{N}$ *and any* $f \in \mathcal{M}^{(n)}$ *with* $\phi(f) \neq 0$*, there exist (commuting) elements* $s_1, \dots, s_r \in \boldsymbol{F}$*,* $r \leq P$*,* $\overline{c}_{ij} \in \mathbb{Z}^k$*,* $i \in [n], j \in [r]$*, such that* $|\overline{c}_{11}| + \dots + |\overline{c}_{nr}| \leq N$ *and*

$$\phi(f)(\overline{x}_1, \dots, \overline{x}_n) = \prod_{j=1}^{r} s_j^{\overline{c}_{1j}\overline{x}_1 + \dots + \overline{c}_{nj}\overline{x}_n}.$$

## 4 Complexity of PCSP and Edge-Path Groups

In this section we apply the results from above to the complexity of the PCSP.

Let again $(\mathbf{A}, \mathbf{B})$ be a PCSP template, and fix a relation $R$ pp-definable in $(\mathbf{A}, \mathbf{B})$ and a polymorphism-stable pair $\mathcal{H}^{\mathbf{A}}, \mathcal{H}^{\mathbf{B}}$ of simplicial complexes on $R^{\mathbf{A}}, R^{\mathbf{B}}$ such that $\mathcal{H}^{\mathbf{B}}$ is connected. If there are $t \in R^{\mathbf{B}}$ and a cycle $C = t_1, \dots, t_m, t_1$ in $\mathcal{H}^{\mathbf{A}}$ such that for any homomorphism $g : \mathbf{A} \to \mathbf{B}$ the cycle $P, g(C), P^{-1}$, where $P$ is a path from $t$ to $g(t_1)$, is not null-homotopic, the template $(\mathbf{A}, \mathbf{B})$ is said to be *non-degenerate with respect to* $R, C$. (Note that as $\mathcal{H}^{\mathbf{B}}$ is connected, the vertex $t$ can be chosen arbitrarily.)

We are now ready to state and prove our main hardness theorem.

**Theorem 7.** *Let* $(\mathbf{A}, \mathbf{B})$ *be a non-degenerate template with respect to* $R, C$*. If* $\pi_1(\mathcal{H}^{\mathbf{B}})$ *is an Abelian-bounded group, then* $\mathrm{PCSP}(\mathbf{A}, \mathbf{B})$ *is NP-hard.*

The proof of Theorem 7 uses Theorem 5 to find a minion homomorphism $\xi$ from $\mathrm{Pol}(\mathbf{A}, \mathbf{B})$ to $\mathrm{Pol}(\mathbb{Z}, \pi_1(\mathcal{H}^{\mathbf{B}}))$ and Theorem 6 to describe its structure. Since $|c_i| \geq 1$ for non-zero coefficients from Theorem 6, the number of essential variables in $\xi(f)$, $f \in \mathrm{Pol}(\mathbf{A}, \mathbf{B})$, cannot be greater than $N$. The result then follows from Theorem 4.

Some properties of the template $(\mathbf{A}, \mathbf{B})$ guarantee that the conditions of Theorem 7 hold.

---

[3] As is easily seen, this condition is equivalent to the following one: $\mathbf{F}$ is torsion-free and every of its Abelian subgroup is finitely generated. However, in order to obtain the results below it cannot be relaxed by dropping the requirement that Abelian subgroups are finitely generated.

**Lemma 6.** *The group $\pi_1(\mathcal{H}^{\mathbf{B}})$ is free if any two maximal faces of $R^{\mathbf{B}}$ have at most one common vertex.*

We now introduce some additional conditions on PCSP templates. A template $(\mathbf{A}, \mathbf{B})$ is said to be a *$\mu$-template* if there are permutations $\mu^{\mathbf{A}}, \mu^{\mathbf{B}}$ on $R^{\mathbf{A}}$, $R^{\mathbf{B}}$ respectively, such that

(M1) $\mu^{\mathbf{A}}, \mu^{\mathbf{B}}$ preserve faces, that is, for any faces $\sigma, \sigma'$ of $\mathcal{H}^{\mathbf{A}}, \mathcal{H}^{\mathbf{B}}$, respectively, $\mu^{\mathbf{A}}(\sigma), \mu^{\mathbf{B}}(\sigma')$ are also faces of $\mathcal{H}^{\mathbf{A}}, \mathcal{H}^{\mathbf{B}}$, respectively.

(M2) $\mu^{\mathbf{A}}, \mu^{\mathbf{B}}$ permute with polymorphisms, i.e., for any $n$-ary $f \in \mathrm{Pol}(\mathbf{A}, \mathbf{B})$, $f(\mu^{\mathbf{A}}(t_1), \ldots, \mu^{\mathbf{A}}(t_n)) = \mu^{\mathbf{B}}(f(t_1, \ldots, t_n))$ for any $t_1, \ldots, t_n \in R^{\mathbf{A}}$.

(M3) There is $\ell > 1$, called the order of the pair $\mu^{\mathbf{A}}, \mu^{\mathbf{B}}$, such that for any faces $\sigma$, $\sigma'$ of $\mathcal{H}^{\mathbf{A}}, \mathcal{H}^{\mathbf{B}}$, respectively, $(\mu^{\mathbf{A}})^{\ell}(\sigma) = \sigma, (\mu^{\mathbf{B}})^{\ell}(\sigma') = \sigma'$, and $(\mu^{\mathbf{A}})^{i}(\sigma) \neq \sigma, (\mu^{\mathbf{B}})^{i}(\sigma') \neq \sigma'$ for $i \in [\ell - 1]$.

The simplicial complex $\mathcal{H}^{\mathbf{B}}$ of the $\mu$-structure $\mathbf{B}$ is said to be *$\mu$-connected* if for any vertex $t$ in $R^{\mathbf{B}}$ there is a path from $t$ to $\mu^{\mathbf{B}}(t)$ in $G(\mathcal{H}^{\mathbf{B}})$. Combining Theorem 7 with the concept of $\mu$-connectedness we obtain the following theorem.

**Theorem 8.** *Let $(\mathbf{A}, \mathbf{B})$ be a $\mu$-template, $\mathcal{H}^{\mathbf{A}}$ $\mu$-connected, and $G(\mathcal{H}^{\mathbf{B}})$ connected. If any two maximal faces in $\mathcal{H}^{\mathbf{B}}$ have at most one vertex in common, then* $\mathrm{PCSP}(\mathbf{A}, \mathbf{B})$ *is NP-hard.*

## 5 Applications

In this section we list several applications of our techniques. Some of them are known, some are new.

**The Absence of Minion Homomorphisms.** Some of the known NP-hard proofs of PCSP problems, such as $\mathrm{PCSP}(\mathbf{C}_{2k+1}, \mathbf{K}_3)$ [28], $\mathrm{PCSP}(\mathbf{C}_{2k+1}, \mathbf{K}_4)$ [2], and $\mathrm{PCSP}(\mathbf{LO}_3, \mathbf{LO}_4)$ [19] are based on finding a minion homomorphism from the polymorphisms of the PCSP template to $\mathrm{Pol}(\mathbb{Z}, \mathbf{G})$ for some group $\mathbf{G}$. We prove that this approach does not work for AGCP. A similar property of topological maps associated with polymorphisms was also mentioned in [19].

**Proposition 1.** *For $k \geq 3, t \geq k^3$, any non-trivial group $\mathbf{G}$, any minion homomorphism $\xi : \mathrm{Pol}(\mathbf{K}_k, \mathbf{K}_t) \to \mathrm{Pol}(\mathbb{Z}, \mathbf{G})$, and any $f \in \mathrm{Pol}(\mathbf{K}_k, \mathbf{K}_t)$, the function $\xi(f)$ is constant.*

**Constructing $\mu$-Templates.** We start with an example of how a $\mu$-template can be constructed. A relation $R$ is said to be *cyclic* if for any $(a_1, \ldots, a_r) \in R$ the tuple $(a_r, a_1, \ldots, a_{r-1})$ also belongs to $R$. Let $(\mathbf{A}, \mathbf{B})$ be a PCSP template and a relation $R$ such that $R^{\mathbf{A}}, R^{\mathbf{B}}$ are cyclic is pp-definable in $(\mathbf{A}, \mathbf{B})$. Let a pair $\mathcal{H}^{\mathbf{A}}, \mathcal{H}^{\mathbf{B}}$ of simplicial complexes on $R^{\mathbf{A}}, R^{\mathbf{B}}$ be defined as follows: The faces of $\mathcal{H}^{\mathbf{A}}$ ($\mathcal{H}^{\mathbf{B}}$) are the sets of tuples of the form $A_1 \times \cdots \times A_r \subseteq R^{\mathbf{A}}$ (respectively, $B_1 \times \cdots \times B_r \subseteq R^{\mathbf{B}}$), which is the standard way of defining simplicial complexes in the literature and also in Lemma 4. For tuples $t =$

$(a_1, \ldots, a_r) \in R^{\mathbf{A}}, t' = (a'_1, \ldots, a'_r) \in R^{\mathbf{B}}$, we define the action of $\mu^{\mathbf{A}}$ and $\mu^{\mathbf{B}}$ as follows: $\mu^{\mathbf{A}}(t) := (a_r, a_1, \ldots, a_{r-1})$ and $\mu^{\mathbf{B}}(t') := (a'_r, a'_1, \ldots, a'_{r-1})$. A tuple $(a_1, \ldots, a_r)$ is called *periodic* if for some $k \in [r-1]$, we have $a_i = a_{(i+k) \bmod r}$ for any $i \in [r]$. (Note that $a_0 = a_r$). For example, any constant tuple is periodic, and if $r$ is a prime number, then only constant tuples are periodic. Observe that if $R^{\mathbf{A}}$ has no periodic tuples, then for any face $\sigma$ and $i \in [r-1]$, we have $\mu^i(\sigma) \neq \sigma$. (If $\mu^i(\sigma) = \sigma$ for some $1 < i < r$, then by Lemma 4 there exists a tuple $t \in \sigma$ such that $\mu^i(t) = t$). Moreover, $\mu^r(\sigma) = \sigma$ for any face $\sigma$. The same property holds for $R^{\mathbf{B}}$, and $\mu$ satisfies condition (M3). Conditions (M1) and (M2) are straightforward. $\mu$-template of this type have been intensively studied in the literature including that on the PCSP (see, e.g., [28]). The majority of the results fit in this framework for $r = 2$ and [19] considers such a construction for $r = 3$.

**The Hardness of** PCSP$(\mathbf{C}_{2k+1}, \mathbf{K}_3)$. Undirected graphs without loops provide a prime example of $\mu$-templates, see, e.g., [28] and [19] for a more general case. This allows us to use Theorem 8 to obtain some hardness results for graph PCSP. In particular, the NP-hardness of PCSP$(\mathbf{C}_{2k+1}, \mathbf{K}_3)$, [28,29] follows from Theorem 8. Indeed, if we define $\mathcal{H}^{\mathbf{C}_{2k+1}}$ and $\mathcal{H}^{\mathbf{K}_3}$ as after Lemma 3, the conditions of Theorem 8 are easy to verify. In a similar way, if a graph $\mathbf{G}$ does not have $\mathbf{K}_{2,2}$ as a subgraph, then any maximal face in $\mathcal{H}^{\mathbf{G}}$ is of the form $\mathbf{K}_{1,r}$ for some $r \geq 1$. So any two maximal faces of $\mathcal{H}^{\mathbf{G}}$ have at most one tuple in common. The NP-hardness of PCSP$(\mathbf{C}_{2k+1}, \mathbf{G})$ ( [28]), $k \geq 1$, again follows from Theorem 8.

**The Hardness of** PCSP$(\mathbf{H}_2, \mathbf{E})$. Let $\mathbf{H}_i = \{[i], R^{\mathbf{H}_i}\}$ be the relational structure where $R^{\mathbf{H}_i}$ is a ternary relation that contains all tuples except for the constant tuples. The NP-hardness of PCSP$(\mathbf{H}_2, \mathbf{H}_k)$ was proved in [18] for any $k \geq 2$. Let also $\mathbf{E} = (\{1,2,3\}; R^{\mathbf{E}})$, where $R^{\mathbf{E}} = R^{\mathbf{H}_2} \cup \{(a,b,c) \mid |\{a,b,c\}| = 3\}$. The NP-hardness of PCSP$(\mathbf{H}_2, \mathbf{E})$ was first proved in [18][4], but it can also be concluded from Theorem 8 by studying the faces of $\mathcal{H}^{\mathbf{E}}$. The six maximal faces of $\mathcal{H}^{\mathbf{E}}$ are obtained from $\{(1,2,1), (1,2,2), (1,2,3)\}$ by permutations of the coordinate positions. Then any two maximal faces in $\mathcal{H}^{\mathbf{E}}$ have at most 1 common tuple. The structures $\mathbf{H}_2$ and $\mathbf{E}$ are both connected and $\mu$-connected. There is no periodic tuple in both $R^{\mathbf{H}_2}$ and $R^{\mathbf{E}}$. So PCSP$(\mathbf{H}_2, \mathbf{E})$ is NP-hard by Theorem 8.

**The Hardness of** PCSP$(\mathbf{A}, \mathbf{A}_3)$. Let $\mathbf{A}_n = (\{0, 1, \ldots, n-1\}; R^{\mathbf{A}_n})$ be a relational structure for $n \geq 2$ where $R^{\mathbf{A}_n}$ is a ternary relation containing all tuples $(a, b, c)$ such that the set $\{a, b, c\}$ has a unique maximum element, see also [30]. Let $\mathbf{A} = (\{0,1,2\}; R^{\mathbf{A}})$ be a relational structure where $R^{\mathbf{A}}$ is a ternary relation given by $R^{\mathbf{A}} = R^{\mathbf{A}_3} \setminus \{(1,1,2), (1,2,1), (2,1,1), (1,0,2), (0,2,1), (2,1,0)\}$. The maximal faces of $\mathcal{H}^{\mathbf{A}_3}$ can be found in Fig. 1(a) (the edges and shaded rhombuses). The NP-hardness of PCSP$(\mathbf{A}, \mathbf{A}_3)$ was proved in [27], but it can also be concluded from Theorem 8 by studying the faces of $\mathcal{H}^{\mathbf{A}}$ and $\mathcal{H}^{\mathbf{A}_3}$. As is easily seen, any two faces in $\mathcal{H}^{\mathbf{A}_3}$ have at most 1 common tuple. It is also true for $\mathbf{A}$ since the set of tuples of $R^{\mathbf{A}}$ is a subset of that of $R^{\mathbf{A}_3}$. The structures $\mathbf{A}$ and $\mathbf{A}_3$ are both connected. There is no periodic tuple in both $R^{\mathbf{A}}$ and $R^{\mathbf{A}_3}$. So PCSP$(\mathbf{A}, \mathbf{A}_3)$ is NP-hard by Theorem 8.

[4] Note that the result of [18] is stronger than that.

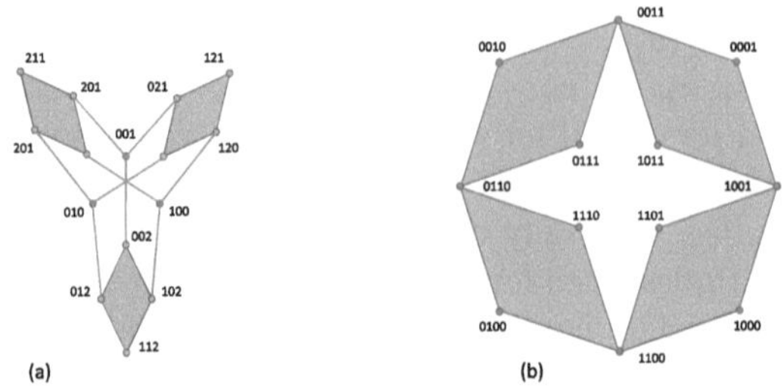


**Fig. 1.** .

**The Hardness of** PCSP($\mathbf{B}_n, \mathbf{D}_n$). A tuple $t = (t_1, \ldots, t_n)$ on $\{0, 1\}$ is said to be a *cyclic tuple* if there exist $i, j$ with $1 \leq i \leq j \leq n$ and $j - i < n - 1$ such that either $t_k = 1$ for any $i \leq k \leq j$ and $t_k = 0$ otherwise, or $t_k = 0$ for any $i \leq k \leq j$ and $t_k = 1$ otherwise. In the first case, $t$ is said to be the $(i, j)$-cyclic tuple, and in the second case the $(j, i)$-cyclic tuple. If the number of 1's in $t$ is equal to $r$, then $t$ is called an $r$-cyclic tuple. Now, let $\mathbf{B}_n = (\{0, 1\}; R^{\mathbf{B}_n})$ and $\mathbf{D}_n = (\{0, 1\}; R^{\mathbf{D}_n})$ be relational structures with one relations of arity $n \geq 3$ where $R^{\mathbf{B}_n}$ only contains all 1-cyclic and 2-cyclic tuples, and $R^{\mathbf{D}_n}$ contains all cyclic tuples. Figure 1(b) shows the simplicial complex of the structure $\mathbf{D}_4$. We now show that PCSP($\mathbf{B}_n, \mathbf{D}_n$) is NP-hard by studying the faces of $\mathcal{H}^{\mathbf{B}_n}$ and $\mathcal{H}^{\mathbf{D}_n}$. The structures $\mathbf{B}_n$ and $\mathbf{D}_n$ are both connected (and therefore $\mu$-connected), and there is no periodic tuple in both $R^{\mathbf{B}_n}$ and $R^{\mathbf{D}_n}$. To prove the NP-hardness of PCSP($\mathbf{B}_n, \mathbf{D}_n$) for $n \geq 3$, it remains to show that any two maximal faces in $\mathcal{H}^{\mathbf{D}_n}$ have at most 1 tuple in common. First, we define an operator $\oplus_n$ on $[n]$ where $a \oplus_n b := a + b \bmod n$ where 0 and $n$ are identified. Similarly, we define an operator $\ominus$ on $[n]$ where $a \ominus_n b := a - b \bmod n$ where 0 and $n$ are identified. For any $i, j$ with $1 \leq i \leq j \leq n$ and $j - i < n - 2$, let $\sigma_{i,j}$ be the face that contains the $(i, j)$-cyclic, $(i, j \oplus_n 1)$-cyclic, $(i \ominus_n 1, j)$-cyclic, and $(i \ominus_n 1, j \oplus_n 1)$-cyclic tuples. Suppose $\sigma_{j,i}$ be the face where all 0's and 1's in all tuples of $\sigma_{i,j}$ are swapped. It is not hard to see that $\sigma_{i,j}$ and $\sigma_{j,i}$ for $1 \leq i \leq j \leq n$ and $j - i < n - 2$ are all maximal faces of $\mathcal{H}^{\mathbf{D}_n}$ and any two maximal faces in $\mathcal{H}^{\mathbf{D}_n}$ have at most 1 common tuple. Hence PCSP($\mathbf{B}_n, \mathbf{D}_n$) is NP-hard for any $n \geq 3$ by Theorem 8.

**The Hardness of** PCSP($\mathbf{L}, \mathbf{D}_3$). Let $\mathbf{L} = (\{0, 1, 2\}; R^{\mathbf{L}})$ be a ternary relational structures with one relation where $R^{\mathbf{L}}$ contains $(0, 0, 1), (0, 0, 2), (0, 1, 2)$ and all permutations of their elements. The structures $\mathbf{L}$ and $\mathbf{D}_3$ are both connected (and therefore $\mu$-connected), and there is no periodic tuple in both $R^{\mathbf{L}}$ and $R^{\mathbf{D}_3}$. The NP-hardness of PCSP($\mathbf{L}, \mathbf{D}_3$) is obtained since any two maximal faces in $\mathcal{H}^{\mathbf{D}_3}$ have at most 1 tuple in common. So PCSP($\mathbf{L}, \mathbf{D}_3$) is NP-hard by Theorem 8.

## References


1. Austrin, P., Guruswami, V., Håstad, J.: $(2+\epsilon)$-Sat is NP-hard. SIAM J. Comput. **46**(5), 1554–1573 (2017). https://doi.org/10.1137/15M1006507
2. Avvakumov, S., Filakovský, M., Opršal, J., Tasinato, G., Wagner, U.: Hardness of 4-colouring G-colourable graphs. In STOC, pp. 72–83 (2025). https://doi.org/10.1145/3717823.3718154
3. Barto, L.: Promises make finite (constraint satisfaction) problems infinitary. In LICS, pp. 1–8 (2019)
4. Barto, L., Bulín, J., Krokhin, A.A., Opršal, J.: Algebraic approach to promise constraint satisfaction. J. ACM, **68**(4), 28:1–28:66 (2021). https://doi.org/10.1145/3457606
5. Barto, L., Krokhin, A.A., Willard, R.: Polymorphisms, and how to use them. In: The Constraint Satisfaction Problem: Complexity and Approximability, pp. 1–44 (2017)
6. Beikmohammadi, A., Bulatov, A.A.: Discrete homotopy and promise constraint satisfaction problem. CoRR, abs/2512.05120 (2025). https://doi.org/10.48550/arXiv.2512.05120
7. Brakensiek, J., Guruswami, V.: Promise constraint satisfaction: algebraic structure and a symmetric Boolean dichotomy. SIAM J on Comp. **50**(6), 1663–700 (2021). https://doi.org/10.1137/19M128212X
8. Brakensiek, J., Guruswami, V., Sandeep, S.: SDPs and robust satisfiability of promise CSP. In: STOC, pp. 609–622 (2023). https://doi.org/10.1145/3564246.3585180.
9. Brakensiek, J., Guruswami, V., Wrochna, M., Zivný, S.: The power of the combined basic linear programming and affine relaxation for promise constraint satisfaction problems. SIAM J. Comp., **49**(6), 1232–1248 (2020). https://doi.org/10.1137/20M1312745
10. Brandts, A., Wrochna, M., Zivný, S.: The complexity of promise SAT on non Boolean domains. ACM Trans. Comput. Theory, **13**(4), 26:1–26:20 (2021). https://doi.org/10.1145/3470867
11. Bulatov, A.A.: A dichotomy theorem for nonuniform CSPs. In: FOCS, pp. 319–330 (2017). https://doi.org/10.1109/FOCS.2017.37.
12. Bulatov, A.A., Jeavons, P., Krokhin, A.A.: Classifying the complexity of constraints using finite algebras. SIAM J. Comput. **34**(3), 720–742 (2005). https://doi.org/10.1137/S0097539700376676
13. Bulín, J., Krokhin, A.A., Opršal, J.: Algebraic approach to promise constraint satisfaction. In: STOC, pp. 602–613 (2019). https://doi.org/10.1145/3313276.3316300.
14. Ciardo, L., Zivný, S.: The Sherali-Adams hierarchy for promise CSPs through tensors. CoRR, abs/2203.02478 (2022)
15. Ciardo, L., Živn'y, S.: Approximate graph colouring and the hollow shadow. In: STOC, pp. 623–631 (2023)
16. Ciardo, L., Zivný, S.: CLAP: a new algorithm for promise CSPS. SIAM J. Comput. **52**(1), 1–37 (2023). https://doi.org/10.1137/22M1476435
17. Dinur, I., Mossel, E., Regev, O.: Conditional hardness for approximate coloring. In: STOC, pp. 344–353 (2006). https://doi.org/10.1145/1132516.1132567.
18. Dinur, I., Regev, O., Smyth, C.D.: The hardness of 3-uniform hypergraph coloring. Comb. **25**(5), 519–535 (2005)
19. Filakovský, M., Nakajima, T.-V., Opršal, J., Tasinato, G., Wagner, U.: Hardness of linearly ordered 4-colouring of 3-colourable 3-uniform hypergraphs. ACM Trans. Comput. Theory (2023). https://doi.org/10.1145/3779121

20. Garey, M.R., Johnson, D.S.: The complexity of near-optimal graph coloring. J. ACM **23**(1), 43–49 (1976). https://doi.org/10.1145/321921.321926
21. Guruswami, V., Khanna, S.: On the hardness of 4-coloring a 3-colorable graph. SIAM J. Discret. Math. **18**(1), 30–40 (2004). https://doi.org/10.1137/S0895480100376794
22. Guruswami, V., Sandeep, S.: D-to-1 hardness of coloring 3-colorable graphs with O(1) colors. In: ICALP, volume 168, pp. 62:1–62:12 (2020). https://doi.org/10.4230/LIPIcs. ICALP.2020.62
23. Hatcher, A.: Algebraic topology. Cambridge University Press (2001)
24. Huang, S.: Improved hardness of approximating chromatic number. In APPROX-RANDOM'2013, volume 8096 of LNCS, pp. 233–243 (2013). https://doi.org/10.1007/978-3-642-40328-6_17
25. Khanna, S., Linial, N., Safra, S.: On the hardness of approximating the chromatic number. Comb. **20**(3), 393–415 (2000). https://doi.org/10.1007/s004930070013
26. Krokhin, A.A., Opršal, J.: An invitation to the promise constraint satisfaction problem. ACM SIGLOG News **9**(3), 30–59 (2022). https://doi.org/10.1145/3559736.3559740
27. Krokhin, A.A., Vagnozzi, D.: Approximating 1-in-3 SAT by linearly ordered hypergraph 3-colouring is NP-hard. CoRR, abs/2508.14606 (2025)
28. Krokhin, A.A., Opršal, J., Wrochna, M., Živn'y, S.: Topology and adjunction in promise constraint satisfaction. SIAM J. Comp. **52**(1), 38–79 (2023). https://doi.org/10.1137/20M1378223
29. Krokhin, A.A., Opršal, J.: The complexity of 3-coloring H-colorable graphs. FOCS, pp. 1227–1239 (2019). https://doi.org/10.1109/FOCS.2019.00076.
30. Nakajima, T.-V., Zivný, S.: Linearly ordered colourings of hypergraphs. ACM Trans. on Comput. Theory **14**(3–4), 1–9 (2023). https://doi.org/10.1145/3570909
31. Rotman, J.: An Introduction to the Theory of Groups, volume 148 of Graduate Texts in Mathematics. Springer-Verlag, 4 edition (1995)
32. Singer, I.M., Thorpe, J.A.: Lecture Notes on Elementary Topology and Geometry (1967)
33. Spanier, E.H.: Algebraic topology. Springer Sci. Bus. Media (1989)
34. Wrochna, M., Zivný, S.: Improved hardness for H -colourings of G-colourable graphs. In: SODA, pp. 1426–1435 (2020)
35. Zhuk, D.: A proof of the CSP dichotomy conjecture. JACM, **67**(5), 30:1–30:78 (2020). https://doi.org/10.1145/3402029.

# Local Homophily on Bicolored Graphs is P-Complete

Pablo Concha-Vega(✉)

Aix Marseille Université, CNRS, LIS, Marseille, France
pablo.concha-vega@lis-lab.fr

**Abstract.** We propose a local transformation on bicolored graphs, which we call local homophily, inspired by adaptive networks and based on majority dynamics and homophily. In this transformation, a vertex updates its color to match the majority of its neighbors, while neighbors of the same color become connected and neighbors of the opposite color become disconnected.

We show how to simulate Boolean circuits using local homophily and establish that determining whether a given pair of vertices becomes connected under iterative applications of local homophily is **P**-complete under logspace reductions.

**Keywords:** Adaptive Networks · Computational Complexity · Majority Dynamics · Homophily

## 1 Introduction

Adaptive networks are systems in which the colors of vertices and the network topology coevolve over time, with vertex colors and edges updated according to rules that depend on the current network configuration [3,9]. A central example is consensus formation via majority dynamics, where each vertex updates its color according to the majority of its neighbors [1,4,8]. Homophily, the tendency of vertices (agents) with similar colors (opinions) to preferentially connect, often guides the rewiring of edges [6,7,10].

In this work, we study a concrete local transformation on bicolored graphs. Given a vertex $v$, the transformation proceeds as follows: $v$ changes its color to match the majority color of its neighbors; neighbors of $v$ that have the same color become connected, while neighbors of the opposite color become disconnected.

From a computational perspective, a central task in combinatorics is to "test" or "probe" specific combinations of elements within a combinatorial object. Motivated by this, we consider the following problem: given a bicolored graph and a pair of special vertices, does iteratively applying the vertex transformation eventually connect the special pair?

We show that this problem is **P**-complete under logspace reductions via a reduction from the Circuit Value Problem (CVP). A key structural lemma


Y. Li et al. (Eds.): COCOON 2026, LNCS 16835, pp. 273–287, 2027.
https://doi.org/10.1007/978-981-92-3309-0_21

describing the evolution of the graph under the transformation underlies the correctness of the reduction and the proof of the main theorem. Thus, while adaptive networks are often studied from a dynamical or statistical perspective, we investigate them from the viewpoint of computational complexity.

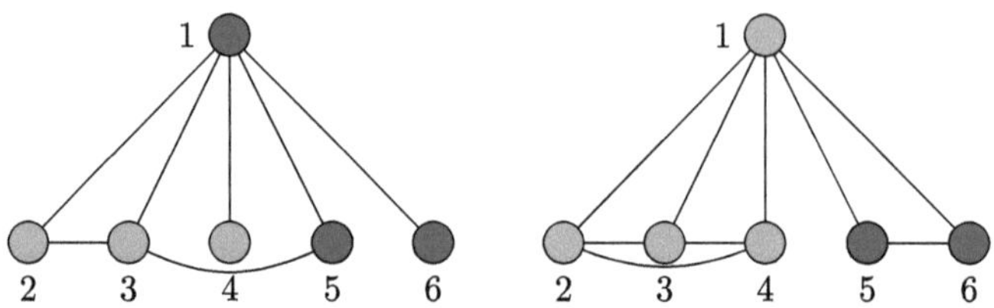


**Fig. 1.** Example of local homophily. **Left:** the original bicolored graph $B$. **Right:** the bicolored graph after applying the transformation at vertex 1, i.e., $\Phi_1(B)$.

## 2 Preliminaries

We consider finite, simple graphs. Let $G$ be a graph. The set of vertices of $G$ is denoted $V(G)$, and the set of edges by $E(G) \subseteq V(G) \times V(G)$ ($\subseteq \binom{V(G)}{2}$ for undirected graphs). When $G$ is undirected, the neighborhood of a vertex $v$ is denoted by $N_G(v)$. Given a set $X \in V(G)$, $G[X]$ denotes the subgraph induced by $X$. For a finite set $X$, we denote by $X^*$ the set of all finite words over $X$, including the empty word $\varepsilon$. We use the terms *sequence* and *word* interchangeably. A word $w \in X^*$ of length $n$ is written as $w = (w_1, w_2, \ldots, w_n)$, where $w_i \in X$, or simply as $w_1 w_2 \ldots w_n$ when the meaning is clear from the context. We denote by $[n]$ the set of the first $n$ positive integers, i.e., $[n] = \{1, \ldots, n\}$ and $[k, n] = \{k, \ldots, n\}$. A *bicolored graph* is a pair $B = (G, c)$, where $G$ is an undirected graph and $c : V(G) \to \{-1, +1\}$ is a binary coloring function.

*Local Homophily Transformation* (Fig. 1). Let $B = (G, c)$ be a bicolored graph. For $v \in V(G)$, the *local homophily transformation* at $v$ is

$$\Phi_v(B) = (G', c'),$$

where $c'(u) = c(u)$ for all $u \neq v$, and

$$c'(v) := \begin{cases} \operatorname{sign}\left(\sum_{u \in N(v)} c(u)\right), & \text{if } \sum_{u \in N(v)} c(u) \neq 0, \\ c(v), & \text{otherwise.} \end{cases}$$

The edge set of $G'$ is obtained from $G$ by replacing the subgraph induced by $N(v)$ with a graph in which $xy \in E(G')$ if and only if $c(x) = c(y)$ for all distinct $x, y \in N(v)$. All other edges remain unchanged.

For a word $w = v_1 v_2 \dots v_k \in V(G)^*$, we define

$$\Phi_w := \Phi_{v_k} \circ \cdots \circ \Phi_{v_1} \quad \text{and} \quad \Phi_\varepsilon := \text{id}.$$

Accordingly, $\Phi_w(B)$ denotes the bicolored graph obtained by applying the local homophily transformation to the vertices of $w$ from left to right.

Given a bicolored graph $B$ and a sequence of vertices $w \in V(G)^*$, the transformation $\Phi_w(B)$ completely determines the colors of the vertices and the edges among neighbors affected by the sequence. A natural computational question is whether two given vertices become adjacent after applying such a sequence. This leads to the following decision problem:

*Local Homophily Evaluation* (LHE).

**Input:** A bicolored graph $B = (G, c)$, two vertices $s, t \in V(G)$, and a word $w \in V(G)^*$.

**Question:** Is $st \in E(G_w)$, where $\Phi_w(B) = (G_w, c_w)$?

### 2.1 P-Completeness Theory

In order to contextualize the results, we give a brief introduction to **P**-completeness theory and its main concepts.

*Boolean Circuits.* A *Boolean circuit* is a directed acyclic graph whose vertices (called *gates*) are either inputs, constant values, or logical operations (such as AND, OR, NOT). A designated vertex is the *output gate*. Each gate computes a Boolean value from its predecessors according to its operation. A Boolean circuit is *monotone* if it contains only AND and OR gates, i.e., it does not have any NOT gates.

*Complexity Classes.* A problem is in **P** if there exists a deterministic Turing machine that decides it in time polynomial in the size of the input. A function $f$ is *logspace computable* if there exists a deterministic Turing machine with a read-only input tape, a write-only output tape, and a read-write work tape, such that on every input $x$ it outputs $f(x)$ while using at most $O(\log |x|)$ cells on the work tape. The space used on the input and output tapes is not counted.

*Hardness and Completeness.* Let **C** be a class of decision problems, and let $R$ be a type of reduction (such as logspace reductions). A problem $A$ is said to be **C**-*hard* under $R$ if every problem in **C** can be reduced to $A$ using a reduction of type $R$.

If $A$ is both **C**-hard under $R$ and belongs to **C**, then $A$ is called **C**-*complete* under $R$.

*Circuit Value Problem (CVP).* The *Circuit Value Problem* is as follows: given a Boolean circuit and an assignment of its input values, decide whether the output gate evaluates to TRUE. CVP is known to be **P**-complete under logspace reductions [5]. Moreover, several restricted versions of CVP remain **P**-complete, including:

- the *monotone* CVP, where only monotone gates (AND and OR) are allowed;
- the *synchronous* CVP, where a circuit is said to be *synchronous* if, for every gate $v$, all its input vertices have $\mathsf{level}(u) = \mathsf{level}(v) - 1$, with $\mathsf{level}(v)$ defined as the length of the longest directed path from an input vertex to $v$;
- versions with fan-in and fan-out at most 2.

Furthermore, the version of CVP that combines all of these restrictions is also **P**-complete [2]. Although these restricted versions have their own names in the literature, from now on we will simply refer to CVP as the version that is monotone, synchronous, and has fan-in and fan-out at most 2.

## 3 Hardness of LHE

In this section, we prove the main result of this article:

**Theorem 1.** *LHE is* **P***-complete under logspace reductions.*

To prove this, we give a logspace reduction from the CVP. Intuitively, we encode the evaluation of a Boolean circuit using the local homophily transformation, so that the output gate evaluates to TRUE if and only if a specific edge appears in the final graph. Note that LHE is trivially in **P**, as it can be solved by sequentially applying the transformations.

*Outline of the Proof.* The proof proceeds along the following steps:

- We first prove a structural lemma that will be used in the reduction.
- We then present the gadgets corresponding to circuit elements: AND, OR, signal duplicator.
- Next, we describe how to connect these gadgets to encode an entire Boolean circuit, and argue why the sequence of transformations propagates the computation correctly.
- Finally, we discuss why the construction can be performed in logspace.

### 3.1 Flower Graphs

**Definition 1 (Flower graph (Fig. 2)).** *We define a* flower graph $F_{n,m}$ *as follows: start with a clique* $K_n$ *(the* center*) with vertices colored* $+1$*, and for each vertex* $v \in K_n$*, attach a disjoint clique* $K_m^{(v)}$ *(the* petals*) colored* $-1$*, connecting* $v$ *to every vertex of* $K_m^{(v)}$*. No other edges are added.*

**Lemma 1.** *Let* $n, m \in \mathbb{N}$ *with* $m \geq n$*, and let* $F_{n,m}$ *be a flower graph with central vertices* $[n]$*. For any integer* $0 < k \leq n$*, the following hold for* $\Phi_{1\cdots k}(F_{n,m})$*:*

1. *Each central vertex* $i \leq k$ *has its color flipped.*
2. *For each* $i < k$*, vertex* $i$ *is connected to all the vertices of the petal of vertex* $i + 1$*.*

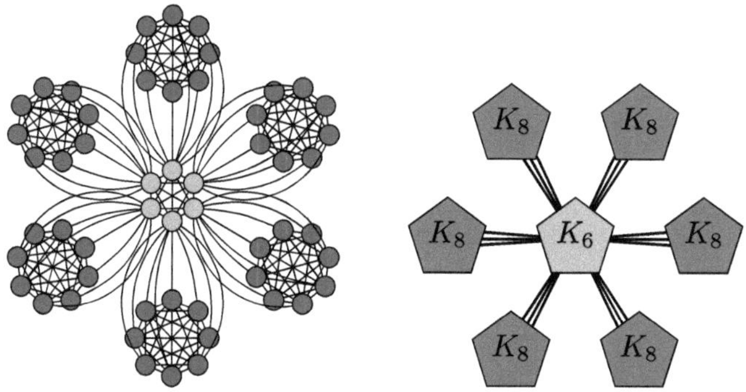


**Fig. 2.** Example of a flower graph. **Left:** the flower graph $F_{6,8}$. **Right:** a succinct representation of $F_{6,8}$.

3. *The subgraph induced by* $[k]$ *is the path* $P_k$.
4. *For all* $i < k$, *vertex* $i$ *has no edges to any central vertex* $> k$.
5. *The subgraph induced by* $[k, n]$ *is* $K_{n-k+1}$.

*Proof.* We proceed by induction on $k$.

Vertex 1 flips its color when applying $\Phi_1$, because in the central clique it has $n - 1$ neighbors of its initial color $+1$, while in its petal it is connected to $m \geq n$ vertices of the opposite color $-1$. Therefore, the majority color in its neighborhood is $-1$, and the flip occurs.

Conditions 2–5 are easily verified for $k = 1$:

- Condition 2 is vacuously satisfied since there are no vertices $i < 1$.
- Condition 3: the subgraph induced by $\{1\}$ is trivially $P_1$.
- Condition 4: there are no vertices $i < 1$, so vacuously satisfied.
- Condition 5: the subgraph induced by $[1, n]$ is the clique $K_n$ as in the original flower graph.

**Inductive Step.** Assume the lemma holds for some $k < n$, i.e., after applying $\Phi_{1\cdots k}$. Now consider $\Phi_{1\cdots(k+1)} = \Phi_{k+1} \circ \Phi_{1\cdots k}$.

**Color Flip:** Vertex $k+1$ flips its color because the majority of its neighbors is $-1$: it has $n - k + 1$ neighbors in the central clique of color $+1$, one of color $-1$ (vertex $k$) and $m \geq n$ neighbors in its petal of color $-1$.

**Connections with Petals:** By the definition of $\Phi$, vertex $k$ is now connected to all vertices of the petal of $k + 1$, while the previous connections of vertices $i < k$ remain unchanged.

**Path Among First** $k+1$ **Vertices:** The subgraph induced by $[k+1]$ forms the path $P_{k+1}$: vertices 1 through $k$ already induce $P_k$ by the inductive hypothesis.

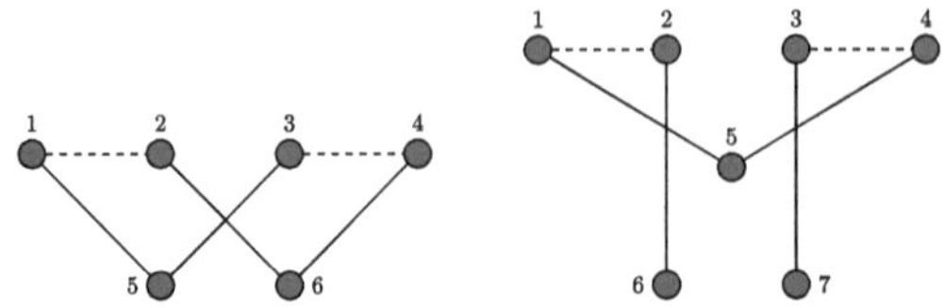


**Fig. 3.** OR and AND gadgets. Dashed lines indicate the positions of the inputs.

Also by the inductive hypothesis there is no vertex $< k$ connected to vertices $> k$, which includes $k+1$. Therefore, no vertex $i < k$ is connected to $k+1$.

**No Edges from** $[1, k]$ **to Vertices** $> k+1$**:** The operation $\Phi_{k+1}$ only affects the neighborhood of vertex $k+1$, which consists of $[k, n]$ together with its petal. Since vertex $k$ changed color in the previous step, it becomes disconnected from all vertices $> k+1$, while vertices $i < k$ remain disconnected from vertices $> k+1$ by the inductive hypothesis.

**Clique Among Remaining Vertices:** The subgraph induced by $[k+1, n]$ remains a clique $K_{n-k}$, as $\Phi_{k+1}$ does not remove edges among vertices $> k+1$ since they are all of their initial color, with the exception of $k+1$. However by definition $\Phi_{k+1}$ does not change its neighborhood. □

### 3.2 Implementation of Logical Gates via $\Phi$

In this subsection we construct the gadgets used in the reduction from the CVP. We implement logical AND and OR gates, as well as a signal duplicator, within our bicolored graph framework. Boolean values are encoded through the presence or absence of specific edges, and the operation $\Phi$ propagates these values across the construction.

Each gadget consists of a bicolored graph $B$ together with a fixed sequence of vertices $w$, written as a pair $(B, w)$. The sequence $w$ specifies the order in which $\Phi$ is applied to the vertices of the gadget, ensuring that the outputs behave as intended given the inputs. In other words, $\Phi_w(B)$ evaluates the gadget correctly according to the logical operation it is meant to simulate.

We start with the OR gadget (see Fig. 3 left), defined as the pair $(B_\vee, w_\vee)$, where $B_\vee = (G_\vee, c_\vee)$ is the bicolored graph with $V(G_\vee) = \{1, \dots, 6\}$, $E(G_\vee) = \{(1,5), (3,5), (2,6), (4,6)\}$, and $c_\vee(v) = -1$ for all $v \in V(G_\vee)$. The fixed sequence of updates is $w_\vee = (1, 4, 2, 3)$. The inputs are encoded via the potential edges $(1,2)$ and $(3,4)$, and the output corresponds to the edge $(5,6)$. The operation of this gadget is illustrated in Appendix A Fig. 7. Since it is an OR gate, the edge $(5,6)$ is absent if and only if both edges $(1,2)$ and $(3,4)$ are absent in the initial configuration.

On the other hand, the AND gadget (see Fig. 3 right) is defined as the pair $(B_\wedge, w_\wedge)$, where $B_\wedge = (G_\wedge, c_\wedge)$ is the bicolored graph with $V(G_\wedge) = \{1, \dots, 7\}$, $E(G_\wedge) = \{(1,5), (2,6), (3,7), (4,5)\}$, and $c_\wedge(v) = -1$ for all $v \in V(G_\wedge)$. The fixed sequence of updates is $w_\wedge = (2,3,1,4,5)$. The inputs are encoded via the potential edges $(1,2)$ and $(3,4)$, and the output corresponds to the edge $(6,7)$. The operation of this gadget is illustrated in Appendix A Fig. 8. Since it is an AND gate, the edge $(6,7)$ is present if and only if both edges $(1,2)$ and $(3,4)$ are present in the initial configuration.

Although we now have OR and AND gadgets, for our reduction we require all gadgets to have outdegree at most 2. As is clear, our current gadgets have a single output, so we need to introduce an additional gadget capable of duplicating a Boolean value. This means the gadget has one input and two outputs, each of which will be TRUE if and only if the input was initially TRUE.

The duplicator gadget is the most complex gadget in our construction, at least among the ones we could find. It consists of several cliques and, unlike the logical gadgets, it has an additional parameter $k$, which we will discuss later.

Concretely, the gadget contains vertices labeled 1 through 11, with vertex 1 connected to the center of a flower graph $F_{k,k+2}$.

The duplicator gadget (see Fig. 4) is defined as the pair $(B_D, w_D)$, where $B_D = (G_D, c_D)$ is the bicolored graph with $V(G_D) = \{1,\ldots,11\} \cup V(F_{k,k+2})$, and vertex 1 is connected to the center of the flower graph $F_{k,k+2}$, which we assume are labeled from 12 to $11+k$. The edges outside the flower are given by:

$$E(G_D) \setminus E(F_{k,k+2}) = \{(1,3),(1,4),(1,6),(2,5),(2,7),\\ (3,6),(4,8),(4,9),(4,10),(5,11)\}.$$

The coloring of the vertices is defined as

$$c_D(v) = \begin{cases} +1 & \text{for } v = 4,5 \text{ and } v \in [12, 11+k], \\ -1 & \text{for all other vertices.} \end{cases}$$

The fixed update sequence is $w_D = (1,2,12,\ldots,11+k,3,1,4,5,4)$. The single input is encoded via the potential edge $(1,2)$, and the two outputs correspond to the edges $(6,7)$ and $(10,11)$. The operation of this gadget is depicted in Figs. 5 and 6. Both outputs are TRUE if and only if the input edge is initially present.

Note that upon applying $\Phi_1$, the center of the flower becomes connected to vertex 4. Subsequently, after applying $\Phi_2$, this connection is maintained. At this point, the flower together with vertices 1 and 4 induces a subgraph consisting of a flower $F_{k,k+2}$ and two additional +1-colored vertices adjacent to every vertex of its center.

Applying $\Phi_{(12,\ldots,11+k)}$ affects the flower exactly as described in Lemma 1. It remains to determine the adjacency of vertices 1 and 4. Observe that whenever the transformation is applied to a center vertex $i$, vertices 1 and 4 become disconnected from vertex $i-1$, since $i-1$ is then colored $-1$. Therefore, as the sequence progresses, they lose their adjacency to the center vertices one by one. Consequently, after applying $\Phi_{(12,\ldots,11+k)}$, vertices 1 and 4 are adjacent only to vertex $11+k$. The remaining transformations can be carried out without difficulty.

The duplicator gadget also satisfies several important properties that are crucial for our construction:

1. Vertices belonging to different outputs are never connected.
2. Vertices of the flower are never connected to the outputs.
3. The output vertices are all colored −1.

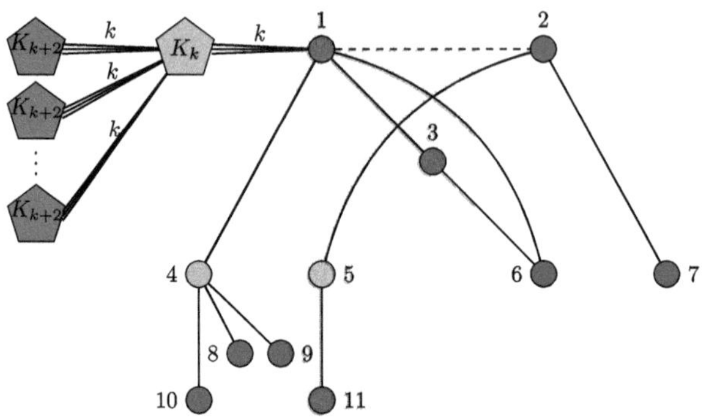


**Fig. 4.** Duplicator gadget.

### 3.3 Simulating Boolean Circuits

Given a monotone Boolean circuit, we construct a corresponding network of gadgets as follows. For each circuit input, we introduce a duplicator gadget. If an input is TRUE, the corresponding input edge of its duplicator is added to the initial configuration.

For each AND and OR gate, we introduce the corresponding logical gadget and connect it to a duplicator. Connecting two gadgets means identifying the pair of output vertices of one gadget with the predefined input vertices of the next.

Let the level of a gate be the length of the shortest path from an input to that gate. The construction is organized in layers according to the level: a layer of duplicators (inputs), followed by a layer of gates, then duplicators, and so on. The global update sequence is obtained by concatenating the fixed sequences of all gadgets in increasing order of their level.

A key issue is the propagation of edges across layers. After a gadget is evaluated, its output vertices may acquire new edges. Since these vertices serve as inputs to gadgets in the next layer, such edges accumulate towards lower levels.

This is where the parameter $k$ of the duplicator becomes crucial. Vertex 1 is connected to the center of a flower of size $k$ colored +1, to vertex 4 colored +1, to vertices 3 and 6 colored −1, and, when the gadget is initialized to TRUE, to vertex 2 of color −1. To ensure that $\Phi_1$ flips the color of vertex 1, the number of −1 colored neighbors potentially attached to it from upper layers must be strictly smaller than $k - 2$.

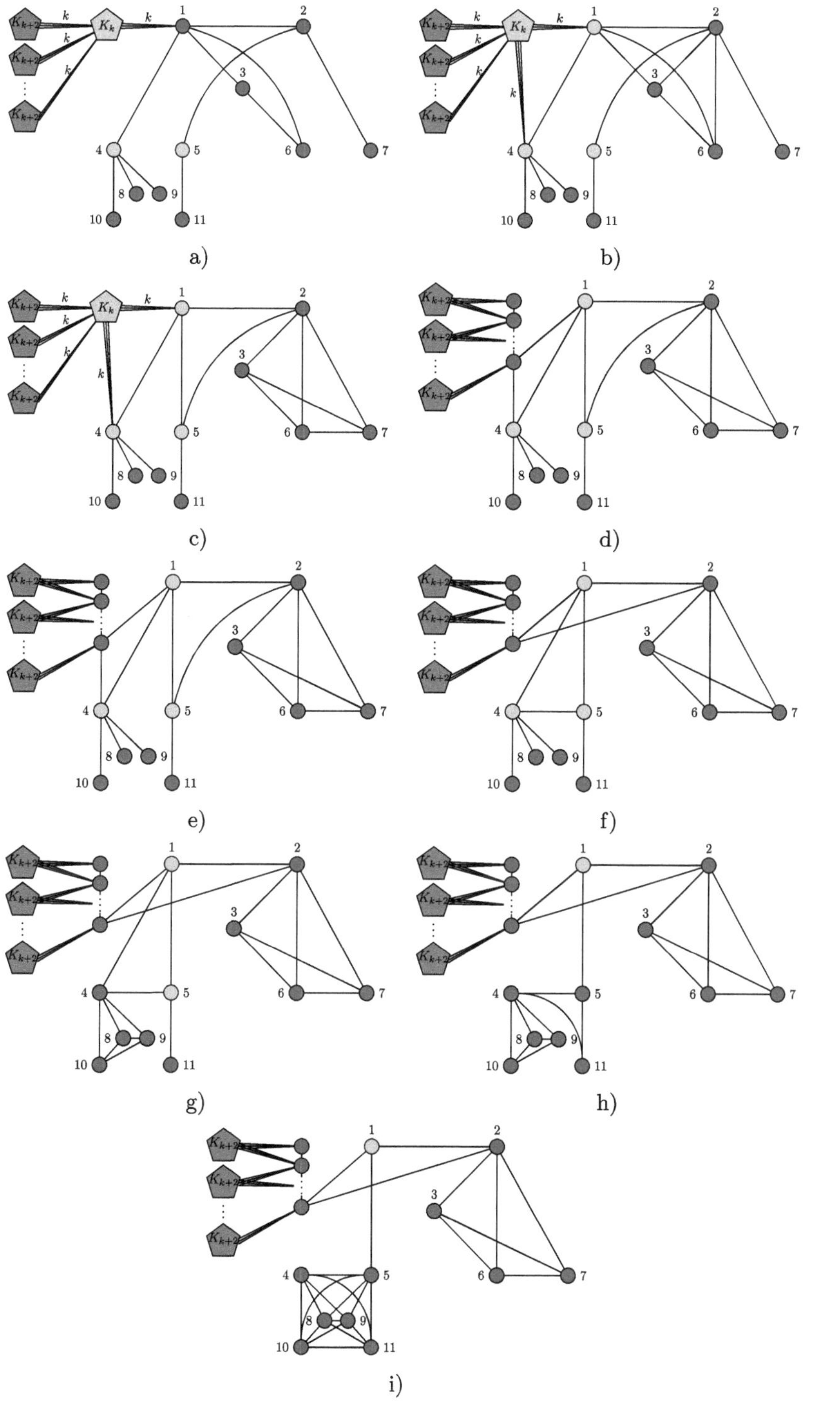


**Fig. 5. a)** The duplicator with input set to TRUE. **b)–i)** Evolution of the gadget under $\Phi_{w_D}$. The transition from **c)** to **d)** follows from Lemma 1.

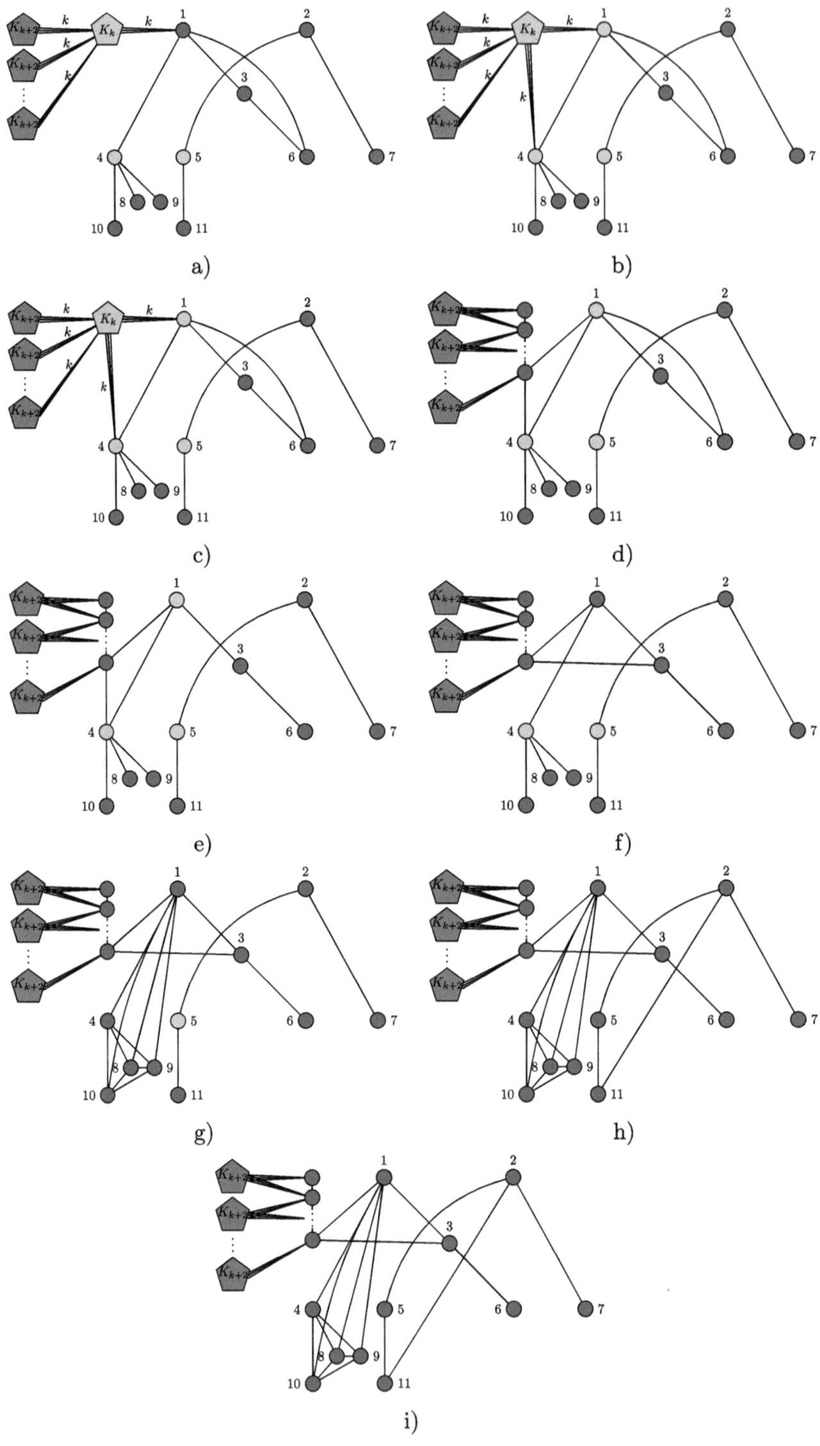


**Fig. 6.** **a)** The duplicator with input set to FALSE. **b)–i)** Evolution of the gadget under $\Phi_{w_D}$. The transition from **c)** to **d)** follows from Lemma 1.

An upper bound on this number is

$$7n_\wedge + 6n_\vee + 9(n_\wedge + n_\vee) + 2,$$

where $n_\wedge$ and $n_\vee$ denote the number of AND and OR gates, respectively. Choosing $k$ strictly larger than this quantity guarantees that the accumulated influence from upper layers cannot prevent the intended color change of vertex 1.

**Theorem 2.** *Let $C$ be a monotone Boolean circuit and let $(B_C, w_C)$ be the bicolored graph and update sequence obtained by the above construction. For every assignment to the input gates of $C$, the designated output edge of $B_C$ is present after applying $w_C$ if and only if the output gate of $C$ evaluates to TRUE.*

*Proof.* We prove the statement by induction on the level of the circuit.

For level 0 (input gates), each input gate is represented by a duplicator gadget. By construction, the presence or absence of its designated input edge encodes the Boolean value assigned to that gate. By correctness of the duplicator gadget, its output edges are present if and only if the input edge is present. Hence the duplicator correctly encodes the value of each input gate.

Assume now that for every gate at level at most $\ell$, the corresponding gadget in $B_C$ produces an output edge that is present if and only if the gate evaluates to TRUE. Let $g$ be a gate at level $\ell+1$. By construction, the input vertices of the gadget corresponding to $g$ are identified with the output vertices of gadgets at level $\ell$. By the induction hypothesis, these vertices encode exactly the Boolean values of the predecessors of $g$ in the circuit.

Since the AND and OR gadgets were shown to compute the correct Boolean function on their designated input edges, the output edge of the gadget corresponding to $g$ is present after applying its update sequence if and only if the gate $g$ evaluates to TRUE.

It remains to verify that propagated edges from upper levels do not alter the intended behavior of duplicators. By the choice of $k$, the number of additional $-1$ colored neighbors that may accumulate at any duplicator is strictly smaller than the size of the flower center. Therefore, the application of $\Phi_1$ produces the same color change as in the isolated analysis of the duplicator, and its outputs depend only on its designated input.

Finally, since $w_C$ is defined as the concatenation of the update sequences of all gadgets in increasing order of their level, every gadget is evaluated only after all gadgets at smaller levels have been evaluated. Hence the above argument applies to all levels.

Therefore, the designated output edge of $B_C$ is present after applying $w_C$ if and only if the output gate of $C$ evaluates to TRUE. □

### 3.4 The Construction is Computable in LOGSPACE

The parameter $k$ can be computed in logarithmic space by counting the number of AND and OR gates and applying $k > 7n_\wedge + 6n_\vee + 9(n_\wedge + n_\vee)$, using $O(\log n)$ bits for the counters.

The vertex set of $B_C$ consists of gadgets associated with each gate, as well as duplicator gadgets. Although the duplicator gadget depends on a parameter $k = O(n)$, each vertex can be identified by a pair (gate index, local gadget index), which requires $O(\log n)$ space. Edges are generated on-the-fly by iterating over gates and their connections in the input circuit. For each output edge, the corresponding input vertex of the next gadget is reconstructed from its gate index and local index, so there is no need to store entire layers of outputs.

The coloring $c_C$ is determined locally by gadget type and local index, and is written simultaneously when generating vertices. The update sequence $w_C$ is generated by iterating over gates in topological order and writing each gadget's fixed sequence in order. Since the construction of each gadget only requires $O(\log n)$ space for indices and counters, the entire construction $(B_C, w_C)$ can be computed in logarithmic space. This concludes Theorem 1.

## 4 Conclusions

In this work, we introduced a local graph transformation, which we call local homophily, inspired by adaptive networks and based on the principles of majority dynamics and homophily. We defined the class of flower graphs and proved a key structural lemma that underlies the functioning of the duplication gadget. We then presented the construction of the gadgets, explained how to assemble them into circuits, and proved the correctness of the overall construction. Finally, we discussed how the construction can be computed in logspace, leading to our main theorem establishing the **P**-completeness of the LHE.

Several directions for future research emerge from this work. One natural question is to further study the dynamics of the local homophily transformation itself, for example by characterizing the set of graphs reachable from a given class of initial graphs. Potential applications could include consensus or other complex processes on adaptive networks. It would also be interesting to analyze the computational complexity of other local transformations, or to consider complexity questions on local homophily itself, such as reachability: "given two bicolored graphs, can one be reached from the other via local homophily?" Finally, one could explore richer algebraic structures associated with the transformation, which may provide additional insights into its behavior and computational properties.

# A Full Behavior of the Gates

This appendix provides figures illustrating the full behavior of the OR and AND gadgets.

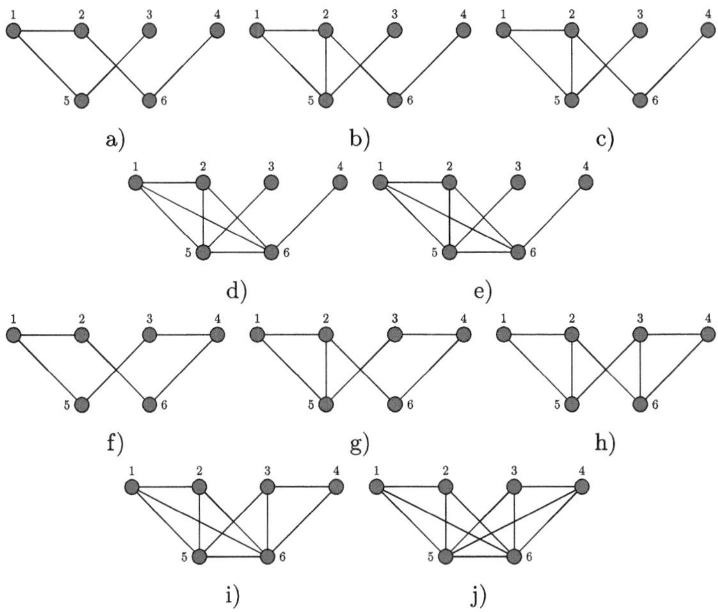


**Fig. 7.** Behavior of the OR gadget: **a)** OR gadget with one input TRUE and one input FALSE. **b)–e)** Evolution according to $w_\vee$. **f)** OR gadget with both inputs TRUE. **g)–j)** Evolution according to $w_\vee$. The case with both inputs FALSE is trivial. The case with inputs FALSE and TRUE is symmetrical to TRUE and FALSE.

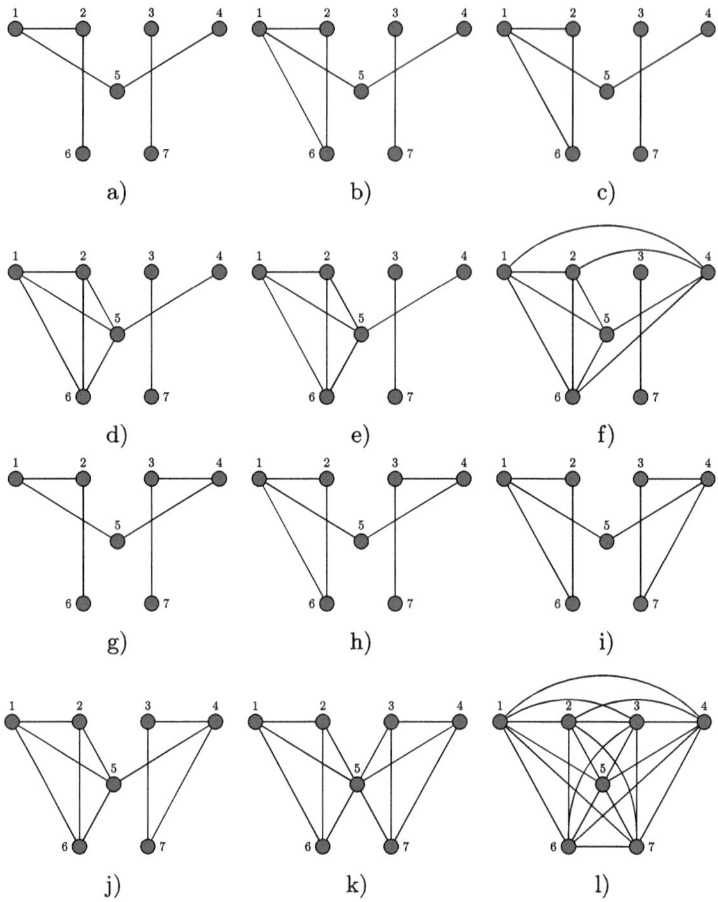


**Fig. 8.** Behavior of the AND gadget: **a)** AND gadget with one input TRUE and one input FALSE. **b)–f)** Evolution according to $w_\wedge$. **g)** AND gadget with both inputs TRUE. **h)–l)** Evolution according to $w_\wedge$. The case with both inputs FALSE is trivial. The case with inputs FALSE and TRUE is symmetrical to TRUE and FALSE.

## References

1. Cruciani, E., Mimun, H.A., Quattropani, M., Rizzo, S.: Phase transitions of the kmajority dynamics in a biased communication model. In: Proceedings of the 22nd International Conference on Distributed Computing and Networking, pp. 146–155 (2021)
2. Greenlaw, R., Hoover, H.J., Ruzzo, W.L.: Limits to Parallel Computation: P-completeness Theory. Oxford University Press (1995)
3. Gross, T., Blasius, B.: Adaptive coevolutionary networks: a review. J. R. Soc. Interface **5**(20), 259–271 (2008)
4. Kozma, B., Barrat, A.: Consensus formation on adaptive networks. Phys. Rev. E Stat. Nonlinear Soft Matter Phys. **77**(1), 016102 (2008)

5. Ladner, R.E.: The circuit value problem is log space complete for p. ACM SIGACT News **7**(1), 18–20 (1975)
6. Loveland, D., Koutra, D.: Unveiling the impact of local homophily on GNN fairness: In-depth analysis and new benchmarks. In: Proceedings of the 2025 SIAM International Conference on Data Mining (SDM), pp. 608–617. SIAM (2025)
7. McPherson, M., Smith-Lovin, L., Cook, J.M.: Birds of a feather: homophily in social networks. Ann. Rev. Sociol. **27**(1), 415–444 (2001)
8. Nguyen, V.X., Xiao, G., Xu, X.J., Wu, Q., Xia, C.Y.: Dynamics of opinion formation under majority rules on complex social networks. Sci. Rep. **10**(1), 456 (2020)
9. Sayama, H., et al.: Modeling complex systems with adaptive networks. Comput. Math. Appl. **65**(10), 1645–1664 (2013)
10. Talaga, S., Nowak, A.: Homophily as a process generating social networks: insights from social distance attachment model. J. Artif. Soc. Soc. Simul. **23**(2), 6 (2020). https://doi.org/10.18564/jasss.4252, http://jasss.soc.surrey.ac.uk/23/2/6.html

# On the Complexity of $k$-Colorable Perfect Matching

Toranosuke Kokai[1(✉)], Akira Suzuki[2], Yuma Tamura[1], and Xiao Zhou[1]

[1] Graduate School of Information Sciences, Tohoku University, Sendai, Japan
kokai.toranosuke.s6@dc.tohoku.ac.jp, {tamura,zhou}@tohoku.ac.jp
[2] Center for Data-driven Science and Artificial Intelligence, Tohoku University, Sendai, Japan
akira@tohoku.ac.jp

**Abstract.** The $k$-Colorable Perfect Matching ($k$-CPM) problem asks whether the vertex set of a graph can be partitioned into $k$ sets, each of which induces a matching. In this paper, we investigate the (parameterized) complexity of $k$-CPM on restricted graphs. Our main results are threefold. First, we show that $k$-CPM is NP-complete for bipartite graphs for any $k \geq 2$, contrasting with the polynomial-time solvability of a standard perfect matching and coloring on bipartite graphs. Second, we prove that 3-CPM is NP-complete for planar graphs. This completes the complexity classification of $k$-CPM on planar graphs: the problem is NP-complete for $2 \leq k \leq 3$ and polynomial-time solvable for $k \geq 4$. Third, we analyze the problem with respect to the parameterized complexity. We prove that $k$-CPM, where $k$ is part of the input, is W[1]-hard when parameterized by clique-width, but becomes fixed-parameter tractable (FPT) when parameterized by both clique-width and $k$. Additionally, we provide an XP algorithm when parameterized by clique-width and an FPT algorithm for chordal graphs when parameterized by $k$.

**Keywords:** Graph algorithm · Perfect Matching · Coloring

## 1 Introduction

Graph coloring is a central topic in graph theory with a wide range of applications in computer science. In its classical definition, a *vertex coloring* of a graph $G = (V, E)$ is an assignment of colors to the vertices such that no two adjacent vertices receive the same color. For a positive integer $k$, a graph is said to be *$k$-colorable* if it can be colored using at most $k$ colors. In this setting, for each color $i \in \{1, \ldots, k\}$, the set of vertices $V_i \subseteq V$ assigned color $i$, called a *color class*, forms an independent set, and the collection $V_1, \ldots, V_k$ forms a partition of $V$.

Several generalizations have been studied in which the subgraphs induced by each color class may contain edges. Cowen et al. introduced the concept of

This work was partially supported by JSPS KAKENHI Grant Numbers JP25K14980 and JP25K21148.


Y. Li et al. (Eds.): COCOON 2026, LNCS 16835, pp. 288–300, 2027.
https://doi.org/10.1007/978-981-92-3309-0_22

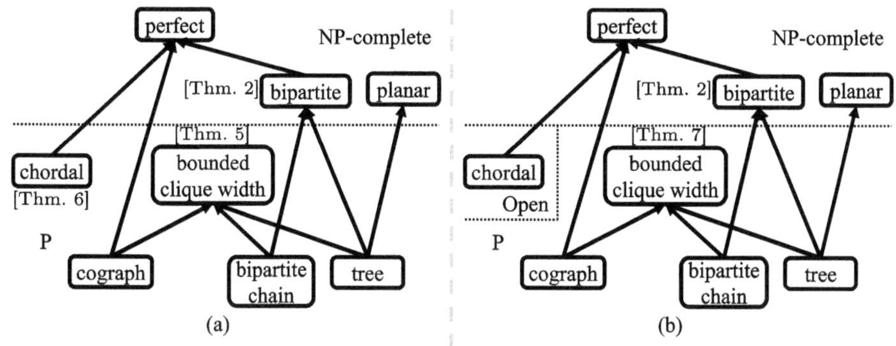


**Fig. 1.** Known and our results with respect to graph classes. Each arrow $A \to B$ means that the graph class $A$ is proper subclass of the graph class $B$. Note that, for planar graphs, NP-completeness for $k = 2$ and polynomial-time solvability for $k \geq 4$ were shown in [3], whereas NP-completeness for $k = 3$ is proved in Theorem 4. (a) The case where $k$ is treated as a constant. (b) The case where $k$ is given as part of the input.

*defective coloring* (or $(k, d)$-coloring), where the vertex set is partitioned into $k$ sets such that each color class induces a subgraph of maximum degree at most $d$ [2]. This relaxation provides a flexible framework for modeling applications in which weak interference within each color class is permissible.

In this paper, we focus on a specific and structured variant of such colorings in which each vertex has degree exactly one within each color class. Formally, for a positive integer $k$, a *$k$-colorable perfect matching* is a partition of the vertex set $V$ into $k$ sets $V_1, \ldots, V_k$ such that each $V_i$ induces a matching rather than an independent set. The $k$-Colorable Perfect Matching ($k$-CPM) problem asks whether a given graph has a $k$-colorable perfect matching.

*Known Results.* The complexity of $k$-CPM has been investigated in several contexts. Schaefer first showed that 2-CPM is NP-complete for general graphs [10]. More recently, Demaine et al. strengthened this result by proving that 2-CPM remains NP-complete even for 2-connected 3-regular planar graphs [3]. They also showed that $k$-CPM is NP-complete for general graphs for any fixed $k \geq 2$. On the positive side, they provided polynomial-time algorithms for $k$-CPM when $k \geq 4$, restricted to either 3-regular graphs or planar graphs.

*Our Contribution.* This paper provides a detailed study of $k$-CPM from the viewpoint of restricted graph classes and parameterized complexity. (See Fig. 1.)

First, we investigate the problem on bipartite graphs. While finding a standard perfect matching is solvable in $O(n^{2.5})$ time [7], $k$-CPM on bipartite graphs is expected to be more complex due to the "harder" constraint of induced matchings; finding a maximum induced matching is NP-hard even in bipartite graphs of maximum degree 4 [11]. We settle the complexity by proving that, in fact, $k$-CPM is NP-complete for bipartite graphs for any $k \geq 2$.

Second, we prove that 3-CPM is NP-complete for planar graphs. This result completes the complexity classification of $k$-CPM on planar graphs; the problem is NP-complete for $2 \leq k \leq 3$ and polynomial-time solvable for $k \geq 4$.

Finally, we analyze the problem through the lens of parameterized complexity. We focus on *clique-width* as a structural parameter. Clique-width is a more general parameter than treewidth and is particularly useful for handling dense graph classes such as cographs and distance-hereditary graphs. We show that $k$-CPM is W[1]-hard when parameterized by clique-width. On the positive side, we prove that the problem is fixed-parameter tractable (FPT) when parameterized by both clique-width and $k$. We also present an XP algorithm parameterized by clique-width. Furthermore, for chordal graphs, we prove that the problem is FPT when parameterized by $k$ alone.

Due to the space limitation, proofs marked $(*)$ are omitted.

## 2 Preliminaries

For a positive integer $n$, we write $[n] = \{1, \dots, n\}$. Let $G = (V, E)$ be a graph: we also denote by $V(G)$ and $E(G)$ the vertex set and the edge set of $G$, respectively. All the graphs considered in this paper are finite, simple, and undirected. For a vertex subset $V' \subseteq V$, let $G[V']$ denote the subgraph induced by $V'$. For a vertex $v$ of $G$, we denote by $N_G(v)$ and $N_G[v]$ the open and closed neighborhoods of $v$ in $G$, respectively, that is, $N_G(v) = \{u \in V \mid uv \in E(G)\}$ and $N_G[v] = N_G(v) \cup \{v\}$. We sometimes drop the subscript $G$ if it is clear from the context. The *degree* $\deg_G(v)$ of $v$ is the size of $N_G(v)$, that is, $\deg_G(v) = |N_G(v)|$. The *maximum degree* of $G$ is defined as $\max_{v \in V} \deg_G(v)$. A vertex subset $C \subseteq V(G)$ is called a *clique* if $uv \in E(G)$ for any two distinct vertices $u, v \in C$. A vertex subset $I \subseteq V(G)$ is called an *independent set* if $uv \notin E(G)$ for any two vertices $u, v \in I$. A graph is *bipartite* if there exists a partition $(L, R)$ of $V$ such that both $L$ and $R$ are independent sets. A bipartite graph with a partition $(L, R)$ is *complete* if every pair of $\ell \in L$ and $r \in R$ is adjacent. The complete bipartite graph with $|L| = m$ and $|R| = n$ is denoted by $K_{m,n}$. A graph is *planar* if it can be embedded in the plane without crossing edges.

For a positive integer $k$, a *$k$-coloring* of a graph $G$ is a mapping $c : V(G) \to [k]$ such that $c(u) \neq c(v)$ whenever $uv \in E(G)$. Thus, for each $i \in [k]$, the vertex set $c^{-1}(i) = \{u \in V(G) \mid c(u) = i\}$ is an independent set, and $c^{-1}(1), \dots, c^{-1}(k)$ form a partition of $V$. We call $c(u)$ the *color* of $u$. The *chromatic number* of $G$, denoted by $\chi(G)$, is the smallest number $k$ such that $G$ has a $k$-coloring.

A *matching* $M$ is a subset of $E(G)$ such that each vertex of $G$ is incident to at most one edge of $M$. A matching $M$ is called *perfect* if every vertex of $G$ is incident to exactly one edge of $M$. An *induced matching* $S$ is a subset of $V(G)$ such that every vertex of $G[S]$ has degree exactly 1.

For a positive integer $k$, a *$k$-colorable perfect matching* of a graph $G$ is a mapping $c_{\mathrm{pm}} : V(G) \to [k]$ such that each vertex $u \in V(G)$ has exactly one neighbor with the same color as itself. In other words, for each $i \in [k]$, the vertex set $c_{\mathrm{pm}}^{-1}(i) = \{u \in V(G) \mid c(u) = i\}$ is an induced matching, and $c_{\mathrm{pm}}^{-1}(1), \dots, c_{\mathrm{pm}}^{-1}(k)$

form a partition of $V$. The *$k$-chromatic perfect matching number* of $G$, denoted by $\chi_{\mathrm{pm}}(G)$, is the smallest number $k$ such that $G$ has a $k$-colorable perfect matching. For a vertex subset $U \subseteq V(G)$, let $c_{\mathrm{pm}}(U) = \{c_{\mathrm{pm}}(u) \mid u \in U\}$.

The $k$-Colorable Perfect Matching ($k$-CPM) problem is as follows.

> **$k$-Colorable Perfect matching ($k$-CPM)**
>
> **Input:** A graph $G = (V, E)$.
> **Output:** Does $G$ admit a $k$-colorable perfect matching?

We now turn to the notion of the clique-width of a graph. For a positive integer $w$, a *$w$-labeled graph* is a graph whose vertices are labeled with integers from $[w] = \{1, 2, \ldots, w\}$. We consider the following four operations on $w$-labeled graphs.

**Introduce** $i(v)$ : Create a graph consisting of a single vertex $v$ labeled with $i \in [w]$.
**Union** $\oplus$ : Take the disjoint union of two $w$-labeled graphs.
**Relabel** $\rho_{i \to j}$ : Replace every label $i$ with $j$.
**Join** $\eta_{i,j}$ : Add all possible edges between vertices labeled $i$ and $j$.

The *clique-width* $cw(G)$ of a graph $G$ is the smallest integer $w$ such that a $w$-labeled graph isomorphic to $G$ can be obtained from a sequence of these operations. The sequence can be represented by a rooted tree, called a *$w$-expression tree* $T$ of $G$, whose nodes are classified according to the above operations, namely, *introduce nodes*, *union nodes*, *relabel nodes*, and *join nodes*, respectively. It is known that, given a graph $G$ of clique-width at most $w$, there exists an algorithm that computes a $(2^{w+1} - 1)$-expression tree for $G$ in time $O(|V(G)|^3)$ [6,8,9].

## 3 Hardness Results

In this section, we establish several hardness results for the $k$-CPM problem.

### 3.1 $k$-CPM on Bipartite Graphs

We begin by describing the source problem for our reduction. Let $\varphi$ be a conjunctive normal form (CNF) formula over Boolean variables $\mathcal{X} = \{x_1, \ldots, x_n\}$, given by a conjunction of clauses $\mathcal{C} = \{C_1, \ldots, C_m\}$, that is, $\varphi = C_1 \wedge \cdots \wedge C_m$. A formula $\varphi$ is *NAE-satisfiable* if there is a truth assignment $A : \mathcal{X} \to \{\text{True}, \text{False}\}$ such that no clause in $\mathcal{C}$ has all its literals assigned the same value under $A$. A *positive 3-CNF formula* is a CNF formula in which each clause in $\mathcal{C}$ consists of exactly three positive literals. The Positive NAE 3-SAT problem asks whether a given positive 3-CNF formula $\varphi$ is NAE-satisfiable. This problem is known to be NP-complete [10].

We now prove the following theorem regarding the complexity of 2-CPM.

**Theorem 1.** *2-CPM is NP-complete even for bipartite graphs.*

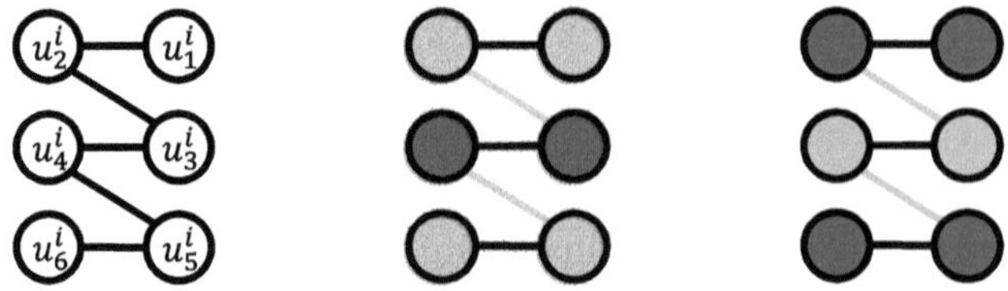


(a) Variable Gadget (b) True (c) False

**Fig. 2.** (a) The variable gadget $U_i$. If the variable $x_i$ is assigned True (resp. False), then the corresponding 2-colorable perfect matching is indicated in (b) (resp. (c)).

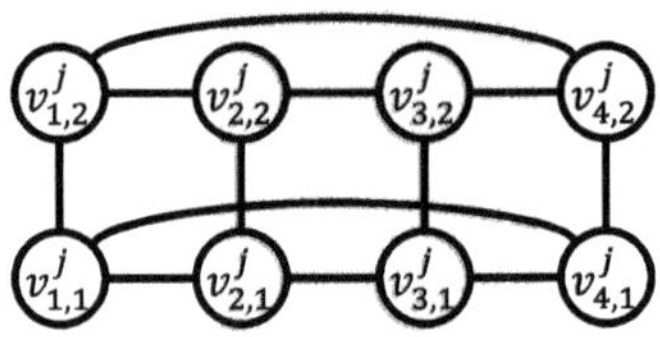


**Fig. 3.** The clause gadget $H_j$.

It is easy to verify that $k$-CPM belongs to the class NP. To prove Theorem 1, we provide a polynomial-time reduction from POSITIVE NAE 3-SAT to 2-CPM. Let $\varphi$ be an instance of POSITIVE NAE 3-SAT. We construct an instance $G$ of 2-CPM from $\varphi$ using the following gadgets.

**Variable Gadget.** For each Boolean variable $x_i \in \mathcal{X}$, we construct a variable gadget $U_i$ consisting of a path of six vertices $\langle u_1^i, \ldots, u_6^i \rangle$ as illustrated in Fig. 2(a). The gadget $U_i$ admits a unique perfect matching such that $M = \{u_1^i u_2^i, u_3^i u_4^i, u_5^i u_6^i\}$. With respect to this matching, there are exactly two valid 2-colorable perfect matchings defined as follows.

$$c_{\text{true}} : \{u_1^i, \ldots, u_6^i\} \to \{1, 2\} \text{ such that } c_{\text{true}}(u_\ell^i) = \begin{cases} 1 & \text{if } \ell \in \{1, 2, 5, 6\}, \\ 2 & \text{otherwise.} \end{cases}$$

$$c_{\text{false}} : \{u_1^i, \ldots, u_6^i\} \to \{1, 2\} \text{ such that } c_{\text{false}}(u_\ell^i) = \begin{cases} 1 & \text{if } \ell \in \{3, 4\}, \\ 2 & \text{otherwise.} \end{cases}$$

Assigning the value True (resp. False) to the variable $x_i$ corresponds to coloring the vertices of $U_i$ by $c_{\text{true}}$ (resp. $c_{\text{false}}$).

**Clause Gadget.** The clause gadget $H_j$ for a clause $C_j \in \mathcal{C}$ consists of the vertices $V(H_j) = \{v_{p,q}^j \mid 1 \le p \le 4, 1 \le q \le 2\}$ and the edges $E(H_j) = \{v_{p,1}^j v_{p,2}^j \mid 1 \le p \le 4\} \cup \{v_{p,q}^j v_{p+1,q}^j \mid 1 \le p \le 3, 1 \le q \le 2\} \cup \{v_{1,1}^j v_{4,1}^j, v_{1,2}^j v_{4,2}^j\}$. The clause gadget is illustrated in Fig. 3.

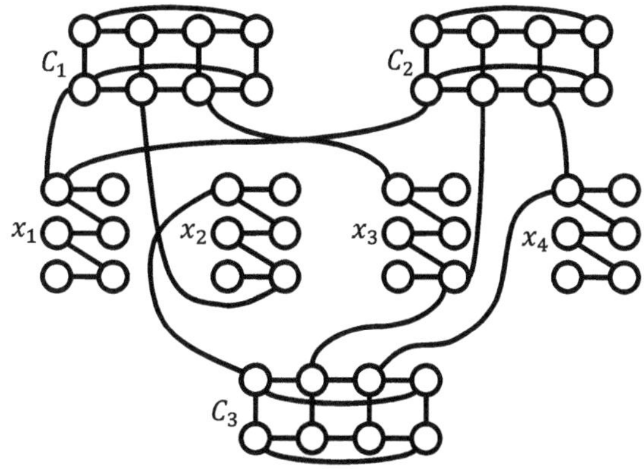


**Fig. 4.** An example illustrating the graph $G$ obtained from the positive 3-CNF formula $\varphi = (x_1 \vee x_2 \vee x_3) \wedge (x_1 \vee x_3 \vee x_4) \wedge (x_2 \vee x_3 \vee x_4)$.

**Overall Construction.** Using the gadgets introduced above, we construct a graph $G$ for 2-CPM from $\varphi$. We first place the variable gadget $U_i$ and the clause gadget $H_j$ corresponding to each variable $x_i \in \mathcal{X}$ and each clause $C_j \in \mathcal{C}$, respectively. Then, for a clause $C_j = (x \vee y \vee z)$, we refer to $x, y$, and $z$ as the *first literal*, *second literal*, and *third literal*, respectively. Finally, for each pair of $i \in [n]$ and $j \in [m]$, we add the edges $E^* = \{u_2^i v_{1,1}^j \mid x_i \text{ is the first literal of } C_j\} \cup \{u_5^i v_{2,1}^j \mid x_i \text{ is the second literal of } C_j\} \cup \{u_2^i v_{3,1}^j \mid x_i \text{ is the third literal of } C_j\}$. Figure 4 shows the graph $G$ constructed from $\varphi$ by the above procedure.

It is clear that the graph $G$ can be obtained in polynomial time. Obviously, the variable gadgets and the clause gadgets are bipartite. Furthermore, we connect the variable gadget to the clause gadget such that no odd cycles are introduced. Therefore, $G$ is a bipartite graph. To complete the proof of Theorem 1, it remains to show the correctness of the reduction, which is provided in the following lemma.

**Lemma 1.** *The instance $\varphi$ of* Positive NAE 3-SAT *is NAE-satisfiable if and only if the constructed graph $G$ has a 2-colorable perfect matching.*

*Proof.* (Only-if direction.) Suppose that $\varphi$ is NAE-satisfiable, that is, there is a truth assignment $A : \mathcal{X} \to \{\text{True}, \text{False}\}$ such that no clause in $\mathcal{C}$ has all its literals assigned the same value under $A$. If $A(x_i) = \text{True}$ (resp. $A(x_i) = \text{False}$), we color the vertices in $U_i$ according to $c_{\text{true}}$ (resp. $c_{\text{false}}$). Note that, since $\varphi$ is NAE-satisfiable, the three vertices adjacent to each clause gadget $H_j$ do not all share the same color. For any assignment of colors to these three vertices, $H_j$ admits a 2-colorable perfect matching, as illustrated in Fig. 5. Therefore, if $\varphi$ is NAE-satisfiable, then $G$ has a 2-colorable perfect matching.

(If direction.) Suppose that there exists a 2-colorable perfect matching $c_{\text{pm}} : V(G) \to \{1, 2\}$. For each $i \in [n]$, since the vertices $u_1^i$ and $u_6^i$ in the variable gadget $U_i$ have degree 1, it holds that $c_{\text{pm}}(u_1^i) = c_{\text{pm}}(u_2^i)$ and $c_{\text{pm}}(u_5^i) = c_{\text{pm}}(u_6^i)$.

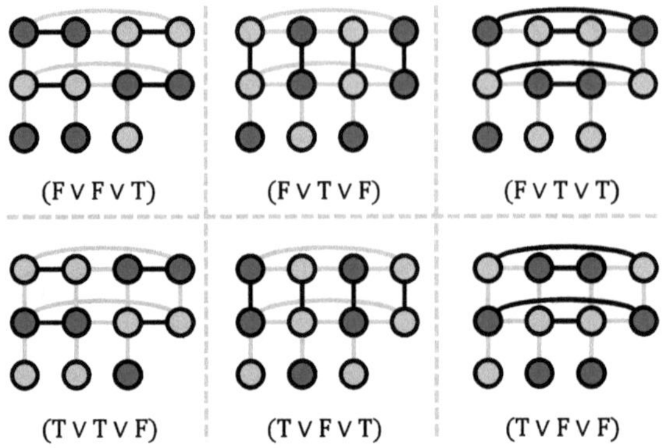


**Fig. 5.** All possible 2-colorable perfect matchings of a clause gadget corresponding to all valid truth assignments to a clause $C = (x \vee y \vee z)$.

Moreover, we claim that $c_{\mathrm{pm}}(u_2^i) = c_{\mathrm{pm}}(u_5^i)$. Suppose otherwise, and assume that $c_{\mathrm{pm}}(u_2^i) = 1$ and $c_{\mathrm{pm}}(u_5^i) = 2$ without loss of generality. Then, $c_{\mathrm{pm}}(u_3^i) = 2$ and $c_{\mathrm{pm}}(u_4^i) = 1$ holds. However, both neighbors of $u_3^i$, namely $u_2^i$ and $u_4^i$, are assigned colors different from that of $u_3^i$, which contradicts the fact that $c_{\mathrm{pm}}$ is a 2-colorable perfect matching of $G$.

We define a truth assignment $A : \mathcal{X} \to \{\text{True, False}\}$ such that for each $i \in [n]$, $A(x_i) = $ True (resp. $A(x_i) = $ False) if $c_{\mathrm{pm}}(u_2^i) = c_{\mathrm{pm}}(u_5^i) = 1$ (resp. $c_{\mathrm{pm}}(u_2^i) = c_{\mathrm{pm}}(u_5^i) = 2$). No clause in $\mathcal{C}$ can have all its literals assigned the same value under $A$; otherwise, some clause gadget would have three neighbors with the same color, making it impossible for $c_{\mathrm{pm}}$ to be a 2-colorable perfect matching. Therefore, if $G$ has a 2-colorable perfect matching, then $\varphi$ is NAE-satisfiable. □

The following theorem can be proved by the reduction from 2-CPM on bipartite graphs.

**Theorem 2** (∗). *For any $k \geq 2$, $k$-CPM is NP-complete even for bipartite graphs.*

### 3.2 $k$-CPM Parameterized by Clique-Width

**Theorem 3.** *When $k$ is part of the input, $k$-CPM is W[1]-hard when parameterized by clique-width.*

We prove Theorem 3 by a parameterized reduction from the Coloring problem, which asks whether $G$ admits a $k$-coloring, where the integer $k$ is part of the input. This problem is known to be W[1]-hard when parameterized by clique-width [4]. Let $(G, k)$ be an instance of Coloring. We construct an instance $(G', k)$ of $k$-CPM from $G$, when $k$ is part of the input.

Suppose that $V(G) = \{v_1, \ldots, v_n\}$, where $n$ is an integer. Let $G'$ be the graph obtained from $G$ by adding a vertex $u_i$ of degree 1 such that $N_{G'}(u_i) = \{v_i\}$ for each $i \in [n]$. The following two lemmas complete the proof of Theorem 3.

**Lemma 2 (*).** $cw(G') \leq cw(G) + 1$.

**Lemma 3 (*).** *The instance* $(G, k)$ *has a solution to* Coloring *if and only if the instance* $(G', k)$ *has a solution to* $k$*-CPM.*

### 3.3 3-CPM for Planar Graphs

The 3-Coloring problem is known to be NP-complete even for planar graphs [5]. By applying the same reduction as in Sect. 3.2 with $k = 3$, we can reduce 3-Coloring to 3-CPM on planar graphs. Combined with the known results that for planar graphs, 2-CPM is NP-complete and $k$-CPM is solvable in polynomial time for any $k \geq 4$ [3], we obtain the complexity classification of $k$-CPM on planar graphs.

**Theorem 4.** *For planar graphs,* $k$*-CPM is NP-complete for* $2 \leq k \leq 3$ *and polynomial-time solvable for any* $k \geq 4$.

## 4 Positive Results

### 4.1 FPT Algorithms

In this section, we study the fixed-parameter tractability of $k$-CPM.

**Clique-Width.** The property that $G$ has a $k$-colorable perfect matching is expressible in monadic second-order logic, called $\mathrm{MSO}_1$. The result of Courcelle et al. directly implies Theorem 5.

**Theorem 5 (*).** *Let* $G$ *be a graph with* $n$ *vertices and clique-width* $\mathsf{cw}$. *For a positive integer* $k$, $k$*-CPM can be solved in time* $f(k, \mathsf{cw}) \cdot n$, *where* $f$ *is some computable function.*

**Chordal Graphs.** A graph is *chordal* if it does not contain any cycle of length at least four as an induced subgraph. From Theorem 5 and the properties of chordal graphs, the following theorem can be obtained.

**Theorem 6 (*).** *Let* $G$ *be a chordal graph with* $n$ *vertices. For a positive integer* $k$, $k$*-CPM can be solved in time* $f(k) \cdot n$ *for chordal graphs, where* $f$ *is some computable function.*

### 4.2 XP Algorithms

$k$-CPM was shown to be W[1]-hard when parameterized by clique-width in Theorem 3. Moreover, $k$-CPM admits an FPT algorithm when parameterized by clique-width and $k$ in Theorem 5. A natural question is whether $k$-CPM belongs to XP when parametrized solely by clique-width. This section shows the following theorem.

**Theorem 7.** *Given a $w$-expression tree for $G$, $\chi_{pm}(G)$ can be computed in time $O(64^w w(n+1)^{2 \cdot 16^w + 1})$.*

To show Theorem 7, we present an algorithm over a given $w$-expression tree $\mathcal{T}$. Let $t$ be a node in $\mathcal{T}$. We denote by $G_t = (V_t, E_t)$ the labeled graph constructed by operations in the subtree rooted at $t$. We compute candidate solutions on $G_t$ for each node $t$ of $\mathcal{T}$ in a bottom-up manner. Let $[w]$ be the set of labels and let $\mathcal{P} = 2^{[w]}$ denote its power sets. We denote by $L_i$ the set of vertices labeled by $i \in [w]$. For each $\alpha \in \mathcal{P}$, define $L_\alpha = \bigcup_{i \in \alpha} L_i$.

Consider a colorable perfect matching $c : V(G) \to [n]$ of $G$. In the restriction $c_t$ to $V_t$, each vertex has at most one neighbor with the same color as itself. To obtain an XP algorithm for clique-width, this information is managed using labels from $[w]$ instead of $c_t$. For a certain color $s$ in $c_t$, denote by $J_s$ the set of vertices with $s$, that is, $J_s = \{u \in V_t \mid c_t(u) = s\}$. Moreover, let $I_s \subseteq J_s$ be a vertex subset such that no vertex in $I_s$ is adjacent to any other vertex of the same color in $c_t$. Here, we prove the following lemma to update a candidate solution on the $w$-expression tree $\mathcal{T}$.

**Lemma 4.** *Let $c$ be a colorable perfect matching of $G$, and let $c_t$ be the restriction of $c$ to $G_t$, where $t$ is a node in $\mathcal{T}$. For each color $s$ and each label $i \in [w]$, the restriction $c_t$ satisfies the following two claims:*

(a) $|I_s \cap L_i| \leq 1$; and
(b) if $|I_s \cap L_i| = 1$, then $|J_s \cap L_i| = 1$.

For each color $s$ in $c_t$ and each pair $(\alpha, \beta) \in \mathcal{P} \times \mathcal{P}$, we say that a color $s$ is *compatible with* $(\alpha, \beta)$ if

- $\alpha = \{i \in [w] \mid J_s \cap L_i \neq \emptyset\}$, and
- $\beta = \{i \in [w] \mid I_s \cap L_i \neq \emptyset\}$.

That is, $\alpha$ represents a set of labels associated with at least one vertex of color $s$, and each label in $\beta$ corresponds to a set of vertices that contains an unpaired vertex of color $s$. Consequently, whenever the color $s$ is compatible with $(\alpha, \beta)$, we have $\beta \subseteq \alpha$. A function $f : \mathcal{P} \times \mathcal{P} \to [n]$ is *valid* in $G_t$ if there exists a mapping $c_t : V_t \to [n]$ for $G_t$ such that every pair $(\alpha, \beta) \in \mathcal{P} \times \mathcal{P}$ satisfies $f(\alpha, \beta) = \ell$, where $\ell$ is the number of colors compatible with $(\alpha, \beta)$.

For each node $t \in \mathcal{T}$, we define $F_t$ as the set of all valid functions $f$ in $G_t$. At the root node $r$ of $\mathcal{T}$, the desired mapping $c$ must be a colorable perfect matching of $G$. Therefore, we look up functions $f : \mathcal{P} \times \mathcal{P} \to [n]$ in $F_r$ such that $f(\alpha, \beta) = 0$ for every pair $(\alpha, \beta) \in \mathcal{P} \times \mathcal{P}$ with $\beta \neq \emptyset$. Let $F_{\text{pm}}$ be the set of such functions $f$. Then $\chi_{\text{pm}}(G)$ is determined by

$$\chi_{\text{pm}}(G) = \min_{f \in F_{\text{pm}}} \sum_{\alpha \in \mathcal{P}} f(\alpha, \emptyset).$$

In the following, we demonstrate how to compute $F_t$ according to the type of a node $t$ in $\mathcal{T}$.

**Introduce Node.** When a vertex $v$ with label $i$ is introduced, the vertex $v$ is assigned a certain color. Therefore, we put the following function $f$ in $F_t$:

$$f(\alpha, \beta) = \begin{cases} 1 & \text{if } \alpha = \beta = \{i\} \\ 0 & \text{otherwise} \end{cases}$$

**Join Node.** Suppose that node $t$ is labeled with $\eta_{i,j}$ and has a child node $t'$. Let $c_t$ be the restriction of a colorable perfect matching $c$ of $G$, and consider a certain color $s$ that appears in both $L_i$ and $L_j$. Since there is an edge between every vertex of $L_i$ and every vertex of $L_j$ in $G_t$, there are unique vertices $u \in J_s \cap L_i$ and $v \in J_s \cap L_j$. Moreover, $u$ (resp. $v$) has no neighbor of the same color other than $v$ (resp. $u$). Therefore, for every pair $(\alpha, \beta) \in \mathcal{P} \times \mathcal{P}$ with $\{i, j\} \subseteq \alpha$, there is no color compatible with $(\alpha, \beta)$ if $\beta \cap \{i, j\} \neq \emptyset$. Otherwise, if $\beta \cap \{i, j\} = \emptyset$, in the restriction $c_{t'}$ of $c$ to $G_{t'}$, the color $s$ is compatible with $(\alpha, \beta \cap \{i, j\})$.

Suppose next that $J_s \cap L_i = \emptyset$ or $J_s \cap L_j = \emptyset$ in the restriction $c_t$. In this case, the color $s$ compatible with a pair $(\alpha, \beta)$ is also compatible with $(\alpha, \beta)$ in the restriction $c_{t'}$. In summary, a function $f$ is valid if there exists a valid function $f' \in F_{t'}$ such that the following equation holds for every $(\alpha, \beta) \in \mathcal{P} \times \mathcal{P}$:

$$f(\alpha, \beta) = \begin{cases} 0 & \text{if } \{i, j\} \subseteq \alpha \wedge \beta \cap \{i, j\} \neq \emptyset \\ f'(\alpha, \beta \cup \{i, j\}) & \text{if } \{i, j\} \subseteq \alpha \wedge \beta \cap \{i, j\} = \emptyset \\ f'(\alpha, \beta) & \text{otherwise} \end{cases}$$

We include the valid function $f$ in $F_t$ if and only if this condition holds.

**Relabel Node.** Suppose that node $t$ has a child node $t'$ and the vertices with label $i$ are relabeled to $j$. Let $c_{t'}$ be the restriction of a colorable perfect matching $c$ of $G$ to $G_{t'}$, and consider a certain color $s$.

Suppose that the color $s$ is compatible with $(\alpha, \beta) \in \mathcal{P} \times \mathcal{P}$ such that $\{i, j\} \subseteq \alpha$. If $\beta \cap \{i, j\} \neq \emptyset$, then $c_{t'}$ cannot be extended to the restriction $c_t$ of $c$ to $G_t$ due to the relabeling of $i$ to $j$ and Lemma 4. Therefore, we only consider a valid function $f' \in F_{t'}$ that satisfies $f'(\alpha, \beta) = 0$ for every pair $(\alpha, \beta) \in \mathcal{P} \times \mathcal{P}$ such that $\{i, j\} \subseteq \alpha$ and $\beta \cap \{i, j\} \neq \emptyset$. Let $F^*_{t'} \subseteq F_{t'}$ be the set of such functions.

Since $G_t$ has no vertex with label $i$, there is no color compatible with $(\alpha, \beta) \in \mathcal{P} \times \mathcal{P}$ such that $i \in \alpha$. Furthermore, every color in $c_{t'}$ compatible with $(\alpha, \beta)$ with $i \notin \alpha$ and $j \notin \alpha$ is compatible with $(\alpha, \beta)$ in $c_t$.

The nontrivial case is when $(\alpha, \beta)$ satisfies $i \notin \alpha$ and $j \in \alpha$. Let $s$ be a color appearing in $c_t$ compatible with $(\alpha, \beta)$. It is necessary to consider whether a vertex with $s$ originates from $L_i$ or $L_j$ in node $t'$. For a set $\gamma \in \mathcal{P}$, let $\gamma_{i \to j} = \gamma \cup \{j\} \setminus \{i\}$ if $i \in \gamma$; otherwise, let $\gamma_{i \to j} = \gamma$. We denote by $\Gamma(\alpha, \beta)$ the set of pairs $(\alpha', \beta') \in \mathcal{P} \times \mathcal{P}$ that corresponds to $(\alpha, \beta)$ after the relabeling. Formally,

$$\Gamma(\alpha, \beta) = \{(\alpha'_{i \to j}, \beta'_{i \to j}) \mid (\alpha', \beta') \in \mathcal{P} \times \mathcal{P}\}.$$

After relabeling, the number of colors compatible with $(\alpha, \beta)$ is equal to the total number of colors compatible with pairs in $\Gamma(\alpha, \beta)$. Therefore, a function $f$

is valid if there exists a valid function $f' \in F^*_{t'}$ such that the following equation holds for every $(\alpha, \beta) \in \mathcal{P} \times \mathcal{P}$:

$$f(\alpha, \beta) = \begin{cases} 0 & \text{if } i \in \alpha \\ f'(\alpha, \beta) & \text{if } i \notin \alpha \text{ and } j \notin \alpha \\ \sum_{(\alpha', \beta') \in \Gamma(\alpha, \beta)} f'(\alpha', \beta') & \text{otherwise} \end{cases}$$

We include the valid function $f$ in $F_t$ if and only if this condition holds.

**Union Node.** Let $\ell$ and $r$ be the two child nodes of $t$. We specify functions to be included in $F_t$ from fixed functions $f_\ell \in F_\ell$ and $f_r \in F_r$. This operation is performed for each pair $(f_\ell, f_r) \in F_\ell \times F_r$.

First, we introduce additional notation and terminology. Let $c_\ell$ and $c_r$ be color assignments corresponding to $f_\ell$ and $f_r$, respectively. We denote by $c_\ell \oplus c_r$ the corresponding color assignment of the vertices in $G_t = G_\ell \oplus G_r$. Then a color $s_\ell$ in $c_\ell$ and a color $s_r$ in $c_r$ can be *merged*, that is, the two colors are identified. The merge itself is represented by the pair $(s_\ell, s_r)$.

We use a function $g$ to denote the number of merges $(s_\ell, s_r)$ such that $s_\ell$ and $s_r$ are compatible with $(\alpha_\ell, \beta_\ell)$ and $(\alpha_r, \beta_r)$, respectively. Here, we assume that each color is involved in at most one merge. This is guaranteed by the fact that any color in a coloring of $G_t$ can be partitioned into at most one color from $G_\ell$ and at most one from $G_r$. Consequently, the total number of merges involving $s_\ell$ (resp. $s_r$) is bounded above by $f_\ell(\alpha_\ell, \beta_\ell)$ (resp. $f_r(\alpha_r, \beta_r)$). Formally, $g : \mathcal{P}^4 \to \{0, \ldots, n\}$ is a function satisfying the following conditions:

$$\forall (\alpha_\ell, \beta_\ell) \in \mathcal{P} \times \mathcal{P}, \quad \sum_{(\alpha_r, \beta_r) \in \mathcal{P} \times \mathcal{P}} g(\alpha_\ell, \beta_\ell, \alpha_r, \beta_r) \le f_\ell(\alpha_\ell, \beta_\ell),$$

$$\forall (\alpha_r, \beta_r) \in \mathcal{P} \times \mathcal{P}, \quad \sum_{(\alpha_\ell, \beta_\ell) \in \mathcal{P} \times \mathcal{P}} g(\alpha_\ell, \beta_\ell, \alpha_r, \beta_r) \le f_r(\alpha_r, \beta_r).$$

Note that we define $g(\alpha_\ell, \beta_\ell, \alpha_r, \beta_r) = 0$ if $\alpha_\ell$ or $\alpha_r$ is empty.

Given the function $g$, we now compute the number of colors compatible with $(\alpha, \beta) \in \mathcal{P} \times \mathcal{P}$ at node $t$ using $f_\ell$ and $f_r$. First, Lemma 4 implies that we must have $\alpha_\ell \cap \beta_r = \emptyset$ and $\alpha_r \cap \beta_\ell = \emptyset$. Therefore, any pair $(f_\ell, f_r) \in F_\ell \times F_r$ violating these conditions is discarded. Next, note that the total number of merged colors originating from $f_\ell(\alpha, \beta)$ is given by $\sum_{(\alpha_r, \beta_r) \in \mathcal{P} \times \mathcal{P}} g(\alpha, \beta, \alpha_r, \beta_r)$. Thus, the number of unmerged colors among the $f_\ell(\alpha, \beta)$ colors is equal to $f_\ell(\alpha_\ell, \beta_\ell) - \sum_{(\alpha_r, \beta_r)} g(\alpha, \beta, \alpha_r, \beta_r)$. Similarly, the number of unmerged colors among the $f_r(\alpha, \beta)$ colors is $f_r(\alpha, \beta) - \sum_{(\alpha_\ell, \beta_\ell)} g(\alpha_\ell, \beta_\ell, \alpha, \beta)$. Moreover, for each pairs $(\alpha_\ell, \beta_\ell)$ and $(\alpha_r, \beta_r)$ such that $\alpha_\ell \cup \alpha_r = \alpha$ and $\beta_\ell \cup \beta_r = \beta$, a color compatible with $(\alpha_\ell, \beta_\ell)$ and one compatible with $(\alpha_r, \beta_r)$ is merged into a single color compatible with $(\alpha, \beta)$. Consequently, the function $f$ is added to

$F_t$ according to the following equation:

$$\forall(\alpha,\beta),\quad f(\alpha,\beta) = f_\ell(\alpha,\beta) - \sum_{(\alpha_r,\beta_r)\in\mathcal{P}\times\mathcal{P}} g(\alpha,\beta,\alpha_r,\beta_r) + f_r(\alpha,\beta) - \sum_{(\alpha_\ell,\beta_\ell)\in\mathcal{P}\times\mathcal{P}} g(\alpha_\ell,\beta_\ell,\alpha,\beta) + \sum_{\substack{(\alpha_\ell,\beta_\ell)\in\mathcal{P}\times\mathcal{P}\\ (\alpha_r,\beta_r)\in\mathcal{P}\times\mathcal{P}\\ \alpha_\ell\cup\alpha_r=\alpha \text{ and } \beta_\ell\cup\beta_r=\beta}} g(\alpha_\ell,\beta_\ell,\alpha_r,\beta_r).$$

**Running Time.** The number of possible pairs $(\alpha,\beta)\in\mathcal{P}\times\mathcal{P}$ is bounded by $4^w$. The function $f$ independently assigns an integer from 0 up to $n$ to each pair $(\alpha,\beta)$, and hence the number of possible functions is $(n+1)^{4^w}$. Therefore, the size of $F_t$ is $O((n+1)^{4^w})$. The set $F_t$ of functions can be computed in time $O((n+1)^{4^w})$ for an introduce node, $O(4^w(n+1)^{4^w})$ for a join node, and $O(4^w \cdot 4^w(n+1)^{4^w}) = O(16^w(n+1)^{4^w})$ for a relabel node. The number of possible 4-tuple $(\alpha_\ell,\beta_\ell,\alpha_r,\beta_r)\in\mathcal{P}^4$ is bounded by $16^w$. Consider a union node. There are $O((n+1)^{4^w}\cdot(n+1)^{4^w}) = O((n+1)^{2\cdot 4^w})$ possible pairs $(f_\ell,f_r)\in F_\ell\times F_r$. The function $g$ independently assigns an integer from 0 up to $n$ to each 4-tuple, and hence the number of possible functions is $(n+1)^{16^w}$. For fixed $f_\ell$, $f_r$, and $g$, the value $f(\alpha,\beta)$ can be computed in $O(16^w w)$ time. Therefore, $F_t$ can be computed in time $O(4^w\cdot 16^w w\cdot(n+1)^{2\cdot 4^w}\cdot(n+1)^{16^w}) = O(64^w w(n+1)^{2\cdot 16^w})$ for a union node. Since the $w$-expression consists of $O(n)$ nodes [1], the total running time is $O(64^w w(n+1)^{2\cdot 16^w+1})$.

## 5 Future Work

Several directions remain open. For chordal graphs, we showed that $k$-CPM is FPT when parameterized by $k$. However, the complexity of $k$-CPM on chordal graphs when $k$ is part of the input remains open. Since $k$-CPM is NP-complete for bipartite graphs and W[1]-hard when parameterized by clique-width, it is natural to ask whether tractability holds for subclasses of bipartite graphs that have unbounded clique-width, such as chordal bipartite graphs and induced grids. It would also be interesting to determine whether the XP algorithm for clique-width can be improved. Another natural question concerns the approximability of $\chi_{\mathrm{pm}}(G)$: while we have focused on the decision version, the optimization variant of minimizing $k$ deserves further investigation.

**Acknowledgments.** We are grateful to Takahiro Suzuki and Yohei Tamiya for valuable discussions with them. We thank anonymous reviewers for their valuable comments and suggestions, which greatly helped to improve the presentation of this paper.

## References


1. Courcelle, B., Makowsky, J.A., Rotics, U.: Linear time solvable optimization problems on graphs of bounded clique-width. Theory Comput. Syst. **33**(2), 125–150 (2000). https://doi.org/10.1007/S002249910009
2. Cowen, L., Goddard, W., Jesurum, C.E.: Defective coloring revisited. J. Graph Theory **24**(3), 205–219 (1997). https://doi.org/10.1002/(SICI)1097-0118(199703)24:3<205::AID-JGT2>3.0.CO;2-T
3. Demaine, E.D., Karntikoon, K., Pitimanaaree, N.: 2-colorable perfect matching is NP-complete in 2-connected 3-regular planar graphs. Theory Comput. Syst. **69**(2), 22 (2025). https://doi.org/10.1007/S00224-025-10221-2
4. Fomin, F.V., Golovach, P.A., Lokshtanov, D., Saurabh, S.: Intractability of clique-width parameterizations. SIAM J. Comput. **39**(5), 1941–1956 (2010). https://doi.org/10.1137/080742270
5. Garey, M.R., Johnson, D.S.: Computers and Intractability: A Guide to the Theory of NP-Completeness. W. H. Freeman (1979)
6. Hlinený, P., Oum, S.: Finding branch-decompositions and rank-decompositions. SIAM J. Comput. **38**(3), 1012–1032 (2008). https://doi.org/10.1137/070685920
7. Hopcroft, J.E., Karp, R.M.: An $n^{5/2}$ algorithm for maximum matchings in bipartite graphs. SIAM J. Comput. **2**(4), 225–231 (1973). https://doi.org/10.1137/0202019
8. Oum, S.: Approximating rank-width and clique-width quickly. ACM Trans. Algorithms **5**(1), 10:1-10:20 (2008). https://doi.org/10.1145/1435375.1435385
9. Oum, S., Seymour, P.D.: Approximating clique-width and branch-width. J. Comb. Theory B **96**(4), 514–528 (2006). https://doi.org/10.1016/j.jctb.2005.10.006
10. Schaefer, T.J.: The complexity of satisfiability problems. In: Proceedings of the 10th Annual ACM Symposium on Theory of Computing, pp. 216–226. ACM (1978). https://doi.org/10.1145/800133.804350
11. Stockmeyer, L.J., Vazirani, V.V.: NP-completeness of some generalizations of the maximum matching problem. Inf. Process. Lett. **15**(1), 14–19 (1982). https://doi.org/10.1016/0020-0190(82)90077-1

# Online Fault-Tolerant Bin Packing Problem Revised

Yaojun Liu, Xin Han(✉), HanBin Yang, Yong Zhou, and Hao Lu

School of Software Technology, Dalian University of Technology, Dalian 116000, China
{hanxin,zy_dut}@dlut.edu.cn, {yanghanbin,luhao}@mail.dlut.edu.cn

**Abstract.** In this paper, we study a fault-tolerant bin packing problem abstracted from server consolidation in resource allocation. The online setting is adopted to model sequential item arrivals without knowledge of future workloads. Viewing servers possessing uniform capacity as bins and services with heterogeneous sizes as items, this problem aims to minimize the number of required bins while tolerating at most one bin failure, i.e., ensuring that all items in the failed bin can be shifted to some designated bins without overloading bins.

By adopting the classical Refined Harmonic strategy, we develop a new algorithm for the fault-tolerant online bin packing problem and prove that it achieves an asymptotic competitive ratio less than 1.566, improving on the previous best upper bound of 1.599. In addition, we prove a new general lower bound of 1.447, surpassing the former best bound of 1.428. These new bounds further tighten the current theoretical gap for the problem.

**Keywords:** Competitive analysis · bin packing problem · fault tolerance · online algorithm · server consolidation

## 1 Introduction

Resource efficiency and system robustness are central concerns in modern cloud computing. On the efficiency side, each physical server offers a fixed amount of computational capacity and is typically shared by multiple co-located services. Since the aggregate workload hosted on a server cannot exceed its capacity [1], cloud providers rely on server consolidation to place services onto as few machines as possible, thereby reducing operational cost and energy consumption [3,13]. On the robustness side, cloud systems must continue to deliver service despite hardware or software faults, i.e., failures that prevent a component from operating normally [12,17]. Designing allocation methods that improve utilization while preserving fault tolerance is therefore fundamental to building dependable, cost-effective cloud infrastructures.

Motivated by this fact, we study an *online fault-tolerant bin packing problem* that abstracts server consolidation with single-server-failure tolerance: Bins of


Y. Li et al. (Eds.): COCOON 2026, LNCS 16835, pp. 301–314, 2027.
https://doi.org/10.1007/978-981-92-3309-0_23

uniform capacity represent servers, and items of heterogeneous sizes represent services with different workloads [14,16]. Items arrive over time, and an online algorithm irrevocably places each arriving item without knowing future arrivals. Upon the arrival of an item of size $s \in (0, 1)$, the workload is split evenly into two replicas of size $s/2$, labeled red and blue and placed in two distinct bins. The packing must tolerate any single bin failure: When a bin fails to serve its contents, the replica of each affected service is migrated to the surviving bin that hosts its other replica, increasing the occupied size there from $s/2$ to $s$. A packing is valid if, both before and after any such failure-induced migrations, the total occupied size in every surviving bin does not exceed its capacity. The objective is to minimize the number of used bins while maintaining a valid packing.

To evaluate online algorithms in this setting, we use the asymptotic competitive ratio, hereafter competitive ratio, a standard performance measure for online packing algorithms. Formally, for an online algorithm $A$ and an input sequence $L$, let $A(L)$ denote the number of bins used by $A$ and let $\mathrm{OPT}(L)$ denote the minimum number of bins in an optimal (offline) solution. The competitive ratio of $A$ is defined as

$$r(A) = \lim_{\mathrm{OPT}(L)\to\infty} \sup_{L} \left[\frac{A(L)}{\mathrm{OPT}(L)}\right].$$

Classical online bin packing heuristics provide an important algorithmic foundation for the fault-tolerant server consolidation problem [10], and we briefly review them here. In the classical online bin packing problem, Next-Fit maintains only one open bin and achieves a competitive ratio of 2 [7], whereas First-Fit and Best-Fit place each item according to remaining capacities of previously opened bins and attain a competitive ratio of 1.7 [5,6]. More sophisticated Harmonic algorithm partitions items into size classes and packs them class by class. While such strategy achieves 1.691 [9], it may leave substantial empty space because each item in the largest-size class occupies a single bin alone. Refinements that allow mixing of large items effectively reduce this waste: The Refined Harmonic and Advanced Harmonic algorithms achieve competitive ratios 1.636 and 1.578 [2], respectively, with the latter being the best known ratio for online bin packing.

Beyond the classical problem, fault-tolerant variants have also been studied under stronger failure assumptions. Recently, Li and Tang proposed a model allowing up to $f \geq 1$ concurrent server failures [11]. In this model, each service is copied into $f + 1$ replicas: The largest is primary and the other $f$ replicas are standby. Moreover, all $f+1$ replicas of the same service are placed in distinct bins. When at most $f$ servers fail, for each primary replica in a failed bin, a surviving standby is promoted to primary so that the service remains available. In this model, Li and Tang presented a Harmonic-based algorithm with competitive ratio 2, which was subsequently improved to 1.75 by Kamali and Nikbakht [8]. Our prior work further tightened this bound to 1.694, approaching the theoretical lower bound of the classical Harmonic algorithm.

Our focus, however, is on the single-server-failure model defined before. Indeed, the online fault-tolerant bin packing problem under this setting has been investigated for decades. Schaffner et al. introduced an early single-faulty-server bin-packing formulation in multi-tenant database systems and proposed the Best-Fit-based Mirroring and Interleaving algorithms [15]. Later, Daudjee et al. proved that these two approaches admit asymptotic competitive ratios no better than 2, and proposed the Horizontal Harmonic algorithm, which improves the competitive ratio to the range from 1.597 to 1.599 and remains the state-of-the-art for the single-server-failure model [4]. This work also shows that no algorithm for the online fault-tolerant server consolidation problem can achieve a competitive ratio below 1.428.

The gap between the best-known upper bound and the general lower bound motivates further algorithmic refinement. Accordingly, we propose a new approach that combines the Refined Harmonic and Shifting strategies. The Refined Harmonic strategy extends the classical Harmonic framework by allowing large items from designated classes to share bins, thereby improving space utilization. Meanwhile, Shifting guarantees that any two bins share replicas of at most one service. As a result, after a bin failure, each correct bin receives at most one additional replica, reducing the reserved capacity needed for fault tolerance.

Our main contributions are listed below:

(1). A novel algorithm called Refined-Harmonic-Shifting is proposed for the online fault-tolerant server consolidation problem;
(2). We prove that the new algorithm achieves an asymptotic competitive ratio less than 1.566, surpassing the prior state-of-the-art result of 1.599;
(3). Through a refined sequence construction and rigorous theoretical analysis, we elevate the general lower bound from 1.428 to 1.447 for the online fault-tolerant server consolidation problem with single faulty server.

In sum, our efforts contract the gap between the best achieved upper bound and general lower bound from $1.599 - 1.428 = 0.171$ to $1.566 - 1.447 = 0.119$, further validating the effectiveness and competitiveness of our proposed algorithm.

## 2 Refined-Harmonic-Shifting Algorithm

Upon receiving a service, the proposed Refined-Harmonic-Shifting algorithm determines its classification and then implements the corresponding packing method. This section presents the introduced algorithm following the framework: (1). Establish a classification scheme for services based on the size of their replicas. (2). Define mixed and pure services, and respectively provide packing strategies for each.

### 2.1 Service Classification

We determine the class of services by dividing the interval $\left(0, \frac{1}{2}\right]$ into 157 disjoint subintervals: $J_k$ for $k \in \{1, 2, \ldots, 155\}$, $J_x$, and $J_y$, whose definitions are specifically shown in Table 1. Note that for $3 \leq k < 155$, $J_k = \left(\frac{1}{k+2}, \frac{1}{k+1}\right]$, while

**Table 1.** Service classes and replica intervals

| Service class | Replica size |
|---|---|
| 1 | $J_1 = \left(0.361,\ \frac{1}{2}\right]$ |
| $x$ | $J_x = \left(\frac{1}{3},\ 0.361\right]$ |
| 2 | $J_2 = \left(0.278,\ \frac{1}{3}\right]$ |
| $y$ | $J_y = \left(\frac{1}{4},\ 0.278\right]$ |
| $3 \leq k < 155$ | $J_k = \left(\frac{1}{k+2},\ \frac{1}{k+1}\right]$ |
| 155 | $J_{155} = \left(0,\ \frac{1}{156}\right]$ |

$J_1 \cup J_x = \left(\frac{1}{3}, \frac{1}{2}\right]$ and $J_2 \cup J_y = \left(\frac{1}{4}, \frac{1}{3}\right]$. In what follows, a replica is termed a $J_k$-replica if its size lies in $J_k$, and the corresponding service is assigned to the $k$-th class, where $k \in \{1, 2, \ldots, 155\} \cup \{x, y\}$.

### 2.2 Packing Methods

The packing strategy allows services from $x$-th and $y$-th classes to be mixed in the same bin, while services in other classes ($k \in \{1, 2, \ldots, 155\}$) can exclusively be packed with those from the identical class. Thus, class-$x$ and class-$y$ services are termed *mixed*, and other services *pure*. Generally, the proposed algorithm maintains the following packing principles: (1). Replicas of same color are packed together, respectively forming blue and red bins; (2). For each service, the blue replica is placed before the red one; (3). In each bin, the reserved space is kept for the size expansion of only one replica; (4). Whenever two services share a blue bin, their red replicas are assigned to distinct red bins.

The overall packing executions are summarized in Algorithm 1, where $c_q = \{c_{q,o}\}$ represents the $q$-th released service consisting of two replicas. Here $o \in \{b, r\}$ indicates the replica color, and $b$ and $r$ represent blue and red, respectively.

**Algorithm 1. Refined-Harmonic-Shifting algorithm**

**input:** A sequence $\sigma = \langle c_1, c_2, \ldots, c_n \rangle$ of services
**output:** An online fault-tolerant packing of $\sigma$
**for** $q \leftarrow 1$ **to** $n$ **do**
  determine the class $k$ of $c_q$ according to Table 1
  **if** $k \in \{1, 2, \ldots, 154\}$ **then** $PackPure_1(k, c_q)$
  **else if** $k = 155$ **then** $PackPure_2(c_q)$
  **else** $PackMix(c_q)$
**end**

As shown in Algorithm 1, after classifying the input service, the algorithm branches into three distinct schemes for packing pure services and mixed services. We begin with the packing of pure services.

I. Packing pure services

For services in $k$-th class ($1 \leq k < 155$), their replicas are packed into a set of bin groups, each consisting of $k$ blue bins and $k$ red bins. Within a group, blue replicas are placed sequentially following Next-Fit discipline: Replicas first fill the first blue bin, and once a blue bin hosts $k$ replicas, subsequent replicas are placed into the next blue bin. For the $i$-th blue replica in $j$-th blue bin ($1 \leq i, j \leq k$), its corresponding red replica is placed as the $j$-th replica in the $i$-th red bin.

Procedure 1 specifies the detailed packing steps for pure services in $k$-th class, $1 \leq k < 155$. In this procedure, a *bin* is *full* when it contains exactly $k$ $J_k$-replicas. Furthermore, a *bin group* turns to *full* if all included bins reach the full state, and at this point, it is closed and a new bin group for class-$k$ services is opened.

**Procedure 1.** $PackPure_1(k, c_q)$

```
if g is empty or full then        //g is the current bin group hosting class-k services
   g ← an array of 2k empty bins;           // a new bin group for class-k services
   i_{k,b} ← 1;            // the index of the bin packing c_{q,b} in g
   i_{k,r} ← k + 1          // the index of the bin packing c_{q,r} in g
 else if i_{k,r} > 2k then          // now the g[i_{k,b}] blue bin is full
         i_{k,r} ← k + 1; i_{k,b} ← i_{k,b} + 1
place c_{q,b} into bin g[i_{k,b}];
place c_{q,r} into bin g[i_{k,r}]
i_{k,r} ← i_{k,r} + 1
end
```

As for the services belonging to 155-th class, the algorithm separately aggregates their blue and red replicas into blue and red blocks. Once these two blocks reach a size in $J_{11} = (1/13, 1/12]$, they are considered *full*[1] and treated as the way that $J_{11}$-replicas are treated, that is, the blocks are packed in groups consisting of 11 blue and 11 red bins, with each full bin containing 11 blocks. Notably, these blocks are never mixed with regular $J_{11}$-replicas, in accordance with the rule that pure services are packed only with those from the same class. The detailed packing process is presented in Procedure 2.

II. Packing mixed services

By leveraging both Shifting and Refined-Harmonic methods, we propose the packing strategy for mixed services. The Shifting technique is reflected in the rule that, for services sharing blue replicas in the same bin, their red replicas should be allocated to distinct bins. In doing so, an important term legal bin is introduced here.

*legal bin*: For a mixed service $c_q$, a red bin $B$ is *legal* for $c_{q,r}$ if $B$ contains no service sharing the same blue bin with $c_q$.

Maintaining the setting in Refined Harmonic, our method allows some class-$y$ services to mix with class-$x$ services, while packing other class-$y$ services solely

[1] Since the two blocks respectively host blue and red replicas of same services, they always keep the same size and thus achieve full state simultaneously.

**Procedure 2.** *PackPure*$_2(c_q)$

**if** the blue and red blocks are empty or full **then**
  build a new blue and a red block;
  $s \leftarrow 0$; // block size
pack $c_{q,b}$ in blue block;
pack $c_{q,r}$ in red block;
$s \leftarrow s + s(c_{q,b})$ // $s(c_{q,b})$ is the size of $c_{q,b}$
**if** $s > 1/13$ **then**
  call Procedure 1 to pack the blue (red) block as the blue (red) replica of class-11 services.
**end**

with those from the same class. Hence, we generally place mixed services in five types of bins $B_h : h \in \mathbb{H}$, where $\mathbb{H} = \{x, y, xy, yy, y'\}$. For $p, q \in \{x, y\}$, a $B_p$ bin contains a single $J_p$-replica, whereas a $B_{pq}$ bin contains one $J_p$-replica along with one $J_q$-replica. In addition, a $B_{y'}$ bin also contains one $J_y$-replica, but is designated to evolve into a $B_{yy}$ bin. Moreover, let $B_{h,o}$ represent a $B_h$ bin that packs color-$o$ replicas, and denote $N_{h,o}$ as the number of $B_{h,o}$ bins during the packing process, where $h \in \mathbb{H}$ and $o \in \{b, r\}$.

The packing procedure of mixed services is presented in Procedure 1. In this procedure, whenever a bin is created or its type changes, the corresponding $N_{h,o}$ is updated accordingly: Building a new $B_{h,o}$ bin increases $N_{h,o}$ by one, while transforming a bin from type $B_{h,o}$ to $B_{h',o}$ decreases $N_{h,o}$ by one and increases $N_{h',o}$ by one. Note that as the number of released class-$y$ services grows, the algorithm guarantees a fixed growth relation: Every increment of 185 in $N_{yy,b}$ is accompanied by an increment of 26 in $N_{v,b}$, where $N_{v,b} = N_{xy,b} + N_{y,b}$. A specific example shown in Appendix[2] is built to clarify the executions of mixed services in Procedure 3.

## 3 Competitiveness of Algorithm

We analyze the competitive ratio via a *weighting* argument, where each replica's weight reflects its proportional bin cost. The analysis proceeds in three steps: (1) Bound the bins used by our algorithm by the sum of all replica weights plus an additive constant; (2) Define the weight functions and show that the competitive ratio is at most the maximum total weight of any single bin in an optimal packing; (3) Enumerate all cases of bins in the optimal solution to derive the explicit upper bound of competitive ratio.

### 3.1 Bin Cost by the Proposed Algorithm and Weight Function

We define $A(L)$ as the number of bins used by our algorithm to pack an input list $L$, $u_{\text{pure}}$ and $u_{\text{mix}}$ as the number of bins hosting pure services and mixed services at the end of the packing process, respectively. It follows directly that

[2] All appendices can be found in the journal version of this paper.

$A(L) = u_{\text{pure}} + u_{\text{mix}}$. To establish an upper bound for $A(L)$, we first analyze the individual components $u_{\text{pure}}$ and $u_{\text{mix}}$ separately.

**Procedure 3.** *PackMix*($c_q$)

```
if c_q is the first arriving mixed service then
   N_{h,o} ← 0      //the number of B_{h,o}, with h ∈ {x, y, xy, yy, y'} and o ∈ {b, r}
if c_q is a class-x service then
   //pack the blue replica c_{q,b}:
      if there exists a B_{y,b} then
         pack c_{q,b} into the earliest opened B_{y,b}, forming a B_{xy,b}
      else place c_{q,b} in a new (empty) bin, building a B_{x,b}
   //pack the red replica c_{q,r}:
      if there exists a legal B_{y,r} for c_{q,r} then
         pack c_{q,r} into the earliest opened one, forming a B_{xy,r}
      else place c_{q,r} in a new bin, building a B_{x,r}
else
   //pack the blue replica c_{q,b}:
      if there exists a B_{y',b} then              // B_{y',o} means the half-full B_{yy,o}
         pack c_{q,b} into it, forming a B_{yy,b}
      else if 26N_{yy,b} < 185N_{v,b} then          //N_{v,b} = N_{xy,b} + N_{y,b}
            place c_{q,b} to a new bin, building a B_{y',b}
         else if a B_{x,b} exists then
               place c_{q,b} into the earliest opened B_{x,b}, forming a B_{xy,b}
            else place c_{q,b} into a new bin, building a B_{y,b}
   //pack the red replica c_{q,r}:
      if c_{q,b} is contained in a B_{xy,b} or B_{y,b} then
         if there exists a legal bin in B_{x,r} for c_{q,r} then
            pack c_{q,r} into the earliest opened one, forming a B_{xy,r}
         else place c_{q,r} in a new bin, building a B_{y,r}
      else if there exists one legal B_{y',r} for c_{q,r} then
            pack c_{q,r} into earliest opened one, forming a B_{yy,r}
         else place c_{q,r} into a new bin, building a B_{y',r}
 end
```

Note that a $B_{y,b}$ and a $B_{x,b}$ bin never coexist during the packing process, namely, $N_{x,b} \cdot N_{y,b} = 0$ holds at all times. Thus

$$u_{x,b} \cdot u_{y,b} = 0, \tag{3.1}$$

where $u_{x,o}$ ($u_{y,o}$) denotes the final value of $N_{x,o}$ ($N_{y,o}$) after packing finishes.

Assume $l_k$ is the total number of blue and red $J_k$-replicas, $k \in \{1, 2, \ldots, 155\} \cup \{x, y\}$ and $s_{155}$ represents the total size of all $J_{155}$-replicas, we can derive the theorem below.

**Theorem 1.** *If* $u_{x,b} = 0$, *then*

$$A(L) < \sum_{k=1}^{154} \frac{l_k}{k} + \frac{13}{11} s_{155} + \frac{211}{396} l_y + O(1). \tag{3.2}$$

*Else,*

$$A(L) < \sum_{k=1}^{154} \frac{l_k}{k} + \frac{13}{11} s_{155} + l_x + \frac{185}{396} l_y + O(1). \tag{3.3}$$

This theorem follows directly from the sum of upper bounds of $u_{\text{pure}}$ and $u_{\text{mix}}$, and the specific proof is provided in Appendix.

Recall that the *weight* of a replica refers to the proportion of bin it requires in packing, and thus can be derived from Eqs. (3.2) and (3.3), which reveal the marginal increase of total bin number induced by a replica. Here we define two weight functions $h_1(x)$ and $h_2(x)$ for a replica of size $x$ as follows:

$$\begin{aligned} h_i(x) &= \frac{1}{k}, && \text{if } x \in J_k \text{ and } 1 \le k \le 154, \\ &= \frac{13x}{11}, && \text{if } x \in J_{155}, \\ &= \begin{cases} \frac{211}{396}, & i = 1, \\ \frac{185}{396}, & i = 2, \end{cases} && \text{if } x \in J_y, \\ &= \begin{cases} 0, & i = 1, \\ 1, & i = 2, \end{cases} && \text{if } x \in J_x, \end{aligned}$$

where $i = 1$ and $i = 2$ respectively corresponds to $u_{x,b} = 0$ and $u_{x,b} > 0$, in which case $u_{y,b} = 0$ by Eq. (3.1)

### 3.2 The Upper Bound of Competitive Ratio

In what follows, we demonstrate how weighting scheme serves as an efficient tool for deriving the competitive ratio of our algorithm. Assume the optimal packing uses $l^*$ bins, and let $w_{i,l}$ be the total weight of replicas in the $l$-th bin under weight function $h_i$, where $i \in \{1, 2\}$ and $1 \le l \le l^*$. Then, define $H_i = \max_{1 \le l \le l^*} w_{i,l}$, where $i \in \{1, 2\}$.

**Lemma 1.** $H = max\,(H_1, H_2)$ *is an upper bound for the competitive ratio of proposed algorithm.*

The proof is shown in Appendix.

**Lemma 2.** $H < 1.566$.

*Proof.* The density of a replica is defined as its weight divided by its size. In following analysis, we focus on density bounds for $J_k$-replicas with $k \ge 2$, whose density is fixed no matter given $h_1$ or $h_2$. Since a $J_2$-replica has weight 1/2 and size in $J_2 = (0.278, 1/3]$, its density is thereby less than $\frac{1/2}{0.278} < 1.799$. For $3 \le k \le 154$, a $J_k$-replica has weight $1/k$ and size greater than $1/(k+2)$, and thus its density is less than $\frac{1/k}{1/(k+2)} = \frac{k+2}{k}$, which decreases as $k$ increases. All replicas in $J_{11}, \ldots, J_{155}$ have density at most 13/11, since $J_k$-replicas with $11 \le k \le 154$ have density less than 13/11, and $J_{155}$-replicas have density exactly 13/11.

Assume that the largest replica in $B$ lies in $J_{k^*}$ interval. To avoid overloading bins, the total available space of $B$ is no more than one minus the lower endpoint of $J_{k^*}$ interval. We now distinguish five cases according to the value of $k^*$ in $B$ and analyze $w_1$ and $w_2$ in each case, where $w_i$ is the total weight of replicas under weight function $h_i$ with $i \in \{1, 2\}$.

**Case 1: $k^* = 1$.** In this case, the total available space for replicas is less than $1 - 0.361 = 0.639$, which may simultaneously involve a $J_1$ and $J_y$-replica. Two situations are specifically analyzed as follows:

(i). $B$ contains a $J_y$-replica, the remaining space for smaller replicas is at most $0.278 - \frac{1}{4} = 0.028$. Therefore, the $J_{34}$-replicas or smaller replicas can be additionally placed, with the density lower than $\frac{13}{11}$. Add the weight of $J_1$ and $J_y$-replicas, then $w_2 < w_1 < 1 + \frac{211}{396} + 0.028 \cdot \frac{13}{11} \approx 1.5659$.

(ii). No $J_y$-replica exists. In this condition, remaining replicas are in $J_k$ intervals with $k \ge 3$ and thus have the density less than $\frac{5}{3}$, and we have $w_1 = w_2 < 1 + 0.278 \cdot \frac{5}{3} \approx 1.4633$.

**Case 2: $k^* = x$.** Then the available space for packing is no more than $1 - \frac{1}{3} = \frac{2}{3}$, which enables the mix of a $J_x$ and $J_2$-replica. Clearly, the following four conditions exist:

(i). $B$ hosts a $J_2$-replica. Then, the total remaining space is no more than $1 - \frac{2}{3} - 0.278 < 0.0554$, which can involve the largest replica from the $J_{17}$ interval. Thus, one can claim that replicas in the residual space have a density less than $\frac{13}{11}$. Hence, we conclude that $w_1 < w_2 < 1 + \frac{1}{2} + 0.0554 \cdot \frac{13}{11} \approx 1.5655$.

(ii). $B$ hosts no $J_2$-replica but a $J_y$-replica. Then the remaining space is less than $1 - \frac{2}{3} - \frac{1}{4} = \frac{1}{12}$, in which the largest replica is in $J_{11}$ interval. Therefore, the density of all replicas in such space is at most $\frac{13}{11}$. Consequently, we have $w_1 < w_2 < 1 + \frac{185}{396} + \frac{1}{12} \cdot \frac{13}{11} \approx 1.5657$.

(iii). $B$ has neither $J_2$ nor $J_y$-replica but one $J_3$-replica. The residual space for other replicas is smaller than $1 - \frac{2}{3} - \frac{1}{5} = \frac{2}{15}$, which can further accommodate replicas from $J_6$, with the density less than $\frac{4}{3}$. Hence, $w_1 < w_2 < 1 + \frac{1}{3} + \frac{2}{15} \cdot \frac{4}{3} \approx 1.5111$.

(iv). $B$ involves neither $J_2$, $J_y$ nor $J_3$-replica. It follows that replicas other than the $J_x$-replicas cover a capacity less than $1 - \frac{2}{3} = \frac{1}{3}$, and thus have a density below $\frac{3}{2}$. It is not difficult to obtain that $w_1 < \frac{1}{3} \cdot \frac{3}{2} = 0.5000$ and $w_2 < 1 + \frac{1}{3} \cdot \frac{3}{2} = 1.5000$.

**Case 3: $k^* = 2$.** Here, the total available space is less than $1 - 0.278 = 0.722$. The bin $B$ involves at most two $J_2$-replicas, suggesting two subcases discussed below.

(i). $B$ hosts one $J_2$-replica and one $J_y$-replica, then the remaining available space for other replicas is smaller than $1 - 2 \cdot 0.278 - \frac{1}{4} = 0.194$. Since $0.194 \in J_4$, the density of replicas placed in such space is less than $\frac{3}{2}$. Obviously, $w_2 < w_1 < \frac{1}{2} + \frac{211}{396} + 0.194 \cdot \frac{3}{2} \approx 1.3238$.

(ii). In other conditions, the available space excluding one $J_2$-replica is less than $1 - 2 \cdot 0.278 = 0.444$. The replicas in such space have density less than 1.799, because a second $J_2$-replica may exist in the bin. Thus, $w_1 = w_2 < \frac{1}{2} + 1.799 \cdot 0.444 \approx 1.2988$.

**Case 4: $k^* = y$.** It holds that the total available space is at most $1 - \frac{1}{4} = \frac{3}{4}$. Given that at most two $J_y$-replicas can be packed in $B$, we consider two possible subcases.

(i). $B$ has two $J_y$-replicas. In this case, other replicas occupy total space less than $1 - 3 \cdot \frac{1}{4} = \frac{1}{4}$, which belongs to the $J_3$ interval. One can derive that replicas packed in such space have density less than $\frac{5}{3}$. Then, $w_2 < w_1 < 2 \cdot \frac{211}{396} + \frac{1}{4} \cdot \frac{5}{3} \approx 1.4823$.

(ii). $B$ has only one $J_y$-replica. The remaining space of at most $1 - \frac{2}{4} = \frac{1}{2}$ can additionally host replicas lying in $J_k$ intervals, where $k \geq 3$. Hence, $w_2 < w_1 < \frac{211}{396} + \frac{1}{2} \cdot \frac{5}{3} \approx 1.3662$.

**Case 5: $k^* \geq 3$.** The density of $J_k$-replicas with $k < 11$ exceeds $\frac{13}{11}$, whereas all other replicas have density at most $\frac{13}{11}$. This fact naturally leads to the following two cases.

(i). $k^* \leq 10$. $B$ has the total available space less than $1 - \frac{1}{k+2}$, and the density of all contained replicas is less than $\frac{k+2}{k}$. Thus, $w_1 = w_2 \leq \left(1 - \frac{1}{k+2}\right) \cdot \frac{k+2}{k} = 1 + \frac{1}{k} \leq 1.3333$.

(ii). $11 \leq k^* \leq 155$. The largest density value of all contents in $B$ is at most $\frac{13}{11}$. Thus, $w_1 = w_2 \leq \frac{13}{11} \cdot 1 \approx 1.1818$.

Finally, we have $H_1 < 1.566$ and $H_2 < 1.566$, and thus $H = max\,(H_1, H_2) < 1.566$ is proved. □

**Theorem 2.** *The proposed algorithm has a competitive ratio less than 1.566.*

The theorem follows directly from Lemma 2.

## 4 A Refined General Lower Bound

In this section, we establish a new general lower bound on the competitive ratio of any online algorithm for the considered fault-tolerant server consolidation problem. More specifically, we enhance the lower bound from 1.428 in [4] to 1.447.

We design a specific input sequence comprising $\frac{3}{4}n$ services of size $\frac{1}{6} - 6\epsilon$, $\frac{n}{2}$ services of size $\frac{1}{2}+2\epsilon$, and $\frac{9}{16}n$ services of size $\frac{2}{3}+2\epsilon$, where $n$ is a sufficiently large integer divisible by 16 and $\epsilon$ is a small positive constant. Since each service is split into two equal-sized replicas which are placed in distinct bins, the corresponding replica sequence $\gamma$ can be expressed by $\gamma = \gamma_1\gamma_2\gamma_3$, where $\gamma_1$ contains $\frac{3}{2}n$ replicas of size $x = \frac{1}{12} - 3\epsilon$, $\gamma_2$ involves $n$ replicas whose size is $y = \frac{1}{4} + \epsilon$, and $\gamma_3$ has $\frac{9}{8}n$ replicas of size $z = \frac{1}{3} + \epsilon$. For convenience, we thereafter refer to replica of size $i$ as $i$-replica, where $i \in \{x, y, z\}$.

**Lemma 3.** $\mathrm{OPT}(\gamma_1) \leq \frac{3}{22}n + c_1, \mathrm{OPT}(\gamma_1\gamma_2) \leq \frac{n}{2} + c_2$, *and* $\mathrm{OPT}(\gamma_1\gamma_2\gamma_3) \leq \frac{9}{8}n + c_3$.

Its proof is discussed in Appendix.

**Theorem 3.** *The competitive ratio of any online algorithm A for the considered online fault-tolerant bin packing problem is at least* $\frac{55}{38}$.

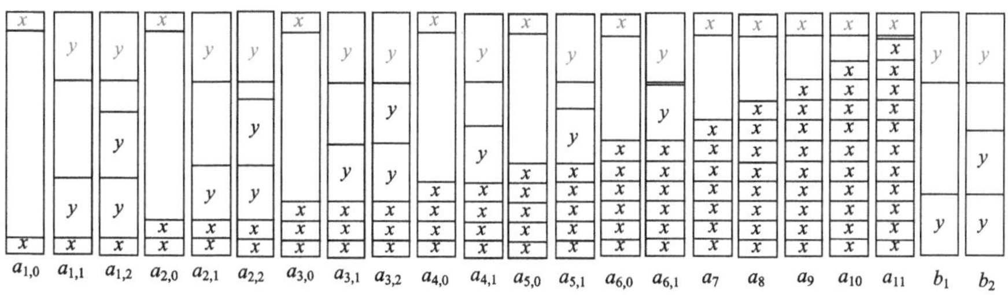

**Fig. 1.** All bin types may arise after processing $\gamma_1\gamma_2$. In any feasible fault-tolerant packing, each bin keeps the reserved space as large as the biggest replica it contains, the size of which is shown in gray $x$ or $y$. For simplicity, each replica is labeled by its size $x$ or $y$.

Fix an arbitrary online algorithm $A$. At the time that $A$ finishes packing $\gamma_1\gamma_2$, we define some bin-count variables as follows according to the contents in bins. Let $a_{i,j}$ denote the number of bins containing exactly $i$ $x$-replicas and $j$ $y$-replicas. A valid packing implies that $i \leq 11$, $j \leq 2$ for $i \in \{1, 2, 3\}$, $j \leq 1$ for $i \in \{4, 5, 6\}$, and $j = 0$ for $i \in \{7, 8, 9, 10, 11\}$. In particular, when $i \geq 7$, we denote $a_i$ as the number of bins that exclusively contain $i$ $x$-replicas, as shown in Fig. 1. Accordingly, given that at most two $y$-replicas stay in a same bin, let $b_1$ and $b_2$ respectively be the numbers of bins that contain only one $y$-replica and only two $y$-replicas.

For any input sequence $\sigma$, let $A(\sigma)$ be the number of bins used by algorithm $A$ to pack $\sigma$. Then, the packing generated by $A$ satisfies five following constraints:

Algorithm $A$ packing $\gamma_1$ generates bins only involving $x$ replicas and thus uses the number of bins expressed by

$$A(\gamma_1) = \sum_{i=1}^{3}\sum_{j=0}^{2} a_{i,j} + \sum_{i=4}^{6}\sum_{j=0}^{1} a_{i,j} + \sum_{i=7}^{11} a_i. \tag{4.1}$$

Moreover, it is not difficult to see that

$$A(\gamma_1\gamma_2) = A(\gamma_1) + b_1 + b_2. \tag{4.2}$$

Summing the number of $x$-replicas over all bin types after placing $\gamma_1\gamma_2$ gives

$$\frac{3n}{2} = \sum_{i=1}^{3} i \sum_{j=0}^{2} a_{i,j} + \sum_{i=4}^{6} i \sum_{j=0}^{1} a_{i,j} + \sum_{i=7}^{11} i a_i. \tag{4.3}$$

Similarly, the total number of $y$-replicas is given by

$$n = \sum_{i=1}^{6} a_{i,1} + 2\sum_{i=1}^{3} a_{i,2} + b_1 + 2b_2. \tag{4.4}$$

For bins containing $i$ $x$-replicas and one $z$-replica, we have $ix + z \le 1 - z$, implying $i \le 4$. Thus, a bin containing more than four $x$-replicas is not available for a $z$-replica. Combining the fact that bins can be fully utilized with one $x$-replica, one $y$-replica and one $z$-replica, we conclude that among all bins, only those counted by $a_{i,0}$ $(1 \le i \le 4)$, $a_{1,1}$ and $b_1$ can additionally pack a $z$-replica. Therefore, it is not hard to see that

$$\frac{9}{8}n \le a_{1,1} + \sum_{i=1}^{4} a_{i,0} + b_1 + b_z,$$

where $b_z$ is the number of bins only involving $z$-replicas at the end of packing $\gamma_1\gamma_2\gamma_3$. As a result, we derive that

$$\begin{aligned} A(\gamma_1\gamma_2\gamma_3) &= A(\gamma_1\gamma_2) + b_z \\ &\ge \sum_{i=5}^{6} a_{i,0} + \sum_{i=2}^{6} a_{i,1} + \sum_{i=1}^{3} a_{i,2} + \sum_{i=7}^{11} a_i + b_2 + \frac{9}{8}n. \end{aligned} \tag{4.5}$$

Let $r_A$ denote the competitive ratio of $A$, then there exists a constant term $c'$ such that $A(\sigma) \le r_A \cdot OPT(\sigma) + c'$ for any input $\sigma$. Therefore, by Lemma 3 and Eqs. (4.1), (4.2) and (4.5), we obtain

$$r_A \cdot \frac{3}{22}n + O(1) \ge \sum_{i=1}^{3}\sum_{j=0}^{2} a_{i,j} + \sum_{i=4}^{6}\sum_{j=0}^{1} a_{i,j} + \sum_{i=7}^{11} a_i, \tag{4.6}$$

$$r_A \cdot \frac{n}{2} + O(1) \ge \sum_{i=1}^{3}\sum_{j=0}^{2} a_{i,j} + \sum_{i=4}^{6}\sum_{j=0}^{1} a_{i,j} + \sum_{i=7}^{11} a_i + b_1 + b_2, \tag{4.7}$$

$$r_A \cdot \frac{9}{8}n + O(1) \ge \sum_{i=5}^{6} a_{i,0} + \sum_{i=2}^{6} a_{i,1} + \sum_{i=1}^{3} a_{i,2} + \sum_{i=7}^{11} a_i + b_2 + \frac{9}{8}n. \tag{4.8}$$

Then, to derive a lower bound on $r_A$, we consider a weighted sum of Eqs. (4.3), (4.4), (4.6), (4.7), (4.8). Specifically, first multiply (4.3) by $-1$, (4.4) by

$-4$, (4.6) by 3, and (4.7) and (4.8) by 4, then add them together and finally we obtain the following inequality:

$$\begin{aligned} & r_A\left(\frac{9}{22}+2+\frac{9}{2}\right)n-\frac{3n}{2}-4n+c \\ & \geq 6a_{1,0}+2a_{1,1}+2a_{1,2}+5a_{2,0}+5a_{2,1}+a_{2,2} \\ & \quad +4a_{3,0}+4a_{3,1}+3a_{4,0}+3a_{4,1}+6a_{5,0}+2a_{5,1} \\ & \quad +5a_{6,0}+a_{6,1}+4a_7+3a_8+2a_9+a_{10}+\frac{9n}{2}, \end{aligned} \tag{4.9}$$

where $c$ on the left side represents the constant term after summation. Since all variables on the right-hand side are nonnegative, and the constant term $c$ can be ignored in asymptotic calculations, Eq. (4.9) implies that

$$r_A\left(\frac{9}{22}+2+\frac{9}{2}\right)-\frac{3}{2}-4\geq\frac{9}{2}$$

and we have $r_A \geq \frac{55}{38}$.

## 5 Conclusions

In this work, we propose a Refined-Harmonic-Shifting algorithm for the online fault-tolerant bin packing problem with single faulty server. Through a delicate weighting argument, we prove that the proposed algorithm achieves an asymptotic competitive ratio below 1.566, which is the best known result among existing algorithms. Besides, the general lower bound of the considered problem is enhanced from $10/7 \approx 1.428$ to $55/38 \approx 1.447$. These results significantly narrow the theoretical gap between existing algorithms and the optimal offline algorithm. In the future, we can extend the Refined Harmonic framework to multi-failure scenarios with adaptive replica counts.

**Acknowledgement.** This work was supported by the National Natural Science Foundation of China (12471338, 12461011, and 12371363), and the LiaoNing Revitalization Talents Program (XLYC2403125).

## References

1. Ayyadevara, N., Dabas, R., Khan, A., Sreenivas, K.V.N.: Near-optimal algorithms for stochastic online bin packing. ACM Trans. Algorithms **21**(2), 1–39 (2025). https://doi.org/10.1145/3728642
2. Balogh, J., Békési, J., Dósa, G., Epstein, L., Levin, A.: A new and improved algorithm for online bin packing. In: Azar, Y., Bast, H., Herman, G. (eds.) 26th Annual European Symposium on Algorithms (ESA 2018). Leibniz International Proceedings in Informatics (LIPIcs), vol. 112, pp. 5:1–5:14. Schloss Dagstuhl – Leibniz-Zentrum für Informatik, Dagstuhl (2018). https://doi.org/10.4230/LIPIcs.ESA.2018.5

3. Bastos, R.R., Paz de Moura, B.M., Lucca, G., Santos, H.S., Yamin, A.C., Reiser, R.H.S.: Hybrid-FLBCC: virtual machine consolidation in cloud infrastructures exploring flexible computing. In: 2025 IEEE International Conference on Fuzzy Systems (FUZZ), pp. 1–6. IEEE (2025). https://doi.org/10.1109/fuzz62266.2025.11197675
4. Daudjee, K., Kamali, S., López-Ortiz, A.: On the online fault-tolerant server consolidation problem. In: Proceedings of the 26th ACM Symposium on Parallelism in Algorithms and Architectures, SPAA 2014, pp. 12–21. Association for Computing Machinery, New York (2014). https://doi.org/10.1145/2612669.2612686
5. Dósa, G., Sgall, J.: First fit bin packing: a tight analysis. In: Portier, N., Wilke, T. (eds.) 30th International Symposium on Theoretical Aspects of Computer Science (STACS 2013). Leibniz International Proceedings in Informatics (LIPIcs), vol. 20, pp. 538–549. Schloss Dagstuhl – Leibniz-Zentrum für Informatik, Dagstuhl (2013). https://doi.org/10.4230/LIPIcs.STACS.2013.538
6. Dósa, G., Sgall, J.: Optimal analysis of best fit bin packing. In: Esparza, J., Fraigniaud, P., Husfeldt, T., Koutsoupias, E. (eds.) ICALP 2014. LNCS, vol. 8572, pp. 429–441. Springer, Heidelberg (2014). https://doi.org/10.1007/978-3-662-43948-7_36
7. Johnson, D.S., Demers, A., Ullman, J.D., Garey, M.R., Graham, R.L.: Worst-case performance bounds for simple one-dimensional packing algorithms. SIAM J. Comput. **3**(4), 299–325 (1974). https://doi.org/10.1137/0203025
8. Kamali, S., Nikbakht, P.: On the fault-tolerant online bin packing problem. In: D'Angelo, G., Michail, O. (eds.) ALGOCLOUD 2021. LNCS, vol. 13084, pp. 1–17. Springer, Cham (2021). https://doi.org/10.1007/978-3-030-93043-1_1
9. Lee, C.C., Lee, D.T.: A simple on-line bin-packing algorithm. J. ACM **32**(3), 562–572 (1985). https://doi.org/10.1145/3828.3833
10. Li, B., et al.: Algorithms for online fault tolerance server consolidation. Digit. Commun. Netw. **11**(2), 514–523 (2025). https://doi.org/10.1016/j.dcan.2024.06.007
11. Li, C., Tang, X.: On fault-tolerant bin packing for online resource allocation. IEEE Trans. Parallel Distrib. Syst. **31**(4), 817–829 (2020). https://doi.org/10.1109/tpds.2019.2948327
12. Malik, S., Huet, F.: Adaptive fault tolerance in real time cloud computing. In: 2011 IEEE World Congress on Services, pp. 280–287. IEEE, Washington (2011). https://doi.org/10.1109/services.2011.108
13. Marzolla, M., Babaoglu, O., Panzieri, F.: Server consolidation in clouds through gossiping. In: 2011 IEEE International Symposium on a World of Wireless, Mobile and Multimedia Networks, pp. 1–6. IEEE, Lucca (2011). https://doi.org/10.1109/wowmom.2011.5986483
14. Ren, R., Tang, X., Li, Y., Cai, W.: Competitiveness of dynamic bin packing for online cloud server allocation. ACM Trans. Network. **25**(3), 1324–1331 (2017). https://doi.org/10.1109/tnet.2016.2630052
15. Schaffner, J., et al.: RTP: robust tenant placement for elastic in-memory database clusters. In: Luo, M., Zhang, L.J. (eds.) Proceedings of the 2013 ACM SIGMOD International Conference on Management of Data, SIGMOD 2013, pp. 773–784. ACM, New York (2013). https://doi.org/10.1145/2463676.2465302
16. Speitkamp, B., Bichler, M.: A mathematical programming approach for server consolidation problems in virtualized data centers. IEEE Trans. Serv. Comput. **3**(4), 266–278 (2010). https://doi.org/10.1109/tsc.2010.25
17. Zheng, Z., Zhou, T.C., Lyu, M.R., King, I.: Component ranking for fault-tolerant cloud applications. IEEE Trans. Serv. Comput. **5**(4), 540–550 (2012). https://doi.org/10.1109/tsc.2011.42

# Permanental Energy of Graphs

Priyanshu Pant(✉) and Ranveer Singh

Indian Institute of Technology Indore, Indore, India
priyanshupant03@gmail.com, ranveer@iiti.ac.in

**Abstract.** For a simple graph $G$ with adjacency matrix $A(G)$, let $\pi(G,x) := \mathrm{per}(xI - A(G))$ be its permanental polynomial with roots $\mu_1, \ldots, \mu_n \in \mathbb{C}$, and define the *permanental energy* $\mathcal{E}_{\mathrm{per}}(G) := \sum_{i=1}^{n} |\mu_i|$. We prove a sharp universal lower bound: for every $m$-edge graph $G$, $\mathcal{E}_{\mathrm{per}}(G) \geq 2\sqrt{m}$, with equality if and only if $G$ is a star together with isolated vertices. We also prove the general upper bound $\mathcal{E}_{\mathrm{per}}(G) \leq n\rho(G)$, where $\rho(G)$ is the spectral radius, and we study $\mathcal{E}_{\mathrm{per}}(G)$ on several graph families.

**Keywords:** permanental polynomial · graph energy · extremal graph theory · permanent

## 1 Introduction

Let $G$ be a finite simple graph on $n$ vertices, with adjacency matrix $A(G)$ and eigenvalues $\lambda_1, \ldots, \lambda_n$. The *energy* of $G$ is defined by

$$\mathcal{E}(G) = \sum_{i=1}^{n} |\lambda_i|.$$

Introduced by Gutman [8], $\mathcal{E}(G)$ has become a central invariant in spectral graph theory and mathematical chemistry. Its original motivation comes from the Hückel molecular orbital (HMO) model, where eigenvalues of molecular graphs are used to approximate the total $\pi$-electron energy of conjugated hydrocarbons; see [13]. More generally, spectral quantities such as $\mathcal{E}(G)$ provide concise descriptors of graph structure; see [4] for background on graph spectra.

A bridge from linear algebra to graph invariants is via the *characteristic polynomial*

$$\chi(G,x) = \det(xI - A(G)),$$

whose roots are exactly the eigenvalues $\lambda_1, \ldots, \lambda_n$. Since the determinant can be computed in $O(n^{\omega})$ arithmetic operations, where $\omega$ is the matrix-multiplication exponent [3], this bridge is useful not only conceptually but also computationally. In particular, invariants such as $\mathcal{E}(G)$ have a rich theory and admit efficient computation.


Y. Li et al. (Eds.): COCOON 2026, LNCS 16835, pp. 315–328, 2027.
https://doi.org/10.1007/978-981-92-3309-0_24

The permanent looks deceptively similar to the determinant. For an $n \times n$ matrix $M = (m_{ij})$,

$$\det(M) = \sum_{\sigma \in S_n} \operatorname{sgn}(\sigma) \prod_{i=1}^{n} m_{i,\sigma(i)}, \qquad \operatorname{per}(M) = \sum_{\sigma \in S_n} \prod_{i=1}^{n} m_{i,\sigma(i)},$$

where $S_n$ is the symmetric group on $[n] := \{1, 2, \ldots, n\}$ and $\operatorname{sgn}(\sigma) \in \{+1, -1\}$ denotes the sign of the permutation $\sigma$. The only difference is the sign factor, yet the consequences are dramatic. Valiant proved that computing $\operatorname{per}(M)$ is $\#P$-complete, even for 0–1 matrices [25], making the permanent a central object in theoretical computer science.

The Pólya Permanent Problem [22] asks when the permanent of a matrix can be transformed into the determinant of a related matrix by suitable sign changes. McCuaig [18] showed that this problem is equivalent to several combinatorial and graph-theoretic problems, including counting perfect matchings in a graph. This motivates studying which structural and spectral properties are shared by the permanent and determinant, despite the hardness of the permanent.

Analogous to the characteristic polynomial, the *permanental polynomial* of a graph $G$ is

$$\pi(G, x) := \operatorname{per}(xI - A(G)).$$

Introduced by Turner [24], $\pi(G, x)$ has been studied as a permanent-based spectral invariant in graph theory and chemical graph theory; see [11,19]. In particular, its coefficients and zeros have been used as structural descriptors and computed for several chemically motivated families. Because computing permanents is hard in general, much of the literature focuses on structural properties and efficient computation for special graph families; see [9,10,14]. Computational studies suggest that *copermanental* graphs (nonisomorphic graphs with the same permanental polynomial) are rare, especially compared with cospectrality for the characteristic polynomial, so $\pi(G, x)$ may be a strong isomorphism heuristic [16]. Related work develops the theory of permanental spectra [15,21,26].

**Permanental Energy.** Let $\mu_1, \ldots, \mu_n$ be the roots of $\pi(G, x)$ (in general $\mu_i \in \mathbb{C}$), and write $|\mu_i|$ for their modulus. We define the *permanental energy* of $G$ as

$$\mathcal{E}_{\text{per}}(G) = \sum_{i=1}^{n} |\mu_i|.$$

Thus $\mathcal{E}_{\text{per}}(G)$ is a single number that summarizes the permanental roots, in the same spirit as the usual graph energy. However, permanental roots are often complex, so many standard eigenvalue techniques do not apply. Notably, Dehmer *et al.* [5] studied graph descriptors built from the moduli $|\mu_i|$ like $\sum_i |\mu_i|$ (that is, $\mathcal{E}_{\text{per}}(G)$), $\sum_i |\mu_i|^2$, and more generally $\sum_i |\mu_i|^p$ for various $p$, and reported that these quantities empirically distinguish networks well in practice. However, to the best of our knowledge, little general theory is known for such modulus-based permanental descriptors.

Since computing the permanent is #$P$-complete, exactly computing $\pi(G,x)$ and its roots is infeasible in general; consequently, one should not expect efficient exact computation of $\mathcal{E}_{\text{per}}(G)$ for arbitrary graphs. This makes general bounds and extremal characterizations especially valuable, because they provide information about $\mathcal{E}_{\text{per}}(G)$ without requiring explicit root computation.

Despite the hardness of computing $\pi(G,x)$ exactly, the quantity $\mathcal{E}_{\text{per}}(G)$ admits sharp universal extremal behavior. We prove that among all graphs with $m$ edges, the minimum possible permanental energy is exactly $2\sqrt{m}$, attained only by a star plus isolated vertices. We prove the general upper bound $\mathcal{E}_{\text{per}}(G) \le n\rho(G)$ and derive basic corollaries (Theorem 3 and Corollaries 3–4). We also give sharper information for several graph families, in Sect. 4.

The remainder of the paper is structured as follows. Section 2 introduces the necessary definitions, notations, and preliminary results. Section 3 proves upper and lower bounds on $\mathcal{E}_{\text{per}}(G)$ and characterizes the extremal graphs. Section 4 studies $\mathcal{E}_{\text{per}}(G)$ for several graph families. Section 5 lists future directions.

## 2 Preliminaries

For an $n \times n$ matrix $A$ and index sets $I, J \subseteq [n]$, let $A[I,J]$ denote the submatrix of $A$ formed by rows indexed by $I$ and columns indexed by $J$. In particular, for $S \subseteq [n]$, we write $A[S,S]$ for the principal submatrix indexed by $S$.

Throughout this paper, graphs are finite, undirected, and simple. Let $G$ be a graph with $V(G) = [n]$ and adjacency matrix $A(G)$, and for $S \subseteq [n]$ write $A(G)[S] := A(G)[S,S]$. Let $\Delta(G)$ denote the maximum degree of a vertex of $G$. We write $\sqcup$ for disjoint union of graphs. Standard graphs are denoted by $K_n$ (complete graph on $n$ vertices), $K_{1,m}$ (star with $m$ leaves), $K_1$ (isolated vertex), $P_n$ (path on $n$ vertices), and $C_n$ (cycle on $n$ vertices). Write $[n] := \{1,2,\dots,n\}$. We write $i$ for the imaginary unit, so $i^2 = -1$.

We collect below several basic lemmas on permanental polynomials and their roots that will be used throughout the paper. First recall a standard principal-submatrix expansion for $\text{per}(xI - A)$; see [20].

**Lemma 1.** *Let $A \in \mathbb{R}^{n\times n}$ and define its permanental polynomial*

$$\pi(A,x) := \text{per}(xI - A) = \sum_{i=0}^{n} c_i\, x^{n-i}.$$

*Then $c_0 = 1$, and for each $1 \le i \le n$,*

$$c_i = (-1)^i \sum_{\substack{S\subseteq[n]\\ |S|=i}} \text{per}\big(A[S,S]\big).$$

Applying Lemma 1 to $A(G)$ yields the first coefficients of the permanental polynomial $\pi(G,x) = \text{per}(xI - A(G))$.

**Lemma 2.** *Let $G$ be a simple graph on $n$ vertices with $m$ edges and $t$ triangles. Write*

$$\pi(G, x) = \sum_{k=0}^{n} c_k\, x^{n-k}.$$

*Then $c_0 = 1$, $c_1 = 0$, $c_2 = m$, and $c_3 = -2t$.*

*Proof.* By Lemma 1, we have

$$c_k = (-1)^k \sum_{\substack{S \subseteq [n] \\ |S| = k}} \mathrm{per}(A(G)[S]) \qquad (0 \le k \le n).$$

For $k = 1$, every $1 \times 1$ principal submatrix equals $(0)$, hence $c_1 = 0$. For $k = 2$, $A(G)[S] = \left(\begin{smallmatrix} 0 & 1 \\ 1 & 0 \end{smallmatrix}\right)$ if and only if $S$ is an edge, and then $\mathrm{per}(A(G)[S]) = 1$, otherwise $\mathrm{per}(A(G)[S]) = 0$; thus $c_2 = m$. For $k = 3$, since $G$ has no loops, a nonzero contribution to $\mathrm{per}(A(G)[S])$ can only come from the two 3-cycle permutations. These contribute exactly when $G[S] \cong K_3$, in which case each contributes 1. Hence $\mathrm{per}(A(G)[S]) = 2$ iff $G[S] \cong K_3$ and otherwise 0, so $c_3 = -\sum_{|S|=3} \mathrm{per}(A(G)[S]) = -2t$.

We will use the following Newton identities to express coefficients of a polynomial in terms of power sums of its roots.

**Lemma 3** ([17]). *Let $p(x)$ be a monic polynomial of degree $n$ with roots $\mu_1, \ldots, \mu_n$, and write*

$$p(x) = x^n + a_1 x^{n-1} + a_2 x^{n-2} + \cdots.$$

*Then*

$$\sum_{i=1}^{n} \mu_i = -a_1, \qquad \sum_{i=1}^{n} \mu_i^2 = a_1^2 - 2a_2.$$

**Corollary 1.** *Let $G$ be a simple graph with $m$ edges and permanental roots $\mu_1, \ldots, \mu_n$. Then*

$$\sum_{i=1}^{n} \mu_i = 0, \qquad \sum_{i=1}^{n} \mu_i^2 = -2\,m.$$

*Proof.* Combine Lemmas 3 and 2.

We will need the following nonstandard inequality (including its equality conditions) in proving the lower bound for $\mathcal{E}_{\mathrm{per}}(G)$.

**Lemma 4.** *Let $z_1, \ldots, z_n \in \mathbb{C}$ satisfy $\sum_{i=1}^{n} z_i = 0$. Then*

$$\Big(\sum_{i=1}^{n} |z_i|\Big)^2 \ge 2 \sum_{i=1}^{n} |z_i|^2. \tag{1}$$

*Moreover, equality holds iff either $z_1 = \cdots = z_n = 0$, or there exist distinct indices $p \ne q$ and $\alpha \ne 0$ such that $z_p = \alpha$, $z_q = -\alpha$, and $z_i = 0$ for all $i \notin \{p, q\}$.*

*Proof.* Let $s := \sum_{i=1}^{n} |z_i|$. If $s = 0$, then $|z_i| = 0$ for all $i$, hence $z_1 = \cdots = z_n = 0$. Assume $s > 0$. By $\sum_{i=1}^{n} z_i = 0$ we have $z_i = -\sum_{j \neq i} z_j$, and therefore

$$|z_i| \leq \sum_{j \neq i} |z_j| = s - |z_i|.$$

Thus $|z_i| \leq s/2$ for every $i$. Multiplying by $|z_i|$ gives $|z_i|^2 \leq (s/2)|z_i|$, and summing over $i$ yields

$$\sum_{i=1}^{n} |z_i|^2 \leq \frac{s}{2} \sum_{i=1}^{n} |z_i| = \frac{s^2}{2}. \tag{2}$$

Rearranging (2) gives (1). For the equality case, suppose equality holds in (1), equivalently in (2). Then

$$\sum_{i=1}^{n} \left( \frac{s}{2}|z_i| - |z_i|^2 \right) = \frac{s^2}{2} - \sum_{i=1}^{n} |z_i|^2 = 0.$$

Since each summand is nonnegative, we must have $|z_i|^2 = (s/2)|z_i|$ for every $i$, hence $|z_i| \in \{0, s/2\}$. Since the sum of all moduli is $s$, exactly two of the numbers $|z_i|$ are equal to $s/2$, and all the others are zero. Thus there exist distinct indices $p \neq q$ with $|z_p| = |z_q| = s/2$, while $z_i = 0$ for all $i \notin \{p, q\}$. Since $\sum_{i=1}^{n} z_i = 0$, we have $z_p + z_q = 0$, hence $z_q = -z_p$. Writing $z_p = \alpha$ gives $z_q = -\alpha$ with $\alpha \neq 0$.

Conversely, if $z_p = \alpha$, $z_q = -\alpha$, and all other $z_i = 0$, then $\sum_{i=1}^{n} z_i = 0$ and

$$\left( \sum_{i=1}^{n} |z_i| \right)^2 = (2|\alpha|)^2 = 4|\alpha|^2 = 2\big(|\alpha|^2 + |\alpha|^2\big) = 2 \sum_{i=1}^{n} |z_i|^2,$$

so equality holds in (1).

# 3 Bounds and Extremal Graphs

In this section we establish universal lower and upper bounds on $\mathcal{E}_{\text{per}}(G)$ and characterize the graphs attaining equality.

## 3.1 Lower Bound

**Theorem 1.** *Let $G$ be a simple graph with $m$ edges and permanental roots $\mu_1, \ldots, \mu_n$. Then*

$$\mathcal{E}_{\text{per}}(G) = \sum_{i=1}^{n} |\mu_i| \ \geq \ 2\sqrt{m}.$$

*Proof.* By Corollary 1, $\sum_{i=1}^{n} \mu_i = 0$ and $\sum_{i=1}^{n} \mu_i^2 = -2m$. Applying Lemma 4 to $z_i = \mu_i$ gives

$$\left( \sum_{i=1}^{n} |\mu_i| \right)^2 \geq 2 \sum_{i=1}^{n} |\mu_i|^2. \tag{3}$$

Moreover, since $|\mu_i|^2 = |\mu_i^2|$,

$$\sum_{i=1}^{n} |\mu_i|^2 = \sum_{i=1}^{n} |\mu_i^2| \geq \left|\sum_{i=1}^{n} \mu_i^2\right| = 2m. \tag{4}$$

Combining (3) and (4) yields $\mathcal{E}_{\mathrm{per}}(G)^2 \geq 4m$, hence $\mathcal{E}_{\mathrm{per}}(G) \geq 2\sqrt{m}$.

**Theorem 2.** *Let $G$ be a simple graph on $n$ vertices with $m$ edges. Then $\mathcal{E}_{\mathrm{per}}(G) = 2\sqrt{m}$ if and only if $G$ is a star graph on $m+1$ vertices together with $n-m-1$ isolated vertices, that is,*

$$G \cong K_{1,m} \sqcup (n-m-1)K_1.$$

*Proof.* We first prove the forward direction. Assume $\mathcal{E}_{\mathrm{per}}(G) = 2\sqrt{m}$ and let $\mu_1, \ldots, \mu_n$ be the roots of $\pi(G, x)$. If $m = 0$, then $G$ has no edges, so $A(G) = 0$ and hence $\pi(G, x) = \mathrm{per}(xI) = x^n$, which implies $G \cong nK_1$. Thus assume $m \geq 1$. Equality in Theorem 1 forces equality in (3). Since also $\sum_i \mu_i = 0$ by Corollary 1, the equality case of Lemma 4 implies that there exist distinct indices $p \neq q$ and $\alpha \neq 0$ such that

$$\mu_p = \alpha, \qquad \mu_q = -\alpha, \qquad \mu_i = 0 \ \text{ for all } i \notin \{p, q\}.$$

Using Corollary 1 again, we get

$$-2m = \sum_{i=1}^{n} \mu_i^2 = \alpha^2 + (-\alpha)^2 = 2\alpha^2,$$

so $\alpha^2 = -m$ and hence $\alpha = \pm i\sqrt{m}$. Therefore

$$\pi(G, x) = x^{n-2}(x^2 + m) = x^n + mx^{n-2}. \tag{5}$$

From (5) the coefficient of $x^{n-3}$ is 0, hence Lemma 2 gives $t = 0$, i.e., $G$ is triangle-free. Also, for every $k \geq 4$ the coefficient of $x^{n-k}$ in (5) is 0. By Lemma 1,

$$\sum_{\substack{S \subseteq [n] \\ |S| = k}} \mathrm{per}(A(G)[S]) = 0 \qquad (k \geq 4).$$

Since each $\mathrm{per}(A(G)[S]) \geq 0$, it follows that

$$\mathrm{per}(A(G)[S]) = 0 \qquad \text{for every } S \subseteq [n] \text{ with } |S| \geq 4. \tag{6}$$

We claim that $G$ has no two vertex-disjoint edges. Indeed, if $\{a, b\}$ and $\{c, d\}$ are disjoint edges and $S = \{a, b, c, d\}$, then the permutation $(a\,b)(c\,d)$ contributes 1 to $\mathrm{per}(A(G)[S])$, contradicting (6). Hence any two edges of $G$ share a common endpoint.

Let $c$ be a vertex of maximum degree $\Delta \geq 1$. If $\Delta = 1$, then $G$ has at most one edge, so $G \cong K_{1,1} \sqcup (n-2)K_1$, which matches the claim for $m = 1$. Assume $\Delta \geq 2$ and choose two distinct neighbors $u$ and $v$ of $c$. If there were an edge $e$

not incident to $c$, then $e$ must meet both $\{c, u\}$ and $\{c, v\}$. Since $e$ avoids $c$, this forces $e = \{u, v\}$, creating a triangle $cuv$, a contradiction. Therefore every edge of $G$ is incident to $c$, so the non-isolated part of $G$ is a star with center $c$ and $m$ edges. Hence $G \cong K_{1,m} \sqcup (n-m-1)K_1$.

For the converse direction, if $G \cong K_{1,m} \sqcup (n-m-1)K_1$, then $\pi(G,x) = x^{n-2}(x^2+m)$ and the permanental roots are 0 (with multiplicity $n-2$) and $\pm i\sqrt{m}$, so $\mathcal{E}_{\text{per}}(G) = 2\sqrt{m}$.

**Corollary 2.** *If $G$ is connected on $n \geq 2$ vertices, then*

$$\mathcal{E}_{\text{per}}(G) \geq 2\sqrt{n-1},$$

*with equality iff $G \cong K_{1,n-1}$.*

*Proof.* Let $G$ have $m$ edges. Since $G$ is connected, $m \geq n-1$, so Theorem 1 gives

$$\mathcal{E}_{\text{per}}(G) \geq 2\sqrt{m} \geq 2\sqrt{n-1}.$$

If equality holds, then $m = n-1$ and Theorem 2 forces $G$ to be a star, hence $G \cong K_{1,n-1}$. Conversely, if $G \cong K_{1,n-1}$, then $\pi(G,x) = x^{n-2}(x^2+n-1)$ and hence $\mathcal{E}_{\text{per}}(G) = 2\sqrt{n-1}$.

### 3.2 Upper Bounds

For a square matrix $M$, let $\rho(M)$ be its spectral radius, that is, the largest absolute value among its eigenvalues. In particular, for a graph $G$, we write $\rho(G) := \rho(A(G))$. We use a standard bound of Brenner and Brualdi [2] on the roots of $\text{per}(xI - A)$ to upper bound $\mathcal{E}_{\text{per}}(G)$.

**Lemma 5 (Brenner–Brualdi [2]).** *Let $A \geq 0$ be an $n \times n$ matrix. Every root $\mu$ of $\text{per}(xI - A)$ satisfies $|\mu| \leq \rho(A)$.*

**Theorem 3.** *Let $G$ be a simple graph on $n$ vertices with spectral radius $\rho = \rho(G)$. Then*

$$\mathcal{E}_{\text{per}}(G) \leq n\rho.$$

*Proof.* Let $\mu_1, \ldots, \mu_n$ be the roots of $\pi(G,x) = \text{per}(xI - A(G))$. By Lemma 5 (applied to $A(G) \geq 0$), we have $|\mu_i| \leq \rho$ for all $i$. Summing gives $\mathcal{E}_{\text{per}}(G) \leq n\rho$.

Thus, any upper bound on $\rho(G)$ immediately yields a corresponding upper bound on $\mathcal{E}_{\text{per}}(G)$ via Theorem 3.

**Corollary 3.** *Let $G$ be a simple graph on $n$ vertices with $m$ edges. Then*

$$\mathcal{E}_{\text{per}}(G) \leq \frac{n(\sqrt{8m+1}-1)}{2}.$$

*Proof.* Combine Theorem 3 with Stanley's bound $\rho(G) \leq (\sqrt{8m+1}-1)/2$ [23].

**Corollary 4.** *For every simple graph $G$ on $n \geq 2$ vertices,*

$$\mathcal{E}_{\text{per}}(G) \leq n\Delta(G) \leq n(n-1).$$

*Proof.* Use $\rho(G) \leq \Delta(G) \leq n-1$ in Theorem 3.

*Remark 1 (Tightness of the upper bound).* Theorem 3 is usually not tight, since it upper bounds all permanental roots by $\rho(G)$. For instance, $\mathcal{E}_{\text{per}}(K_{1,n-1}) = 2\sqrt{n-1}$, while Theorem 3 gives $\mathcal{E}_{\text{per}}(K_{1,n-1}) \leq n\sqrt{n-1}$.

*Comparison with Adjacency Energy.* It is well known that $2\sqrt{m} \leq \mathcal{E}(G) \leq \sqrt{2mn}$ and both bounds are tight ; see [8]. Theorem 1 shows that the same sharp lower bound $2\sqrt{m}$ holds for $\mathcal{E}_{\text{per}}(G)$, but the upper bound $\sqrt{2mn}$ does not extend to $\mathcal{E}_{\text{per}}(G)$: for $G = K_3$, $\pi(K_3, x) = x^3 + 3x - 2$ has roots $\mu_1 \approx 0.5961$ and $\mu_{2,3} \approx -0.2980 \pm 1.8073\,i$, hence $\mathcal{E}_{\text{per}}(K_3) \approx 4.2596 > \sqrt{18} \approx 4.2426$.

This motivates the extremal problem of maximizing $\mathcal{E}_{\text{per}}(G)$ over all graphs on $n$ vertices. Based on computations for all graphs up to $n \leq 10$, we observe that the complete graph is the maximizer; see Sect. 4.4.

# 4 Special Families

In this section we discuss graph families for which $\mathcal{E}_{\text{per}}(G)$ admits sharper information than the universal bounds of Sect. 3.

## 4.1 Bipartite Families

For some bipartite graph classes, the permanental polynomial can be written in terms of the characteristic polynomial of an associated matrix. This can force $\mathcal{E}_{\text{per}}(G)$ to coincide with the usual adjacency energy $\mathcal{E}(G)$ and can also yield stronger upper bounds for such classes.

If $G$ is bipartite and has no cycle whose length is divisible by 4, then Borowiecki [1] proved the following relation between the permanental and characteristic polynomials.

**Theorem 4.** *If $G$ is bipartite and contains no cycle of length $4k$ for any $k \geq 1$, then*

$$\pi(G, x) = i^{-n}\chi(G, ix).$$

*Equivalently, the permanental roots satisfy $\{\mu_1, \dots, \mu_n\} = \{-i\lambda_1, \dots, -i\lambda_n\}$, where $\lambda_1, \dots, \lambda_n$ are the adjacency eigenvalues (as a multiset).*

**Corollary 5.** *If $G$ is bipartite and contains no cycle of length $4k$ for any $k \geq 1$, then $\mathcal{E}_{\text{per}}(G) = \mathcal{E}(G)$.*

*Proof.* By Theorem 4, the permanental roots are $\{-i\lambda_j\}_{j=1}^{n}$ (with multiplicities), hence $|\mu_j| = |\lambda_j|$ and $\mathcal{E}_{\text{per}}(G) = \mathcal{E}(G)$.

An *orientation* assigns a direction to each edge. Since $G$ is bipartite, every cycle of $G$ has even length. We say that a cycle is *oddly oriented* in an orientation $\sigma$ if, when traversing the cycle, an odd number of its edges are directed along the traversal. Given an orientation $G^\sigma$, let $S(G^\sigma)$ be the matrix with $S_{uv} = 1$ if $u \to v$ is an arc of $G^\sigma$, $S_{uv} = -1$ if $v \to u$ is an arc, and $S_{uv} = 0$ otherwise. Zhang and Li [27] showed that if $G$ admits an orientation in which every cycle is oddly oriented, then the permanental polynomial has an exact determinantal description.

**Theorem 5** ([27]). *Let $G$ be bipartite. If $G$ admits an orientation $\sigma$ in which every cycle is oddly oriented, then*

$$\pi(G,x) = \operatorname{per}(xI - A(G)) = \det\big(xI - S(G^\sigma)\big).$$

This gives a McClelland-type upper bound for this class.

**Theorem 6.** *Let $G$ be a bipartite graph on $n$ vertices with $m$ edges. Suppose that $G$ admits an orientation $\sigma$ in which every cycle of $G$ is oddly oriented. Then*

$$\mathcal{E}_{\text{per}}(G) \le \sqrt{2mn}.$$

*Proof.* Write $S := S(G^\sigma)$. By Theorem 5, $\pi(G,x) = \det(xI - S)$. Set $H := -iS$. Since $S^\mathsf{T} = -S$ and $S$ is real, $H$ is Hermitian and

$$\pi(G,x) = \det(xI - iH).$$

Thus the roots of $\pi(G,x)$ are $i\lambda_1, \ldots, i\lambda_n$, where $\lambda_1, \ldots, \lambda_n \in \mathbb{R}$ are the eigenvalues of $H$. Hence

$$\mathcal{E}_{\text{per}}(G) = \sum_{j=1}^{n} |\lambda_j|.$$

By Cauchy–Schwarz,

$$\mathcal{E}_{\text{per}}(G)^2 \le n \sum_{j=1}^{n} \lambda_j^2 = n \operatorname{tr}(H^2).$$

Moreover,

$$\operatorname{tr}(H^2) = \sum_{u,v} |h_{uv}|^2 = \sum_{u,v} |s_{uv}|^2 = 2m,$$

because $S$ has exactly $2m$ off-diagonal entries equal to $\pm 1$. Therefore $\mathcal{E}_{\text{per}}(G)^2 \le 2mn$, that is, $\mathcal{E}_{\text{per}}(G) \le \sqrt{2mn}$.

## 4.2 Forests and Tree Extremals

Forests are bipartite and contain no cycles, hence satisfy Theorem 4. Therefore, for every forest $F$ one has $\mathcal{E}_{\text{per}}(F) = \mathcal{E}(F)$.

**Corollary 6.** *Among all trees $T$ on $n$ vertices,*

$$\mathcal{E}_{\text{per}}(K_{1,n-1}) \leq \mathcal{E}_{\text{per}}(T) \leq \mathcal{E}_{\text{per}}(P_n),$$

*with equality on the left if and only if $T \cong K_{1,n-1}$ and equality on the right if and only if $T \cong P_n$.*

*Proof.* Since every tree is a forest, we have $\mathcal{E}_{\text{per}}(T) = \mathcal{E}(T)$. Apply the classical extremal theorem for adjacency energy on trees [8].

### 4.3 Cycles

Cycles can be handled explicitly. The next theorem gives $\mathcal{E}_{\text{per}}(C_n)$, with different behavior for even and odd $n$.

**Theorem 7.** *Let $n \geq 3$.*

1. *If $n$ is even, then*

$$\mathcal{E}_{\text{per}}(C_n) = \frac{4}{\sin(\pi/n)}.$$

2. *If $n$ is odd, then*

$$\lim_{\substack{n\to\infty \\ n \text{ odd}}} \frac{\mathcal{E}_{\text{per}}(C_n)}{n} = \frac{4}{\pi}.$$

*Proof.* We use the following explicit expression for $\pi(C_n, x)$ due to Li and Zhang [12]:

$$\pi(C_n, x) = \begin{cases} \displaystyle\prod_{t=1}^{n}\left(x + 2i\sin\frac{(2t-1)\pi}{n}\right), & \text{if } n \text{ is even,} \\ \displaystyle\prod_{t=1}^{n}\left(x + 2i\cos\frac{t\pi}{n+1}\right) + \prod_{t=1}^{n-2}\left(x + 2i\cos\frac{t\pi}{n-1}\right) - 2, & \text{if } n \text{ is odd.} \end{cases}$$

First suppose that $n$ is even. Then the roots are

$$\mu_t = -2i\sin\frac{(2t-1)\pi}{n}, \qquad t = 1, \ldots, n.$$

Therefore

$$\mathcal{E}_{\text{per}}(C_n) = 2\sum_{t=1}^{n}\left|\sin\frac{(2t-1)\pi}{n}\right| = 4\sum_{t=1}^{n/2}\sin\frac{(2t-1)\pi}{n}.$$

Using the standard identity [6]

$$\sum_{j=1}^{m}\sin((2j-1)\theta) = \frac{\sin^2(m\theta)}{\sin\theta}$$

with $m = n/2$ and $\theta = \pi/n$, we get

$$\sum_{t=1}^{n/2} \sin\frac{(2t-1)\pi}{n} = \frac{\sin^2(\pi/2)}{\sin(\pi/n)} = \frac{1}{\sin(\pi/n)}.$$

Hence $\mathcal{E}_{\text{per}}(C_n) = 4/\sin(\pi/n)$. Now suppose that $n$ is odd. We use the closed form [11]

$$\pi(C_n, x) = \lambda_+^n + \lambda_-^n + 2(-1)^n, \qquad \lambda_\pm = \frac{x \pm \sqrt{x^2+4}}{2}.$$

Let $a = \log(1+\sqrt{2})$. Since $n$ is odd, $\lambda_- = -1/\lambda_+$ and $(-1)^n = -1$. Writing $\lambda = \lambda_+$, the equation $\pi(C_n, x) = 0$ becomes

$$\lambda^n - \lambda^{-n} - 2 = 0.$$

Thus, if $y = \lambda^n$, then $y - y^{-1} = 2$, so $y^2 - 2y - 1 = 0$. Taking $y = 1 + \sqrt{2} = e^a$, we obtain the roots

$$\mu_k = 2\sinh\Bigl(\frac{a + 2\pi i k}{n}\Bigr), \qquad k = 0, 1, \ldots, n-1.$$

Let $u = a/n$ and $\theta_k = 2\pi k/n$. Since $|\sinh(u+i\theta)|^2 = \sinh^2 u + \sin^2\theta$, we have

$$\frac{1}{n}\mathcal{E}_{\text{per}}(C_n) = \frac{2}{n}\sum_{k=0}^{n-1}\sqrt{\sinh^2(a/n) + \sin^2\theta_k}.$$

As $\sinh(a/n) = O(1/n)$, this gives

$$\frac{1}{n}\mathcal{E}_{\text{per}}(C_n) = \frac{2}{n}\sum_{k=0}^{n-1}|\sin\theta_k| + o(1).$$

The sum is a Riemann sum for

$$\frac{1}{2\pi}\int_0^{2\pi}|\sin t|\,dt = \frac{2}{\pi}.$$

Therefore

$$\lim_{\substack{n\to\infty \\ n \text{ odd}}} \frac{\mathcal{E}_{\text{per}}(C_n)}{n} = \frac{4}{\pi}.$$

## 4.4 Complete Graphs

The general bound $\mathcal{E}_{\text{per}}(G) \le n\rho(G)$ suggests that graphs with large spectral radius may also have large permanental energy. In particular, the complete graph $K_n$ is a natural candidate. Let $D_n$ denote the number of derangements of $[n]$, that is, permutations $\sigma \in S_n$ with $\sigma(i) \ne i$ for all $i \in [n]$.

**Lemma 6.** *For $n \geq 1$, $\mathrm{per}(A(K_n)) = D_n$.*

*Proof.* In $A(K_n)$ the diagonal entries are 0 and all off-diagonal entries are 1. Hence a permutation $\sigma$ contributes 1 to $\mathrm{per}(A(K_n))$ iff $\sigma(i) \neq i$ for all $i$, that is, iff $\sigma$ is a derangement.

**Lemma 7.** *For every $n \geq 1$,*

$$\mathcal{E}_{\mathrm{per}}(K_n) \;\geq\; n\, D_n^{1/n}.$$

*Proof.* Let $\mu_1, \ldots, \mu_n$ be the roots of the monic polynomial $\pi(K_n, x)$. Since $\pi(K_n, 0) = \mathrm{per}(-A(K_n)) = (-1)^n \,\mathrm{per}(A(K_n))$, we have

$$\prod_{i=1}^{n} \mu_i = (-1)^n \pi(K_n, 0) = (-1)^n(-1)^n \,\mathrm{per}(A(K_n)) = \mathrm{per}(A(K_n)) = D_n$$

by Lemma 6. Taking absolute values gives $\prod_{i=1}^{n} |\mu_i| = D_n$. Applying AM–GM to $|\mu_1|, \ldots, |\mu_n|$ yields

$$\frac{1}{n}\sum_{i=1}^{n} |\mu_i| \;\geq\; \Big(\prod_{i=1}^{n} |\mu_i|\Big)^{1/n} = D_n^{1/n},$$

which implies $\mathcal{E}_{\mathrm{per}}(K_n) = \sum_{i=1}^{n} |\mu_i| \geq n D_n^{1/n}$.

**Corollary 7.** *As $n \to \infty$,*

$$\mathcal{E}_{\mathrm{per}}(K_n) \;\geq\; \Big(\frac{1}{e} - o(1)\Big) n^2.$$

*In particular, $\mathcal{E}_{\mathrm{per}}(K_n) = \Omega(n^2)$.*

*Proof.* By Lemma 7, $\mathcal{E}_{\mathrm{per}}(K_n) \geq n\, D_n^{1/n}$. It is standard that $D_n = \frac{n!}{e} + O(1)$ (see [7]), hence $D_n^{1/n} = \big(\frac{n!}{e}\big)^{1/n} (1 + o(1))$. By Stirling's formula, $(n!)^{1/n} = \big(1 + o(1)\big) \frac{n}{e}$, so $D_n^{1/n} = \big(1 + o(1)\big) \frac{n}{e}$. Therefore $\mathcal{E}_{\mathrm{per}}(K_n) \geq \big(\frac{1}{e} - o(1)\big) n^2$.

As a simple consequence, $K_n$ already dominates every $n$-vertex graph whose spectral radius is at most $D_n^{1/n}$.

**Theorem 8.** *Let $G$ be a simple graph on $n$ vertices. If $\rho(G) \leq D_n^{1/n}$, then*

$$\mathcal{E}_{\mathrm{per}}(G) \leq \mathcal{E}_{\mathrm{per}}(K_n).$$

*Proof.* By Theorem 3, $\mathcal{E}_{\mathrm{per}}(G) \leq n\rho(G) \leq n D_n^{1/n}$. By Lemma 7, $\mathcal{E}_{\mathrm{per}}(K_n) \geq n D_n^{1/n}$. Thus $\mathcal{E}_{\mathrm{per}}(G) \leq \mathcal{E}_{\mathrm{per}}(K_n)$.

*Remark 2.* Exhaustive enumeration for all graphs up to $n \leq 10$ indicates that $K_n$ is the unique maximizer of $\mathcal{E}_{\mathrm{per}}(G)$ among $n$-vertex graphs. Moreover, for $3 \leq n \leq 8$, the best non-complete graph is $K_n$ with one edge deleted and in the dense regime $m = \binom{n}{2} - k$ the maximizer appears to be the clique with a matching of size $k$ deleted.

## 5 Future Directions

Several interesting questions remain open. On the algorithmic side, it would be interesting to determine the complexity of computing $\mathcal{E}_{\text{per}}(G)$ exactly, and more realistically to understand the complexity of approximating $\mathcal{E}_{\text{per}}(G)$ within additive error $\varepsilon n$ or relative error $1 \pm \varepsilon$. On the extremal side, our general upper bound $\mathcal{E}_{\text{per}}(G) \leq n\rho(G)$ is often not tight; finding universal upper bounds that improve on this in nontrivial regimes seems particularly worthwhile. Structurally, beyond the bipartite classes in Sect. 4, it remains to characterize broad graph families for which $\mathcal{E}_{\text{per}}(G) = \mathcal{E}(G)$, or to identify clear obstructions to equality. Finally, developing general constraints on the location and multiplicity pattern of permanental roots (forced zeros, symmetry, stability phenomena, etc.) could provide new ways to control $\mathcal{E}_{\text{per}}(G)$ without explicitly computing permanental roots.

**Acknowledgments.** The authors thank the anonymous reviewers for their helpful comments and suggestions. Priyanshu Pant is supported by the CSIR–UGC NET JRF Fellowship. This work is also supported by the ANRF Grant ANRF/ARGM/2025/002341/TS.

**Disclosure of Interests.** The authors have no competing interests to declare that are relevant to the content of this article.

## References

1. Borowiecki, M.: On spectrum and per-spectrum of graphs. Publ. Inst. Math. (Beograd) **38**, 31–33 (1985). http://elib.mi.sanu.ac.rs/files/journals/publ/58/n052p031.pdf
2. Brenner, J.L., Brualdi, R.A.: Eigenschaften der Permanentefunktion. Arch. Math. **18**, 585–586 (1967). https://doi.org/10.1007/BF01898864
3. Bunch, J.R., Hopcroft, J.E.: Triangular factorization and inversion by fast matrix multiplication. Math. Comput. **28**(125), 231–236 (1974). https://doi.org/10.1090/S0025-5718-1974-0331751-8
4. Cvetković, D., Doob, M., Sachs, H.: Spectra of Graphs: Theory and Application. Academic Press, New York (1980)
5. Dehmer, M., Emmert-Streib, F., Hu, B., Shi, Y., Stefu, M., Tripathi, S.: Highly unique network descriptors based on the roots of the permanental polynomial. Inf. Sci. **408**, 176–181 (2017). https://doi.org/10.1016/j.ins.2017.04.041
6. Gradshteyn, I.S., Ryzhik, I.M.: Table of Integrals, Series, and Products, 8th edn. Academic Press (2014)
7. Graham, R.L., Knuth, D.E., Patashnik, O.: Concrete Mathematics: A Foundation for Computer Science, 2nd edn. Addison-Wesley (1994)
8. Gutman, I.: The energy of a graph. Chem. Phys. Lett. **57**, 358–361 (1978)
9. Gutman, I., Cash, G.G.: Relations between the permanental and characteristic polynomials of fullerenes and benzenoid hydrocarbons. MATCH Commun. Math. Comput. Chem. **45**, 55–70 (2002). https://match.pmf.kg.ac.rs/electronic_versions/Match45/match45_55-70.pdf

10. Huo, Y., Liang, H., Bai, F.: An efficient algorithm for computing permanental polynomials of graphs. Comput. Phys. Commun. **175**(3), 196–203 (2006). https://doi.org/10.1016/j.cpc.2006.03.002
11. Kasum, D., Trinajstić, N., Gutman, I.: Chemical graph theory. III. On the permanental polynomial. Croatica Chemica Acta **54**(3), 321–328 (1981). https://hrcak.srce.hr/file/286568
12. Li, W., Zhang, H.: The permanental polynomials of certain graphs. MATCH Commun. Math. Comput. Chem. **68**(3), 871–888 (2012). https://match.pmf.kg.ac.rs/electronic_versions/Match68/n3/match68n3_871-888.pdf
13. Li, X., Shi, Y., Gutman, I.: Graph Energy. Springer, New York (2012). https://doi.org/10.1007/978-1-4614-4220-2
14. Liang, H., Tong, H., Bai, F.: Computing the permanental polynomial of C60 in parallel. MATCH Commun. Math. Comput. Chem. **60**, 349–358 (2008). https://match.pmf.kg.ac.rs/electronic_versions/Match60/n2/match60n2_349-358.pdf
15. Liu, S., Zhang, H.: On the characterizing properties of the permanental polynomials of graphs. Linear Algebra Appl. **438**(1), 157–172 (2013). https://doi.org/10.1016/j.laa.2012.08.026
16. Liu, S., Ren, J.: Enumeration of copermanental graphs. arXiv preprint arXiv:1411.0184 (2015). https://doi.org/10.48550/arXiv.1411.0184
17. Marden, M.: Geometry of Polynomials, Mathematical Surveys, vol. 3. American Mathematical Society (1966). https://www.ams.org/books/surv/003/
18. McCuaig, W.: Pólya's permanent problem. Electron. J. Combinatorics **11**(1), R79 (2004). https://doi.org/10.37236/1832
19. Merris, R., Rebman, K.R., Watkins, W.: Permanental polynomials of graphs. Linear Algebra Appl. **38**, 273–288 (1981). https://doi.org/10.1016/0024-3795(81)90026-4
20. Minc, H.: Permanents, Encyclopedia of Mathematics and its Applications, vol. 6. Cambridge University Press (1984). https://www.cambridge.org/core/books/permanents/ED9F2795FFAD02D8058ADC1DEAAAEB4D
21. Pant, P., Chakrabartty, S., Singh, R.: A permanental analog of the rank-nullity theorem for symmetric matrices. In: 43rd International Symposium on Theoretical Aspects of Computer Science (STACS 2026). Leibniz International Proceedings in Informatics (LIPIcs), vol. 364, pp. 70:1–70:12. Schloss Dagstuhl – Leibniz-Zentrum für Informatik, Dagstuhl, Germany (2026). https://doi.org/10.4230/LIPIcs.STACS.2026.70
22. Pólya, G.: Aufgabe 424. Archiv der Mathematik und Physik **20**, 271 (1913)
23. Stanley, R.P.: A bound on the spectral radius of graphs with $e$ edges. Linear Algebra Appl. **87–88**, 267–271 (1987). https://doi.org/10.1016/0024-3795(87)90172-8
24. Turner, J.: Generalized matrix functions and the graph isomorphism problem. SIAM J. Appl. Math. **16**(3), 520–526 (1968). https://doi.org/10.1137/0116041
25. Valiant, L.G.: The complexity of computing the permanent. Theoret. Comput. Sci. **8**(2), 189–201 (1979). https://doi.org/10.1016/0304-3975(79)90044-6
26. Wu, T., Lai, H.J.: On the permanental nullity and matching number of graphs. Linear Multilinear Algebra **66**(3), 516–524 (2018). https://doi.org/10.1080/03081087.2017.1302403
27. Zhang, H., Li, W.: Computing the permanental polynomials of bipartite graphs by PFAFFIAN orientation. Discret. Appl. Math. **160**(13), 2069–2074 (2012). https://doi.org/10.1016/j.dam.2012.04.007

# A Competitive Algorithm for the Online Stochastic Resource Allocation Problem with Departures

Yusuf Amidu[1], Khaled Elbassioni[2], and Adriana F. Gabor[1(✉)]

[1] Department of Mathematics, Khalifa University, Abu Dhabi, United Arab Emirates
{100060537,adriana.gabor}@ku.ac.ae

[2] Department of Computer Science, Khalifa University, Abu Dhabi, United Arab Emirates
khaled.elbassioni@ku.ac.ae

**Abstract.** This paper introduces a competitive algorithm for the online stochastic resource allocation problem with departures. In the problem setting, random requests with apriori known probability distributions arrive sequentially over time, and upon arrival of each request, its realized values (reward, size, time interval) on each resource are revealed. The algorithm must decide immediately whether to accept or reject the request and, if accepted, assign it to one of the available resources. The objective is to maximize the expected total reward without violating the capacity of any resource. Under the assumptions that the arriving requests are statistically independent and that each request demands service upon arrival, we show that our online algorithm achieves a constant competitive ratio relative to the expected offline optimum.

**Keywords:** Online Knapsack Problems · Stochastic Algorithm · Competitive Ratio

## 1 Introduction

Many real-world problems involve allocating limited resources to competing requests that arrive randomly over time. Online resource allocation problems appear in a wide range of applications, including online advertising, cloud computing, and job scheduling. Resource allocation problems are typically NP-hard, even in the offline setting, where all the input requests are presented in advance.

In this paper we consider the stochastic version of the online resource allocation (also known as the multiple knapsack) problem with departures (OSMKD). In this variant, requests (items) for capacity arrive over time, and the sizes, rewards, and the duration of requests are stochastic, following a *known* joint probability distribution. Each resource has limited capacity. The objective of the online algorithm is to assign requests to resources such that the expected total reward obtained is maximized over the time horizon, without violating


Y. Li et al. (Eds.): COCOON 2026, LNCS 16835, pp. 329–341, 2027.
https://doi.org/10.1007/978-981-92-3309-0_25

the capacity of any resource. We propose a randomized online algorithm for the stochastic version with a constant competitive ratio. As in several previous results [1,2], our algorithm relies on solving an offline "prophet" linear program (LP) to decide a routing strategy for each request upon its arrival. Under the assumptions that the arriving requests are independent and that each request demands service upon arrival, we show that the competitive ratio (CR) of our algorithm is constant.

The remainder of this paper is structured as follows. In Sect. 2, we review some related work. Section 3 contains the description of the online problem and assumptions. In Sect. 4, we present the offline problem, prophet LP and introduce some notation. Section 5 presents the online algorithm for OSMKD and Sect. 6 contains the analysis of its CR. We conclude in Sect. 7. Proofs omitted due to lack of space can be found in the Appendix.

## 2 Related Work

The online (single/multiple) knapsack problem (OMK) has been widely studied within the framework of competitive analysis [3–6]. For the case of infinitesimal item sizes and fluctuation (ratio between maximum and minimum) of the item value density bounded by $\bar{\theta}$, [4] proposed a threshold-based algorithm for OMK with a CR of $\ln(\bar{\theta}) + 1$ and showed that no online algorithm can achieve a significantly lower CR. [5] was the first to study the online multiple knapsack problem with departures (OMKD), where it was shown that an extension of threshold-based policy for OMK attains a tight CR of $O(\log(\bar{d} \cdot \bar{\theta}))$ with $\bar{d}$ being the maximum duration fluctuation. A similar CR for OMKD was obtained via the online primal-dual approach in [7].

The online stochastic knapsack problem where items arrive over time according to a known probability distribution and both sizes and rewards are random with known distributions has been extensively studied in operations research, theoretical computer science, and algorithmic game theory. The dynamic and stochastic version of the knapsack problem was introduced in [8], where objects with random sizes and rewards arrive sequentially with a known probability distribution and assignment of objects to resources must be made in real-time. The model is motivated by classical applications in transportation and scheduling. A closely related model is the online stochastic generalized assignment problem studied in [9]. In this model, items of several types arrive sequentially and must be assigned to $m$ bins, each with a limited capacity. Each item type is characterized by a value and a size distribution, which may vary depending on the bin to which the item is assigned. While the probability distributions governing types, values, and sizes (not necessarily i.i.d) are known in advance, the exact size realization of an item is observed only after it has been placed into a bin. The objective is to determine an assignment of items to bins that maximizes the total value while respecting the capacity constraints. The model assumes that items arrive in adversarial order, but their stochastic properties are known. Under the large-capacity assumption that no item occupies more than a $\frac{1}{k}$ ($k > 0$) fraction of any bin's capacity, the authors designed a $1 - \frac{1}{\sqrt{k}}$ competitive algorithm. [10] studied online resource allocation problem in which requests arrive sequentially in an online fashion, and at each time step, a request is sampled independently from an unknown distribution (requests are i.i.d.s). They proposed algorithms that achieve a $(1 - \varepsilon)$-approximation of the optimal offline solution, without prior knowledge of the distribution, under the assumption that the maximum request-size to capacity ratio is $o(\varepsilon^2)$. Moreover, they introduced the adversarial stochastic input model, for which they proposed algorithms attaining a $(1 - \varepsilon)$-fraction of the optimal profit relative to the worst-case sequence of distributions.

Recent study has significantly improved the achievable competitive ratios in the online stochastic knapsack problem. For instance, [1] show that a competitive ratio of 0.32 can be obtained for a special case where customers of different types arrive according to nonhomogeneous Poisson processes, the size of their requests depends on the customer type, the allocated resource, and the value of a request is proportional to the size of the request. A tighter analyses based on tracking the distribution of capacity utilization rather than partitioning items by size have led to improved guarantees relative to the LP relaxation. For example, [2] studied the online contention resolution scheme (OCRS) and demonstrated that the best possible competitive ratio in the general knapsack setting is $\frac{1}{3+e^{-2}} \approx 0.319$, when size and value (reward) distributions are known in advance (note that this is the special case of OSMKD without departures). This result was further improved for a unit-density of knapsack problem to achieve 0.35 for the multi-resource appointment scheduling problem of [1].

The OSMKD problem is closely related to reusable resource allocation problems due to the finite duration of resource usage. However, it differs from classical rental or assortment models because in the OSMKD, resources may have general capacity consumptions whereas in many reusable rental models, consumers select a rental product and typically consume a single unit of capacity [11]. Also, in reusable resource settings, a customer may simultaneously consume multiple resources for different durations [12].

**Our Contribution.** To the best of our knowledge, this paper is the first to give an online algorithm for the stochastic online multiple knapsack problem with departures (OSMKD) with a constant CR. In our model, we consider stochastic reward, size and duration and assume that arriving requests demand to be serviced immediately (assumption (A1) below). As in several previous results [1,2], our algorithm is based on rounding the solution to a prophet linear program (LP) that upper bounds the expected optimal offline solution. Our rounding technique is inspired by the approach used for the offline Unsplittable Flow Problem [13]. Under the assumptions of independence, we show that the competitive ratio of our algorithm is a constant (at least $\frac{1}{32}$), which improves as the minimum capacity of the resources increases (reaching $\frac{1}{20}$ in the limit).

## 3 Problem Description

We consider an online resource allocation problem with requests arriving over time to a set of $K$ resources where each resource $k \in K$ has a capacity $C_k \geq 0$.

Without loss of generality, we assume that exactly one request arrives per time unit. If request $n$ is assigned to resource $k \in K$, it yields a stochastic reward $v_{nk} \geq 0$ and consumes a stochastic size $w_{nk} > 0$ units of the capacity of resource $k$ during its period of stay. Let $T$ be the time horizon and denote the time interval request $n$ demands to stay in resource $k$ by $T_{nk} = \{s_{nk}, s_{nk}+1, \ldots, s_{nk}+d_{nk}-1\}$, where $s_{nk}$ denotes the starting time and $d_{nk}$ denotes the duration of request $n$.

Each request $n$ is associated with a random tuple $\mathbf{u}_n = (\mathbf{v}_n, \mathbf{w}_n, \mathbf{T}_n)$, where $\mathbf{v}_n = (v_{nk} : k \in K)$, $\mathbf{w}_n = (w_{nk} : k \in K)$ and $\mathbf{T}_n = (T_{nk} : k \in K)$. We assume that $\mathbf{u}_n$ is drawn from a *known discrete* probability distribution $\mathbf{p}_n$: $p_n(\tilde{\mathbf{u}}_n) = \Pr[\mathbf{u}_n = \tilde{\mathbf{u}}_n]$ for a realization $\tilde{\mathbf{u}}_n$ of $\mathbf{u}_n$.

The objective is to design an online policy that decides, for each arriving request, whether to accept or reject it and, if accepted, which resource to assign it to, so as to maximize the expected total collected reward, subject to the capacity constraints of all resources over time.

We shall make the following assumptions:

(A1) For any requests $n, n' \in N$ such that $n < n'$, the following holds for all $k \in K$:

$$\max_{\tilde{\mathbf{u}}_n : \mathbf{p}_n(\tilde{\mathbf{u}}_n) > 0} s_{nk} \leq \min_{\tilde{\mathbf{u}}_{n'} : \mathbf{p}_{n'}(\tilde{\mathbf{u}}_{n'}) > 0} s_{n'k}.$$

(A2) For all $n \in N$, $k \in K$ and $\tilde{\mathbf{u}}_n$, $\tilde{w}_{nk} \leq 1$.

(A3) For all $k \in K$, $C_k \geq 1$ and hence $C_{\min} = \min_{k \in K} C_k \geq 1$.

(A4) The random variables $\mathbf{u}_1, \ldots, \mathbf{u}_n$ are statistically independent.

In particular, assumption (A1) holds if the consumption of any request must start upon its arrival. We call such case the "extension" model as we can think of each admitted request as initially occupying only one unit of the resource, then it requests an extension (on the same resource) with some positive probability. Note that (A2) and (A3) can be assumed without loss of generality by scaling.

In the following, we distinguish a random variable $y$ from a realization of $y$ by using $\tilde{y}$ for the realization.

## 4 The Offline Problem and Prophet LP

In the offline problem, all requests are revealed in advance. Given a realization $\tilde{I}$ of the random input $I$, the problem can be formulated as the following integer program (IP):

$$V^{\text{off}}(\tilde{I}) = \max_{\mathbf{x}} \sum_{n \in N} \sum_{k \in K} \tilde{v}_{nk} x_{nk} \qquad (1)$$

$$\text{s.t.} \sum_{n \in N : t \in \tilde{T}_{nk}} \tilde{w}_{nk} x_{nk} \leq C_k, \qquad \forall k \in K,\ \forall t \in T, \qquad (2)$$

$$\sum_{k \in K} x_{nk} \leq 1, \qquad \forall n \in N, \qquad (3)$$

$$x_{nk} \in \{0, 1\}, \qquad \forall n \in N,\ \forall k \in K. \qquad (4)$$

The objective of the IP is to maximize the total reward obtained from the allocation of requests to resources. Constraints (2) ensure that for each resource and at each time period, the total demand of all active requests that are assigned to a resource does not exceed the capacity of the resource. Constraints (3) guarantee that each request is assigned to at most one resource.

The prophet's value is denoted by $\mathbb{E}_{I\sim\mathcal{H}}\big[V^{\text{off}}(I)\big]$, where, $I = \big(\mathbf{u}_n : n \in N\big)$, and $\mathcal{H} = (\mathbf{p}_n : n \in N)$ denotes the vector of distributions for the requests.

*Prophet LP.* For each request $n \in N$ and resource $k \in K$, let $x_{nk}(\tilde{\mathbf{u}}_n)$ denote the (probabilistic) decision of the prophet after observing the realization $\tilde{\mathbf{u}}_n$ of request $n$. Following [2], we use the following linear program (LP) to upper bound the prophet's value:

$$z^*(\mathcal{H}) = \max_{\mathbf{x}} \sum_{n\in N}\sum_{k\in K}\sum_{\tilde{\mathbf{u}}_n} p_n(\tilde{\mathbf{u}}_n)\,\tilde{v}_{nk}\,x_{nk}(\tilde{\mathbf{u}}_n) \tag{5}$$

$$\text{s.t.} \sum_{n\in N}\sum_{\tilde{\mathbf{u}}_n : t\in\tilde{T}_{nk}} p_n(\tilde{\mathbf{u}}_n)\,\tilde{w}_{nk}\,x_{nk}(\tilde{\mathbf{u}}_n) \le C_k, \quad \forall k\in K,\ \forall t\in T, \tag{6}$$

$$\sum_{k\in K} x_{nk}(\tilde{\mathbf{u}}_n) \le 1, \quad \forall n\in N,\ \forall \tilde{\mathbf{u}}_n, \tag{7}$$

$$x_{nk}(\tilde{\mathbf{u}}_n) \ge 0, \quad \forall n\in N,\ \forall k\in K,\ \forall \tilde{\mathbf{u}}_n. \tag{8}$$

**Lemma 1.** *For all problem setups $\mathcal{H}$, it holds that $\mathbb{E}_{I\sim\mathcal{H}}\big[V^{\text{off}}(I)\big] \le z^*(\mathcal{H})$.*

As in several previous works [1] (see also [13]), we classify each observed realization of a request into "small" and "large" based on the demand, and categorize the resources accordingly to those serving large requests and those serving small requests, based on the contributions of each request in the optimal LP solution.

*Preprocessing via LP Solution.* We first solve the upper-bound LP (Prophet LP) to obtain an optimal solution $\mathbf{x}^\star$. Fix parameters $\delta, \alpha, \beta \in [0,1]$ to be determined later.

*Classification of Realizations.* For each request $n \in N$ and resource $k \in K$, define $L_{nk}(\delta) = \big\{\tilde{\mathbf{u}}_n : \tilde{w}_{nk} \ge \delta\, C_k\big\}$, and $S_{nk}(\delta) = \big\{\tilde{\mathbf{u}}_n : \tilde{w}_{nk} < \delta\, C_k\big\}$ as the sets of large and small realizations respectively.

*Classification of Resources.* For convenience of notation let us write $V^*_{n,k}(\tilde{\mathbf{u}}_n) = p_n(\tilde{\mathbf{u}}_n)\tilde{v}_{nk}\,x^\star_{nk}(\tilde{\mathbf{u}}_n)$ and for each resource $k \in K$, define $V^\star_k = \sum_{n\in N}\sum_{\tilde{\mathbf{u}}_n} V^*_{nk}(\tilde{\mathbf{u}}_n)$. Note that $z^*(\mathcal{H}) = \sum_{k\in K} V^*_k$. Define further the set of large-type requests (contributions from large realizations dominate) and the set of small-type requests (contributions from small realizations dominate) as

$$N_k^L(\delta) = \left\{ n\in N \;\middle|\; \sum_{\tilde{\mathbf{u}}_n\in L_{nk}(\delta)} V^*_{n,k}(\tilde{\mathbf{u}}_n) \ge \sum_{\tilde{\mathbf{u}}\in S_{nk}(\delta)} V^*_{n,k}(\tilde{\mathbf{u}}_n) \right\}, \text{ and } N_k^S(\delta) = N \setminus N_k^L(\delta),$$

respectively. We also define total reward from large-type requests under large realizations and total reward from small-type request over small realizations as

$$V_k^{LL}(\delta) = \sum_{n \in N_k^L(\delta)} \sum_{\tilde{\mathbf{u}}_n \in L_{nk}(\delta)} V_{nk}^*(\tilde{\mathbf{u}}_n), \tag{9}$$

$$V_k^{SS}(\delta) = \sum_{n \in N_k^S(\delta)} \sum_{\tilde{\mathbf{u}}_n \in S_{nk}(\delta)} V_{nk}^*(\tilde{\mathbf{u}}_n). \tag{10}$$

We classify each resource $k \in K$ as either *large* or *small* according to these contributions, and let

$$K^L(\delta) = \{k \in K \mid V_k^{LL}(\delta) \geq V_k^{SS}(\delta)\}, \quad \text{and } K^S(\delta) = K \setminus K^L(\delta)$$

denote the set of large and small resources, respectively. We will make use of the following simple observation.

**Lemma 2.** *$V_k^{LL}(\delta) \geq \frac{V_k^*}{4}$ for $k \in K^L(\delta)$, and $V_k^{SS}(\delta) \geq \frac{V_k^*}{4}$ for $k \in K^S(\delta)$.*

## 5 Stochastic Online Algorithm

The stochastic online algorithm is described in Algorithm 1 below. The algorithm first computes an optimal fractional solution to the prophet LP. For each arriving request $n$, the algorithm observes the realization of the request and randomly routes the request to a given resource $k$ with probability proportional to the LP solution (lines 3-4). The request is then admitted with some constant probability only if it matches the resource's type (large or small) and provided that it does not violate capacity constraints given the current capacity consumption of the resource (lines 5-9).

**Algorithm 1.** Stochastic Online Algorithm for Resource Allocation Problem with Departures

1: **Solve** the upper-bound LP (UP-LP) and obtain an optimal solution $\mathbf{x}^\star$
2: **for** each arriving request $n \in N$ **do**
3: Observe the realization $\tilde{\mathbf{u}}_n$
4: Randomly route request $n$ to a resource $k \in K$ with probability $x_{nk}^*(\tilde{\mathbf{u}}_n)$
5: **if** $\tilde{\mathbf{u}}_n \in L_{nk}(\delta)$ and $k \in K^L(\delta)$ **then**
6: admit request $n$ on resource $k$ with probability $\alpha$ if it does not result in capacity violation
7: **end if**
8: **if** $\tilde{\mathbf{u}}_n \in S_{nk}(\delta)$ and $k \in K^S(\delta)$ **then**
9: admit request $n$ on resource $k$ with probability $\beta$ if it does not result in capacity violation
10: **end if**
11: **end for**

**Theorem 1.** *Under assumptions (A1)-(A4), the competitive ratio of Algorithm 1 is* $\max_{\alpha,\beta,\delta\in[0,1]:\beta+\delta\leq 1} f(\alpha,\beta,\delta)$*, where*

$$f(\alpha,\beta,\delta)=\frac{1}{4}\min\left\{\alpha\left(1-\frac{\alpha}{\delta}\right),\beta\left(1-\min\left\{\frac{\beta}{1-\delta},\left(\frac{e^{\frac{1-\delta}{\beta}}-1}{\left(\frac{1-\delta}{\beta}\right)^{\frac{1-\delta}{\beta}}}\right)^{\beta\cdot C_{\min}}\right\}\right)\right\}.$$

It can be checked that, for $C_{\min}=1$, the maximum of $f(\alpha,\beta,\delta)=0.03125$ is attained at $\alpha=\frac{1}{4}$, $\beta=\frac{1}{4}$ and $\delta=\frac{1}{2}$. This yields a competitive ratio of 0.03125. Table 1 below gives the competitive ratios for different values of $C_{\min}$. From the Table, we observe that as $C_{\min}$ increases, the competitive ratio increases from 0.03125 up to approximately 0.0478 for $C_{\min}=1000$ (it can be easily seen that the CR approaches 0.05 as $C_{\min}\to\infty$).

**Table 1.** Optimized parameters and competitive ratio for selected $C_{\min}$.

| $C_{\min}$ | $\alpha$ | $\beta$ | $\delta$ | CR |
|---|---|---|---|---|
| 1 | 0.2500 | 0.2500 | 0.5000 | 0.031250 |
| 50 | 0.3347 | 0.1914 | 0.6694 | 0.041838 |
| 100 | 0.3514 | 0.1925 | 0.7028 | 0.043924 |
| 200 | 0.3640 | 0.1936 | 0.7280 | 0.045501 |
| 400 | 0.3735 | 0.1947 | 0.7469 | 0.046682 |
| 800 | 0.3805 | 0.1957 | 0.7610 | 0.047561 |
| 1000 | 0.3823 | 0.1960 | 0.7647 | 0.047793 |

## 6 Analysis of the CR of the Algorithm

Our analysis of the CR is inspired by the analysis of the approximation ratio for the (offline) *unsplittable flow* problem on line graphs in [13].

For each request $n\in N$, resource $k\in K$, let us define the following indicator random variables:

$$I_{nk}=\begin{cases}1, & \text{if there is enough capacity in resource } k \text{ to accept request } n \text{ at } k,\\ 0, & \text{otherwise,}\end{cases}$$

$$X_{nk}=\begin{cases}1, & \text{if request } n \text{ is routed to resource } k,\\ 0, & \text{otherwise,}\end{cases}$$

$$Y_{nk}=\begin{cases}1, & \text{if request } n \text{ is admitted on resource} k,\\ 0, & \text{otherwise.}\end{cases}$$

Let us also define the random variables $V_{nk}$ to be the reward obtained from request $n$ if it is admitted on resource $k$. The total reward obtained by the online algorithm can then be written as $\text{ALG} = \sum_{n\in N}\sum_{k\in K} V_{nk}$.

The expected value of the output of the algorithm, over the random variables $\mathbf{u}_n$ and the random choices of the algorithm satisfies

$$\mathbb{E}[\text{ALG}] = \sum_{n\in N}\sum_{k\in K}\mathbb{E}[V_{nk}].$$

We aim to show that there exists a constant $c > 0$ such that, for all $n \in N_k^L(\delta)$ and $k \in K^L(\delta)$, we have

$$\mathbb{E}[V_{nk}] \geq c \sum_{\tilde{\mathbf{u}}_n \in L_{nk}(\delta)} V_{n,k}^*(\tilde{\mathbf{u}}_n), \tag{11}$$

and, similarly, for all $n \in N_k^S(\delta)$ and $k \in K^S(\delta)$, we have

$$\mathbb{E}[V_{nk}] \geq c \sum_{\tilde{\mathbf{u}}_n \in S_{nk}(\delta)} V_{n,k}^*(\tilde{\mathbf{u}}_n), \tag{12}$$

which would imply that

$$\begin{aligned}\mathbb{E}[\text{ALG}] &\geq c \sum_{k\in K^L(\delta)}\sum_{n\in N_k^L(\delta)}\sum_{\tilde{\mathbf{u}}_n\in L_{nk}(\delta)} V_{n,k}^*(\tilde{\mathbf{u}}_n) + c\sum_{k\in K^S(\delta)}\sum_{n\in N_k^S(\delta)}\sum_{\tilde{\mathbf{u}}_n\in S_{nk}(\delta)} V_{n,k}^*(\tilde{\mathbf{u}}_n)\\ &= c\sum_{k\in K^L(\delta)} V_k^{LL}(\delta) + c\sum_{k\in K^S(\delta)} V_k^{SS}(\delta) \geq \frac{c}{4}\sum_{k\in K} V_k^* = \frac{c}{4} z^*(\mathcal{H}) \geq \frac{c}{4}\cdot \mathbb{E}_{I\sim\mathcal{H}}\left[V^{\text{off}}(I)\right],\end{aligned}$$

where the last two inequalities follow by Lemmas 2 and 1, respectively. Thus, Theorem 1 follows from the following two lemmas.

**Lemma 3.** *Under assumption (A1), for $k \in K^L(\delta)$ and $n \in N_k^L(\delta)$, it holds that*

$$\mathbb{E}[V_{nk}] \geq \alpha\left(1-\frac{\alpha}{\delta}\right)\sum_{\tilde{\mathbf{u}}_n\in L_{nk}(\delta)} V_{n,k}^*(\tilde{\mathbf{u}}_n).$$

**Lemma 4.** *Under assumptions (A1)-(A4) and $\beta+\delta \leq 1$, for $k \in K^S(\delta)$ and $n \in N_k^S(\delta)$, it holds that*

$$\mathbb{E}[V_{nk}] \geq \beta\left(1-\min\left\{\frac{\beta}{1-\delta}, \left(\frac{e^{\frac{1-\delta}{\beta}}-1}{\left(\frac{1-\delta}{\beta}\right)^{\frac{1-\delta}{\beta}}}\right)^{\beta\cdot C_{\min}}\right\}\right)\cdot \sum_{\tilde{\mathbf{u}}_n\in S_{nk}(\delta)} V_{n,k}^*(\tilde{\mathbf{u}}_n).$$

*Proof of Lemma 3 (case of large resources).* Fix a resource $k \in K^L(\delta)$ and a request $n \in N_k^L(\delta)$. Then, $k \in K^L(\delta)$ implies that any request $n'$ admitted on resource $k$ must have one of its large realizations observed, that is, $\tilde{w}_{n'k} \geq \delta C_k$

if realization $\tilde{\mathbf{u}}_{n'}$ was observed upon receiving request $n'$. From the capacity constraint (6) in the prophet LP, it follows that for any time slot $t$,

$$\sum_{n' \in N} \sum_{\tilde{\mathbf{u}}_{n'} \in L_{n'k}(\delta): t \in \tilde{T}_{n'k}} p_{n'}(\tilde{\mathbf{u}}_{n'}) \, \tilde{w}_{n'k} \, x^{\star}_{n'k}(\tilde{\mathbf{u}}_{n'}) \; \leq \; C_k.$$

As $\tilde{w}_{n'k} \geq \delta C_k$ for any $\tilde{\mathbf{u}}_{n'} \in L_{n'k}(\delta)$ when $n'$ is admitted on resource $k$, the above inequality implies that

$$\sum_{n' \in N} \sum_{\tilde{\mathbf{u}}_{n'} \in L_{n'k}(\delta): t \in \tilde{T}_{n'k}} p_{n'}(\tilde{\mathbf{u}}_{n'}) \, x^{\star}_{n'k}(\tilde{\mathbf{u}}_{n'k}) \; \leq \; \frac{1}{\delta}, \qquad \forall t \in T. \tag{13}$$

By step 4 of the algorithm, $\Pr[X_{nk} = 1 \mid \mathbf{u}_n = \tilde{\mathbf{u}}_n] = x^*_{nk}(\tilde{\mathbf{u}}_n)$ and by step 6,

$$\Pr[Y_{nk} = 1 \mid \mathbf{u}_n = \tilde{\mathbf{u}}_n, X_{nk} = 1, I_{nk} = 1] = \begin{cases} \alpha, & \text{if } \tilde{\mathbf{u}}_n \in L_{nk}(\delta) \\ 0, & \text{otherwise.} \end{cases}$$

By the (probability) chain rule:

$$\begin{aligned} \mathbb{E}[V_{nk}] &= \sum_{\tilde{\mathbf{u}}_n} \mathbb{E}[V_{nk} \mid \mathbf{u}_n = \tilde{\mathbf{u}}_n] p_n(\tilde{\mathbf{u}}_n) = \sum_{\tilde{\mathbf{u}}_n} \tilde{v}_{nk} \Pr[Y_{nk} = 1 \mid \mathbf{u}_n = \tilde{\mathbf{u}}_n] p_n(\tilde{\mathbf{u}}_n) \\ &= \sum_{\tilde{\mathbf{u}}_n} \tilde{v}_{nk} \Pr[Y_{nk} = 1, X_{nk} = 1, I_{nk} = 1 \mid \mathbf{u}_n = \tilde{\mathbf{u}}_n] p_n(\tilde{\mathbf{u}}_n) \\ &= \sum_{\tilde{\mathbf{u}}_n} \tilde{v}_{nk} \Pr[Y_{nk} = 1 \mid \mathbf{u}_n = \tilde{\mathbf{u}}_n, X_{nk} = 1, I_{nk} = 1] \\ &\qquad \cdot \Pr[I_{nk} = 1 \mid X_{nk} = 1, \mathbf{u}_n = \tilde{\mathbf{u}}_n] \Pr[X_{nk} = 1 \mid \mathbf{u}_n = \tilde{\mathbf{u}}_n] p_n(\tilde{\mathbf{u}}_n) \\ &= \sum_{\tilde{\mathbf{u}}_n \in L_{nk}(\delta)} \tilde{v}_{nk} \Pr[I_{nk} = 1 \mid X_{nk} = 1, \mathbf{u}_n = \tilde{\mathbf{u}}_n] \alpha x^*_{nk}(\tilde{\mathbf{u}}_n) p_n(\tilde{\mathbf{u}}_n). \end{aligned} \tag{14}$$

Further, note that a lower-bound of $\mathbb{E}[V_{nk}]$ can be obtained by finding an upper-bound $\Pr[I_{nk} = 0 \mid X_{nk} = 1, \mathbf{u}_n = \tilde{\mathbf{u}}_n]$. Conditional on $X_{nk} = 1$ and $\mathbf{u}_n = \tilde{\mathbf{u}}_n$, having $I_{nk} = 0$ implies that there must exist a request $n'$ arriving before $n$ such that its observed realization $\tilde{T}_{n'k}$ overlaps with $\tilde{T}_{nk}$, and $n'$ was admitted to resource $k$:

$$\begin{aligned} \Pr[I_{nk} = 0 \mid X_{nk} = 1, \mathbf{u}_n = \tilde{\mathbf{u}}_n] \leq \Pr\big[&\exists\, n' \in N, \tilde{\mathbf{u}}_{n'} \in L_{n'k}(\delta): \\ & n' < n, \mathbf{u}_{n'} = \tilde{\mathbf{u}}_{n'}, s_{nk} \in \tilde{T}_{n'k}, Y_{n'k} = 1\big], \end{aligned}$$

where we have made use of assumption (A1) which implies that any previously admitted request $n'$ which overlaps with $\tilde{T}_{nk}$ must have a realization $\tilde{T}_{n'k}$ that overlaps with the starting time of $\tilde{T}_{nk}$.

Thus, by applying the union bound and using (13), we get

$$\begin{aligned} \Pr[I_{nk} = 0 \mid X_{nk} = 1, \mathbf{u}_n = \tilde{\mathbf{u}}_n] &\leq \sum_{n' < n \in N} \sum_{\tilde{\mathbf{u}}_{n'} \in L_{n'k}(\delta): s_{nk} \in \tilde{T}_{n'k}} \Pr[\mathbf{u}_{n'} = \tilde{\mathbf{u}}_{n'}, Y_{n'k} = 1] \\ &= \sum_{n' < n} \sum_{\tilde{\mathbf{u}}_{n'} \in L_{n'k}(\delta): s_{nk} \in \tilde{T}_{n'k}} \Pr[Y_{n'k} = 1 \mid \mathbf{u}_{n'} = \tilde{\mathbf{u}}_{n'}] \Pr[\mathbf{u}_{n'} = \tilde{\mathbf{u}}_{n'}] \\ &\leq \sum_{n' < n} \sum_{\tilde{\mathbf{u}}_{n'} \in L_{n'k}(\delta): s_{nk} \in \tilde{T}_{n'k}} \alpha\, x^{\star}_{n'k}(\tilde{\mathbf{u}}_{n'}) \, p_{n'}(\tilde{\mathbf{u}}_{n'}) \leq \frac{\alpha}{\delta}, \end{aligned} \tag{15}$$

where for (15) we used a similar reasoning as in (14), to show that the admission criterion in step 6 implies that

$$\Pr[Y_{n'k} = 1 \mid \mathbf{u}_{n'} = \tilde{\mathbf{u}}_{n'}] \leq \alpha x^*_{n'k}(\tilde{\mathbf{u}}_n) \Pr[I_{n'k} = 1 \mid X_{n'k} = 1, \mathbf{u}_{n'}] \leq \alpha x^*_{n'k}(\tilde{\mathbf{u}}_n).$$

From (14) and (15) we obtain

$$\begin{aligned}\mathbb{E}[V_{nk}] &\geq \sum_{\tilde{\mathbf{u}}_n \in L_{nk}(\delta)} \tilde{v}_{nk}(1 - \Pr[I_{nk} = 0 \mid X_{nk} = 1, \mathbf{u}_n = \tilde{\mathbf{u}}_n])\alpha x^*_{nk}(\tilde{\mathbf{u}}_n) p_n(\tilde{\mathbf{u}}_n) \\ &\geq \sum_{\tilde{\mathbf{u}}_n \in L_{nk}(\delta)} \tilde{v}_{nk}\left(1 - \frac{\alpha}{\delta}\right) \alpha x^*_{nk}(\tilde{\mathbf{u}}_n)\, p_n(\tilde{\mathbf{u}}_n) = \alpha\left(1 - \frac{\alpha}{\delta}\right) \sum_{\tilde{\mathbf{u}}_n \in L_{nk}(\delta)} V^*_{nk}(\tilde{\mathbf{u}}_n).\end{aligned} \tag{16}$$

This concludes the proof of Lemma 3. □

*Proof of Lemma 4 (case of small resources).* Fix a resource $k \in K^S(\delta)$ and a request $n \in N^S_k(\delta)$. Then, $k \in K^S(\delta)$ implies that any request $n'$ admitted on resource $k$ must have one of its small realizations observed. In particular,

$$\tilde{w}_{nk} < \delta\, C_k, \tag{17}$$

if realization $\tilde{\mathbf{u}}_n$ was observed upon receiving request $n$.

By step 4 of the algorithm, $\Pr[X_{nk} = 1 \mid \mathbf{u}_n = \tilde{\mathbf{u}}_n] = x^*_{nk}(\tilde{\mathbf{u}}_n)$ and by step 9,

$$\Pr[Y_{nk} = 1 \mid \mathbf{u}_n = \tilde{\mathbf{u}}_n, X_{nk} = 1, I_{nk} = 1] = \begin{cases} \beta, & \text{if } \tilde{\mathbf{u}}_n \in S_{nk}(\delta) \\ 0, & \text{otherwise.} \end{cases}$$

We proceed as in the proof of Lemma 3 and obtain

$$\mathbb{E}[V_{nk}] = \sum_{\tilde{\mathbf{u}}_n \in S_{nk}(\delta)} \tilde{v}_{nk} \Pr[I_{nk} = 1 \mid X_{nk} = 1, \mathbf{u}_n = \tilde{\mathbf{u}}_n] \beta x^*_{nk}(\tilde{\mathbf{u}}_n) p_n(\tilde{\mathbf{u}}_n). \tag{18}$$

As before, we need to bound the probability that request $n$ was rejected after being routed to resource $k$ when realization $\tilde{\mathbf{u}}_n$ was observed, i.e., $\Pr[I_{nk} = 0 \mid X_{nk} = 1, \mathbf{u}_n = \tilde{\mathbf{u}}_n]$. Under assumption (A1) and by (17), a rejection of request $n$ on resource $k$ can occur only if the total load contributed by previously admitted requests on resource $k$ at the start of interval $\tilde{T}_{nk}$ is sufficiently large. But the feasibility of $\mathbf{x}^*$ for the prophet LP implies that the expectation of this total load is small. This allows us to use concentration inequalities to bound the probability of deviation from the mean.

*Bounding the Expected Load.* We say that request $n' \in N^S_k(\delta)$ is considered for admission on resource $k$ in line 9 of the algorithm when it is considered right before checking the condition $I_{n'k} = 1$. It will be useful to think of the execution of line 9 as first considering $n'$ for admission on resource $k$ with probability $\beta$, then admitting it or not, based on whether $I_{n'k}$ is 1 or 0.

For $n' \in N_k^S(\delta)$, and $\tilde{\mathbf{u}}_{n'} \in S_{n'k}(\delta)$, define the indicator random variable:

$$Z_{n'k}(\tilde{\mathbf{u}}_{n'}) = \begin{cases} 1, & \text{if } n' \text{ is considered for admission on resource } k \text{ and } \mathbf{u}_{n'} = \tilde{\mathbf{u}}_{n'}, \\ 0, & \text{otherwise.} \end{cases}$$

Let the random variable $Z_t$ represent the total load considered for admission (but not necessarily admitted) on resource $k$ at time $t$ due to previously arriving requests:

$$Z_t = \sum_{n'<n} \sum_{\tilde{\mathbf{u}}_{n'} \in S_{nk}(\delta):\ t \in \tilde{T}_{n'k}} \tilde{w}_{n'k} Z_{n'k}(\tilde{\mathbf{u}}_{n'}). \tag{19}$$

As in (14), we have

$$\begin{aligned}\mathbb{E}[Z_{n'k}(\tilde{\mathbf{u}}_{n'})] &= \Pr[Z_{n'k}(\tilde{\mathbf{u}}_{n'}) = 1] = \Pr[Z_{n'k} = 1 |\ \mathbf{u}_{n'} = \tilde{\mathbf{u}}_{n'}] \cdot \Pr[\mathbf{u}_{n'} = \tilde{\mathbf{u}}_{n'}] \\ &\le \beta \cdot x^*_{n'k}(\tilde{\mathbf{u}}_n) p_{n'}(\tilde{\mathbf{u}}_{n'}).\end{aligned}$$

It then follows that

$$\begin{aligned}\mathbb{E}[Z_t] &= \sum_{n'<n} \sum_{\tilde{\mathbf{u}}_{n'} \in S_{n'k}(\delta): t \in \tilde{T}_{n'k}} \tilde{w}_{n'k} \cdot \mathbb{E}[Z_{n'k}(\tilde{\mathbf{u}}_{n'})] \\ &\le \sum_{n'<n} \sum_{\tilde{\mathbf{u}}_{n'} \in S_{n'k}(\delta): t \in \tilde{T}_{n'k}} \beta \cdot p_{n'}(\tilde{\mathbf{u}}_{n'})\, \tilde{w}_{n'k}\, x^\star_{n'k}(\tilde{\mathbf{u}}_{n'}) \\ &\le \beta C_k, \end{aligned} \tag{20}$$

where the last inequality follows from the feasibility of $\mathbf{x}^*$.

*Using Markov's Inequality.* Let $Z'_t$ be the admitted load on resource $k$ at time $t$. Then, obviously, $Z'_t \le Z_t$. Conditional on the facts that $X_{nk} = 1$ and $\mathbf{u}_n = \tilde{\mathbf{u}}_n$, having $I_{nk} = 0$ means that admitting request $n$ on resource $k$ would violate the capacity of that resource, that is, $Z'_t + \tilde{w}_{nk} > C_k$ for $t = s_{nk}$, implying by (17) that $Z_t \ge Z'_t > (1-\delta)C_k$. Thus, by Markov's inequality, applied to the nonnegative R.V. $Z_t$ and using (20):

$$\begin{aligned}\Pr[I_{nk} = 0 \mid X_{nk} = 1, \mathbf{u}_n = \tilde{\mathbf{u}}_n] \le \Pr[Z_t \ge (1-\delta)C_k] &\le \frac{\mathbb{E}[Z_t]}{(1-\delta)C_k} \\ &\le \frac{\beta C_k}{(1-\delta)C_k} = \frac{\beta}{1-\delta}.\end{aligned} \tag{21}$$

*Using Chernoff Bound.* Note that $\sum_{\tilde{\mathbf{u}}_{n'} \in S_{n'k}(\delta)} Z_{n'k}(\tilde{\mathbf{u}}_{n'}) \le 1$ and hence the variables $Z_{n'k}(\tilde{\mathbf{u}}_{n'k})$, for $n' \in N_k^S(\delta)$ and $\tilde{\mathbf{u}}_{n'} \in S_{n'k}(\delta)$, are *negatively correlated*[1]

[1] Recall that Bernoulli random variables $Z_1, \ldots, Z_m$ are negatively correlated if for any subset $S \subseteq \{1, \ldots, m\}$,

$$\Pr\left[\bigwedge_{i \in S} Z_i = 1\right] \le \prod_{i \in S} \Pr[Z_i = 1].$$

.

by assumption (A4). Thus, by (22), $Z_t$ is the weighted sum of negatively correlated R.V.s with weights $\tilde{w}_{n'k} \in [0,1]$ (by assumption (A2)). By the Chernoff bound for negatively correlated R.V.s [14], for $\gamma = \frac{1-\delta}{\beta} - 1 \geq 0$, and using (20) at $t = s_{nk}$:

$$\Pr[I_{nk} = 0 \mid X_{nk} = 1, \mathbf{u}_n = \tilde{\mathbf{u}}_n] \leq \Pr[Z'_t \geq (1-\delta)C_k] \leq \Pr[Z_t \geq (1+\gamma)\beta C_k]$$
$$\leq \left(\frac{e^{\gamma}}{(1+\gamma)^{1+\gamma}}\right)^{\beta C_k} = \left(\frac{e^{\frac{1-\delta}{\beta}-1}}{\left(\frac{1-\delta}{\beta}\right)^{\frac{1-\delta}{\beta}}}\right)^{\beta C_k}. \tag{22}$$

By combining (18), (21) and (22), we obtain

$$\mathbb{E}[V_{nk}] \geq \sum_{\tilde{\mathbf{u}}_n \in S_{nk}(\delta)} \tilde{v}_{nk}(1 - \Pr[I_{nk} = 0 \mid X_{nk} = 1, \mathbf{u}_n = \tilde{\mathbf{u}}_n])\beta x^*_{nk}(\tilde{\mathbf{u}}_n) p_n(\tilde{\mathbf{u}}_n)$$
$$\geq \sum_{\tilde{\mathbf{u}}_n \in S_{nk}(\delta)} \tilde{v}_{nk}\,(1-\kappa)\,\beta \cdot x^{\star}_{nk}(\tilde{\mathbf{u}}_n)\, p_n(\tilde{\mathbf{u}}_n) = \beta\,(1-\kappa) \sum_{\tilde{\mathbf{u}}_n \in S_{nk}(\delta)} V^*_{nk}(\tilde{\mathbf{u}}_n),$$

where $\kappa = \min\left\{\frac{\beta}{1-\delta}, \left(\frac{e^{\frac{1-\delta}{\beta}-1}}{\left(\frac{1-\delta}{\beta}\right)^{\frac{1-\delta}{\beta}}}\right)^{\beta \cdot C_{\min}}\right\}$. This concludes the proof of Lemma 4. □

## 7 Conclusion

We gave a randomized online algorithm for the online stochastic multiple knapsack problem with departures, under natural assumptions ((A1) and (A4)). We showed that the CR of the algorithm is at least 1/32. Getting rid of the assumptions and/or improving the CR are obvious research directions for future consideration.

## References

1. Stein, C., Truong, V.-A., Wang, X.: Advance service reservations with heterogeneous customers. Manage. Sci. **66**(7), 2929–2950 (2020)
2. Jiang, J., Ma, W., Zhang, J.: Tight guarantees for multi-unit prophet inequalities and online stochastic knapsack. In: Proceedings of the 2022 Annual ACM-SIAM Symposium on Discrete Algorithms (SODA), SIAM, pp. 1221–1246 (2022)
3. Marchetti-Spaccamela, A., Vercellis, C.: Stochastic on-line knapsack problems. Math. Program. **68**(1), 73–104 (1995)
4. Chakrabarty, D., Zhou, Y., Lukose, R.: Online knapsack problems. In: Workshop on Internet and Network Economics (WINE), pp. 1–9 (2008)
5. Zhang, Z., Li, Z., Wu, C.: Optimal posted prices for online cloud resource allocation. Proc. ACM Meas. Anal. Comput. Syst. **1**(1), 1–26 (2017)

6. Yang, L., Zeynali, A., Hajiesmaili, M.H., Sitaraman, R.K., Towsley, D.: Competitive algorithms for online multidimensional knapsack problems. Proc. ACM Meas. Anal. Comput. Syst. **5**(3), 1–30 (2021)
7. Amidu, Y., Elbassioni, K., Gabor, A.F.: Online multiple resource allocation problems with departures via the primal-dual approach CoRR abs/2510.04737 (2025)
8. Papastavrou, J.D., Rajagopalan, S., Kleywegt, A.J.: The dynamic and stochastic knapsack problem with deadlines. Manage. Sci. **42**(12), 1706–1718 (1996)
9. Alaei, S., Hajiaghayi, M., Liaghat, V.: The online stochastic generalized assignment problem. In: Raghavendra, P., Raskhodnikova, S., Jansen, K., Rolim, J.D.P. (eds.) International Workshop on Approximation Algorithms for Combinatorial Optimization, pp. 11–25. Springer (2013). https://doi.org/10.1007/978-3-642-40328-6_2
10. Devanur, N.R., Jain, K., Sivan, B., Wilkens, C.A.: Near optimal online algorithms and fast approximation algorithms for resource allocation problems. J. ACM (JACM) **66**(1), 1–41 (2019)
11. Feng, Y., Niazadeh, R., Saberi, A.: Near-optimal Bayesian online assortment of reusable resources. In: Proceedings of the 23rd ACM Conference on Economics and Computation, pp. 964–965 (2022)
12. Zhang, X., Cheung, W.C.: Online resource allocation for reusable resources, arXiv preprint arXiv:2212.02855 (2022)
13. Chakrabarti, A., Chekuri, A., Gupta, C., Kumar, A.: Approximation algorithms for the unsplittable flow problem, Algorithmica **49**(4), 308–323 (2007)
14. Panconesi, A., Srinivasan, A.: Randomized distributed edge coloring via an extension of the Chernoff-Hoeffding bounds. SIAM J. Comput. **26**(2), 350–368 (1997)

# Envy-Free School Redistricting Between Two Groups

Daisuke Shibatani and Yutaro Yamaguchi(✉)

Osaka University, Osaka, Japan
yutaro.yamaguchi@ist.osaka-u.ac.jp

**Abstract.** We study an application of fair division theory to school redistricting. Procaccia, Robinson, and Tucker-Foltz (SODA 2024) recently proposed a mathematical model to generate redistricting plans that provide theoretically guaranteed fairness among demographic groups of students. They showed that an almost proportional allocation can be found by adding $O(g \log g)$ extra seats in total, where $g$ is the number of groups. In contrast, for three or more groups, adding $o(n)$ extra seats is not sufficient to obtain an almost envy-free allocation in general, where $n$ is the total number of students. In this paper, we focus on the case of two groups. We introduce a relevant relaxation of envy-freeness, termed *1-relaxed envy-freeness*, which limits the capacity violation not in total but at each school to at most one. We show that there always exists a 1-relaxed envy-free allocation, which can be found in polynomial time.

## 1 Introduction

### 1.1 Background

The public school a student attends is typically determined by their place of residence. Even within the same municipality, significant disparities in school quality may exist, which makes the assignment of school attendance zones a crucial issue for students. Due to several factors, municipalities must periodically restructure these zones. However, school redistricting is often controversial and can sometimes cause severe conflicts.

To mitigate such turmoil, Procaccia, Robinson, and Tucker-Foltz [11] recently proposed a mathematical model to generate redistricting plans that provide theoretically guaranteed fairness among demographic groups based on fair division theory. As noted in [2,5], problems related to fair division are ubiquitous, encompassing scenarios such as cake cutting, inheritance division, and chore allocation. The problem of fair division has a very long history, and there are two primary concepts of fairness: proportionality and envy-freeness. An allocation is considered *proportional* if, given $n$ agents, every agent perceives their share to be worth at least $1/n$ of the total value. An allocation is *envy-free* if no agent strictly prefers another agent's share to their own. While early research on fair


Y. Li et al. (Eds.): COCOON 2026, LNCS 16835, pp. 342–354, 2027.
https://doi.org/10.1007/978-981-92-3309-0_26

division primarily focused on infinitely divisible goods, many recent studies have addressed fair division problems involving indivisible goods.

Procaccia et al. [11] applied fair division theory to school redistricting for the first time, defining relaxations of proportionality and envy-freeness specifically for this problem. They showed that an almost proportional allocation can always be found by adding $O(g \log g)$ seats in total, where $g$ is the number of groups; furthermore, when $g$ is constant, such an allocation can be found in polynomial time. In contrast, they showed that envy-freeness is difficult to achieve by demonstrating for $g \geq 3$ that adding $o(n)$ seats is not sufficient to obtain an almost envy-free allocation in general, where $n$ is the number of students.

### 1.2 Our Contribution

In this study, we focus on the case where there exist two groups (when $g = 2$) and aim to establish a method to obtain an envy-free allocation. Even in this case, as school seats are indivisible, we need to consider relaxation of envy-freeness. Specifically, we first introduce another reasonable relaxation of envy-freeness for the school redistricting problem, termed *1-relaxed envy-freeness* (Definition 1), which only allows the capacity violation in *each* school by at most one while the *total* violation is bounded by a parameter $t$ in [11]; their relation is explained in more detail after the definition in Sect. 2. Although a 1-relaxed envy-free allocation does not necessarily exist when $g \geq 3$ as in the previous case [11], we show that when $g = 2$, it always exists and can be computed in polynomial time (Theorem 1). The proof is based on the integrality of a network flow problem and ad-hoc transformation of solutions that are not 1-relaxed envy-free.

### 1.3 Related Work

As reviewed by Suksompong [14], fair division has been extensively studied under various constraints. However, none of these models are directly applicable to the setting of [11]. In fair division with several constraints, the allocation problem becomes significantly more complex—or even impossible—when the number of agents is three or more. For instance, in the continuous resource model (i.e., cake cutting), Stromquist [13] proved that calculating a connected envy-free allocation for three or more agents using a finite number of queries is impossible. For indivisible goods, under cardinality constraints with monotonic utility functions, Kyropoulou, Suksompong, and Voudouris [9] proved the existence of an *EF1 (envy-free up to one item)* allocation for two agents, whereas the case of three or more agents remains an open problem. Suksompong [14] outlines the differences between the cases of two agents and three or more agents under various other settings, including indivisible goods on a graph, graphical cake cutting, geometric constraints, and conflict constraints. This illustrates that restricting the problem to two agents can sometimes enable the discovery of almost envy-free allocations that are intractable in the general case.

As mentioned above, [11] is pioneering work on fair districting in the context of school redistricting. Several other studies have addressed school redistricting, primarily focusing on optimization approaches. For example, Allman, Ashlagi, Lo, Love, Mentzer, Ruiz-Sets, and O'Connell [1] proposed an optimization framework aimed at preventing racial re-segregation and achieving diverse student demographics.

Closely related theoretical frameworks can also be found in [3,4], which consider matchings in weighted bipartite graphs with agents on one side and goods on the other. Compared to these models, the setting in [11] (as well as ours) is simpler in that all agents share identical valuations for the schools. However, it introduces significant challenges because every student must be assigned to one of their accessible schools defined by geographical constraints.

Subsequent to [11], Cembrano, Moraga, and Verdugo [6] also investigated envy-freeness in the context of school redistricting. However, their relaxation of envy-freeness simply compares utilities under a specific allocation, without seat-subset conditions. Therefore, their definition is fundamentally different from the concept of envy-freeness employed in [11] and in our present study.

## 2 Model and Result

An instance of the *school redistricting problem* is described by the following components:

- A set of *students* $N = \{1, 2, \ldots, n\}$;
- A partition of the students into $g$ *groups* $N = N_1 \cup N_2 \cup \cdots \cup N_g$;
- A set of *schools* $M = \{1, 2, \ldots, m\}$, where each school $k$ has a *capacity* $c_k$ and a (common) *value* $v_k$;
- A bipartite graph $\mathcal{G} = (N \cup M, \mathcal{E})$ between students and schools, where the edge set $\mathcal{E}$ represents which students can be assigned to (i.e., can commute to) which schools.

An *allocation* is a function $A\colon N \to M$ such that $\{j, A(j)\} \in \mathcal{E}$ for every student $j \in N$. Let $A^{-1}(k) = \{j \in N \mid A(j) = k\}$ and $A_i^{-1}(k) = A^{-1}(k) \cap N_i$. The *utility* of group $i$ under an allocation $A$ is defined as $u(i, A) := \sum_{j \in N_i} v_{A(j)}$.

The formulation up to this point is identical to that in [11]. In our model, we assume an *initial* allocation $B$ is given, and the capacity of each school is set to $c_k = |B^{-1}(k)|$. This $B$ can be interpreted as the current allocation or a tentative allocation only caring the number of students assigned to each school. In either case, our goal is to correct unfairness of $B$, where it is desirable to assign almost the same number of students to each school as $B$. In particular, we say that an allocation $A$ is *amount-preserving* if $|A^{-1}(k)| = c_k$ for all $k \in M$.

Even when there are two groups, the indivisibility of school seats requires a relaxation of envy-freeness. We define 1-relaxed envy-freeness as follows.

**Definition 1.** An allocation $A$ is 1-*relaxed envy-free* if it satisfies

$$\max_{k \in M} \left| |A^{-1}(k)| - c_k \right| \le 1 \tag{1}$$

and, for any pair of groups $(i_1, i_2)$, no other allocation $A'$ simultaneously satisfies the following three inequalities:

$$u(i_1, A') > u(i_1, A), \tag{2}$$

$$|A'^{-1}_{i_1}(k)| \leq |A^{-1}_{i_2}(k)| \quad (\forall k \in M), \tag{3}$$

$$\max_{k \in M} \left| |A'^{-1}(k)| - c_k \right| \leq n \cdot \max_{k \in M} \left| |A^{-1}(k)| - c_k \right|. \tag{4}$$

First, (1) states that a capacity deviation of up to 1 is allowed in each school under allocation $A$. An allocation $A'$ satisfying (2)–(4) is considered to cause envy of group $i_1$ to $i_2$ in the allocation $A$, and we say $i_1$ *envies* $i_2$ if there exists such an $A'$:

- (2) indicates that the utility of group $i_1$ strictly increases.
- (3) means that the seats assigned to $i_1$ under $A'$ can be regarded as a subset of the seats assigned to $i_2$ under $A$.
- (4) may look complicated and artificial rather than the first two conditions. Since we allow a capacity deviation in $A$ as (1), it is natural to do so in $A'$. Nevertheless, if $A$ does not have a capacity deviation in any school, then a potential envy based on $A'$ that has a capacity deviation in some school can be refuted by claiming that $A$ is a strictly more consistent allocation than $A'$. In other words, if $A$ is amount-preserving, then envy can be justified only by another amount-preserving allocation $A'$, and otherwise this is not the case. Note that $A$ can only have a capacity deviation of at most one per school, but $A'$ can have an arbitrarily large deviation in each school due to the $n$-factor in the right-hand side of (4).

Compared with our definition, in the definition of $t$-envy-freeness in [11],

- only the total capacity violation of $A$ is bounded by $t$ (only from above), whereas (1) imposes per-school bounds (both from above and below),
- (2) is strengthened by adding a $\Theta(t)$ term in the right-hand side, which requires a large utility gap (depending on $t$) to justify envy of $i_1$,
- (3) is imposed in the same way, and
- it is not allowed for $A'$ to have any capacity violation (to the above) in contrast to our (4).

Thus, our definition is basically stronger (where envy is justified more easily) and in particular provides the following implication: if the capacity of each school is defined in the same way, a 1-relaxed envy-free allocation in our definition implies $(m/2)$-envy-freeness in the sense of [11]. Also, using essentially the same argument as in the proof of [11, Theorem 3.1], we can observe that a 1-relaxed envy-free allocation does not necessarily exist when $g \geq 3$.

The main result of this paper is stated as follows:

**Theorem 1.** *For any instance of the school redistricting problem with two groups, a 1-relaxed envy-free allocation always exists. Furthermore, such an allocation can be constructed in polynomial time.*

# 3 Proofs

In this section, we prove Theorem 1. We prove it separately for the cases where the sizes of two groups are different (in Sect. 3.1) and the same (in Sect. 3.2).

## 3.1 Easy Case: When Two Groups Have Different Sizes

When $|N_1| \neq |N_2|$, the following lemma completes the proof.

**Lemma 1.** *If the two groups have different sizes, an amount-preserving allocation maximizing the utility of the smaller group is always 1-relaxed envy-free. Furthermore, such an allocation can be computed in polynomial time.*

*Proof.* In this setting, since an initial allocation is given and gives the capacity of each school, every instance is feasible. Let group 1 be the smaller group and group 2 be the larger group among the two groups. Let $A^*$ be a utility-maximizing amount-preserving allocation for group 1; that is, $A^*$ is an allocation that maximizes $u(1, A^*)$ subject to $|{A^*}^{-1}(k)| = c_k$ for all $k \in M$.

First, we show that group 2 (larger) does not envy group 1 (smaller). From (3) in Definition 1, if group 2 envies group 1, there exists an allocation $A'$ satisfying

$$|{A'}_2^{-1}(k)| \leq |{A^*}_1^{-1}(k)| \quad (\forall k \in M).$$

By summing this up, we obtain

$$|N_2| = \sum_{k \in M} |{A'}_2^{-1}(k)| \leq \sum_{k \in M} |{A^*}_1^{-1}(k)| = |N_1|,$$

but this contradicts the fact that the size of group 2 is strictly greater than the size of group 1. Thus, group 2 cannot envy group 1.

Next, we show that group 1 does not envy group 2. From (2) and (4) in Definition 1, if group 1 envies group 2, there exists an amount-preserving allocation $A'$ satisfying

$$u(1, A') > u(1, A^*),$$

but this contradicts that $A^*$ maximizes the utility of group 1 under the capacity constraint. Thus, group 1 cannot envy group 2.

From the above, we have shown that the allocation $A^*$ is 1-relaxed envy-free. Furthermore, as in [11], such an ideal allocation $A^*$ for group 1 can be computed in polynomial time using the Hungarian method [8,10] (by reducing to the so-called weighted $b$-matching problem; see, e.g., [12]). □

## 3.2 Main Case: When Two Groups Have the Same Size

In what follows, we assume $|N_1| = |N_2|$. We first show a lemma that guarantees the existence of a symmetric allocation for any not 1-relaxed envy-free amount-preserving allocation. Here, for a given allocation $A$, an allocation $A'$ is called a *perfectly-swapped* allocation with respect to $A$ if it satisfies $|{A'}_1^{-1}(k)| = |A_2^{-1}(k)|$ and $|{A'}_2^{-1}(k)| = |A_1^{-1}(k)|$ for all $k \in M$.

**Lemma 2.** *Let $A$ be an amount-preserving allocation. If there is no perfectly-swapped allocation $A'$ with respect to $A$, then $A$ is 1-relaxed envy-free.*

*Proof.* We prove the contrapositive; that is, if the allocation $A$ is not 1-relaxed envy-free, then there exists a perfectly-swapped allocation $A'$. Suppose that $A$ is not 1-relaxed envy-free. By symmetry, we assume without loss of generality that group 1 envies group 2. Let this envy in allocation $A$ be caused by the existence of some allocation $A'$ that simultaneously satisfies (2)–(4) in Definition 1. Since $A$ is amount-preserving, this should also be true for $A'$ by (4). Furthermore, as the sizes of the two groups are equal, the following holds:

$$\sum_{k \in M} |{A'}_1^{-1}(k)| = |N_1| = |N_2| = \sum_{k \in M} |A_2^{-1}(k)|.$$

This implies that (3) holds with equality for all $k \in M$, i.e.,

$$|{A'}_1^{-1}(k)| = |A_2^{-1}(k)| \quad (\forall k \in M). \tag{5}$$

Also, the total number of students assigned to each school is the same in both allocations $A$ and $A'$ (as they are both amount-preserving), yielding the following:

$$|A_1^{-1}(k)| + |A_2^{-1}(k)| = c_k = |{A'}_1^{-1}(k)| + |{A'}_2^{-1}(k)| \quad (\forall k \in M). \tag{6}$$

From (5) and (6), we have the following:

$$|{A'}_2^{-1}(k)| = |A_1^{-1}(k)| \quad (\forall k \in M).$$

Thus, $A'$ is a perfectly-swapped allocation with respect to $A$. □

Let $B$ be the initial allocation. By Lemma 2, if there is no perfectly-swapped allocation with respect to $B$, then $B$ is 1-relaxed envy-free. Finding such an allocation is simply reduced to the maximum flow problem (more specifically, the so-called $b$-matching problem; see, e.g., [12]) and solved in polynomial time [7]. Thus, we may assume that there exists a perfectly-swapped allocation $B'$. The following lemma enables us to make a stronger assumption: there exists an amount-preserving allocation $A$ and a perfectly-swapped allocation $A'$ such that

$$|A_1^{-1}(k)| - |A_2^{-1}(k)| = |{A'}_2^{-1}(k)| - |{A'}_1^{-1}(k)| \in \{-1, 0, 1\} \quad (\forall k \in M).$$

**Lemma 3.** *Given a perfectly-swapped allocation $B'$ with respect to the initial allocation $B$, one can compute an amount-preserving allocation $A$ such that $\big||A_1^{-1}(k)| - |A_2^{-1}(k)|\big| \le 1$ for all $k \in M$.*

*Proof.* Let $N = \{i_1, i_2, \dots, i_n\}$ be the set of students, and let $M = \{s_1, s_2, \dots, s_m\}$ be the set of schools. Let $g(j) \in \{1, 2\}$ denote the group of each student $j \in N$. We construct an instance of the network flow problem as follows (see Fig. 1):

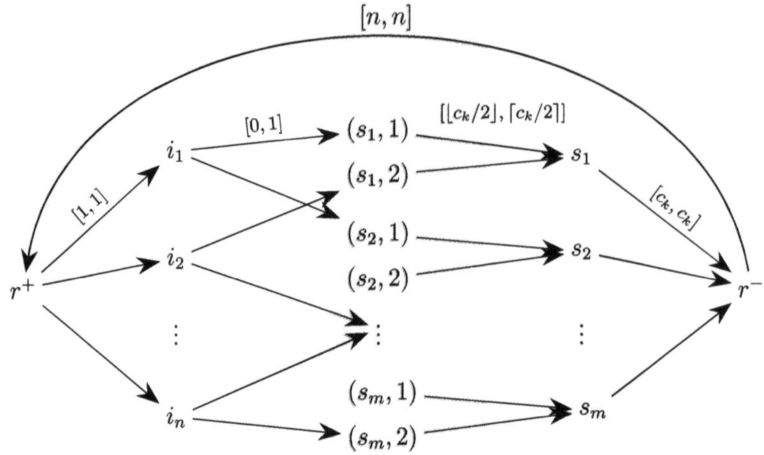


**Fig. 1.** Conceptual diagram of the network in Lemma 3.

- Vertex set $V = \{r^+\} \cup N \cup (M \times \{1,2\}) \cup M \cup \{r^-\}$:
  $r^+$: source, $j \in N$: student vertices, $(k,1),(k,2) \in M \times \{1,2\}$: school-group pair vertices, $k \in M$: school vertices, $r^-$: sink.
- Edge set $E = E_s \cup E_N \cup E_G \cup E_M \cup E_r$ and capacity (flow lower bound $\ell$ and upper bound $u$):

- From source $r^+$ to each student:
  * $E_s = \{(r^+, j) \mid j \in N\}$;
  * $\ell(e) = u(e) = 1$.
- From each student to school-group pairs:
  * $E_N = \{(j, (k, g(j))) \mid j \in N,\ k \in \{B(j), B'(j)\}\}$ (if $B(j) = B'(j)$, we allow multiple edges);
  * $\ell(e) = 0$, $u(e) = 1$.
- From school-group pairs to each school:
  * $E_G = \{((k,h),k) \mid k \in M,\ h \in \{1,2\}\}$;
  * $\ell(e) = \lfloor c_k/2 \rfloor$, $u(e) = \lceil c_k/2 \rceil$.
- From each school to sink $r^-$:
  * $E_M = \{(k, r^-) \mid k \in M\}$;
  * $\ell(e) = u(e) = c_k$.
- From sink $r^-$ to source $r^+$:
  * $E_r = \{(r^-, r^+)\}$;
  * $\ell(e) = u(e) = n$.

In the following, we consider a *circulation* in this network, which is a function $f\colon E \to \mathbb{R}$ satisfying the following:

**Capacity constraint:** $\ell(e) \le f(e) \le u(e)$ for all edges $e \in E$;

**Flow conservation:** $\sum_{e \in \delta^+(v)} f(e) = \sum_{e \in \delta^-(v)} f(e)$ for all vertices $v \in V$, where $\delta^+(v)$ and $\delta^-(v)$ denote the sets of edges outgoing from and incoming to $v$, respectively.

As $B$ and $B'$ are both amount-preserving allocations, we can construct a circulation $f$ as follows:

- $f(e) = 1$ for each $e \in E_s$;
- $f(e) = 1/2$ for each $e \in E_N$;
- $f(e) = c_k/2$ for each $e \in E_G$;
- $f(e) = c_k$ for each $e \in E_M$;
- $f(e) = n$ for each $e \in E_r$.

The capacity constraint is obviously satisfied, and the flow conservation is confirmed by regarding the assignment of student $j$ to school $k$ under allocation $A \in \{B, B'\}$ as a circulation of value 1/2 along a directed cycle $r^+ \to j \to (k, g(j)) \to k \to r^- \to r^+$ (note that $f$ is the sum of these circulations).

Consequently, by the integrality of the network flow problem (cf. [12, Theorem 11.2]), we conclude that an integer circulation $\tilde{f}\colon E \to \mathbb{Z}$ exists in the same network. Furthermore, such an integer circulation can be found by a single maximum-flow computation in an auxiliary network (cf. [12, Theorem 11.3]); thus, it can be computed in polynomial time [7]. By the definition of the network ($E_s$ and $E_r$ in particular), the obtained integer circulation $\tilde{f}$ is decomposed into $n$ circulations, each of value 1 along a directed cycle of form $r^+ \to j \to (k, g(j)) \to k \to r^- \to r^+$ as above. Then, an allocation $A$ is naturally determined so that each student $j$ is assigned to school $k$ along the unique relevant cycle. By the definition of capacity on $E_G$ and $E_M$, under $A$, each school has exactly $\lfloor c_k/2 \rfloor$ students of one group and exactly $\lceil c_k/2 \rceil$ students of the other group, whose difference is at most 1. This completes the proof. □

Let $A$ be the allocation obtained by Lemma 3. If a perfectly-swapped allocation $A'$ does not exist, then $A$ is already a 1-relaxed envy-free allocation by Lemma 2. Thus, we assume that such an $A'$ exists. Then, by appropriately modifying $A$ and $A'$, we can obtain a 1-relaxed envy-free allocation as follows, which completes the proof of Theorem 1:

**Lemma 4.** *Given an amount-preserving allocation $A$ and a perfectly-swapped allocation $A'$ such that $\left||A_1^{-1}(k)| - |A_2^{-1}(k)|\right| = \left||A'^{-1}_1(k)| - |A'^{-1}_2(k)|\right| \leq 1$ for all $k \in M$, one can compute an allocation $X$ such that $\left||X^{-1}(k)| - c_k\right| \leq 1$ and $|X_1^{-1}(k)| = |X_2^{-1}(k)|$ for all $k \in M$, which is 1-relaxed envy-free.*

*Proof.* Let us define $\Delta_{A,k} := |A_1^{-1}(k)| - |A_2^{-1}(k)| \in \{-1, 0, 1\}$. We call a school with $\Delta_{A,k} = -1$ a *deficient* school, and a school with $\Delta_{A,k} = 1$ an *excess* school.

We obtain a desired allocation $X$ by Algorithm 1. Starting with $X = A$, this algorithm resolves pairs of excess and deficient schools one by one by moving students of group 1. To do this, considering only group 1, we construct a directed graph $G_X = (M, E_X)$ on the set of schools by

$$E_X := \{e_j = (X(j), A'(j)) \mid j \in N_1\}, \tag{7}$$

**Algorithm 1.** Adjustment to a balanced allocation

**Input:** Allocations $A$ and $A'$ satisfying the condition in Lemma 4.
**Output:** An allocation $X$ satisfying the condition in Lemma 4.
**Step 1 (Initialization):**
Set $X \leftarrow A$ and construct the directed graph $G_X$.
**Step 2 (Search and update):**
Repeat the following operations until $S_X$ becomes empty:
(a) Select an excess school $s \in S_X$.
(b) Find a directed path $P = (s = v_0, v_1, \ldots, v_\ell = t)$ in $G_X$ from $s$ to some deficient school $t \in T_X$.
(c) For each edge $e_j = (v_i, v_{i+1})$ on $P$, update $X(j) \leftarrow A'(j)$ (originally, $X(j) = v_i$ and $A'(j) = v_{i+1}$). After that, update $G_X$ (as well as $S_X$ and $T_X$) with respect to the new $X$.
**Step 3 (Termination):**
Return $X$.

where $G_X$ may contain a self-loop when $X(j) = A'(j)$ for some $j \in N_1$. We move students along a directed path in $G_X$. A student $j \in N$ moved in each iteration is fixed to their destination school; that is, we set $X(j) \leftarrow A'(j)$, who will never be moved further. Let $S_X$ and $T_X$ denote the sets of excess schools and deficient schools, respectively, with respect to the currect allocation $X$. The proof is completed as follows: Lemma 5 guarantees that there always exists a path $P$ from any $s \in S_X$ to $T_X$ in $G_X$ when $S_X \neq \emptyset$. After that, we see that the algorithm terminates in polynomial time in Lemma 6 and that its output $X$ is indeed a desired allocation in Lemma 7. □

**Lemma 5.** *Let $X$ be the allocation during an iteration of Algorithm 1. Fix any excess school $s \in S_X$, and define the set of schools reachable from $s$ in $G_X$ as*

$$R := \{k \in M \mid s \rightsquigarrow k\}.$$

*Then, $R$ always contains a deficient school in $T_X$.*

*Proof.* Recall that $\Delta_{X,k} = |X_1^{-1}(k)| - |X_2^{-1}(k)|$, and by definition of $G_X$, the out-degree $d_X^+(k)$ and in-degree $d_X^-(k)$ of each school $k \in M$ can be written as follows:

$$d_X^+(k) = |X_1^{-1}(k)|, \quad d_X^-(k) = |A'^{-1}_1(k)|. \tag{8}$$

Since $A'$ is a perfectly-swapped allocation with respect to $A$ and the students of group 2 are not moved, we have

$$|A'^{-1}_1(k)| = |A_2^{-1}(k)| = |X_2^{-1}(k)|. \tag{9}$$

From (8) and (9), we obtain the following:

$$d_X^+(k) - d_X^-(k) = |X_1^{-1}(k)| - |X_2^{-1}(k)| = \Delta_{X,k}. \tag{10}$$

Suppose for the sake of contradiction that $R$ does not contain a deficient school. Then, we have

$$\Delta_{X,s} = 1, \quad \Delta_{X,k} \geq 0 \quad (\forall k \in R). \tag{11}$$

From (10) and (11), as $s \in R$, we obtain

$$\sum_{k \in R} \left(d_X^+(k) - d_X^-(k)\right) = \sum_{k \in R} \Delta_{X,k} \geq 1, \tag{12}$$

which can be rephrased as

$$\sum_{k \in R} d_X^+(k) > \sum_{k \in R} d_X^-(k). \tag{13}$$

On the other hand, by definition of $R$, no edge in $G_X$ leaves from $R$ to outside. Thus, counting the edges incident to $R$, we obtain

$$\sum_{k \in R} d_X^+(k) \leq \sum_{k \in R} d_X^-(k),$$

which contradicts (13). Therefore, we have shown that $R$ contains at least one deficient school. □

**Lemma 6.** *Algorithm 1 terminates in polynomial time.*

*Proof.* From Lemma 5, in each iteration of Step 2 of Algorithm 1, there exists a path from $s$ to some $t \in T_X$ in $G_X$, which is easily found in linear time. By moving students of group 1 along the path $P$, the value $\Phi_X := \sum_{k \in M} |\Delta_{X,k}|$ decreases by 2 as follows. For each inner vertices $v_i$ on $P$, exactly one student of group 1 is moved out and exactly one is moved in, so $|X_1^{-1}(v_i)|$ does not change before and after the update in (c). In contrast, for the end vertices $s$ and $t$, exactly one student of group 1 is moved out and moved in, respectively, so $|X_1^{-1}(s)|$ decreases by one and $|X_1^{-1}(t)|$ increases by one, which makes $|\Delta_{X,s}|$ and $|\Delta_{X,t}|$ from 1 to 0. Thus, $\Phi_X$ becomes 0 in at most $\Phi_A/2 \leq m/2$ iterations. Thus, Algorithm 1 terminates in polynomial time. □

**Lemma 7.** *The output $X$ of Algorithm 1 satisfies $\left||X^{-1}(k)| - c_k\right| \leq 1$ and $|X_1^{-1}(k)| = |X_2^{-1}(k)|$ for all $k \in M$, which is 1-relaxed envy-free.*

*Proof.* Recall that at the beginning of Algorithm 1, $X = A$ is amount-preserving and satisfies $\Delta_{X,k} \in \{-1, 0, 1\}$ for all $k \in M$. As described in the proof of Lemma 6, in each iteration of Step 2, the number of students of group 1 decreases by one at the start vertex $s$ of the path $P$, increases by one at the goal vertex $t$, and remains unchanged at the inner vertices. Since each school $k$ with $|\Delta_{X,k}| = 1$ is chosen as an end vertex of $P$ exactly once and any student of group 2 is not moved in the algorithm, we have $\left||X^{-1}(k)| - c_k\right| \leq 1$ for all $k \in M$. Also, at the end of Algorithm 1, the allocation $X$ satisfies $\Delta_{X,k} = 0$ for all $k \in M$, which means that $|X_1^{-1}(k)| = |X_2^{-1}(k)|$ for all $k \in M$.

Consequently, the utilities of the two groups become equal:

$$u(1, X) = u(2, X). \tag{14}$$

Suppose for the sake of contradiction that $X$ is not 1-relaxed envy-free. This means that one group envies the other. By symmetry, we can assume without loss of generality that group 1 envies group 2. Let this envy in allocation $X$ be caused by the existence of some allocation $X'$ that simultaneously satisfies (2)–(4) in Definition 1; in particular, (2) and (3) are written as follows:

$$u(1, X') > u(1, X), \tag{15}$$

$$|{X'}_1^{-1}(k)| \leq |X_2^{-1}(k)| \quad (\forall k \in M). \tag{16}$$

Since the two groups have the same size, we have the following:

$$\sum_{k \in M} |{X'}_1^{-1}(k)| = \sum_{k \in M} |X_1^{-1}(k)| = \sum_{k \in M} |X_2^{-1}(k)|. \tag{17}$$

From (16) and (17), we obtain

$$|{X'}_1^{-1}(k)| = |X_2^{-1}(k)| \quad (\forall k \in M). \tag{18}$$

Thus, by (14) and (18) (as the utility is just defined by the sum of the values of assigned schools), the following holds:

$$u(1, X') = u(2, X) = u(1, X), \tag{19}$$

which contradicts (15). Therefore, $X$ is a 1-relaxed envy-free allocation. □

# 4 Conclusion and Future Work

In this study, we have addressed the fair division problem in school redistricting. While Procaccia et al. [11] showed for three or more groups that adding $o(n)$ extra seats in total and relaxing how to compare the utilities are not sufficient to guarantee the existence of an envy-free allocation in general, we have proved for the case of two groups that reasonable envy-freeness is achieved with at most one seat deviation in each school. Specifically, we have introduced the 1-relaxed envy-freeness as a relaxation of envy-freeness tailored to the setting where we are given an initial allocation of the students to the schools. We have shown that such a 1-relaxed envy-free allocation always exists and can be computed in polynomial time.

Although we have shown positive results for two groups, the setting may be considered restrictive in the following senses:

- In both our model and the previous work [11], the value of each school is the same for all students. We can relax this assumption so that the value of each school is the same for all students in each group (which can be different over the groups), but it is still restrictive because the students' preferences may be individually different even in the same group.

- In both our model and the previous work [11], envy of group $i_1$ to group $i_2$ is justified only by another allocation where the seats for $i_1$ in every school is included by the seats for $i_2$ in the school under the current allocation (cf. (3) in Definition 1). This makes envy too difficult to occur; in particular, a larger group $i_1$ cannot envy a smaller group $i_2$ (cf. the proof of Lemma 1).
- In our problem setting, the capacity of each school is defined as the number of students in the initial allocation. The previous work [11] considers redistricting scenarios driven by demographic changes or capacity fluctuations due to school opening or closing. Our present results can be applied after computing a tentative allocation $B$ that only cares the number of students assigned to each school, but it does not give any direct implication to their setting in general.

It is a possible direction of future work to formulate and investigate a wider reasonable setting of envy-free school redistricting to address these restrictive aspects.

**Acknowledgments.** We would like to thank the reviewers for giving helpful comments. This work was supported by JSPS KAKENHI Grant Number JP25H01114, and JST CRONOS Japan Grant Number JPMJCS24K2, and JST ASPIRE Japan Grant Number JPMJAP2520.

## References

1. Allman, M., et al.: Designing school choice for diversity in the San Francisco unified school district. In: Proceedings of the 23rd ACM Conference on Economics and Computation, pp. 290–291 (2022)
2. Amanatidis, G., Birmpas, G., Filos-Ratsikas, A., Voudouris, A.A.: Fair division of indivisible goods: a survey. In: Proceedings of the 31st International Joint Conference on Artificial Intelligence, pp. 5385–5393(2022)
3. Benabbou, N., Chakraborty, M., Elkind, E., Zick, Y.: Fairness towards groups of agents in the allocation of indivisible items. In: Proceedings of the 28th International Joint Conference on Artificial Intelligence, pp. 95–101 (2019)
4. Benabbou, N., Chakraborty, M., Igarashi, A., Zick, Y.: Finding fair and efficient allocations for matroid rank valuations. In: Proceedings of the 13th International Symposium on Algorithmic Game Theory, pp. 32–46 (2020)
5. Brams, S.J., Taylor, A.D.: Fair Division: From Cake-cutting to Dispute Resolution, Cambridge University Press (1996)
6. Cembrano, J., Moraga, A., Verdugo, V.: Near-feasible fair allocations in two-sided markets. In: Proceedings of the 26th Conference on Economics and Computation, pp. 898–915 (2025)
7. Ford, L.R., Jr., Fulkerson, D.R.: Maximal flow through a network. Can. J. Math. **8**, 399–404 (1956)
8. Kuhn, H.W.: The Hungarian method for the assignment problem. Naval Res. Logistics Quarterly **2**(1–2), 83–97 (1955)
9. Kyropoulou, M., Suksompong, W., Voudouris, A.A.: Almost envy-freeness in group resource allocation. Theoret. Comput. Sci. **841**, 110–123 (2020)

10. Munkres, J.: Algorithms for the assignment and transportation problems. J. Soc. Ind. Appl. Math. **5**(1), 32–38 (1957)
11. Procaccia, A., Robinson, I., Tucker-Foltz, J.: School redistricting: wiping unfairness off the map. In: Proceedings of the 2024 Annual ACM-SIAM Symposium on Discrete Algorithms, pp. 2704–2724 (2024)
12. Schrijver, A.: Combinatorial Optimization: Polyhedra and Efficiency. Springer (2003)
13. Stromquist, W.: Envy-free cake divisions cannot be found by finite protocols. Electron. J. Combin. **15**(1), R11 (2008)
14. Suksompong, W.: Constraints in fair division. SIGecom Exchanges **19**(2), 46–61 (2021)

# On the Arithmetic Complexity of Euler Tours

Nikhil Balaji[1], Prasad Chaugule[2(✉)], and Nitin Saurabh[3]

[1] Indian Institute of Technology, Delhi, India
nbalaji@cse.iitd.ac.in
[2] Chennai Mathematical Institute, Chennai, India
pchaugule@cmi.ac.in
[3] Indian Institute of Technology, Hyderabad, India
nitin@cse.iith.ac.in

**Abstract.** Counting problems on graphs are a rich source of polynomials in algebraic complexity. Our work is motivated by the following question: *If a counting problem is easy, does it admit an algebraization that is easy, and similarly, if a counting problem is hard, does its algebraization remain hard?* For example, counting spanning trees is easy via the matrix-tree theorem [1] and the corresponding spanning tree polynomial is also computable in VBP [10]. Similarly, counting perfect matchings is #P-complete and its algebraic counterpart, the perfect matching polynomial, is also VNP-complete.

We investigate this relationship between counting problems and algebraic complexity from the perspective of *Euler orientations* and *Euler tours* polynomials. We show that:

- Over fields of characteristic zero, the commutative (resp. noncommutative) Complete Euler Orientation polynomial is VNP-complete (resp. $\mathsf{VNP}_{nc}$-complete) under linear $p$-projections and the commutative Euler tour polynomial is VNP-complete under linear $p$-projections.
- There exists a commutative polynomial encoding of directed Euler tours which is VNP-complete under $p$-projections. This is surprising since counting Euler tours on directed graphs is in $\mathsf{NC}^2$ via the BEST theorem [1].

**Keywords:** Algebraic Complexity · Counting Complexity · Euler Tours

## 1 Introduction

The central goal of algebraic complexity is to understand what is the most efficient way to compute a given multivariate polynomial. Counting problems on graphs are a rich source of such polynomials. Typically, one associates formal variables with the vertices and edges of a graph, and encodes a combinatorial property of interest as a monomial in these variables. The resulting


Y. Li et al. (Eds.): COCOON 2026, LNCS 16835, pp. 355–369, 2027.
https://doi.org/10.1007/978-981-92-3309-0_27

polynomial, aggregates as its monomials, all subgraphs satisfying the combinatorial property. For example, in order to encode Hamiltonian cycles on $n$ vertex graphs, one starts with the complete graph $K_n$ whose edges are encoded by variables, $X = \{x_{i,j}\}_{1\leq i<j\leq n}$ and a Hamiltonian cycle is captured by the cycle structure of a permutation, $\sigma \in S_n$ and this is encoded as the monomial $x_{1,\sigma(1)}x_{2,\sigma(2)}\cdots x_{n,\sigma(n)}$. The Hamiltonian Cycle polynomial ($\mathsf{HC}_n$) is then the sum over all monomials arising from permutations $\sigma \in S_n$ corresponding to a Hamiltonian cycle. It is easily observed that by suitably substituting the edge variables by constants 0/1, one can easily count the number of Hamiltonian cycles in any given graph from $\mathsf{HC}_n(X)$.

In this work, we are motivated by the following question: if a counting problem is "easy", does it admit an algebraisation that is "easy", and similarly, if a counting problem is "hard", is every possible algebraization of this problem hard? For example, counting spanning trees is easy via the matrix-tree theorem [1] and the corresponding spanning tree polynomial is also computable in VBP [10]. In this paper, we investigate this relationship between counting problems and algebraic complexity from the perspective of Euler tours.

An Euler tour of an (undirected/directed) graph $G$ is a closed walk in $G$ which traverses every edge of $G$ exactly once. While deciding if a (directed or undirected) graph admits an Euler tour has a well-known linear time algorithm due to Euler, the problem of counting the number of Euler tours varies greatly in complexity. A remarkable theorem due to de Bruijn, Ehrenfest, Smith and Tutte (the so-called BEST theorem [21,23]) reduces counting Euler tours in directed graphs to a determinant computation, thereby placing it in $\mathsf{NC}^2$. Counting undirected Euler tours is known to be in polynomial time for restricted graph classes [7]; However, the problem is known to be #P-complete [9] on general graphs. Indeed, obtaining a fully polynomial randomised approximation scheme (FPRAS) for counting Euler tours on undirected graphs is an outstanding open problem [14] in the area of Markov chain Monte Carlo methods. While $\mathsf{HC}_n(X)$ was proven to be VNP-complete over all fields in Valiant's seminal work on algebraic complexity classes [22], to the best of our knowledge, there has been no work that has attempted to capture Euler tours as a formal polynomial.

An approach to encoding Euler tours similar to the Hamiltonian cycle polynomials hits several difficulties: First, naïvely encoding Euler tours through (commuting) formal edge variables (akin to Hamiltonian cycles) would result in all Euler tours being encoded by a single monomial, namely $\prod_{1\leq i<j\leq n} x_{ij}$. Second, unlike Hamiltonicity, projections can destroy Eulerianity, i.e., for a given $n$ number of vertices, if we define our Euler tour polynomial over a complete graph $K_n$ (as in the case of Hamiltonian cycle polynomial), merely setting the variables of the edges absent in the subgraph $H$ of $K_n$ to 0 will not preserve the correct count of the number of Euler tours in subgraph $H$. Therefore, it is crucial to define the Euler tour polynomial carefully such that for any given $n$, the definition captures the count of Euler tours of each possible subgraph of graph $K_n$.

Euler tours naturally provide an ordering on edge variables and hence seem readily interpretable as *noncommutative polynomials*. Indeed, if the edge variables $X$ are noncommutative, one can uniquely encode every Euler tour of a graph (up to a fixed starting edge for the tour) using a single monomial. Noncommutative polynomials have been a remarkable success story in algebraic complexity. Starting with the seminal work of Nisan [19], noncommutative models of computation [2] have enriched and influenced the toolkit for proving algebraic circuit lower bounds [20]. Over the past decade substantial progress [3,11,15–17] has been made in understanding the $\mathsf{VP}_{nc}$ vs $\mathsf{VNP}_{nc}$ question. Nevertheless, the question of separating $\mathsf{VP}_{nc}$ from $\mathsf{VNP}_{nc}$ remains open and lies at the frontier of algebraic complexity.

**Related Work.** Unlike the commutative world, there is a paucity of polynomials complete for $\mathsf{VP}_{nc}$ and $\mathsf{VNP}_{nc}$. Arvind et al. [4] exhibit polynomials inspired by formal language theory that are hard for noncommutative $\mathsf{VBP}_{nc}, \mathsf{VP}_{nc}, \mathsf{VNP}_{nc}$ under a variety of reductions. A series of papers over the last two decades [5,8,12] have established that the noncommutative determinant is as hard as the permanent. Engels and Rao [13] give a combinatorial characterisation of the #P-hardness of the Cayley Permanent. In this work, we study Euler orientations and Euler tours and show the following:

**Theorem 1 (Informal).** *Over fields of characteristic zero, the commutative (resp. noncommutative) Complete Euler Orientation polynomial is* $\mathsf{VNP}$*-complete (resp.* $\mathsf{VNP}_{nc}$*-complete) under linear p-projections.*

However, we are unable to prove a similar noncommutative hardness for the corresponding Euler tour polynomials. Instead, we have the following

**Theorem 2 (Informal).** *Over fields of characteristic zero, the commutative Euler tour polynomial is* $\mathsf{VNP}$*-complete under linear p-projections.*

Finally, we partially answer our motivating question raised earlier by showing that there exists a suitable algebraisation of BEST theorem that leads to a $\mathsf{VNP}$-complete polynomial family that captures Euler tours on directed graphs. This is surprising since it is easy to count Euler tours on directed graphs.

**Theorem 3 (Informal).** *There exists a commutative polynomial encoding of directed Euler tours which is* $\mathsf{VNP}$*-complete under p-projections.*

## 2 Preliminaries

**Notation.** Throughout the paper, unless stated otherwise, we denote by $\mathbb{F}$ the underlying field and assume it has characteristic 0. By $\mathbb{F}[X]$ we denote the commutative polynomial ring over a finite set of variables $X = \{x_1, \ldots, x_n\}$ and by $\mathbb{F}\langle X\rangle$ the noncommutative polynomial ring with coefficients from field $\mathbb{F}$.

**Definition 1 (Algebraic Circuit).** *An algebraic circuit $C$ over the field $\mathbb{F}$ and the set of variables $X = \{x_1, \ldots, x_n\}$ is a* directed acyclic graph *(DAG), where the vertices of in-degree* 0 *are called the* input gates. *There is a special vertex of*

*out-degree* 0 *called the* output gate. *All the vertices have in-degree* 2. *The input vertices are labelled either with a field constant from* $\mathbb{F}$ *or an element from the variable set* $X$. *Every other vertex is labelled by either* $\times$ *or* $+$. *The input gate labelled by* $\alpha \in \mathbb{F} \cup X$ *computes the polynomial* $\alpha$. *The polynomial computed by a* $+$ *gate (resp.* $\times$*) is the sum (resp. the product) of the polynomials computed by its children. The polynomial computed by the circuit is the polynomial computed at the output gate. The* size *and* depth *of an algebraic circuit refer to the number of vertices and the longest path from the input gate to the output, respectively, in the underlying DAG.*

*Furthermore, if the algebraic circuit is noncommutative, multiplication is associative but not (necessarily) commutative, and each* $\times$ *gate has a designated left child and a designated right child and computes the product of the polynomials computed by its children in left-to-right order.*

**Definition 2** (VP, $\mathsf{VP}_{nc}$)**.** *Fix a field* $\mathbb{F}$. *A family of polynomials* $\{f_n\}$ *over* $\mathbb{F}$ *is p-bounded if there exists some polynomial* $t : \mathbb{N} \to \mathbb{N}$ *such that for every* $n$, *both the number of variables in* $f_n$ *and the degree of* $f_n$ *are at most* $t(n)$. *The class* VP *(resp.* $\mathsf{VP}_{nc}$*) consists of all p-bounded families over* $\mathbb{F}$ *that can be computed by algebraic circuits (resp. noncommutative algebraic circuits) of polynomial size.*

**Definition 3** (VNP, $\mathsf{VNP}_{nc}$)**.** *A family* $f_n$ *is in* VNP *(resp.* $\mathsf{VNP}_{nc}$*), if there exist polynomially bounded functions* $p(n)$ *and* $t(n)$ *and a family* $g_n \in \mathsf{VP}$ *(resp.* $\mathsf{VP}_{nc}$*) such that*

$$f_n = \sum_{y_1,\ldots,y_{t(n)} \in \{0,1\}} g_n(x_1, \ldots, x_{p(n)}, y_1, y_2, \ldots, y_{t(n)})$$

**Proposition 1 (Valiant's Criterion [10, Proposition 2.20]).** *Suppose* $\phi : \{0,1\}^* \to \mathbb{N}$ *is a function in the class* #P/poly. *Then the family* $f_n$ *of polynomials is in* VNP *where*

$$f_n(x_1, \ldots, x_n) = \sum_{e \in \{0,1\}^n} \phi(e) x_1^{e_1} \ldots x_n^{e_n}$$

**Definition 4 (**$p$**-projection, Linear** $p$**-projection).** *A polynomial* $f(x_1, \ldots, x_n)$ *is a projection of* $g(y_1, \ldots, y_m)$, *denoted* $f \leq g$, *if* $f$ *can be obtained from* $g$ *by substituting each* $y_i$ *by either a variable from* $\{x_1, \ldots, x_n\}$ *or a field constant. In the noncommutative setting, we require that the substitutions preserve multiplication order. A family* $\{f_n\}$ *is a p-projection of* $\{g_n\}$, *denoted* $f \leq_p g$, *if there exists a polynomially bounded function* $m(n)$ *such that* $f_n \leq g_{m(n)}$ *for all* $n$. *A family* $\{f_n\}$ *is a linear p-projection of* $\{g_n\}$, *denoted* $f \leq_p^\ell g$, *if there exists a polynomially bounded function* $m(n)$ *and field constants* $\lambda_1, \ldots, \lambda_{m(n)}$ *such that for every* $n$, $f_n \leq \sum_{i=1}^{m(n)} \lambda_i, g_{m(n)}^{(i)}$ *where the polynomials* $g_{m(n)}^{(i)}$ *are defined on disjoint variable sets.*

**Definition 5 (Perfect Matching polynomial).** *Let $G = (V_1 \cup V_2, E)$ be the complete bipartite graph with $|V_1| = |V_2| = n$. Let $V_1 = \{u_i | 1 \le i \le n\}$ and $V_2 = \{u_j | 1 \le j \le n\}$. Let $X = \{x_{i,j} | 1 \le i, j \le n\}$. Let $\Phi : E \rightarrow X$ be a function, where $\Phi(u_i, v_j) = x_{i,j}$. Let $\mathcal{M}$ denote the set of all perfect matchings of $G$. Then the Perfect Matching polynomial* $\mathsf{PM}(X)$ *is defined as*

$$\mathsf{PM}_n(X) = \sum_{m \in \mathcal{M}} \prod_{(u_i, v_j) \in m} x_{i,j}$$

The Perfect Matching $\mathsf{PM}_n$ polynomial is VNP-complete under $p$-projections for all fields of characteristic $\neq 2$ ([10,22]). The polynomial $\mathsf{CPerm}_n(Y) \in \mathbb{F}\langle X \rangle$ defined below is a noncommutative variant of the Perfect Matching polynomial where the multiplication in each monomial uses the row order of the matrix.

**Definition 6 (Cayley Permanent [13]).** *Let $Y = (y_{ij})_{1 \le i,j \le n}$ be a $n \times n$ matrix of noncommuting formal variables. Then the Cayley permanent is defined as follows:*

$$\mathsf{CPerm}_n(Y) = \sum_{\sigma \in S_n} y_{1\sigma(1)} y_{2\sigma(2)} \cdots y_{n\sigma(n)}$$

**Definition 7 (Euler Tours and Euler Orientation).** *An Euler tour of an (undirected/directed) graph $G$ is a closed walk in $G$ which traverses every edge of $G$ exactly once. A graph is* Eulerian *if it admits an Euler tour. Given an undirected graph $G = (V, E)$, an orientation $\phi$ is a function that assigns directions to edges. We denote by $G^{\phi}$ the directed graph obtained from the undirected graph $G$ by applying the orientation $\phi$. An orientation $\phi$ is said to be an Euler orientation if for every vertex $v \in V(G^{\phi})$, the in-degree of $v$ is equal to the out-degree of $v$.*

**Definition 8 (Arborescence [1]).** *Let $T = (V, E)$ is a directed graph and $r$ a vertex. We say that $T$ is an arborescence converging to $r$ if there is a directed path from any $v \neq r$ to $r$, and the out-degree of every vertex $v \neq r$ in $T$ is* 1 *and* 0 *for $r$. This implies, of course, that there is exactly one such path from any vertex $v$ to $r$. Given a directed graph $G = (V, E)$, a subgraph $T \subseteq G$ is called a* spanning arborescence *converging to $r$ if $T$ is an arborescence towards $r$, and $V(T) = V(G)$.*

**Theorem 4 (BEST theorem [1]).** *Let $G = (V, E)$ be a directed, connected Eulerian graph. Let $f(G)$ denote the total number of Euler tours of graph $G$. Let $deg^{+}(u)$ denote the out-degree (which equals the in-degree in an Eulerian graph) of vertex $u$ in $G$. Let $Arb(G, s)$ denote the set of arborescences (see Definition 8) of $G$ rooted at $s$. Then,*

$$f(G) = \left( \prod_{u \in V(G)} (deg(u) - 1)! \right) \times |Arb(G, s)|$$

**Lemma 1 (Univariate Interpolation).** *Let $\mathbb{F}$ be a field of size at least $d+1$. Let $f(X,t) = c_0 + c_1 t + c_2 t^2 + \ldots + c_d t^d$ be a polynomial of degree $d$ in variable $t$, where $c_0, c_1, \ldots, c_d \in \mathbb{F}[X]$. Let $\alpha_0, \alpha_1, \ldots, \alpha_d$ be distinct constants from $\mathbb{F}$. Then for every $i \in \{0, 1, \ldots, d\}$, there exists constants $\beta_{i0}, \beta_{i1}, \ldots, \beta_{id} \in \mathbb{F}$ such that, $c_i = \sum_{j=0}^{d} \beta_{ij} f(X, \alpha_j)$.*

**Lemma 2 (Lagrange interpolation with central evaluation points).** *Let $R$ be a (not necessarily commutative) ring with centre $Z(R)$. Consider*

$$f(t) = \sum_{i=0}^{d} c_i t^i \qquad (c_i \in R).$$

*Fix scalars $\alpha_0, \ldots, \alpha_d \in Z(R)$, and define the evaluations*

$$y_j := f(\alpha_j) = \sum_{i=0}^{d} c_i \alpha_j^i \in R \qquad (j = 0, \ldots, d).$$

*Let $V = (\alpha_j^i)_{0 \le j, i \le d}$ be the $(d+1) \times (d+1)$ Vandermonde matrix with entries in $Z(R)$. If $V$ is invertible in $M_{d+1}(Z(R))$ (equivalently, $\det V$ is a unit in $Z(R)$), then the coefficient vector*

$$(c_0, \ldots, c_d)^\top$$

*is uniquely determined by the evaluations, namely*

$$\begin{pmatrix} c_0 \\ \vdots \\ c_d \end{pmatrix} = V^{-1} \begin{pmatrix} y_0 \\ \vdots \\ y_d \end{pmatrix}.$$

*In particular, each $c_i$ is a $Z(R)$-linear combination of the $y_j$.*

*Proof (Sketch).* Because each $\alpha_j \in Z(R)$ commutes with all $c_i$, the evaluation equations can be written in matrix form as

$$y = Vc,$$

with $y = (y_0, \ldots, y_d)^\top$ and $c = (c_0, \ldots, c_d)^\top$. Since $V^{-1} \in M_{d+1}(Z(R))$ exists by hypothesis, we can multiply on the left to obtain

$$c = V^{-1} y.$$

Thus the coefficients are uniquely recovered as $Z(R)$-linear combinations of the evaluations. □

## 3 Euler Orientation and Euler Tour Polynomials

In this section, we study the hardness of the Euler orientation and Euler tour polynomials.

### 3.1 Euler Orientation Polynomials

We first capture Euler orientations as a noncommutative polynomial.

Let $X = \{x_{ij} | 1 \leq i, j \leq n\}$ be a set of non-commuting variables encoding the edges of the complete undirected graph $K_n$. We fix a lexicographic ordering of the variables in $X$, i.e., $x_{11} < x_{12} \ldots, < x_{1n} < x_{21} \cdots < x_{2n} < x_{n1} \ldots, < x_{nn}$.

**Definition 9 (Euler Orientation polynomial).** *For an undirected graph $H$ that is a subgraph of $K_n$, let $\mathcal{O}_H$ denote the set of all Euler orientations of $H$. For every edge $\{i, j\} \in E(H)$, we associate a set of two variables $\{x_{ij}, x_{ji}\} \subseteq X$ and the monomial corresponding to an orientation includes exactly one of these.*

*The noncommutative Euler Orientation Polynomial of $H$ is given by*

$$\mathsf{ncEO}_H(X) = \sum_{\phi \in \mathcal{O}_H} \prod_{(u,v) \in E(H^\phi)} x_{uv}$$

*where each monomial is ordered according to the lexicographic ordering of variables in $X$.*

*Let $\mathcal{S}$ denote the set of all subgraphs of $K_n$. The Complete Euler Orientation polynomial is defined as follows:*

$$\mathsf{ncCEO}_n(X) = \sum_{H \in \mathcal{S}} \mathsf{ncEO}_H = \sum_{H \in \mathcal{S}} \sum_{\phi \in \mathcal{O}_H} \prod_{(u,v) \in E(H^\phi)} x_{uv}$$

Note that the lexicographic ordering on the variable set of the complete graph enables a canonical way to map digraphs to monomials of $\mathsf{ncCEO}_n(X)$. We are now ready to prove $\mathsf{VNP}_{nc}$-completeness of $\mathsf{ncCEO}_n(X)$. Towards this, we reduce from $\mathsf{CPerm}_n(Y)$ (See Definition 6 in Sect. 2):

**Theorem 5.** $\mathsf{CPerm}_n \leq_p^\ell \mathsf{ncCEO}_n$.

The proof of Theorem 5 closely follows a parsimonious reduction between perfect matchings and Euler orientations due to Mihail and Winkler [18]. The following gadget is central to the reduction.

**The Gadget.** Let $G = (V_1 \cup V_2, E)$ be the complete bipartite graph with $V_1(G) = \{u_i | 1 \leq i \leq n\}$ and $V_2(G) = \{v_i | 1 \leq i \leq n\}$. We associate a unique variable $y_{i,j}$ to every edge $(u_i, v_j)$ of graph $G$.

**Converting Graph. $G$ to $\widehat{G}$.** We add two new vertices $s$ and $t$ to $G$. For every vertex $u \in V_1(G)$, we add $n-2$ edges between $s$ and $u$. Recall that $deg(u)$ is the degree of vertex $u$ in $G$. Similarly, for each vertex $v \in V_2(G)$, we add $n-2$ edges between $v$ and $t$. Observe that the total number of edges added between $s$ and the vertices in $V_1(G)$ is equal to the total number of edges added between the vertices in $V_2(G)$ and $t$, we denote this number by $m = n(n-2)$. We finally add $m$ parallel edges, say $\mathcal{E}_1, \mathcal{E}_2, \ldots, \mathcal{E}_m$ between $s$ and $t$.

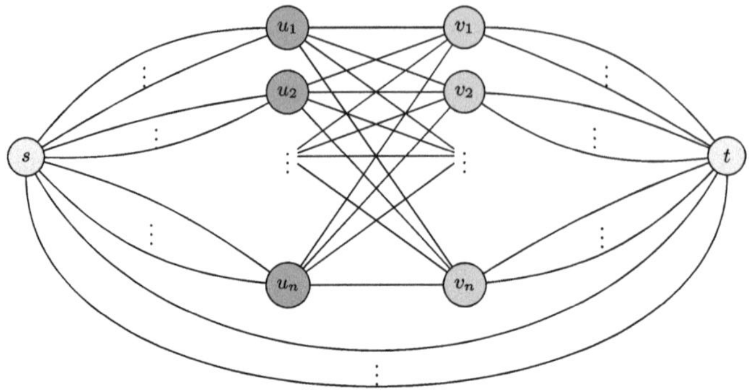


**Fig. 1.** Reduction: $\mathsf{CPerm}(Y) \leq \mathsf{ncEO}(X)$

**Getting Rid of Parallel Edges.** Let $u$ and $v$ be two vertices of $\widehat{G}$ such that there are more than one edge between $u$ and $v$. For every edge $e$ between $u$ and $v$ in $\widehat{G}$, we delete the edge $e$, add a new vertex $\theta_e$ and add edges between $u$ and $\theta_e$ and between $\theta_e$ and $v$. We call this new graph $G'$. See Fig. 1 for a sketch of the reduction (without the edge subdivision).

**Relabelling.** We interpret graph $G$ as a subgraph of the complete undirected graph $K_r$ where $r$ is the number of vertices in $G'$. We relabel the vertices of $G'$ so that vertices $v_i \in V_2(G)$ are labelled as vertices $1, \ldots, n$ of $K_r$ and the remaining vertices $(V(G') \setminus V_2(G))$ are labelled arbitrarily from $n+1, \ldots, r$ where $r$ is polynomially bounded in $n$

*Proof.* (of Theorem 5) We now show that there exists a polynomially bounded function $m : \mathbb{N} \to \mathbb{N}$ and a map $\phi : X \to \mathbb{F} \cup Y$ such that $\mathsf{ncCEO}_r(X)$ under $\phi$ computes $\sum_{k=0}^{m} t^k f_k(Y) \in \mathbb{F}[t]\langle Y \rangle$, where $f_m(Y) = \mathsf{CPerm}_n(Y)$. Along with Lemma 1, this is sufficient to establish the VNP-hardness of $\mathsf{ncCEO}_n(X)$ under linear $p$-projections (see Definition 4). Towards this we start from the complete bipartite graph $G$ and produce the graph $G'$ as described in the gadget construction above. Observe that the edges incident on $\theta_{\mathcal{E}_i}$ (the nodes obtained by subdividing $s-t$ edges in $\widehat{G}$) cannot be both directed towards or away from $\theta_{\mathcal{E}_i}$. Therefore, considering the following two cases suffices:

**Case 1:** For each $i \in [m]$, let the edge between $t$ and $\theta_{\mathcal{E}_i}$ is directed from $t$ to $\theta_{\mathcal{E}_i}$ and the edge between $\theta_{\mathcal{E}_i}$ and $s$ is directed from $\theta_{\mathcal{E}_i}$ and $s$. We now wish to extend this partial orientation to an Euler orientation of graph $G'$. Note that the only way to extend this partial orientation to an Euler orientation is to direct all the edges between $s$ and the vertices in set $V_1(G)$ away from $s$ and towards the vertices in $V_1(G)$ (via the $\theta$ vertices) which ensures that the indegree and outdegree of $s$ are equal. Similarly, the edges between $t$ and the vertices in $V_2(G)$, must be directed away from the vertices in $V_2(G)$ and towards the vertex $t$ (via the $\theta$ vertices). Let $u$ be any vertex in $V_1(G)$. The only way to balance

$u$ is to orient all the edges incident on $u$ in graph $G$ away from $u$ except one. That is, there is exactly one edge incident on $u$ whose tail lies in the vertex set $V_2(G)$. Similarly, for every $v \in V_2(G)$, all the edges incident on $v$ in $G$ must be directed towards $u$, except one. That is, there is exactly one edge incident on $v$ in $G$, whose head lies in $V_1(G)$. The set of edges of graph $G$ directed away from vertices in $V_2(G)$ and whose heads lie in $V_1(G)$ forms a perfect matching in graph $G$. Let $S_1$ denote the set of all Euler orientations of case 1 and let $\mathsf{ncEO}^{(1)}_{G'}(Y)$ denote the corresponding Euler orientation polynomial. Clearly, every monomial of the Euler orientation polynomial $\mathsf{ncEO}^{(1)}_{G'}(Y)$ contains $y_{1\sigma(1)} \cdots y_{n\sigma(n)}$ as a *submonomial* thanks to the lexicographic ordering of the variable set $Y$ resulting from the relabelling. Note that there is a one-to-one correspondence between the set of perfect matchings of $G$ and the set $S_1$. Let

$$\mathsf{ncEO}^{(1)}_{G'}(Y) = \sum_{\phi \in S_1} \prod_{(u,v) \in E(G'^{\phi})} y_{uv}$$

**Case 2:** Let us assume that there exists at least one $j$ such that the edge between $s$ and $\theta_{\mathcal{E}_j}$ is directed from $s$ to $\theta_{\mathcal{E}_j}$ and the edge between $\theta_{\mathcal{E}_j}$ and $t$ is directed from $\theta_{\mathcal{E}_j}$ to $t$. Let $S_2$ denote the set of all Euler orientations of case 2 and $\mathsf{ncEO}^{(2)}_{G'}(Y)$ the corresponding Euler orientation polynomial.

$$\mathsf{ncEO}^{(2)}_{G'}(Y) = \sum_{\phi \in S_2} \prod_{(u,v) \in E(G'^{\phi})} y_{uv}$$

Let $r$ be the total number of vertices of graph $G'$. We now interpret the graph $G'$ as a complete undirected graph on $r$ vertices, $K_r$, where the edges present in $G'$ inherit their weights in $K_r$ and the edges absent in $G'$ are interpreted as weight 0 edges in $K_r$. Let this projection be called as $\Psi$. Hereafter, we assume that the polynomials defined over $K_r$ are under the projection $\Psi$. Note that

$$\mathsf{ncCEO}_r(Y) = \left( \sum_{g \in S \setminus \{G'\}} \mathsf{ncEO}_g(Y) \right) + \mathsf{ncEO}_{G'}(Y)$$

where $S$ is the set of subgraphs of $K_r$. Since the above two cases are exhaustive,

$$\mathsf{ncEO}_{G'}(Y) = \mathsf{ncEO}^{(1)}_{G'}(Y) + \mathsf{ncEO}^{(2)}_{G'}(Y)$$

Therefore,

$$\mathsf{ncCEO}_r(Y) = \left( \sum_{g \in S \setminus \{G'\}} \mathsf{ncEO}_g(Y) \right) + \left( \mathsf{ncEO}^{(1)}_{G'}(Y) + \mathsf{ncEO}^{(2)}_{G'}(Y) \right)$$

Let $S' = S \setminus \{G'\}$. Let $S'' \subseteq S'$ be a set of subgraphs which uses at least one edge in $K_r$ which is set to 0 under $\Psi$. Therefore,

$$\mathsf{ncCEO}_r(Y) = \left( \sum_{g \in S''} \mathsf{ncEO}_g(Y) + \sum_{g \in S' \setminus S''} \mathsf{ncEO}_g(Y) \right) + \left( \mathsf{ncEO}^{(1)}_{G'}(Y) + \mathsf{ncEO}^{(2)}_{G'}(Y) \right) \quad (1)$$

We now extend the projection $\Psi$ of $K_r$. Clearly, $\sum_{g\in S''} \mathsf{ncEO}_g(Y)$ vanishes since every monomial contains an edge that is set to 0 by $\Psi$. Moreover, for every $i$, we set $x_{s\theta_{\mathcal{E}_i}}$ to 0. Therefore, $\mathsf{ncEO}^{(2)}_{G'}(Y)$ also vanishes. The new equation will be as follows.

$$\mathsf{ncCEO}_r(Y) = \left(\sum_{g\in S'\setminus S''} \mathsf{ncEO}_g(Y)\right) + \left(\mathsf{ncEO}^{(1)}_{G'}(Y)\right)$$

We now describe our final projection. We set $x_{\theta_{\mathcal{E}_i}s}$ to a variable $z$ which commutes with the variable set $Y$. We set the variables $x_{s,\theta_{\mathcal{E}_i}}$ to 0. We set the variable $x_{ij}$ to 1 and $x_{ji}$ to $y_{ji}$ associated with the edge between $v_i \in V_2(G)$ and the $u_j \in V_1(G)$. We set all other variables (associated with other edges) to 1. We call the resulting polynomial $\mathsf{ncCEO}_r(Y,z)$. Note that the degree of the variable $z$ in $\mathsf{ncCEO}_r(Y,z)$ associated with the Euler orientation of any subgraph of $G'$ is strictly less than $m$ (recall that $m$ is the number of new vertices introduced in the gadget while converting $G$ to $\widehat{G}$). Therefore,

$$\mathsf{ncCEO}_r(Y,z) = \sum_{j=0}^{m} f_j z^j$$

where $f_m = \mathsf{CPerm}_n(Y)$. Notice that $\mathsf{ncCEO}_r(Y) \in \mathbb{F}\langle Y\rangle[z]$ By Lemma 2, the result immediately follows. □

**Corollary 1.** $\mathsf{ncCEO}_n(X)$ *is* $\mathsf{VNP}_{nc}$*-complete under linear p-projections.*

*Proof.* It suffices to prove that $\mathsf{ncCEO}_n(X) \in \mathsf{VNP}_{nc}$, since $\mathsf{VNP}_{nc}$-hardness follows from Theorem 5. Notice that every valid monomial (which corresponds to a unique Euler orientation of the graph $H$) in $\mathsf{ncCEO}_n(X)$ can occur at most once in the polynomial: when it occurs, it is contributed by a unique Eulerian subgraph of $K_n$. This is in $\mathbf{NP} \subseteq \#\mathbf{P}$, by a nondeterministic machine which guesses the said subgraph and the checks if the given monomial indeed corresponds to a valid Eulerian orientation in this subgraph. Hence by Proposition 1 (Valiant's criterion) it is clear that $\mathsf{ncCEO}_n(X)$ is in $\mathsf{VNP}_{nc}$. □

We now observe that the *commutative* Complete Euler Orientation polynomial defined by encoding Euler tours via commuting edge variables (denoted $\mathsf{CEO}_n(X) \in \mathbb{F}[X]$) is VNP-complete.

$$\mathsf{CEO}_n(X) = \sum_{H\in\mathcal{S}} \mathsf{EO}_H = \sum_{H\in\mathcal{S}} \sum_{\phi\in\mathcal{O}_H} \prod_{(u,v)\in E(H^\phi)} x_{uv}$$

**Corollary 2.** $\mathsf{CEO}_n(X)$ *is* VNP*-complete under linear p-projections.*

*Proof.* It is easy to see that the commutative variant of $\mathsf{CPerm}_n(Y)$, namely the Perfect Matching polynomial $\mathsf{PM}(Y)$ can be expressed as a linear $p$-projection of the commutative complete Euler orientation polynomial $\overline{\mathsf{ncCEO}_n}(X) \in \mathbb{F}[X]$ (obtained by dropping the ordering on the variable set $X$) by exactly the same gadget construction as the one outlined in the proof of Theorem 5. □

The noncommutative Euler orientation polynomials proposed in Definition 9 extends naturally to a noncommutative polynomial for Euler tours. For a graph $H$, we define the Euler tour polynomial $\mathsf{ncET}_H(X)$ and the complete Euler tour polynomial $\mathsf{ncCET}_n(X)$ along similar lines as $\mathsf{ncEO}_H(X)$ and $\mathsf{ncCEO}(X)$, by mapping Euler tours to monomials and summing over all possible Euler tours of subgraphs of $K_n$. A natural way to prove that $\mathsf{ncCET}_n(X)$ is $\mathsf{VNP}_{nc}$-hard would be to express $\mathsf{ncCEO}_n(X)$ as a projection of $\mathsf{ncCET}_n(X)$. While we are able to do so under the assumption that the variables commute, a similar proof for the noncommutative case remains open.

### 3.2 Euler Tour Polynomials

We now define *commutative* Euler tour polynomials for both undirected and directed graphs.

**Definition 10 (Euler Tour polynomial).**
*For a graph $H$, let $\mathcal{T}_H$ denote the set of all Euler tours of $H$. For a given Euler tour $T$ of $H$, we associate a function $\Phi_T : E(H) \to X$, where*

$$\Phi_T(i,j) = \begin{cases} x_{ij} \text{ if edge } (i,j) \text{ is traversed from the vertex } i \text{ to } j \text{ in } T \\ x_{ji} \text{ if edge } (i,j) \text{ is traversed from the vertex } j \text{ to } i \text{ in } T \end{cases}$$

*The Euler Tour polynomial of graph $H$ is defined as follows:*

$$\mathsf{ET}_H(X) = \sum_{T \in \mathcal{T}_H} \prod_{(i,j) \in E(H)} \Phi_T(i,j)$$

*Let $\mathcal{S}$ denote the set of all Eulerian subgraphs of $K_n$. We define the Complete Euler Tour polynomial as follows:*

$$\mathsf{CET}_n(X) = \sum_{H \in \mathcal{S}} \mathsf{ET}_H(X) = \sum_{H \in \mathcal{S}} \sum_{T \in \mathcal{T}_H} \prod_{(i,j) \in E(H)} \Phi_T(i,j)$$

Note that while $\mathsf{ET}_H(X)$ for a directed graph is a single monomial whose coefficient captures the number of directed Euler tours in $H$, for undirected graphs this polynomial can have exponentially many monomials (corresponding to different Euler orientations of the undirected graph). However, $\mathsf{CET}_n(X)$ is the same for both directed and undirected graphs on $n$ vertices since we sum over all possible subgraphs.

**Theorem 6.** $\mathsf{PM}_n \leq_p^{\ell} \mathsf{CET}_n$

*Proof.* We proceed exactly as in the proof of Theorem 5: From the complete bipartite graph $G$ we produce the graph $G'$ described in the gadget in Sect. 3.1 while inheriting the values of the described projection. Let $\mathcal{J}$ denote the set of Euler Orientations of the graph $G'$, and let $\mathcal{J}' \subseteq \mathcal{J} = \{j_1, j_2, \ldots, j_k\}$ denote the set of all Euler orientations of $G'$, where for each $i \in [m]$, the edge between $t$ and $\theta_{\mathcal{E}_i}$ is directed from $t$ to $\theta_{\mathcal{E}_i}$ and the edge between $\theta_{\mathcal{E}_i}$ and $s$ is directed from $\theta_{\mathcal{E}_i}$ to $s$. Since we inherit the projection from Theorem 5, observe that any $j_t \in \mathcal{J} \setminus \mathcal{J}'$ will vanish. Let $u$ be any arbitrary vertex of $G'$. For any $j_i \in \mathcal{J}'$, let $Arb(j_i, u)$ denote the set of arborescences of $j_i$ with root $u$. Observe that, for any $m$, $n \in [k]$ and $m \neq n$, $|Arb(j_m, u)| = |Arb(j_n, u)|$. While this is not true in general, it is true for the graph $G'$ we have constructed. Indeed, in the graph $G'$, the only freedom among the orientations $j_i \in \mathcal{J}'$ lies in the orientation of the edges of the complete bipartite graph $G = (V_1 \cup V_2, E)$, and these orientations correspond bijectively to perfect matchings of $G$. All other edges of $G'$ are oriented identically in every $j_i \in \mathcal{J}'$. For any $j_m, j_n \in \mathcal{J}'$, the corresponding perfect matchings differ by a permutation of the vertices in $V_2$. Since the construction of $G'$ is symmetric under permutations of $V_2$, such a permutation extends to a directed graph automorphism of $G'$ mapping $j_m$ to $j_n$ while fixing the root $u$. Let $\mathcal{X}_{\mathcal{J}'}$ denote the set of all Euler tours of the graph $G'$ respecting some orientation from the set $\mathcal{J}'$. There is a 1-to-$N$ mapping from the set $\mathcal{J}'$ to $\mathcal{X}_{\mathcal{J}'}$ for some fixed $N$. That is, every Euler orientation $\phi$ in $\mathcal{J}'$ of graph $G'$ gives rise to $N$ distinct undirected Euler tours of $G'$ respecting $\phi$ where $N = |Arb(j_i, u)| \prod_{v \in V}(deg^+(v) - 1)!$, by the BEST theorem. Therefore, we have $\mathsf{CET}_r(X, z) = \sum_{j=1}^{m(n)} f_j z^j$ where $m(n)$ is a polynomially bounded function, and $f_m = N \times \mathsf{PM}_n(Y)$ which can be obtained as a linear combination of $\mathsf{CET}_n$ using Lemma 1. Finally, scaling the entire computation by $1/N$, yields the result. □

**Corollary 3.** $\mathsf{CET}_n$ *is* $\mathsf{VNP}$*-complete under linear p-projections.*

*Proof.* $\mathsf{CET}_n(X) \in \mathsf{VNP}$ is straightforward: every monomial encodes a valid Euler Tour and given a monomial, we can guess the specific Eulerian subgraph that contributed it and check if the monomial encodes a valid Euler tour of the subgraph in $\mathsf{NP} \subseteq \#P$ and this yields the $\mathsf{VNP}$ upper bound via Proposition 1. □

### 3.3 Euler Tour Polynomials via BEST Theorem

The BEST theorem (see Theorem 4) is a classical result in graph theory that shows that the number of Euler tours in directed graphs can be computed in polynomial time [1]. In contrast, on undirected graphs the problem is known to be #P-complete [9]. We now present a commutative polynomial encoding Euler Tours in directed graphs inspired by the BEST theorem.

The main idea behind the BEST theorem is that one can fix an arborescence rooted at a specific vertex $s$ for every Euler tour by picking the last edge used to visit a vertex before returning to the root. Now this yields an alternate way to encode Euler tour polynomials as follows:

**Definition 11 (BEST encoding of Euler Tours).** *Let $H = (V, E)$ be a directed graph where $V = \{u_1, u_2, \ldots, u_n\}$. For a given directed Euler tour $T$ of $H$, we associate a function $\Phi_T : E(H) \to [D]$, where $D$ is the maximum out-degree of any vertex in $H$ and $\Phi_T(e = (u_i, u_j)) = m$, if and only if the vertex $u_i$*

*is exited $m^{th}$ time in the tour $T$ via the edge $e = (u_i, u_j)$. The BEST polynomial of $H$ with $f$ as the starting (first) edge is defined as*

$$\mathsf{BEST}_{H,f}(X) = \sum_{T \in \mathcal{T}(H)} \prod_{e \in [E(G)]} x_{e,\Phi_T(e)}$$

Note that different starting edges lead to syntactically different polynomials in our encoding, and therefore require the polynomial to be defined with respect to a starting edge.

A *tournament* $T_n$ is directed graph obtained from the complete undirected graph $K_n$ and an orientation $\phi$ by orienting the edges of $K_n$ according to $\phi$, i.e. $T_n = K_n^{\phi}$. A tournament $T$ is said to be *regular* if the in-degree and the out-degree of every vertex in $T_n$ is the same.

**Theorem 7.** *Let $T_n$ be a sequence of regular tournaments. Then $\mathsf{BEST}_{T_n,e}(X)$ is $\mathsf{VNP}$-complete under p-projections for any edge e.*

*Proof.* Using Proposition 1, it is easy to note that $\mathsf{BEST}_{T_n,e}(X)$ is in $\mathsf{VNP}$. We now show $\mathsf{PM}_n(Y) \leq \mathsf{BEST}_{T_{2n+3},e}(X)$, where $V(T_{2n+3}) = \{u_1, u_2, \ldots, u_{2n+3}\}$. Let the edge between the vertices $u_1$ and $u_2$ in $T_{2n+3}$ is directed from $u_1$ to $u_2$. Let us call $(u_1, u_2)$ as $e$. Assume (without loss of generality) that the edges directed away from $u_1$ are towards the vertices $u_2$, $u_3$, ..., $u_{n+2}$ and the edges directed towards the vertex $u_1$ are from the vertices $u_{n+3}$, $u_{n+4}$, ..., $u_{2n+3}$. We set the weight of variable $x_{e,j}$ to $y_{e,j}$ for all $j \in \{3, 4, \ldots, n+2\}$. We set the weight of variable $x_{e,1}$ and all the other variables to 1. Therefore, we get $c \cdot \mathsf{PM}_n(Y) \leq \mathsf{BEST}_{T_{2n+3},e}(X)$, for some $c$ where $c = \prod_{i \in [n] \setminus \{1\}} (n+1)!$. We can scale $\mathsf{BEST}_{T_{2n+3},e}(X)$ by $1/c$, therefore, the result immediately follows. □

It is easy to see that Theorem 7 yields $\mathsf{VNP}$-completeness of $\mathsf{BEST}_{H_n,e}$ for any graph sequence $\{H_n\}$ that contains a vertex of $\Omega(n)$ degree.

## 4 Discussion

We initiated a study of Euler orientation and Euler tour polynomials, and established $\mathsf{VNP}_{nc}$ and $\mathsf{VNP}$-completeness under linear $p$-projections. However, several intriguing questions remain:

1. We introduced several algebraizations of the Euler tour problem. However, we are unable to separate the directed and undirected cases algebraically. Is there a natural algebraization (that distinguishes tours, unlike a single monomial) under which the directed Euler tour polynomial becomes efficiently computable? On a related note, is the noncommutative Euler tour polynomial $\mathsf{CET}_n(X)$ $\mathsf{VNP}_{nc}$-complete under $p$-projections?
2. Can we show $\mathsf{VNP}$-hardness of $\mathsf{ncET}_H(X), \mathsf{ET}_H(X), \mathsf{ncEO}_H(X)$ and $\mathsf{EO}(X)$ for a *fixed* $H$? [6] shows that counting Euler tours in directed bounded treewidth graphs is in logspace. Can we obtain $\mathsf{VNP}$-hardness of Euler tour polynomials already for a sparse family of graphs? (say planar graphs)? [7]

shows that counting Euler tours is in $\#\mathsf{SAC}^1$ on undirected bounded treewidth graphs. Can this proof be adapted to show that $\mathsf{ET}_H(X)$ is in VP for bounded treewidth $H$?

**Acknowledgment.** N.B is supported by ANRF/ARG/2025/010912/MS and ANRF/ARGM/2025/001463/MTR.

## References

1. Aigner, M.: Combinatorial Theory, vol. 234. Springer Berlin, Heidelberg (2012). https://doi.org/10.1007/978-3-642-59101-3
2. Allender, E., Jiao, J., Mahajan, M., Vinay, V.: Non-commutative arithmetic circuits: depth reduction and size lower bounds. Theoret. Comput. Sci. **209**(1–2), 47–86 (1998)
3. Arvind, V., Chatterjee, A.: On lifting lower bounds for noncommutative circuits using automata. Chic. J. Theor. Comput. Sci. **1**, 1–12 (2025)
4. Arvind, V., Joglekar, P.S., Raja, S.: Noncommutative valiant's classes: structure and complete problems. ACM Trans. Comput. Theory (ToCT) **9**(1), 1–29 (2016)
5. Arvind, V., Srinivasan, S.: On the hardness of the noncommutative determinant. In: Proceedings of the 42nd STOC, pp. 677–686 (2010)
6. Balaji, N., Datta, S.: Bounded treewidth and space-efficient linear algebra. In: Jain, R., Jain, S., Stephan, F. (eds.) TAMC 2015. LNCS, vol. 9076, pp. 297–308. Springer, Cham (2015). https://doi.org/10.1007/978-3-319-17142-5_26
7. Balaji, N., Datta, S., Ganesan, V.: Counting euler tours in undirected bounded treewidth graphs. In: 35th FSTTCS, p. 246 (2015)
8. Bläser, M.: Noncommutativity makes determinants hard. Inf. Comput. **243**, 133–144 (2015)
9. Brightwell, G.R., Winkler, P.: Counting Eulerian circuits is# p-complete. In: ALENEX/ANALCO, pp. 259–262 (2005)
10. Bürgisser, P.: Completeness and Reduction in Algebraic Complexity Theory, volume 7 of Algorithms and Computation in Mathematics. Springer Berlin, Heidelberg (2000). https://doi.org/10.1007/978-3-662-04179-6
11. Carmosino, M.L., Impagliazzo, R., Lovett, S., Mihajlin, I.: Hardness amplification for non-commutative arithmetic circuits. In: 33rd CCC, pp. 12–1. Schloss Dagstuhl–Leibniz-Zentrum für Informatik (2018)
12. Chien, S., Harsha, P., Sinclair, A., Srinivasan, S.: Almost settling the hardness of noncommutative determinant. In: Proceedings of the 43rd STOC, pp. 499–508 (2011)
13. Engels, C., Rao, B.V.R.: On hard instances of non-commutative permanent. Discret. Appl. Math. **277**, 127–138 (2020)
14. Ge, Q., Štefankovič, D.: The complexity of counting Eulerian tours in 4-regular graphs. Algorithmica **63**(3), 588–601 (2012)
15. Hrubeš, P., Wigderson, A., Yehudayoff, A.: Non-commutative circuits and the sum-of-squares problem. In: Proceedings of the 42nd STOC, pp. 667–676 (2010)
16. Lagarde, G., Limaye, N., Srinivasan, S.: Lower bounds and pit for non-commutative arithmetic circuits with restricted parse trees. Comput. Complex. **28**(3), 471–542 (2019)

17. Limaye, N., Malod, G., Srinivasan, S.: Lower bounds for non-commutative skew circuits. Theory Comput. **12**(1), 1–38 (2016)
18. Mihail, M., Winkler, P.: On the number of Eulerian orientations of a graph. Algorithmica **16**, 402–414 (1996)
19. Nisan, N.: Lower bounds for non-commutative computation. In: Proceedings of the 23rd STOC, pp. 410–418 (1991)
20. Nisan, N., Wigderson, A.: Lower bounds on arithmetic circuits via partial derivatives. Comput. Complex. **6**(3), 217–234 (1996)
21. Tutte, W.T., Smith, C.A.B.: On unicursal paths in a network of degree 4. Am. Math. Mon. **48**(4), 233–237 (1941)
22. Valiant, L.G.: Completeness classes in algebra. In: Proceedings of the 11th STOC, pp. 249–261 (1979)
23. van Aardenne-Ehrenfest, T., de Bruijn, N.G.: Circuits and trees in oriented linear graphs. In: Classic Papers in Combinatorics, pp. 149–163 (1987)

# Improved Algorithms for the Maximum Weight Star Packing Problem

Shiming Li[1], Yong Chen[1], Zhaohui Liu[2], Wei Yu[2], and An Zhang[1(✉)]

[1] Department of Mathematics, Hangzhou Dianzi University, Hangzhou 310018, China
{90077,chenyong,anzhang}@hdu.edu.cn

[2] School of Mathematics, East China University of Science and Technology, Shanghai 200237, China
{zhliu,yuwei}@ecust.edu.cn

**Abstract.** Given an edge-weighted complete graph $G = (V, E)$, the maximum weight star packing problem asks for a collection of vertex-disjoint stars in $G$ that maximizes the total weight of the stars. We consider two versions of the problem parameterized by a fixed positive integer $k$. The maximum weight $k^-$-star packing problem (MW$k^-$SP) allows each selected star to contain at most $k$ vertices. The maximum weight $k$-star packing problem (MW$k$SP), under the condition that $|V| = k \times n$ for some integer $n$, requires only stars containing exactly $k$ vertices. For both versions, we present improved approximation algorithms based on local search. Specifically, we develop a $\frac{k}{2k-1}$-approximation algorithm for MW$k^-$SP and a $\frac{1}{2}$-approximation algorithm for MW$k$SP. On $\{1, 2\}$-weighted graphs, we further refine these algorithms to achieve an improved approximation ratio of $\frac{3}{4}$ for the two versions. All proposed algorithms outperform the best known results in the literature.

**Keywords:** Star packing · Approximation algorithm · Local search · Maximum-cost Maximum-flow

## 1 Introduction

The maximum weight star packing problem arises in various practical settings such as transportation problems [1], facility location [20], online carpooling [13] and wireless sensor networks [16]. In general, given a complete graph $G = (V, E)$ with a non-negative weight function $\omega : E \to \mathbb{R}^+$, the problem aims to find a collection of vertex-disjoint stars in $G$ such that the total weight of these stars is maximized. A star in $G$ is referred to as a subgraph of $G$ isomorphic to $K_{1,t-1}$ for some integer $t \geq 1$, consisting of a center incident to all edges and $t - 1$ satellites.

There are two versions with respect to a fixed positive integer $k$ as the parameter, which are mostly studied in the literature. If each star is allowed to contain at most $k$ vertices, then the problem is called the maximum weight $k^-$-star packing problem, denoted as MW$k^-$SP. If each star is restricted to containing


Y. Li et al. (Eds.): COCOON 2026, LNCS 16835, pp. 370–382, 2027.
https://doi.org/10.1007/978-981-92-3309-0_28

exactly $k$ vertices, then the problem is known as the maximum weight $k$-star packing problem, denoted as MW$k$SP, for which it is additionally required that $|V| = k \times n$ for some integer $n$.

### 1.1 Related Works

When $k = 2$, both MW$k^-$SP and MW$k$SP are equivalent to the maximum weight matching problem, which can be solved in $O(|V|^3)$ time [12,14]. For any fixed $k \geq 3$, MW$k^-$SP and MW$k$SP become NP-hard even when the edge weights are restricted to $\{0, 1\}$ or $\{1, 2\}$ [11]. Babenko and Gusakov [2] observed that when the centers of the stars in an optimal solution are predetermined, MW$k^-$SP can be transformed into a network flow problem and thus be solved in polynomial time [8]. Motivated by this observation, they obtained a $\frac{4k}{9(k-1)}$-approximation algorithm for MW$k^-$SP. On the other hand, Kutiel and Rawitz [13] viewed the total weight of the stars in MW$k^-$SP as a set function defined on the sets of candidate centers and established that the function is a non-monotone submodular function. From this perspective, the problem admits a natural $\frac{1}{2}$-approximation algorithm [5,6]. They also developed a local search algorithm achieving the same ratio. These are the current best results for MW$k^-$SP. Similarly, the objective of MW$k$SP can be viewed as a non-monotone submodular set function subject to a cardinality constraint that at most $\frac{|V|}{k} = n$ centers are included in a candidate set. That way, MW$k$SP admits a 0.401-approximation algorithm [7]. For MW$k$SP on metric graphs, i.e., the edge weights satisfy the triangle inequality, Han et al. [9] proposed an improved algorithm with approximation ratio $\frac{k}{2(k-1)}$. For the more special case on $\{1, 2\}$-weighted graphs, they further developed a $\frac{11}{15}$-approximation algorithm for MW4SP. A generalized version of MW$k$SP called the maximum capacitated star packing problem (MCSP) was originally introduced by Arkin et al. [1]. In their setting, all stars have prescribed sizes, $c_1, c_2, \cdots, c_n$, which sum to $|V|$ exactly. They proposed a $\frac{1}{3}$-approximation local search algorithm for MCSP.

By replacing the set of stars with a set of paths or cycles in the problem of MW$k$SP, we come up with the maximum weight $k$-path packing problem (MW$k$PP) and the maximum weight $k$-cycle packing problem (MW$k$CP), respectively. These problems find applications in areas like kidney exchange programs [4], social networks [19] and the maximum quadratic assignment problem [18]. For MW3PP (which coincides with MW3SP), Bar-Noy et al. [3] presented a simple, matching-based $\frac{7}{12}$-approximation algorithm. Recently, Zhao and Xiao [23] improved the ratio to the current best of $\frac{10}{17}$. Hassin and Rubinstein [10] developed a $\frac{3}{4}$-approximation algorithm for MW4PP via matching techniques too. For general $k$, they provided a $\frac{k-1}{k}\alpha$-approximation algorithm [10], where $\alpha$ denotes the ratio for approximating the maximum traveling salesman problem (MaxTSP). For metric graphs, Li and Yu [15] presented a $\frac{3}{4}$-approximation algorithm for MW3PP; Zhao and Xiao [22] proposed a $\frac{14}{17}$-approximation for MW4PP. For $k \in \{6, 8, 10\}$, Zhao and Xiao [22] further designed an approximation algorithm achieving the ratio of $\frac{27k^2-48k+16}{32k^2-36k-24}$.

For the problem of MW$k$CP, Li and Yu [15] presented a $(\frac{k-1}{k})^2\alpha$-approximation algorithm. Thiery and Ward [21] proposed a 0.5599-approximation algorithm for $k = 3$, and Zhao and Xiao [22] gave a $\frac{3}{4}$-approximation for $k = 4$. Zhao and Xiao [22,24] also considered MW$k$CP on metric graphs, where the approximation ratios are improved to $(\frac{7}{8} - \frac{1}{8k})(1 - \frac{1}{k})$ and $\frac{7}{8}(1 - \frac{1}{k} + \frac{1}{k(k-1)})$ for odd and even $k > 5$ respectively, and to $0.66835 - \varepsilon$, $\frac{5}{6}$ and $\frac{7}{10}$ for $k = 3, 4$ and 5 respectively.

When restricting the problems on $\{0, 1\}$-weighted graphs, Bar-Noy et al. [3] presented a $\frac{3}{4}$-approximation algorithm for MW3PP and a $\frac{3}{5}$-approximation algorithm for MW3CP, while Monnot and Toulouse [17] proposed a $\frac{9}{10}$-approximation algorithm for MW4PP. Recently, Zhao and Xiao [22] observed that any $\rho$-approximation algorithm for the $\{0, 1\}$-weighted graphs can be transformed into a $\frac{\rho+1}{2}$-approximation algorithm for the corresponding $\{1, 2\}$-weighted graphs. With this fact, they succeeded to improve the approximation ratios on $\{1, 2\}$-weighted graphs, e.g., they obtained a $\frac{9}{11}$-approximation algorithm for MW3CP and a $\frac{7}{8}$-approximation algorithm for MW4CP on $\{1, 2\}$-weighted graphs.

### 1.2 Our Contribution

In this paper, we first present an algorithm for the problem of MW$k^-$SP that achieves an approximation ratio $\frac{k}{2k-1}$, which slightly improves the best known $\frac{1}{2}$-approximation given by Kutiel and Rawitz [13]. Next, we develop a $\frac{1}{2}$-approximation algorithm for MW$k$SP, which beats the previous 0.401-approximation straightforwardly derived from the submodularity of the problem [7,13]. Using the fact revealed by Zhao and Xiao [22], our $\frac{1}{2}$-approximation algorithm for MW$k$SP also implies a $\frac{3}{4}$-approximation for MW$k$SP on $\{1, 2\}$-weighted graphs. This improves upon the existing $\frac{11}{15}$-approximation [9] too. Notice that the same approach cannot be directly applied to MW$k^-$SP on $\{1, 2\}$-weighted graphs. We then devise a simple idea to achieve the $\frac{3}{4}$-approximation for this case. All our algorithms are based on local search where the set of centers is iteratively updated by solving a maximum-cost maximum-flow problem.

The rest of the paper is organized as follows. In Sect. 2, we introduce some definitions and notations as preliminaries. Section 3 and Sect. 4 are devoted to MW$k^-$SP and MW$k$SP respectively, where we describe our algorithms and establish their approximation ratios. In Sect. 5, we refine the algorithms for MW$k^-$SP and MW$k$SP on $\{1, 2\}$-weighted graphs. Finally, we draw our conclusion in Sect. 6.

## 2 Preliminaries

Formally, we are given a complete graph $G = (V, E)$ with a non-negative weight function on the edge set $\omega : E \to \mathbb{R}^+$. For a subgraph $H$ of $G$, let $V(H)$ and $E(H)$ be the set of vertices and the set of edges in it. Define the weight of a subgraph $H$ as $\omega(H) = \sum_{e \in E(H)} \omega(e)$. A star in $G$ is a specific subgraph of $G$

that is isomorphic to $K_{1,t-1}$ for some $t \geq 1$. In other words, it consists of one center vertex and $t-1$ satellite vertices so that every edge in the star is incident to the center and one of the satellites. We refer to a $k(k^-)$-star as a star with exactly (at most) $k$ vertices.

If a collection $\mathcal{S} = \{S_1, S_2, \ldots, S_m\}$ of subgraphs of $G$ satisfies (i) each $S_i$ is a star, (ii) $V(S_i) \cap V(S_j) = \emptyset$ for any $i \neq j$, and (iii) $\bigcup_{i=1}^{m} V(S_i) \subseteq V(G)$, then it is called a star packing of $G$. The maximum weight star packing problem is to find a star packing of the given graph with the maximum total weight, i.e., to maximize $\omega(\mathcal{S}) = \sum_{S_i \in \mathcal{S}} \omega(S_i)$. In particular, when the star packing is restricted to containing only $k$-stars (or $k^-$-stars), it is called a $k$-star packing (or a $k^-$-star packing), and the corresponding maximum weight star packing problem is denoted as MW$k$SP (or MW$k^-$SP). Note that in the problem of MW$k$SP, it is usually assumed that $|V| = k \times n$.

For an instance of MW$k^-$SP or MW$k$SP, we use $OPT$ to denote the optimal solution, where the stars in $OPT$ are represented as $S_1^*, \ldots, S_m^*$, and use *opt* to denote the optimal value, i.e., $opt = \sum_{i=1}^{m} \omega(S_i^*)$. Similarly, let $SOL$ denote the solution obtained by an algorithm in the subsequent discussions, where the stars in $SOL$ are represented as $S_1, \ldots, S_p$, and let *sol* denote the total weight of the stars in $SOL$. For a given solution $SOL$ and a vertex $v \in V$, we use $touch(v)$ to denote the total weight of all edges in $SOL$ that are incident to $v$. Accordingly, we have $sol = \sum_{v \in c(SOL)} touch(v) = \sum_{v \in s(SOL)} touch(v)$, where $c(SOL)$ and $s(SOL)$ denote the sets of centers and satellites in $SOL$ respectively.

## 3 Approximate the Problem of MW$k^-$SP

In this section, we develop a local search based algorithm Approx1 for the problem of MW$k^-$SP, outperforming the previous $\frac{1}{2}$-approximation algorithm which is derived from the non-monotone submodularity [13]. In Approx1, we may frequently compute the "gain" – an estimated increase in the objective value when adding a candidate set $V'$ of centers to the current solution $SOL$. This gain serves as a lower bound on the actual increase. For the sake of clarity, we describe the computation procedure of this gain as a subroutine, namely, Gain$(V', SOL)$.

### 3.1 A Subroutine Computing the Gain

Given a candidate set $V' \subseteq V$ of centers and the current solution $SOL$, the subroutine Gain$(V', SOL)$ returns the gain achievable by reassigning some vertices in $V \setminus V'$ to the centers in $V'$, denoted as $\omega(\text{Gain})$, as well as the new solution achieving this gain, denoted as $SOL_{\text{Gain}}$. Gain$(V', SOL)$ first computes a maximum-cost maximum-flow in the following constructed network $G'$.

- $G'$ consists of a source node $s$, a sink node $t$, and a bipartite graph between $V'$ and $V \setminus V'$.
- There is a directed edge from $s$ to each vertex in $V'$ with capacity $k-1$ and cost 0.

- There is a directed edge from each vertex in $V \setminus V'$ to $t$ with capacity 1 and cost 0.
- There is a directed edge from $u \in V'$ to $v \in V \setminus V'$ if and only if $\omega(u, v) - touch(v) > 0$. In case the edge exists, let its capacity be 1 and its cost be $\omega(u, v) - touch(v)$.

After solving the maximum-cost maximum-flow problem on $G'$ in $O(|V|^3)$ time [8], we obtain the gain $\omega(\text{GAIN})$ as the cost of the maximum-cost maximum-flow minus the loss of $V'$ itself, i.e., $\sum_{v \in V'} touch(v)$. The corresponding maximum flow in $G'$ also defines a new $k^-$-star packing solution $SOL_{\text{GAIN}}$. In fact, all the edges between $V'$ and $V \setminus V'$ with non-zero flows together form a set of $k^-$-stars centered at $V'$, and by removing the vertices included in these stars, the remaining stars in $SOL$ are reserved. One sees that when computing the gain $\omega(\text{GAIN})$, the weight of an edge in $SOL$ may be subtracted twice. This leads to an underestimation of the actual increase from the initial solution $SOL$ to the new solution $SOL_{\text{GAIN}}$.

The following figure (Fig. 1) shows a construction example from the given graph $G$ (the left graph) to the network $G'$ (the directed graph on the right). The solid edges in $G$ give the current solution $SOL$, while the dashed edges are those with non-zero weights. The weight is labeled on each edge. The network $G'$ is constructed under $SOL$ and $V' = \{b, e\}$. Each directed edge is marked with a binary vector, where the first and second term represent the capacity and the cost of the edge respectively. In this example, the maximum-cost maximum-flow of $G'$ attains a cost of 12, implying that the gain $\omega(\text{GAIN}) = 12 - touch(b) - touch(e) = 1$; the corresponding maximum flow contains four edges between $V'$ and $V \setminus V'$ with non-zero flows, $bc, bd, ea$ and $ef$, which together form two 3-stars in the new solution $SOL_{\text{GAIN}}$. It is also easy to see that the actual increase from $SOL$ to $SOL_{\text{GAIN}}$ is equal to 19, much larger than the gain.

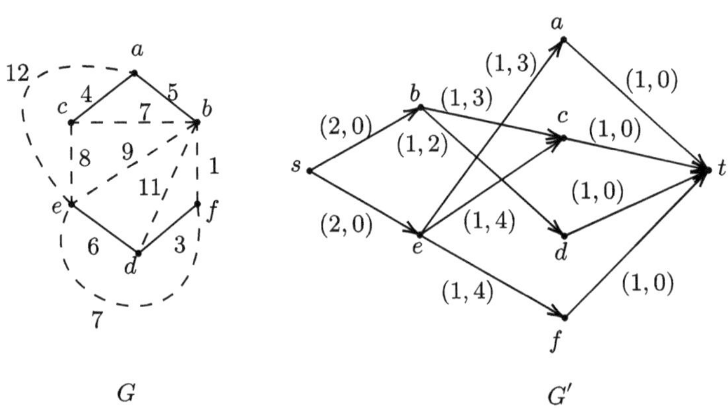


**Fig. 1.** Illustration for constructing the network $G'$ from $G$.

### 3.2 The Local Search Algorithm

Our local search algorithm Approx1 for MW$k^-$SP begins with a feasible solution $SOL$ and an arbitrarily selected star $S$ in it. It then runs the subroutine Gain on a modified solution $SOL' = SOL \setminus \{S\}$ for each subset $V' \subseteq V$ with cardinality no more than $k$. The current solution $SOL$ will switch to $SOL_{\text{Gain}(V',SOL')}$ if the resulting gain $\omega(\text{Gain}(V', SOL')) > \omega(S)$. In other words, the solution is updated whenever the total weight strictly increases. We give a detailed description in the following.

---

**Approx1: A local Search Algorithm for MW$k^-$SP**

---

**Input:** An undirected complete graph $G = (V, E)$ with a non-negative weight function $\omega : E \rightarrow \mathbb{R}^+$.
**Output:** A $k^-$-star packing $SOL$ of $G$.
1: Construct an arbitrary feasible solution $SOL$.
2: **repeat**
3:   **for** each star $S \in SOL$ **do**
4:     Let $target = \omega(S)$ be the weight of the star $S$.
5:     Remove $S$ from $SOL$, obtaining a modified solution $SOL' = SOL \setminus \{S\}$.
6:     **for** each subset $V' \subseteq V$ with $|V'| \leq k$ **do**
7:       Run the subroutine Gain$(V', SOL')$, and compute $\omega(\text{Gain}(V', SOL'))$ and $SOL_{\text{Gain}(V',SOL')}$.
8:       **if** $\omega(\text{Gain}(V', SOL')) > target$ **then**
9:         Update $SOL \leftarrow SOL_{\text{Gain}(V',SOL')}$ and go to line 2.
10:       **end if**
11:     **end for**
12:   **end for**
13: **until** no improvement is found after examining all stars $S \in SOL$ and all subsets $V' \subseteq V$ with $|V'| \leq k$
14: **return** $SOL$;

---

We claim that for any fixed $k$, the above algorithm can be implemented to run in polynomial time. Note that in each iteration, the algorithm enumerates all stars in the current solution $SOL$ and all subsets of $V$ with cardinality no more than $k$. For each such $V'$, it invokes the subroutine Gain, which computes a maximum-cost maximum flow in $O(|V|^3)$ time. Therefore, each iteration of the algorithm requires at most $O(|V|^{k+4})$ time. If the edge weights are polynomially bounded by the input size, then the total weight increase must be polynomially bounded too. This ensures a polynomial number of iterations as each iteration strictly increases the total weight of the solution. In fact, using the standard technique introduced in [13], the edge weights can be rounded into polynomially many values with only a negligible loss in the approximation ratio. In summary, the algorithm Approx1 can be made to run in polynomial time for any fixed $k$.

Now let's analyze the approximation ratio of the algorithm. For each star $S \in SOL$, define a bundle of optimal stars $\mathcal{B}_S = \{S^* \in OPT : V(S^*) \cap V(S) \neq \emptyset\}$.

Since a star in any feasible solution of MW$k^-$SP contains at most $k$ vertices, it can intersect at most $k$ stars in any other solution. Accordingly, we must have $|\mathcal{B}_S| \leq k$ and each star $S^* \in OPT$ appears in at most $k$ such bundles. Based on the construction of $\mathcal{B}_S$ and the properties of the subroutine GAIN, we can obtain the following two inequalities.

**Lemma 1.** *For any star $S \in SOL$ and its corresponding $\mathcal{B}_S$, we have*

$$\sum_{S^* \in \mathcal{B}_S} \omega(S^*) - \sum_{v \in V(\mathcal{B}_S) \setminus V(S)} touch(v) \leq \omega(S). \tag{1}$$

*Proof.* Consider the following operation. Remove $S$ from $SOL$ to obtain a new solution $SOL'$, and take the centers of all stars in $\mathcal{B}_S$ as the candidate set $V'$. Note in $SOL'$, we have $touch(v) = 0$ for every vertex $v \in V(S)$, while for any other vertex $v$, the value of $touch(v)$ remains the same as in $SOL$. According to the algorithm, the output solution $SOL$ is locally optimal, which means that $\text{GAIN}(V', SOL') \leq \omega(S)$. Because all stars in $\mathcal{B}_S$ together form a maximum flow in the subroutine GAIN, the cost of this flow is no less than $\sum_{S^* \in \mathcal{B}_S} \omega(S^*) - \sum_{v \in V(\mathcal{B}_S) \setminus V(S)} touch(v)$. Consequently, we obtain the gain $\text{GAIN}(V', SOL') \geq \sum_{S^* \in \mathcal{B}_S} \omega(S^*) - \sum_{v \in V(\mathcal{B}_S) \setminus V(S)} touch(v)$. This completes the proof.

**Lemma 2.** *For any star $S^* \in OPT$, we can conclude that*

$$\omega(S^*) \leq \sum_{v \in V(S^*)} touch(v). \tag{2}$$

*Proof.* For any star $S^* \in OPT$, consider taking its center $c^*$ as a single candidate set. By the local optimality condition, applying the subroutine $\text{GAIN}(\{c^*\}, SOL)$ cannot yield an improvement either. This follows that $\omega(S^*) \leq \sum_{v \in V(S^*)} touch(v)$.

Lemma 1 and Lemma 2 give the upper bound of the weight of $S^* \in OPT$ and the lower bound of the weight of $S \in SOL$, respectively. To derive the approximation ratio, we rewrite Eq. (1) as

$$\sum_{S^* \in \mathcal{B}_S} \omega(S^*) \leq \omega(S) + \sum_{v \in V(\mathcal{B}_S)} touch(v) - \sum_{v \in V(S)} touch(v). \tag{3}$$

Now we count each star in $OPT$ exactly $k$ times in the following way.

- For each $S \in SOL$, every bundle $\mathcal{B}_S$ is counted once via Eq. (3).
- If any optimal star $S^* \in OPT$ appears fewer than $k$ times, we repeatedly apply Eq. (2) until it has been counted exactly $k$ times.

Summing all these inequalities, the left-hand side becomes $k \cdot opt$. On the right-hand side, each $\omega(S)$ (for $S \in SOL$) appears exactly once from Eq. (3), contributing a total of $sol$. We now explain why each vertex $v \in V$ contributes its $touch(v)$ exactly $k-1$ times on the right-hand side after summing all inequalities. The contribution of $touch(v)$ comes from the following three sources.

- From $\sum_{v \in V(\mathcal{B}_S)} touch(v)$ in Eq. (3): For each $S \in SOL$, if $v \in V(\mathcal{B}_S)$, then $touch(v)$ is counted once. Let $\alpha_v$ be the number of stars $S \in SOL$ such that $v \in V(\mathcal{B}_S)$. Then this source contributes $\alpha_v$ copies of $touch(v)$.
- From $-\sum_{v \in V(S)} touch(v)$ in Eq. (3): Since $v$ belongs to exactly one star in $SOL$, it is subtracted exactly once. This contributes -1 copy of $touch(v)$.
- From Eq. (2): Let $S^*$ be the star in $OPT$ that contains $v$. To ensure that $S^*$ is counted exactly $k$ times in total (across both Eq. (2) and Eq. (3)), we apply Eq. (2) exactly $k - \alpha_v$ times. Each such application contributes one copy of $touch(v)$.

Thus, for any $v \in V$, by summing all contributions of $touch(v)$ from the three sources, the total number of $touch(v)$ appears is $\alpha_v - 1 + (k - \alpha_v) = k - 1$. Hence we can obtain the following inequality and get the approximation ratio:

$$k \cdot opt \leq sol + (k-1) \cdot \sum_{v \in V} touch(v) = sol + 2(k-1) \cdot sol,$$

where the last equation is from $\sum_{v \in V} touch(v) = 2 \cdot sol$.

**Theorem 1.** Approx1 *is a* $\frac{k}{2k-1}$*-approximation algorithm for* $MWk^{-}SP$.

## 4 Approximate the Problem of MW$k$SP

In this section, we present a local search algorithm Approx2 for MW$k$SP that achieves an approximation ratio of $\frac{1}{2}$. Once the set of centers is fixed, the optimal assignment of satellites to these centers can be determined by a network flow algorithm. Therefore, our algorithm iteratively updates the current center set by changing up to $k$ vertices at each step. Details are shown in Approx2.

First, we give the time complexity of Approx2. In each iteration, the algorithm enumerates all subsets $R \subseteq c(SOL)$ of size $k$ and all subsets $A \subseteq V \setminus c'$ of size $k$. The number of such combinations is at most $C_n^k \cdot C_{|V|}^k$, which is $O(n^{2k} \cdot k^k)$ for fixed $k$. For each candidate center set $c_{\text{new}}$, the optimal assignment of satellites is computed via the network flow algorithm in [1]. This reduces to a maximum-cost maximum flow problem in a bipartite graph with $k \cdot n$ vertices and $k \cdot n \cdot (n-1)$ edges, which can be solved in $O((k \cdot n)^3)$. Since each improving iteration strictly increases the total weight of the solution. If the edge weights of $G$ are polynomially bounded, the algorithm runs in polynomial time.

We now analyze the approximation ratio of the algorithm. Although the exchange operation is defined with a fixed size $k$, in the analysis we allow exchanges of size less than $k$, as long as $R \cap A \neq \emptyset$. To facilitate the analysis, we classify the stars in $OPT$ according to their intersection with the center set $c(SOL)$ of the current local optimum solution $SOL$.

- $\mathcal{O}_1$: the set of stars in $OPT$ that contain at least one vertex from $c(SOL)$;
- $\mathcal{O}_2$: the set of stars in $OPT$ that contain no vertex from $c(SOL)$.

**APPROX2: A local Search Algorithm for MWkSP**

**Input:** An undirected complete graph $G = (V, E)$ with $|V| = k \times n$, and a non-negative weight function $\omega : E \rightarrow \mathbb{R}^+$.
**Output:** A $k$-star packing $SOL$ of $G$.
Construct an arbitrary feasible $k$-star packing $SOL$ of $G$, consisting of stars $\{S_1, S_2, \ldots, S_n\}$. Let $c(SOL)$ denote the set of centers in $SOL$.
**repeat**
  **for** each subset $R \subseteq c(SOL)$ with $|R| = k$ **do**
    Remove the $k$ stars centered at vertices in $R$ from $SOL$. Let $c' = c(SOL) \setminus R$.
    **for** each subset $A \subseteq V \setminus c'$ with $|A| = k$ **do**
      Construct a new candidate center set $c_{\text{new}} = c' \cup A$.
      Compute the optimal assignment of satellites to centers in $c_{\text{new}}$ via the maximum-cost maximum-flow algorithm shown in [1], obtaining a new solution $SOL_{\text{new}}$.
      **if** $\omega(SOL_{\text{new}}) > \omega(SOL)$ **then**
        Update $SOL \leftarrow SOL_{\text{new}}$ and go to line 2.
      **end if**
    **end for**
  **end for**
**until** no improvement is found after examining all possible $R \subseteq c(SOL)$ of size $k$.
**return** $SOL$;

For each star $S \in \mathcal{O}_1$, let $i_S = |V(S) \cap c(SOL)|$, i.e., the number of centers of $SOL$ that belong to $S$. Note that $1 \leq i_S \leq k$. We then arbitrarily select $i_S - 1$ distinct stars from $\mathcal{O}_2$ and group them together with $S$ to form a bundle $\mathcal{B}_S$.

We claim that such a grouping can be arranged so that every star in $OPT$ appears in exactly one bundle. For stars in $\mathcal{O}_1$, this holds by construction. For stars in $\mathcal{O}_2$, we need to show that they can be assigned to bundles without overlap and that all of them are used. Observe that $|c(SOL)| = n$, since $SOL$ consists of $n$ stars each with exactly one center. The stars in $\mathcal{O}_1$ collectively contain all vertices of $c(SOL)$. Therefore, we have $\sum_{S \in \mathcal{O}_1} i_S = n$. Consequently, $\sum_{S \in \mathcal{O}_1} (i_S - 1) = n - |\mathcal{O}_1|$. On the other hand, since $OPT$ contains $n$ stars, we have $|OPT| = n$ and $|\mathcal{O}_2| = n - |\mathcal{O}_1| = \sum_{S \in \mathcal{O}_1} (i_S - 1)$. This shows that the total number of stars in $\mathcal{O}_2$ exactly equals the total number of "slots" required to form the bundles. By assigning distinct stars from $\mathcal{O}_2$ to each bundle arbitrarily, we can ensure that every star in $\mathcal{O}_2$ appears in exactly one bundle, with no star reused. Thus, we obtain $|\mathcal{O}_1|$ disjoint bundles that form a partition of $OPT$, where each bundle contains one star $S_j$ from $\mathcal{O}_1$ and $i_{S_j} - 1$ stars from $\mathcal{O}_2$.

Similarly, we construct a corresponding partition of $SOL$ into $|\mathcal{O}_1|$ disjoint bundles. For each bundle $\mathcal{B}_s$ (which contains the star $S \in \mathcal{O}_1$), consider the set of centers $V(S) \cap c(SOL)$. These are exactly the $i_S$ centers of $SOL$ that belong to $S$. The stars in $SOL$ centered at these vertices form a natural group, which we denote by $\mathcal{B}'_S$. It is easy to see that $|\mathcal{B}'_S| = |\mathcal{B}_S|$, and the collection $\{\mathcal{B}'_S : S \in \mathcal{O}_1\}$

forms a partition of $SOL$. Based on the construction of $\mathcal{B}_S$ and $\mathcal{B}'_S$, we have the following observation:

**Observation 1.** *All vertices in $V(\mathcal{B}_S) \setminus V(\mathcal{B}'_S)$ are satellites in $SOL$.*

Based on the local optimality condition, no exchange involving fewer than $k$ stars can improve the total weight of $SOL$. We can draw the following conclusions.

**Lemma 3.** *For any bundle $\mathcal{B}_S$ consisting of stars in $OPT$, we have*

$$\sum_{T\in\mathcal{B}_S} \omega(T) \leq \sum_{T\in\mathcal{B}'_S} \omega(T) + \sum_{v\in V(\mathcal{B}_S)\setminus V(\mathcal{B}'_S)} touch(v). \quad (4)$$

*Proof.* Consider the following exchange operation: replace the centers of the stars in a bundle $\mathcal{B}'_S$ (which are all from $c(SOL)$) with the centers of the stars in the corresponding bundle $\mathcal{B}_S$.

Although the exact configuration after the exchange may differ, we can at least obtain a feasible solution that includes all stars in $\mathcal{B}_S$. In this new solution, the total weight contributed by these stars is $\sum_{T\in\mathcal{B}_S} \omega(T)$. Meanwhile, we would lose the stars originally in $\mathcal{B}'_S$, whose total weight is $\sum_{T\in\mathcal{B}'_S} \omega(T)$. Additionally, we need to account for the edges incident to vertices in $V(\mathcal{B}_S) \setminus V(\mathcal{B}'_S)$ that are currently present in $SOL$. The total weight of these edges is denoted by $\sum_{v\in V(\mathcal{B}_S)\setminus V(\mathcal{B}'_S)} touch(v)$. Since the exchange does not yield an improvement, we have $\sum_{T\in\mathcal{B}_S} \omega(T) \leq \sum_{T\in\mathcal{B}'_S} \omega(T) + \sum_{v\in V(\mathcal{B}_S)\setminus V(\mathcal{B}'_S)} touch(v)$.

Lemma 3 provides an upper bound for the weight of every bundle in $OPT$. Summing the Eq. (4) over all bundles $\mathcal{B}$, we have

$$\sum_{S\in\mathcal{O}_1}\sum_{T\in\mathcal{B}_S} \omega(T) \leq \sum_{S\in\mathcal{O}_1}\sum_{T\in\mathcal{B}'_S} \omega(T) + \sum_{S\in\mathcal{O}_1}\sum_{v\in V(\mathcal{B}_S)\setminus V(\mathcal{B}'_S)} touch(v). \quad (5)$$

Since the bundles $\{\mathcal{B}_S\}_{S\in\mathcal{O}_1}$ partition $OPT$ and $\{\mathcal{B}'_S\}_{S\in\mathcal{O}_1}$ partition $SOL$ the left-hand side equals *opt* and the first term on the right-hand side equals *sol*.

For the second term, according to Observation 1, each vertex in $V(\mathcal{B}_S)\setminus V(\mathcal{B}'_S)$ is a satellite in $SOL$. Each satellite belongs to exactly one $\mathcal{B}_S$. Therefore,

$$\sum_{S\in\mathcal{O}_1}\sum_{v\in V(\mathcal{B}_S)\setminus V(\mathcal{B}n'_S)} touch(v) \leq \sum_{v\in s(SOL)} touch(v) = sol. \quad (6)$$

Combining Eq. (5) and (6), we have $opt \leq sol + \sum_{v\in V(\mathcal{B}_S)\setminus V(\mathcal{B}'_S)} touch(v) \leq 2sol$ and derive the following theorem.

**Theorem 2.** APPROX2 *is a $\frac{1}{2}$-approximation algorithm for the MWkSP.*

## 5 Refine the Algorithms for $\{1,2\}$-Weighted Graphs

Recall that any $\rho$-approximation algorithm for problem MW$k$PP on $\{0,1\}$-weighted graphs can be directly converted to a $\frac{1+\rho}{2}$-approximation algorithm on $\{1,2\}$-weighted graphs [22]. We observe the same transformation can be applied to the problem of MW$k$SP too. Therefore, the algorithm APPROX2 (for $\{0,1\}$-weighted graphs) presented in previous section can directly yield a $\frac{3}{4}$-approximation algorithm for MW$k$SP on $\{1,2\}$-weighted graphs.

**Theorem 3.** APPROX2 *is a* $\frac{3}{4}$*-approximation algorithm for MW*$k$*SP on* $\{1,2\}$*-weighted graphs.*

However, when considering the MW$k^-$SP problem, the transformation of approxiamtion algorithms from $\{0,1\}$-weighted graphs to $\{1,2\}$-weighted graphs becomes invalid. This is because the number of edges within stars of a feasible solution $SOL$ and an optimal solution $OPT$ of MW$k^-$SP might not be equal, violating the key condition of the transformation [22]. Nevertheless, by including the trivial 1-stars in each solution, we see the following observation holds trivially.

**Observation 2.** *For any feasible solution* $SOL$ *to the MW*$k^-$*SP problem on graph* $G$, $|E(SOL)| = |V(G)| - |SOL|$.

From Observation 2, the numbers of edges within stars of $SOL$ and $OPT$ could be equal if $SOL$ and $OPT$ have the same number of stars, i.e., $|SOL| = |OPT|$. Consequently, we refine our algorithm APPROX2 by enumerating, before it starts, the number of stars in an optimal solution, which takes $O(|V|)$ time. Then we apply APPROX2 to output a fixed number of $k^-$-stars of maximum weight. Here the number is set to the guessed $|OPT|$. One may see from the proof of Theorem 2 that APPROX2 can approximate this problem within the same ratio of $\frac{1}{2}$ as the original one. Accordingly, the refined APPROX2 can be transformed to solve MW$k^-$SP on $\{1,2\}$-weighted graphs, which gives the following theorem.

**Theorem 4.** *There exists a* $\frac{3}{4}$*-approximation algorithm for MW*$k^-$*SP on* $\{1,2\}$*-weighted graphs.*

## 6 Conclusion

In this paper, we studied the maximum weight star packing problem parameterized by a fixed positive integer $k$. For MW$k^-$SP and MW$k$SP, we presented a $\frac{k}{2k-1}$-approximation algorithm and a $\frac{1}{2}$-approximation algorithm respectively. When restricting the two problems on $\{1,2\}$-weighted graphs, we refined the algorithms to achieve a better approximation ratio of $\frac{3}{4}$. All our algorithms are based on local search and outperform the previous known results.

**Acknowledgements.** This research is supported by the NSFC Grants (No. 12371316, 12471301, 12571337, 92567201), the Zhejiang Provincial NSF Grant (No. LZ25A010001), and the NSF Grant of Shanghai (No. 24ZR1416900).

## References


1. Arkin, E.M., Hassin, R., Rubinstein, S., Sviridenko, M.: Approximations for maximum transportation problem with permutable supply vector and other capacitated star packing problems. Algorithmica **39**(2), 175–187 (2004)
2. Babenko, M., Gusakov, A.: New exact and approximation algorithms for the star packing problem in undirected graphs. In: Proceedings of the 28th Symposium on Theoretical Aspects of Computer Science, pp. 519–530 (2011)
3. Bar-Noy, A., Peleg, D., Rabanca, G., Vigan, I.: Improved approximation algorithms for weighted 2-path partitions. Discret. Appl. Math. **239**, 15–37 (2018)
4. Biro, P., Manlove, D.F., Rizzi, R.: Maximum weight cycle packing in directed graphs, with application to kidney exchange programs. Discret. Math. Algorithms Appl. **1**(4), 499–517 (2009)
5. Buchbinder, N., Feldman, M., Seffi, J., Schwartz, R.: A tight linear time (1/2)-approximation for unconstrained submodular maximization. SIAM J. Comput. **44**(5), 1384–1402 (2015)
6. Buchbinder, N., Feldman, M.: Deterministic algorithms for submodular maximization problems. ACM Trans. Algorithms **14**(3), 1–20 (2018)
7. Buchbinder, N., Feldman, M.: Constrained submodular maximization via new bounds for DR-submodular functions. In: Proceedings of the 56th Annual ACM Symposium on Theory of Computing, pp. 1820–1831 (2024)
8. Ford, L. R., Fulkerson, D. R.: Flows in Networks. Princeton University Press (1963)
9. Han, N., Yu, W., Liu, Z.: Approximation algorithms for the metric maximum-weight $k$-star partition problem. Accepted for publication in COCOA 2025 (2025)
10. Hassin, R., Rubinstein, S.: An approximation algorithm for maximum packing of 3-edge paths. Inf. Process. Lett. **63**(2), 63–67 (1997)
11. Kirkpatrick, D.G., Hell, P.: On the complexity of general graph factor problems. SIAM J. Comput. **12**(3), 601–609 (1983)
12. Korte, B., Vygen, J.: Combinatorial Optimization: Theory and Algorithms, 6th edn. Springer, New York (2018)
13. Kutiel, G., Rawitz, D.: Local search algorithms for the maximum carpool matching problem. Algorithmica **82**(11), 3165–3182 (2020)
14. Lawler, E.L.: Combinatorial Optimization: Networks and Matroids. Holt, Rinehart and Winston, New York (1976)
15. Li, S., Yu, W.: Approximation algorithms for the maximum-weight cycle/path packing problems. Asia-Pacific J. Oper. Res. **40**(4), 2340003 (2023)
16. Lin, C., Cui, L., Coit, D.W., Lv, M.: Performance analysis for a wireless sensor network of star topology with random nodes deployment. Wireless Pers. Commun. **97**(3), 3993–4013 (2017)
17. Monnot, J., Toulouse, S.: Approximation results for the weighted $P_4$ partition problem. J. Discret. Algorithms **6**(2), 299–312 (2008)
18. Nagarajan, V., Sviridenko, M.: On the maximum quadratic assignment problem. Math. Oper. Res. **34**(4), 859–868 (2009)
19. Palsetia, D., Patwary, M.M.A., Hendrix, W., Agrawal, A., Choudhary, A.: Clique guided community detection. In: 2014 IEEE International Conference on Big Data (Big Data), pp. 500–509 (2014)
20. Shmoys, D.B., Tardos, E., Aardal, K.: Approximation algorithms for facility location problems. In: Proceedings of the 29th Annual ACM Symposium on Theory of Computing, pp. 265–274 (1997)

21. Thiery, T., Ward, J.: An improved approximation for maximum weighted $k$-set packing. In: Proceedings of the 2023 Annual ACM-SIAM Symposium on Discrete Algorithms, pp. 1138–1162 (2023)
22. Zhao, J., Xiao, M.: Approximation algorithms for cycle and path partitions in complete graphs. Theoret. Comput. Sci. **1029**, 115049 (2025)
23. Zhao, J., Xiao, M.: An improved approximation algorithm for maximum weight 3-path packing. arXiv preprint arXiv:2512.14457 (2025)
24. Zhao, J., Xiao, M.: A deterministic approximation algorithm for metric triangle packing. Theoret. Comput. Sci. **1010**, 114699 (2024)

# Six Standard Playing Cards Are Sufficient for All Three-Input Boolean Functions

Masanori Kabutomori[1] and Takaaki Mizuki[2](✉)

[1] School of Engineering, Tohoku University, Sendai 980–8578, Japan
[2] Cyberscience Center, Tohoku University, Sendai 980–8578, Japan
mizuki+lncs@tohoku.ac.jp

**Abstract.** This paper deals with secure computation using a standard deck of playing cards. Since the first protocol using playing cards was devised by Niemi and Renvall in 1999, several secure computation protocols have been proposed. In 2022, Haga et al. proposed a generic protocol that securely computes three-input Boolean functions using six playing cards. However, this did not cover all three-input Boolean functions, and determining whether there exist six-card protocols for all such functions remained an open problem. In this paper, we construct protocols using six playing cards for each three-input Boolean function for which a protocol has not yet been built, thereby resolving this open problem.

**Keywords:** Card-based cryptography · Secure computation · Playing cards

## 1 Introduction

The method of realizing secure computation and other cryptographic tasks using a physical deck of cards is referred to as *card-based cryptography* [6,17]. In many existing card-based protocols, a special deck of cards, called a "two-color deck," is used, in which their front sides are $\boxed{\heartsuit}$ and $\boxed{\clubsuit}$, and their back sides $\boxed{?}$ are indistinguishable. On the other hand, there are also several existing studies using commercially available playing cards (like $\boxed{2\clubsuit}\boxed{6\diamondsuit}\boxed{4\spadesuit}$), and this paper deals with secure computation protocols using such a standard deck of playing cards.

### 1.1 Protocols Using Playing Cards

Secure computation protocols using commercially available playing cards were first proposed by Niemi and Renvall [20] in 1999. Since there are 52 unique playing cards (excluding jokers), determined by the combination of a rank (from 1 to 13) and a suit ($\clubsuit, \spadesuit, \heartsuit, \diamondsuit$), a deck of playing cards can be mapped to integers from 1 to 52, so that we have 52 numbered cards $\boxed{1}\boxed{2}\boxed{3}\cdots$ whose backs $\boxed{?}$ are all identical. Niemi and Renvall encoded a one-bit value using a pair of cards $\boxed{i}$ and $\boxed{j}$ with $1 \le i < j \le 52$ as follows:

$$\boxed{i}\boxed{j} = 0, \quad \boxed{j}\boxed{i} = 1.$$


Y. Li et al. (Eds.): COCOON 2026, LNCS 16835, pp. 383–396, 2027.
https://doi.org/10.1007/978-981-92-3309-0_29

That is, if the card on the left is smaller, it represents 0; if the card on the left is larger, it represents 1. When a bit $x \in \{0,1\}$ is represented with $\boxed{i}$ and $\boxed{j}$ placed face down, these two cards are called a *commitment* to $x$ and are written as:

$$\underbrace{\boxed{?}\,\boxed{?}}_{[x]^{\{i,j\}}},$$

where the set $\{i, j\}$ is called the *base* of the commitment, and this notation is sometimes omitted.

Secure computation protocols are usually constructed using commitments defined above as input. For example, a secure computation of the NOT operation can be realized easily: given a commitment to $x$, swapping the left and right cards of the commitment yields a commitment to $\overline{x}$:

$$\underbrace{\boxed{?}\,\boxed{?}}_{[x]^{\{i,j\}}} \quad \rightarrow \quad \boxed{?} \rightleftharpoons \boxed{?} \quad \rightarrow \quad \underbrace{\boxed{?}\,\boxed{?}}_{[\overline{x}]^{\{i,j\}}}.$$

## 1.2 Previous Research and Open Problem

The aforementioned Niemi and Renvall [20] specifically proposed an AND protocol:

$$\underbrace{\boxed{?}\,\boxed{?}}_{[a]^{\{1,2\}}}\underbrace{\boxed{?}\,\boxed{?}}_{[b]^{\{3,4\}}}\boxed{5} \rightarrow \cdots \rightarrow \underbrace{\boxed{?}\,\boxed{?}}_{[a \wedge b]}.$$

That is, given two commitments to $a, b \in \{0,1\}$, it produces a commitment[1] to $a \wedge b$. This protocol uses 5 cards and 7.5 shuffles (expected value), the outline of which will be presented in Sect. 2.4. Niemi and Renvall also constructed XOR and copy protocols[2].

Following this research, several protocols have been devised. The progress regarding AND and XOR protocols is shown in Table 1. As can be seen from this table, protocols using four cards exist for both AND and XOR. Since the two-bit input is given as two commitments, four cards are necessary, making these protocols optimal in terms of the number of cards. Furthermore, protocols for all other two-input Boolean functions besides AND and XOR can also be constructed with four cards by modifying the AND or XOR protocol (along with the NOT computation). Thus, the problem of finding *card-minimal* protocols for all two-input Boolean functions was already resolved.

Next, we look at three-input Boolean functions $f : \{0,1\}^3 \rightarrow \{0,1\}$. How about the card-minimality problem for three inputs? We want to construct a

---

1 Such a protocol that produces a commitment as output (without leaking any information) is called a *committed-format* protocol; this paper only considers committed-format protocols.

2 This implies that any Boolean function can be securely computed (provided that sufficient numbers of cards and shuffles are available) because we can construct a protocol for it by combining the AND, XOR, and copy protocols based on its circuit.

**Table 1.** Existing protocols for two-input Boolean functions (where #Cards and #Shuffles mean the numbers of required cards and shuffles, respectively).

| Function | #Cards | #Shuffles | Authors |
|---|---|---|---|
| AND | 5 | 7.5 (exp.) | Niemi & Renvall [20] |
| | 8 | 4 | Mizuki [15] |
| | 4 | 6 (exp.) | Koch et al. [7] |
| XOR | 4 | 7 (exp.) | Niemi & Renvall [20] |
| | 4 | 1 | Mizuki [15] |
| | 4 | 1 | Koyama et al. [10] |

**Table 2.** Existing protocols for three-input Boolean functions (#Cards and #Shuffles mean the numbers of required cards and shuffles, respectively). For details on the "140 functions," see Sect. 3.1.

| Function | #Cards | #Shuffles | Authors |
|---|---|---|---|
| 3-AND | 6 | 8.5 (exp.) | Koyama et al. [9] |
| 140 functions | 6 | 8.5 (exp.) | Haga et al. [2] |

protocol using only three input commitments to $a, b, c \in \{0, 1\}$, i.e., only six cards:

$$\underbrace{\boxed{?}\boxed{?}}_{[a]^{\{1,2\}}}\underbrace{\boxed{?}\boxed{?}}_{[b]^{\{3,4\}}}\underbrace{\boxed{?}\boxed{?}}_{[c]^{\{5,6\}}} \rightarrow \cdots \rightarrow \underbrace{\boxed{?}\boxed{?}}_{[f(a,b,c)]}.$$

In 2021, Koyama et al. [9] constructed a three-input AND protocol (with six cards) with an expected number of 8.5 shuffles. Subsequently, by extending this protocol, Haga et al. [2] constructed six-card protocols for 140 out of 256 three-input Boolean functions. These are listed in Table 2. Thus, the previous studies did not fully cover three-input Boolean functions.

Therefore, whether six-card protocols can be constructed for the remaining 116 three-input Boolean functions is considered an open problem, and we tackle this problem.

### 1.3 Our Contribution

The main contribution of this paper is to show that six-card protocols can be constructed for all 116 of the three-input Boolean functions previously unaddressed, thereby completely resolving this open problem.

Since dealing with all 256 three-input Boolean functions individually is tedious, we consider *NPN equivalence classes*. In NPN equivalence classes, functions that can be transformed into each other by negation of input variables (Negation), permutation of input variable order (Permutation), and negation of the output result (Negation) are considered to be in the same equivalence class. In card-based protocols, the NOT operation and variable swapping are trivial,

**Table 3.** Number of shuffles for six-card three-input Boolean function protocols

| | And3 | XorAnd | OrAnd | Onehot | Majority | Equality | Dot | Mux | AndXor | Xor3 |
|---|---|---|---|---|---|---|---|---|---|---|
| Koyama et al. [9] | 8.5 | — | — | — | — | — | — | — | — | — |
| Haga et al. [2] | 8.5 | 8.5 | 8.5 | — | 8.5 | 8.5 | — | 8.5 | 8.5 | — |
| Reducing to 2-input | — | 7 | — | — | — | — | — | — | 7 | 2 |
| This paper | — | — | — | 10.5 | — | — | 10.5 | — | — | — |

so if a secure computation protocol exists for a certain function, a protocol also exists for all functions in the same NPN equivalence class (with the same numbers of cards and shuffles). Therefore, for each equivalence class, we only need to construct a protocol for a single representative function.

It is known that there are a total of 14 NPN equivalence classes for three-input Boolean functions [23]. We list the representative functions[3] for the 10 equivalence classes excluding the trivial ones (i.e., 0, $a$, $a \wedge b$, and $a \oplus b$):

$$\begin{aligned}
\mathsf{And3}(a,b,c) &= a \wedge b \wedge c \\
\mathsf{XorAnd}(a,b,c) &= a \wedge (b \oplus c) \\
\mathsf{OrAnd}(a,b,c) &= a \wedge (b \vee c) \\
\mathsf{Onehot}(a,b,c) &= (a \wedge \overline{b} \wedge \overline{c}) \oplus (\overline{a} \wedge b \wedge \overline{c}) \oplus (\overline{a} \wedge \overline{b} \wedge c) \\
\mathsf{Majority}(a,b,c) &= (a \wedge b) \vee (b \wedge c) \vee (a \wedge c) \\
\mathsf{Equality}(a,b,c) &= (a \wedge b \wedge c) \oplus (\overline{a} \wedge \overline{b} \wedge \overline{c}) \\
\mathsf{Dot}(a,b,c) &= a \oplus (c \vee (a \wedge b)) \\
\mathsf{Mux}(a,b,c) &= (a \wedge b) \vee (\overline{a} \wedge c) \\
\mathsf{AndXor}(a,b,c) &= a \oplus (b \wedge c) \\
\mathsf{Xor3}(a,b,c) &= a \oplus b \oplus c\,.
\end{aligned}$$

Among these 10 representatives, the ones that cannot be handled by the method of Haga et al. [2] are three: Onehot, Dot, and Xor3. Since Xor3 can be realized by repeating existing two-input XOR protocols [15,20] twice, the truly unresolved ones are Onehot and Dot. For these, we construct six-card protocols in this paper, whose number of shuffles is 10.5 (expected value). Table 3 summarizes the previous research and the results of this paper. Thus, this paper proves that there always exists a six-card protocol for every three-input Boolean function, successfully closing the open problem.

### 1.4 Related Work

Closely related to the setting of this paper, partial opening actions on playing cards were devised in [14], followed by [4,5]; efficient protocols have been

[3] The names of the functions are partially based on literature [12].

designed. If private operations are allowed, efficient protocols can be obtained [11,19].

Aside from secure computations, Ruangwises [22] developed zero-knowledge proof protocols for Sudoku using playing cards. Such zero-knowledge proof protocols for puzzles have been constructed with the help of a two-color deck, e.g., [1,3,21].

### 1.5 Organization of This Paper

The remainder of this paper is organized as follows. In Sect. 2, we describe the computational model of card-based protocols, and introduce some kinds of shuffles and previous methods. In Sect. 3, we classify the protocols of Haga et al. [2] into NPN equivalence classes. In Sect. 4, we present our protocols to resolve the open problem. Finally, Sect. 5 provides a conclusion.

## 2 Preliminaries

In this section, we briefly introduce the computational model of card-based protocols, two kinds of shuffles, and existing methods.

### 2.1 Computational Model of Card-Based Protocols

Card-based protocols are formally defined via abstract machines [16]. In the computational model, a protocol applies a series of three actions, turn, perm, and shuf, to a sequence of cards. We briefly explain these three actions below.

**Permute.** Apply a certain permutation $\pi \in S_\ell$ to a sequence of cards. Here, $S_\ell$ represents the symmetric group of degree $\ell$, and this action is written as $(\mathsf{perm}, \pi)$:

$$\overset{1}{\boxed{?}}\,\overset{2}{\boxed{?}}\cdots\overset{\ell}{\boxed{?}} \xrightarrow{(\mathsf{perm},\pi)} \overset{\pi^{-1}(1)}{\boxed{?}}\ \overset{\pi^{-1}(2)}{\boxed{?}}\ \cdots\ \overset{\pi^{-1}(\ell)}{\boxed{?}}\ .$$

**Turn.** Turn over the $t$-th card from the left of a sequence. This action is written as $(\mathsf{turn}, \{t\})$:

$$\overset{1}{\boxed{?}}\,\overset{2}{\boxed{?}}\cdots\overset{t}{\boxed{?}}\cdots\overset{\ell}{\boxed{?}} \xrightarrow{(\mathsf{turn},\{t\})} \overset{1}{\boxed{?}}\,\overset{2}{\boxed{?}}\cdots\overset{t}{\boxed{3}}\cdots\overset{\ell}{\boxed{?}}.$$

**Shuffle.** For a sequence of cards, apply a permutation $\pi \in \Pi$ chosen uniformly at random from a certain set of permutations $\Pi \subseteq S_\ell$. This action is written as $(\mathsf{shuf}, \Pi)$:

$$\overset{1}{\boxed{?}}\,\overset{2}{\boxed{?}}\cdots\overset{\ell}{\boxed{?}} \xrightarrow{(\mathsf{shuf},\Pi)} \overset{\pi^{-1}(1)}{\boxed{?}}\ \overset{\pi^{-1}(2)}{\boxed{?}}\ \cdots\ \overset{\pi^{-1}(\ell)}{\boxed{?}}\ .$$

We here assume that nobody knows which permutation was applied among the permutations included in $\Pi$.

### 2.2 Random Cut

A random cut is a shuffle that cyclically shifts a sequence of cards. When a random cut is applied to a sequence of $\ell$ cards, it becomes one of the $\ell$ possible sequences, each with a probability of $1/\ell$, written as follows:

$$\left\langle \overset{1}{\boxed{?}}\overset{2}{\boxed{?}}\cdots\overset{\ell-1}{\boxed{?}}\overset{\ell}{\boxed{?}} \right\rangle \rightarrow \begin{cases} \overset{1}{\boxed{?}}\overset{2}{\boxed{?}}\cdots\overset{\ell-1}{\boxed{?}}\overset{\ell}{\boxed{?}} \\ \overset{2}{\boxed{?}}\overset{3}{\boxed{?}}\cdots\overset{\ell}{\boxed{?}}\overset{1}{\boxed{?}} \\ \qquad\vdots \\ \overset{\ell-1}{\boxed{?}}\overset{\ell}{\boxed{?}}\cdots\overset{\ell-3}{\boxed{?}}\overset{\ell-2}{\boxed{?}} \\ \overset{\ell}{\boxed{?}}\overset{1}{\boxed{?}}\cdots\overset{\ell-2}{\boxed{?}}\overset{\ell-1}{\boxed{?}} \end{cases}.$$

Formally, it can be written as $(\mathsf{shuf}, \{(1\,2\,\ldots\,\ell)^i \mid 1 \le i \le \ell\})$, where $(1\,2\,\ldots\,\ell)$ represents a cyclic permutation.

### 2.3 Finding a Specific Card by Random Cut

Here, we show the procedure for finding a card with a specific number from a sequence of face-down cards using the random cut [20].

Suppose that there are four face-down cards

$$\boxed{?}\boxed{?}\boxed{?}\boxed{?}$$

known to be composed of $\boxed{1}\boxed{2}\boxed{3}\boxed{4}$ (whose order is secret), and we want to identify $\boxed{1}$. Then, it suffices to repeatedly apply a random cut and turn over the first card until the revealed card becomes $\boxed{1}$:

$$\boxed{?}\boxed{?}\boxed{?}\boxed{?} \rightarrow \left\langle \boxed{?}\boxed{?}\boxed{?}\boxed{?} \right\rangle \rightarrow \boxed{2}\boxed{?}\boxed{?}\boxed{?} \rightarrow \left\langle \boxed{?}\boxed{?}\boxed{?}\boxed{?} \right\rangle \rightarrow \boxed{1}\boxed{?}\boxed{?}\boxed{?}.$$

By virtue of the randomization provided by the random cut, no information other than the fact that the first card is $\boxed{1}$ leaks. The expected number of shuffles (i.e., random cuts) required is four.

When applying this method to identify one of $k$ cards from a sequence of $\ell$ cards, the expected number of shuffles is $\ell/k$. As seen in the next subsection, this method plays an important role in the Niemi–Renvall AND protocol [20].

### 2.4 Niemi–Renvall AND Protocol

As mentioned in Sect. 1.2, the Niemi–Renvall AND protocol takes

$$\underbrace{\boxed{?}\boxed{?}}_{[a]^{\{1,2\}}}\underbrace{\boxed{?}\boxed{?}}_{[b]^{\{3,4\}}}\boxed{5}$$

as input. Let us swap the second and third cards; then, the five-card sequence changes as follows:

| $(a,b)$ | Sequence | | $(a,b)$ | Sequence |
|---|---|---|---|---|
| $(0,0)$ | 1 2 3 4 5 | | $(0,0)$ | 1 3 2 4 5 |
| $(0,1)$ | 1 2 4 3 5 | $\rightarrow$ | $(0,1)$ | 1 4 2 3 5 |
| $(1,0)$ | 2 1 3 4 5 | | $(1,0)$ | 2 3 1 4 5 |
| $(1,1)$ | 2 1 4 3 5 | | $(1,1)$ | 2 4 1 3 5 |

Using the method explained in Sect. 2.3, find $\boxed{2}$ and $\boxed{3}$ by an expected number of $(2.5+4)$ random cuts, and remove them; then, we have a three-card sequence $\boxed{?}\boxed{?}\boxed{?}$ satisfying:

| $(a,b)$ | Sequence | | | | |
|---|---|---|---|---|---|
| $(0,0)$ | 1 4 5 | or | 5 1 4 | or | 4 5 1 |
| $(0,1)$ | 1 4 5 | or | 5 1 4 | or | 4 5 1 |
| $(1,0)$ | 1 4 5 | or | 5 1 4 | or | 4 5 1 |
| $(1,1)$ | 1 5 4 | or | 5 4 1 | or | 4 1 5 |

After applying a random cut, reveal the first card; then, we obtain:

$$\boxed{1}\ \underbrace{\boxed{?}\boxed{?}}_{[a\wedge b]^{\{4,5\}}} \quad \text{or} \quad \boxed{5}\ \underbrace{\boxed{?}\boxed{?}}_{[a\wedge b]^{\{1,4\}}} \quad \text{or} \quad \boxed{4}\ \underbrace{\boxed{?}\boxed{?}}_{[\overline{a\wedge b}]^{\{1,5\}}},$$

as desired (remember that the NOT operation is trivial).

This is the Niemi–Renvall AND protocol [20], enhanced by Koch, Schrempp, and Kirsten [7].

### 2.5 Random Bisection Cut

A random bisection cut [18] is a shuffle that transforms a sequence of $2\ell$ cards into one of the following two states with a probability of $1/2$:

$$\left[\overset{1}{\boxed{?}}\cdots\overset{\ell}{\boxed{?}}\,\middle|\,\overset{\ell+1}{\boxed{?}}\cdots\overset{2\ell}{\boxed{?}}\right] \rightarrow \begin{cases} \overset{1}{\boxed{?}}\cdots\overset{\ell}{\boxed{?}}\,\overset{\ell+1}{\boxed{?}}\cdots\overset{2\ell}{\boxed{?}} \\ \overset{\ell+1}{\boxed{?}}\cdots\overset{2\ell}{\boxed{?}}\,\overset{1}{\boxed{?}}\cdots\overset{\ell}{\boxed{?}} \end{cases}.$$

Formally, it can be written as $(\mathsf{shuf}, \{\mathsf{id},\ (1\ \ell+1)(2\ \ell+2)\ ...\ (\ell\ 2\ell)\})$, where $\mathsf{id}$ is the identity permutation.

## 3 Analyzing Haga et al's Protocols by NPN Equivalence Classes

In this section, for a total of 256 three-input Boolean functions, we identify the functions already solved by existing research by Haga et al. [2], based on the NPN equivalence classes.

**Table 4.** Haga et al.'s results and NPN equivalence class classification

| $h$ \ $g$ | $0$ | $a \wedge b$ | $a \wedge \overline{b}$ | $a$ | $\overline{a} \wedge b$ | $b$ | $a \oplus b$ | $a \vee b$ | $\overline{a \vee b}$ | $\overline{a \oplus b}$ | $\overline{b}$ | $a \vee \overline{b}$ | $\overline{a}$ | $\overline{a} \vee b$ | $\overline{a \wedge b}$ | $1$ |
|---|---|---|---|---|---|---|---|---|---|---|---|---|---|---|---|---|
| $0$ | #1 | #2 | #2 | #3 | #2 | #3 | #4 | #5 | #2 | #4 | #3 | #5 | #3 | #5 | #5 | #6 |
| $a \wedge b$ | #2 | #3 | #4 | #5 | #4 | #5 | #10 | #8 | #9 | #7 | #10 | #11 | #10 | #11 | #12 | #5 |
| $a \wedge \overline{b}$ | #2 | #4 | #3 | #5 | #9 | #10 | #7 | #11 | #4 | #10 | #5 | #8 | #10 | #12 | #11 | #5 |
| $a$ | #3 | #5 | #5 | #6 | #10 | #11 | #12 | #5 | #10 | #12 | #11 | #5 | #13 | #10 | #10 | #3 |
| $\overline{a} \wedge b$ | #2 | #4 | #9 | #10 | #3 | #5 | #7 | #11 | #4 | #10 | #10 | #12 | #5 | #8 | #11 | #5 |
| $b$ | #3 | #5 | #10 | #11 | #5 | #6 | #12 | #5 | #10 | #12 | #13 | #10 | #11 | #5 | #10 | #3 |
| $a \oplus b$ | #4 | #10 | #7 | #12 | #7 | #12 | #13 | #7 | #10 | #14 | #12 | #10 | #12 | #10 | #7 | #4 |
| $a \vee b$ | #5 | #8 | #11 | #5 | #11 | #5 | #7 | #3 | #12 | #10 | #10 | #4 | #10 | #4 | #9 | #2 |
| $\overline{a \vee b}$ | #2 | #9 | #4 | #10 | #4 | #10 | #10 | #12 | #3 | #7 | #5 | #11 | #5 | #11 | #8 | #5 |
| $\overline{a \oplus b}$ | #4 | #7 | #10 | #12 | #10 | #12 | #14 | #10 | #7 | #13 | #12 | #7 | #12 | #7 | #10 | #4 |
| $\overline{b}$ | #3 | #10 | #5 | #11 | #10 | #13 | #12 | #10 | #5 | #12 | #6 | #5 | #11 | #10 | #5 | #3 |
| $a \vee \overline{b}$ | #5 | #11 | #8 | #5 | #12 | #10 | #10 | #4 | #11 | #7 | #5 | #3 | #10 | #9 | #4 | #2 |
| $\overline{a}$ | #3 | #10 | #10 | #13 | #5 | #11 | #12 | #10 | #5 | #12 | #11 | #10 | #6 | #5 | #5 | #3 |
| $\overline{a} \vee b$ | #5 | #11 | #12 | #10 | #8 | #5 | #10 | #4 | #11 | #7 | #10 | #9 | #5 | #3 | #4 | #2 |
| $\overline{a \wedge b}$ | #5 | #12 | #11 | #10 | #11 | #10 | #7 | #9 | #8 | #10 | #5 | #4 | #5 | #4 | #3 | #2 |
| $1$ | #6 | #5 | #5 | #3 | #5 | #3 | #4 | #2 | #5 | #4 | #3 | #2 | #3 | #2 | #2 | #1 |

### 3.1 Existing Protocols by Haga et al

Haga et al. [2] considered three-input Boolean functions as follows:

$$f(a,b,c) = \begin{cases} g(a,b) & \text{if } c = 1 \\ h(a,b) & \text{if } c = 0 \end{cases} .$$

That is, they represented a three-input Boolean function $f$ using two two-input Boolean functions, $g$ and $h$, and constructed protocols based on this decomposition. In brief, the protocol privately rearranges the four cards of commitments to $a$ and $b$ using a random bisection cut based on the value of commitment to $c$. Then, similar to the Niemi–Renvall AND protocol explained in Sect. 2.4, the protocol finds two specific cards from five cards through repeated random cuts, applies a final random cut, and turns over the first card to obtain an output commitment. The expected number of shuffles is 8.5.

This general-purpose protocol can securely compute the functions highlighted in yellow in Table 4. In this table, a three-input Boolean function $f$ is determined by defining two two-input Boolean functions $g$ and $h$.

Consequently, among the 256 possible functions, six-card protocols have already been constructed for 140 functions. The 116 functions not highlighted in yellow in Table 4 are those that remained unresolved in the existing research by Haga et al. [2].

### 3.2 Analysis Based on NPN Equivalence Classes

In Table 4, we indicate which NPN equivalence class each of the 256 functions belongs to using numbers from #1 to #14. These numbers represent the NPN equivalence classes, defined as shown in Table 5.

**Table 5.** Representative functions of equivalence classes

| Class | #1 | #2 | #3 | #4 | #5 | #6 | #7 | #8 | #9 | #10 | #11 | #12 | #13 | #14 |
|---|---|---|---|---|---|---|---|---|---|---|---|---|---|---|
| Rep. | 0 | And3 | $a \wedge b$ | XorAnd | OrAnd | $a$ | Onehot | Majority | Equality | Dot | Mux | AndXor | $a \oplus b$ | Xor3 |

Recall that Haga et al.'s generic protocol [2] works only for the functions highlighted in yellow in Table 4. Therefore, we find that the NPN equivalence classes not supported by Haga et al.'s generic protocol are #7, #10, and #14 (because these are the numbers not highlighted in yellow across all entries)[4].

Among these three, #14 (namely, $\mathsf{Xor3}(a, b, c) = a \oplus b \oplus c$) can be realized by applying the existing two-input XOR protocol [15] twice. Thus, the truly unresolved classes are #7 (Onehot) and #10 (Dot). In the next section, we construct six-card protocols for these two functions.

Note that for #4 (XorAnd) and #12 (AndXor), protocols can be constructed by combining the existing two-input XOR protocol [15] and two-input AND protocol [7]. The total number of shuffles is 7 (expected value), as shown in Table 3.

Furthermore, #1, #3, #6, and #13 are trivial even without using the protocol by Haga et al. [2]. This is because #1 (0) and #6 ($a$) are a constant and a single-variable function, respectively, requiring no actions; #3 ($a \wedge b$) and #13 ($a \oplus b$) are essentially two-input functions, to which the existing two-input AND protocol [7] or two-input XOR protocol [15] can be applied.

# 4 Proposed Protocols

Recall that the truly unresolved classes are #7 (Onehot) and #10 (Dot). Thus, in this section, we construct a six-card protocol for each of the two functions Onehot and Dot.

## 4.1 Our Protocol for Onehot

In this subsection, we construct a protocol for Onehot. To this end, we exploit the following decomposition:

$$\mathsf{Onehot}(a, b, c) = \begin{cases} b \oplus c & \text{if } a = 0 \\ \overline{b \vee c} & \text{if } a = 1 \end{cases}.$$

Given three commitments to $a, b, c \in \{0, 1\}$, our protocol proceeds as follows.

1. Place the three input commitments as:

$$\underbrace{\boxed{?}\,\boxed{?}}_{[a]^{\{1,2\}}}\;\underbrace{\boxed{?}\,\boxed{?}}_{[b]^{\{3,4\}}}\;\underbrace{\boxed{?}\,\boxed{?}}_{[c]^{\{5,6\}}}.$$

[4] For example, the class #11 has both 'highlighted' and 'non-highlighted' functions, and any non-highlighted function in the class can be computed with six cards by transforming it into any 'highlighted' function in the class.

Then, the six cards (depending on $(a,b,c)$) are as follows:

| $(a,b,c)$ | Sequence | $(a,b,c)$ | Sequence |
|---|---|---|---|
| $(0,0,0)$ | 1 2 3 4 5 6 | $(1,0,0)$ | 2 1 3 4 5 6 |
| $(0,0,1)$ | 1 2 3 4 6 5 | $(1,0,1)$ | 2 1 3 4 6 5 |
| $(0,1,0)$ | 1 2 4 3 5 6 | $(1,1,0)$ | 2 1 4 3 5 6 |
| $(0,1,1)$ | 1 2 4 3 6 5 | $(1,1,1)$ | 2 1 4 3 6 5 |

2. Through steps (a)–(d) below, we swap the third and sixth cards only when $a = 0$ without revealing the value of $a$:
   (a) Permute the sequence by $(\mathsf{perm}, (2\ 3)(4\ 5\ 6))$:

   positions 1 2 3 4 5 6: ? ? ? ? ? ? → positions 1 3 2 6 4 5: ? ? ? ? ? ? .

   (b) Apply a random bisection cut to the leftmost four cards:

   [ ? ? | ? ? ] ? ? → ? ? ? ? ? ? .

   (c) Permute the sequence by $(\mathsf{perm}, (2\ 3)(4\ 6\ 5))$:

   positions 1 2 3 4 5 6: ? ? ? ? ? ? → positions 1 3 2 5 6 4: ? ? ? ? ? ? .

   Note that the first two cards are either 1 2 or 2 1 with equal probability.
   (d) Turn over the first and second cards. If 1 2 appears, permute the sequence by $(\mathsf{perm}, (1\ 2)(3\ 6))$:

   1 2 ? ? ? ? (positions 3 4 5 6) → 2 1 ? ? ? ? (positions 6 4 5 3) .

   Then, the six cards

   2 1 ? ? ? ?

   satisfy:

| $(a,b,c)$ | Sequence | $(a,b,c)$ | Sequence |
|---|---|---|---|
| $(0,0,0)$ | 2 1 6 4 5 3 | $(1,0,0)$ | 2 1 3 4 5 6 |
| $(0,0,1)$ | 2 1 5 4 6 3 | $(1,0,1)$ | 2 1 3 4 6 5 |
| $(0,1,0)$ | 2 1 6 3 5 4 | $(1,1,0)$ | 2 1 4 3 5 6 |
| $(0,1,1)$ | 2 1 5 3 6 4 | $(1,1,1)$ | 2 1 4 3 6 5 |

That is, when $a = 1$, the original arrangement of $b$ and $c$ remains unchanged; in contrast, when $a = 0$, the first card of $b$ and the second card of $c$ are swapped.

3. Using the method explained in Sect. 2.3, find $\boxed{3}$ or $\boxed{6}$ from the last four cards by an expected number of two random cuts.
   (a) If $\boxed{3}$ is found, move $\boxed{1}$ just before the sixth card:

$$\boxed{2}\boxed{1}\;\boxed{3}\boxed{?}\boxed{?}\boxed{?} \;\rightarrow\; \boxed{2}\;\boxed{3}\boxed{?}\boxed{?}\boxed{1}\boxed{?}.$$

   Then, we have:

| $(a,b,c)$ | Sequence | $(a,b,c)$ | Sequence |
|---|---|---|---|
| $(0,0,0)$ | 2 ‖ 3 6 4 1 5 | $(1,0,0)$ | 2 ‖ 3 4 5 1 6 |
| $(0,0,1)$ | 2 ‖ 3 5 4 1 6 | $(1,0,1)$ | 2 ‖ 3 4 6 1 5 |
| $(0,1,0)$ | 2 ‖ 3 5 4 1 6 | $(1,1,0)$ | 2 ‖ 3 5 6 1 4 |
| $(0,1,1)$ | 2 ‖ 3 6 4 1 5 | $(1,1,1)$ | 2 ‖ 3 6 5 1 4 |

   Observing the cyclic order of $\boxed{3}$ and $\boxed{6}$ starting from $\boxed{1}$ reveals that it matches the value of $b \oplus c$ when $a = 0$, and that of $\overline{b \vee c}$ when $a = 1$; so if we remove $\boxed{4}$ and $\boxed{5}$ , we will obtain:

$$\left.\begin{array}{ll} \boxed{1}\;\underbrace{\boxed{?}\boxed{?}}_{[b\oplus c]^{\{3,6\}}} & \text{if } a=0 \\ \boxed{1}\;\underbrace{\boxed{?}\boxed{?}}_{[\overline{b\vee c}]^{\{3,6\}}} & \text{if } a=1 \end{array}\right\} = \boxed{1}\;\underbrace{\boxed{?}\boxed{?}}_{[\mathsf{Onehot}(a,b,c)]}.$$

   (b) If $\boxed{6}$ is found, move $\boxed{1}$ just before the fifth card:

$$\boxed{2}\boxed{1}\;\boxed{6}\boxed{?}\boxed{?}\boxed{?} \;\rightarrow\; \boxed{2}\;\boxed{6}\boxed{?}\boxed{1}\boxed{?}\boxed{?}.$$

   Then, we have:

| $(a,b,c)$ | Sequence | $(a,b,c)$ | Sequence |
|---|---|---|---|
| $(0,0,0)$ | 2 ‖ 6 4 1 5 3 | $(1,0,0)$ | 2 ‖ 6 3 1 4 5 |
| $(0,0,1)$ | 2 ‖ 6 3 1 5 4 | $(1,0,1)$ | 2 ‖ 6 5 1 3 4 |
| $(0,1,0)$ | 2 ‖ 6 3 1 5 4 | $(1,1,0)$ | 2 ‖ 6 4 1 3 5 |
| $(0,1,1)$ | 2 ‖ 6 4 1 5 3 | $(1,1,1)$ | 2 ‖ 6 5 1 4 3 |

   Note that, similar to the case (a) above, removing $\boxed{4}$ and $\boxed{5}$ brings a commitment to $\mathsf{Onehot}(a,b,c)$.
4. Ignoring $\boxed{2}$ , turn over the face-up cards:

$$\boxed{?}\boxed{?}\boxed{?}\boxed{?}\boxed{?}.$$

   Find and remove $\boxed{4}$ and $\boxed{5}$ by using the method explained in Sect. 2.3; the number of random cuts is 6.5 (expected value):

$$\boxed{4}\boxed{5}\;\;\boxed{?}\boxed{?}\boxed{?}.$$

5. Apply a random cut to the face-down three cards:

$$\left\langle \boxed{?}\boxed{?}\boxed{?} \right\rangle \rightarrow \boxed{?}\boxed{?}\boxed{?}.$$

6. Turn over the first card to obtain a commitment to $\mathsf{Onehot}(a, b, c)$ (or its negation) as follows:

$$\boxed{?}\boxed{?}\boxed{?} \xrightarrow{(\mathsf{turn},\{1\})} \begin{cases} \boxed{1}\ \underbrace{\boxed{?}\boxed{?}}_{[\mathsf{Onehot(a,b,c)}]} \\ \boxed{3}\ \underbrace{\boxed{?}\boxed{?}}_{[\overline{\mathsf{Onehot(a,b,c)}}]} \\ \boxed{6}\ \underbrace{\boxed{?}\boxed{?}}_{[\mathsf{Onehot(a,b,c)}]} \end{cases}.$$

This is our six-card protocol for Onehot. The expected number of shuffles is 10.5 in total.

Up to Step 2, our protocol follows the same procedure as Haga et al. [2]. The key difference and novelty lie in the subsequent steps: while Haga et al.'s protocol only identifies and removes two cards, our proposed protocol strategically repositions $\boxed{1}$ after a single card is identified.

### 4.2 Our Protocol for Dot

Similar to our protocol for Onehot presented in the previous subsection, a protocol for Dot can be constructed using six cards, based on the following decomposition:

$$\mathsf{Dot}(a, b, c) = \begin{cases} a \oplus c & \text{if } b = 0 \\ \overline{a} \wedge c & \text{if } b = 1 \end{cases}.$$

Due to page limitations, we omit the details.

## 5 Conclusion

In this paper, we addressed the problems left unresolved in existing research by Haga et al. [2] and showed that secure computation protocols can be constructed for all three-input Boolean functions using six playing cards. The required number of shuffles is summarized in Table 3. Reducing these shuffle counts remains a subject for future work.

Our results imply that the card-minimality problem is resolved for all Boolean functions with up to three inputs. Solving the card-minimality problem for $n$-input Boolean functions with $n \geq 4$ (in the playing-card setting) is also an intriguing direction for future work. It should be noted that, as an upper bound, $2n + 8$ cards have been shown to be sufficient [25].

Recently, the application of card-based cryptography to games such as Old Maid [24], President [13], and Tagiron [8] has attracted growing attention; designing such protocols with only standard playing cards is a promising direction for future study.

**Acknowledgements.** We thank the anonymous reviewers, whose comments have helped us improve the presentation of the paper. This work was supported in part by JSPS KAKENHI Grant Numbers JP24K02938.

## References

1. Dumas, J.-G., Lafourcade, P., Miyahara, D., Mizuki, T., Sasaki, T., Sone, H.: Interactive physical zero-knowledge proof for Norinori. In: Du, D.-Z., Duan, Z., Tian, C. (eds.) COCOON 2019. LNCS, vol. 11653, pp. 166–177. Springer, Cham (2019). https://doi.org/10.1007/978-3-030-26176-4_14
2. Haga, R., Hayashi, Y., Miyahara, D., Mizuki, T.: Card-minimal protocols for three-input functions with standard playing cards. In: Batina, L., Daemen, J. (eds.) AFRICACRYPT 2022. LNCS, vol. 13503, pp. 448–468. Springer, Cham (2022). https://doi.org/10.1007/978-3-031-17433-9_19
3. Hatsugai, K., Asano, K., Abe, Y.: A physical zero-knowledge proof for Sumplete, a puzzle generated by ChatGPT. In: Wu, W., Tong, G. (eds.) Computing and Combinatorics (COCOON). LNCS, vol. 14422, pp. 398–410. Springer, Cham (2024). https://doi.org/10.1007/978-3-031-49190-0_29
4. Honda, Y., Shinagawa, K.: Efficient card-based protocols with a standard deck of playing cards using partial opening. In: Minematsu, K., Mimura, M. (eds.) Advances in Information and Computer Security. LNCS, vol. 14977, pp. 85–100. Springer, Singapore (2024). https://doi.org/10.1007/978-981-97-7737-2_5
5. Honda, Y., Shinagawa, K.: Efficient three-input and four-input AND protocols using playing cards with partial-open actions. In: Kim, Y., Miyaji, A., Tibouchi, M. (eds.) Cryptology and Network Security. LNCS, vol. 16351, pp. 199–212. Springer, Singapore (2025). https://doi.org/10.1007/978-981-95-4434-9_9
6. Koch, A.: The landscape of security from physical assumptions. In: IEEE Information Theory Workshop, pp. 1–6. IEEE, NY (2021). https://doi.org/10.1109/ITW48936.2021.9611501
7. Koch, A., Schrempp, M., Kirsten, M.: Card-based cryptography meets formal verification. New Gener. Comput. **39**(1), 115–158 (2021). https://doi.org/10.1007/s00354-020-00120-0
8. Koizumi, K., Mizuki, T.: An application of secure computation to Tagiron. In: Hartisch, M., Hsueh, C.H., van den Herik, J. (eds.) Advances in Computer Games. LNCS, vol. 16463, pp. 191–204. Springer Nature Switzerland, Cham (2026). https://doi.org/10.1007/978-3-032-23657-9_16
9. Koyama, H., Miyahara, D., Mizuki, T., Sone, H.: A secure three-input AND protocol with a standard deck of minimal cards. In: Santhanam, R., Musatov, D. (eds.) Computer Science – Theory and Applications. LNCS, vol. 12730, pp. 242–256. Springer, Cham (2021). https://doi.org/10.1007/978-3-030-79416-3_14
10. Koyama, H., Toyoda, K., Miyahara, D., Mizuki, T.: New card-based copy protocols using only random cuts. In: ACM ASIA Public-Key Cryptography Workshop, pp. 13–22. ACM, NY (2021). https://doi.org/10.1145/3457338.3458297

11. Manabe, Y., Ono, H.: Card-based cryptographic protocols with a standard deck of cards using private operations. New Gener. Comput. **42**, 305–329 (2024). https://doi.org/10.1007/s00354-024-00257-2
12. Marakkalage, D.S., Testa, E., Riener, H., Mishchenko, A., Soeken, M., De Micheli, G.: Three-input gates for logic synthesis. IEEE Trans. Comput. Aided Des. Integr. Circuits Syst. **40**(10), 2184–2188 (2021). https://doi.org/10.1109/TCAD.2020.3032625
13. Miyahara, D., Lafourcade, P., Mizuki, T., Shinagawa, K.: Playing president with virtual players: how to play multiple cards of a kind. In: Iacono, J. (ed.) Fun with Algorithms. LIPIcs, vol. 366, pp. 34:1–34:15. Schloss Dagstuhl, Dagstuhl, Germany (2026). https://doi.org/10.4230/LIPIcs.FUN.2026.34
14. Miyahara, D., Mizuki, T.: Secure computations through checking suits of playing cards. In: Li, M., Sun, X. (eds.) Frontiers in Algorithmics. LNCS, vol. 13461, pp. 110–128. Springer, Cham (2023). https://doi.org/10.1007/978-3-031-20796-9_9
15. Mizuki, T.: Efficient and secure multiparty computations using a standard deck of playing cards. In: Foresti, S., Persiano, G. (eds.) CANS 2016. LNCS, vol. 10052, pp. 484–499. Springer, Cham (2016). https://doi.org/10.1007/978-3-319-48965-0_29
16. Mizuki, T., Shizuya, H.: A formalization of card-based cryptographic protocols via abstract machine. Int. J. Inf. Secur. **13**(1), 15–23 (2014). https://doi.org/10.1007/s10207-013-0219-4
17. Mizuki, T., Shizuya, H.: Computational model of card-based cryptographic protocols and its applications. IEICE Trans. Fundam. **E100.A**(1), 3–11 (2017). https://doi.org/10.1587/transfun.E100.A.3
18. Mizuki, T., Sone, H.: Six-card secure AND and four-card secure XOR. In: Deng, X., Hopcroft, J.E., Xue, J. (eds.) FAW 2009. LNCS, vol. 5598, pp. 358–369. Springer, Heidelberg (2009). https://doi.org/10.1007/978-3-642-02270-8_36
19. Nakai, T., Iwanari, K., Ono, T., Abe, Y., Watanabe, Y., Iwamoto, M.: Card-based cryptography with a standard deck of cards, revisited: efficient protocols in the private model. New Gener. Comput. **42**, 345–358 (2024). https://doi.org/10.1007/s00354-024-00269-y
20. Niemi, V., Renvall, A.: Solitaire zero-knowledge. Fundam. Inf. **38**(1,2), 181–188 (1999). https://doi.org/10.3233/FI-1999-381214
21. Otsuji, T., Fulla, P., Fukunaga, T.: NP-Completeness and physical zero-knowledge proof of Hotaru Beam. In: Chen, Y., Gao, X., Sun, X., Zhang, A. (eds.) Computing and Combinatorics (COCOON), pp. 239–251. Springer, Singapore (2024). https://doi.org/10.1007/978-981-96-1090-7_20
22. Ruangwises, S.: Two standard decks of playing cards are sufficient for a ZKP for sudoku. In: Chen, C.-Y., Hon, W.-K., Hung, L.-J., Lee, C.-W. (eds.) COCOON 2021. LNCS, vol. 13025, pp. 631–642. Springer, Cham (2021). https://doi.org/10.1007/978-3-030-89543-3_52
23. Sasao, T.: Switching Theory for Logic Synthesis. Kluwer Academic Publishers, Boston (1999)
24. Shinagawa, K., Miyahara, D., Mizuki, T.: How to play old maid with virtual players. Theory Comput. Syst. **69**(1), 13 (2025). https://doi.org/10.1007/s00224-024-10203-w
25. Shinagawa, K., Mizuki, T.: Secure computation of any Boolean function based on any deck of cards. In: Chen, Y., Deng, X., Lu, M. (eds.) FAW 2019. LNCS, vol. 11458, pp. 63–75. Springer, Cham (2019). https://doi.org/10.1007/978-3-030-18126-0_6

# Strong Conflict-Free Vertex-Connection via Twin Cover: Kernelization and Chromatic Bounds

Samuel German(✉)

University of California, San Diego, USA
sgerman@ucsd.edu

**Abstract.** A vertex-coloring of a connected graph $G$ is a strong conflict-free vertex-connection coloring if every two distinct vertices are joined by a shortest path on which some color appears exactly once. The minimum number of colors in such a coloring is the strong conflict-free vertex-connection number $\mathrm{svcfc}(G)$. We study this problem under the parameter twin cover. Let $X$ be a twin cover of $G$ of size $t$, and let $k$ be the target number of colors. In our first result, given $(G, k)$ together with a twin cover $X$, we reduce in polynomial time to an equivalent annotated instance on at most $\max\{2, t+(t+1)k2^{t+k-1}\}$ vertices. Hence the annotated version of Strong CFVC Number, in which a twin cover is supplied as part of the input, is fixed-parameter tractable parameterized by $t+k$. Using this bound, we then obtain a kernel parameterized by $\mathrm{tc}(G)+k$; in particular, for every fixed $k$, the problem is FPT parameterized by the twin-cover number alone. In our second result, we prove every connected graph $G$ with twin cover $X$ of size $t$ satisfies $\chi(G) \leq \mathrm{svcfc}(G) \leq \chi(G)+t$. More generally, if $Y \subseteq X$ intersects every shortest path of length at least 3, then $\mathrm{svcfc}(G) \leq \chi(G) + |Y|$. We also derive an exact expression for the chromatic number on graphs of bounded twin-cover number: for every proper coloring $\varphi$ of $G[X]$, the minimum number of colors needed to extend $\varphi$ to all of $G$ is $K_\varphi = \max_{S\subseteq X}(|\varphi(S)| + m(S))$, and hence $\chi(G) = \min_{\varphi \text{ proper on } G[X]} K_\varphi$. Our results provide the first evidence that twin cover is a useful parameter for strong conflict-free vertex-connection and show that once a twin cover is fixed, the remaining difficulty is concentrated in a bounded additive gap above the chromatic number.

**Keywords:** Conflict-free coloring · strong conflict-free vertex-connection · twin cover · parameterized complexity · kernelization · graph coloring

## 1 Introduction

Conflict-free coloring is a way of coloring in which certain combinatorial objects must contain a uniquely colored element. The notion originated in a geometric setting motivated by frequency assignment in cellular networks and has since


Y. Li et al. (Eds.): COCOON 2026, LNCS 16835, pp. 397–408, 2027.
https://doi.org/10.1007/978-981-92-3309-0_30

developed into a substantial area in combinatorics and algorithms [1,3,10,11]. In graph settings, conflict-free ideas have been adapted to neighborhoods, paths, and several connectivity notions, including conflict-free connection and strong conflict-free connectivity; see [1,2,9]. One particularly natural direction is to combine proper vertex coloring with shortest-path connectivity constraints.

Recently, Hsieh et al. introduced the *strong conflict-free vertex-connection* problem [7]. A vertex-coloring of a connected graph $G$ is a strong conflict-free vertex-connection coloring if every two distinct vertices are linked by a shortest path on which some color appears exactly once. The minimum number of colors in such a coloring is denoted $\mathrm{svcfc}(G)$. This parameter blends ordinary proper coloring with a path-based uniqueness requirement. The initial complexity study already showed that the problem behaves quite differently from classical graph coloring: among other results, STRONG CFVC NUMBER is NP-hard already for the 3-color case on highly restricted graphs, while certain structured graph classes still admit polynomial-time algorithms [7].

The parameterized complexity of the problem has only begun to be understood. A recent follow-up by Feghali, Le, and Le proved that STRONG CFVC NUMBER is fixed-parameter tractable when parameterized by the vertex-cover number, and also established that the 3-color case admits no polynomial kernel under this parameter unless $\mathsf{NP} \subseteq \mathsf{coNP/poly}$ [4]. This naturally suggests moving beyond vertex cover. A canonical candidate is *twin cover*, introduced by Ganian [5]: it strictly generalizes vertex cover, preserves a strong decomposition into twin-cliques outside the parameter set, and can remain small even on dense graphs. These features make twin cover especially attractive for strong CFVC, in which both proper coloring and shortest paths interact tightly with cliques of true twins. From the perspective of coloring, this choice is also natural: twin cover has already proved useful for kernelization in fixed-target graph coloring problems [8].

In this paper, we take a first step in that direction. Our first main result is an explicit kernel bound in the annotated setting where a twin cover is supplied. More precisely, given a valid annotated instance $(G, k, X)$ with $X \subseteq V(G)$ a twin cover of size $t$, we compute in polynomial time an equivalent valid annotated instance $(G', k', X')$ such that $|V(G')| \le \max\{2,\ t + (t+1)k\,2^{t+k-1}\}$. Thus the annotated version of STRONG CFVC NUMBER is fixed-parameter tractable parameterized by $t + k$. We then convert this into an unannotated result parameterized by $\mathrm{tc}(G) + k$: using a twin cover of size at most $2\ \mathrm{tc}(G)$, we obtain a kernel on at most

$$\max\Big\{2,\ 2\ \mathrm{tc}(G) + \big(2\ \mathrm{tc}(G) + 1\big)k\,2^{\,2\,\mathrm{tc}(G)+k-1}\Big\}$$

vertices. In particular, for every fixed constant $k$, STRONG CFVC NUMBER is fixed-parameter tractable parameterized by the twin-cover number alone.

We give a second structural contribution. We prove that every connected graph $G$ with twin cover $X$ of size $t$ satisfies $\chi(G) \le \mathrm{svcfc}(G) \le \chi(G) + t$. More generally, if $Y \subseteq X$ intersects every shortest path of length at least 3, then $\mathrm{svcfc}(G) \le \chi(G) + |Y|$. Thus, once a twin cover is fixed, the possible values of svcfc($G$) lie in a window of width at most $t$ above the ordinary chromatic number. This shifts the viewpoint from an arbitrary target $k$ to a bounded additive slack above $\chi(G)$.

To complement this, we give an exact expression for the chromatic number on graphs of bounded twin-cover number: for every proper coloring $\varphi$ of the twin cover $G[X]$, we show that the minimum number of colors needed to extend $\varphi$ to all of $G$ is $K_\varphi = \max_{S \subseteq X}\big(|\varphi(S)| + m(S)\big)$, where $m(S)$ is the maximum size of a twin-clique with neighborhood $S$ in $X$. Consequently, $\chi(G) = \min_{\varphi \text{ proper on } G[X]} K_\varphi$. This formula identifies the precise contribution of the twin-cover core and the outside twin-cliques to ordinary coloring.

Taken together, our results show that twin cover is a meaningful parameter for strong CFVC. Algorithmically, we obtain positive evidence that the problem remains tractable beyond the vertex-cover setting. Structurally, we isolate the remaining difficulty: after fixing a twin cover, computing svcfc($G$) amounts to resolving a bounded gap above the chromatic number. In this sense, our results place strong CFVC closer to the broader body of coloring problems that are well behaved under twin-cover parameterization, while also highlighting the additional difficulty created by the shortest-path conflict-free requirement [4,8]. We view this as being useful evidence that twin cover is the right framework in which to study the next phase of the problem.

## 2 Preliminaries and Definitions

All graphs considered herein are finite, simple, undirected, and connected unless stated otherwise.

### 2.1 Graphs, Paths, and Colorings

For a graph $G$, we write $V(G)$ and $E(G)$ for its vertex set and edge set, respectively. For a set $X \subseteq V(G)$, we write $G[X]$ for the subgraph of $G$ induced by $X$; we adittionally write $G - X := G[V(G) \setminus X]$. For a vertex $v \in V(G)$, its open neighborhood is $N_G(v) := \{u \in V(G) : uv \in E(G)\}$, and its closed neighborhood is $N_G[v] := N_G(v) \cup \{v\}$. For a set $X \subseteq V(G)$, we write $N_G(X) := \left(\bigcup_{v \in X} N_G(v)\right) \setminus X$. We omit the subscript $G$ whenever the graph to which the neighborhood applies is clear from the context.

Herein all paths are simple paths. If $P = v_0 v_1 \cdots v_\ell$ is a path, then the *length* of $P$ is $\ell$. For vertices $u, v \in V(G)$, the *distance* between $u$ and $v$, denoted by $d_G(u, v)$, is the minimum length of a $u$-$v$ path in $G$. A $u$-$v$ path of length $d_G(u, v)$ is a *shortest* $u$-$v$ path.

A *clique* is a set of vertices for which any two vertices therein are adjacent.

A (vertex) *coloring* of $G$ is a function $c\colon V(G) \to \mathbb{N}$. We say that $c$ is a $k$-*coloring* if $c(V(G)) \subseteq [k]$. A coloring $c$ is *proper* if $c(u) \neq c(v)$ for every edge $uv \in E(G)$. The *chromatic number* of $G$, denoted by $\chi(G)$, is the minimum integer $k$ such that $G$ admits a proper $k$-coloring.

For a coloring $c$ and a vertex set $X \subseteq V(G)$, we write $c(X) := \{c(v) : v \in X\}$. If $C$ is a clique and $c$ is proper, then necessarily $|c(C)| = |C|$.

### 2.2 Strong Conflict-Free Vertex-Connection

Let $c$ be a coloring of $G$, and let $P = v_0v_1 \cdots v_\ell$ be a path in $G$. We say that $P$ is *conflict-free with respect to* $c$ if there exists a color $\alpha$ such that $\alpha$ appears on exactly one vertex of $P$, that is,

$$\left|\{i \in \{0,1,\ldots,\ell\} : c(v_i) = \alpha\}\right| = 1$$

for some color $\alpha$.

A coloring $c$ of $G$ is a *strong conflict-free vertex-connection coloring*, or briefly a *strong CFVC coloring*, if for every two distinct vertices $u, v \in V(G)$ there exists a conflict-free shortest $u$-$v$ path in $G$.

The *strong conflict-free vertex-connection number* of $G$, denoted by $\mathrm{svcfc}(G)$, is the minimum number of colors in a strong CFVC coloring of $G$.

We consider the following decision problem.

Strong CFVC Number

*Input:* A connected graph $G$ and an integer $k \geq 1$.

*Question:* Is $\mathrm{svcfc}(G) \leq k$?

Annotated Strong CFVC Number

*Input:* A connected graph $G$, an integer $k \geq 1$, and a set $X \subseteq V(G)$.

*Parameter:* $k + |X|$.

*Promise:* $X$ is a twin cover of $G$.

*Question:* Is $\mathrm{svcfc}(G) \leq k$?

We note that the promise can be verified in polynomial time: it suffices to check, for every edge $uv$ of $G - X$, that $N_G[u] = N_G[v]$.

A color that is not used elsewhere in the coloring under consideration will be called a *fresh color*.

### 2.3 Twins, Twin Cover, and Twin-Cliques

Two distinct vertices $u, v \in V(G)$ are *true twins* if $N_G[u] = N_G[v]$. Equivalently, $u$ and $v$ are adjacent and satisfy $N_G(u) \setminus \{v\} = N_G(v) \setminus \{u\}$. An edge $uv \in E(G)$ is a *twin edge* if its endpoints $u$ and $v$ are true twins. A set $X \subseteq V(G)$ is a *twin cover* of $G$ if every edge of $G - X$ is a twin edge. The *twin-cover number* of $G$, denoted by $\mathrm{tc}(G)$, is the minimum size of a twin cover of $G$. Throughout the paper, whenever a twin cover $X$ is fixed, we write $t := |X|$. Let $X$ be a fixed twin cover of $G$. A connected component of $G - X$ will be called a *twin-clique*. By the definition of twin cover, every twin-clique is a clique. This is an immediate consequence of the definition of twin cover. Indeed, if $uv \in E(G - X)$, then neither endpoint lies in $X$, and therefore the edge $uv$ must be a twin edge; equivalently, $u$ and $v$ are true twins. Now let $v_0v_1 \cdots v_r$ be a path contained in one connected component of $G - X$. Since each consecutive pair $v_i, v_{i+1}$ is joined by an edge of $G - X$, we have $N_G[v_i] = N_G[v_{i+1}]$ for all $i$, and hence, by transitivity, all vertices $v_0, \ldots, v_r$ have the same closed neighborhood in $G$. In particular, they have the same neighborhood in $X$, and they are pairwise adjacent. Thus every connected component of $G - X$ is a clique, and all vertices of such a component have the same neighborhood in $X$; compare also Observation 1 of [5]. Hence, if $C$ is a twin-clique, we may define $N_X(C) := N_G(v) \cap X$ for any $v \in C$. For $S \subseteq X$ and $s \in \mathbb{N}$, we write

$$\mathcal{C}_{S,s} := \{\, C : C \text{ is a twin-clique of } G - X,\ N_X(C) = S,\ |C| = s \,\}.$$

We refer to the pair $(S, s)$ as the *type* of a twin-clique in $\mathcal{C}_{S,s}$. If $c$ is a coloring and $C$ is a twin-clique, we write $\mathrm{col}_c(C) := c(C)$ for the set of colors used on $C$. For each $S \subseteq X$, we also define

$$m(S) := \max\{\, |C| : C \text{ is a twin-clique of } G - X \text{ with } N_X(C) = S \,\},$$

with the convention that $m(S) = 0$ if no such twin-clique exists. If $\varphi$ is a proper coloring of $G[X]$, we write $\varphi(S) := \{\varphi(x) : x \in S\}$ for the set of colors appearing on $S$, and we define $K_\varphi := \max_{S \subseteq X} \big(|\varphi(S)| + m(S)\big)$. The quantity $K_\varphi$ will be used later in our treatment of proper colorings of graphs of bounded twin-cover number.

### 2.4 Parameterized Complexity

We use standard terminology from parameterized complexity. A parameterized problem is *fixed-parameter tractable* (FPT) if instances of size $n$ with parameter value $\kappa$ can be solved in time $f(\kappa)\, n^{O(1)}$ for some computable function $f$.

A *kernelization* for a parameterized problem is a polynomial-time algorithm which maps each instance $(I, \kappa)$ to an equivalent instance $(I', \kappa')$ such that

$$|I'| + \kappa' \leq g(\kappa)$$

for some computable function $g$. The reduced instance is called a *kernel.* If $g$ is bounded by a polynomial in $\kappa$, then the problem admits a *polynomial kernel.*

For Annotated Strong CFVC Number, we call a triple $(G, k, X)$ *valid* if $X$ is a twin cover of $G$; as noted above, this can be checked in polynomial time. The parameter is

$$\kappa := k + |X|.$$

A kernelization for this annotated problem is therefore a polynomial-time algorithm which maps each valid instance $(G, k, X)$ to an equivalent valid instance $(G', k', X')$ such that $X'$ is a twin cover of $G'$ and

$$|V(G')| + k' + |X'| \leq h(\kappa)$$

for some computable function $h$.

Since our reductions are graph reductions, we will usually state kernel bounds in terms of the number of vertices of the reduced graph. Thus, when we say that Annotated Strong CFVC Number admits a kernel on at most $h(\kappa)$ vertices, we mean that the output valid instance can be chosen so that $|V(G')| \le h(\kappa)$. In our construction, either we output the fixed valid no-instance $(K_2, 1, V(K_2))$, or we keep $k' = k$ and $X' = X$; hence such a vertex bound immediately yields a standard kernel in the usual encoding-size sense.

## 3 Basic Structural Properties

Throughout this section, let $G$ be a connected graph and let $X \subseteq V(G)$ be a fixed twin cover of size $t$.

**Lemma 1.** *Every strong CFVC coloring is proper.*

*Proof.* Let $c$ be a strong CFVC coloring of $G$, and let $uv \in E(G)$. The unique shortest $u$-$v$ path is the edge $uv$ itself. Hence that path must be conflict-free, which is possible only if $c(u) \neq c(v)$. Therefore $c$ is proper. □

**Lemma 2.** *Let $P = v_0v_1 \cdots v_r$ be a shortest path in $G$, and let $C$ be a twin-clique. If at least one endpoint of $P$ lies outside $C$, then $P$ contains at most one vertex of $C$.*

*Consequently, if the two endpoints of $P$ do not belong to the same twin-clique, then $P$ contains at most one vertex from each twin-clique, meets at most $t+1$ twin-cliques, and has length at most $2t$.*

*Proof.* Suppose first that at least one endpoint of $P = v_0v_1 \cdots v_r$ lies outside $C$, and assume for contradiction that $P$ contains at least two vertices of $C$. Let $i$ be the first index such that $v_i \in C$, and let $j$ be the last index such that $v_j \in C$. Then $i < j$.

Because at least one endpoint of $P$ lies outside $C$, we have either $i > 0$ or $j < r$. Assume that $j < r$; the case $i > 0$ is symmetric. Then $v_{j+1} \notin C$. Since $v_jv_{j+1} \in E(G)$ and all vertices of $C$ have the same neighborhood outside $C$, it follows that $v_iv_{j+1} \in E(G)$. Therefore replacing the subpath

$$v_iv_{i+1} \cdots v_jv_{j+1}$$

by the single edge $v_iv_{j+1}$ yields a shorter path, a contradiction. Thus $P$ contains at most one vertex of $C$.

For the consequence, assume that the endpoints of $P$ do not lie in the same twin-clique. Then the first part applies to every twin-clique, so $P$ contains at most one vertex from each twin-clique. Since distinct twin-cliques are distinct connected components of $G - X$, there are no edges between them. Hence every vertex of $P$ that lies in $V(G) \setminus X$ has all its neighbors on $P$ (if any) in $X$. In particular, the vertices of $P \setminus X$ appear on the path as isolated vertices separated by vertices of $X$. Therefore

$$|V(P) \setminus X| \le |V(P) \cap X| + 1 \le t + 1.$$

Each vertex of $V(P) \setminus X$ lies in a distinct twin-clique, so $P$ meets at most $t+1$ twin-cliques. Also, since $P$ is simple, it contains at most $t$ vertices of $X$. Hence

$$|V(P)| = |V(P) \cap X| + |V(P) \setminus X| \le t + (t+1) = 2t + 1.$$

Therefore the number of edges of $P$ is at most $2t$, as claimed. □

**Corollary 1.** *Every shortest path of length at least* 2 *contains a vertex of* $X$.

*Proof.* Let $P$ be a shortest path of length at least 2. Its endpoints cannot belong to the same twin-clique, because every twin-clique is a clique. If $P$ avoided $X$, then $P$ would lie entirely in $G \setminus X$, hence inside a single connected component of $G \setminus X$, which is a clique. But then $P$ would have length at most 1, a contradiction. Therefore $P$ contains a vertex of $X$. □

## 4 An FPT Kernel for the Combined Parameter $t + k$

In this section, we first prove a kernel bound for Annotated Strong CFVC Number, in which the input is accompanied by a twin cover $X$ of size $t$. We then derive, in Corollary 2, the corresponding unanotated result parameterized by $\mathrm{tc}(G) + k$. Let $(G, k, X)$ be a valid instance of Annotated Strong CFVC Number, and let $t := |X|$.

By Lemma 1, if some twin-clique has size greater than $k$, then $(G, k, X)$ is immediately a no-instance. Hence, from now on, we may assume that every twin-clique has size at most $k$.

**Lemma 3.** *Let* $S \subseteq X$ *and let* $s \in [k]$. *If* $C, D \in \mathcal{C}_{S,s}$, *then every bijection* $\beta\colon C \to D$ *extends to an automorphism of* $G$ *that fixes every vertex in* $V(G) \setminus (C \cup D)$.

*Proof.* Define a permutation $\pi$ of $V(G)$ by

$$\pi(v) = \begin{cases} \beta(v), & \text{if } v \in C, \\ \beta^{-1}(v), & \text{if } v \in D, \\ v, & \text{otherwise.} \end{cases}$$

Since $C$ and $D$ are cliques of the same size, there are no edges between $C$ and $D$, and every vertex of $C \cup D$ has neighborhood exactly $S$ in $X$ and no neighbors outside $X \cup C \cup D$, the map $\pi$ preserves adjacency. Hence $\pi$ is an automorphism of $G$. □

We now state the kernelization rule. The intuition is that, because any shortest path intersects at most $t{+}1$ twin-cliques by Lemma 2, having $t{+}2$ twin-cliques with the same size, neighborhood in $X$, and color set guarantees that at least one spare clique remains untouched by the path and can act as a substitute.

**Reduction Rule.** Let $S \subseteq X$ and let $s \in [k]$. If $|\mathcal{C}_{S,s}| > (t+1)\binom{k}{s}$, then delete an arbitrary twin-clique $C \in \mathcal{C}_{S,s}$.

**Lemma 4.** *The reduction rule is safe: if an application of the rule transforms a valid instance* $(G, k, X)$ *into* $(G - C, k, X)$, *then* $(G, k, X)$ *is a yes-instance if and only if* $(G - C, k, X)$ *is a yes-instance.*

*Proof (Proof sketch).* In the interest of space, we present only a proof sketch here, with the full proof occurring in the appendix of the arXiv full version of this paper [6].

Let $C \in \mathcal{C}_{S,s}$ be deleted and choose $D^* \in \mathcal{C}_{S,s} \setminus \{C\}$. The key observation is that $d_{G-C}(u,v) = d_G(u,v)$ for all $u, v \in V(G) \setminus C$: if a shortest $u$-$v$ path in $G$ uses a vertex of $C$, then by Lemma 2 it uses exactly one, which can be replaced by any vertex of $D^*$.

For ($\Leftarrow$), extend a strong CFVC $k$-coloring of $G - C$ to $C$ by copying colors from $D^*$ via a bijection $C \to D^*$.

For ($\Rightarrow$), among the more than $(t+1)\binom{k}{s}$ cliques of type $(S, s)$, choose $t+2$ with the same color set. Any shortest path meets at most $t+1$ twin-cliques, so one such clique is disjoint from the path; replacing the unique vertex of $C$ on the path by the matching vertex in that spare clique preserves both length and color multiset.

□

We can now bound the size of the reduced instance.

**Theorem 1.** *Given a valid instance $(G, k, X)$ of* Annotated Strong CFVC Number *with $t := |X|$, one can in polynomial time compute an equivalent valid instance $(G', k', X')$ such that*

$$|V(G')| \leq \max\{2,\ t + (t+1)k\,2^{t+k-1}\}.$$

*In particular,* Annotated Strong CFVC Number *admits a kernel and is fixed-parameter tractable parameterized by $t + k$.*

*Proof.* If some twin-clique of $G - X$ has size greater than $k$, then by Lemma 1 the instance is a no-instance. We output the fixed valid no-instance $(K_2, 1, V(K_2))$, which has two vertices and therefore satisfies the stated bound. This proves the theorem in this case.

Assume from now on that every twin-clique has size at most $k$. For each pair $(S, s)$ with $S \subseteq X$ and $s \in [k]$, apply the reduction rule exhaustively until $|\mathcal{C}_{S,s}| \leq (t+1)\binom{k}{s}$. By Lemma 4, each application is safe. The exhaustive application can be implemented in polynomial time by computing the twin-cliques of $G - X$, their sizes, and their neighborhoods in $X$.

Let $G'$ denote the resulting graph. Since we only delete vertices from $V(G) \setminus X$, the same set $X$ is a twin cover of $G'$. We output the valid annotated instance $(G', k, X)$.

For each $S \subseteq X$ and each $s \in [k]$, the graph $G'$ contains at most $(t+1)\binom{k}{s}$ twin-cliques in $\mathcal{C}_{S,s}$. Hence

$$|V(G') \setminus X| \leq \sum_{S \subseteq X} \sum_{s=1}^{k} s \cdot (t+1)\binom{k}{s} = (t+1)2^t \sum_{s=1}^{k} s\binom{k}{s}.$$

Using the identity $\sum_{s=1}^{k} s\binom{k}{s} = k2^{k-1}$, we obtain

$$|V(G') \setminus X| \leq (t+1)2^t \cdot k2^{k-1} = (t+1)k\,2^{t+k-1}.$$

Adding the $t$ vertices of $X$ yields

$$|V(G')| \le t + (t+1)k\,2^{t+k-1} \le \max\{2,\ t + (t+1)k\,2^{t+k-1}\}.$$

Thus, in all cases, we compute an equivalent valid instance satisfying the stated bound. This proves the theorem. □

We now convert the annotated kernel of Theorem 1 into a standard parameterized result in terms of $\mathrm{tc}(G) + k$.

**Corollary 2.** Strong CFVC Number *admits a kernel parameterized by* $\mathrm{tc}(G) + k$. *More precisely, every instance* $(G, k)$ *can be reduced in polynomial time to an equivalent instance on at most*

$$\max\Big\{2,\ 2\ \mathrm{tc}(G) + \big(2\ \mathrm{tc}(G) + 1\big)k\,2^{\,2\,\mathrm{tc}(G)+k-1}\Big\}$$

*vertices.*

*Proof.* Let $G^\dagger$ be the graph obtained from $G$ by deleting all twin edges. By Lemma 2 of [5], the vertex-cover number of $G^\dagger$ is exactly $\mathrm{tc}(G)$.

Compute a maximal matching $M$ in $G^\dagger$, and let $Y$ be the set of endpoints of the edges of $M$. Since $M$ is maximal, $Y$ is a vertex cover of $G^\dagger$. Moreover,

$$|Y| = 2|M| \le 2\ \mathrm{vc}(G^\dagger) = 2\ \mathrm{tc}(G).$$

Because every vertex cover of $G^\dagger$ is a twin cover of $G$, the set $Y$ is a twin cover of $G$ of size at most $2\ \mathrm{tc}(G)$. Applying Theorem 1 to the annotated instance $(G, k, Y)$ therefore yields, in polynomial time, an equivalent valid annotated instance whose underlying graph has at most $\max\{2,\ |Y| + (|Y|+1)k\,2^{|Y|+k-1}\}$ vertices. Forgetting the annotation, we obtain an equivalent instance of Strong CFVC Number on at most the same number of vertices.

Since $|Y| \le 2\ \mathrm{tc}(G)$, this is at most

$$\max\Big\{2,\ 2\ \mathrm{tc}(G) + \big(2\ \mathrm{tc}(G) + 1\big)k\,2^{\,2\,\mathrm{tc}(G)+k-1}\Big\}.$$

Hence Strong CFVC Number admits a kernel parameterized by $\mathrm{tc}(G)+k$. □

**Corollary 3.** *For every fixed integer* $k \ge 1$*, deciding whether* $\mathrm{svcfc}(G) \le k$ *is fixed-parameter tractable parameterized by* $\mathrm{tc}(G)$.

*Proof.* By Corollary 2, Strong CFVC Number is fixed-parameter tractable parameterized by $\mathrm{tc}(G) + k$. For every fixed integer $k$, this is fixed-parameter tractability parameterized by $\mathrm{tc}(G)$ alone. □

# 5 Bounding the Strong CFVC Number via the Chromatic Number

In this section, we show that for a graph equipped with a twin cover $X$ of size $t$, the strong conflict-free vertex-connection number differs from the chromatic number by at most $t$. We also give an exact formula for $\chi(G)$ in terms of a fixed twin cover.

Throughout this section, let $G$ be a connected graph and let $X \subseteq V(G)$ be a fixed twin cover of size $t$.

## 5.1 A $\chi(G) + t$ Upper Bound

We begin with a slightly more general statement than the bound we will ultimately use.

**Theorem 2.** *Let $Y \subseteq X$ be such that every shortest path in $G$ of length at least 3 contains a vertex of $Y$. Then* $\text{svcfc}(G) \le \chi(G) + |Y|$.

*Proof.* Let $\varphi$ be a proper $\chi(G)$-coloring of $G$. Construct a new coloring $\psi$ as follows: for every vertex $y \in Y$, assign a fresh color $\alpha_y$, where the colors $\alpha_y$ are pairwise distinct and do not appear on any vertex of $V(G) \setminus Y$; for every vertex $v \in V(G) \setminus Y$, set $\psi(v) := \varphi(v)$.

The coloring $\psi$ uses at most $\chi(G) + |Y|$ colors. Moreover, $\psi$ is proper: on $V(G) \setminus Y$ it agrees with the proper coloring $\varphi$, and every vertex of $Y$ receives a fresh color distinct from all other colors.

We claim that $\psi$ is a strong CFVC coloring. Let $u, v \in V(G)$ be distinct.

If $d_G(u, v) = 1$, then the edge $uv$ is a shortest $u$-$v$ path. Since $\psi$ is proper, that edge is conflict-free.

If $d_G(u, v) = 2$, then every shortest $u$-$v$ path has the form $u - w - v$. Because $\psi$ is proper, the middle vertex $w$ has a color different from the colors of $u$ and $v$. Hence the color $\psi(w)$ appears exactly once on the path, and the path is conflict-free.

Finally, assume that $d_G(u, v) \ge 3$. Let $P$ be any shortest $u$-$v$ path. By the assumption on $Y$, the path $P$ contains some vertex $y \in Y$. By construction, the color $\alpha_y = \psi(y)$ appears nowhere else in $G$. Therefore it appears exactly once on $P$, so $P$ is conflict-free.

Thus every two vertices of $G$ are joined by a conflict-free shortest path under $\psi$. Hence $\psi$ is a strong CFVC coloring, and $\text{svcfc}(G) \le \chi(G) + |Y|$. □

We obtain the promised bound by taking $Y = X$.

**Corollary 4.** *For every connected graph $G$ with twin cover $X$ of size $t$, $\chi(G) \le$* $\text{svcfc}(G) \le \chi(G) + t$. *In particular, the additive gap* $\text{svcfc}(G) - \chi(G)$ *is at most $t$.*

*Proof.* The lower bound follows immediately from Lemma 1. For the upper bound, Corollary 1 shows that every shortest path of length at least 3 contains a vertex of $X$. Hence Theorem 2 applies with $Y = X$. □

### 5.2 An Exact Formula for the Chromatic Number

We now show that, once the coloring of the twin cover is fixed, the chromatic number of the whole graph is determined exactly by the quantities $m(S)$ and $|\varphi(S)|$.

**Theorem 3.** *Let $\varphi$ be a proper coloring of $G[X]$. Then the minimum number of colors needed by a proper coloring of $G$ that extends $\varphi$ is exactly*

$$K_\varphi = \max_{S \subseteq X}\big(|\varphi(S)| + m(S)\big).$$

*Proof.* We first prove the lower bound. Let $c$ be any proper coloring of $G$ that extends $\varphi$.

Fix a subset $S \subseteq X$. The coloring $c$ uses all colors from $\varphi(S)$ on the vertices of $S$, and therefore uses at least $|\varphi(S)|$ colors in total.

If $m(S) = 0$, then this already gives $|c(V(G))| \geq |\varphi(S)| = |\varphi(S)| + m(S)$.

Assume now that $m(S) > 0$. Let $C$ be a twin-clique with $N_X(C) = S$ and $|C| = m(S)$. Every vertex of $C$ is adjacent to every vertex of $S$, so no color which appears on $S$ may be used on any vertex of $C$. Moreover, $C$ is a clique of size $m(S)$, so $c$ uses exactly $m(S)$ pairwise distinct colors on $C$. Consequently,

$$|c(V(G))| \geq |\varphi(S)| + m(S).$$

Since $S \subseteq X$ was arbitrary, we conclude that every proper extension $c$ of $\varphi$ satisfies

$$|c(V(G))| \geq \max_{S \subseteq X}\big(|\varphi(S)| + m(S)\big) = K_\varphi.$$

We now prove the matching upper bound. Let

$$K := K_\varphi = \max_{S \subseteq X}\big(|\varphi(S)| + m(S)\big).$$

Because $K \geq |\varphi(X)|$, after renaming colors if necessary we may assume that $\varphi(X) \subseteq [K]$.

We construct a proper $K$-coloring of $G$ extending $\varphi$. Keep the colors of the vertices of $X$ fixed according to $\varphi$. Now let $C$ be any twin-clique with neighborhood $S := N_X(C)$ and size $s := |C|$. Since $K - |\varphi(S)| \geq m(S) \geq s$, there are at least $s$ colors in the set $[K] \setminus \varphi(S)$. Choose any $s$ such colors and assign them injectively to the vertices of $C$.

This coloring is proper on $C$ because $C$ is a clique and its vertices receive distinct colors. It is also proper between $C$ and $S$, because no color used on $C$ belongs to $\varphi(S)$. There are no edges from $C$ to vertices of $X \setminus S$. Since different twin-cliques are pairwise anticomplete, the color choices for distinct twin-cliques may be made independently.

Thus we obtain a proper coloring of $G$ extending $\varphi$ and using only the colors in $[K]$. Therefore the minimum number of colors needed by a proper extension of $\varphi$ is at most $K_\varphi$.

Combining the two bounds yields the claim. □

As an immediate consequence, we obtain an exact formula for the chromatic number.

**Corollary 5.** *For every connected graph $G$ with fixed twin cover $X$,*

$$\chi(G) = \min_{\varphi \text{ proper on } G[X]} K_\varphi = \min_{\varphi \text{ proper on } G[X]} \max_{S \subseteq X} \big(|\varphi(S)| + m(S)\big).$$

*Proof.* Every proper coloring of $G$ restricts to a proper coloring $\varphi$ of $G[X]$. By Theorem 3, every proper extension of $\varphi$ uses at least $K_\varphi$ colors, and there exists a proper extension using exactly $K_\varphi$ colors. Taking the minimum over all proper colorings $\varphi$ of $G[X]$ yields the formula. □

*Remark 1.* Corollary 4 and Corollary 5 show that, once a twin cover $X$ is fixed, the remaining difficulty in determining svcfc($G$) lies in the bounded additive gap above $\chi(G)$, which is at most $|X| = t$.

**Disclosure of Interests.** The author has no competing interests to declare.

## References


1. Chang, H., Huang, Z.: A survey on conflict-free connection coloring of graphs. Discret. Appl. Math. **352**, 88–104 (2024). https://doi.org/10.1016/j.dam.2024.03.021
2. Czap, J., Jendroľ, S., Valiska, J.: Conflict-free connections of graphs. Discussiones Mathematicae Graph Theor. **38**(4), 911–920 (2018). https://doi.org/10.7151/dmgt.2036
3. Even, G., Lotker, Z., Ron, D., Smorodinsky, S.: Conflict-free colorings of simple geometric regions with applications to frequency assignment in cellular networks. SIAM J. Comput. **33**(1), 94–136 (2003). https://doi.org/10.1137/S0097539702431840
4. Feghali, C., Le, H.O., Le, V.B.: The parameterized complexity of strong conflict-free vertex-connection colorability. Discret. Appl. Math. **383**, 85–93 (2026). https://doi.org/10.1016/j.dam.2025.12.025
5. Ganian, R.: Improving vertex cover as a graph parameter. Discrete Math. Theor. Comput. Sci. **17**(2), 77–100 (2015). https://doi.org/10.46298/dmtcs.2136
6. German, S.: Strong conflict-free vertex-connection via twin cover: kernelization and chromatic bounds (2026). arXiv:2605.13299. Full version with appendix. Latest version available at https://arxiv.org/abs/2605.13299
7. Hsieh, S.Y., Le, H.O., Le, V.B., Peng, S.L.: The complexity of strong conflict-free vertex-connection k-colorability. In: Computing and Combinatorics - 30th International Conference, COCOON 2024, Proceedings. LNCS, vol. 15161, pp. 289–300 (2025). https://doi.org/10.1007/978-981-96-1090-7_24
8. Jansen, B.M.P., Pieterse, A.: Optimal data reduction for graph coloring using low-degree polynomials. Algorithmica **81**(10), 3865–3889 (2019). https://doi.org/10.1007/s00453-019-00578-5
9. Ji, M., Li, X., Zhu, X.: (strong) conflict-free connectivity: algorithm and complexity. Theoret. Comput. Sci. **804**, 72–80 (2020). https://doi.org/10.1016/j.tcs.2019.10.043
10. Pach, J., Tardos, G.: Conflict-free colourings of graphs and hypergraphs. Comb. Probab. Comput. **18**(5), 819–834 (2009). https://doi.org/10.1017/S0963548309990290
11. Smorodinsky, S.: Conflict-free coloring and its applications. In: Geometry—Intuitive, Discrete, and Convex, Bolyai Society Mathematical Studies, vol. 24, pp. 331–389. Springer (2013). https://doi.org/10.1007/978-3-642-41498-5_12

# The Path-Extremal Conjecture for Zero Forcing: Distance-Hereditary Graphs and a Split-Decomposition Reduction

Samuel German(✉)

University of California, San Diego, USA
sgerman@ucsd.edu

**Abstract.** For an $n$-vertex graph $G$, let $z(G;k)$ denote the number of zero forcing sets of size $k$. A conjecture of Boyer et al. asserts that the path $P_n$ maximizes these numbers coefficientwise among all $n$-vertex graphs; equivalently, the zero forcing polynomial of every $n$-vertex graph should be coefficientwise dominated by that of $P_n$. We prove this path-extremal conjecture for distance-hereditary graphs. This extends the previously known tree case to a much larger class that includes, in particular, all trees and all cographs.

We then use canonical split decomposition to push the argument one step beyond the distance-hereditary setting. Specifically, we show that if a split-prime graph $H$ and all of its induced subgraphs are path-extremal, then every connected graph whose canonical split decomposition has a unique prime bag whose label graph is isomorphic to $H$ is also path-extremal. As a corollary, for each fixed $m$, if every induced subgraph of every split-prime graph on at most $m$ vertices is path-extremal, then so is every connected graph whose canonical split decomposition has a unique prime bag of size at most $m$ (Corollary 4). Thus, on these classes, the conjecture reduces to a finite verification problem on bounded-order prime cores.

Our proofs combine two counting mechanisms for non-forcing sets—fort obstructions arising from twin pairs and a leaf recurrence—with the accessibility description of graph-labelled trees in the canonical split decomposition. This yields a new positive instance of the path-extremal conjecture and identifies a natural structural frontier for further progress.

**Keywords:** zero forcing · zero forcing polynomial · distance-hereditary graph · split decomposition · graph-labelled tree

## 1 Introduction

Zero forcing is a deterministic propagation process on a graph: starting from an initial blue set $S \subseteq V(G)$, a blue vertex with exactly one white neighbor forces that neighbor to become blue. Introduced in connection with the maximum nullity and minimum rank problems for matrices described by graphs, zero forcing


Y. Li et al. (Eds.): COCOON 2026, LNCS 16835, pp. 409–422, 2027.
https://doi.org/10.1007/978-981-92-3309-0_31

has become a standard meeting point of graph theory and linear algebra [1,9]. The surrounding theory has also expanded to related zero forcing parameters and minimum-rank questions, including positive semidefinite zero forcing [3]. Beyond its original linear-algebraic role, zero forcing has been connected to propagation time [11], strong structural controllability [15], a priori sensor placement and error amplification in linear recovery [13], and even logic-circuit constructions based on forcing gadgets [5]. Probabilistic variants have also attracted attention, beginning with probabilistic zero forcing [12] and continuing with work on random graphs and expected propagation time [8].

A natural refinement of the zero forcing number is to count forcing sets by their size. For an $n$-vertex graph $G$, let $z(G;k)$ denote the number of zero forcing sets of size $k$, and consider the zero forcing polynomial $\mathcal{Z}(G;x) = \sum_{k=1}^{n} z(G;k)x^k$. Boyer et al. introduced this polynomial and initiated the systematic study of the counting problem, establishing structural properties of $\mathcal{Z}(G;x)$ such as extremal coefficients, multiplicativity, unimodality questions, and recognizability phenomena [4]. The counting viewpoint is also probabilistically natural: the ratio $z(G;k)/\binom{n}{k}$ is the probability that a uniformly random $k$-subset of $V(G)$ is zero forcing, while recent work has studied closely related models in which vertices are sampled independently at random [7]. In this framework, Boyer et al. formulated a striking coefficientwise extremal conjecture: among all graphs on $n$ vertices, the path $P_n$ should maximize the number of zero forcing sets of every size, that is, $z(G;k) \leq z(P_n;k) \qquad \text{for all } 0 \leq k \leq n$. Equivalently, the path should maximize the zero forcing polynomial coefficientwise [4].

This path-extremal conjecture has recently seen significant progress. Menon and Singh developed a graph-operation framework for the numbers $z(G;k)$ and used it to prove the conjecture for outerplanar graphs and threshold graphs, obtaining the tree case as a corollary [14]. Their work makes clear that the conjecture is especially amenable on graph classes with canonical recursive structure. At the same time, the random-set perspective of Curtis et al. further underscores the importance of coefficientwise bounds by studying the probability that a random initial set is zero forcing [7]. The present paper continues this decomposition-driven approach.

Our first main result proves the path-extremal conjecture for distance-hereditary graphs (Theorem 1). This class is a natural next target for several reasons. First, distance-hereditary graphs form a large and classical graph class: they admit a one-vertex extension characterization via pendant, false-twin, and true-twin additions [2], and, equivalently, they are exactly the totally decomposable graphs for split decomposition, namely those whose canonical graph-labelled tree has only clique and star bags [10]. Second, these structural descriptions match the two basic counting mechanisms that now underpin many positive results on the conjecture: twin pairs produce small forts and hence many non-forcing sets, while leaves give recursive lower bounds on the number of non-forcing sets [4,14]. In this sense, distance-hereditary graphs are the largest standard class for which the "twin/leaf" strategy is expected to work without any prime obstruction.

Our second main result pushes this perspective one step beyond the distance-hereditary setting. Using the canonical split decomposition, we prove a conditional extension for graphs with a unique prime bag (Theorem 2): if a fixed split-prime graph $H$ and all of its induced subgraphs are path-extremal, then every connected graph whose canonical split decomposition has a unique prime bag whose label graph is isomorphic to $H$ is also path-extremal. As a corollary, for each fixed $m$, if every induced subgraph of every split-prime graph on at most $m$ vertices is path-extremal, then so is every connected graph whose canonical split decomposition has a unique prime bag of size at most $m$ (Corollary 4). This gives a clean reduction from an infinite family of graphs to finitely many bounded-order prime cores, expressed in the natural graph-labelled-tree language of split decomposition [10].

These results are significant in three ways. First, Theorem 1 gives a substantial new positive instance of the path-extremal conjecture, extending the previously known tree case to the much larger distance-hereditary class, which in particular contains all trees, all cographs, and many graphs built by repeated pendant and twin extensions [2,10,14]. Second, Theorem 2 identifies a precise structural frontier at which the purely distance-hereditary argument stops and shows how far it can be pushed once a single prime component is allowed. Third, Corollary 4 suggests a concrete hybrid strategy for future work: combine structural induction on split decomposition with finite verification of bounded prime bases. This reduction is not only combinatorially natural but also algorithmically appealing, since graph-labelled trees provide a standard framework for manipulating split decompositions [10].

At a technical level, the proofs combine three ingredients: the fort obstruction arising from twin pairs, the leaf recurrence for non-forcing sets, and the accessibility description of canonical split decomposition [4,10,14]. Together these ingredients explain both why distance-hereditary graphs are a natural positive class and why unique-prime-bag families form the next meaningful level of generality.

## 2 Definitions and Preliminaries

All graphs in this paper are finite, simple, and undirected. For a graph $G$, we write $V(G)$ and $E(G)$ for its vertex set and edge set, respectively, and we let $n := |V(G)|$. For a vertex $v \in V(G)$, the *open neighborhood* of $v$ is $N_G(v) := \{u \in V(G) : uv \in E(G)\}$, the *closed neighborhood* is $N_G[v] := N_G(v) \cup \{v\}$, and the degree of $v$ is $\deg_G(v) := |N_G(v)|$. When the ambient graph is clear, we write $N(v)$ and $\deg(v)$. For a set $X \subseteq V(G)$, the induced subgraph on $X$ is denoted by $G[X]$, and $G - X$ denotes the induced subgraph $G[V(G) \setminus X]$. For vertices $u, v \in V(G)$, we write $u \sim v$ if $uv \in E(G)$ and $u \nsim v$ otherwise. The path on $n$ vertices is denoted by $P_n$. A vertex of degree 1 is called a *leaf* or *pendant vertex*.

### 2.1 Zero Forcing

Let $G$ be a graph and let $S \subseteq V(G)$. We regard the vertices of $S$ as initially blue and the vertices of $V(G) \setminus S$ as initially white. The *zero forcing color-change rule* is the following:
*If a blue vertex has exactly one white neighbor, then it forces that neighbor to become blue.*

Starting from $S$, we repeatedly apply the color-change rule until no further force is possible. The set of vertices that are blue at the end of this process is denoted by $\mathrm{cl}_G(S)$ and is called the *zero forcing closure* of $S$ in $G$.

A set $S \subseteq V(G)$ is a *zero forcing set* of $G$ if $\mathrm{cl}_G(S) = V(G)$. The *zero forcing number* of $G$ is $Z(G) := \min\{|S| : S \subseteq V(G) \text{ is a zero forcing set of } G\}$.

For $0 \le k \le n$, let

$$z(G;k) := \big|\{S \subseteq V(G) : |S| = k \text{ and } S \text{ is a zero forcing set of } G\}\big|$$

denote the number of zero forcing sets of size $k$. We also write $z'(G;k) := \binom{n}{k} - z(G;k)$ for the number of *non-forcing* $k$-subsets of $V(G)$.

**Convention.** For notational convenience, we extend the definitions of $z(G;k)$ and $z'(G;k)$ to all integers $k$ by setting $z(G;k) = z'(G;k) = 0$ whenever $k < 0$ or $k > |V(G)|$. Likewise, throughout the paper we use the standard convention $\binom{a}{b} = 0$ whenever $b < 0$ or $b > a$.

The *zero forcing polynomial* of $G$ is $\mathcal{Z}(G;x) := \sum_{k=1}^{n} z(G;k)x^k$.

For two polynomials $f(x) = \sum_{k \ge 0} a_k x^k$ and $g(x) = \sum_{k \ge 0} b_k x^k$, we write $f(x) \preceq g(x)$ if $a_k \le b_k$ for every $k$. Thus $\mathcal{Z}(G;x) \preceq \mathcal{Z}(H;x)$ means $z(G;k) \le z(H;k)$ for all $k$.

When $|V(G)| = n$, we say that $G$ is *path-extremal* if $z(G;k) \le z(P_n;k)$ for all $0 \le k \le n$. Equivalently, $G$ is path-extremal if $z'(G;k) \ge z'(P_n;k)$ for all $0 \le k \le n$.

### 2.2 Forts and Twins

A set $F \subseteq V(G)$ is a *fort* if every vertex in $V(G) \setminus F$ has either 0 neighbors in $F$ or at least 2 neighbors in $F$. Forts serve as obstructions to zero forcing: if an initial blue set has empty intersection with a fort, then the zero forcing process cannot enter that fort.

Two distinct vertices $u, v \in V(G)$ are *true twins* if $u \sim v$ and $N(u) \setminus \{v\} = N(v) \setminus \{u\}$, and they are *false twins* if $u \nsim v$ and $N(u) = N(v)$. A pair $\{u, v\}$ is called a *twin pair* if $u$ and $v$ are either true twins or false twins. Equivalently, a two-element set $\{u, v\}$ is a fort if and only if $\{u, v\}$ is a twin pair: every vertex outside the pair is adjacent to both or to neither, while $u$ and $v$ may be adjacent or nonadjacent.

### 2.3 Distance-Hereditary Constructions

Let $G$ be a graph and let $v \in V(G)$.

- A *pendant addition at v* is the operation of adding a new vertex $u \notin V(G)$ adjacent to exactly one vertex, namely $v$.
- A *false-twin addition at v* is the operation of adding a new vertex $u \notin V(G)$ such that $u \nsim v$ and $N_{G'}(u) = N_G(v)$, where $G'$ denotes the resulting graph.
- A *true-twin addition at v* is the operation of adding a new vertex $u \notin V(G)$ such that $u \sim v$ and $N_{G'}(u) \setminus \{v\} = N_G(v)$.

A graph is *distance-hereditary* if it can be obtained from the one-vertex graph $K_1$ by a sequence of pendant additions, false-twin additions, and true-twin additions.

### 2.4 Splits and Split Decomposition

From this point onward, whenever split decomposition is discussed, all graphs are assumed to be connected.

A *split* of a connected graph $G$ is a partition $(A, B)$ of $V(G)$ such that $|A|, |B| \geq 2$ and there exist nonempty sets $A_1 \subseteq A$ and $B_1 \subseteq B$ for which

$$ab \in E(G) \iff a \in A_1 \text{ and } b \in B_1$$

for every $a \in A$ and $b \in B$. The displayed condition, for $A, B, A_1, B_1$, just says that all of the edges crossing the cut between $A$ and $B$ constitute exactly the edges of the complete bipartite graph $K_{A_1,B_1}$. A connected graph is *split-prime* if it admits no split and is neither a clique nor a star. Equivalently, in the terminology of canonical split decomposition, split-prime graphs are the nondegenerate no-split graphs that occur as prime bag labels [10].

We use the standard graph-labelled-tree model of the *canonical split decomposition*; see, for example, [10]. Its internal nodes are called *bags*. Each bag carries a label graph, and each internal edge of the decomposition tree corresponds to a distinguished vertex of the label graph, called a *marker vertex*. Our terminology is a compressed version of that in [10, Definitions 2.1–2.2]: their internal tree nodes are our bags, and their leaves of the graph-labelled tree are the vertices of $G$. We suppress the pendant leaf edges and identify each such leaf with the corresponding vertex of the adjacent label graph; these identified label vertices are called *ordinary vertices*, while marker vertices are the label vertices corresponding to internal tree edges. The label of each bag is one of the following:

- a *clique bag*, whose label graph is a clique;
- a *star bag*, whose label graph is a star;
- a *prime bag*, whose label graph is split-prime in the above nondegenerate sense.

Thus clique bags and star bags account for the degenerate cases, and a *prime bag* always means a nondegenerate no-split bag.

A bag is a *leaf bag* if it is a leaf of the tree obtained from the full graph-labelled tree by retaining only the bags and the edges between them. If $B$ is a leaf bag, then exactly one vertex of its label graph is a marker vertex; we denote this vertex by $m_B$ and call it the *marker* of $B$. All other vertices of the label graph of $B$ are called the *ordinary vertices* of $B$.

If $B$ is a star leaf bag, then its label graph has a unique center. We say that $B$ is *center-attached* if $m_B$ is the center of that star, and *leaf-attached* otherwise.

The ordinary vertices appearing in the bag labels are the actual vertices of the original graph $G$; marker vertices are auxiliary. Adjacency in $G$ is defined by the standard *accessibility* relation on the graph-labelled tree. More precisely, if two ordinary vertices lie in the same bag, then they are adjacent in $G$ if and only if they are adjacent in the corresponding label graph. Otherwise, let $u$ and $v$ be ordinary vertices lying in bags $B_0$ and $B_t$, respectively, and let $B_0, B_1, \ldots, B_t$ be the unique path between these bags in the decomposition tree. For $0 \leq i < t$, let $m_i^+$ be the marker vertex of $B_i$ corresponding to the tree edge $B_iB_{i+1}$, and for $1 \leq i \leq t$, let $m_i^-$ be the marker vertex of $B_i$ corresponding to the tree edge $B_{i-1}B_i$. Then $u$ and $v$ are adjacent in $G$ if and only if $u$ is adjacent to $m_0^+$ in the label of $B_0$, $m_i^-$ is adjacent to $m_i^+$ in the label of $B_i$ for every $1 \leq i \leq t-1$, and $m_t^-$ is adjacent to $v$ in the label of $B_t$. We refer to this as the accessibility relation.

A graph-labelled-tree representation of a connected graph will be called *reduced* in the standard split-decomposition sense: every clique bag and every star bag has at least three vertices in its label graph, and no internal edge admits one of the standard degenerate-bag joins, namely a clique-clique join or a star leaf-marker to star center-marker join; see [10, Section 2.2, definition before Theorem 2.9]. For the purposes of this paper, we record the reducedness facts used later.

**Lemma 1.** *Let $T$ be a reduced graph-labelled-tree representation of a connected graph $G$.*

1. *Every clique bag and every star bag of $T$ has at least three vertices in its label graph.*
2. *If $B$ is a clique leaf bag of $T$, then $B$ has at least two ordinary vertices.*
3. *If $B$ is a center-attached star leaf bag of $T$, then $B$ has at least two ordinary leaves.*

*Proof.* Assertion (1) is the degree greater than two condition in the definition of reduced graph-labelled trees in [10, Section 2.2, definition before Theorem 2.9]. Since a leaf bag has exactly one marker vertex, assertions (2) and (3) follow immediately from (1). □

**Lemma 2 (Reducedness constraints on internal edges).** *Let $T$ be a reduced graph-labelled-tree representation of a connected graph. Then:*

1. *no internal tree edge of $T$ joins two clique bags; and*
2. *no internal tree edge of $T$ joins a star bag through a leaf-marker to a star bag through a center-marker.*

*Equivalently, $T$ has no internal edge of type $KK$ and no internal edge of type $S_pS_c$, where $K$ denotes a clique bag, $S_p$ a star bag incident through a leaf-marker, and $S_c$ a star bag incident through its center-marker.*

This is the graph-labelled-tree formulation of the reducedness condition in Cunningham's split-decomposition theorem [6]; in the terminology used here, the condition is stated by Gioan and Paul as the absence of clique-joins and star-joins in a reduced graph-labelled tree [10, Section 2.2, definition before Theorem 2.9].

A connected graph has a *unique prime bag* if its canonical split decomposition contains exactly one prime bag.

For a fixed split-prime graph $H$, we write $\mathcal{C}(H)$ for the class of connected graphs whose canonical split decomposition has exactly one prime bag and whose unique prime bag has label graph isomorphic to $H$. We refer to that bag as the *prime core* of the graph.

For $m \in \mathbb{N}$, we write $\mathcal{C}_{\leq m}$ for the class of connected graphs whose canonical split decomposition has exactly one prime bag of size at most $m$. Here the *size* of a bag means the number of vertices in its label graph.

Finally, a connected graph is distance-hereditary if and only if its canonical split decomposition has no prime bag.

## 3 Distance-Hereditary Graphs Are Path-Extremal

In this section we verify the path-extremal conjecture for distance-hereditary graphs.

We begin with two ingredients from the recent literature: an explicit formula for the coefficients of the zero forcing polynomial of a path, and a recurrence for non-forcing sets in the presence of a leaf.

**Lemma 3 ([4]).** *For every $n \geq 1$ and every $0 \leq k \leq n$, $z'(P_n; k) = \binom{n-k-1}{k}$. Equivalently, $z(P_n; k) = \binom{n}{k} - \binom{n-k-1}{k}$.*

**Lemma 4 ([14]).** *Let $G$ be a graph with a leaf $x$, and let $v$ be the unique neighbor of $x$. Then, for every $k \geq 1$, $z'(G; k) \geq z'(G-x; k) + z'(G-\{x, v\}; k-1)$.*

We also use the standard hereditary property of distance-hereditary graphs.

**Lemma 5 ([2]).** *Every induced subgraph of a distance-hereditary graph is distance-hereditary.*

The next observation records the basic fort obstruction that will be used throughout the proof.

**Lemma 6.** *Let $F \subseteq V(G)$ be a fort. If $S \cap F = \varnothing$, then $S$ is not a zero forcing set of $G$.*

*Proof.* Suppose that $S$ is a zero forcing set. Consider the zero forcing process started from $S$, and let $w \notin F$ be the first blue vertex that forces a vertex of $F$. Immediately before this force occurs, every vertex of $F$ is still white. Since $F$ is a fort, the vertex $w$ has either 0 or at least 2 neighbors in $F$. The first case is impossible because $w$ is forcing a vertex of $F$. In the second case, $w$ has at least two white neighbors, contradicting the color-change rule. Hence no force can ever enter $F$, and $S$ is not a zero forcing set. □

**Lemma 7.** *If $u$ and $v$ form a twin pair in $G$, then $\{u, v\}$ is a fort.*

*Proof.* Let $w \in V(G) \setminus \{u, v\}$. Since $u$ and $v$ are twins, we have $w \sim u \iff w \sim v$. Thus $w$ has either 0 or 2 neighbors in $\{u, v\}$, and so $\{u, v\}$ is a fort. □

**Corollary 1.** *If $G$ contains a twin pair, then $G$ is path-extremal.*

*Proof.* Let $\{u, v\}$ be a twin pair in $G$. By Lemma 7, the set $\{u, v\}$ is a fort. Hence, by Lemma 6, every $k$-subset of $V(G) \setminus \{u, v\}$ is non-forcing. Therefore, if $n = |V(G)|$, then $z'(G; k) \geq \binom{n-2}{k}$ for every $0 \leq k \leq n$. For $k = 0$, this already gives $z'(G; 0) \geq z'(P_n; 0)$. For $k \geq 1$, we have $n - 2 \geq n - k - 1$, and hence $\binom{n-2}{k} \geq \binom{n-k-1}{k} = z'(P_n; k)$ by Lemma 3. Thus $z'(G; k) \geq z'(P_n; k)$ for all $0 \leq k \leq n$. Equivalently, $G$ is path-extremal. □

The next structural lemma is the only place where we use the recursive construction of distance-hereditary graphs.

**Lemma 8.** *Let $G$ be a distance-hereditary graph with at least two vertices. Then $G$ contains either a leaf or a twin pair.*

*Proof.* By definition, $G$ can be obtained from $K_1$ by a sequence of pendant additions, false-twin additions, and true-twin additions. Consider the last operation in such a construction. If the last operation is a pendant addition, then the newly added vertex is a leaf of $G$. If the last operation is a false-twin addition or a true-twin addition, then the newly added vertex forms a twin pair with the vertex to which it was added. In either case, $G$ contains a leaf or a twin pair. □

We now prove the main result of this section.

**Theorem 1.** *Every distance-hereditary graph is path-extremal. Equivalently, if $G$ is a distance-hereditary graph on $n$ vertices, then $\mathcal{Z}(G; x) \preceq \mathcal{Z}(P_n; x)$.*

*Proof.* We argue by induction on $n = |V(G)|$. The statement is immediate for $n \leq 2$.

Now let $n \geq 3$, and let $G$ be a distance-hereditary graph on $n$ vertices. By Lemma 8, the graph $G$ contains either a twin pair or a leaf.

If $G$ contains a twin pair, then the result follows immediately from Corollary 1.

Assume instead that $G$ contains a leaf $x$, and let $v$ be the unique neighbor of $x$. By Lemma 5, both $G - x$ and $G - \{x, v\}$ are distance-hereditary. Since these graphs have fewer than $n$ vertices, the induction hypothesis gives $z'(G - x; k) \geq$

$z'(P_{n-1};k) = \binom{n-k-2}{k}$. for all $0 \leq k \leq n-1$, and $z'(G-\{x,v\};k-1) \geq z'(P_{n-2};k-1) = \binom{n-k-2}{k-1}$ for all $1 \leq k \leq n$, where we used Lemma 3 in both equalities.

Applying Lemma 4, we obtain, for every $1 \leq k \leq n$, $z'(G;k) \geq z'(G-x;k) + z'(G-\{x,v\};k-1) \geq \binom{n-k-2}{k} + \binom{n-k-2}{k-1}$. By Pascal's identity, $\binom{n-k-2}{k} + \binom{n-k-2}{k-1} = \binom{n-k-1}{k} = z'(P_n;k)$, again by Lemma 3. Thus $z'(G;k) \geq z'(P_n;k)$ for all $1 \leq k \leq n$. The case $k=0$ is trivial, so $G$ is path-extremal. □

**Corollary 2.** *Every tree and every cograph is path-extremal.*

*Proof.* Both classes are distance-hereditary. □

*Remark 1.* The proof of Theorem 1 isolates two mechanisms that reappear in more general split-decomposition arguments: a small fort arising from a twin pair, and a recurrence for non-forcing sets arising from a leaf. This modularity is what makes distance-hereditary graphs a natural first test case for the path-extremal conjecture.

## 4 Graphs with a Unique Prime Bag

We now extend Theorem 1 by allowing a single prime bag in the split decomposition. For the inductive proof it is convenient to enlarge the class $\mathcal{C}(H)$ slightly.

For a fixed split-prime graph $H$, let $\mathcal{D}(H)$ denote the class of connected graphs that admit a reduced graph-labelled-tree representation with at most one prime bag, and such that the label graph of the prime bag, if it exists, is isomorphic to an induced subgraph of $H$. In particular, $\mathcal{C}(H) \subseteq \mathcal{D}(H)$. Moreover, if a graph in $\mathcal{D}(H)$ has no prime bag, then it is totally decomposable and hence distance-hereditary [10].

We begin with the basic local consequences of the accessibility relation.

**Lemma 9.** *Let $T$ be a reduced graph-labelled-tree representation of a connected graph $G$, and let $B$ be a non-prime leaf bag of $T$.*

1. *If $B$ is a clique bag, then $G$ contains a twin pair.*
2. *If $B$ is a center-attached star bag, then $G$ contains a twin pair.*
3. *If $B$ is a leaf-attached star bag with center $c$, then every ordinary leaf of $B$ is a leaf of $G$ adjacent to $c$.*

*Proof.* Let $m_B$ be the marker of $B$.

Assume first that $B$ is a clique bag. By Lemma 1, the bag $B$ has at least two ordinary vertices. Any ordinary vertex of $B$ is adjacent to $m_B$ inside the clique, so every ordinary vertex of $B$ sees the rest of the graph through the same marker and therefore has the same neighborhood outside $B$. Since the ordinary vertices of $B$ are pairwise adjacent inside the bag, any two of them form a pair of true twins in $G$.

Next assume that $B$ is a center-attached star bag. Again, Lemma 1 implies that $B$ has at least two ordinary leaves. Each ordinary leaf is adjacent to the marker $m_B$, which is now the center of the star, and no two ordinary leaves are adjacent to one another. Thus any two ordinary leaves have the same neighborhood outside $B$ and are nonadjacent, so they form a pair of false twins in $G$.

Finally, assume that $B$ is a leaf-attached star bag with center $c$. Let $x$ be an ordinary leaf of $B$. Inside $B$, the vertex $x$ is adjacent only to $c$, and it is not adjacent to the marker $m_B$. Consequently, $x$ has no neighbor outside $B$. Therefore $x$ has degree 1 in $G$, and its unique neighbor is $c$. □

**Corollary 3.** *Let $T$ be a reduced graph-labelled-tree representation of a connected graph $G$, and let $B$ be a leaf-attached star bag of $T$. If $B$ has at least two ordinary leaves, then $G$ contains a twin pair.*

*Proof.* Let $c$ be the center of $B$. By Lemma 9, every ordinary leaf of $B$ is a leaf of $G$ adjacent to $c$. Hence any two ordinary leaves of $B$ are nonadjacent and have the same unique neighbor $c$, so they are false twins. □

The next lemma identifies exactly when one can peel a non-prime leaf bag away from the prime bag.

**Lemma 10.** *Let $T$ be a reduced graph-labelled-tree representation of a connected graph $G$, and suppose that $T$ has a unique prime bag $P$. If $T$ is not a star centered at $P$, then there exists a non-prime leaf bag $B$ whose unique neighbor bag is also non-prime.*

*Proof.* Since $T$ is not a star centered at $P$, there exists a bag at distance at least 2 from $P$. Choose a bag $B \neq P$ maximizing $\mathrm{dist}_T(B, P)$. In a tree, every vertex farthest from a fixed vertex is a leaf, so $B$ is a leaf bag. Because $\mathrm{dist}_T(B, P) \geq 2$, the unique neighbor of $B$ is not $P$. As $P$ is the only prime bag, that neighbor bag is non-prime. □

The next lemma shows that, in the non-star case, removing a leaf-attached star bag with a single ordinary leaf preserves membership in $\mathcal{D}(H)$.

**Lemma 11.** *Let $H$ be a split-prime graph, let $G \in \mathcal{D}(H)$, and fix a reduced graph-labelled-tree representation $T$ of $G$ with unique prime bag $P$. Suppose that $T$ is not a star centered at $P$, and let $B$ be a non-prime leaf bag whose unique neighbor bag is non-prime. Assume that $B$ is a leaf-attached star bag with exactly one ordinary leaf $x$ and center $c$. Let $A$ be the unique neighbor bag of $B$, and let $a$ be the marker vertex of $A$ corresponding to the tree edge joining $A$ to $B$. Then:*

1. *$G - x \in \mathcal{D}(H)$;*
2. *$G - \{x, c\} \in \mathcal{D}(H)$.*

*Proof (Proof sketch).* Let $m_B$ be the marker of $B$. Since $B$ is a leaf-attached star bag with exactly one ordinary leaf $x$, its label graph consists of the three vertices $m_B, c, x$, with edges $m_B c$ and $cx$.

Because $B$ is leaf-attached, the marker $m_B$ is a leaf of the star label of $B$. Hence, by Lemma 2, if the neighboring bag $A$ is a star bag, then the corresponding marker $a$ in $A$ cannot be the center of that star; thus $a$ is a leaf whenever $A$ is a star bag.

For (1), delete the bag $B$ and the tree edge $AB$, and reinterpret the marker $a$ of $A$ as an ordinary vertex labelled $c$. By the accessibility relation, this changes neither the adjacencies among the remaining old ordinary vertices nor the neighborhood of $c$, so the resulting graph-labelled tree represents $G-x$. No prime bag label changes, and after the standard reduction operations if necessary, we obtain a reduced graph-labelled-tree representation of $G-x$ with the same unique prime bag label as before. Hence $G - x \in \mathcal{D}(H)$.

For (2), instead delete the bag $B$, the tree edge $AB$, and the marker $a$ from the label graph of $A$. Again by the accessibility relation, the resulting graph-labelled tree represents $G - \{x, c\}$, since any accessibility path using the edge $AB$ necessarily ended at one of the deleted vertices $x$ or $c$. Because $A$ is non-prime and $a$ is either a clique vertex or a leaf of a star, deleting $a$ leaves a clique bag or a star bag; after standard reductions if necessary, the unique prime bag label is preserved. Therefore $G - \{x, c\} \in \mathcal{D}(H)$.

□

We now analyze the complementary case in which every non-prime leaf bag is adjacent to the prime bag.

**Lemma 12.** *Let $H$ be a split-prime graph, let $G \in \mathcal{D}(H)$, and fix a reduced graph-labelled-tree representation $T$ of $G$ whose unique prime bag is $P$. Suppose that $T$ is a star centered at $P$. Then one of the following holds:*

1. *$G$ contains a twin pair; or*
2. *there exists an induced subgraph $Q$ of $G$ isomorphic to the label graph of $P$ such that $G$ is obtained from $Q$ by attaching pendant vertices to vertices of $Q$.*

*Proof.* Let $B$ be any non-prime leaf bag adjacent to $P$. If $B$ is a clique bag or a center-attached star bag, then $G$ contains a twin pair by Lemma 9. If $B$ is a leaf-attached star bag with at least two ordinary leaves, then $G$ contains a twin pair by Corollary 3.

We may therefore assume that every non-prime leaf bag is a leaf-attached star bag with exactly one ordinary leaf. Let the leaf bags be $B_1, \ldots, B_t$. For each $i$, let $m_i$ be the marker of $B_i$, let $c_i$ be the center of $B_i$, let $x_i$ be the unique ordinary leaf of $B_i$, and let $p_i$ be the marker vertex of $P$ corresponding to the tree edge joining $P$ to $B_i$.

Let $O(P)$ denote the set of ordinary vertices of the prime bag $P$, and define $Q := G[\,O(P) \cup \{c_1, \ldots, c_t\}\,]$. We claim that $Q$ is isomorphic to the label graph of $P$. Define a map $\phi : V(Q) \to V(P)$ by fixing each ordinary vertex of $P$ and sending $c_i$ to $p_i$.

We check adjacency. If $u, v \in O(P)$, then $u$ and $v$ are adjacent in $Q$ if and only if they are adjacent in the label graph of $P$, since they lie in the same bag.

If $u \in O(P)$, then $c_i$ is adjacent to $u$ in $G$ if and only if $c_i$ is adjacent to $m_i$ in $B_i$ and $p_i$ is adjacent to $u$ in $P$, by the accessibility relation. Since $c_i \sim m_i$ in $B_i$, this is equivalent to $p_i \sim u$ in $P$. Similarly, for $i \neq j$, the vertices $c_i$ and $c_j$ are adjacent in $G$ if and only if $c_i \sim m_i$ in $B_i$, $p_i \sim p_j$ in $P$, and $m_j \sim c_j$ in $B_j$; again this is equivalent to $p_i \sim p_j$ in $P$. Thus $\phi$ is an isomorphism from $Q$ to the label graph of $P$.

Finally, by Lemma 9, each $x_i$ is a leaf of $G$ adjacent only to $c_i$. Hence $G$ is obtained from $Q$ by attaching the pendant vertices $x_1, \ldots, x_t$ to the vertices $c_1, \ldots, c_t$, respectively. □

The next lemma shows that path-extremality is preserved under such pendant extensions, provided the base graph and all of its induced subgraphs are already path-extremal.

**Lemma 13.** *Let $Q$ be a graph such that every induced subgraph of $Q$ is path-extremal. Let $G$ be a graph obtained from $Q$ by attaching pendant vertices to vertices of $Q$. Then $G$ is path-extremal.*

*Proof.* We argue by induction on the number $t$ of pendant vertices attached to $Q$. The case $t = 0$ is immediate.

Assume $t \geq 1$. If some vertex of $Q$ supports at least two added pendant vertices, then those pendant vertices are false twins in $G$, and so $G$ is path-extremal by Corollary 1.

We may therefore assume that no vertex of $Q$ supports more than one added pendant vertex. Let $x$ be one of the pendant vertices, and let $v \in V(Q)$ be its unique neighbor.

Then $G - x$ is obtained from $Q$ by attaching $t - 1$ pendant vertices, so $G - x$ is path-extremal by the induction hypothesis. Moreover, because $v$ supports no other pendant vertex, the graph $G - \{x, v\}$ is obtained from the induced subgraph $Q - v$ by attaching at most $t - 1$ pendant vertices. Since every induced subgraph of $Q$ is path-extremal, the same is true of $Q - v$, and hence the induction hypothesis implies that $G - \{x, v\}$ is path-extremal.

Applying Lemma 4 to the leaf $x$, we obtain for every $k \geq 1$, $z'(G; k) \geq z'(G - x; k) + z'(G - \{x, v\}; k - 1) \geq z'(P_{n-1}; k) + z'(P_{n-2}; k - 1) = z'(P_n; k)$, where $n = |V(G)|$, and the last equality follows from Lemma 3 and Pascal's identity. The case $k = 0$ is trivial. Therefore $G$ is path-extremal. □

**Theorem 2.** *Let $H$ be a split-prime graph. Suppose that every induced subgraph of $H$ is path-extremal. Then every graph in $\mathcal{C}(H)$ is path-extremal.*

*Proof.* We prove the stronger statement that every graph in $\mathcal{D}(H)$ is path-extremal, by induction on $n = |V(G)|$.

Let $G \in \mathcal{D}(H)$, and fix a reduced graph-labelled-tree representation $T$ of $G$ with at most one prime bag.

If $T$ has no prime bag, then $G$ is distance-hereditary, and the result follows from Theorem 1. Thus we may assume that $T$ has a unique prime bag $P$.

If $T$ has only one bag, then $G$ is isomorphic to the label graph of $P$. Since the label graph of $P$ is isomorphic to an induced subgraph of $H$, the hypothesis on $H$ implies that $G$ is path-extremal.

We now assume that $T$ has more than one bag.

*Case 1: $T$ is not a star centered at $P$.* By Lemma 10, there exists a non-prime leaf bag $B$ whose unique neighbor bag is non-prime.

If $B$ is a clique bag or a center-attached star bag, then $G$ contains a twin pair by Lemma 9, and hence $G$ is path-extremal by Corollary 1. If $B$ is a leaf-attached star bag with at least two ordinary leaves, then $G$ contains a twin pair by Corollary 3, and again $G$ is path-extremal.

We may therefore assume that $B$ is a leaf-attached star bag with exactly one ordinary leaf $x$. Let $c$ be the center of $B$. By Lemma 9, the vertex $x$ is a leaf of $G$ with unique neighbor $c$. Hence Lemma 4 gives $z'(G;k) \geq z'(G-x;k)+z'(G-\{x,c\};k-1)$ for every $k \geq 1$.

By Lemma 11(1), we have $G-x \in \mathcal{D}(H)$, so the induction hypothesis implies that $G-x$ is path-extremal.

Moreover, Lemma 11(2) gives $G-\{x,c\} \in \mathcal{D}(H)$, so the induction hypothesis implies that $G-\{x,c\}$ is path-extremal. Thus both graphs on the right-hand side are path-extremal.

Therefore, for every $k \geq 1$, $z'(G;k) \geq z'(G-x;k) + z'(G-\{x,c\};k-1) \geq z'(P_{n-1};k) + z'(P_{n-2};k-1) = z'(P_n;k)$, where the last equality follows from Lemma 3 and Pascal's identity. The case $k=0$ is trivial, so $G$ is path-extremal.

*Case 2: $T$ is a star centered at $P$.* By Lemma 12, either $G$ contains a twin pair, in which case $G$ is path-extremal by Corollary 1, or there exists an induced subgraph $Q$ of $G$ isomorphic to the label graph of $P$ such that $G$ is obtained from $Q$ by attaching pendant vertices to vertices of $Q$.

Since the label graph of $P$ is isomorphic to an induced subgraph of $H$, the same is true of $Q$. Consequently, every induced subgraph of $Q$ is path-extremal by the hypothesis on $H$. Lemma 13 now implies that $G$ is path-extremal.

This completes the induction. Since $\mathcal{C}(H) \subseteq \mathcal{D}(H)$, the theorem follows. □

**Corollary 4.** *Let $m \in \mathbb{N}$. Suppose that every induced subgraph of every split-prime graph on at most $m$ vertices is path-extremal. Then every graph in $\mathcal{C}_{\leq m}$ is path-extremal.*

*Proof.* Let $G \in \mathcal{C}_{\leq m}$, and let $H$ denote the label graph of the unique prime bag of the canonical split decomposition of $G$. By definition, $|V(H)| \leq m$. Hence every induced subgraph of $H$ is path-extremal by hypothesis, so Theorem 2 implies that $G$ is path-extremal. □

*Remark 2.* Theorem 2 shows that the only genuinely new obstruction beyond the distance-hereditary case occurs when all non-prime bags are attached directly to the prime bag. In that star-centered configuration, the graph either already contains a twin pair or reduces to a split-prime core together with pendant extensions. Corollary 4 therefore reduces the path-extremal conjecture on $\mathcal{C}_{\leq m}$ to a finite verification problem on bounded-order split-prime bases.

**Disclosure of Interests.** The author has no competing interests to declare.

## References

1. AIM Minimum Rank – Special Graphs Work Group: Zero forcing sets and the minimum rank of graphs. Linear Algebra and its Applications **428**(7), 1628–1648 (2008). https://doi.org/10.1016/j.laa.2007.10.009
2. Bandelt, H.J., Mulder, H.M.: Distance-hereditary graphs. Journal of Combinatorial Theory, Series B **41**(2), 182–208 (1986). https://doi.org/10.1016/0095-8956(86)90043-2
3. Barioli, F., Barrett, W., Fallat, S.M., Hall, H.T., Hogben, L., Shader, B.L., van den Driessche, P., van der Holst, H.: Zero forcing parameters and minimum rank problems. Linear Algebra Appl. **433**(2), 401–411 (2010). https://doi.org/10.1016/j.laa.2010.03.008
4. Boyer, K., Brimkov, B., English, S., Ferrero, D., Keller, A., Kirsch, R., Phillips, M., Reinhart, C.: The zero forcing polynomial of a graph. Discret. Appl. Math. **258**, 35–48 (2019). https://doi.org/10.1016/j.dam.2018.11.033
5. Burgarth, D., Giovannetti, V., Hogben, L., Severini, S., Young, M.: Logic circuits from zero forcing. Nat. Comput. **14**(3), 485–490 (2014). https://doi.org/10.1007/s11047-014-9438-5
6. Cunningham, W.H.: Decomposition of directed graphs. SIAM Journal on Algebraic Discrete Methods **3**(2), 214–228 (1982). https://doi.org/10.1137/0603021
7. Curtis, B., Gan, L., Haddock, J., Lawrence, R., Spiro, S.: Zero forcing with random sets. Discret. Math. **347**(5), 113944 (2024). https://doi.org/10.1016/j.disc.2024.113944
8. English, S., MacRury, C., Prałat, P.: Probabilistic zero forcing on random graphs. Eur. J. Comb. **91**, 103207 (2021). https://doi.org/10.1016/j.ejc.2020.103207
9. Fallat, S.M., Hogben, L.: The minimum rank of symmetric matrices described by a graph: A survey. Linear Algebra Appl. **426**(2–3), 558–582 (2007). https://doi.org/10.1016/j.laa.2007.05.036
10. Gioan, E., Paul, C.: Split decomposition and graph-labelled trees: Characterizations and fully dynamic algorithms for totally decomposable graphs. Discret. Appl. Math. **160**(6), 708–733 (2012). https://doi.org/10.1016/j.dam.2011.05.007
11. Hogben, L., Huynh, M., Kingsley, N., Meyer, S., Walker, S., Young, M.: Propagation time for zero forcing on a graph. Discret. Appl. Math. **160**(13–14), 1994–2005 (2012). https://doi.org/10.1016/j.dam.2012.04.003
12. Kang, C.X., Yi, E.: Probabilistic zero forcing in graphs. Bull. Inst. Combin. Appl. **67**, 9–16 (2013)
13. Kenter, F.H.J., Lin, J.C.H.: On the error of a priori sampling: Zero forcing sets and propagation time. Linear Algebra Appl. **576**, 124–141 (2019). https://doi.org/10.1016/j.laa.2018.03.031
14. Menon, K., Singh, A.: Exploring the influence of graph operations on zero forcing sets. Discret. Math. **348**(8), 114516 (2025). https://doi.org/10.1016/j.disc.2025.114516
15. Tréfois, M., Delvenne, J.C.: Zero forcing number, constrained matchings and strong structural controllability. Linear Algebra Appl. **484**, 199–218 (2015). https://doi.org/10.1016/j.laa.2015.06.025

# Algorithms and Complexity of Influence Maximization on Directed Acyclic Graphs

Panfeng Liu and Biaoshuai Tao(✉)

Shanghai Jiao Tong University, Shanghai, China
{liupf22,bstao}@sjtu.edu.cn

**Abstract.** This paper investigates the influence maximization problem under the Independent Cascade (IC) and Linear Threshold (LT) models. While this problem is known to be APX-hard on general graphs, we explore its computational limits by focusing on Directed Acyclic Graphs (DAGs) and more restricted tree structures. Our primary result demonstrates that influence maximization remains APX-hard on DAGs under the LT model, suggesting that the absence of cycles is insufficient to achieve a polynomial-time approximation scheme (PTAS). In contrast, we show that the problem becomes tractable when the topology is further restricted to out-arborescences and in-arborescences. Specifically, for out-arborescences, we show that the IC model and the LT model are equivalent, and we develop exact polynomial-time algorithms based on dynamic programming that leverage the unique path properties of these structures. For in-arborescences, it is known that the problem is polynomial-time solvable under the LT model, and it is NP-hard under the IC model. We complement these results by presenting a fully polynomial-time approximation scheme (FPTAS) for the IC model.

**Keywords:** Influence Maximization · Directed Acyclic Graphs · Arborescence · APX-hardness · Dynamic Programming

## 1 Introduction

The *influence maximization* (InfMax) problem, which is defined to *seed* a set of nodes in the social network to maximize the spreading of the resulting *cascade* [1–3,7,9,11,16–19,22], where a *cascade* is a basic social network process that captures the character of the information diffusion in a social network, in which a number of initially infected seeds process a certain attribute of information and spread this attribute to their neighbor.

Two most well-known cascade models are the independent cascade (IC) model and the linear threshold (LT) model, both introduced in the seminal work of Kempe et al. [9]. These two models are studied almost exclusively in the past literature of this field, and we will focus on these two models in this paper. In the IC model, a newly activated node $u$ attempts to activate each of its inactive

The full version of this paper is available on https://arxiv.org/abs/2606.00585.


Y. Li et al. (Eds.): COCOON 2026, LNCS 16835, pp. 423–436, 2027.
https://doi.org/10.1007/978-981-92-3309-0_32

neighbors $v$ with a fixed probability, independently of other infections (we use the words "activation" and "infection" interchangeably throughout this work). In the LT model, if the graph is unweighted, each non-seed vertex is assigned a threshold randomly and independently from the interval $[0, 1]$. A vertex becomes active when the fraction of its infected neighbors exceeds its threshold. Formal definitions of the two models are available in Sect. 2.

The computational complexity and approximability of InfMax are well-understood in general graphs. For both the IC and LT models, the problem is known to be APX-hard on directed and undirected graphs [9,20]. On the positive side, since the influence function $\sigma(\cdot)$ is submodular under these models [13], a simple greedy algorithm achieves a $(1 - 1/e)$-approximation ratio [9,14]. For undirected networks, this approximation guarantee can be slightly improved [10, 21]. However, for directed graphs under the IC model, the $(1 - 1/e)$ bound remains tight unless P = NP [9]. These hardness results suggest that achieving exact solutions or better approximation ratios requires restricting the graph topology.

In this paper, we focus on Directed Acyclic Graphs (DAGs) and their variants. DAGs represent a natural and significant special case for influence propagation, as influence in the real world often follows a clear hierarchical and unidirectional structure. For instance, in social media or professional networks, such as citation networks, information cascades, influence typically flows from high-profile figures or domain experts to their followers in a top-down, non-recurrent manner. Moreover, DAG-based decompositions are widely used in the analysis of diffusion processes on general graphs. DAGs are among the most fundamental graph classes in algorithm design and complexity theory. The existence of topological orderings often makes problems more tractable on DAGs, providing insight into the boundary between tractable and intractable cases. Despite the absence of cycles, we first present our primary hardness result: InfMax remains APX-hard on DAGs under the LT model, indicating that the problem's inherent difficulty persists even in such structured settings. Motivated by this boundary, we further investigate two more restricted structures: out-arborescences and in-arborescences. We demonstrate that the unique path properties of these trees allow for polynomial-time algorithms or approximation schemes via dynamic programming, thereby providing a complete characterization of the transition from tractability to APX-hardness in hierarchical networks.

## 1.1 Our Results

We first study the approximability of InfMax on directed acyclic graphs. For the IC model, the same proof in Kempe et al. [9] can show that InfMax remains NP-hard to approximate to within a factor of $(1 - 1/e + \varepsilon)$ (for any $\varepsilon > 0$), as the reduction used by Kempe et al. uses a directed acyclic graph. In this paper, we show that InfMax is APX-hard for the LT model for directed acyclic graphs. Specifically, there exists a universal constant $\tau > 0$ such that InfMax is NP-hard to approximate to within a factor of $(1 - \tau)$. See Sect. 3 for details.

Motivated by the hardness of directed acyclic graphs, we then focus on directed trees. For out-arborescences, in Sect. 4, we show that the unique path property permits a polynomial-time dynamic programming algorithm. Crucially, we prove that the LT and IC models are equivalent on this structure, rendering our dynamic programming approach universally applicable to both propagation models in this setting. For in-arborescences, the IC and LT models are no longer equivalent. Wang et al. [23] show that InfMax under LT model admits a polynomial-time algorithm, while Lu et al. [12] show that InfMax under the IC model is still NP-hard. We complement these results by presenting a fully polynomial-time approximation scheme for the IC model in Sect. 5.

## 2 Preliminaries

Throughout this paper, a social network is represented by a weighted directed graph $G = (V, E, P)$, where $V$ is the node (i.e., user) set with $|V| = n$, $E$ is the edge (i.e., the connections between users) set with $|E| = m$ and $P = \{p_e \in (0, 1]\}_{e \in E}$ is the edge weights. For a directed edge $(u, v) \in E$, we say $u$ (resp. $v$) is the incoming (resp. outgoing) neighbor of $v$ (resp. $u$), and $(u, v)$ is the outgoing (resp. incoming) edge of $u$ (resp. $v$).

This paper focuses on the class of *directed acyclic graphs* (DAGs) and two special sub-classes: *in-arborescences* and *out-arborescences.*

**Definition 1.** *Let $G = (V, E)$ be a directed acyclic graph (DAG). For a vertex $v \in V$, an in-arborescence rooted at $v$ is a directed tree in which every vertex has a unique directed path to $v$, i.e., all edges are oriented toward the root $v$. An out-arborescence rooted at $v$ is a directed tree in which there exists a unique directed path from $v$ to every other vertex, i.e., all edges are oriented away from the root.*

*Diffusion Models.* A *diffusion model* $\Gamma$ is a (possibly random) function that maps from a seed set $S$ (the vertices that are initially infected) to a vertex set $\Gamma(S)$ (the set of influenced vertices at the end of the spreading).

**Definition 2 (Independent Cascade Model (IC) [9]).** *Given a social network (directed graph) $G = (V, E, P)$, the* IC *model assigns the state of each node as* active *or* inactive. *On the input seed set $S \subseteq V$,* IC *outputs the set $\Gamma_{\mathrm{IC}}(S)$ as follows:*

1. *At timestamp 0, only nodes in $S$ are active.*
2. *At each timestamp $t = 1, 2, \ldots$, each newly activated node $u$ from the previous timestamp gets one chance to activate its inactive outgoing neighbor $v$ with probability $p_{(u,v)}$. The attempts to activate neighbors are independent of each other. If multiple incoming neighbors of an inactive node attempt to activate it, each attempt is considered separately with its own probability.*
3. *The diffusion process terminates when no additional activation occurs, and* IC *outputs $\Gamma_{\mathrm{IC}}(S)$ as the set of active nodes.*

**Definition 3 (Linear Threshold Model (LT) [9]).** *Given a social network (directed graph) $G = (V, E, P)$ where the edge weights satisfy $\sum_{u \in N(v)} p_{(u,v)} \leq 1$ for each $v \in V$, the* LT *model assigns the state of each node as* active *or* inactive*. Given the input seed set $S \subseteq V$,* LT *outputs the set $\Gamma_{\mathrm{LT}}(S)$ as follows:*

1. *At the beginning, for each vertex $v$, a threshold $\theta_v \in [0, 1]$ is sampled uniformly at random independently.*
2. *At timestamp 0, only nodes in $S$ are active.*
3. *At each timestamp $t = 1, 2, \ldots$, a node $v$ is active if the sum of the weights of edges from $v$'s active in-neighbors to $v$ exceeds the threshold $\theta_v$:*

$$\sum_{u: u \in N(v) \text{ and } u \text{ is active}} p_{(u,v)} \geq \theta_v$$

4. *The diffusion process terminates when no additional activation occurs, and* LT *outputs $\Gamma_{\mathrm{LT}}(S)$ as the set of active nodes.*

**Definition 4 (Influence Maximization (InfMax) [9]).** *Given a directed weighted graph $G = (V, E, P)$, a positive integer $k$ and a diffusion model $\Gamma$, the* InfMax *problem aims to find a seed set $S \subseteq V$ with $|S| \leq k$ that maximizes the expected spread $\sigma_\Gamma(S)$ under the given diffusion model.*

Given a diffusion model $\Gamma$, let $\sigma_\Gamma(S) = \mathbb{E}(|\Gamma(S)|)$ be the expected number of infected vertices. The goal is to find $S$ that maximizes $\sigma_\Gamma(S)$. It is known that computing $\sigma_\Gamma(\cdot)$ is #P-hard for both IC and LT models [4,5,9]. On the other hand, by simple Monte-Carlo samplings, we can easily obtain a fully polynomial-time randomized approximation scheme (FPRAS) for computing $\sigma_\Gamma(\cdot)$. In addition, for directed acyclic graphs, the evaluation of $\sigma_\Gamma(\cdot)$ under the LT model becomes tractable: since the influence propagation is acyclic, given a seed set, we can compute the probability of infection for each vertex one by one following the topological order of the graph [5]. This problem remains #P-hard for the IC model even for directed acyclic graphs [15]. However, as we will see later, the APX-hardness of the influence maximization problem with the IC model on directed acyclic graphs does not come from the #P-hardness of evaluating $\sigma_\Gamma(\cdot)$. For in-arborescences and out-arborescences, computing $\sigma_\Gamma(\cdot)$ for the IC model becomes tractable: we can compute the probability of infection for each vertex in the bottom-up order (for in-arborescences) or the top-down order (for out-arborescences).

In this paper, we omit the subscript $\Gamma$ of $\sigma_\Gamma$ when it is clear from the context.

## 3 APX-Hardness of InfMax on Directed Acyclic Graphs

In the context of propagation modeling, directed acyclic graphs eliminate cyclic feedback, ensuring that the diffusion of influence follows a clear temporal or hierarchical order, which seemingly significantly simplifies the propagation dynamics. However, this section demonstrates that such structural simplification is insufficient to significantly reduce the computational hardness of the influence maximization problem. We will prove that even when the propagation graph is restricted to a DAG, the influence maximization problem remains difficult in the sense of approximation; specifically, the problem is APX-hard.

For the IC model, there is a straightforward reduction from the *max-k-coverage* problem (selecting $k$ subsets of a set with the largest union) to the InfMax problem. Firstly, create a vertex for each subset, and a large number $w$ of vertices for each element. Then, create a directed edge from a vertex representing the subset to each one of the $w$ vertices representing the element if the element is contained in the subset in the max-k-coverage instance, and set the weight of this edge to be 1. Seeding a vertex representing a subset simulates selecting a subset in the max-k-coverage problem. This is obviously an approximation-ratio preserving reduction by setting $w$ to be sufficiently large. Given that the inapproximability ratio $(1-1/e+\varepsilon)$ of max-k-coverage is known due to Feige [8], we have the same inapproximability ratio for InfMax.[1] In addition, the above-mentioned graph is a directed acyclic graph, so the same inapproximability ratio extends to the InfMax problem with directed acyclic graphs. The inapproximability does not come from the #P-hardness of evaluating $\sigma(\cdot)$, as this function is easy to compute in the above instance since all edges have weight 1.

We now complement this result by showing that the InfMax problem on directed acyclic graphs is also APX-hard under the LT model.

**Theorem 1 (APX-Hardness on DAGs).** *There exists a universal constant $\tau > 0$ such that* InfMax *on directed acyclic graphs with the* LT *model is NP-hard to approximate to within a factor of* $(1-\tau)$.

We will use the following inapproximability result for the vertex cover problem. Theorem 2 is a straightforward corollary to Dinur's PCP theorem [6], which states that max-3SAT is APX-hard for instances where each variable appears a constant number of times. Based on Dinur's PCP theorem, Theorem 2 follows from the well-known reduction from 3SAT to vertex cover. The proof is available in the full version of this paper.

**Theorem 2 (APX-Hardness of Vertex Cover).** *There exist a universal constant integer $d$ and a universal constant $\gamma \in (0,1)$ such that, given an even integer $k$ and an undirected graph $G=(V,E)$ where the degree of each vertex is bounded by $d$ and $|V|=\frac{3}{2}k$, it is NP-hard to distinguish between the following two cases:*

- *YES: $G$ has a vertex cover of size $k$;*
- *NO: all vertex covers of $G$ have sizes at least $(1+\gamma)k$.*

As a few remarks, the theorem above requires that the degrees of the vertices are bounded by a constant $d$, which also implies $|E|=O(|V|)$ ($|E|\leq\frac{d}{2}|E|$ to be more precise). In addition, the optimal size of the vertex cover in the yes instance is a constant fraction of the total number of vertices: $k$ versus $|V|=\frac{3}{2}k$.

We prove Theorem 1 in the remaining part of this section.

[1] This is exactly the reduction used in Kempe et al. [9].

### 3.1 Construction and Preliminary Observations

Given a Vertex Cover instance $(G = (V, E), k)$ with $|V| = n = \frac{3}{2}k$ and $|E| = m \leq \frac{d}{2}n$ that satisfies the description in Theorem 2, we construct an influence maximization instance $G'$ where the underlying graph is a DAG. The core idea of the construction is to design a local gadget for every edge in the original graph, such that the selection of endpoints in the original graph directly corresponds to the influence gain obtainable within the gadget.

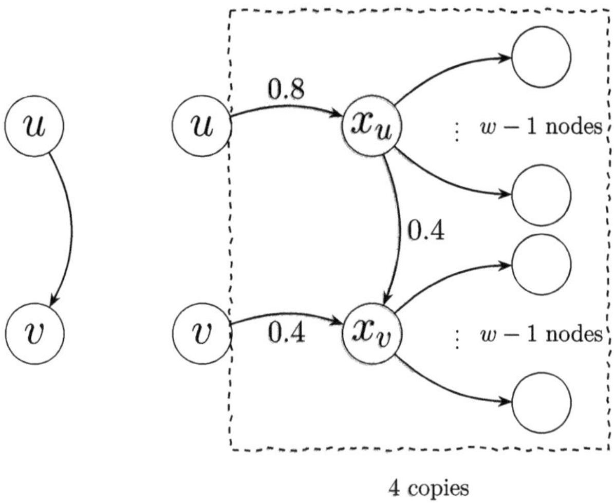


**Fig. 1.** Reduction gadget: Converting an edge $(u, v)$ of the original graph into a gadget for the influence maximization instance.

Specifically, for each undirected edge $(u, v) \in E$ in the original graph, we replace the edge by the gadget shown in Fig. 1 into $G'$. The gadget contains two intermediate nodes $x_u$ and $x_v$, corresponding to the two endpoints of the edge $(u, v)$. A directed edge with weight $b_1 = 0.8$ is added from $u$ to $x_u$, a directed edge with weight $b_3 = 0.4$ is added from $v$ to $x_v$, and a directed edge with weight $b_2 = 0.4$ is added from $x_u$ to $x_v$. Furthermore, $w - 1$ leaf nodes are attached to both $x_u$ and $x_v$; these leaf nodes are activated with probability 1 whenever their respective parent node is activated, thereby amplifying the influence differences within the gadget. Finally, this gadget is duplicated three more times (the vertices $u$ and $v$ in the original graph are not duplicated, the remaining part of the gadget has four identical copies). By repeating this process for all edges, we obtain the influence maximization instance $G'$, which is globally a directed acyclic graph.

Finally, we set the number of seeds $k'$ to be $k' = k + 4m$. We obtain an InfMax instance $(G', k')$.

Below, we list some preliminary observations.

1. If we choose both intermediate-layer vertices $x_u$ and $x_v$ as seeds, all vertices in each copy of the gadget are infected with probability 1. The expected number is $2w$.
2. If one or both of $u$ and $v$ is/are seeded and we carefully choose exactly one of $x_u, x_v$ as a seed, then the expected number of infected vertices in each copy of the gadget reaches $1.8w$. To see this, if $u$ is seeded, we choose $x_v$ as a seed, then $x_u$ is infected with probability 0.8 and $x_v$ is infected with probability 1; if $v$ is seeded, we choose $x_u$ as a seed, then $x_u$ is infected with probability 1 and $x_v$ is infected with probability $0.4+0.4 = 0.8$; if both $u$ and $v$ are seeded, the choice of $x_u$ and $x_v$ can be arbitrary. In all cases, the expected number of infected vertices is $1.8w$.
3. If one or both of $u$ and $v$ is/are seeded and none of $x_u$ and $x_v$ is seeded, the expected number of infected vertices in each copy of the gadget is at most $1.52w$. To see this, even if both $u$ and $v$ are seeded, without seeding $x_u$ and $x_v$, $x_u$ is infected with probability 0.8, and $x_v$ is infected with probability $0.4 + 0.8 \times 0.4 = 0.72$. The expected number of infected vertices is at most $(0.8 + 0.72)w = 1.52w$.
4. If none of $u$ and $v$ is seeded (meaning that the edge $(u, v)$ in the vertex cover instance is uncovered) and we are to choose one seed from $x_u$ and $x_v$, the best choice is $x_u$, and the expected number of infected vertices is $(1+0.4)w = 1.4w$.

*Completeness.* Suppose there exists a vertex cover $S$ of size $k$ in the original graph $G$. We construct a seed set $S'$ in $G'$ as follows: First, include all nodes from $S$ in $S'$. Second, for each edge $(u, v) \in E$, since $S$ is a vertex cover, at least one endpoint belongs to $S$. If $u \in S$, we add node $x_v$ to $S'$; if $v \in S$, we add node $x_u$ to $S'$. If both $u, v \in S$, we choose one arbitrarily. We do this for all four copies in the gadget. The number of seeds chosen is exactly $k' = k + 4m$. By Observation 2, each copy of the gadget has $1.8w$ infected vertices in expectation. Since each gadget has four copies and there are $m$ edges, the total expected number of infected vertices is $k + 4m \cdot 1.8w > 7.2mw$.

*Soundness.* Now, suppose the size of any vertex cover in $G$ is at least $(1+\gamma)k$. We consider the optimal choice $S'$ of the seed set in the InfMax instance $(G', k')$, and we aim to show that $\sigma(S')$ is at most $(1-\delta)7.2mw$ for some constant $\delta$. We first give some characterizations for $S'$.

First of all, notice that $S'$ cannot contain a seed from those $w-1$ leaf nodes (those vertices on the right-hand side of Fig. 1): seeding the corresponding $x_u$ or $x_v$ is much better. Next, we show that there cannot exist a copy of the gadget where both intermediate vertices $x_u$ and $x_v$ are seeded in $S'$.

*Sub-optimality of Doubly-Seeding.* Suppose there exists a vertex pair $(u, v)$ such that both $x_u$ and $x_v$ are seeded in one copy of the gadget. We will show that such a seeding strategy is always sub-optimal. We consider two cases regarding the set of seeds chosen among the vertices in the original vertex cover instance, i.e., $S' \cap V$:

- Case 1: $S' \cap V$ is a vertex cover of $G$, and

– Case 2: $S' \cap V$ is not a vertex cover of $G$.

For Case 1, we must have $|S' \cap V| \geq (1+\gamma)k$. Since $k' = k + 4m$, we can choose at most $4m - \gamma k < 4m$ vertices among those intermediate vertices in the gadgets. If there is one copy $(u, v)$ where both $x_u$ and $x_v$ are seeded, then there must exist another copy $(u', v')$ where none of $x_{u'}$ and $x_{v'}$ is seeded. By replacing a seed from the former copy with a seed in the latter copy, the expected number of infected vertices in the graph increases. To see this, by Observations 1 and 2, the extra seed in the former copy has a $0.2w$ marginal influence; by Observations 2 and 3, adding one seed to the latter copy increases the expected influence by at least $1.8w - 1.52w = 0.28w$. Hence, the exchange gives an increment of $0.08w$ in expected influence. Thus, doubly-seeding is always sub-optimal under Case 1.

We then consider Case 2. Consider an arbitrary uncovered edge $(u, v)$ in the original graph. We first show that all the 8 intermediate vertices in the gadget must be seeded. Suppose this is not the case. If exactly 7 intermediate vertices in the gadget are seeded, then replacing one of them by either $u$ or $v$ improves the expected influence. Before the replacement, by Observations 1 and 4, the expected number of infected vertices in the gadget is $2w+2w+2w+1.4w = 7.4w$. After the replacement, by Observations 1 and 2, the expected number of infected vertices in the gadget is $2w + 2w + 1.8w + 1.8w = 7.6w$. Thus, this replacement is beneficial. If at most 6 intermediate vertices in the gadget are seeded, then replacing any double seed (from this gadget or from another gadget) by either $u$ or $v$ improves the expected influence. By adding one of $u$ and $v$ as seeds and by Observation 2 and 4, the improvement of influence within this gadget is at least $2(1.8w - 1.4w) = 0.8w$. On the other hand, the loss in the expected influence due to selecting one less double seed is at most $2w - 1.4w = 0.6w$ (by Observation 1 and 4). This replacement is also beneficial.

Next, if there are at least 3 copies (from the same gadget, or from different gadgets) where none of the two intermediate vertices is seeded, we show that the existence of an uncovered edge $(u, v)$ where all the 8 intermediate vertices are seeded makes $S'$ sub-optimal. We can instead select only 4 intermediate vertices such that each of the four copies contains only one seeded intermediate vertex, and, for the 4 more seeds, we use one of them to seed $u$ or $v$, and the other 3 to seed the intermediate vertices from the 3 copies where no intermediate seed is chosen. To show that this adjustment is beneficial, we first compute the loss in the expected influence within the gadget $(u, v)$. Before the adjustment, by Observation 1, the expected influence is $2w \times 4 = 8w$. After the adjustment, by Observation 2, it is $1.8w \times 4 = 7.2w$, the loss is $0.8w$. On the other hand, for the 3 seeds put in the other copies, each of them introduces a marginal influence of at least $1.8w - 1.52w = 0.28w$. Therefore, the overall gain is $0.28w \times 3 = 0.84w > 0.8w$. This adjustment is beneficial.

Finally, it remains the case where there are at most 2 copies where none of the two intermediate vertices is seeded, and, in addition, for every edge $(u, v)$ in the original graph that is not covered, all the 8 intermediate vertices are seeded. It is easy to see that, in this case, we have used more than $k' = k + 4m$ seeds, leading to a contradiction. This can be proved by a single counting argument.

Consider the following rearrangement of the seeds: choose any uncovered edge $(u, v)$; among the 8 intermediate seeds, choose (at most) 2 of them to compensate for the (at most) 2 copies where no intermediate vertices are seeded; after this, for each uncovered edge $(u, v)$, at least 6 intermediate vertices are still seeded; then we replace one of the intermediate seed by either $u$ or $v$ to make $(u, v)$ covered. By this rearrangement, all the edges are now covered, and each copy still contains at least one intermediate seed. The total number of seeds is at least $(1 + \gamma)k + 4m > k'$. This concludes the analysis of Case 2.

*Bounding* $\sigma(S')$. Now we compute an upper bound to the expected influence of $S'$. First of all, since we have ruled out double-seeding, in each of the four copies in each gadget, the expected number of infected vertices is at most $1.8w$.

We consider two cases regarding $S' \cap V$:

- Case 1: $|S' \cap V| > (1 + \frac{\gamma}{2})k$, and
- Case 2: $|S' \cap V| \leq (1 + \frac{\gamma}{2})k$.

For the first case, given $k' = k + 4m$, there are at least $\frac{\gamma}{2}k$ copies where no intermediate vertex is seeded. Even if each of the remaining $4m - \frac{\gamma}{2}k$ copies has the maximum number $1.8w$ of infected vertices, the expected total number of infected vertices in the gadgets is at most

$$1.8w \cdot \left(4m - \frac{\gamma}{2}k\right) + \frac{\gamma}{2}k \cdot 1.52w = 7.2mw - 0.14\gamma kw. \tag{1}$$

For the second case, since a vertex cover has size at least $(1+\gamma)k$, at least $\frac{\gamma}{2}k$ edges are not covered. Without double-seeding, the expected number of infected vertices in each gadget is at most $1.4w \times 4 = 5.6w$ (Observation 4). The expected total number of infected vertices in the gadgets is at most

$$1.8w \cdot 4 \cdot \left(m - \frac{\gamma}{2}k\right) + 5.6w \cdot \frac{\gamma}{2}k = 7.2mw - 0.8\gamma kw. \tag{2}$$

Combining (1) and (2), the upper bound to the expected number of infected vertices in the gadgets is $7.2mw - 0.14\gamma kw$. By making $w$ sufficiently large, e.g., $w = n^2$, the number of infected vertices outside those gadgets, i.e., those $n$ vertices in the original graph, is negligible. We can conclude that the expected number of infected vertices in the entire graph is at most $7.2mw - 0.14\gamma kw + o(w)$.

Finally, we conclude Theorem 1 by showing that the gap between $7.2mw$ and $7.2mw - 0.14\gamma kw + o(w)$ is constant. Noticing that $\gamma$ is a constant, we only need to show that $k > cm$ for some constant $c$. This is true, as we have $k = \frac{2}{3}n$ and $m \leq \frac{d}{2}n$.

## 4 Influence Maximization on Out-Arborescence

Let $T = (V, E)$ be an out-arborescence where edges are directed from parents to children. In the case of out-arborescences, we demonstrate that the unique path property facilitates a polynomial-time solution via dynamic programming.

**Theorem 3.** *For the influence maximization problem on out-arborescences, given any seed set $S$, we always have $\sigma_{\mathrm{IC}}(S) = \sigma_{\mathrm{LT}}(S)$. In addition, there exists a polynomial-time algorithm to compute $S$ that maximizes $\sigma_{\mathrm{IC}}(S) = \sigma_{\mathrm{LT}}(S)$.*

We first present the following lemma, which establishes the equivalence between the two models. The proof is straightforward from the definitions of the two models, and is thus omitted.

**Lemma 1.** *In an out-arborescence $T$ under both the* IC *and* LT *models, for any nodes $u$ and $v$, if there exists a unique directed path $p = \langle u = w_0, w_1, \ldots, w_k = v\rangle$, then $h_{u,v} = \prod_{i=0}^{k-1} P_{(w_i,w_{i+1})}$ where $P_{(w_i,w_{i+1})}$ represents the weight (propagation probability) of edge $(w_i, w_{i+1})$ and $h_{u,v}$ denote the probability that $u$ activates $v$ (if $u$ is the unique seed in $T$). If no directed path exists, $h_{u,v} = 0$.*

Lemma 1 gives an effective way to compute the probability of infection for each node $u$ given a seed set $S$. If $u$ does not have any seeded ancestor, then $u$ is infected with probability 0. Otherwise, $u$'s infection probability only depends on the position of the lowest seeded ancestor $s$ (any other seeds, including seeds on the other branches, or ancestor of $s$, play no role in infecting $u$). Then, $u$'s infection probability is $h_{s,u}$ according to Lemma 1. We can compute this for all vertices, and the expected total number of infected vertices is just a summation over all vertices' infection probabilities by linearity of expectation. This gives an effective way to compute $\sigma(S)$ for a seed set $S$. Moreover, this holds for both the IC and LT models. Therefore, the first part of Theorem 3 concludes.

We now consider InfMax on an out-arborescence: Given $T = (V, E)$, edge weights $\{b_{(u,v)}\}$, and a budget $K$, select $K$ seeds to maximize the expected influence. We first convert $T$ to a *binary tree* by introducing additional *virtual* nodes. For example, if $u$ has three children $v_1, v_2, v_3$, we introduce an extra node $u'$ such that $u$ has two children $u'$ and $v_3$, and then $u'$ is the parent of $v_1$ and $v_2$. Set $p_{u',v_1}$ and $p_{u',v_2}$ to be $p_{u,v_1}$ and $p_{u,v_2}$ in the original graph. Set $p_{u,u'} = 1$. We can do this recursively for a node with more than three children. Notice that those virtual nodes cannot be seeded. In the remaining part of this section, we assume $T$ is a binary tree with virtual nodes.

**Definition 5 (Dynamic Programming State).** *For any node $v \in V$ in tree $T = (V, E)$, define the DP state as $I(v, k, p)$, representing the maximum expected influence obtainable within the subtree rooted at $v$, given that at most $k$ seeds are selected within this subtree and node $v$ receives an external influence intensity $p \in [0, 1]$ from its ancestors.*

The parameter $p$ captures the influence transmitted from the parent or the ancestors to $v$. If $v$'s parent $u$ is selected as a seed, $p = p_{(u,v)}$. If $u$ is not a seed but is activated by its own ancestors, the influence decays along the edge, i.e., $p = p_{(u,v)} \cdot p_u$. For the root, $p = 0$. We distinguish two mutually exclusive cases for any internal node $v$:

**$v$ Is Not Selected as a Seed ($I_{\text{no}}$).** The activation of $v$ depends entirely on the external influence $p$, so $v$ contributes $p$ to the expected influence if $v$ is not virtual. All $k$ seeds must be distributed among its children's subtrees. For a binary tree with children $v_l$ and $v_r$:

$$I_{\text{no}}(v,k,p) = \max_{0\leq i\leq k}\Big\{I\big(v_l,i,p\cdot b_{(v,v_l)}\big)+I\big(v_r,k-i,p\cdot b_{(v,v_r)}\big)+p\cdot\mathbb{I}(v \text{ is not virtual})\Big\},$$

where $\mathbb{I}$ is the indicator function.

$v$ **Is Selected as a Seed ($I_{\text{sel}}$).** Node $v$ is then not virtual and is activated with certainty, contributing 1. The remaining $k-1$ seeds are distributed in the subtrees. The children receive influence directly from seed $v$:

$$I_{\text{sel}}(v,k,p) = \max_{0\leq i\leq k-1}\Big\{I\big(v_l,i,b_{(v,v_l)}\big) + I\big(v_r,k-1-i,b_{(v,v_r)}\big) + 1\Big\}.$$

The complete transition equation is:

$$I(v,k,p) = \begin{cases} \max\{I_{\text{no}}(v,k,p),\ I_{\text{sel}}(v,k,p)\} & \text{if } v \text{ is not virtual} \\ I_{\text{no}}(v,k,p) & \text{otherwise} \end{cases}. \tag{3}$$

Then we define the boundary conditions for a leaf node $v$: $I(v,k,p) = 1$ if $k \geq 1$, and $I(v,k,p) = p$ otherwise.

Finally, to ensure the validity of the dynamic programming algorithm, we need to make sure that we only need to compute a polynomial number of $I(v,k,p)$. For the third parameter $p$, we need to make sure, for each node $v$, only a polynomial number of values for $p$ is needed. To see this, we need to compute $I(\text{root},K,0)$ at the end of the day. For a vertex $u$ at the second level, we only need $I(u,k,p)$ for $k = 0,1,\ldots,K$ and $p \in \{0, p_{\text{root},u}\}$. For a vertex $u$ at the third level with parent $v$, we only need $I(u,k,p)$ for $k = 0,1,\ldots,K$ and $p \in \{0, p_{v,u}, p_{v,u}\cdot p_{\text{root},u}\}$. Similarly, for a vertex $u$ at the $i$-th level, we only need $(i+1)$ values for $p$. Therefore, the number of values of $p$ needed for each $I(v,k,p)$ is bounded by the depth of $v$, which is bounded by $O(n)$. The total number of values for $I(v,k,p)$ is bounded by $O(n^2K)$. Computing each recurrence relation requires $O(K)$ time (for enumerating $i$). Thus, the overall time complexity is $O(n^2K^2)$.

## 5 Influence Maximization on In-Arborescence Structures

In this section, we address the InfMax problem under the Independent Cascade (IC) model on in-arborescence structures. While it is known that the problem is solvable in polynomial time under the Linear Threshold (LT) model, it remains NP-hard under the IC model [12,23]. We bridge this gap by establishing the following theorem:

**Theorem 4.** *There exists a Fully Polynomial Time Approximation Scheme (FPTAS) for the influence maximization problem under the IC model on an in-arborescence.*

Let $T = (V, E)$ be an in-arborescence where edges are directed from children to parents. As introduced in Sect. 4, we first transform the in-arborescence $T$ into a binary tree by introducing auxiliary *virtual nodes*. Consider a node $u$ with three children $v_1, v_2$, and $v_3$. We introduce a virtual node $u'$ such that $u$ becomes the parent of $u'$ and $v_3$, while $u'$ becomes the parent of $v_1$ and $v_2$. To preserve the original propagation probabilities, we set the edge weights $(v_1, u')$ and $(v_2, u')$ equal to the original $b_{v_1,u}$ and $b_{v_2,u}$ respectively, and assign a weight of 1 to the edge $(u', u)$. This process is applied recursively to any node with a degree greater than two. It is important to note that these virtual nodes are purely structural and cannot be selected as seeds. In the subsequent analysis, we assume $T$ refers to this transformed binary structure containing virtual nodes.

Let $v_l, v_r$ be the left and right children of $v$, with edge weights $b_l, b_r$ and activation probabilities $p_l, p_r$, correspondingly. The probability that $v$ is activated by its children is given by the non-linear combination:

$$p_v = 1 - (1 - p_l \cdot b_l)(1 - p_r \cdot b_r) \tag{4}$$

Within a subtree $T_v$ rooted at $v$, two quantities are of interest: the total expected influence $\varsigma(v)$ within the subtree $T_v$ and the activation probability $p_v$ of vertex $v$. Locally, we would like to maximize $\varsigma(v)$. Globally, $p_v$ completely controls the influence from $T_v$ to the remaining part of the graph.

To handle the trade-off between local influence $\varsigma$ and upward activation probability $p$, we propose a dynamic programming approach based on the Pareto Frontier. Instead of a single value, we maintain a set of pairs:

$$\mathcal{S}(v, k) = \{(p, \varsigma)\} \tag{5}$$

where $p$ denotes the probability of infecting $v$ and $\varsigma$ represents the expected number of infected nodes in $T_v$ is $\varsigma$. Each pair $(p, \varsigma)$ represents a strategy using at most $k$ seeds in $T_v$.

To guarantee the size of $\mathcal{S}(v, k)$ is polynomially bounded, we need to consider roundings for $p$ and $\varsigma$. Choose a sufficiently large integer $M$ and let $\delta = 1/M$. We will round the values of $p$ and $\varsigma$ downward such that they are integer multiples of $\delta$. Therefore, the range of $p$ is $\{0, \delta, 2\delta, \ldots, 1 - \delta, 1\}$, with size $M + 1$, and the range of $\varsigma$ is a set of size $nM + 1$ (since the number of infected vertices cannot exceed $n$). Thus, $|\mathcal{S}(v, k)| \leq (M+1)(nM+1)$. An alternative way to view $\mathcal{S}(v, k)$ is a $(M + 1) \times (nM + 1)$ Boolean table, where the index of each cell is a pair $(p, \varsigma)$ and the Boolean value indicates if there is a seeding strategy such that $v$ is infected with probability approximately $p$ and the expected number of infected vertices in the subtree $T_v$ is approximately $\varsigma$.

The derivation of the recurrence relation for the dynamic programming is then similar to it is in Sect. 4. The details of the algorithm and the analyses for the approximation guarantee and the time complexity are available in the full version of this paper.

## References


1. Angell, R., Schoenebeck, G.: Don't be greedy: leveraging community structure to find high quality seed sets for influence maximization. In: Devanur, N.R., Lu, P. (eds.) WINE 2017. LNCS, vol. 10660, pp. 16–29. Springer, Cham (2017). https://doi.org/10.1007/978-3-319-71924-5_2
2. Brown, J.J., Reingen, P.H.: Social ties and word-of-mouth referral behavior*. J. Consum. Res. **14**(3), 350–362 (1987). https://doi.org/10.1086/209118
3. Chen, N.: On the approximability of influence in social networks. SIAM J. Discret. Math. **23**(3), 1400–1415 (2009)
4. Chen, W., Wang, C., Wang, Y.: Scalable influence maximization for prevalent viral marketing in large-scale social networks. In: Proceedings of the 16th ACM SIGKDD International Conference on Knowledge Discovery and Data Mining, pp. 1029–1038 (2010)
5. Chen, W., Yuan, Y., Zhang, L.: Scalable influence maximization in social networks under the linear threshold model. In: 2010 IEEE International Conference on Data Mining, pp. 88–97. IEEE (2010)
6. Dinur, I.: The PCP theorem by gap amplification. J. ACM (JACM) **54**(3), 12–es (2007)
7. Domingos, P., Richardson, M.: Mining the network value of customers. In: Proceedings of the Seventh ACM SIGKDD International Conference on Knowledge Discovery and Data Mining, KDD 2001, pp. 57–66. Association for Computing Machinery, New York, NY, USA (2001). https://doi.org/10.1145/502512.502525
8. Feige, U.: A threshold of ln n for approximating set cover. J. ACM **45**(4), 634–652 (1998). https://doi.org/10.1145/285055.285059
9. Kempe, D., Kleinberg, J.M., Tardos, É.: Maximizing the spread of influence through a social network. Theory Comput. **11**, 105–147 (2015)
10. Khanna, S., Lucier, B.: Influence maximization in undirected networks. In: Proceedings of the Twenty-Fifth Annual ACM-SIAM Symposium on Discrete Algorithms, pp. 1482–1496. SIAM (2014)
11. Lerman, K., Ghosh, R.: Information contagion: an empirical study of the spread of news on Digg and Twitter social networks. Proc. Int. AAAI Conf. Web Soc. Media **4**(1), 90–97 (2010). https://doi.org/10.1609/icwsm.v4i1.14021. https://ojs.aaai.org/index.php/ICWSM/article/view/14021
12. Lu, Z., Zhang, Z., Wu, W.: Solution of Bharathi-Kempe-Salek conjecture for influence maximization on arborescence. J. Comb. Optim. **33**, 803–808 (2017)
13. Mossel, E., Roch, S.: Submodularity of influence in social networks: From local to global. SIAM J. Comput. **39**, 2176–2188 (2010). https://doi.org/10.1137/080714452
14. Nemhauser, G.L., Wolsey, L.A., Fisher, M.L.: An analysis of approximations for maximizing submodular set functions—I. Math. Program. **14**, 265–294 (1978)
15. Nguyen, H., Zheng, R.: On budgeted influence maximization in social networks. IEEE J. Sel. Areas Commun. **31**(6), 1084–1094 (2013)
16. Pastor-Satorras, R., Vespignani, A.: Epidemic dynamics and endemic states in complex networks. Phys. Rev. E **63**(6), 066117 (2001)
17. Richardson, M., Domingos, P.: Mining knowledge-sharing sites for viral marketing. In: Proceedings of the Eighth ACM SIGKDD International Conference on Knowledge Discovery and Data Mining, pp. 61–70 (2002)
18. Rigobon, R.: Contagion: how to measure it? In: Preventing Currency Crises in Emerging Markets, pp. 269–334. NBER Chapters, National Bureau of Economic Research, Inc. (2002). https://ideas.repec.org/h/nbr/nberch/10638.html

19. Schoenebeck, G., Tao, B.: Beyond worst-case (in) approximability of nonsubmodular influence maximization. ACM Trans. Comput. Theory (TOCT) **11**(3), 1–56 (2019)
20. Schoenebeck, G., Tao, B.: Influence maximization on undirected graphs: toward closing the (1–1/e) gap. ACM Trans. Econ. Comput. (TEAC) **8**(4), 1–36 (2020)
21. Schoenebeck, G., Tao, B., Yu, F.Y.: Limitations of greed: Influence maximization in undirected networks re-visited (2020). arXiv preprint arXiv:2002.11679
22. Schoenebeck, G., Tao, B., Yu, F.Y.: Think globally, act locally: on the optimal seeding for nonsubmodular influence maximization. Inf. Comput. **285**, 104919 (2022)
23. Wang, A., Wu, W., Cui, L.: On Bharathi-Kempe-Salek conjecture for influence maximization on arborescence. J. Comb. Optim. **31**, 1678–1684 (2016)

# Feedback Set Problems on Bounded-Degree (Planar) Graphs

Tian Bai[1,2], Yixin Cao[3], and Mingyu Xiao[2](✉)

[1] Department of Informatics, University of Bergen, Bergen, Norway
tian.bai@uib.no
[2] University of Electronic Science and Technology of China, Chengdu, China
myxiao@uestc.edu.cn
[3] Hong Kong Polytechnic University, Hong Kong, China
yixin.cao@polyu.edu.hk

**Abstract.** The feedback set problems are about removing the minimum number of vertices or edges from a graph to break all its cycles. As fundamental problems in algorithmic graph theory, their complexity on planar and bounded-degree graphs has been extensively studied. While the exact degree thresholds for undirected graphs were conclusively settled in the 1980s, the analogous question for directed graphs, particularly for planar digraphs, has persisted as a fundamental open problem for nearly half a century, primarily due to the directional nature of arcs and stringent planar embedding constraints that obstruct classical degree-reduction techniques. In this paper, we completely settle this historical question. We also establish tight degree bounds for the connected feedback vertex set problem on undirected (planar) graphs.

## 1 Introduction

In the feedback vertex set problem, we are given a graph $G$ and an integer $k$, and asked whether there exists a set of at most $k$ vertices whose removal from $G$ makes the graph acyclic. The graph may be undirected or directed. The problem has an edge variation, where we are removing edges (undirected graphs) or arcs (digraphs) instead of vertices. They are collectively called feedback set problems, and the solutions are called *feedback vertex (resp., edge, arc) sets*. For undirected graphs, the edge variation is equivalent to the maximum/minimum spanning tree problem, hence easy. All the other variants are NP-complete, and both directed variations appear in Karp's list [9]. The classic reduction for the feedback vertex set problem on digraphs, which was attributed to the Algorithms Seminar at Cornell University, was from the vertex cover problem [9], where we ask for at most $k$ vertices whose removal makes the graph edgeless. The reduction replaces each edge of $G$ with two arcs of opposite directions. The undirected case is handled analogously using parallel edges.

T. Bai—Funded by the European Union, GA#101126560; Bergen research and training program for future AI leaders across the disciplines, LEAD AI.
Y. Cao—Supported by NSFC under grant 62372394.
M. Xiao—Supported by NSFC under grant 62372095.


Y. Li et al. (Eds.): COCOON 2026, LNCS 16835, pp. 437–450, 2027.
https://doi.org/10.1007/978-981-92-3309-0_33

Since feedback set problems have wide applications, a natural line of investigation is to determine how structural restrictions on the input graph affect computational complexity. Two particularly well-studied restrictions are planarity and bounded maximum degree. Indeed, in the very first systematic study of the feedback set problems, Younger [18] conjectured that the feedback arc set problem can be solved in polynomial time on planar graphs. This was later confirmed by Lucchesi and Younger [11,12]; see also [10]. In contrast, the feedback vertex set problem remains NP-hard on planar graphs because the vertex cover problem is NP-hard on planar graphs [6], and the classic reduction maintains planarity.

Degree bounds frequently ascertain the border between tractability and intractability. It has been observed that the vertex degrees are intrinsic in this problem [3]. On the one hand, all variants are polynomial-time solvable when the maximum degree is at most two. On the other hand, since the vertex cover problem remains NP-complete on planar graphs of maximum degree three [6], the feedback vertex set problem is NP-complete on planar graphs of maximum degree six via the classical reduction (see Sect. 2.1). These simple observations left a small but annoying gap.

For undirected graphs, this gap was closed in the 1980s. In Speckenmeyer's Ph.D. thesis [14], he introduced degree-reduction gadgets preserving planarity, showing that the feedback vertex set problem remains NP-complete for planar graphs of maximum degree four (see Sect. 2.1). Moreover, Speckenmeyer [15,16] observed that the feedback vertex set problem and the connected vertex cover problem, where the solution is required to induce a connected subgraph, are equivalent on cubic undirected graphs, i.e., undirected graphs in which every vertex has degree three. Then, subsequent works [5,17] established polynomial-time solvability for graphs of maximum degree at most three. Thus, for undirected graphs, the degree threshold is three, both in the general and planar settings.

In contrast, the situation for digraphs is murkier, particularly for planar digraphs. A natural approach is to adapt Speckenmeyer's gadgets to planar digraphs. However, while we do not need to distinguish edges incident to a vertex in an undirected graph, the arcs in a digraph have directions. As we will see in the next section, the application of Speckenmeyer's approach crucially relies on the *embedding*, i.e., how the graph is drawn on the plane. In particular, if three incoming arcs and three outgoing arcs alternate in the embedding, it seems highly unlikely that such a vertex can be replaced by a planar gadget. (Indeed, the complete bipartite graph $K_{3,3}$ is non-planar.) Consequently, a fundamental question has remained unanswered for nearly half a century:

> What is the maximum degree threshold for NP-completeness of the feedback vertex set problem on planar digraphs, and does it coincide with that for undirected graphs?

*Contributions and Techniques.* We completely classify the complexity of feedback vertex set and feedback arc set problems under degree constraints, for both general and planar graphs.

For general directed graphs, both problems are polynomial-time solvable when the maximum degree $\Delta \leq 2$, and NP-complete when $\Delta \geq 3$.

We show that the feedback vertex set problem is NP-hard on planar digraphs of maximum degree three. Specifically, for each pair of opposite arcs between the same pair of vertices in the classic reduction, we can switch their order independently of other pairs. In other words, we can assign any orientation to the cycle of length two formed by them. We carefully arrange the embedding of the resulting digraph so that the three cycles of each vertex are in different orientations, i.e., one or two clockwise and the other(s) anticlockwise. This ensures that the vertex can be replaced by a planar gadget, and thus the reduction works for planar digraphs of maximum degree three.

The full picture of the complexity is summarized in Table 1. The results on planar digraphs are slightly stronger than alluded to. To relate them, we employ a more precise degree parameter $\Delta^*$, defined as follows. For each vertex, count whichever is smaller: its in-degree or out-degree. Then pick the vertex where that smaller count is as large as possible. Note that $\Delta \leq 3$ implies $\Delta^* \leq 1$, while $\Delta^* \geq 2$ implies $\Delta \geq 4$. Needless to say, all the hardness results remain even if the graphs are required to be bipartite, as we can always subdivide every edge or arc, which has no impact on the minimum solutions.

**Table 1.** Complexity of the feedback set problems on graphs of bounded degree.

| | P | | NPC | |
|---|---|---|---|---|
| Undirected, vertex | $\Delta \leq 3$ | [5,16,17] | $\Delta \geq 4$ | [14] |
| Planar undirected, vertex | $\Delta \leq 3$ | [5,16,17] | $\Delta \geq 4$ | [14] |
| Directed, vertex | $\Delta \leq 2$ | Proposition 1 | $\Delta \geq 3$ | Theorem 1 |
| Directed, arc | $\Delta \leq 2$ | Proposition 1 | $\Delta \geq 3$ | Theorem 1 |
| Planar directed, vertex | $\Delta^* \leq 1$ | Corollary 2 | $\Delta^* \geq 2$ | Theorem 3 |
| Planar directed, arc | always | [11,12] | | |

Garey and Johnson [7] already mentioned degree bounds for the feedback set problems on planar digraphs. However, they provided neither proofs nor references for these claims. We do not know what arguments they had in mind; in particular, our proof of Theorem 1 does not appear to follow directly from their statements, since they listed different degree bounds for the vertex and arc versions. Specifically, it was only claimed that the feedback arc set problem remains NP-complete for digraphs in which both the maximum in-degree and maximum out-degree are at most three.

Additionally, we settle the complexity of the connected variation of the feedback vertex set problem on undirected graphs. In the connected feedback vertex set problem, the solution is required to induce a connected subgraph. While it is trivial on an undirected graph of maximum degree two, it is already NP-hard on planar undirected graphs of maximum degree nine [8]. The main difficulty in narrowing the gap is that we need to design a gadget with small degrees preserving both planarity and connectivity. Revisiting the gadget of Bodlaender et al. [1] on the weighted version of this problem, we show that the problem is already NP-complete on planar undirected graphs of maximum degree three.

Since feedback set problems are frequently used as source problems in reductions, our novel results and techniques will not only be useful for future reductions but might also help improve existing proofs.

## 2 Preliminaries

We follow standard notation from graph theory. Unless stated otherwise, graphs are finite and simple. For an integer $k$ we write $[k] = \{1, 2, \ldots, k\}$.

For a graph $G$, we denote its vertex set and edge (or arc) set by $V(G)$ and $E(G)$. A graph is *planar* if it can be drawn on the plane without edge crossings. For a vertex $v \in V(G)$, let $d(v)$ denote its degree. A graph is *cubic* if the degrees of all its vertices are three. The maximum degree of $G$ is

$$\Delta(G) = \max_{v \in V(G)} d(v).$$

For a digraph $D$, let $d^-(v)$ and $d^+(v)$ denote the indegree and outdegree of $v$, respectively. We define

$$\Delta^*(D) = \max_{v \in V(D)} \min\{d^-(v), d^+(v)\}.$$

For $X \subseteq V(G)$ we use $G[X]$ to denote the subgraph of $G$ *induced* by $X$, and we write $G - X$ for $G[V(G) \setminus X]$. A (directed) path of length $\ell$ is a sequence of distinct vertices $v_1 v_2 \cdots v_\ell$ such that $v_i v_{i+1} \in E(G)$ for all $i \in [\ell - 1]$. A (directed) cycle of length $\ell$ is a path $v_1 v_2 \cdots v_\ell$ with $\ell \geq 3$ together with the edge $v_\ell v_1 \in E(G)$. All cycles considered in this paper are simple. A graph is acyclic if it does not contain a cycle. A vertex subset $S$ is a *vertex cover* of $G$ if every edge of $G$ has at least one endpoint in $S$. A vertex subset $S$ is a *feedback vertex set* of $G$ if $G - S$ is acyclic.

### 2.1 Classical Reductions and Speckenmeyer's Gadgets

We recall two classical reductions that play a central role in the study of feedback vertex and arc set problems, as well as Speckenmeyer's gadgets for undirected graphs of maximum degree four.

The first classic reduction transforms the vertex cover problem into the feedback vertex set problem on digraphs [9]. Given a simple undirected graph $G$, we construct a digraph by

*replacing each edge of $G$ with two arcs of opposite directions.*

These two arcs form a directed cycle of length two, so any feedback vertex set of the resulting digraph must contain at least one endpoint of each edge, corresponding exactly to a vertex cover of $G$.

The second classic reduction, due to Lawler and Karp, transforms the feedback vertex set problem into the feedback arc set problem on digraphs: Given a digraph $D$, we construct a digraph by *replacing each vertex $v \in V(D)$ with two new vertices $v^-$ and $v^+$, connected by an arc $v^-v^+$, and redirect every incoming arc of $v$ to $v^-$ and every outgoing arc from $v$ to $v^+$.*

Removing the arc $v^-v^+$ breaks all directed cycles passing through $v$, and thus has the same effect as removing $v$ in the original digraph.

Throughout this paper, we refer to these constructions as the *doubling operation* and the *splitting operation*. The doubling operation can be adapted to undirected graphs by replacing each edge with two parallel edges. If simple graphs are required, one may subdivide one of the two edges, or equivalently, introduce a new vertex adjacent only to its endpoints.

These two reductions form the basis for proving the hardness of the feedback set problem on planar and bounded-degree graphs. Since vertex cover remains NP-complete on planar graphs of maximum degree three [6], applying the doubling operation shows that the feedback vertex set problem is NP-complete on planar graphs of maximum degree six. To close the remaining gap for undirected graphs, Speckenmeyer [14] introduced planar gadgets to replace vertices of degree five and six[1], as shown in Fig. 1. With these gadgets, the feedback vertex set problem remains NP-complete on planar graphs of maximum degree four, while it becomes polynomial-time solvable for maximum degree three [5,17].

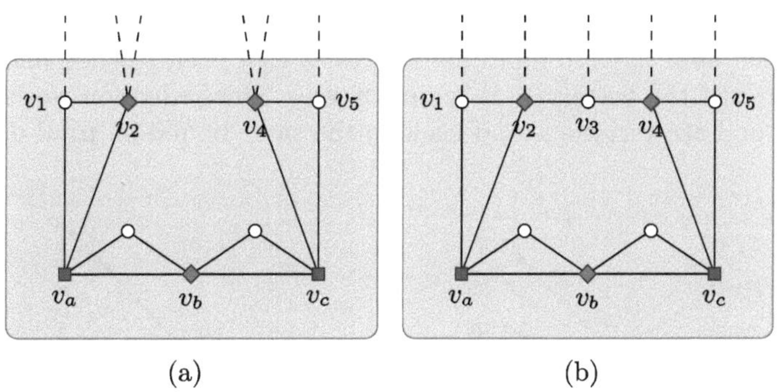


**Fig. 1.** Speckenmeyer's gadgets (a) for a degree-six vertex and (b) for a degree-five vertex [14]. The edges incident to the original vertex are assigned to the dashed lines in cyclic order. Note that a minimum feedback vertex set contains at least two vertices from each gadget (which have to be $v_a$ and $v_c$ if only two), and at most three vertices (no cycle visits any remaining vertex after vertices $v_2$, $v_4$, and $v_b$ are removed).

For planar digraphs of maximum degree three, the feedback vertex set problem coincides with the feedback arc set problem. Vertices with only incoming or only outgoing arcs can be ignored, and vertices with a single incoming or outgoing arc can be handled as in the splitting operation. Since the feedback arc

[1] See the Appendix 5 for a more detailed historical account of these results.

set problem is polynomial-time solvable on planar digraphs [12], the feedback vertex set problem is also polynomial-time solvable in this case.

Finally, by refining the splitting operation, one can construct digraphs with maximum degree three while preserving NP-hardness of both the feedback vertex set and feedback arc set problems. This reduction is surprisingly simple and, to our knowledge, has not been explicitly documented.

## 3 Digraphs of Bounded Degree

It is trivial to solve the feedback set problems on digraphs of maximum degree two. We start with iteratively removing all vertices that have no incoming arcs or no outgoing arcs: they are not visited by any directed cycle. The remaining graph consists of disjoint cycles, and it suffices to take one vertex or arc from each cycle.

**Proposition 1.** *Both feedback set problems can be solved in polynomial time on digraphs having no degree exceeding two.*

On the other hand, the following naïve reduction suffices to pin down the hardness when there are vertices of degree three. The other end of an incoming (resp., outgoing) arc to $v$ is an *in-neighbor* (resp., *out-neighbor*) of $v$. We have seen that splitting a vertex $v$ into $v^-$ and $v^+$, with an arc from $v^-$ to $v^+$, separates in-neighbors and out-neighbors of $v$. If $v$ had more than two in-neighbors, we would further split $v^-$ into multiple vertices so that each receives one incoming arc. We process the vertex $v^+$ in a similar way. This reduction works for both the vertex and arc variations and leads to the same bound on total degrees.

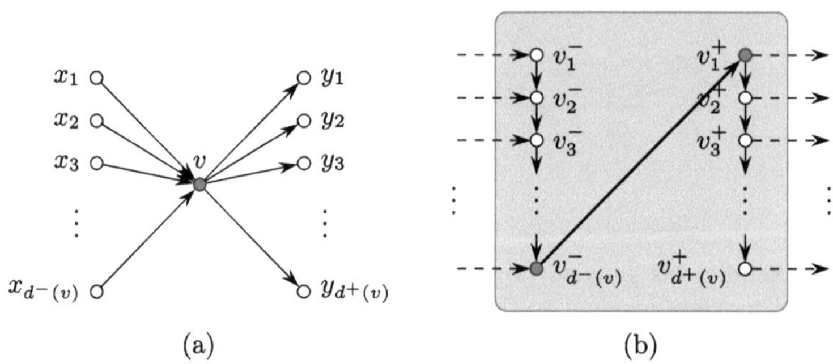


**Fig. 2.** A vertex $v$ in (a) is replaced by a path on $d(v)$ new vertices in (b).

**Theorem 1.** *Both feedback set problems remain* NP*-complete for digraphs having no degree exceeding three.*

*Proof.* Let $D$ be a digraph. We transform $D$ into another digraph $D'$ by conducting the following operations on each vertex $v$ of $D$. We introduce a directed path, denoted as $P(v)$, on $d(v)$ new vertices:

$$v_1^- v_2^- \cdots v_{d^-(v)}^- v_1^+ v_2^+ \cdots v_{d^+(v)}^+.$$

Let the in-neighbors and out-neighbors of $v$ be numbered in an arbitrary way as $\{x_1, x_2, \ldots, x_{d^-(v)}\}$ and $\{y_1, y_2, \ldots, y_{d^+(v)}\}$, respectively. It is possible that $x_i = y_j$ for some $i$ and $j$ with $1 \leq i \leq d^-(v)$ and $1 \leq j \leq d^+(v)$. For $i = 1, 2, \ldots, d^-(v)$, we add an arc $x_i v_i^-$, and for $i = 1, 2, \ldots, d^+(v)$, we add an arc $v_i^+ y_i$. See Fig. 2 for an illustration. Let $D'$ denote the resulting digraph.

If we remove the vertex $v_1^+$ from the gadget $P(v)$, then no cycle can visit the remaining vertices of this gadget. Thus, a minimum feedback vertex set of $D'$ contains at most one vertex from a gadget. Moreover, if a minimum feedback vertex set of $D'$ contains a vertex from a gadget $P(v)$, we can replace it with $v_1^+$. We claim that a set $S \subseteq V(D)$ is a feedback vertex set of $D$ if and only if

$$S' = \{v_1^+ : v \in S\}$$

is a feedback vertex set of $D'$.

For necessity, let $S$ be a feedback vertex set of $D$. Suppose for contradiction that $C'$ is a cycle in $D' - S'$. Since each gadget is acyclic, $C'$ visits vertices from more than one gadget. Moreover, if $C'$ visits vertices on $P(v)$, then $C'$ must visit the arc $v_{d^-(v)}^- v_1^+$. We list the gadgets that $C'$ visits in cyclic order. By the construction of $D'$, if $P(u)$ is followed by $P(v)$, then $uv \in E(D)$. We can thus obtain a cycle of $D$. Since $S$ is a feedback vertex set of $D$, it contains at least one vertex on this cycle, say $v$. But then $v_1^+ \in S'$, a contradiction.

For sufficiency, let $S'$ be a feedback vertex set of $D'$. Suppose that $C$ is a cycle in $D - S$. Let $uv$ be an arc on $C$. Suppose that $u$ is the $p$th in-neighbor of $v$ and $v$ is the $q$th out-neighbor of $u$ (in the numbering of $N^+(u)$ and $N^-(v)$ during the reduction). Hence, $u_q^+ v_p^-$ is an arc of $D'$. We replace $uv$ with the path

$$u_{d^-(u)}^- u_1^+ u_2^+ \cdots u_q^+ v_p^- v_{p+1}^- \cdots v_{d^-(v)}^-.$$

Conducting similar replacements for all the arcs on $C$ leads to a cycle $C'$ of $D'$. Since $S'$ is a feedback vertex set of $D'$, it contains at least one vertex on $C'$, say $v_1^+$. But then $v \in S$, a contradiction.

The same reduction also works for the feedback arc set problem: a vertex set $S \subseteq V(D)$ is a feedback vertex set of $D$ if and only if the edge set $\{v_{d^-(v)}^- v_1^+ : v \in S\}$ is a feedback arc set of $D'$. □

Note that the reduction above does not start from the feedback set problems on digraphs of bounded degree. Theorem 1 is slightly stronger than separate bounds on maximum in- and out-degrees.

**Corollary 1.** *Both feedback set problems remain* NP*-complete for digraphs having no in- or out-degree exceeding two.*

*Proof.* If a vertex has only incoming arcs or only outgoing arcs, then it can be removed from the graph. Afterward, if the total degree of a vertex is three, then one of its in-degree and out-degree is two, and the other is one. □

## 4 Planar Digraphs of Bounded Degree

A sharp-eyed reader may have noticed that the gadget in Fig. 2 does maintain planarity. However, this happens only when the arcs incident to the vertex $v$ are embedded in a certain way. We say that a plane embedding of a planar digraph $D$ is *bipolar* if, for each vertex $v \in V(D)$, the incoming arcs toward $v$ are circularly consecutive (hence the outgoing arcs from $v$ are also circularly consecutive) in the embedding. Note that when applied to such an embedded digraph, the splitting operation ends with a planar digraph.

**Theorem 2.** *The feedback vertex set problem can be solved in polynomial time in planar digraphs admitting bipolar embeddings.*

*Proof.* Let $D$ be a planar digraph that admits a bipolar embedding. Let $D'$ denote the resulting digraph by the splitting operation to $D$; note that it is planar. Then a subset $S \subseteq V(D)$ is a feedback vertex set of $D$ if and only if $\{v^-v^+ : v \in S\}$ is a feedback arc set of $D'$ [9]. Since $D'$ is planar, the feedback arc set problem can be solved in polynomial time. The statement follows. □

It may be worth mentioning that the algorithm in Theorem 2 does not require a bipolar embedding of the input graph given. It suffices to apply the splitting operation and then find a plane embedding of the resulting digraph. A planar digraph $D$ with $\Delta^*(D) \leq 1$ trivially admits a bipolar embedding: for every vertex $v$, either $d^-(v) \leq 1$ or $d^+(v) \leq 1$. This is always the case when $\Delta(D) \leq 3$.

**Corollary 2.** *The feedback vertex set problem can be solved in polynomial time on planar digraphs $D$ with $\Delta^*(D) \leq 1$.*

**Corollary 3.** *The feedback vertex set problem can be solved in polynomial time on planar digraphs $D$ with $\Delta(D) \leq 3$.*

In the rest, we show that both corollaries are tight. We say that a digraph $D$ is *3-regular* if $d^-(v) = d^+(v) = 3$ for every vertex $v \in V(D)$. Since the vertex cover problem remains NP-complete on undirected cubic planar graphs [6], the reduction by the doubling operation implies that the feedback vertex set problem remains NP-complete on 3-regular planar digraphs. A natural attempt is to devise planar gadget(s) à la Speckenmeyer to replace the vertices one by one. However, we have to respect the cyclic ordering of the arcs incident to each embedded vertex, which is not always easy. In particular, the natural attempt seems very unlikely to succeed if the incoming and outgoing arcs incident to a vertex alternate in the embedding.

If we use "−" and "+" to denote an incoming arc and an outgoing arc, respectively, then the cyclic ordering of the six arcs incident to any vertex can be written as $(-,-,-,+,+,+)$ in a bipolar embedding. Likewise, we write $(-,+,-,+,-,+)$ if they alternate. The other possible cyclic orderings of the arcs incident to a 3-regular digraph are

$$(-,-,+,+,-,+) \text{ and } (+,+,-,-,+,-).$$

Note that they are symmetric. We say that a plane embedding of a 3-regular planar digraph $D$ is *irregular* if for each vertex $v \in V(D)$, the arcs incident to $v$ are in the circular order of either $(-,-,+,+,-,+)$ or $(+,+,-,-,+,-)$. Interestingly, we can always construct an irregular embedding for a 3-regular planar digraph obtained by the doubling operation. Note that this is not true for general 3-regular planar digraphs; a classic result states that if the underlying graph is three-connected, the digraph admits an essentially unique embedding. The trick here is that we can freely switch the order of any pair of opposite arcs between the same pair of vertices.

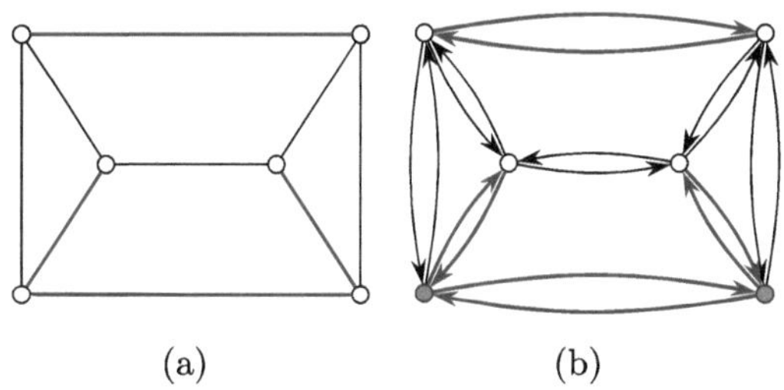


**Fig. 3.** (a) An undirected cubic planar graph $G$, where the edges in $F$ are represented as thick purple lines, and (b) an irregular embedding of the digraph obtained from $G$ by the doubling operation. Note that the two shadowed vertices have $(-,-,+,+,-,+)$ embedding, while all the others $(+,+,-,-,+,-)$.

**Lemma 1.** *Let $G$ be an undirected cubic planar graph. The digraph $D$ obtained by the doubling operation admits an irregular embedding, and such an embedding can be constructed in polynomial time.*

*Proof.* We fix an arbitrary plane embedding of $G$. According to Duncan et al. [4], $E(G)$ can be covered by two linear forests (the union of disjoint paths), and they can be found in linear time. Let $F$ be one of the linear forests. We do the doubling operation as follows. We place the opposite arcs from an edge $e$ of $G$ so that the directed cycle formed by them is clockwise if and only if $e \in F$ (see Fig. 3). Let $D$ denote the resulting digraph, which is clearly a planar digraph: the construction actually ends with an embedding. To see that the embedding is irregular, note that each vertex $v$ is incident to one or two edges in $F$. If all the three edges incident to $v$ belong to $F$, then $F$ is not a linear forest; if all of them are disjoint from $F$, then another linear forest cannot cover the three edges. If $v$ is incident to exactly one edge from $F$, then the embedding is $(+,+,-,-,+,-)$; it is $(-,-,+,+,-,+)$ otherwise. This concludes the proof. □

Irregular embeddings allow us to group the pair of consecutive incoming arcs and the pair of outgoing arcs for the gadget; see Fig. 4.

**Theorem 3.** *The feedback vertex set problem remains* NP*-complete for planar digraphs having no in- or out-degree exceeding two.*

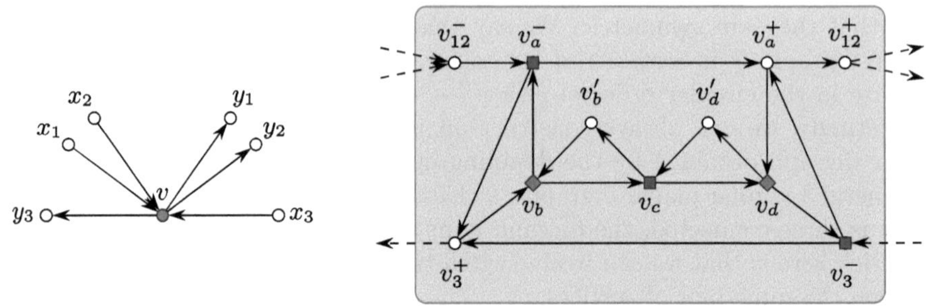


(a) (b)

**Fig. 4.** (a) A vertex $v$ with $(-,-,+,+,-,+)$ embedding; (b) the gadget for $v$.

*Proof.* Let $D$ be the digraph derived from an undirected planar cubic graph by the doubling operation, and $k$ an integer. Note that it is NP-complete to decide whether $(D, k)$ is a yes-instance of the feedback vertex set problem. We use Lemma 1 to construct an irregular embedding of $D$. We replace each vertex $v$ in $V(D)$ whose embedding is $(-,-,+,+,-,+)$ with 11 vertices

$$v_{12}^-, v_{12}^+, v_3^-, v_3^+, v_a^-, v_a^+, v_b, v_b', v_c, v_d, v_d',$$

and the following 16 arcs:

- an arc $v_3^- v_3^+$, a directed path $v_{12}^- v_a^- v_a^+ v_{12}^+$; and
- four directed triangles $v_b v_c v_b'$, $v_c v_d v_d'$, $v_a^- v_3^+ v_b$, and $v_3^- v_a^+ v_d$.

The gadget is denoted as $H(v)$. Finally, we reassign the arcs incident to $v$ as

$$x_1 v_{12}^-, x_2 v_{12}^-, v_{12}^+ y_1, v_{12}^+ y_2, x_3 v_3^-, \text{ and } v_3^+ y_3.$$

See Fig. 4 for an illustration. We replace each vertex $v$ in $V(D)$ with embedding $(+,+,-,-,+,-)$ in a symmetric manner. Let $D'$ denote the resulting digraph. Note that $D'$ is a planar digraph.

Let $n = |V(G)| = |V(D)|$ and $k' = 2n + k$. We argue that $(D, k)$ is a yes-instance of the feedback vertex set problem if and only if $(D', k')$ is a yes-instance.

For necessity, suppose that $S$ is a feedback vertex set of $D$. We claim that

$$S' = \{v_b, v_d : v \in V(D) \setminus S\} \cup \{v_a^-, v_c, v_3^- : v \in S\}$$

is a feedback vertex set of $D'$. Note that

$$|S'| = 2|V(D) \setminus S| + 3|S| = 2|V(D)| + |S| = 2n + k.$$

After removing either $\{v_b, v_d\}$ or $\{v_a^-, v_c, v_3^-\}$ from the gadget $H(v)$, no directed cycle can visit the remaining vertices from $H(v)$. Thus, $D' - S'$ is acyclic.

For sufficiency, suppose that $S'$ is a feedback vertex set of $D'$. We claim that

$$S = \{v : S' \text{ contains more than two vertices from } H(v)\}$$

is a feedback vertex set of $D$. Since the triangles $v_a^- v_b v_3^+$ and $v_3^- v_a^+ v_d$ are disjoint, $S'$ contains at least two vertices from each gadget. Thus,

$$|S'| \geq 3|S| + 2|V(D) \setminus S| = 2n + |S|,$$

and hence $|S| \leq k$.

Suppose for contradiction that $C$ is a cycle in $D - S$. Let $uvw$ be a sub-path of $C$ (possibly $u = w$). Since $v \notin S$, the feedback vertex set $S'$ contains $v_b$ and $v_d$ and no other vertex in $H(v)$. Then there are paths from $v_i^-$ to $v_j^+$ in $H(v)$ for all pairs of $i, j \in \{12, 3\}$ via one of the following

$$v_{12}^- v_a^- v_a^+ v_{12}^+, \qquad v_{12}^- v_a^- v_3^+, \qquad v_3^- v_a^+ v_{12}^+, \quad \text{or} \quad v_3^- v_3^+$$

Therefore, we can concatenate them to form a cycle of $D' - S'$, a contradiction. The proof is now complete. □

## 5 The Connected Feedback Vertex Set Problem

The study of the connected feedback vertex set problem has been exclusively focused on undirected graphs, and so is ours. Again, it is trivial to solve this problem in polynomial time when the maximum degree is two. On the other hand, since the connected vertex cover problem remains NP-hard even for undirected planar graphs with maximum degree four [6], the same reduction (by doubling edges) implies the NP-hardness of the connected feedback vertex set problem on undirected planar graphs of maximum degree eight. Bodlaender et al. [1] managed to show that the weighted version of the connected feedback vertex set problem is NP-hard on planar graphs of maximum degree four (even with only two different weights allowed).

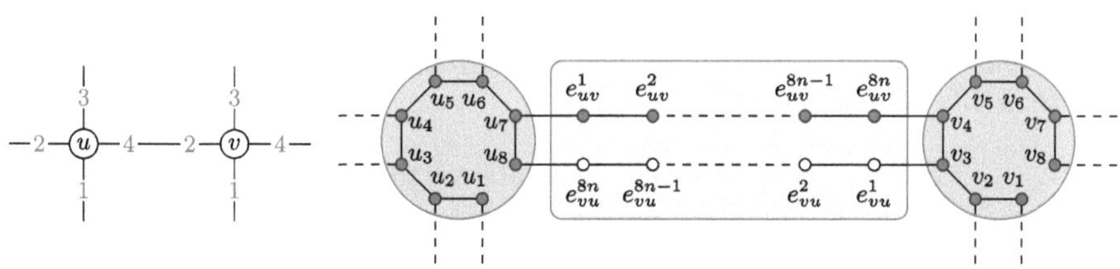


(a) (b)

**Fig. 5.** (a) Two adjacent vertices of $G$ and edges incident to them, where the numbers on edges denote their cyclic order. For example, the edge $uv$ is the fourth of $u$ and the second of $v$. (b) The gadgets $P(u)$, $P(uv)$, and $P(v)$, which comprise 8, $16n$, and 8 vertices, respectively.

**Theorem 4.** *The connected feedback vertex set problem remains* NP*-complete on undirected planar graphs of maximum degree three.*

*Proof.* Let $G$ be an undirected planar graph having no vertices of degree more than four, and let $n = |V(G)|$. We may assume without loss of generality that $G$ is connected, and it contains at least two edges. For each vertex $v \in V(G)$, we introduce a path $P(v)$ on eight new vertices $v_1 v_2 \cdots v_8$, arranged in clockwise order. For each edge $uv \in E(G)$, we introduce two disjoint paths each on $8n$ new vertices:

$$e^1_{uv} e^2_{uv} \cdots e^{8n}_{uv} \quad \text{and} \quad e^1_{vu} e^2_{vu} \cdots e^{8n}_{vu},$$

denoted as $P(uv)$. We fix an arbitrary embedding of $G$ and connect these gadgets as follows. Suppose the neighbors of $v$ are $x_1$, $x_2$, ..., $x_{d(v)}$ in the clockwise order, where $d(v) \leq 4$. For $i = 1, 2, \ldots, d(v)$, we add edges $v_{2i-1} e^1_{vx_i}$ and $v_{2i} e^{8n}_{x_i v}$. See Fig. 5 for an illustration.

Let $G'$ denote the resulting graph. It is clear from the construction that $G'$ is a connected planar graph of maximum degree three. We claim that $(G, k)$ is a yes-instance of the connected vertex cover problem if and only if $(G', k')$ is a yes-instance of the connected feedback vertex set problem, where $k' = 8k + 8n(k-1)$.

For necessity, suppose $S$ is a minimum connected vertex cover of size at most $k$ in $G$. We may assume that $|S| = k$: we can always add vertices to it because $n > k$. Since $G[S]$ is connected, we can find a spanning tree $T$ of $G[S]$; we root it at an arbitrary vertex. We claim that

$$S' = \{v_1, v_2, \ldots, v_8 : v \in S\} \cup \{e^1_{uv}, e^2_{uv}, \ldots, e^{8n}_{uv} : u \text{ is the parent of } v\}$$

is a connected feedback vertex set of $G'$. Note that

$$|S'| = 8|S| + 8n(|S| - 1) = 8k + 8n(k-1) = k',$$

and the subgraph of $G'$ induced by $S'$ is connected. Since $S$ is a vertex cover of $G$, a component $C$ of $G' - S'$ either is the path $e^1_{vu} e^2_{vu} \cdots e^{8n}_{vu}$ for some edge $uv \in E(G)$, or comprises $P(v)$ and a subset of $\bigcup_{uv \in E(G)} P(vu)$. In either case, $C$ is acyclic. Thus, $S'$ is a connected feedback vertex set of $G'$.

For sufficiency, let $S'$ be a minimum connected feedback vertex set of size at most $k'$ in $G'$. We show that

$$S = \{v : S' \text{ contains at least one vertex from } P(v)\}$$

is a connected vertex cover of $G$ of size at most $k$. Any edge $uv$ is mapped to a distinct cycle

$$u_{2p-1} e^1_{uv} e^2_{uv} \cdots e^{8n}_{uv} v_{2q} v_{2q-1} e^1_{vu} e^2_{vu} \cdots e^{8n}_{vu} u_{2p},$$

where $v$ is the $p$th neighbor of $u$ and $u$ is the $q$th neighbor of $v$. The solution $S'$ needs to contain at least one vertex from this cycle. By the assumption that $G$ has at least two edges, there are at least two such cycles. Since $G'[S']$ is connected, at least one of the four vertices $u_{2p-1}$, $u_{2p}$, $v_{2q-1}$, $v_{2q}$ needs to be in $S'$. Thus, at least one of $u$ and $v$ is in $S$, implying that $S$ is a vertex cover of $G$.

Next, we show by contradiction that the subgraph $G[S]$ is connected. Suppose that $X$ and $Y$ are two components of $G[S]$. Let $Z$ be the set of neighbors of $X$, and let $Z'$ denote the set of vertices of $G'$ derived from $Z$, i.e., $Z' = \bigcup_{v \in Z} P(v)$. There must be a vertex $x' \in S' \cap P(x)$ for some $x \in X$ and a vertex $y' \in S' \cap P(y)$ for some $y \in Y$. By construction, $S'$ is disjoint from $Z'$. Note that $x'$ and $y'$ belong to different components of $G' - Z'$. We have a contradiction.

It remains to verify $|S| \leq k$. We argue that if $S'$ contains any vertex from $P(uv)$, say, $e^i_{uv}$ for some $i$ with $1 \leq i \leq 8n$, then it contains all the vertices $e^1_{uv}$, $e^2_{uv}$, ..., $e^{8n}_{uv}$. Suppose for contradiction that $S'$ contains $e^i_{uv}$ but not $e^{i+1}_{uv}$ for some $i$ with $1 \leq i < 8n$. Since $G[S]$ is connected, $S$ must contain $e^1_{uv}$ and its neighbor in $P(u)$ (again, we use the assumption that $G$ has at least two edges). But this contradicts the minimality of $S'$ because $S' \setminus \{e^i_{uv}\}$ would remain a connected feedback vertex set of $G'$. Therefore, the number of edges $e$ of $G$ such that $S'$ contains vertices from $P(e)$ is at most

$$\left\lfloor \frac{k'}{8n} \right\rfloor \leq \left\lfloor \frac{8k + 8n(k-1)}{8n} \right\rfloor = (k-1) + \left\lfloor \frac{k}{n} \right\rfloor = k - 1.$$

Since $S'$ induces a connected subgraph, it can contain vertices from $P(v)$ for at most $k$ vertices $v$ of $G$. This concludes the proof. □

## Appendix: Related Work and Historical Remarks

Speckenmeyer uploaded a scanned copy of his thesis to https://www.researchgate.net/publication/269029032 on March 12, 2015 (retrieved on May 26, 2023). Before that, he had not published the gadgets in Fig. 1 or the corresponding reduction, except for a brief announcement at the end of his paper [16] (the reference numbers are updated to refer to the reference of the current paper):

> Garey and Johnson [7] have shown that the problem of determining a maximum nsis [nonseparating independent set] of a connected planar graph of degree at most 4 is NP-hard and in [14] the problem of determining a minimum fvs [feedback vertex set] for the same class of graphs is shown to be NP-hard, too.

Only a brief statement in Speckenmeyer's paper addressed the reduction, providing limited information. In particular, the statement did not clarify the underlying construction. The paper [16] was devoted to the relationship between feedback vertex sets and connected vertex covers. Without access to the original source [14], it is natural to suppose that the claimed reduction is from the connected vertex cover problem on planar graphs of maximum degree four, which, however, is not the case.

Due to the lack of an explicit construction, alternative reductions were later published, even three decades after Speckenmeyer's thesis. In 2009, Rizzi [13] devised two gadgets for replacing degree-six and degree-five vertices, respectively. Another reduction, directly from the satisfiability problem, was reported by Brandstädt et al. [2, Theorem 1]. Both reductions of [2,13] differ from Speckenmeyer's in that they do not preserve planarity. The complexity question continued to generate discussion, as evidenced by several posts on https://cstheory.

stackexchange.com, among others, asking about the complexity of the feedback vertex set problem on undirected graphs of maximum degree four.

## References

1. Bodlaender, H.L., Feremans, C., Grigoriev, A., Penninkx, E., Sitters, R., Wolle, T.: On the minimum corridor connection problem and other generalized geometric problems. Comput. Geom. **42**(9), 939–951 (2009)
2. Brandstädt, A., Brito, S., Klein, S., Nogueira, L.T., Protti, F.: Cycle transversals in perfect graphs and cographs. Theor. Comput. Sci. **469**, 15–23 (2013)
3. Cao, Y.: A naive algorithm for feedback vertex set. In: Proceedings of the 1st SIAM Symposium on Simplicity in Algorithms (SOSA). OASICS, vol. 61, pp. 1:1–1:9. Schloss Dagstuhl - Leibniz-Zentrum fuer Informatik (2018)
4. Duncan, C.A., Eppstein, D., Kobourov, S.G.: The geometric thickness of low degree graphs. In: Proceedings of the 20th ACM Symposium on Computational Geometry, pp. 340–346. ACM (2004)
5. Furst, M.L., Gross, J.L., McGeoch, L.A.: Finding a maximum-genus graph imbedding. J. ACM **35**(3), 523–534 (1988)
6. Garey, M., Johnson, D.S.: The rectilinear Steiner tree problem is NP-complete. SIAM J. Appl. Math. **32**(4), 826–834 (1977)
7. Garey, M.R., Johnson, D.S.: Computers and Intractability: A Guide to the Theory of NP-Completeness. Freeman, San Francisco (1979)
8. Grigoriev, A., Sitters, R.: Connected feedback vertex set in planar graphs. In: Graph-Theoretic Concepts in Computer Science. LNCS, vol. 5911, pp. 143–153 (2009)
9. Karp, R.M.: Reducibility among combinatorial problems. In: Complexity of Computer Computations. The IBM Research Symposia Series, pp. 85–103. Plenum Press, New York (1972)
10. Lovász, L.: On two minimax theorems in graph. J. Comb. Theory Ser. B **21**(2), 96–103 (1976)
11. Lucchesi, C.L.: A minimax equality for directed graphs. Ph.D. thesis, University of Waterloo, Waterloo, Ontario (1976)
12. Lucchesi, C.L., Younger, D.H.: A minimax theorem for directed graphs. J. London Math. Soc. **s2-17**(3), 369–374 (1978)
13. Rizzi, R.: Minimum weakly fundamental cycle bases are hard to find. Algorithmica **53**(3), 402–424 (2009)
14. Speckenmeyer, E.: Untersuchungen zum Feedback Vertex Set Problem in ungerichteten Graphen. Ph.D. thesis, Universität Paderborn, Paderborn, Germany (1983)
15. Speckenmeyer, E.: Bounds on feedback vertex sets of undirected cubic graphs. In: Algebra, Combinatorics and Logic in Computer Science, Colloquia Mathematica Societatis János Bolyai, vol. 42, pp. 719–729. North-Holland (1986)
16. Speckenmeyer, E.: On feedback vertex sets and nonseparating independent sets in cubic graphs. J. Graph Theory **12**(3), 405–412 (1988)
17. Ueno, S., Kajitani, Y., Gotoh, S.: On the nonseparating independent set problem and feedback set problem for graphs with no vertex degree exceeding three. Discret. Math. **72**, 355–360 (1988)
18. Younger, D.H.: Feedback in a directed graph. Ph.D. thesis, Columbia University, New York City, New York (1963)

# On the Border Complexity of Sums of ROFs

Pranjal Dutta[1(✉)] and Bhargav Thankey[2]

[1] Nanyang Technological University, Singapore, Singapore
pranjal.dutta@ntu.edu.sg
[2] Google, Bengaluru, India

**Abstract.** Border complexity – central to algebraic complexity and to Geometric Complexity Theory (GCT) – captures polynomials lying in the Zariski closure of low-complexity classes; equivalently, those obtainable as limits (degenerations) of efficient computations. Notably, the best upper bounds on the matrix-multiplication exponent come via low *border* tensor rank. *Debordering* is the task of proving an upper bound on some non-border complexity measure in terms of a border complexity measure, thus getting rid of limits. Debordering is central to understanding the difference between Valiant's determinant vs. permanent conjecture and the Mulmuley-Sohoni's GCT framework via border determinantal complexity. Recent work has established qualitative debordering and efficient hitting sets for several border models.

In this work, we initiate the study of debordering the border of sums of Read-Once Formulas (ROFs). Our first main result is a quantitative debordering theorem: every polynomial in the border of the sum of two homogeneous read-once formulas (ROFs) admits an exact representation as a sum of $O(n)$ homogeneous ROFs. As a second main result, we construct a quasi-polynomial time hitting set for the border of sums of two homogeneous depth-5 ROFs over large fields. Finally, we show that the class of sums of $k$ ROFs, denoted $\Sigma_k$ROF is *not closed* under taking limits: for $2 \leq k \leq n/5$, the elementary symmetric polynomial $\mathsf{ESym}_{n,n-k+1}$ lies in the border of $\Sigma_k$ROF but not in the class itself.

**Keywords:** De-bordering · Sums of ROFs · PIT

## 1 Introduction

A central goal of theoretical computer science is to understand the computational resources required to solve algorithmic problems. Complexity theory formalizes this by defining classes of problems according to resource bounds – e.g., **P**, **NP**, and #**P** – and investigating their relationships. The most famous of these questions is the **P** vs. **NP** problem.

In parallel to the Boolean setting, *algebraic complexity theory* studies the cost of computing multivariate polynomials over a field using +, ×, and field

A full version of the paper can be found at this link.


Y. Li et al. (Eds.): COCOON 2026, LNCS 16835, pp. 451–464, 2027.
https://doi.org/10.1007/978-981-92-3309-0_34

constants. This viewpoint underlies many problems in symbolic computation, algebraic geometry, invariant theory, optimization, and numerical analysis.

**Arithmetic Formulas.** An *arithmetic formula* over variables $x_1, \ldots, x_n$ is a rooted tree whose leaves are labeled by variables or field constants, and whose internal nodes are labeled by $+$ or $\times$. It computes a polynomial bottom-up in the natural way; its *size* is the number of edges and its *depth* is the longest root-to-leaf path.

**Definition 1 (Read-Once Formula (ROF)).** *An arithmetic formula* $\mathsf{C}$ *is* read-once *if each variable labels at most one leaf of* $\mathsf{C}$. *We identify each gate with the polynomial it computes, and* $\mathsf{C}$ *with the polynomial at the root. W.l.o.g.* $\mathsf{C}$ *alternates* $+$ *and* $\times$ *layers, every internal gate has fan-in at least two, and every child of a* $\times$*-gate computes a non-constant polynomial. We also assume no leaf and no wire is labeled by* 0; *hence every variable occurring in* $\mathsf{C}$ *also occurs in the computed polynomial, i.e. it lies in* $\mathrm{var}(f)$.

The *product-depth* of a ROF $\mathsf{C}$, denoted $\Delta$, is the number of $\times$-gates on a longest root-to-leaf path. For a gate $G$, its product-depth is the number of $\times$-gates on the path from the root to $G$, excluding $G$. We call $\mathsf{C}$ $+$*-rooted* (resp. $\times$*-rooted*) if its root is a $+$-gate (resp. $\times$-gate).

**Definition 2** ($\mathrm{ROF}_0$). *A constant leaf is an* additive constant *if it is a child of a* $+$*-gate. An ROF is* additive-constant-free *if it has no additive constants; denote this class by* $\mathrm{ROF}_0$. *If* $\mathsf{C} \in \mathrm{ROF}_0$ *uses* $n$ *variables, we write* $\mathsf{C} \in \mathrm{ROF}_0(n)$.

A polynomial computed by a ROF is called a Read-Once Polynomial (ROP for short). It is easy to see that ROPs are multilinear. ROFs have been studied in both the Boolean and arithmetic settings [8–10,25,36,37] for their structural properties, algorithmic applications, and links to algebraic complexity. Read-once *oblivious* algebraic branching programs (ROABPs) generalize ROFs and form a standard testbed for blackbox PIT [2,20,23].

**Some Known Results on ROFs.** ROFs are a standard model for studying sums of restricted formulas: every multilinear polynomial can be written as a sum of ROPs, and the sum of ROFs model includes several other restricted circuit classes. Mahajan–Tawari [29] analyzed the number of required summands, proving tight lower bounds for explicit polynomials and a strict hierarchy that sum of $k$-many ROFs[1] is *strictly contained* in sum of $(k+1)$-many ROFs: $\Sigma_k\mathrm{ROF} \subsetneq \Sigma_{k+1}\mathrm{ROF}$, for $k \leq \lceil n/2 \rceil$. From a structural viewpoint, Volkovich [38] proved the following: a multilinear polynomial is read-once if and only if all its three-variable restrictions are read-once.

**Polynomial Identity Testing.** Since ROFs form a very restricted model of computation, they are a natural testbed for designing efficient polynomial identity testing algorithms. *Polynomial Identity Testing* (PIT) asks whether a succinctly represented polynomial (e.g., by a circuit/formula) is identically zero.

---

[1] We shall denote the class of polynomials computed by sum of $k$ ROFs as $\sum_k \mathrm{ROF}$. In addition, we shall use $\sum_k \mathrm{ROF}(n)$ to denote the set of all polynomials computed by the sum of $k$ many ROFs in $n$ variables.

The *Polynomial Identity* Lemma [13,34,35,39] gives an efficient randomized algorithm for PIT. In the *blackbox* setting, one is not given the full description of the circuit $C$ but only allowed blackbox (oracle) access to $C$. One of the central open problems in algebraic complexity is to *derandomize* blackbox PIT by constructing explicit and efficient hitting sets (or hitting-set generators) for natural circuit classes. After a series of works [4,37], Minahan and Volkovich designed a deterministic polynomial-time blackbox PIT algorithm for ROFs [30]. Progress on PIT is deeply intertwined with algebraic circuit lower bounds and hardness-vs-randomness tradeoffs [1,5,6,17,22,26,27], and also connects to invariant theory and Noether Normalization [3,19,31,32]. For more details, refer to the recent survey [16] and the references within.

### 1.1 Border Complexity and GCT

Many algebraic complexity measures $\Gamma$ (e.g., circuit size, ABP width, Waring rank) admit a *border* analogue: we say $f$ has *border $\Gamma$-complexity* at most $s$ (we write $\overline{\Gamma}(f) \leq s$) if there exists a polynomial $g(\mathbf{x}, \epsilon)$ of $\Gamma$-complexity $\leq s$ over the field $\mathbb{F}(\epsilon)$ such that $g$ approximates $f$, that is $g(\mathbf{x}, \epsilon) = f(\mathbf{x}) + \epsilon \cdot h(\mathbf{x}, \epsilon)$, for some polynomial $h(\mathbf{x}, \epsilon)$ (equivalently, $f = \lim_{\epsilon \to 0} g$ over fields like $\mathbb{C}$ or $\mathbb{R}$).

Border notions are central in complexity and geometry (e.g., tensor border rank and orbit-closure questions in geometric complexity theory (GCT)), and they also arise in derandomization contexts such as PIT. A basic goal is *debordering*: given a border representation of $f$, output an explicit *exact* representation of $f$ in the underlying model with small parameter blow-up. We write $\overline{\mathcal{C}}$ for the *border class* of $\mathcal{C}$, i.e., the set of all polynomials that are approximated by polynomials in $\mathcal{C}$. Loosely speaking, in the above definition, $g \in \mathcal{C}_{\mathbb{F}(\epsilon)} \implies f \in \overline{\mathcal{C}}$ (equivalently, the Zariski/Eudlidean closure of $\mathcal{C}$ in the space of coefficients).

**A Motivating Question.** Let $\mathcal{C}$ be a Zariski-closed algebraic class (so $\overline{\mathcal{C}} = \mathcal{C}$). What is the structure of its *sum border* $\overline{\mathcal{C} + \mathcal{C}}$? Even when $\mathcal{C}$ admits a clean algebraic/algorithmic description, $\overline{\mathcal{C} + \mathcal{C}}$ is typically harder to analyze. Two examples:

- $\mathcal{C} = \text{ROABP}(w, n, d)$, the $n$-variate degree-$d$ polynomials computable by a width-$w$ ROABP in some variable order. It is known (via Nisan's characterization) that $\overline{\text{ROABP}(w, n, d)} = \text{ROABP}(w, n, d)$ [18,33], yet the structure of $\overline{\text{ROABP} + \text{ROABP}}$ remains open.[2]
- $\mathcal{C} = \prod_{i=1}^{d} \ell_i$ (products of linear forms): $\mathcal{C}$ is closed, but $\overline{\mathcal{C} + \mathcal{C}}$ is much richer; recent work places it inside **VBP** (polynomial-size ABPs) [14].

In this work we focus on $\mathcal{C} = \text{ROF}(n)$.[3] One can show that ROF is *Zariski-closed* (i.e. $\overline{\text{ROF}} = \text{ROF}$; for a proof, see Sect. 2.2). Let $\Sigma_2\text{ROF}$ denote the sum of two read-once formulas. We ask:

[2] The two ROABPs may use different variable orders, so Nisan's characterization does not directly apply. In the log-variate regime, [7] gives a polynomial-time HSG without explicitly debordering the model.

[3] Observe that the size and degree of a $C \in \text{ROF}(n)$ are both at most $n$.

*Which polynomials lie in $\overline{\Sigma_2\text{ROF}}$? How does this border compare to the exact class?*

To the best of our knowledge, no algebraic characterization of $\overline{\Sigma_2\text{ROF}}$ is known. Such a description could potentially lead to stronger derandomization and lower bounds.

## 1.2 Our Contributions

We study the border of sums of $k$ ROFs, for constant $k$, denoted $\overline{\Sigma_k\text{ROF}}$, and some restrictions of this model. We make significant progress along three complementary axes.

An ROF is *additive-constant-free* if it has no additive-constants (for a detailed definition, please refer to a full version of the paper.). We shall denote the class of additive-constant-free $n$-variate ROFs by $\text{ROF}_0(n)$. It is easy to see that additive-constant-free ROFs *subsume* homogeneous ROFs. Our first result is the efficient debordering of $\overline{\text{ROF}_0 + \text{ROF}_0}$, denoted $\overline{\sum_2 \text{ROF}_0}$. For a detailed proof, we refer the reader to the full version of this paper.

**Theorem 1 (Debordering the border of sum of 2 ROFs).** *Over fields of characteristic other than 2, $\overline{\sum_2 \text{ROF}_0(n)} \subseteq \sum_{O(n)} \text{ROF}_0(n)$.*[4]

*Remark 1.* Even though the additive-constant-free/homogeneous assumption may appear to simplify the setting, it does not make the problem trivial. Substantial cancellations can still occur in the homogeneous regime, so the resulting limit can be dramatically different and remains genuinely nontrivial. Even in the basic warm-up case of the sum of two homogeneous ROFs—namely, depth-3, fan-in-2 homogeneous multilinear circuits where each product is over variable-disjoint linear forms– the task of debordering is far from obvious, and a naive application of prior techniques [14,15] yields only an ABP. In contrast, our argument (implicit in the paper, but apparent when the technique is followed step-by-step) actually shows that the limit can be computed as a sum of $O(n)$ terms, each term being a product of variable-disjoint linear forms!

At higher depths ($\geq$5), the situation becomes even more intricate, and past techniques no longer apply, necessitating a deeper, case-by-case analysis.

Next, we design a quasi-polynomial-time hitting set for the border of sums of two *homogeneous depth-5* ROFs. This advances PIT for border versions of structured circuits and complements the debordering result above. Our results hold over any field $\mathbb{F}$ of size poly($n$) and characteristic other than 2.

**Theorem 2 (Hitting set for the border of sum of 2 homogeneous depth-5 ROFs).** *There is an $n^{O(\log n)}$ time computable hitting set for the border of sums of two homogeneous depth-5 $n$-variate ROFs.*

[4] Unfortunately, our proof does not work for $\overline{\sum_2 \text{ROF}(n)}$; see Remark 2 in Sect. 3.

Finally, we show an explicit separation between sums of ROFs and border of sums of ROFs. To show that, we recall the definition of elementary symmetric polynomial $\mathsf{ESym}_{n,d}$:

$$\mathsf{ESym}_{n,d} := \sum_{S \subseteq [n] | S| = d} \prod_{i \in S} x_i .$$

We show $\mathsf{ESym}_{n,n-k+1} \in \overline{\Sigma_k\text{ROF}} \setminus \Sigma_k\text{ROF}$ for any $2 \leq k \leq n/5$. Our work also extends the lower bound of [29] where it was only established that $\mathsf{ESym}_{n,n-1} \notin \Sigma_{\lceil n/2 \rceil - 1}\text{ROF}$. For a detailed proof, please see the full version of this paper.

**Theorem 3 (Sum of ROFs not closed under border).** *For any $n \in \mathbb{N}$, $n \geq 10$ and $2 \leq k \leq \frac{n}{5}$, $\sum_k \text{ROF}(n) \subsetneq \overline{\sum_k \text{ROF}(n)}$ over any field.*

We exploit structural properties of $\overline{\Sigma_2\text{ROF}}$ to obtain debordering, efficient hitting sets, and lower bounds. Although $\Sigma_k$ROABP, $\overline{\Sigma_k\text{ROABP}}$, and several of their restrictions have been investigated in multiple settings [7,11,12,21,24,28], a general debordering theorem for $\overline{\Sigma_k\text{ROABP}}$ remains open for all $k \geq 2$.

## 2 Preliminaries

**Notations.** $[n] = \{1, \dots, n\}$. We shall use $\mathbb{F}$ to denote a field. Capital letters like $C, R, T, Q, \mathsf{C}, \mathsf{D}$ will be used to denote arithmetic circuits, and $\mathbf{x}, \mathbf{y}, \mathbf{z}$ to denote variable sets of polynomials computed by these circuits. We shall use $\epsilon$ to denote a fresh formal variable; when we say a circuit is in the border of some circuit class, the circuit will be defined over $\mathbb{F}(\epsilon)$. We use small case Greek letters like $\alpha, \beta, \gamma$ to denote elements of $\mathbb{F}(\epsilon)$. For a polynomial $f \in \mathbb{K}[\mathbf{x}]$, $\text{var}(f)$ will denote all variables in $\mathbf{x}$ present in $f$; here $\mathbb{K}$ can be $\mathbb{F}, \mathbb{F}(\epsilon)$, or $\mathbb{F}[\epsilon]$.

Throughout this work, whenever we say that $\mathsf{C}$ is a circuit over $\mathbb{F}(\epsilon)$, we can assume without loss of generality that all $\mathbb{F}(\epsilon)$-elements in it are of the form $\epsilon^N \cdot \gamma$ for some $\gamma \in \mathbb{F}[\epsilon]$. For an $\alpha \neq 0$, $\alpha = \sum_{i \geq M} \alpha_i \epsilon^i$, where $M \in \mathbb{Z}$, and $\alpha_M \neq 0$, the valuation $\mathsf{val}_\epsilon(\alpha) := M$. We assume $\mathsf{val}_\epsilon(0) := \infty$. For a $g \in \mathbb{F}(\epsilon)[\mathbf{x}]$, $\mathsf{val}_\epsilon(g)$ is the minimum valuation of a coefficient of any monomial of $g$. For an $\alpha \in \mathbb{F}[\epsilon]$, $\alpha(0) \in \mathbb{F}$ denotes the constant term of $\alpha$. Throughout the paper, whenever we use $\mathsf{val}(\cdot)$, we will usually mean $\mathsf{val}_\epsilon$ unless specified otherwise.

### 2.1 ROFs

Observe that the class of homogeneous ROFs is subsumed by additive-constant-free ROFs. For an ROF $\mathsf{C}$ and $x, y \in \mathbf{x}$, $\text{fca}(x, y)$ denotes the first common ancestor gate of $x, y$ in $\mathsf{C}$. Because $\mathsf{C}$ is an ROF, the first common ancestor is unique for any pair of variables. The notion of a gate graph of an ROF, defined below, is crucial to proving our results.

**Definition 3 (Gate graph).** *For an ROF $\mathsf{C} \in \mathbb{F}[\mathbf{x}]$, its gate graph $G = (\mathbf{x}, E)$, where*

$$E := \{\{x, y\} : \text{fca}(x, y) \textit{ is a } \times \textit{ gate}\}.$$

**Proposition 1.** *[37]* $E = \left\{\{x, y\} : \frac{\partial^2 \mathsf{C}}{\partial x \partial y} \neq 0\right\}$.

### 2.2 Border of $\mathrm{ROF}_0$

Here we show that for only one summand, it is *closed* under debordering, i.e. $\overline{\mathrm{ROF}_0} = \mathrm{ROF}_0$. Before proving this, we state the following folklore claim which follows from Nisan's characterisation of ROABPs [33].

*Claim.* $\overline{\mathrm{ROABP}} = \mathrm{ROABP}$.

It is also known that $\overline{\mathrm{ROF}} = \mathrm{ROF}$. However, we need a similar statement for additive-constant-free ROFs.

*Claim.* $\overline{\mathrm{ROF}_0} = \mathrm{ROF}_0$.

*Proof.* By induction on the number of variables $n$ in a $\mathsf{C} \in \overline{\mathrm{ROF}_0}$. For $n = 1$, $f = \alpha x + O(\epsilon)$ for some $\alpha \in \mathbb{F}(\epsilon)$. Since $\alpha x + O(\epsilon) \in \mathbb{F}[\epsilon]$, $\alpha \in \mathbb{F}[\epsilon]$. Thus, $f = \alpha(0) \cdot x$ and the claim is true. Let the claim be true for all $f' \in \overline{\mathrm{ROF}_0(n-1)}$ and let $f \in \overline{\mathrm{ROF}_0(n)}$; say it is $\mathsf{C} + O(\epsilon)$. Note that $\mathsf{C} \in \mathbb{F}[\epsilon][\mathbf{x}]$.

If the top gate of $\mathsf{C}$ is a $+$ gate then $\mathsf{C} = T_1 + T_2$, where $T_i$s are ROFs over $\mathbb{F}(\epsilon)$. They are also non-constant, variable disjoint, and additive-constant-free. Hence, they must be ROFs over $\mathbb{F}[\epsilon]$. As they have fewer than $n$ variables, from the induction hypothesis $T_i(\epsilon = 0)$ is in $\mathrm{ROF}_0$ and $f = T_1(\epsilon = 0) + T_2(\epsilon = 0) \in \mathrm{ROF}_0$. Otherwise, $\mathsf{C} = Q_1 Q_2$ where $Q_i$ are non-constant, variable disjoint, additive-constant-free ROFs over $\mathbb{F}(\epsilon)$. Without loss of generality, $\mathsf{val}(Q_1) \leq \mathsf{val}(Q_2)$. As $\mathsf{C} \in \mathbb{F}[\epsilon][\mathbf{x}]$ and $Q_1, Q_2$ are variable disjoint, $\mathsf{val}(Q_1) + \mathsf{val}(Q_2) \geq 0$. Let $\ell := \max\{0, -\mathsf{val}(Q_1)\}$ and $Q_1' := \epsilon^{\ell} Q_1$, $Q_2' := \epsilon^{-\ell} Q_2'$. Note that $Q_1', Q_2' \in \mathbb{F}[\epsilon][\mathbf{x}]$. As they have fewer than $n$ variables, the induction hypothesis gives that, $Q_1'(\epsilon = 0)$ and $Q_2'(\epsilon = 0)$ are in $\mathrm{ROF}_0$. Thus, $f = Q_1'(\epsilon = 0) Q_2'(\epsilon = 0)$ is also in $\mathrm{ROF}_0$.

**Remark.** The above proof also holds for ROF.

## 3 Detailed Proof Ideas

In this section, we sketch the proof ideas of the main theorems. We will use the following notions called the *first common ancestor gate* (fca) and the *gate graph* (see Definition 3) . For an ROF $\mathsf{C}$ and $x, y \in \mathbf{x}$, $\mathrm{fca}(x, y)$ denotes the first common ancestor gate (fca) of $x, y$ in $R$. Because $R$ is an ROF, the first common ancestor is *unique* for any pair of variables. A *gate graph* is a graph whose vertices are variables in $\mathbf{x}$ and the edge set is $E = \{\{x, y\} : \mathrm{fca}(x, y) \text{ is a } \times \text{ gate}\}$, equivalently $\{x, y\} \in E \iff \partial^2 \mathsf{C}/\partial x\, \partial y \not\equiv 0$.

### 3.1 Proof Idea of Theorem 1

Let $f \in \mathbb{F}[\mathbf{x}]$ with $f + O(\epsilon) = R_1(\mathbf{x}, \epsilon) + R_2(\mathbf{x}, \epsilon)$ where each $R_i \in \mathrm{ROF}_0$ over $\mathbb{F}(\epsilon)$. We prove by induction on $n = |\mathbf{x}|$ that $f$ admits a representation as a sum of $O(n)$ members of $\mathrm{ROF}_0$. At a high level, the induction breaks down $R_1$ or $R_2$

as a sum of multiple ROFs, showing that all but one have a limit. *Peeling* off such a summand strictly reduces the variable set.

*Setup and Case Split.* Fix a *deepest* gate $G$ in $R_1$ and distinguish whether $G$ is a product or a sum gate. (We use that $R_i \in \mathrm{ROF}_0$ and basic properties of first-common-ancestor $\mathrm{fca}(\cdot,\cdot)$ from Sect. 2.)

**Case 1** (multiplicative $G$). Here $G = x_1 x_2 \cdots x_m$ with $m \geq 2$. We further divide into two subcases.

Case 1.1 ($\mathrm{fca}(x_1, x_2)$ is $+$ in $R_2$). Then

$$\partial_{x_1} f + O(\epsilon) = \partial_{x_1} R_1 + \partial_{x_1} R_2.$$

It is not hard to see that every monomial of $\partial_{x_1} R_1$ contains $x_2$, while no monomial of $\partial_{x_1} R_2$ contains $x_2$; hence there is no cancellation between the two summands. Therefore, it follows that $\partial_{x_1} R_2 \in \mathbb{F}[\epsilon][\mathbf{x}]$. Since, $\overline{\mathrm{ROF}_0} = \mathrm{ROF}_0$ (see Sect. 2.2), $x_1 \cdot (\partial_{x_1} R_2)(\epsilon = 0)$ is an $\mathrm{ROF}_0$ term we can peel off from $f$. Using a similar argument, $\partial_{x_2} R_2 \in \mathbb{F}[\epsilon][\mathbf{x}]$ and $x_2 \cdot (\partial_{x_2} R_2)(\epsilon = 0)$ can also be peeled off. Then we replace the factor $x_1 x_2$ in $R_1$ by a fresh variable to drop one variable and recurse. More details can be found in the full version of this paper.

Case 1.2 ($\mathrm{fca}(x_1, x_2)$ is $\times$ in $R_2$.) Assume (by adding a dummy top $+$ if needed) that the top-most gate of $R_2$ is a $+$ gate. Using multilinearity expand

$$R_2 \;=\; R_2(x_1 = 0, x_2 = 0) \;+\; x_1 \cdot \Big(\partial_{x_1} R_2\Big)(x_2 = 0) \;+\; x_2 \cdot \Big(\partial_{x_2} R_2\Big)(x_1 = 0) \;+\; x_1 x_2 \cdot \partial^2_{x_1 x_2} R_2.$$

Using the same no-cancellation argument as in Case 1.1, the first-order components are in $\mathbb{F}[\epsilon][\mathbf{x}]$. Let

$$R_3 \;:=\; (x_1 \cdot (\partial_{x_1} R_2)\,(x_2 = 0))\,(\epsilon = 0), \qquad R_4 \;:=\; \big(x_2 \cdot \big(\partial_{x_2} R_2\big)(x_1 = 0)\big)\,(\epsilon = 0);$$

we have $R_3, R_4 \in \mathrm{ROF}_0$. The main part of the analysis in this case is showing that $R_3, R_4 \in \mathrm{ROF}_0$ implies at least one of $R_2(x_1 = 0, x_2 = 0)$ and $x_1 x_2 \cdot \big(\partial^2_{x_1 x_2} R_2\big)$ is in $\mathbb{F}[\epsilon][\mathbf{x}]$; for more details we refer the reader to the full version of this paper.

Thus,

$$f + O(\epsilon) \;=\; (R_1 + R_2') \;+\; R_3 \;+\; R_4 \;+\; R_5,$$

where $R_5$ is either $R_2(x_1 = 0, x_2 = 0)(\epsilon = 0)$ or $x_1 x_2 \cdot \big(\partial^2_{x_1 x_2} R_2\big)\,(\epsilon = 0)$. In the first case, $x_1, x_2$ appear in the same monomial in $R_2'$ while in the second case they do not appear in $R_2'$. We peel off $R_3, R_4, R_5$. As in Case 1.1, replace $x_1 x_2$ in the deepest product $G = x_1 x_2 \cdots x_m$ in $R_1$ by a fresh $y \cdot x_3 \cdots x_m$ to eliminate one variable and recurse.

**Case 2** (additive $G$). Since G is one of the deepest gates in $R_1$, it must compute a linear form. Write $G = \sum_{j=1}^{m} \alpha_j(\epsilon)\, x_j$ and (after rescaling) normalize $\alpha_1(0) = 1$. Set $\alpha := \alpha_2(0)$ and make the invertible substitution $x_1 \leftarrow x_1 - \alpha x_2$ to obtain

$f', R_1', R_2'$ from $f, R_1, R_2$ respectively. Notice that $R_1'$ is independent of $x_2$, but $R_2'$ need not be an $\mathrm{ROF}_0$ over $\mathbb{F}(\epsilon)$ and can contain $x_2$ in two places possibly making it a degree 2 polynomial in $x_2$. We now analyze $\partial_{x_2} f + O(\epsilon) = \partial_{x_2} R_2'$ in the following two cases.

Case 2.1 $\mathrm{fca}(x_1, x_2)$ is a $+$ gate in $R_2$. If $x_1$ and $x_2$ are directly connected to this common $+$ gate, then $\partial_{x_2} R_2'$ is an ROF over $\mathbb{F}(\epsilon)$, so we can peel off $x_2 \cdot \partial_{x_2} R_2'$ and recurse. Otherwise, we argue that

$$\partial_{x_2} R_2' = -\alpha \cdot \partial_{x_1} R_2 + \partial_{x_2} R_2,$$

and that there can be no cancellations between the two summands (see the full version of this paper for details). Thus both are in $\mathbb{F}[\epsilon][\mathbf{x}]$. We can peel off $(x_2 \cdot \partial_{x_2} R_2')(\epsilon = 0) \in \Sigma_2\mathrm{ROF}_0$ and recurse on $f'' := \big(R_1' + R_2'(x_2 = 0)\big)(\epsilon = 0) \in \overline{\Sigma_2\mathrm{ROF}_0}(n-1)$.

Case 2.2. $\mathrm{fca}(x_1, x_2)$ is a $\times$ gate in $R_2$. Then we can write $R_2'$ as

$$R_2' = R_2'(x_2 = 0) + x_2 \cdot \partial_{x_2} R_2'(x_2 = 0) + \frac{1}{2} x_2^2 \cdot \partial^2_{x_2^2} \cdot R_2'.$$

Since $R_1'$ does not contain $x_2$, $x_2 \cdot \partial_{x_2} R_2'(x_2 = 0), \frac{1}{2} \cdot x_2^2 \cdot \partial^2_{x_2^2} R_2' \in \mathbb{F}[\epsilon][\mathbf{x}]$. We then recurse on $f'' + O(\epsilon) := R_1' + R_2'(x_2 = 0) \in \overline{\sum_2 \mathrm{ROF}_0(n-1))}$ and get an $R \in \sum_{O(n-1)} \mathrm{ROF}_0(n-1)$ such that $f' = R + (x_2 \cdot \partial_{x_2} R_2'(x_2 = 0))\,(\epsilon = 0) + \left(\frac{1}{2} \cdot x_2^2 \cdot \partial^2_{x_2^2} R_2'\right)(\epsilon = 0)$. Note that $R$ does not have $x_2$. Thus by replacing $x_1$ by $x_1 + \alpha x_2$ in $f'$ we get $f$ while keeping $R \in \sum_{O(n-1)} \mathrm{ROF}_0(n)$. We show that this replacement will cause a quadratic term in $x_2$ to appear in $(x_2 \cdot \partial_{x_2} R_2'(x_2 = 0))\,(\epsilon = 0)$ and this will be exactly $-\frac{1}{2} \cdot x_2^2 \cdot \partial^2_{x_2^2} R_2'$; see the full version of this paper for details. Thus we are left with $f \in \sum_{O(n)} \mathrm{ROF}_0(n)$.

*Final Blowup.* Each peeling step in cases 1 and 2 adds $O(1)$ summands and reduces the variable count by 1; after at most $n$ steps we obtain $f = \sum_{i=1}^{O(n)} Q_i$ with each $Q_i \in \mathrm{ROF}_0$, completing the debordering.

*Remark 2.* Our proof *does not* work for $\overline{\Sigma_2\mathrm{ROF}}$. The way we show that there is no cancellation between $-\alpha \cdot \partial_{x_1} R_2$ and $\partial_{x_2} R_2$ in Case 2.1 is by arguing that every monomial in one of the summands must contain a variable from a certain $\mathbf{z} \subset \mathbf{x}$ which can not be present in any monomial of the other summand.[5] If we allow $R_2$ to have additive constants, then in some of the monomials, these constants can replace the variables in $\mathbf{z}$, and there can be cancellation between the summands. A similar (and more intricate) argument is also required in Case 2.2.

[5] $\mathbf{z}$ is either $\{z : \partial^2_{x_1,z} R_2 \neq 0, \partial^2_{x_2,z} R_2 = 0\}$ or $\{z : \partial^2_{x_2,z} R_2 \neq 0, \partial^2_{x_1,z} R_2 = 0\}$. $\mathbf{z}$ can be shown to be non-empty when at least one of the $x_1, x_2$ is not directly connected to $\mathrm{fca}(x_1, x_2)$.

### 3.2 Proof Idea of Theorem 2

For ease of exposition, we shall give an overview of the proof of Theorem 2 for the special case of the border of sum of two homogeneous depth 4 ROFs. Let $f \in \mathbb{F}[\mathbf{x}]$ with $f + O(\epsilon) = R_1(\mathbf{x}, \epsilon) + R_2(\mathbf{x}, \epsilon) \neq 0$ where each $R_i$ is a homogeneous depth 4 ROF over $\mathbb{F}(\epsilon)$. A hitting set for $f$ can be easily obtained from a hitting set for $\frac{\partial f}{\partial x_i}$ for any $i \in [n]$ and $f \neq 0$ if and only if $\frac{\partial f}{\partial x_i}$ for some $i \in [n]$. So by taking derivatives if required, we can assume without loss of generality that the top-most gates of $R_1, R_2$ are $\times$ gates. Let

$$R_1 = \prod_{i \in [k]} p_i, \text{ where } p_i = \sum_{j \in [k_i]} \alpha_{i,j} m_{i,j} \quad \text{and} \quad R_2 = \prod_{i \in [\ell]} q_i, \text{ where } q_i = \sum_{j \in [\ell_i]} \beta_{i,j} \mu_{i,j}.$$

Here $\alpha_{i,j}, \beta_{i,j} \in \mathbb{F}(\epsilon)$ and $m_{i,j}, \mu_{i,j}$ are monomials. The crucial observation underlying our proof is the following: If $k = \ell$ and if for all $i \in [k]$, there exists a $j \in [k]$ such that $\{m_{i,j} : j \in [k_i]\} = \{\mu_{i,j} : j \in [\ell_i]\}$, then $R_1$ and $R_2$ have ROABPs *with the same variable order*. Let us call a $f$ in the border of the sum of two homogeneous depth-4 ROFs for which

$$\{m_{i,j} : j \in [k_i]\} = \{\mu_{i,j} : j \in [\ell_i]\}$$

a "good" circuit. Thus, for a good $f$, $f \in \overline{\text{ROABP}} = \text{ROABP}$, and we can use the quasi-polynomial hitting set for ROABPs from [2,20].

Let $\mathcal{H}$ be a hitting set for both the class of ROABPs and $\Sigma_2$ROF. We know a quasi-polynomial time hitting set exists [2,20,30,37]. Our proof starts with an arbitrary $f$ in the border of the sum of two homogeneous depth-4 ROFs and iteratively shows that either a hitting set for $f$ can be easily obtained from $\mathcal{H}$, or some parts of $f$ are zero and removing these parts, $f$ moves *closer* to a good circuit. In the following paragraphs, we describe this iterative approach.

As a first step towards converting $f$ into a good circuit, we show that

$$\{m_{i,j} : i \in [k], j \in [k_i]\} = \{\mu_{i,j} : i \in [\ell], j \in [\ell_i]\}. \tag{1}$$

Suppose not. Then there are three cases.

**Case 1.** There exists a variable $x$ which is present in $R_1$, but not in $R_2$, without loss of generality $x$ is in $m_{1,1}$. As $f$ is a homogeneous ROF, it is also an additive-constant-free ROF. It is easy to see that the derivative of an $\text{ROF}_0$, wrt to a variable, remains additive-constant-free. Thus $\frac{\partial f}{\partial x} = \frac{\partial R_1}{\partial x} + O(\epsilon) \in \overline{\text{ROF}_0} = \text{ROF}_0$. Notice that $\mathcal{H}$ is a hitting set for $\frac{\partial f}{\partial x}$. If $\frac{\partial f}{\partial x}$ is non-zero, then we can easily obtain a set $\mathcal{H}_1$ from $\mathcal{H}$ such that $f(\mathcal{H}_1) \neq 0$, and we are done. Otherwise, we can remove $\alpha_{1,1} m_{1,1} \cdot p_2 \cdots p_k = \frac{\partial f}{\partial x} + O(\epsilon)$ from $R_1$. Observe that this brings us closer to achieving the goal mentioned in Eq. 1.

If $f$ doesn't satisfy the condition in Case 1, then there must exist a pair of variables $x, y$ such that they are in the same monomial in $R_1$, but in different monomials in $R_2$ (or vice versa). Without loss of generality, $x, y$ are in $m_{1,1}$.

**Case 2.** fca$(x, y)$ in $R_2$ is a $+$ gate. Then, $\frac{\partial^2 f}{\partial x \partial y} = \frac{\partial^2 R_1}{\partial x \partial y} + O(\epsilon) \in \overline{\text{ROF}} = \text{ROF}$. Again $\mathcal{H}$ is a hitting set for $\frac{\partial^2 f}{\partial x \partial y}$. Much like in Case 1, if $\frac{\partial^2 f}{\partial x \partial y}(\mathcal{H}) \neq 0$, then a hitting set $\mathcal{H}_2$ for $f$ can be easily obtained from $\mathcal{H}$. Else $\alpha_{1,1} m_{1,1} \cdot p_2 \cdots p_k$ can be removed from $R_1$ and we move closer to achieving the goal mentioned in Eq. 1.

**Case 3.** fca$(x, y)$ in $R_2$ is a $\times$ gate. Without loss of generality, $x$ is in $\mu_{1,1}$ and $y$ is in $\mu_{2,1}$. Observe that $\frac{\partial f}{\partial x}(y = 0) = \frac{\partial R_2}{\partial x}(y = 0) + O(\epsilon) \in \overline{\text{ROF}} = \text{ROF}$. Similar to the above two cases, we can either remove $\beta_{1,1}\mu_{1,1}(q_2 - \beta_{2,1}\mu_{2,1})q_3 \cdots q_\ell$ from $R_2$ or we get a hitting set $\mathcal{H}_3$ for $f$.

By repeating the argument outlined in the three cases above, we get that either $f(\mathcal{H}_1 \cup \mathcal{H}_2 \cup \mathcal{H}_3) \neq 0$ or $f$ has a circuit satisfying the condition in Eq. 1. Since we are done in the former case, we now focus on the latter and show how to convert such an $f$ into a good circuit.

Suppose $f$ is not a good circuit. Without loss of generality for all $i \in [k]$, $\mathsf{val}(\alpha_{i,1}) \leq \mathsf{val}(\alpha_{i,j})$ for all $j \in [k_i]$ and for all $i \in [m]$, $\mathsf{val}(\beta_{i,1}) \leq \mathsf{val}(\beta_{i,j})$ for all $j \in [\ell_i]$.[6] Also, without loss of generality, $m_{1,1} = \mu_{1,j}$ for some $j \in [\ell_1]$. Suppose that some $\mu_{1,j'}$ is not in $p_1$; without loss of generality $\mu_{1,j'} = m_{2,j''}$. Then observe that $\alpha_{1,1} m_{1,1} \cdot \alpha_{2,j''} m_{2,j''} \cdot p_3 \cdots p_k \in \mathbb{F}[\epsilon][\mathbf{x}]$. But this means that $\mathsf{val}(\alpha_{1,1}) + \mathsf{val}(\alpha_{2,j''}) + \mathsf{val}(p_3 \cdots p_k) \geq 0$. As $\mathsf{val}(\alpha_{1,1}) \leq \mathsf{val}(\alpha_{1,j})$ for all $j \in [k_1]$, this means $\mathsf{val}(p_1) + \mathsf{val}(\alpha_{2,j''}) + \mathsf{val}(p_3 \cdots p_k) \geq 0$. So, $\alpha_{2,j''} m_{2,j''} p_1 \cdot p_3 \cdots p_k \in \mathbb{F}[\epsilon][\mathbf{x}]$. But then so is $\beta_{1,j'}\mu_{1,j'} q_2 \cdots q_\ell$. Thus

$$(\alpha_{2,j''} m_{2,j''} p_1 \cdot p_3 \cdots p_k + \beta_{1,j'}\mu_{1,j'} q_2 \cdots q_\ell)\,(\epsilon = 0)$$

is in $\sum_2 \text{ROF}_0$. Thus for all $x \in \mu_{1,j'} = m_{2,j''}$, $\frac{\partial f}{\partial x} \in \sum_2 \text{ROF}$. If any one of these is non-zero, then a we can easily obtain a set $\mathcal{H}_4$ from $\mathcal{H}$ such that $f(\mathcal{H}_4) \neq 0$. Otherwise, we can remove

$$(\alpha_{2,j''} m_{2,j''} p_1 \cdot p_3 \cdots p_k + \beta_{1,j'}\mu_{1,j'} q_2 \cdots q_\ell)$$

from $f$ and $f$ is now closer to being a good circuit than it was earlier. Repeatedly arguing in this was we either get that $\mathcal{H}_4$ is a hitting set for $f$ or $f$ is good and thus $\mathcal{H}$ is a hitting set for $f$. Thus we have shown that at least one of $\mathcal{H}_1, \mathcal{H}_2, \mathcal{H}_3, \mathcal{H}_4$, or $\mathcal{H}$ is a hitting set for $f$.

### 3.3 Proof Idea of Theorem 3

Let $d := n - k + 1 \geq 3$.

[6] As far as border complexity is concerned, we can always assume without loss of generality that an $\alpha \in \mathbb{F}(\epsilon)$ present in a circuit is of the form $\epsilon^N \cdot \beta$, where $\beta \in \mathbb{F}[\epsilon]$ has a non-zero constant term. Then the *valuation* $\mathsf{val}(\alpha) := N$. For a $g \in \mathbb{F}(\epsilon)[\mathbf{x}]$, $\mathsf{val}(g)$ is the minimum valuation of a coefficient of any monomial of $g$.

*Border Membership.* It is easy to see that the following identity holds:

$$\mathsf{ESym}_{n,d} + O(\epsilon) = \epsilon^d \prod_{j\in[n]} \left(\frac{x_j}{\epsilon} + 1\right) - \sum_{i=1}^{n-d} \frac{1}{\epsilon^i} \cdot \mathsf{ESym}_{n,d+i}.$$

Based on this identity, one can prove a stronger identity (by induction) showing that there exist $f_i(\epsilon), g_i(\epsilon)$ with $\mathrm{val}_\epsilon(f_i) = \mathrm{val}_\epsilon(g_i) = 0$ (i.e. $f_i, g_i \in \mathbb{F}[\epsilon]$ with $f_i(0), g_i(0) \neq 0$) such that

$$\mathsf{ESym}_{n,d} + O(\epsilon) = \epsilon^d \prod_{j\in[n]} \left(\frac{x_j}{\epsilon} + 1\right) + \sum_{i=1}^{n-d} \frac{1}{\epsilon^{2i-1}} \cdot \frac{f_i(\epsilon)}{g_i(\epsilon)} \cdot \epsilon^{(d+i)2i} \prod_{j\in[n]} \left(\frac{x_j}{\epsilon^{2i}} + 1\right),$$

a sum of $(n-d+1)$ read-once formulas over $\mathbb{F}(\epsilon)$ converging coefficient-wise to $\mathsf{ESym}_{n,d}$. Hence $\mathsf{ESym}_{n,n-k+1} \in \overline{\Sigma_k\mathrm{ROF}}$. For detailed inductive analysis, we refer the reader to the full version of this paper.

*Separation from $\Sigma_k$ROF.* Assume $\mathsf{ESym}_{n,n-k+1} = C_1 + \cdots + C_k$ with ROFs $C_i$.

By a reduction, after at most $k-1$ steps of (a) differentiating by a variable missing in some $C_i$ or (b) taking a mixed partial $\partial^2/(\partial x\, \partial y)$ when $\mathrm{fca}(x,y) = +$ in some $C_i$, we can obtain

$$C'_1 + \cdots + C'_\ell = \mathsf{ESym}_{n',\, n'-k+1}$$

on $n' \geq n - 2(k-1)$ variables, where $C'_1, \ldots, C'_\ell$ now share the *same* gate graph. In this case, we can assume the common gate graph to be complete, otherwise some pair $(x,y)$ has $\partial^2 C'_j/\partial x\, \partial y \equiv 0$ for all $j$, contradicting that $\partial^2 \mathsf{ESym}_{n',\, n'-k+1}/\partial x\, \partial y = \mathsf{ESym}_{n'-2,\, n'-k-1} \not\equiv 0$ for $d' = n' - k + 1 \geq 3$.

We show that an ROF with a complete gate graph can not compute $\mathsf{ESym}_{n',\, n'-k+1}$ in. The proof involves repeatedly translating variables by constants in such a way that every translation makes at least $C'_i$ 0 till we are left with only 2 ROFs. Then we use Theorem 1 from [29] to argue that a sum of two ROFs can not compute the resulting polynomial.

Therefore $\mathsf{ESym}_{n,n-k+1} \in \overline{\Sigma_k\mathrm{ROF}} \setminus \Sigma_k\mathrm{ROF}$ for $2 \leq k \leq n/5$.

## 4 Conclusion

Finally, we state a few open problems for further study

1. Can we drop the additive-constant-free assumption in Theorem 1 and deborder the border of sums of two ROFs?
2. Can Theorem 1 be extended to sums of constantly many ROFs?
3. We only give PIT for the border of sums of two homogeneous, depth-5 ROFs; can Theorem 2 be extended to the border of sums of two (general) ROFs?

**Acknowledgment.** PD is supported by the SUG Grant (#025774-00001), funded by Nanyang Technological University. Part of the manuscript was prepared while PD was a Jane Street fellow at the Simons Institute in the program "Complexity and Linear Algebra" and BT was employed by Folium Labs Private Limited. The work was initiated when BT was a student at the Indian Institute of Science, where he was supported by the Prime Minister's Research Fellowship.

## References

1. Agrawal, M.: Proving lower bounds via pseudo-random generators. In: Sarukkai, S., Sen, S. (eds.) FSTTCS 2005. LNCS, vol. 3821, pp. 92–105. Springer, Heidelberg (2005). https://doi.org/10.1007/11590156_6
2. Agrawal, M., Gurjar, R., Korwar, A., Saxena, N.: Hitting-sets for ROABP and sum of set-multilinear circuits. SIAM J. Comput. **44**(3), 669–697 (2015)
3. Allen-Zhu, Z., Garg, A., Li, Y., Oliveira, R., Wigderson, A.: Operator scaling via geodesically convex optimization, invariant theory and polynomial identity testing. In: Proceedings of the 50th Annual ACM SIGACT Symposium on Theory of Computing, pp. 172–181 (2018)
4. Anderson, M., van Melkebeek, D., Volkovich, I.: Deterministic polynomial identity tests for multilinear bounded-read formulae. Comput. Complex. **24**(4), 695–776 (2015). Conference Version Appeared in the Proceedings of CCC 2011
5. Andrews, R.: Algebraic hardness versus randomness in low characteristic. In: Saraf, S. (ed.) 35th Computational Complexity Conference, CCC 2020, 28–1, July 2020, Saarbrücken, Germany (Virtual Conference). LIPIcs, vol. 169, pp. 37:1–37:32. Schloss Dagstuhl - Leibniz-Zentrum für Informatik (2020)
6. Andrews, R.: On matrix multiplication and polynomial identity testing. In: 63rd IEEE Annual Symposium on Foundations of Computer Science, FOCS 2022, Denver, CO, USA, 31 October–3 November 2022. pp. 356–365. IEEE (2022)
7. Bisht, P., Saxena, N.: Blackbox identity testing for sum of special ROABPs and its border class. Comput. Complex. **30**(1), 8 (2021)
8. Bshouty, D., Bshouty, N.H.: On interpolating arithmetic read-once formulas with exponentiation. J. Comput. Syst. Sci. **56**(1), 112–124 (1998)
9. Bshouty, N.H., Cleve, R.: Interpolating arithmetic read-once formulas in parallel. SIAM J. Comput. **27**(2), 401–413 (1998)
10. Bshouty, N.H., Hancock, T.R., Hellerstein, L.: Learning arithmetic read-once formulas. SIAM J. Comput. **24**(4), 706–735 (1995). Conference Version Appeared in the Proceedings of STOC 1992
11. Chatterjee, P., Ghosal, U., Mukhopadhyay, P., Sinhababu, A.: IPS lower bounds for formulas and sum of ROABPs. In: FSTTCS 2025 (2025)
12. Chatterjee, P., Kush, D., Saraf, S., Shpilka, A.: Lower bounds for set-multilinear branching programs. In: Santhanam, R. (ed.) 39th Computational Complexity Conference, CCC 2024, 22–25 July 2024, Ann Arbor, MI, USA. LIPIcs, vol. 300, pp. 20:1–20:20. Schloss Dagstuhl - Leibniz-Zentrum für Informatik (2024)
13. DeMillo, R.A., Lipton, R.J.: A probabilistic remark on algebraic program testing. Inf. Process. Lett. **7**(4), 193–195 (1978)
14. Dutta, P., Dwivedi, P., Saxena, N.: Demystifying the border of depth-3 algebraic circuits. In: 62nd IEEE Annual Symposium on Foundations of Computer Science, FOCS 2021, Denver, CO, USA, 7–10 February 2022, pp. 92–103. IEEE (2021)

15. Dutta, P., Gesmundo, F., Ikenmeyer, C., Jindal, G., Lysikov, V.: Fixed-parameter debordering of waring rank. In: Beyersdorff, O., Kanté, M.M., Kupferman, O., Lokshtanov, D. (eds.) 41st International Symposium on Theoretical Aspects of Computer Science, STACS 2024 (2024)
16. Dutta, P., Ghosh, S.: Advances in polynomial identity testing. SIGACT News **55**(2), 53–88 (2024)
17. Dvir, Z., Shpilka, A., Yehudayoff, A.: Hardness-randomness tradeoffs for bounded depth arithmetic circuits. SIAM J. Comput. **39**(4), 1279–1293 (2009). Conference Version Appeared in the Proceedings of STOC 2008
18. Forbes, M.: Some concrete questions on the border complexity of polynomials. Presentation Given at the Workshop on Algebraic Complexity Theory WACT 2016 in Tel Aviv (2016). https://www.youtube.com/watch?v=1HMogQIHT6Q
19. Forbes, M.A., Shpilka, A.: Explicit Noether normalization for simultaneous conjugation via polynomial identity testing. In: Raghavendra, P., Raskhodnikova, S., Jansen, K., Rolim, J.D.P. (eds.) APPROX/RANDOM -2013. LNCS, vol. 8096, pp. 527–542. Springer, Heidelberg (2013). https://doi.org/10.1007/978-3-642-40328-6_37
20. Forbes, M.A., Shpilka, A.: Quasipolynomial-time identity testing of non-commutative and read-once oblivious algebraic branching programs. In: 54th Annual IEEE Symposium on Foundations of Computer Science, FOCS 2013, 26–29 October 2013, Berkeley, CA, USA, pp. 243–252. IEEE Computer Society (2013)
21. Forbes, M.A., Shpilka, A., Tzameret, I., Wigderson, A.: Proof complexity lower bounds from algebraic circuit complexity. Theory Comput. **17**(1), 1–88 (2021)
22. Guo, Z., Kumar, M., Saptharishi, R., Solomon, N.: Derandomization from algebraic hardness. SIAM J. Comput. **51**(2), 315–335 (2022)
23. Gurjar, R., Korwar, A., Saxena, N.: Identity testing for constant-width, and any-order, read-once oblivious arithmetic branching programs. Theory Comput. **13**(1), 1–21 (2017). Conference Version Appeared in the Proceedings of CCC 2016
24. Gurjar, R., Korwar, A., Saxena, N., Thierauf, T.: Deterministic identity testing for sum of read-once oblivious arithmetic branching programs. Comput. Complex. **26**(4), 835–880 (2017). Conference Version Appeared in the Proceedings of CCC 2015
25. Hancock, T.R., Hellerstein, L.: Learning read-once formulas over fields and extended bases. In: Warmuth, M.K., Valiant, L.G. (eds.) Proceedings of the Fourth Annual Workshop on Computational Learning Theory, COLT 1991, Santa Cruz, California, USA, 5–7 August 1991, pp. 326–336. Morgan Kaufmann (1991)
26. Heintz, J., Schnorr, C.: Testing polynomials which are easy to compute (extended abstract). In: Miller, R.E., Ginsburg, S., Burkhard, W.A., Lipton, R.J. (eds.) Proceedings of the 12th Annual ACM Symposium on Theory of Computing, 28–30 April 1980, Los Angeles, California, USA, pp. 262–272. ACM (1980)
27. Kabanets, V., Impagliazzo, R.: Derandomizing polynomial identity tests means proving circuit lower bounds. Comput. Complex. **13**(1-2), 1–46 (2004). Conference Version Appeared in the Proceedings of STOC 2003
28. Kayal, N., Nair, V., Saha, C.: Separation between read-once oblivious algebraic branching programs (ROABPs) and multilinear depth three circuits. In: 33rd Symposium on Theoretical Aspects of Computer Science (STACS 2016), pp. 46–1. Schloss Dagstuhl–Leibniz-Zentrum für Informatik (2016)
29. Mahajan, M., Tawari, A.: Sums of read-once formulas: how many summands are necessary? Theor. Comput. Sci. **708**, 34–45 (2018)

30. Minahan, D., Volkovich, I.: Complete derandomization of identity testing and reconstruction of read-once formulas. ACM Trans. Comput. Theory **10**(3), 10:1–10:11 (2018). Conference Version Appeared in the Proceedings of CCC 2017
31. Mukhopadhyay, P.: Depth-4 identity testing and Noether's normalization lemma. In: Kulikov, A.S., Woeginger, G.J. (eds.) CSR 2016. LNCS, vol. 9691, pp. 309–323. Springer, Cham (2016). https://doi.org/10.1007/978-3-319-34171-2_22
32. Mulmuley, K.D.: Geometric complexity theory V: efficient algorithms for Noether normalization. J. Amer. Math. Soc. **30**(1), 225–309 (2017). Extended Abstract Appeared in the Proceedings of FOCS 2012
33. Nisan, N.: Lower bounds for non-commutative computation (extended abstract). In: Koutsougeras, C., Vitter, J.S. (eds.) Proceedings of the 23rd Annual ACM Symposium on Theory of Computing, 5–8 May 1991, New Orleans, Louisiana, USA, pp. 410–418. ACM (1991)
34. Ore, O.: Über höhere Kongruenzen. Norsk Mat. Forenings Skrifter Ser. **I**(7), 15 (1922)
35. Schwartz, J.T.: Fast probabilistic algorithms for verification of polynomial identities. J. ACM **27**(4), 701–717 (1980)
36. Shpilka, A., Volkovich, I.: On reconstruction and testing of read-once formulas. Theory Comput. **10**, 465–514 (2014). Conference Version Appeared in the Proceedings of STOC 2008
37. Shpilka, A., Volkovich, I.: Read-once polynomial identity testing. Comput. Complex. **24**(3), 477–532 (2015). Conference Versions Appeared in the Proceedings of STOC 2008 and APPROX-RANDOM 2009
38. Volkovich, I.: A guide to learning arithmetic circuits. In: Feldman, V., Rakhlin, A., Shamir, O. (eds.) COLT 2016, vol. 49, pp. 1540–1561. JMLR.org (2016)
39. Zippel, R.: Probabilistic algorithms for sparse polynomials. In: ISSAC 1979, pp. 216–226 (1979)

# Author Index




Y. Li et al. (Eds.): COCOON 2026, LNCS 16835, pp. 465–466, 2027.
https://doi.org/10.1007/978-981-92-3309-0

MIX
Papier aus verantwortungsvollen Quellen
Paper from responsible sources
FSC® C105338

If you have any concerns about our products,
you can contact us on
**ProductSafety@springernature.com**

In case Publisher is established outside the EU,
the EU authorized representative is:
**Springer Nature Customer Service Center GmbH**
**Europaplatz 3, 69115 Heidelberg, Germany**

Printed by Libri Plureos GmbH
in Hamburg, Germany